Canadian Democracy

Second Edition

Canadian Democracy

A Concise Introduction

Stephen Brooks
Marc Ménard

OXFORD
UNIVERSITY PRESS

Oxford University Press is a department of the University of Oxford.
It furthers the University's objective of excellence in research, scholarship,
and education by publishing worldwide. Oxford is a registered trade mark of
Oxford University Press in the UK and in certain other countries.

Published in Canada by
Oxford University Press
8 Sampson Mews, Suite 204,
Don Mills, Ontario M3C 0H5 Canada

www.oupcanada.com

Library and Archives Canada Cataloguing in Publication

Brooks, Stephen, 1956–

Canadian democracy : a concise introduction / Stephen Brooks, Marc Ménard.

Includes bibliographical references and index.

ISBN 978-0-19-902165-9

1. Canada—Politics and government—Textbooks.

2. Democracy—Canada—Textbooks. I. Ménard, Marc,

1956-, II. Title.

JL75.B749 2017   320.971   C2017-900141-8

Oxford University Press is committed to our environment.
Wherever possible, our books are printed on paper which comes from
responsible sources.

Printed and bound in the United States of America

1 2 3 4 — 20 19 18 17

Brief Contents

Contents

1 An Introduction to Political Life   1

PART I The Societal Context of Politics   29

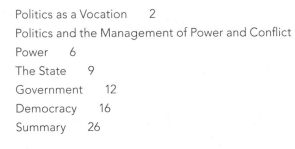

2 Political Culture   30

3 The Social and Economic Setting   65

PART II The Structure
of Governance   173

8   How Parliamentary Government Works in Canada   266

PART III Participation in Politics   317

9   Parties and Elections   318

10   Interest Groups   360

11 The Media 392

12 Conclusion: Canada in the World 421

Figures, Tables, and Boxes

Figures

Tables

Boxes

Democracy Watch

Canadian Spotlight

Inside Politics

Media Beat

Preface

Writing the second edition of *Canadian Democracy: A Concise Introduction* reminded us of the many challenges faced by those who teach and study Canadian politics. Perhaps the most daunting challenge is staying current, because change in the twenty-first century appears to be occurring at a pace best described as turbo-charged and in "revolutions per minute." In just the past four years, for instance, Canadians have witnessed countless and unparalleled technological advancements in all areas of our lives. We've seen changes in the influence of social media on politics, new laws, new interpretations of existing laws, and changes in immigration and refugee patterns, not to mention changes in the nature of terrorism and of globalization. And then, to top it all off, we've experienced changes in government at the municipal, provincial, and federal levels. Every new government means new personalities, new values, new ideas, and new policies. So, how do we ensure that, with all of this change, we do not succumb to confusion, frustration, and despair? Is there an antidote to this perpetual, turbo-charged change? What methods and approaches can we use to identify trends, make generalizations, and predict outcomes?

As we wrote this edition, it seemed to us that the simplest and most direct way of dealing with the challenge of change is to use a disciplined and methodological approach to learning. This must be a constant: *our society and its politics may change, but critical thinking, evidence based learning and the social sciences approach remain the same.*

Another challenge we have tried to address in this edition is the increasing diversity of Canadian classrooms. My classrooms are a mix of native-born Canadians, new Canadians, landed immigrants, and international students. Students may have varying levels of ability in English. They may hold different values and beliefs based on their culture or experience. They may have varying levels of exposure to Canadian history, geography, politics, culture, and education. They practice different religions and have diverse cultural mores. They may have different sexual orientations. They may have functional limitations because of a disability. They may also hate reading. A multi-faceted approach to learning works because it recognizes diversity and also addresses individual learning styles. As we stated above, it is important to remember that aside from helping students learn about Canadian society, our main objective is to encourage them to practice critical thinking skills and apply the social sciences approach to learning and analysis.

Many students learn best by doing, and so we have included at the end of every chapter a debate section with topics that can be used to stimulate discussion in the classroom. Nothing gets students more interested in Canadian politics than an opportunity to argue about things that matter to them in an open and safe learning environment. As well, this textbook can be used with *Political Argument: A Guide to Researching, Writing and Debating* (Oxford University Press, 2016).

Yet another challenge of teaching of teaching Canadian politics, one which we alluded to in the preface of the first edition—one that is connected to the first two challenges—is that our system of government is not easily taught or grasped. This is likely due to the fact that the Canadian political system is a hybrid and an amalgam of laws, institutions, and conventions that were born out of economic, social, geographic, historical, and political necessity. We have discovered through trial and error that students learn best when the teacher and the textbook offer early, clear, and frequent explanations of the "why" of Canadian politics, followed immediately by theoretical models, examples, audio and video clips, and illustrations: in short, with a multi-faceted approach to learning. This text offers several ways of conveying essential information including illustrations, marginal definitions, additional readings, exercises, Internet links, and charts and models that make the text accessible both visually and verbally.

This second concise edition has been re-organized with the following two questions in mind: What do students need to keep learning about Canadian democracy? And what order do they need them in? We came up with a five-part approach that mirrors how people learn: first, we introduce the subject; second, we provide context; third, we outline how Canadian democracy works; fourth, we examine how citizens access and participate in Canadian democracy; and finally, we look at Canadian democracy in the global context.

The introduction, Chapter 1, begins with an explanation of why politics and Canadian democracy are best studied by using definitions, theories, and social sciences methods. Fundamental concepts such as power, the state, and democracy provide the building blocks for the discussion that continues throughout the book.

Political scientists often refer to political systems as though they were living and breathing organisms, constantly evolving eco-systems. For this reason, part I of the textbook is devoted to understanding the societal context in which Canadian democracy has evolved and continues to evolve. Therefore, each chapter describes the environment and the factors that have shaped Canadian society and its political system.

Chapter 2 discusses political culture with particular attention to Canadian values, ideologies, and political institutions. Chapter 3 is an examination of the influence of economics on Canadian democracy. Chapter 4 discusses the effects of geography and regionalism on our Constitution and our political institutions. And Chapter 5 deals with the complex issue of diversity and pluralism by looking at certain facets of Canadian society: language politics, immigration and multiculturalism; equality and gender issues; and the relationship between Aboriginal peoples and the Canadian state.

Part II deals with the structural elements, the accommodations and political arrangements that have made it possible for Canadians to adapt to change and to manage their affairs in relative peace for a century and a half. The first chapter of this section, Chapter 6, deals with the Constitution, and the rules of the "game," the relationships between the branches of government, and the Canadian system of liberty, rights, and freedoms.

The idea of sharing power between a central government and smaller regional governments—federalism—was considered by the Fathers of Confederation to be a great compromise without which there would be no Canada. This is the central theme of Chapter 7.

When studying Canadian politics, students are often surprised at how very different the Canadian system of government is from the American system, in spite of them both being democracies. As such, Chapter 8's comparison of the two countries' machinery of government is often illustrative and educational. It is also interesting to see, in a democracy, the extent to which the machinery of government is shaped by the values and the expectations of its citizens.

Part III is an exploration of how Canadians access and participate in the political system. If Canadians live in a democracy, what is the nature of their participation in the country's politics, and how do they access politicians and the levers of government? Chapter 9 discusses these matters, as well as the role that elections and political parties play in the democratic process. Organizations such as interest groups also have a role to play in a democracy, and Chapter 10 is devoted to an analysis and breakdown of the interest group system in Canada.

Chapter 11 looks at some important questions about the role of the media as an agent of change. The quality of the information provided by the media and the images portrayed therein can significantly affect how people interact with each other and the political system.

Finally, the conclusion, Chapter 12, is a brief look at Canada's international presence. Chapter 12 also allows us to reflect on the perceptions, values, and expectations that shape Canadian democracy but also influence Canada's role on the world stage.

What Stephen Brooks wrote in the preface of the seventh edition of *Canadian Democracy* is worth repeating: we hope to encourage the readers to think about Canadian politics in ways that will enable them to assess fairly and realistically the performance of Canada's political system. We also hope that this book will help build the reader build a foundation for lifelong learning and participation in Canadian democracy.

Acknowledgements

I would like to thank my co-author, Stephen Brooks at the University of Windsor, and Katherine Skene, Acquisition Editor at Oxford University Press, for once again giving me the opportunity to work on this second edition of *Canadian Democracy: A Concise Introduction*. It is impossible to quantify how much I have learned from the writing about Canadian politics. I am a much better teacher for the experience. I recommend it for anyone that has a passion for teaching and for a particular subject matter.

Where would we be without editors? Thank you again to development editor Meg Patterson and copy editor Leslie Saffrey for their assistance and support.

I would also like to thank Claire Moane, Chair of the School of English and Liberal Studies, Seneca College of Applied Arts and Technology, as well as the library staff at Seneca Libraries. I also received countless suggestions and thoughtful comments from my colleagues, Alka Bushan, George Faclaris, Janet Loveday, Mark Rubinstein, and Ken Sproul, all of them social science professors at Seneca College.

And finally, I would like to acknowledge the contributions and encouragement from my partner, Liz, daughters, Laura, Catherine, and Carolyn, and other family members.

Marc Ménard, Professor, School of English and Liberal Studies,
Seneca College, Toronto, Ontario

1 An Introduction to Political Life

Understanding politics and government requires a tool kit of fundamental concepts and terms that are useful in analyzing political life. This chapter will equip you with such tools by examining the following concepts:

- politics
- power
- the state
- government
- authority
- legitimacy
- democracy

↑ When we hear "politics" we may automatically think of Parliament Hill or politicians, but, because the core of politics is the management of power and conflict, it touches on nearly all parts of our daily lives.

Source: Dennis McColeman/Getty Images.

We all have an idea of what politics involves, but few of us actually think about its purpose until something goes wrong with our home, community, or society. The most important thing to know about politics is its purpose: politics keeps our society civilized by determining who should have and who should yield power and by helping citizens resolve conflicts over resources and over values. Essentially, politics is the management of power and conflict. When a society's political institutions function well, as we have experienced in Canada with its democratic political institutions for some 150 years, life tends to be peaceful and prosperous. The reverse is also true: societies with dysfunctional political institutions tend to be less prosperous and in some cases dangerous for their citizens. This book is dedicated to using a political science approach to understanding how Canadian democracy manages power and resolves conflict for its citizens.

The term "political science" may be less familiar and, in some ways, more puzzling. The problem may arise from the word "science" and images of hard facts, measurements, and laboratories, and from the fact that some experts consider politics an art, which defies experimentation and measurement. Can there be such a thing as political science?

Yes, within limits. Political science is considered a "soft" rather than a "hard" science. Like the natural and applied sciences, political science rests on a bedrock of empirical analysis—analysis that seeks to formulate laws and make predictions about the world of politics and government based on verifiable observation and, in some cases, experimentation. Like the practitioners of the hard sciences, those who study politics and government seek to do so objectively, attempting to understand the way things are and how they may be changed. Political scientists generally have to make do with observing behaviour and the functioning of institutions in less controlled circumstances than might be found in laboratories or computer simulations.

No matter where politics and government are studied, the core concepts and analytical methods are the same. Power, authority, identity, participation, bureaucracy, integration, stability, and equality are just some of the core concepts that are relevant to understanding the politics of any country.

Politics as a Vocation

If you want a job that earns you the respect of your fellow citizens, become a firefighter, a nurse, a teacher, or a police officer, but do not become a politician. This is the conclusion that emerges from a 2013 *Reader's Digest* poll conducted by Harris/Decima. Politicians came in thirtieth out of 31 professions ranked according to trust—behind taxi drivers, lawyers, and real-estate agents.[1]

The image of politicians as untrustworthy, and of their calling as low and dishonest, is not entirely fair. There is no hard evidence that politicians are more likely to be dishonest or have lower moral standards than those in other occupations. Indeed, many, if not most, people who run for and are elected to public office are motivated by a desire to serve and to improve the lives of those they represent. Many politicians make significant financial and personal sacrifices by holding public office. Yet Canadians do not trust them.

To understand why, we need to think about the nature of the politician's craft in societies with democratic forms of government. In liberal democracies such as Canada, not everyone shares the same opinions or has identical interests. To win elections, politicians and political parties need to appeal to a range of interests and values. Once elected, politicians and parties must do the same: balance competing demands and points of view. Moreover, politicians may find that their ability to do certain things—things that may be popular or that they believe are the right thing to do—is limited by circumstances beyond their control. Politicians make promises that cannot be kept, or perhaps are kept, but not quite in the form or according to the timetable that was expected. And perhaps politicians knew or suspected this all along, saying things and making promises with a reckless disregard for the truth or the realistic likelihood of achieving those goals, in the hope of being elected.

It is the messy activity of politics—the compromises, the occasional evasiveness, the failure to deliver on promises made, the recent cases of election fraud and politicians' misspending, as well as the sense that those elected to public office do not faithfully represent those who put them there—leads to cynicism about politicians and political parties. This may also help explain why Canadians lack confidence in their politicians and why most Canadians do not

GEOFF ROBINS/AFP/Getty Images

City of Toronto mayor Rob Ford was arguably one of the most controversial politicians in Canadian politics. His supporters felt that he was a politician who kept his word; his critics blamed him for tarnishing the image of politicians even further and turning the politics of Canada's largest city into a circus. Whatever might be said of the late Mr. Ford, his presence did increase citizens' awareness of the importance of local politics.

Listen to the "Political Corruption in Canada: It's Not as Bad as You Think!" podcast at www. oup.com// BrooksConcise2e.

participate in political life or follow politics very closely. Canadians are not alone in their negativity. In fact, in no established democracy do a majority of people say they have a lot of confidence in political parties.[2] Surveys of Canadians also show that younger voters tend to be the least interested in politics and are less likely to participate than middle-aged and older citizens.

A healthy dose of cynicism about politics is probably a good thing, at least if the cynicism is fuelled by knowledge. But cynicism based on ignorance or coupled with apathy may not be healthy for democracies. Whether you are a hardened cynic or an enthusiastic fan of Canadian politics, no judgment about how well the political system works is helpful unless it is informed.

Politics and the Management of Power and Conflict

As indicated earlier, politics is the messy business of managing power and conflict within a society, and is considered by many to be both an art and a science. It arises from the fact of

© Dale Cummings/Artizans

In the 2011 Canadian federal election, the voter turnout was just 61.4 per cent. And, in 2015, the voter turnout was 68.3 per cent, the highest in two decades. Why do you think a large percentage of eligible voters chose not to cast ballots? Are voters increasingly skeptical about their politicians? What qualities are voters looking for that they are not finding in today's politicians? Should voters expect their politicians to fulfill all their promises?

scarcity and involves skills in the use of *power* and the resolution of *conflicts*. There are limits to wealth, privacy, clean air and water, social recognition, and so on. In the real world, it is not possible to fully satisfy every person's needs and desires. Conflicts take place between rival claimants and generally occur for two reasons: over **values** (personal beliefs in what is right or wrong, important or not important, valuable or not valuable); and over **resources** (things we need for survival or desire for comfort). These conflicts explain why politics exists. But more than this, politics is also about how rival claims are settled. **Politics**, then, is the management of power and conflict and an activity by which rival claims are settled by public authorities.

What distinguishes politics from the conflicts, struggles, and rivalries in such settings as the family, the workplace, social organizations, and the marketplace is the public nature of political disputes and the use of public authority—embodied in the state—to deal with them. Political philosophers sometimes call the **public realm** the sphere of what is considered to be political; its boundary is located at the limits of the state's authority. Beyond this line is the **private realm**, where the state's authority does not extend.

Political theorists agree that politics is about the exercise of power. However, as Box 1.1 shows, theorists disagree about what *power relations* count as political ones. Michel Foucault, Karl Marx and Friedrich Engels, and the feminist movement define politics in ways that would include, for example, the relations between bosses and workers in a corporation, between parents and children in a family, and between teachers and students in a school. And in a sense they are right. In the words of American political scientist Charles Merriam, "obviously there is governance everywhere—government in heaven; government in hell; government and law among outlaws; government in prison."[3] John Locke and David Easton both offer a more limited definition of politics, one that goes back to Aristotle's conception of the Greek polis. They argue that what is distinctive about politics is its association with a system for settling disputes that is both public and binding on the whole community. At the centre of this system is the state, or government.

These definitions disagree in another important way. Marxist, postmodernist, and feminist definitions associate politics with a pervasive pattern of oppression. For them, politics is fundamentally about how inequalities are generated and reinforced through the power relations that exist between classes and gender groups at all levels of society.

Does it matter, in the end, how we define politics? We would argue that in labelling as "political" everything that involves any and all social interactions we lose sight of the boundary that separates the public and private realms. This boundary may not be very distinct, but it is crucial for understanding the politics of any society. Moreover, such a boundary is necessary in order to protect the freedoms that most of us believe to be important features of a democratic society. Political conflict is largely about where exactly this boundary between public and private should be drawn: what should be public matters and state decisions, and what should remain private. We can agree that power relations are everywhere without taking the next step of claiming that politics also has no bounds.

But there is, perhaps, another reason for adopting the more limited definition of politics that we have put forward. Only those power relations that take place in the public realm can legitimately be associated with the use of force in its most naked, punitive forms. While compulsion, punishment, and violence may take place in all sorts of social settings, only the public

values personal beliefs in what is right or wrong, important or not important, valuable or not valuable

resources things we need for survival or desire for comfort

politics the management of power and conflict and an activity by which rival claims are settled by public authorities

public realm the sphere of what is considered to be political; its boundary is located at the limits of the state's authority

private realm the areas of life where the state's authority does not extend

Inside Politics

BOX 1.1 | Some Important Definitions of Politics and Power

A political system can be designated as those interactions through which values are authoritatively allocated for a society.

—David Easton, *A Systems Analysis of Political Life*, 1965

Political power, then, I take to be a right of making laws with penalties of death and, consequently, all less penalties for the regulating and preserving of property, and of employing the force of the community in the execution of such laws and in the defense of the commonwealth from foreign injury; and all this only for the public good.

—John Locke, *The Second Treatise of Government*, 1690

Political power, properly so called, is merely the organized power of one class for oppressing another.

—Karl Marx and Friedrich Engels, *The Communist Manifesto*, 1848

Basically power is less a confrontation between two adversaries or the linking of one to the other than a question of government. This word must be allowed the very broad meaning which it had in the sixteenth century. "Government" did not refer only to political structures or to the management of states; rather it designated the way in which the conduct of individuals or of groups might be directed: the government of children, of souls, of communities, of families, of the sick. It did not cover only the legitimately constituted forms of political or economic subjection, but also modes of action . . . which were destined to act upon the possibilities of action of other people. To govern, in this sense, is to structure the possible field of action of others.

—Michel Foucault, *The Subject and Power*, 1982

The personal is political.

—Slogan of the feminist movement

authorities—those who wield the power of the state—have the *legitimate right* to back up their decisions with the full power of society. All other power relations are more limited. The reason for this difference is that the state is the only institution that can reasonably claim to speak and act on behalf of the entire community, and its unique function is to ensure the conditions for some degree of *social order*. This social order is necessary for all other social activities; without order there is no peaceful basis for reconciling conflicts in society.

Power

In order to understand both politics and society, one must also understand power. Philosopher and Nobel Prize laureate Bertrand Russell wrote that "the fundamental concept in social science is Power, in the same sense in which Energy is the fundamental concept in physics." We are all attracted to power because power is the ability to influence what happens. This includes the ability to change others' actions and behaviours. According to Russell, power holds a greater attraction for people than wealth:

> When a moderate degree of comfort is assured, both individuals and communities will pursue power rather than wealth: they may seek wealth as a means to power, or they may forgo an increase of wealth in order to secure an increase in power, but in the former case as in the latter, their fundamental motive is not economic . . .[4]

Power is an agent of social change that takes many forms and is found in all sorts of settings, not just political ones. Social scientists like to unpack the concept of power, breaking it down into species that are distinguished from one another according to the reason why the compliant party obeys. Compliance may result from the ability of A to convince B that a particular action is reasonable or otherwise in B's best interests (influence); from the recognition by the compliant party that the person or organization issuing a command has the right to do so and should be obeyed (authority); or from the threat or use of force (coercion). Politics involves all these faces of power—influence, authority and, coercion—at various times and in different circumstances. Figure 1.1 shows the relationship between politics and power, and some of the many forms power can take, ranging from the "softer" forms of power—influence and authority—to its "harder" form—coercion.

Democratic politics relies primarily on the two softer, non-coercive species of power. But coercion is also used in legitimate ways, and no democracy can function without its system of courts, police, and prisons. Democratic states must strive to maintain a balance between civil rights and the legitimate use of coercion in order to maintain social order. How far coercion and democracy are compatible, however, is an open question. This point is illustrated by a famous and timeless exchange between Prime Minister Pierre Trudeau and CBC journalist Tim Ralfe in October 1970,[5] a few days after the Liberal government had suspended civil liberties by invoking the War Measures Act because of the Front de libération du Québec (FLQ) crisis in Quebec. Ralfe asked, "Sir, what is it with all these men with guns around here?" and said that he was ". . . worried about living in a town that's full of people with guns running around." Trudeau responded:

> Why? Have they done anything to you? Have they pushed you around or anything? . . . there are a lot of bleeding hearts around who just don't like to see people with helmets and guns. All I can say is, go on and bleed, but it is more important to keep law and order in the society than to be worried about weak-kneed people. . . . I think the society must take every means at its disposal to defend itself against the emergence of a parallel power which defies the elected power in this country, and I think that goes to any distance.

Was Trudeau right? One of the great ironies of democracy is that, unlike other political systems, it requires that dissenting points of view and opposition to those in power be

power
the ability to influence what happens

influence the ability of A to convince B that a particular action is reasonable or otherwise in B's best interests

authority
the recognition by the compliant party that the person or organization issuing a command has the right to do so and should be obeyed

coercion the threat or use of force

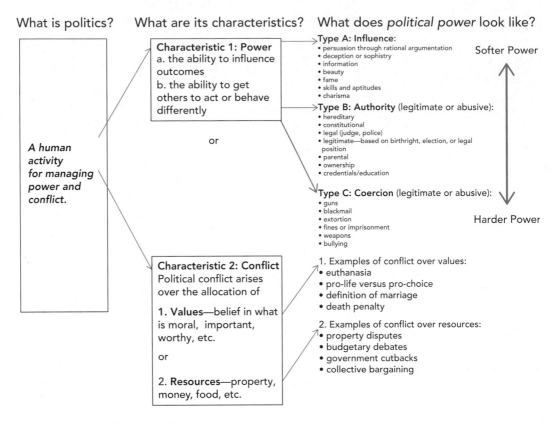

What is politics?   What are its characteristics?   What does *political power* look like?

Type A: Influence:
- persuasion through rational argumentation
- deception or sophistry
- information
- beauty
- fame
- skills and aptitudes
- charisma

Softer Power

Characteristic 1: Power
a. the ability to influence outcomes
b. the ability to get others to act or behave differently

Type B: Authority (legitimate or abusive):
- hereditary
- constitutional
- legal (judge, police)
- legitimate—based on birthright, election, or legal position
- parental
- ownership
- credentials/education

or

Type C: Coercion (legitimate or abusive):
- guns
- blackmail
- extortion
- fines or imprisonment
- weapons
- bullying

Harder Power

A human activity for managing power and conflict.

Characteristic 2: Conflict
Political conflict arises over the allocation of

1. Values—belief in what is moral, important, worthy, etc.

or

2. Resources—property, money, food, etc.

1. Examples of conflict over values:
- euthanasia
- pro-life versus pro-choice
- definition of marriage
- death penalty

2. Examples of conflict over resources:
- property disputes
- budgetary debates
- government cutbacks
- collective bargaining

FIGURE 1.1 What Is Politics?

respected. Whether the issue is invocation of the War Measures Act in 1970 or the measures taken to combat terrorism since 11 September 2001, the eternal trade-off is the same. Arresting people suspected of terrorist acts is, most would agree, necessary to protect democratic government. At some point, however, protecting law and order may exact a high cost in terms of personal freedoms. For example, after the 9/11 terrorist attacks on the World Trade Center and the Pentagon, access to public buildings became more restricted, border crossings became more time-consuming and stressful, airport security was tightened, and measures were taken to curb the rights of immigrants. Some of these changes proved to be temporary, but many—such as the air travel security tax imposed on all Canadian travellers since 2002; the Anti-terrorism Act, which came into effect in December 2001; and the "no-fly list," which came into effect in 2007—have been enduring. The terror-related killing of soldier Patrice Vincent, followed by the attack on Parliament Hill in which soldier Nathan Cirillo was killed, both in October 2014, resulted in the passing of the controversial Anti-terrorism Act of 2015, which granted many more surveillance powers to state security agencies. In a democracy, those in power must justify use of coercion as necessary to maintain such values as freedom, equality, justice, and the rule of law. Inevitably, however, people will disagree over the meaning and relative importance of these values and over how much coercion is acceptable.

Alleged protesters at the June 2010 G20 summit in Toronto, Ontario, are detained at the intersection of Queen Street and Spadina Avenue. Security measures at the summit, including a five-tier screening process and a temporary extension of police powers, were criticized by some as excessive infringement on citizens' personal freedoms such as the right to peaceful assembly. Five years later, a senior officer of the Toronto Police Service was found guilty of misconduct in ordering the mass arrests of G20 protesters.

The State

The existence of the state, we argued earlier, is a necessary condition for the existence of politics. But what is the "state"? To this point we have used the terms "state" and "government" as though they meant the same thing. This lack of distinction can lead to serious confusion. For example, to argue that the government is corrupt or wasteful, or that its policies are undesirable, does not necessarily call into question the state's legitimacy. It does, however, challenge the authority of the people who control the levers of the governmental system. Political activity in a democracy is far more likely to be directed at influencing and changing the government than at reforming the state.

Canadian political scientist Leo Panitch provides this definition of the **state**:

> [The state is] a broad concept that includes government as the seat of legitimate authority in a territory but also includes bureaucracy, judiciary, the Armed Forces and internal police, structures of legislative assemblies and administration, public corporations, regulatory boards, and ideological apparatuses such as the education establishment and publicly owned media. The distinguishing characteristic of the state is its monopoly over the use of force in a given territory.[6]

state the set of institutions that manage power and conflict for a society within a geographically defined territory

According to this definition, the state has three main characteristics:

1. territorial boundaries beyond which it has limited or no legal authority
2. a complex set of institutions that wield public authority, including the courts, the police, the educational system, an elected legislature, and a bureaucracy
3. what Max Weber called a "monopoly of the legitimate use of physical force in the enforcement of its order"

As we see in Box 1.2, there are many other definitions of "state," which raise important questions about the purposes and the interests of those who wield the power of the state.

Some definitions of the state offer answers to these questions. The Marxist and Leninist definitions in Box 1.2 characterize the state as an instrument of class oppression. Marx argued that the end of class conflict would sound the death knell for the state. It would "wither away," no longer having any function. Contemporary Marxists, except for a few diehards, no longer predict the state's demise and the ascent of a social utopia. Some feminists view the state as a patriarchal institution, reinforcing and perpetuating the social superiority of men over women. Many political scientists would argue that the state is responsive to any group with enough political clout to persuade policy makers that it is in their interest to meet the group's demands for public actions on private wants.

Inside Politics

BOX 1.2 | Alternative Definitions of the State

The executive of the modern State is but a committee for managing the common affairs of the whole bourgeoisie.

—Marx and Engels, *The Communist Manifesto*

The state is that fiction by which everyone seeks to live at the expense of everyone else.

—French economist Frédéric Bastiat, *C*. 1840

L'Etat, c'est moi. [I am the state.]

—Attributed to Louis XIV of France, 1638–1715

[The state is that institution which] successfully upholds a claim to the monopoly of the legitimate use of physical force in the enforcement of its order . . . within a given territorial area.

—Max Weber, *The Theory of Social and Economic Organization*

All state-based political systems are patriarchal—that is, in no country in the world are women equal participants in the institutions of the state or equal beneficiaries in its distribution of power or in the norms and values sanctioned in law and enforced by those institutions.

—Jill Vickers, *Reinventing Political Science*

Theoretical Approaches to Understanding the Role of the State

Political science offers four main approaches to answering the question: On whose behalf and in whose interests is the state's authority exercised? These approaches include pluralism, class analysis, feminism, and postmodernism.

Pluralism Approach

Some political theorists espouse **pluralism** and see politics as fundamentally a competition between different interests. They believe that the state responds chiefly to the demands of those groups that are best organized, have superior financial resources, can claim to speak on behalf of large segments of the population, and are successful in associating their special interests with the general interests of society. The pluralist model assumes various forms. The *society-centred* variants emphasize the impact of groups in society on the state, while the *state-centred* variants place greater emphasis on the ability of public officials to act on their own preferences and according to their own interests. Those who work within this perspective argue that groups do not compete on a level playing field, and cite business interests as occupying a privileged position within this competition.

pluralism
the understanding of politics as fundamentally a competition between different interests

Class Analysis Approach

According to the **class analysis** approach, economics shapes politics. Beginning with Karl Marx, class analysis theorists see the state in capitalist societies as an instrument through which small minorities control most of society's wealth to maintain their social and economic dominance. They may disagree on how this dominance is achieved, but they all seem to agree that the state is complicit in perpetuating inequalities rooted in the economic system. They note that the state decision makers are influenced by the demands and interests of certain classes more than others. They cite as examples the state's vulnerability to declines in business confidence, the control of the dominant class over the mass media and popular culture, and a lack of class consciousness among even the least-privileged groups in society, which they argue stems from the widespread acceptance of capitalist and individualistic values.

class analysis
a theoretical approach that sees the state in capitalist societies as an instrument through which small minorities control most of society's wealth to maintain their social and economic dominance

Feminism Approach

In the **feminism** approach the state is seen as an inherently patriarchal institution, where politics is not neutral or gender free. This means that the state, its structures, and its laws all serve to institutionalize male dominance. Feminists see the need to increase the representation of women in elected legislatures, the bureaucracy, and the courts, and to create governmental bodies and programs that recognize women as a group with interests and needs that are not identical to those of men. Feminists also indicate that power relationships between men and women differ greatly in poorer and richer economies. Most feminist political theorists insist that a state-centred political system will continue to be patriarchal unless there is a change in

feminism
a theoretical approach that views the state as an inherently patriarchal institution, where politics is not neutral or gender free

the hierarchical nature of authority embodied in the state. Like Karl Marx's famous prediction that the state would "wither away" once classes were abolished, many feminists argue that eliminating gender discrimination would cause the state, as we know it, to disappear.

Postmodernism Approach

postmodernism
a theoretical approach that sees the state as an essentially oppressive and even repressive institution

In **postmodernism** the state is viewed as an essentially oppressive and even repressive institution. But unlike class analysis and feminism, postmodernism is much more eclectic in the forms of oppression that it associates with the state and public authority. Groups may be oppressed based on their race, gender, ethnicity, sexual preference, or some other trait. This trait excludes them from the dominant group that controls the levers of state power and whose values and identity are reflected in the institutions, language, and mores of the society. Postmodernists view the state as repressive in that its structures, laws, and activities repress the expression of some values while they legitimize and nurture others. Those who embrace this approach constitute what is sometimes called the New Left. The Old Left wished to see the overthrow of the capitalist state and its transformation into a socialist utopia without property, money, or status. Postmodernists, however, are more dubious about the revolutionary visions associated with class analysis and the Old Left, believing that the problem of the state is not simply its relationship to economic power but, as well, to forms of oppression and repression more generally.

Government

government
the organization of the state and the system of institutions and agencies used to exercise its authority

A distinction should now be made between the state and the government. The **government** is the organization of the state and the system of institutions and agencies used to exercise its authority. In a democratic political system, where governments are chosen and removed through elections, the term "government" usually refers to those who have been elected to power. In a democracy, a government is seen as more personal than the state, being associated with a particular group of people such as a political party. In an election, the rules and procedures by which a government is formed are part of the state system. And like the rest of the state, they are less likely to generate political controversy and to undergo change than are the current government and its policies.

legitimacy
the rules and institutions that constitute the state and determine how governments are chosen are accepted by most people as being reasonable

Underlying this distinction between state and government is an important practical difference in how each compels the obedience of the citizens, corporations, and associations within its jurisdiction. The willingness of individuals and groups to obey the decisions of government—decisions they may vigorously disagree with, and may not have voted for—is based on their view that the state's authority is legitimate. **Legitimacy** means that the rules and institutions that constitute the state, and which determine how governments are chosen, are accepted by most people as being reasonable. The legitimacy of the state, therefore, is based on the *consent* of those who are governed. Legitimacy depends not on coercion—an ever-present fear of penalties for disobeying the law—but rather on an implicit acceptance of the rules of the political game.

Canadian Spotlight

BOX 1.3 Timeline: Important Dates in the Evolution of Canadian Democracy up to Confederation

1759 The gradual conquest of New France by the British culminates in a victory at the Plains of Abraham outside Quebec City.

1763 The Treaty of Paris ends French rule in Canada. The British Royal Proclamation of 1763 creates the colony of Quebec and recognizes Aboriginal land rights.

1774 The Quebec Act recognizes the French civil code of law and the Roman Catholic religion in the colony. This is the first significant instance of "accommodation" in Canadian history.

1776 The American War of Independence prompts a flood of Loyalist refugees. An estimated one-third of the American colonies' population moves north and settles in what are now Nova Scotia, New Brunswick, Prince Edward Island, Quebec, and Ontario.

1791 The Constitution Act of 1791 creates Lower Canada (Quebec) and Upper Canada (Ontario). *Representative government* is established in both colonies. The colonies are also given permission to keep their taxes.

1837 and 1838 Armed rebellions occur in both Upper and Lower Canada because of corruption, poverty, social divisions, and disaffection with the ruling elites.

1839 Lord Durham reports on the causes of the rebellions and recommends implementing a parliamentary style of government similar to Britain's; his model includes the concept of *responsible government*. To reduce political conflict between English and French Canadians, he recommends a policy of assimilation of the French Canadians, and that Upper Canada and Lower Canada be united so that the assembly can be dominated by the English-Canadian majority.

1841 Upper and Lower Canada are united through the Act of Union.

1856 Ottawa becomes Canada's capital.

1867 The Dominion of Canada is created under the British North America Act (BNA Act) passed by the British Parliament. Sir John A. Macdonald becomes Canada's first prime minister. Initially, the Dominion includes Ontario, Quebec, Nova Scotia, and New Brunswick, but within six years, Prince Edward Island, Manitoba, and British Columbia join.

Government popularity and state legitimacy are not the same. Democracy requires some measure of stability and respect for rules, including those rules that determine who has the right to govern and how and when that right ends. A particular government or prime minister may be deeply unpopular, but people continue to obey the law and refrain from storming the legislature (although they may organize protests and even throw some tomatoes) because of their implicit acceptance of the state's legitimacy. Government may be upheld by consent or by force. In fact, it is usually upheld by both.

What sets Canada's political system apart from many around the world is that, according to their Constitution, Canadians have a peaceful opportunity to change the government at least every five years. Some states, such as Haiti, Zimbabwe, or Syria, are considered failed states precisely because changes of government are either very difficult or, when they do occur, violent.

The state's authority is sometimes questioned by individuals or by organized interests. When this happens, as Trudeau argued in October 1970 regarding the FLQ's apparent disregard for that authority, the public authorities may resort to force in order to maintain their ability to govern or to crush civil disobedience.

The question of when citizens may be justified in resisting the law, through either passive disobedience of public authority or violence, is an old one. Two of the world's greatest democracies, the United States and France, trace their modern origins to bloody revolutions undertaken in defence of principles that the revolutionaries believed warranted violence against the state. Some, such as American writer and libertarian thinker Henry David Thoreau, India's Mahatma Gandhi, and American civil rights leader Martin Luther King Jr, developed a philosophy of non-violent civil disobedience that has been influential around the world. Others, like American political activist Malcolm X, some leaders of the 1960s American student movement, and the French students whose 1968 demonstrations helped end the Charles de Gaulle presidency, acted on the premise that fighting oppression and injustice through violent opposition to the law and its enforcers is consistent with democracy.

The debate over civil disobedience—when is it justified and what forms may it take in a democracy?—has resurfaced in recent years, principally around issues associated with globalization and income inequality. Since what the media dubbed the "Battle in Seattle," when 1999 meetings of the World Trade Organization were disrupted by thousands of protesters, and scenes of violent confrontations with the police were broadcast live around the world, organized protest is expected near any meeting of policy makers from the world's wealthiest countries. The street tactics used at anti-globalization protests in Seattle, Genoa, and Quebec City, and more recently during the G20 meeting in Toronto and the Occupy Movement protests that started in 2011 have produced, somewhat ironically, a service industry that specializes in providing activist groups with advice and training on confrontations with the police, effective use of the media, and general strategies and tactics for gaining influence through civil disobedience. The oppression and violence that the state may inflict on members of the society, the argument goes, warrant self-defence on the part of victims.

Government that relies primarily on threats and violence to maintain its rule is generally unstable. Even the most repressive political authorities usually come to realize that popular consent is a firmer basis on which to govern. In some societies, the popular consent that legitimizes political rule may emerge from the uncoordinated activities of the various social institutions

© Pictorial Press Ltd / Alamy

Bettman/Getty Images

Mahatma Gandhi (left) and Malcolm X (right) had very different approaches to protest and resisting the law. What are the pros and cons to each approach—Gandhi's civil disobedience and Malcolm X's engaged opposition?

that influence the values and beliefs of citizens: the media, the schools, the family, and governments. In other societies, the state's legitimacy is deliberately and assiduously cultivated through official propaganda.

The active mobilization of society by the state, the deliberate manipulation of public attitudes, and the ruthless suppression of dissent by the public authorities are not features that most of us associate with democracy. The calculated fostering of consent through propaganda is a characteristic feature of totalitarian rule. **Totalitarianism** is a system of government that suppresses all dissent in the name of some supreme goal. This goal may be tied to the destiny of the "race," as it was in Nazi Germany, or to "class struggle," as it was in the Soviet Union under Stalin. Distinctions between the state, government, and society lose all meaning—indeed, they are considered to be subversive—under totalitarianism.

The way in which legitimacy is generated in political democracies is more subtle than under totalitarian rule, and depends primarily on social institutions and the vote. Every vote

totalitarianism
a system of government that suppresses all dissent in the name of some supreme goal

in a democratic society is an endorsement of the democratic way of life and is an act that confers legitimacy on the political system. Moreover, the mass media, religious institutions, and the educational system, when not directly under the control of the state, also generate legitimacy. For example, even public broadcasters and public educators in democracies enjoy a measure of free choice not experienced by their counterparts in totalitarian regimes. Thus legitimacy appears to be based on the free choice of individuals: an appearance that some argue is an illusion. For example, both Marxists and feminists believe government by "popular consent" is a sham that conceals the fundamentally undemocratic character of society and politics. Some Marxist critics use the term **cultural hegemony** to signify the ability of society's dominant class to have its values and beliefs accepted as the conventional wisdom in society at large.

cultural hegemony
the ability of society's dominant class to have its values and beliefs accepted as the conventional wisdom in society at large

Democracy

"Democracy is like pornography," says classical historian and political commentator Victor Davis Hanson, "we know it when we see it."[7] Hanson's observation seems commonsensical. Most of us would agree that a country in which free elections are held is almost certainly more democratic than one where they are not. *Freedom* seems to be an important element of democracies. But when we see a persistent lack of freedom and violations of human rights, or a lack of accountability on the part of those who govern, we are likely to believe that such countries are undemocratic. Many countries, including Canada, the United States, the Democratic People's Republic of Korea, the People's Republic of China, and the Islamic Republic of Iran, claim to be democracies. Obviously they cannot all be democratic unless they meet certain requirements; otherwise the concept of democracy becomes meaningless.

Defining democracy is not an easy task. The word "democracy" comes to us from two words in ancient Greek: "demos"—"people (the many)" and "kratos"—"rule." Most simply, therefore, "democracy" means "rule by the people."

In a book published at the height of the Cold War, Canadian political philosopher C.B. Macpherson argued that there are in fact three different types of democracy in the modern world.[8] Only one, *liberal democracy*, is characterized by competition between political parties. What Macpherson calls the *developmental* and *communist* versions of democracy do not have competitive elections and probably would not be considered democratic by most Canadians. But they both claim to attach greater importance to the social and economic equality of individuals than do liberal democracies, in addition to recognizing the formal political equality of citizens. If democracy is about equality, Macpherson argues, the developmental and communist versions are at least as democratic as the liberal version of democracy found in the capitalist world.

As Table 1.1 shows us, there are many words in politics that end with "-cracy." Each word refers to a political system where different groups and/or group sizes control the state and the levers of government.

TABLE 1.1 Types of Political Systems

Political System or Regime	Number of Participants in Control	Definition
Autocracy	One	Absolute control of the state by one person—monarchy, despotic regime, or dictatorship
Plutocracy	A few	Control of the state by the wealthy
Oligarchy	A few	Control of the state by the powerful
Aristocracy	A few	Control of government by an elite class of citizens (the best) or by a hereditary class (nobility)
Ochlocracy	Many	Rule by the mob—rule or tyranny of the majority (majoritarianism)
Democracy	Many	Control of the state by the people (direct democracy) or with the consent of the people (representative democracy)

If we accept Macpherson's argument that there are three types of democracy, each with a legitimate claim to the label, the world looks very democratic. Leaving aside personal and military dictatorships, and the odd monarchy like the Kingdom of Saudi Arabia or the Sultanate of Brunei, most of what is left would seem to qualify. While common sense suggests that democracy is not so widespread, Macpherson challenges us to reflect on what makes politics and society democratic or not. Is democracy a system of government? Or does democracy connote a type of society? Was Canada democratic before women received the vote? Does the persistence of poverty and large inequalities in wealth and social status in Canada mean that Canadian society is less than democratic?

About the only thing that everyone can agree on is that democracy is based on equality. Agreement breaks down over how much equality in what spheres of life is necessary for a society to qualify as democratic. Majority rule, government by popular consent, "one person–one vote," and competitive elections are usually associated with democratic government. But we

Democracy Watch

BOX 1.4 Is Canada's Democracy Broken?

In March 25, 2015, *CBC Asks* hosted an Oxford-style debate on the question "Is Politics Broken?" Low voter turnout and recent political scandals pertaining to election fraud and misspending by politicians were given as evidence that all is not well with Canada's democratic system.[9]

often see that the operation of democratic political institutions can result in oppressive government unless there are ways to safeguard some freedoms. In order to safeguard the rights and freedoms of individuals and minorities against what Alexis de Tocqueville called "democratic despotism," constitutional limits on the state's power over its citizens may be set or the political status of particular social groups may be entrenched in the formal rules and informal procedures of politics. Democracies have police forces, courts, and jails. But unlike other forms of government, they do not depend on coercion and violence, and they give citizens an opportunity to choose who will govern them.

Perhaps even more important than constitutional guarantees and political practices are a society's social and cultural values. Tocqueville argued that the best protection against the *tyranny of the majority* is the existence of multiple group identities in society. When individuals perceive themselves as belonging to particular social groups—such as religious denominations, ethnic or language groups, regional communities, or interest groups—in addition to sharing a common citizenship with everyone else—the democratic state is less likely to be turned to oppressive ends.

Some twentieth-century writers argue that cultural values represent the main bulwark against the tyranny of the majority. Democratic government, they suggest, depends on popular tolerance of diversity. As discussed in Chapter 5, the existence of multiple group identities (diversity and multiculturalism) is an important feature of Canadian democracy. In *The Civic Culture*, American political scientists Gabriel Almond and Sidney Verba contend that democratic government is sustained by cultural attitudes.[10] According to this *political culture* approach, determining a society's degree of democracy involves examining the population's attitudes and beliefs. This, rather than the existence of apparently democratic political institutions, is argued to be the true test of democracy and the key to sustaining it.

The civic culture thesis has recently enjoyed a renaissance through work on what is called **social capital**: norms of interpersonal trust, a sense of civic duty, and a belief that one's involvement in politics and in the life of the community matters. Where levels of social trust are low, public authorities must invest more in institutions and policies that rely on repression and force to maintain social order. Social capital is argued to have an economic value, but the main argument for policies, practices, and institutions that promote social capital is that citizens will be happier and have greater control over their own lives.

Not everyone agrees. Socialists argue that a society in which the poor are excluded from full participation in political life because they are preoccupied with the problem of feeding and housing themselves decently cannot be described as democratic. The formal equality of citizens that democratic government confers and even most people's endorsement of democratic values do not alter the fact that social inequalities produce inequalities in political power. Some critics go even further in dismissing the democratic claims of capitalist societies. They argue that inequality results simply from a very small proportion of the population—the capitalist class—controlling the vast majority of the means of economic production and distribution. This inequality in property ownership, Marxists have long argued, far outweighs the

social capital
norms of interpersonal trust, a sense of civic duty, and a belief that one's involvement in politics and in the life of the community matters

importance of "one person–one vote" and competitive elections in determining the real political influence of different classes in society.

Inequalities such as those between bosses and workers, parents and children, men and women, and one ethnic or language community over another, it is often claimed, undermine the democratic character of societies whose formal political institutions are based on the equality of citizens. Indeed, if we use any of the all-inclusive definitions of politics examined earlier in this chapter, it is impossible to resist the logic of this argument. Inequalities confront us wherever we turn, and true democracy seems elusive. Even if we define politics more narrowly to include only those activities that focus on the state, it is obvious that even in the most egalitarian societies a small proportion of citizens dominates public life. Most of us participate in politics in short bursts of attention, particularly around election time. Is it reasonable to speak of democratic government when the levers of state power are in the hands of an elite?

Direct Democracy and Representative Democracy

The short answer to the question above is, "It depends on what we expect from democracy." If we expect that all citizens should have the opportunity to participate in the law-making process, we are bound to be disappointed. With some historical exceptions like the Greek polis and the township democracies of seventeenth- and eighteenth-century America, examples of **direct democracy**—government of the citizens by the citizens—are scarce. Direct democracy survives in some isolated pockets such as the couple of Swiss cantons where the *Landsgemeinde*—citizens gathering outdoors each spring to vote on important public questions—still exists. Modern technology, however, creates the possibility of direct democracy from people's living rooms in all advanced industrial societies. Television programs such as *Canadian Idol* or *So You Think You Can Dance Canada* show us how participatory democracy could work. There is no physical or technological reason why making popular choices by pressing telephone keys or clicking your computer's mouse could not be adapted to political decision making. There may, however, be other reasons for rejecting what modern technology makes possible.

direct democracy government of the citizens by the citizens

Perhaps the most commonly advanced reason for skepticism about direct democracy via the Internet and public opinion polls is that many citizens are poorly informed about important public issues. Does it make sense to ask citizens about a particular government policy when the majority may be grossly misinformed or know little about it?

Thomas Jefferson provided a famous answer to this question: "Every government degenerates when trusted to the rulers of the people alone. The people themselves therefore are [democracy's] only safe depositories."[11] Members of the public, Jefferson acknowledged, are often poorly informed or wrong in their opinions on public matters. However, Jefferson believed the solution lay not in excluding the public from determining public affairs but by creating an informed citizenry through the press and public education.

We often hear that the information explosion generated by satellite communication, television, social media, and the Internet has made us the best-informed generation of all time. But as Neil Postman observes, this conceit fails to address why most people are unable to explain even the most basic elements of issues. This ignorance does not prevent pollsters from asking people for their opinion on matters that they may barely understand and clearly renders poll results that are meaningless but send signals to politicians looking for waves to ride. Postman blames modern education, and especially the television media, for this ignorance:

> What is happening here is that television is altering the meaning of "being informed" by creating a species of information that might properly be called *disinformation*. . . . Disinformation does not mean false information. It means misleading information—misplaced, irrelevant, fragmented or superficial information—information that creates the illusion of knowing something but which in fact leads one away from knowing. . . . [W]hen news is packaged as entertainment, that is the inevitable result.[12]

We live in an age of information and yet the pillars that Jefferson counted on to support democratic government have rotted, according to Postman.

All modern democracies are **representative democracies**, where government is carried out by elected legislatures that represent the people. Citizens delegate law-making authority to their representatives, holding them responsible for their actions through periodic elections. Representative democracies sometimes include decision-making processes that provide opportunities for greater and more frequent citizen participation. Examples of democratic institutions that allow for citizen participation in public affairs include **plebiscites** and **referendums** (direct votes of citizens on important public questions), frequent elections, electing judges and administrative officials, and formal procedures for removing elected officials before the end of their term (through voter petitions and "recall" elections).

The appearance of increased participation may be deceiving. In countries like the United States and Switzerland, where referendums are a normal part of the political process, voter turnout is usually very low. Partly because of this, and partly because vested interests are quick to spend money on advertising and mobilizing their supporters, critics charge that referendums may produce outcomes that are far from democratic.[13]

Respect for rights and freedoms is generally considered a distinguishing feature of democratic government. Which rights and freedoms warrant protection and in what circumstances they may legitimately be limited by government are matters of dispute. Many argue that government that levies heavy taxes on citizens is undemocratic because individual choice is reduced when government decides how a large share of people's income will be spent. Others argue that taxation actually promotes freedom by giving disadvantaged groups opportunities that they would not have in a "free" market. Even a value as central to democracy as freedom of speech is sometimes argued to have undemocratic side effects. For example, some believe

representative democracy government carried out by an elected legislature that represents the people

plebiscite or **referendum** direct vote of citizens on an important public question

that any person or organization should have the right to spend money on advertising a particular political point of view during an election. Others argue that unlimited freedom of speech during elections campaigns is undemocratic when well-financed individuals or groups can pay for greater exposure.

Measuring Democracy

Most of us believe that rights and freedoms are important in democracies, but everyone except extreme libertarians believes that protecting these rights or freedoms can sometimes produce undemocratic outcomes. There is no surefire test that will tell us when democracy is promoted or impaired by protecting a right or freedom. Indeed, this quandary is one of the greatest sources of conflict in modern democracy, sometimes portrayed as a struggle between the competing pulls of *individualism* (the private realm) and *collectivism* (the public realm). A private realm that is beyond the legitimate reach of the state is a necessary part of a free society. Democracy cannot exist where the individual's right to be protected from the state is obliterated by the state's right to impose its will on the individual.

A country may claim to be a democracy through having free elections, a constitution that protects rights and freedoms, and a media system that permits the expression of diverse points of view and criticism of the powerful. But if pervasive corruption allows individuals and organizations to buy special treatment, nepotism is rampant, or the law applies to different people in different ways depending on who they are and who they know, a society's claim to be democratic is undermined. In a democracy, however, such behaviours are considered unlawful or at least unethical, depending on how egregiously they violate the rule of law.

So how democratic is Canada? According to Freedom House's World Democracy Audit in 2014, Canada is one of the most democratic countries in the world, but it ranked twenty-sixth behind some of the Scandinavian and Northern European democracies.[14] In ranking countries, Freedom House *operationalizes* the concept of democracy, defining it in measurable ways so that scores can be assigned to each country. As we see in Box 1.5, the criteria used in the Freedom House survey and ranking of the world's political systems combine measures of political rights, civil liberties, press freedom, public corruption, and the rule of law.

The **rule of law** may truly be said to be the foundation of democratic government, on which all else rests. "It means," said Eugene Forsey (1904–1991), one of Canada's foremost constitutionalists of the twentieth century, "that everyone is subject to the law; that no one, no matter how important or powerful, is above the law."[15] It means that no public official has the legitimate right to exercise any powers other than those assigned to his or her office by the law. And if someone in a position of public trust attempts to go beyond his or her legal authority, then it is up to the courts to check that abuse of power. An independent judiciary is, therefore, necessary to democratic governance.

rule of law
the idea that no public official has the legitimate right to exercise any powers other than those assigned to his or her office by the law

Inside Politics

BOX 1.5 | Measuring Freedom

Freedom House uses certain criteria in its "democracy index" to determine how well countries respect and protect political rights and civil liberties. Here are some of the criteria:

Political Rights Criteria

A. Electoral Process

- free and fair elections of heads of government and representatives
- fair electoral laws
- fair and transparent electoral framework
- open and intimidation-free discussion of issues

B. Political Pluralism and Participation

- the right to organize competing political parties as well as the opportunity for the opposition to gain power through elections

- people's choices free from external or internal domination or threats
- full rights and participation of minorities

C. Functioning of Government

- elected representatives and heads of government freely determine government policies
- decision making is transparent, free from pervasive corruption, and accountable to the electorate between elections

Civil Liberties Criteria

D. Freedom of Expression and Belief

- free and independent media and other forms of cultural expression
- free religious institutions and practice in public and in private

majoritarianism the belief that the opinion of the majority should almost always be considered in decision making

This is all fine theory, but inequalities and circumstances can sometimes undermine democratic values and processes. There is also an ever-present tension between majoritarianism— the belief that the opinion of the majority should almost always be considered in decision making— and competing visions of democracy. Let us consider the following questions: In a democracy, who gets heard and why? Is democracy a process or an outcome?

Who Gets Heard and Why?

As we see in Chapters 9, 10, and 11, access to political decision makers and the ability to influence public opinion are not equally distributed in society. If the president of the Royal Bank of Canada places a telephone call to the federal minister of Finance, this call will be returned. Your call or mine probably will not (try it!). Since the beginning of elections in Canadian politics, individuals and organizations have made financial contributions to political parties and their candidates. For

- academic freedom
- open, free private discussion in the social media and private communications

E. Associational and Organizational Rights

- freedom of assembly, demonstration, and open public discussion
- free non-governmental organizations
- free professional and private organizations
- free trade unions, peasant organizations, or equivalents, as well as collective bargaining
- open and free discussion in social media and private communications

F. Rule of Law

- independent judiciary
- rule of law in civilian and criminal matters
- police under direct civilian control

- protection from political terror including unjustified imprisonment, exile, or torture
- freedom from war and insurgencies
- equality of treatment

G. Personal Autonomy and Individual Rights

- Free choice of residence, employment, and education
- Property rights
- Private business rights
- Social freedoms including gender equality, marriage partnership, and family size
- Equal opportunity and freedom from economic exploitation

Source: Adapted from Freedom House, "Checklist of Questions," https://freedomhouse.org/report/freedom-world-2016/methodology.

the relatively modest sum of $1200 per year you can join the Liberal Party's Laurier Club. Among other things, this contribution buys an invitation to party functions across the country, where you might be able to speak directly with the party leader. Corporations are banned from buying memberships, but their CEOs, presidents, board members, and so on are not.

Between election campaigns, interest groups of all sorts are active in many ways, trying to influence the actions of government and the climate of public opinion. Much of the activity of lobbying costs money—often a lot of money. A public relations campaign that uses a well-connected lobbying firm, polling, and focus groups, followed by some combination of electronic and print media advertising, may cost hundreds of thousands of dollars or more. Although there is no guarantee that this money will produce favourable outcomes, there is a well-founded belief that such an investment may yield impressive returns.

But it is not as simple as spending money. The issues that get onto the **public agenda**—the matters identified by opinion leaders in the media and in government as warranting some

public agenda
the matters identified by opinion leaders in the media and in government as warranting some policy response

FREEDOM OF THE PRESS IS THE CORNERSTONE OF DEMOCRACY.

PRESS

In the lead-up to the 2011 spring federal election, Canadian prime minister Stephen Harper limited his daily encounters with the media to just five questions. Some speculated that he was minimizing the risk of making any public gaffes during the campaign, while others felt he was shunning reporters who held different social values than those of his Conservative government. What are the advantages and disadvantages of the press having unrestricted access to the country's top politicians?

policy response, even if that response is a decision not to act—are not determined by the spending of self-interested groups alone. The American journalist H.L. Mencken once said that the proper role of his profession was to "bring comfort to the afflicted and afflict the comfortable." Some in the media, in Canada and elsewhere, take Mencken's counsel to heart. In Canada, as in other capitalist democracies, there is a debate over whether the media—an important segment of the opinion-shaping class—do better at afflicting or at comforting the privileged and the powerful. But whether their reporting "afflicts the comfortable" or not, it is undeniable that the values and beliefs of those who shape public opinion—including teachers, journalists, and writers—influence the stories they tell and how they are told.

On one point, however, the evidence is clear: interests and points of view that are not those of the wealthy and the well-connected do find their way into the public conversation.

Is Democracy a Process or an Outcome?

Tocqueville warned about the tyranny of the majority: that the multitude might show little concern for the rights and interests of minorities and see little wrong in imposing the force of their superior numbers on people whose values and behaviour differ from those of the majority. Most people agree that majoritarianism needs to be tempered by protections for individual and group rights. That is why constitutions like Canada's include express guarantees of rights and freedoms.

But when the rights claims of a minority are upheld by the courts, despite unsympathetic or divided public opinion, and when elected officials are unwilling to legislate such protection, often some argue that this situation is undemocratic. What is undemocratic, these critics charge, is that unelected public officials—judges in this case—have usurped policy-making prerogatives that in a democracy should be exercised by the people's elected representatives. For example, when Ottawa and the provincial governments agreed to the Charter of Rights and Freedoms in 1981, its equality section (s. 15) did not include sexual orientation among the banned grounds for discrimination. This omission was deliberate. The case for including sexual orientation had been made during the hearings on the Charter, but had been almost unanimously rejected by representatives of the federal and provincial governments. Several years later, however, the Supreme Court of Canada decided that discrimination on the basis of sexual orientation was *analogous* to discrimination based on religion, race, or colour, which are prohibited by section 15 of the Charter.

Whether you agree or disagree with the Supreme Court's decision, the point is that cases like this raise contentious issues about what may or may not be democratic in Canadian society. Even if many support such decisions, should citizens consider it a problem when unelected officials such as judges make decisions that could significantly alter their society? Are there some issues that by their very nature or importance should be resolved only by those who have been elected to govern? Does democracy involve a particular process, and if so, what is that process? Or is democracy more about producing socially desirable outcomes regardless of whether elected or appointed officials make the decisions?

Defining Democracy

On reflection, most of us would probably agree that democracy involves both a legitimizing process for resolving rival claims and a means of producing socially desirable outcomes, whether through appointed officials or elected representatives. Throughout this book we argue that formal institutions are only part of what makes a society's politics democratic or not. The activities of the media, interest groups, and political parties are at least as crucial to the quality of democracy. Likewise, the socio-economic and ideological backgrounds of democratic government have important effects on how the formal and informal aspects of the political system operate.

democracy
a political system based on the formal political equality of all citizens, in which there is a realistic possibility that voters can replace the government, and in which certain basic rights and freedoms are protected

Listen to the "Nouveau Politics" podcast on parties, branding, and political ideology at www.oupcanada.com/BrooksConcise2e.

Defining the term "democracy" is a perilous task. Democracy cannot be reduced to either a simple constitutional formula or some particular vision of social equality. Someone is bound to disagree either with what is included in the definition or with what has been left out. In recognition of these hazards, we define **democracy** as a political system based on the formal political equality of all citizens, in which there is a realistic possibility that voters can replace the government, and in which certain basic rights and freedoms are protected.

In the chapters that follow, we will discuss some of the prominent features of Canadian democracy, including how our democratic system of governance manages to overcome the political fault lines that are part of the Canadian historical and social fabric. These include the rift between French- and English-speaking Canada, the relationships with the United States and the United Kingdom, regionalism, and a host of other fault lines, such as class conflict, religious conflict, the rural–urban split, ethnicity, age, Aboriginal rights, and gender.

Summary

This chapter had two purposes: first, to introduce concepts that are essential to the study of politics in general, including the concepts of politics, power, the state, government, authority, legitimacy, and democracy; and second, to lay the groundwork for the study of Canadian political life and democracy in particular. We saw that politics arises from the fact of scarcity and is the activity by which rival claims are settled. Not surprisingly, the two constant features of politics are power—the ability to influence what happens—and conflict—the settling of rival claims over values and over resources. In essence, when conducted for the greater good, politics keeps life civilized.

Throughout Canadian history, Canadians have devised particular institutions and processes to settle rival claims. Whether these institutions and processes can properly be called democratic and whether they work are some of the things political scientists seek to understand.

We also defined and discussed the role of the state and the difference between the terms "state" and "government," particularly in the context of democracies. Theoretical approaches to explaining the state were discussed: pluralism, class analysis, feminism, and postmodernism. Specific characteristics that set democracy apart from other forms of government were examined, as well as some of the issues typically debated in democratic societies, and in particular, Canadian society. We differentiated between direct democracy and representative democracy. And, finally, for the purposes of this book, "democracy" was defined.

Review Exercises

1. Which country is more democratic, Canada or the United States? Canada or Sweden? What criteria have you used in arriving at your conclusions, and how would you set about measuring whether a society has more or fewer of the attributes that you

associate with democracy? In order to guide your thinking about how the concept of democracy can be operationalized, go to the Freedom House website: www .freedomhouse.org. Does Freedom House's ranking of Canada seem reasonable to you?

2. This chapter introduced some concepts and issues relevant to Canadian political life. An easy way to tell what political issues are current in Canada is to look at the political cartoons included in Canadian print journalism. Find a Canadian political cartoon that relates to a political issue with which you are familiar. One of the best sources is www.artizans.com. Click on "Political Cartoons—CDN." What message do you think each cartoonist is trying to communicate? Do you think the cartoonist's treatment of the subject is fair or biased? In what ways and why?

Up for Debate

1. Is democracy possible when only 68.3 per cent of eligible voters cast ballots, as in the 2015 Canadian federal election? Why or why not?
2. Do you agree or disagree that elected representatives should always follow the will of the majority?
3. Do you agree or disagree that politicians should always keep their promises?
4. Should officials such as judges and Crown prosecutors be elected or appointed?

Starting Points for Research

Crick, Bernard. *Democracy: A Very Short Introduction.* New York: Oxford, 2002.

MacLean, George, and Duncan Wood. *Politics: An Introduction*, 2nd edn. Toronto: Oxford University Press, 2014

Vickers, Jill. *Reinventing Political Science: A Feminist Approach.* Halifax: Fernwood, 1997.

World Values Survey. www.worldvaluessurvey.org.

CBC Archives and TVO's *The Agenda*

Visit the companion website for *Canadian Democracy: A Concise Introduction* to follow links to audio and video footage related to the main themes of the chapter: www.oupcanada.com/BrooksConcise2e.

Relevant Websites

Visit the companion website for *Canadian Democracy: A Concise Introduction* to browse a collection of websites featuring material related to the key themes of the chapter (an excellent starting point for research): www.oupcanada.com/BrooksConcise2e.

PART I
The Societal Context of Politics

Every society has issues and divisions, or socio-political fault lines, and studying these fault lines help us understand a society's politics and government. Canadian society and its democratic system of government have had to manage a broad range of fault lines including ideologies, the French–English split, regionalism, economic class, ethnicity, and age and gender differences, as well as external influences from other countries and from globalization. For example, the fact that English and French are spoken by large portions of the population and that the French-speaking population is concentrated largely in one region, with a history that pre-dates the anglophone majority in Canada, continues to influence the politics of the country. Another example is the relatively recent arrival of millions of immigrants from countries outside of Europe, which has changed Canadian demography and is having a significant impact on Canadian politics. Yet another influence on Canadian politics and government is the country's long-standing relationship to the United States, a relationship that involves a complex web of interconnections through trade, investment, population, culture, and foreign policy. In short, the societal context within which political life unfolds is crucial to understanding both the nature of any country's politics and the distribution of power and influence.

Some argue, however, that the actions of the state and their impacts on society are at least as important as, if not more so than, the effects of societal forces on the policies and institutions of government. State actors, including key political leaders and bureaucrats, often have a powerful influence on what happens in politics, shaping the contours of the political conversation, determining which interests and voices are listened to, and thus steering the outcomes that ensue. But only rarely are elected and appointed officials able to ignore the pressure of values, ideas, and interests from the society around them. These values, ideas, and interests, including a society's significant *political identities*, its economic structure, and the major fault lines that cut across its landscape, provide the broader context within which political behaviour and policy making take place. These societal factors are the subject of part I of the book.

← Thousands celebrate Canada Day near Canada Place in Vancouver. Canadian politics is embedded in specific values, ideologies, and institutions; only rarely are elected and appointed officials able to ignore the societal context of politics.
Source: George Rose/Getty Images.

2 Political Culture

Ideas and the values they stem from constitute an important element of political life. Values, which are one's personal beliefs about what is good or bad, right or wrong, important or trivial, valuable or worthless, and so on, are at the root of the ideas citizens have about their society and their expectations of their system of government. This chapter surveys some key issues pertaining to the role of values and ideas in Canadian politics, and discusses the main political ideas and political culture of Canadians. After reading this chapter, you should be able to

1. explain the relationship among the values, ideologies, and institutions that govern Canadian society
2. differentiate among the main ideologies in Canadian politics by using specific models and concepts
3. define and explain the role political culture plays in Canadian democracy

↑ Prime Minister Justin Trudeau participates in a traditional sunrise ceremony on National Aboriginal Day in Gatineau, Quebec. Part of Canada's unique political culture is the relationship between the federal government and the Aboriginal people who live within Canada.
Source: REUTERS/Chris Wattie.

4. apply theoretical models to explain the basis of Canadian political ideas and political institutions
5. outline the values, attitudes, and expectations of Canadians with respect to the ideas of community, freedom, equality, and the role of the state
6. compare the values, ideas, and expectations of Canadians with those of Americans

Canadian Values and Canadian Culture

There is no greater Canadian pastime than reflecting on what it means to be Canadian. Unlike the Chinese, the Russians, and the Americans, to name a few, Canadians have long been obsessed with the **values** and beliefs that make them distinctive. In fact, this perennial search for the cultural essence of the Canadian condition has most often been about explaining the ways in which the values and beliefs of Canadians are different from those of Americans.

Various answers about what Canadians value have been given over the years. Until the latter half of the twentieth century, these answers essentially boiled down to this: Canadians believed in a more orderly, less individualistic society than that of the United States. The Canadian state was expected to engage in activities that promote the welfare of society and the development of an independent Canada. The affective tie to Great Britain remained strong well into the middle of the century, and indeed many Canadians, particularly in English-speaking Canada, thought of themselves as British and of their country as more British than American in its values, institutions, and heritage.

This answer to the question of what it means to be a Canadian has seemed less plausible as Canada has become less British over the last couple of generations. Many still believe, however, that Canadian values continue to be less individualistic and less hostile to government than those of the United States. Such words as "tolerant," "compassionate," and "caring" are often used in comparisons between the two countries, always suggesting that Canadians have more of these qualities than Americans. As the bonds joining Canada to the United States economically and culturally have multiplied and deepened, the question of what it means to be a Canadian continues to be a sort of national obsession.

This is not true, however, in French-speaking Canada, whose centre of gravity is Quebec, where over 90 per cent of Canadian francophones live. Insulated from American cultural influences by language and for much of their history by the strongly Catholic character of their society, French Canadians have been less likely to define themselves and their history with reference to the United States. They have long worried about assimilation and the anglicizing influences on their language and culture. But they have tended to see the challenge as coming chiefly from within Canada, with its English-speaking majority, rather than from the United

values
personal beliefs about what is good or bad, right or wrong, important or trivial, valuable or worthless, and so on

States. This perceived challenge has provided the basis for the rise of, first, French-Canadian nationalism and, more recently, of Quebec nationalism. Lately, as non-traditional sources of immigration have become increasingly important in Quebec, the question of what it means to be Québécois has received greater attention. But in answering it, few French-speaking Canadians would think of using as a starting point the United States and what are believed to be American values and beliefs.

Values, Ideologies, and Institutions

Ideas assume various forms in political life. When they take the form of a set of interrelated values and beliefs about how society is organized and how it ought to function—an interpretative map for understanding the world—they constitute an **ideology**. An ideology spills beyond the boundaries of politics to embrace beliefs and judgments about other social relationships, including economic ones. This holistic character of ideologies distinguishes them from more limited political value systems. People tend not to be aware of their own ideological leanings, and might be puzzled or even startled at being labelled a "conservative," "liberal," or "socialist." However, this does not mean that ideology is irrelevant to their political beliefs and actions. When the politics of a society is described as "pragmatic" and "non-ideological," these terms may simply indicate that a particular ideology dominates to such a degree that it has become the conventional wisdom. Someone who regularly and consciously thinks about political matters and other social relationships in ideological terms is an ideologue: a person who is consciously committed to a particular interpretive map of society. Most people are not ideological in this sense of the word.

If ideology is the currency of the political activist, political culture is the medium of the general population. A **political culture** consists of the characteristic values, beliefs, and behaviours of a society's members in regard to politics. The importance that people place on such values as personal freedom, equality, social order, and national prestige is one aspect of political culture. Citizens' expectations of their government, their participation in public life, patterns of voter turnout, party activism, social movement activities, and other politically relevant forms of behaviour are another. So is the pattern of knowledge about political symbols, institutions, actors, and issues. Obviously, people do not hold identical views on these matters, nor does their participation in politics conform to a single template. It is reasonable, nevertheless, to speak of a society, even one with a number of significant political fault lines, as having certain core values or a belief system that is shared by most of its members.

In Canada, research on political culture has focused primarily on the differences between the politically relevant values, attitudes, and beliefs of French-speaking and English-speaking Canadians, and on the question of whether English-speaking Canada is characterized by regional political cultures. To determine whether these differences are significant, political scientists have attempted to measure such things as levels of political knowledge and participation, feelings of **political efficacy** (people's sense of whether their

ideology a set of interrelated values and beliefs about how society is organized and how it ought to function

political culture the characteristic values, beliefs, and behaviours of a society's members in regard to politics

political efficacy people's sense of whether their participation in politics matters

alienation apathy, estrangement from the political system, or the belief that politics is systematically biased against one's interests and values

participation in politics matters) and **alienation** (variously defined as apathy, estrangement from the political system, or the belief that politics is systematically biased against one's interests and values), attitudes toward political authority and government, and the sense of belonging to a particular regional or linguistic community.

Another way in which ideas are relevant for politics is through individual *personality traits* and *attitudes* about things political. One of the most often repeated claims about Canadians—one that we examine later—is that they are more deferential and less likely to question and challenge authority than are Americans. Several questions used in studies of political culture, such as those dealing with political efficacy and trust in public officials, tap politically relevant dimensions of personality. Research on the political consequences of individual personality traits has often focused on the relationship between a person's general attitudes toward authority and non-conformity, as well as their political attitudes on issues like the protection of civil liberties and tolerance of minority rights. The main conclusion of this research is that personality traits show up in an individual's political ideas and actions.

While most people are not ideologues, they do have beliefs about how society is organized and ought to function. What is your vision of how society should be organized and function? Is this ideology similar to that of your parents? Why might your values and beliefs be different from theirs?

Left-Wing and Right-Wing Values, Ideas, and Ideologies

One popular way of categorizing political ideas is to describe them as being left wing, right wing, or centrist/moderate. **Right wing** and **left wing** are labels often used to classify the political ideas that lie behind an action, opinion, or statement. These labels are also used to group ideas or political parties that are in opposition to each other. **Left** refers to collectivist and social justice ideas and ideologies, and political parties that advocate social reform, whereas **right** refers to ideas and ideologies that advocate social order, protection of private property, economic freedom, and support for capitalism (see Figure 2.1). For example, newspaper editorials proposing tax cuts for the affluent or the elimination of public funding for abortions are often characterized as right wing. Alternatively, editorials advocating increasing the minimum wage, banning the use of replacement workers during a strike or lockout, or increasing spending on assistance for developing countries are likely to be described as left wing. Centrist or moderate positions, as these terms suggest, fall between the right and left wings of the political spectrum. They attempt to achieve some middle ground between the arguments and principles

right wing / left wing labels often used to classify the political ideas that lie behind an action, opinion, or statement

Left collectivist and social justice ideas and ideologies, and political parties that advocate social reform

Right ideas and ideologies that advocate social order, protection of private property, economic freedom, and support for capitalism

FIGURE 2.1 Left–Right Socio-Economic Spectrum

centre
the mainstream of a society's politics

of left and right. The **centre** is, virtually by definition, the mainstream of a society's politics, and those who occupy this location on the political spectrum are likely to view themselves as being non-ideological and pragmatic.

"Right" and "left" are shorthand labels for conflicting values and belief systems. These beliefs include basic notions about how society, the economy, and politics operate, as well as ideas about how these matters should be dealt with by government and by society. To be on the right in Anglo-American societies generally means that one subscribes to an *individualistic* belief system (see Figure 2.1). Such a person is likely to believe that their achievements in life are principally due to their own efforts—that the welfare of society is best promoted by allowing individuals to pursue their own interests, and that modern government is too expensive and intrusive. To be on the left, however, is to prefer a set of beliefs that may be described as *collectivist*. A leftist is likely to attribute greater weight to social and economic circumstances as determinants of one's opportunities and achievements. Those on the left have greater faith in the ability of government to intervene and promote the common good and have doubts about the economic efficiency and social fairness of free markets. Although those on the left may be critical of government actions or institutions, they reject the claim that government needs to be smaller and less influential. Smaller government, they argue, works to the advantage of the affluent and privileged at the expense of the disadvantaged.

In reality, the politics of left and right is more complicated than these simplified portraits suggest. Perhaps this is complicated by the fact that, in addition to socio-economic issues, there are also issues pertaining to how much freedom individuals should have and how much control (power) governments should have (see Figure 2.2). For example, lowering taxes, less government intervention in the economy, and increased property rights are considered right-wing stances on the economy. However, opinions on social issues such as opposition to abortion, same-sex marriage, and euthanasia are also generally viewed as right-wing positions, and many who subscribe to all the elements of right-wing politics may support these policies.

libertarianism
an ideology based on the belief that individuals should be allowed the largest possible margin of freedom in all realms of life, including moral choices

The left–right model has other pitfalls. The fact that members of the Tea Party movement in the United States, sometimes labelled **libertarians**, are in the same American Republican party as the social conservatives is not well explained by this theoretical model. Libertarians believe that individuals should be allowed the largest possible margin of freedom in all realms of life, including moral choices. Social conservatives, on the other hand, support more government control in, for example, banning abortion and same-sex marriage, support capital punishment and stiffer jail sentences, and reject forms of pluralism, which they believe corrode traditional values and social order. Their conservative roots are quite different from those of libertarianism, but their shared antipathy for aspects of the modern welfare state brings libertarians and social conservatives together on the right. The fissures in this alliance and the limitations of the right–left categorization of political ideas become apparent when the issue is personal morality (e.g., abortion, homosexuality, religious teachings in public schools).

Despite these limitations, the right–left spectrum taps a crucial and enduring truth of modern politics: the character of the good society and how best to achieve it. We have said that the underlying struggle is essentially one between collectivist and individualist visions of the good society. These visions differ in how they view the conditions that promote the

Political arguments are often described in simple terms as "left" or "right." While this may be easy to understand and to explain, politics is more complicated than that.

social good and in how much power is exercised by the state. This difference is illustrated in Figure 2.2, where we see that too much oppression can lead to totalitarian regimes, in which citizens may be asked to sacrifice a great deal, even their lives, for the sake of a social goal or social order, or the opposite situation, whereby too little state control can lead to anarchy.

The recent controversy in Canadian politics over Bill C-51—an anti-terrorism law passed in response to two terrorist attacks against Canadian military personnel in 2014—is an example

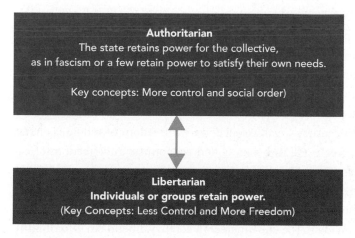

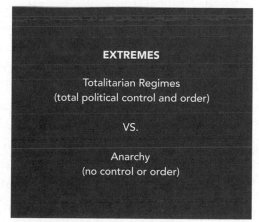

FIGURE 2.2 Political Power Spectrum

This model shows us that ideologies are also about how much political power the state should have in maintaining order for the collective and how much freedom the individual should retain.

Content

of the ongoing debate over the balance between the state having enough power to keep its citizens safe and limiting the state's encroachment on civil liberties.

Ideologies in Canadian Democracy

Socialism, liberalism, and conservatism are the trio of ideologies that have greatly influenced the politics of Western societies since the American and French Revolutions. The importance of these ideologies in defining the contours of political life is seen in major and minor political parties in many Western democracies, including Canada, continuing to use the names "liberal," "conservative," and "socialist."

Liberalism is based on the belief that the state must protect individual liberty, personal choice, and the right to private property. Concepts usually associated with liberalism include inalienable rights, individualism, constitutional protection for rights and freedoms, protection of private property, and liberal democracy.

Conservatism is an ideology based on the belief that traditions and social order are important and that gradual change is best. Concepts usually associated with conservatism include social stability, family values, continuity, right-wing politics, and maintaining social and religious institutions.

Socialism is an ideology based on the collective or state ownership of the means of production and the belief in the state's ability to provide social justice, redistribute wealth, and fix social problems. Concepts usually associated with socialism include equality, redistribution of wealth, left-wing politics, complete or partial ownership of the means of production, social programs, and bigger government.

In Canada, the two parties that have dominated national politics for most of the country's history are the Liberal Party and the Conservative Party. They have their roots in the ideological divisions of the nineteenth century. Over time, however, the labels have lost much, if not all, of their informative value. Today, the ideological distance between a Liberal and a Conservative seems small. Both parties and their supporters share in the dominant liberal tradition that pervaded Canada and the United States. It may be said of all Canadian political parties, including the New Democratic Party (NDP), the Bloc Québécois, and the Green Party, that they traditionally believed in similar core liberal values. At the heart of this tradition was the primacy of individual freedom. **Classical liberalism**—liberalism as it was understood until the middle of the nineteenth century—was associated with freedom of religious choice and practice, free enterprise and free trade in business and economics, and freedom of expression and association in politics. These liberal values constituted a sort of national ethos in the United States, where they were enshrined in the Declaration of Independence during the American Revolution (1776) and in the Bill of Rights (1791). In the colonies of British North America, which would become Canada in the late nineteenth century, liberalism's dominance was somewhat more tentative. This was due to the streak of conservatism kept alive by some elites in colonial society, notably officials of the Catholic Church and the Church of England, and the British colonial authorities.

liberalism
an ideology based on the belief that the state must protect individual liberty, personal choice, and the right to private property

conservatism
an ideology based on the belief that traditions and social order are important and that gradual change is best

socialism
an ideology based on the collective or state ownership of the means of production and the belief in the state's ability to provide social justice, redistribute wealth, and fix social problems

classical liberalism
liberalism as it was understood until the middle of the nineteenth century, associated with freedom of religious choice and practice, free enterprise and free trade in business and economics, and freedom of expression and association in politics

Classical conservatism was an ideology rooted in the ideas of the Irish statesman and political philosopher Edmund Burke, whose writings were a reaction to the disorder caused by the French and American Revolutions; he emphasized the importance of tradition and social order. Classical conservatism accepted human inequality—social, political, and economic—as part of the natural order of things. Conservatives believed in the importance of continuity with the past and the preservation of law and order. They were wary of innovation and opposed to such basic liberal reforms as equal political rights for all men (even liberals did not come around to the idea of equal political rights for women until the twentieth century). Unlike liberals, who located the source of all just rule in the people, conservatives maintained that God and tradition were the true founts of political authority. Consequently, they supported an established Church and were strong defenders of the Crown's traditional prerogatives against the rival claims of elected legislatures.

Although no party having the label "socialist" has ever achieved the status of even a minor important national party in either Canada or the United States, socialist ideology has been influential in various ways. **Classical socialism** was based on the principle of equality of condition and radical egalitarianism that distinguished socialist doctrine from liberalism's advocacy of equality of opportunity. Socialists supported a vastly greater role for the state in directing the economy, providing better working conditions and greater rights for workers vis-à-vis their employers, and instituting reforms like public health care, unemployment insurance, income assistance for the indigent, public pensions, and universal access to public education, which became the hallmarks of the twentieth-century welfare state.

The usefulness of these three "isms" as benchmarks for reading the political map is disappearing (see Table 2.1), for two main reasons. First, the labels of all three classical ideologies, and especially of liberalism and conservatism, mean something quite different today from what they meant 100–200 years ago. For example, contemporary liberalism does not place individual freedom above all else. Instead, modern liberals are distinguished by their belief that governments can and should act to alleviate hardships experienced by the poor and the oppressed. They are more likely to worry about minority group rights than individual freedoms, in the sense that they see protecting disadvantaged minorities as a necessary step in achieving real freedom for the members of these groups. Modern liberalism has also become associated with support for multiculturalism and openness toward non-traditional lifestyles and social institutions.

The doctrine of classical conservatism has disappeared from contemporary democracies, leaving what has been called the conservative outlook or "conservative mind."[1] Modern conservatives tend to embrace the economic beliefs that once were characteristic of liberals. Like classical liberals, they defend the principle of equality of opportunity and are more likely to place the protection of personal freedoms before the advancement of minority rights. As in earlier times, conservatism is generally viewed as the ideology of the privileged in society. It is worth noting, however, that conservative politicians and political parties receive much of their support from middle-class voters whose hands are far from the levers of economic power and social influence.

classical conservatism an ideology based on the importance of tradition and social order and which accepted human inequality—social, political, and economic—as part of the natural order of things

classical socialism an ideology based on the principle of equality of condition and radical egalitarianism

TABLE 2.1 Kay Lawson's Summary of Ideologies

General Issues	Communism and Some Forms of Socialism	Social Democrats/ Feminism	Liberalism	Conservatism	Fascism
1. Means of change	Revolution	Persuasion and democratic elections			Coup/coercion
2. Human nature	Unselfish and social	Selfish and social			Selfish and unsocial
3. Role of the state	Economic redistribution	Protect individual liberty			Control
4. Values	Economic equality	Freedom and political equality			Social order
5. Positions	Far left	Left	Centre	Right	Far right

This table shows how the values of most present-day ideologies are very similar.

Source: Adapted from Kay Lawson, *The Human Polity: A Comparative Introduction to Political Science* (New York: Wadsworth, 2002).

Listen to the "To Leap or Not to Leap? The 2016 NDP Convention" podcast at www.oup.com// BrooksConcise2e.

Of the three classical ideologies, the meaning of "socialism" has changed the least. There is today, however, much less confidence among socialists that state ownership of the means of economic production and distribution is desirable. Modern socialists, or *social democrats* as they often call themselves, temper their advocacy of an egalitarian society with an acceptance of capitalism and the inequalities that inevitably are generated by free-market economies. Defending the rights of society's least-well-off elements is today carried out largely under the banner of other "isms" including feminism, multiculturalism, and environmentalism. These collectivist–egalitarian belief systems have more impact on Canadian and American politics than does socialism. Even the *Leap Manifesto*, a 2015 document intended to redirect the NDP from its shift toward the political centre, calls "… for a Canada based on caring for the Earth and one another," suggesting that the NDP, Canada's socialist party is concerned about more "isms" than socialism.[2] Some might argue that NDP leader Thomas Mulcair was voted out in a party leadership review in 2016 because he was not "feminist," "multiculturalist," "environmentalist," and "socialist" enough.

A second reason why the traditional trio of "isms" is no longer a reliable guide to politics has to do with the character of political divisions in modern society. The aristocracy of land and title and the deferential social norms that nurtured classical conservatism belong to the past.

Some commentators dismiss the traditional "isms" and the left–centre–right ideological grid as outmoded ways of thinking about politics. It is a mistake, however, to underestimate the continuing importance of ideology in politics. Although the traditional ideologies now must jostle with feminism, environmentalism, multiculturalism, and other "isms" on a more crowded playing field, and despite the changes in the meanings of the classical ideological labels, they continue to be useful, but not infallible, guides to understanding political ideas.

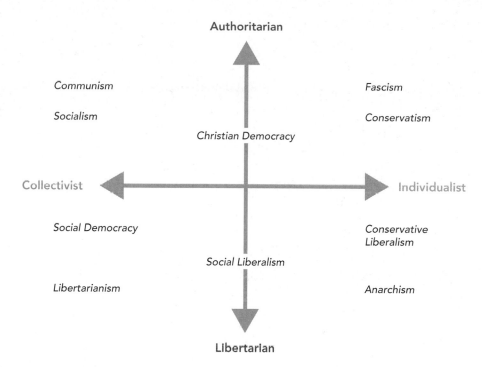

FIGURE 2.3 The Political Compass

When Figures 2.1 and 2.2 are combined as they are here, we get a fairly sophisticated model for categorizing ideologies and political parties according to their values, ideas, and policies.

Canadian Spotlight

BOX 2.1   Canadian Political Parties, 2015

Politicalcompass.org interpreted the ideological position of Canadian political parties during the 2015 general election as follows:

Seldom loved, Prime Minister Stephen Harper is either respected or loathed. Certainly during the last nine years, this most polarising of Canadian prime ministers has shifted Canada's economics to a harsher strain of neoliberalism, and adopted the draconian C-51 "security" bill. The Harper administration has also moved a considerable distance towards making foreign policy a tool of trade policy. Nowhere is this more in evidence than in the country's uncharacteristic assertiveness abroad on behalf of Canadian mining interests. The question is to what extent Harper has taken the population with him.

The Liberals' Justin Trudeau speaks for a gentler Canada, though hugging the so-called centre is increasingly precarious as the political fulcrum shifts relentlessly

Continued

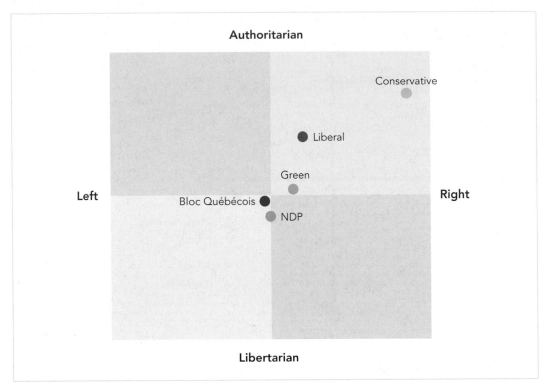

FIGURE 2.4 Ideological Positions of Canadian Political Parties in 2015

Source: www.politicalcompass.org

rightward. During the era of his father's Liberal administration, the party was more genuinely centrist. In those days, the Conservatives occupied a similar space on The Political Compass to where today's Liberals have positioned themselves. While the non-Conservative public might recall Liberal plans for National Child Care and other provisions ditched by the Conservatives, Justin Trudeau nevertheless hardly created any clear blue water between his party and the Conservatives by allowing the passage of the deeply unpopular C-51 bill—not to mention his support for the sellout of strategic energy resources to China, the Keystone XL pipeline and other Conservative initiatives.

Anti-Conservative voters would seem to hold less enthusiasm for Conservative Lite, which might help explain the swell in support for Thomas Mulcair's traditionally left-leaning NDP. But Mulcair, too, has setup his economic tent in centreground, in keeping with the directions of most other social democratic parties today. Indeed, the NDP's tax policy is now generally more conservative than that of the Liberals. The Liberals' recent promise to run an anti-austerity deficit is in surprising contrast to the NDP's neoliberal commitment to balance the budget. While the Greens are considerably more conservative than their sister parties just about everywhere else, they have in Elizabeth May an articulate and persuasive leader. The Greens would probably work well in an NDP coalition that might, in all likelihood, require Liberal participation.

Source: "Canada 2015 Election," https://www.politicalcompass.org/canada2015.

Explaining Canadian Ideas, Political Culture, and Institutions

Explanations of Canadians' political ideas, and of the institutions that embody them, can be grouped into three main approaches: the *fragment theory* approach, the role of *formative events* approach, and the *economic or class analysis* approach. Each of these perspectives stresses a different set of causes and forces in the origins and shaping of Canadians' political ideas and institutions.

The Fragment Theory Approach: European Parents and Cultural Genes

According to the fragment theory approach, Canada, along with other New World soci-eties, was founded by immigrants from Europe. Aboriginal communities already existed, of course, but the sort of society that developed in Canada had its roots and inspiration in the values and practices of European civilization. New World societies were "fragments" of the European societies that gave birth to them. They were fragment societies because they represented only a part of the socio-economic and cultural spectrum of the European soci-ety from which they originated, and also because their creation coincided with particular ideological epochs.

According to this approach, the timing of settlement is crucial. Along with their material possessions, immigrants brought their *cultural baggage*: values, beliefs, and practices acquired in Europe and transplanted into the New World.

Canada has been characterized as a two-fragment society. French Canada was founded by immigrants from France who brought with them their Catholicism and *feudal* ideas about social and political relations. Feudal society is characterized by fairly rigid social classes con-nected by a web of traditional mutual rights and duties, and by the exclusion of most people from the full right to participate in politics. According to French-Canadian historian Fer-nand Ouellet, this was the ideological and social condition of New France when the colony was conquered by British forces in 1759.[3] Cut off from the social and political developments unleashed by the French Revolution in 1789, when emigration from France virtually dried up, French Canada's ideological development was shaped by its origins as a feudal fragment of pre-revolutionary France. Institutions, chiefly the Catholic Church, the dominant social institution in French Canada until well into the twentieth century, maintained this pre-lib-eral inheritance.

The "cultural genes" of English Canada are very different. English Canada was origin-ally populated by immigrants from the United States. These were the so-called "Loyalists" who found themselves on the losing side of the American War of Independence (1776). They migrated north to British colonies that were overwhelmingly French speaking. Al-though there is some debate about their "cultural baggage," the general view seems to be that

© Simon Fraser University/John Larter

Despite the victory of the "No" side in the 1995 Quebec sovereignty referendum, the ideological differences between French and English Canada can be traced back to the eighteenth century. Do you think it is possible for descendants of different societies to build a nation together based on a single vision?

Loyalists held predominantly eighteenth-century liberal political values and beliefs centred on individual freedom in politics, religion, and economic relations. A crucial political tenet of this liberalism was the idea that government was based on the consent of the people. So why did the Loyalists leave the United States, a society whose political independence was founded on liberal beliefs?

The defenders of fragment theory offer different answers. Some argue that the liberalism of the Loyalists was diluted by conservative or **Tory** political beliefs: deference toward established authority and institutions, acceptance of inequality between classes as the natural condition of society, and a greater stress on preserving social order than on protecting individual freedoms.[4] Others reject the view that Tory values were ever a legitimate part of English Canada's political culture, arguing that this belief system had no roots in the pre-revolutionary Thirteen Colonies and therefore could not have been exported to English Canada through the Loyalist migration.[5] The Loyalists were "anti-American Yankees" who rejected American independence because of their loyalty to the British Empire and to the monarchy, and their dislike of republican government (or, as they were more likely to put it, "mob rule"). Their support for liberal ideas was shown by the fact that they immediately clamoured for elected assemblies and the political rights they had been used to in America. Bell and Tepperman argue that

> "The typical Canadian," an Englishman observed a hundred years ago, "tells you that he is not, but he is a Yankee—a Yankee in the sense in which we use the term at home, as synonymous with everything that smacks of democracy." The Loyalist in Canada is thereafter always a paradox, an "anti-American Yankee." Only one path leads out of his dilemma: creating a myth that helps him survive. In this myth, he insists that he is British.[6]

The debate over how important non-liberal values were among the Loyalists is not merely academic. Contemporary analyses of English Canada as a more deferential and conservative society than the United States often trace this alleged difference back to the original ideological mixtures of the two societies. A second reason why the debate matters involves the explanation for Canadian socialism. Some who contend that conservative values were an important and legitimate component of English Canada's original cultural inheritance go on to argue that socialism emerged in Canada first because liberalism failed to achieve the status of an unchallenged national creed (as it did in the United States), and second because social class was not a foreign concept in English Canada.[7] According to this view, conservatism and socialism are two varieties of collectivism.

Of course, not everyone agrees with the fragment theory approach. Most importantly, it ignores the cultural influence of Canada's Indigenous populations. Contemporary Canadian philosopher and writer John Ralston Saul suggests that Canadian society has been more successful than others at integrating a multitude of cultures due to the influence of Aboriginal culture. According to Ralston Saul, Canada is a métis civilization deeply influenced by Aboriginal culture in the early years of immigration from Europe.

Tory a person who believes in deference toward established authority and institutions, acceptance of inequality between classes as the natural condition of society, and a greater stress on preserving social order than on protecting individual freedoms

The Formative Events Approach: Counter-Revolution and the Conquest

Societies, like human beings, are marked by certain major events at critical periods in their development. These events are "formative" in the sense that they influence a society to evolve along particular lines. In politics, these formative events are associated both with ideas and with institutions. For example, the American Revolution was fought in the name of liberal values and was followed by the adoption of a constitution and government structures that enshrined a preference for dispersed political power, a weak executive, and guarantees for individual rights. The institutions embodied eighteenth-century liberal values of individual freedom and limited government that shaped the subsequent pattern of American politics.

Formative events theorist and American sociologist Seymour Martin Lipset argues that the political development of the United States has been shaped by its *revolutionary origins*, while that of English Canada has been shaped by its *counter-revolutionary origins*. Lipset writes,

> Americans do not know but Canadians cannot forget that two nations, not one, came out of the American Revolution. The United States is the country of the revolution, Canada of the counterrevolution. These very different formative events set indelible marks on the two nations. One celebrates the overthrow of an oppressive state, the triumph of the people, a successful effort to create a type of government never seen before. The other commemorates a defeat and a long struggle to preserve a historical source of legitimacy: government's deriving its title-to-rule from a monarchy linked to church establishment. Government power is feared in the south; uninhibited popular sovereignty has been a concern in the north.[8]

The Loyalists thus were the founders of an English-speaking society that originated in its rejection of the American republic. This rejection would be repeated several times: in the War of 1812; in the defeat of the American-style democratic reforms advocated by the losers in the 1837–8 rebellions in Lower and Upper Canada; and in the 1867 decision to establish a new country with a system of government similar to that of Great Britain. The political history of Canada, including many of its major economic and cultural policies, reads largely as a series of refusals in the face of Americanizing pressures.

Is rejection of American political values and institutions proof of the greater strength of conservative values in English Canada? Some who agree with Lipset do not agree that counter-revolutionary gestures signify *ideological conservatism*. Bell and Tepperman argue that the Loyalists were not anti-government, and that Canadians ever since appear to have been more willing to use the state for social, economic, and cultural purposes than were their American neighbours. But, they claim, a fondness for government is not inconsistent with liberal values. It is only in the United States, where the revolution was about the tyranny of government, that liberalism acquired an anti-government character.[9]

What 1776 represents for English Canada's political development, the British Conquest of New France in 1759 represents for that of French Canada. The Conquest has always occupied a central place in French-Canadian nationalism, testifying to French Canadians' own awareness of its significance. The motto on Quebec licence plates, "Je me souviens" ("I remember"), is in fact a reference to the time before the Conquest, when French-speaking Canadians presumably were free from the oppression of Ottawa and English Canadians. Particularly under Parti Québécois governments in Quebec it has been common for the Conquest to be mentioned in official government documents on subjects ranging from language to the economy and constitutional reform.

History did not, of course, stop at the Conquest. The crushed 1837 rebellion in Lower Canada (Quebec) signalled the defeat of the politically liberal *patriotes* and consolidated the dominance of the conservative ideology in French Canada. This ideology would ultimately collapse by the end of the 1950s, finally brought down by the weight of the enormous social and economic transformations that the conservatives had ignored and even denied. Since then, conservative ideology has had little credibility in Quebec, but the memory of the Conquest continues to be a favourite starting point for Quebec nationalists. The protests generated in 2008 by plans (later cancelled) to re-enact the 1759 Battle of the Plains of Abraham, as part of Quebec's four-hundredth anniversary celebration, showed how raw this nerve remains.

The Class Analysis Approach: Economic Structure and Political Ideas

From a class analysis perspective, both fragment theory and the formative events explanation are "hopelessly idealistic."[10] This is because these two approaches suggest that political values and institutions are primarily based on ideas—the "cultural baggage" of fragment theory and the cultural mindset and symbols associated with the notion of formative events. An economic interpretation, by contrast, explains a culture and its institutions as the products of class relations. These class relations are rooted in the particular system of economic production and distribution—the *mode of production* as Marxists call it—that is found in a society at any point in time. Ideas and institutions change in response to transformations in the economic system and in the class relations associated with this system. The dominant ideas and political arrangements of a society are not, however, merely the shadows cast by economic phenomena. But what sets this explanation apart from the other two is the belief that culture and institutions are the embodiments of power relations whose sources lie in the economic system.

By whom, for whom, and how is political culture produced? And what are the effects? Those who approach political values and institutions from the angle of economically determined class relations argue that a society's dominant ideas are inevitably those of its most powerful class (those who control the system of economic production and distribution). The important means of forming and spreading ideas and information, such as the privately owned mass media, are controlled by the dominant class. Others, including the schools, mainstream religious organizations, and the state, accept and spread the values of this class for reasons more subtle than ownership. Chief among these reasons is their support for *social order* and their rejection of tendencies and ideas that fundamentally challenge the status quo. The predominant institutions and social values are not class neutral.

Richard Lautens/Getty Images

In fall 2011, the international Occupy movement, which had a significant presence in Halifax, Toronto, Calgary, and Vancouver, emerged to protest economic and social inequality. "We are the 99%" became the movement's slogan, referring to the concentration of wealth and power among 1 per cent of American income earners. One of the goals of the mass movement was to bring an end to the corrupting influence of money on politics. What examples can you think of that indicate your federal government is acting in the best interests of the public versus those of the corporate world?

Why would the members of subordinate classes embrace the values and beliefs of a self-interested dominant class? The class analysis perspective offers a two-part answer. First, those who belong to the non-dominant class—essentially most people—may be the victims of *false consciousness*. This concept, first used by Karl Marx, describes the inability of the subordinate classes to see where their real interests lie. In feudal societies, for example, deference to established authority and belief in a hereditary aristocracy's "natural right to rule" are ideas that uphold the privileges of the dominant class. In liberal societies, the widespread belief that hard work opens socio-economic opportunities is another example of an idea promoted to reinforce the dominance of a small wealthy minority who control the economy. We learn in school, in the media, and in other ways, that equality of opportunity is a characteristic feature of our society. Yet, abundant empirical evidence shows that significant barriers to socio-economic mobility exist, that poverty is often passed on from generation to generation, and that those at the top of the socio-economic pyramid constitute a largely self-perpetuating elite.

The second reason why members of subordinate classes accept the ideas of the dominant class as "common sense" is that to some extent these ideas conform to their personal experience. For instance, democratic claims about the fundamental equality of all persons have a false ring in societies where some people are denied a share of this equality because of ethnicity. However, claims about equality may be valid in a society in which citizens enjoy equal protection under the constitution, there is universal suffrage, and there are no second-class citizens. Or, consider the liberal belief, discussed earlier, that opportunities to acquire wealth and social standing are relatively open. While some people never escape the socio-economic circumstances they are born into, many do. The 2008 election of Barack Obama as president of the United States—the son of a Kenyan goatherd!—is evidence in mythic proportions. There is enough proof that hard work, intelligence, or both result in material success to make liberalism's claims credible. As Patricia Marchak observes, "the propagation of an ideology cannot occur in a vacuum of experience; there must be a fair amount of congruence between personal experience and ideological interpretation for the propaganda [dominant ideology] to be successful."[11] Where this congruence is either weak or totally absent, the dominant class must rely on force to uphold its rule.

This idea is important: a society's dominant values and beliefs must be compatible with the experience of most of its members; otherwise the ideas of the dominant class will be exposed as pure self-interest. It means that what some have called false consciousness cannot be totally false. Looking at Quebec and the ideological changes associated with its "Quiet Revolution" of the 1960s helps us understand this better.

As recently as the 1950s, the dominant ideology in French-speaking Quebec was conservativism. It was an ideology based on the concept of *la survivance* (survival): conserving French Canada's religious and linguistic heritage in the face of assimilationist pressures. While possessing the formal structures of political democracy, Quebec's political life was dominated by autocratic politicians, rampant patronage, and social institutions—notably the Roman Catholic Church and conservative newspapers—that encouraged submission to established authority.[12] Functions like education and social services that in virtually all industrial democracies were already under state control were still in the hands of the Church in Quebec. Even the province's francophone labour unions were predominantly "confessional"—linked to a Church whose ideas about industrial relations were shaped largely by its concern for preserving social harmony.

This conservatism, linked to the Church's social dominance and to a sharply limited role for the provincial state, was increasingly out of step with the industrial society that had been evolving in Quebec throughout the twentieth century. Those who advocated reforms that entailed a more interventionist role for the Quebec state, such as public control over education and social assistance, and saw Quebec as a secular industrial society found themselves in

la survivance conserving French Canada's religious and linguistic heritage in the face of assimilationist pressures

Listen to the "The Death of Quebec Separatism?" podcast at www. oup.com// BrooksConcise2e.

conflict with the spokespersons for the conservative ideology. By the 1950s, however, the typical Québécois was a city-dweller who worked in a factory, store, or office,[13] and a new middle class of university-educated francophone professionals was becoming larger.[14] This new middle class was the leading force behind the expansion of the state in the early to mid-1960s. Ultimately, the lack of congruence between the values of the conservative ideology and the personal experience of most Québécois brought about the collapse of the one dominant ideology. It was replaced by one in tune with the new and growing groups like the middle class and the francophone business community, which have dominated Quebec politics since the Quiet Revolution.

The Values, Ideas, and Attitudes of Canadians

What do Canadians believe about politics? Is it true that they value social order more, and individual freedom less, than do their American counterparts? Does French Canada, and more particularly French-speaking Quebec, constitute a "distinct society" in terms of its values and beliefs? Is it reasonable to talk about the political ideas of English-speaking Canadians, or are the regional differences in political culture too great to warrant such an approach?

In the following pages we will organize our analysis of political culture and public attitudes and expectations under four themes: community, freedom, equality, and expectations of the state. These tap crucial dimensions of political culture while allowing us to explore the differences and similarities between French- and English-speaking Canadians, between different regions, and between Canadians and Americans.

Canadian Political Community and Its Challenges

"Canadians," someone has said, "are the only people who regularly pull themselves up by the roots to see whether they are still growing." As this remark suggests, the obsessive and often insecure introspection of Canadians may be one of the chief characteristics of the Canadian identity in English Canada, at least. The search for a national identity unites successive generations of Canadians.

The American War of Independence, as explained earlier, was followed by the emigration of Loyalists from the United States to the British colonies that would become Canada. Founded by those who rejected the republican democracy to the south, English Canada would constantly compare itself to that society and seek to explain and justify its separate existence.

More recently these two historical strands of Canada's identity "crisis" have been joined by newer challenges to the political community. These have come from Aboriginal Canadians and from some ethnic minorities who reject their marginalization. Lacking a confident unifying sense of national identity, Canadian society has been buffeted by identity politics and often irreconcilable definitions of Canada.

The term **political community** implies, quite simply, a shared sense of belonging to a country whose national integrity is worth preserving. This is something less than **nationalism**, which defines a community by its language, ethnic origins, traditions, or unique history. And it is not quite the same as **patriotism**, which one associates with a more fervent and demonstrative love of country and its symbols than is usually considered seemly in Canada. Political community is rather what historian W.L. Morton once described as "a community of political allegiance alone."[15] National identity is essentially political—a sense of common citizenship in a country whose members have more in common with one another than with the citizens of neighbouring states and who believe that there are good reasons for continuing to live together as a single political nation. The term "political nationality" is used by Donald Smiley to refer to precisely this sort of non-ethnic, non-racial sense of political community.[16]

Canada's sense of community often seems fragile, threatened by French–English tensions, Western grievances against Central Canada, and most recently, conflicts between Aboriginal Canadians and the federal and provincial governments. But this apparent fragility needs to be viewed alongside evidence suggesting that the country has been relatively successful in managing such tensions. The Constitution dates from 1867, making it one of the oldest and most durable in the world. Moreover, the country's territorial integrity has (so far) remained unshaken by either civil war or secession. This is not to understate the importance of the rifts in Canada's sense of community. But the problems of Canadian unity and identity should be viewed from a broader perspective.

A History of Accommodation

There are four major challenges to the Canadian political community: French–English relations, Aboriginal demands for self-government, American influence on Canadian culture, and regional tensions. The first two are occasionally associated with political violence and calls for redrawing territorial boundaries. They represent clear challenges to the Canadian political community. The challenge of American influence assumes forms that are less territorial; nevertheless, its impact on the Canadian political community has been great. We will examine American influences separately in Chapter 3.

The fourth challenge, regional tensions, has been an important factor in Canadian politics from the country's inception. We would argue, however, that regional grievances and conflicts have never threatened Canada's territorial integrity. Westerners and, less stridently, Atlantic Canadians have long complained about policies and institutions that favour the interests of Ontario and Quebec. But their resentment has never boiled over to produce politically significant separatist movements nor popular defection from the idea of Canada. The importance of regionalism will be discussed in Chapter 4.

For most of Canada's history, relations between the francophone and anglophone communities have not posed a threat to the political community. The differences and tensions between Canada's two major language groups have been managed through political accommodations between their political elites. This practice of accommodating differences arguably

political community
a shared sense of belonging to a country whose national integrity is worth preserving

nationalism
a sense of a community defined by its language, ethnic origins, traditions, or unique history

patriotism
fervent and demonstrative love of country and its symbols

goes back to the Quebec Act of 1774. Official protection was extended to the Roman Catholic Church and Quebec's civil law system just when the British authorities were worried about the prospect of political rebellion in the American colonies spreading north.

The tradition of deal making between French and English Canada acquired a rather different twist in the couple of decades prior to Confederation, when the current provinces of Ontario and Quebec were united with a common legislature. The practice of dual ministries—having a leader from each of Canada East (Quebec) and Canada West (Ontario)—quickly developed, as did the convention that a bill needed to be passed by majorities from both East and West in order to become law. The federal division of powers that formed the basis of the 1867 Confederation continued this deal-making tradition. Provincial jurisdiction over education, property, civil rights, and local matters was shaped by Quebec politicians' insistence on controlling matters involving cultural differences.

This tradition of elitist deal making has continued throughout Canada's history at two different levels. Nationally, the federal cabinet and national political parties, particularly the Liberal Party of Canada, have been important forums where Quebec's interests could be represented. But as a more aggressive Quebec-centred nationalism arose in the 1960s, the ability to represent the interests of French and English Canada within national institutions became less important than whether compromises could be reached between the governments of Canada and Quebec.

There have been many political arrangements between First Nations communities and the Canadian community since the arrival of the European settlers some four hundred years ago. However, two issues have figured prominently in defining these arrangements: property rights and the relationship of the First Nations to the state. For instance, under French colonial rule, France did not recognize Aboriginal rights to the land, but Aboriginals who converted to Christianity were given the status and rights of French citizens. When the French territories were taken over by the British, a new relationship ensued. The Royal Proclamation of 1763 and subsequent treaties sought to organize and stabilize the relationship of the British state and the Aboriginal North Americans in matters of trade and land use. There were also two underlying assumptions embedded in these documents. First, the First Nations were under the protective stewardship of the British. And second, First Nations had some rights to the land, with some right to compensation for land taken by European settlers. In order to ensure that colonial growth was not impeded, the British Crown "reserved" lands for Aboriginal populations. To this day, the Royal Proclamation of 1763 is still important in settling land-claims disputes between First Nations and a provincial or the federal government.

The notion of protective stewardship, as well as the practice of reserving land for First Nations, continued after Confederation and the passing of the Indian Act in 1876. The Indian Act gave First Nations on the reserves control over their economy and society but very limited powers of self-government. For almost a century after Confederation, it was assumed that the First Nations would be absorbed into mainstream Canadian society. Indeed, there were many attempts through government practices, laws, and policies, including the extension of voting rights to First Nations peoples, to speed up this integration. Nevertheless, the First Nations remain distinct in respect of their culture, legal and social status, and civil rights. And the issues of land claims and self-government continue to capture most of the headlines in news coverage of First Nations' issues.

Freedom

Individual freedom is said to be central to the American political creed, symbolized in such icons as the Declaration of Independence, the Bill of Rights, and the Statue of Liberty. Canadians, it is usually claimed, are more willing than Americans to limit individual freedom in pursuit of social order or group rights. Is this true?

In the US political culture, Americans' pride in their system of government and their patriotism exceeding that of most other democracies have coexisted with a mistrust of government rooted in both the revolutionary experience and in the individualistic spirit. The greater stress on individual freedom and suspicion of government control in the United States compared to Canada is corroborated by many types of evidence. There is no Canadian equivalent to Henry David Thoreau, whose writings about civil disobedience and the need to resist the demands of society as the price to be paid for a life of virtue and freedom have significantly influenced the libertarian tradition in American politics. Hollywood's portrayal of the "loner," whose virtue and appeal lie in indifference to laws and social conventions, has long been one of the most successful and popular film genres.

Americans' passionate love affair with freedom is evident in the very different character of the gun control debate in Canada and in the United States. When Liberals proposed tougher restrictions on gun ownership and a national registry for all firearms in 1993, opposition in Canada focused on such matters as whether the legislation would really reduce the use of guns in committing crimes and whether the legislation reflected urban Canada's insensitivity and even hostility to the values and lifestyles of hunters and rural communities. Even during the 2010 debate over the Conservative government's proposal to dismantle it, few Canadians argued that a fundamental freedom was jeopardized by a long-gun registry.

However, in the US, proposals to restrict the sale and ownership of firearms invariably face objections from those who see these restrictions threatening individual freedom. Many Americans believe gun ownership is a right, not a privilege; in fact, one sometimes hears the argument that restrictions on gun ownership would leave citizens helpless to defend themselves, not simply against criminals but against the state! Thus, many Americans understand the argument that government may be the problem and the enemy, and that citizens have a right to defend themselves without relying on government. This argument would be met with blank stares of incomprehension in Canada. And very few Canadians would agree with the "open-carry" gun laws that allow an average citizen to walk into a Burger King or Walmart with a loaded firearm.

Seymour Martin Lipset observes, "If [Canada] leans towards **communitarianism**—the public mobilization of resources to fulfill group objectives the [United States] sees **individualism**—private endeavour—as the way an 'unseen hand' produces optimum, socially beneficial results [emphasis added for definition]."[17] Canadian writer Pierre Berton makes the same point in maintaining that "[w]e've always accepted more governmental control over our lives than . . . [Americans] have—and fewer civil liberties."[18]

communitarianism the belief that active co-operation, including the public mobilization of resources to fulfill group objectives and the recognition of the equality of communities and communal identities, are essential to individual dignity and the maintenance of truly democratic societies

Canadians are frequently portrayed as less assertive about their rights as individuals and more concerned than Americans with social order. While attitudinal data provide some support for these claims, some people object to these characterizations on the grounds that Americans' understanding of "freedom" as "the absence of restraint on individual behaviour"—what is sometimes called "negative freedom"—actually denies real freedom to many people. Canadians' greater willingness to permit government restrictions on individual behaviour means not that they value freedom less, but that they are more likely than Americans to believe that real freedom often requires that government interfere with individual property rights and economic markets. Moreover, Canadians tend to believe that governments should guarantee access to such things as public education and universal health care to help equalize the opportunities available to both the well off and the less privileged. Canadians, some argue, have what might be characterized as a "positive" conception of freedom, one that requires that government act rather than get out of the way. Canadians were more likely than Americans to express the belief that government does more to help people move up the economic ladder (46 per cent of Canadians agreeing, compared to 36 per cent of Americans), whereas Americans were more likely than Canadians to believe that government did more to hurt mobility (46 per cent versus 39 per cent). This is, admittedly, not a particularly large gap between the beliefs of Canadians and Americans.[19]

And from the attitudinal data and other evidence about cultural values, one gets the sense that the defence of individual freedom can be a harder sell in Canada than in the United States. In the wake of the terrorist attacks of 11 September 2001, the American and Canadian governments both passed laws that placed greater restrictions on individual rights and freedoms. Public opinion polls showed that Canadians were considerably less likely than Americans to believe that such restrictions were necessary, but at the same time polls showed that Canadians were about as accepting of security measures that involved some loss of privacy safeguards as were Americans.[20] The post-9/11 spike in American support for measures that appeared to purchase security at the cost of reduced freedoms and rights for some has dissipated over time. Some argued that a role reversal was taking place and that Canada was the society more concerned with individual rights while Americans were obsessed with threats to their national security. Moreover, opposition to limitations on freedoms and rights existed in the United States from the moment the Patriot Act was passed in 2001; this opposition gained strength and won victories in both Congress and the courts as time went on. In fact, Canadians may now be more concerned with their security after two attacks by homegrown terrorists in the fall of 2014, one on Parliament Hill, resulted in the deaths of two military personnel. Canadians subsequently appeared to be more willing to accept the tenets of the anti-terrorism measures of Bill C-51, which allows judges to permit security agencies to override constitutional rights.

Equality

A long line of sociologists, political scientists, and historians, going back to Alexis de Tocqueville, have generally agreed that America's political culture is more egalitarian and Canada's more hierarchical. Canadians are more likely than Americans to value *equality of condition* (or equality of results), whereas Americans are more likely than their northern neighbours to value *equality of opportunity*. Numerous cross-national attitudinal surveys confirm this observation.[21] In Canada, egalitarianism has its roots in a more collectivist tradition; in the United States it draws on a more individualistic tradition. This seems to be the conclusion of Michael Ignatieff, an academic and a former journalist, who was the leader of the Liberal Party of Canada when he wrote

> America and Canada are both free nations. But our freedom is different: There is no right to bear arms north of the 49th parallel, and no capital punishment either; we believe in collective rights to language and land, and in our rights and culture; these can trump individual rights. Not so south of the border. Rights that are still being fought over south of the border—public health for example—have been ours for generations.[22]

The value differences between the two societies are not starkly contrasting. Nevertheless, they help to explain Canadians' apparently greater tolerance—at least historically—for state measures targeted at disadvantaged groups and regions.

This difference between the two societies, however, should not be exaggerated. If Americans care more about equality of opportunity and Canadians about equality of condition, then we would expect to find greater acceptance of economic inequalities among Americans. But the evidence is unclear. In 2013 the average CEO of a Fortune 500 company in the United States made 331 times what the average American worker made. In Canada, the gap was smaller at 171 to 1.[23] Canadians and Americans almost exactly agree about what would constitute a "fair" ratio of maximum-to-minimum earnings: respondents from both countries say that it should be about 10 to 1.[24] A 2013 Pew Research Center survey found almost identical percentages of Canadians (58 per cent) and Americans (61 per cent) agreeing that the economic system favoured the wealthy. And 71 per cent of Americans and 68 per cent of Canadians agree that it is more important to ensure a fair chance than to reduce inequality.[25] If indeed Canadians are more concerned with equality of results rather than equality of opportunity, then one would expect to find a greater gap in these values. Yet, as Miles Corak notes, "Both Americans and Canadians feel strongly that individual characteristics, like hard work, ambition, and [education], lead to upward economic mobility. In both countries, factors external to the individual, outside of his or her control, ranked much lower."[26]

Canadian "Mosaic" versus American "Melting Pot": Is This a Myth?

In Canada, more than in the United States, debates over equality historically have been about group rights and equality between different groups in society, not about equality between individuals. This difference goes back to the founding of the two societies. While the American Constitution made no distinction between groups of citizens, the Quebec Act of 1774 incorporated protection for religious rights, and the British North America Act of 1867 provided protections for both religious and language rights.

As discussed in Chapter 5, a by-product of Canada's long tradition of recognizing group rights, many have argued, is greater tolerance of *cultural diversity* than one finds in the United States. This is the familiar, if exaggerated, theme of the Canadian "mosaic" versus the American "melting pot." Although there is considerable historical evidence to suggest that non-French, non-British groups have felt less pressure to abandon their language and customs in Canada than have non-English-speaking groups in the United States, rates of cultural assimilation have been high in both societies. Moreover, Canadian governments have shown themselves to be as capable as their American counterparts of discriminating against ethnic and religious communities. For example, in both countries during World War II, people of Japanese origin were deprived of their property and confined to camps. The religious practices of Doukhobors, Hutterites, Mennonites, and Jehovah's Witnesses have at various times brought them into conflict with either Ottawa or provincial governments. And although no longer the case, both countries' immigration policies have historically discriminated against non-white, non-European peoples.

Despite these similarities, the treatment of Canada's Aboriginal peoples, for example, has been less harsh and less violent than that of America's Aboriginal minorities. And nothing in Canada's history compares to the official discrimination and the physical violence directed against American blacks. An official policy of multiculturalism has existed in Canada since 1971 and was entrenched in the Constitution in 1982.[27] **Multiculturalism** is the idea that cultural diversity not only is good for society, it should also be encouraged. Moreover, Canada's Constitution appears to provide a firmer basis for affirmative action programs and other state activities that ameliorate the conditions of disadvantaged individuals or groups.[28]

And, despite the fact that cultural assimilation seems historically to have been part of the American ethos, a combination of government policies and court decisions in that country has steered it away from the melting pot and toward a mosaic society. Affirmative action policies such as university admission quotas began earlier and arguably have been taken further in the United States. Universities and other schools in the United States also pioneered the concept and practice of minority-oriented curricula (African American studies, for example).

At the same time, the idea of multiculturalism and the programs and structures that seek to implement the mosaic model have tended to go unchallenged in Canada, but there is some dissent. Neil Bissoondath's bestselling book *Selling Illusions: The Cult of Multiculturalism in Canada*,[29] Reginald Bibby's *Mosaic Madness: The Poverty and Potential of Life in Canada*,[30] and Salim Mansur's *Delectable Lie: A Liberal Repudiation of Multiculturalism*[31] are three of the salvoes launched against official multiculturalism (as opposed to tolerance of expressions of diversity and pluralism that are not sponsored and reinforced by the state). Moreover, it is increasingly clear that not all groups in Canadian society have been treated equitably, as seen, for example, in the suggestion (accusation) put forth in the 2015 report of the Truth and Reconciliation Commission (TRC), *Honouring the Truth: Reconciling for the Future,* that the Canadian government might actually have committed **cultural genocide**—defined by the TRC

multiculturalism
the idea that cultural diversity not only is good for society, it should also be encouraged

cultural genocide
the destruction of those structures and practices that allow a group to continue as a group

as the destruction of those structures and practices that allow a group to continue as a group.

In *The Illusion of Difference*, Jeffrey Reitz and Raymond Breton test the proposition that Canadians are more tolerant of diversity than their allegedly more assimilationist neighbours to the south. They review existing studies of the mosaic versus melting pot thesis and examine a number of comparative surveys and census data from the two countries. They conclude that the differences between Canada and the United States are "more apparent than real." The Canadian style, they argue, "is more low-key than the American; moreover, Canadians have a conscious tradition of 'tolerance' that Americans do not have." These differences in the way multiculturalism and ethnic diversity have been thought of in the two societies "have not produced less pressure towards conformity in Canada, or less propensity to discriminate in employment or housing."[32] Reitz and Breton conclude that there is almost no empirical basis for Canadians' cherished self-image of their society as being more tolerant and less assimilationist than that of the United States.

Residential schools were part of an orchestrated policy by the Canadian government to "Take the Indian out of the Indian." This photo depicts young Aboriginal boys saying their Christian prayers at bedtime in a residential school dormitory.

Shingwauk Residential Schools Centre, Algoma University

Gender equality is another dimension of group rights that has acquired prominence in recent decades. In both Canada and the United States attitudes concerning the appropriate roles and behaviour of men and women have changed sharply in the direction of greater equality. The visible signs of this change are everywhere, including laws on pay equity, easier access to abortion, affirmative action to increase the number of women employed in male-dominated professions, more positive portrayal of females in the media, and greater female participation in politics. While these are all indirect measures of attitudes toward gender equality, we might reasonably infer from the actions of governments and private organizations that these values do exist.

Comparing Canada to the United States using such measures, we come up with a changing scorecard that see increasing greater representation by women in Canada than in the United States. As of 2014, women were slightly better represented on the boards of directors of corporations in the Canada (21 per cent) than in the US (19 per cent).[33] This represents a significant reversal from 2012, when the US had more women on boards of directors than Canada. The percentage of female elected officials in each country's federal legislature is slightly greater in Canada: in 2015 about 26 per cent of members elected to Canada's House of Commons were female, while 20 per cent of those elected to the US House of Representatives and Senate were female.

As with other dimensions of equality, there is no evidence to support the claim that Canadians value equality less than Americans do. Indeed, in terms of recognizing group rights, it is fair to say that Canadian governments have gone at least as far as their American counterparts. In one important respect, however, Canadians are unequivocally more committed to an egalitarian society: racial equality. Although it is tempting to infer from the statistics on such matters as racial segregation, income differences associated with race, and crime and sentencing data that Americans tend to be more racist than Canadians, such an inference may not be warranted. For example, should one infer from the election of a black American as president in 2008, while no black has ever been the leader of a Canadian political party, that Americans are more tolerant of racial difference? Or does the fact that a much higher percentage of blacks hold public office or are CEOs of the largest companies in the United States than in Canada, suggest that the United States is the more racially tolerant society? The answer, most would agree, is no. The enormous differences in the historical circumstances shaping race relations in the two societies and the much greater relative size of the black population in the United States are reasons to be wary of drawing such conclusions. And these two factors ensure that race and racism are far more central to American than to Canadian political life.

Before we jump to conclusions about current attitudes toward race in both societies, we should keep in mind that the average incomes of black Canadians are about 80 per cent of those for white Canadians, roughly the same as in the United States, and that the likelihood of blacks and whites intermarrying is about the same (5 per cent) in both societies. As well, if our focus is the degree of racial and ethnic tolerance in majority populations (and these "majorities" are dwindling), we also would need to examine other groups—South Asians, Aboriginal peoples, Chinese, Hispanics, etc.—using numerous demographic variables.

Canadians' Expectations of the State

It is often argued that Canadians are more likely than Americans to look to government to meet their needs. They are also more likely to accept, rather than mobilize against, government actions they dislike.

The view of Canadians as more demanding of the state (more statist) and more passive or deferential toward it appears to be well entrenched. On the expectations side, it may have been accurate at one time to say that Canadian governments do more than American ones to redistribute wealth between individuals and regions of the country. The evidence suggests that the attitudes in both countries have converged about what a citizen can expect from their governments. Canadian governments' resistance to the expansion of private involvement in health care and post-secondary education continues but recently may have weakened somewhat. They continue to own corporations whose activities range from electricity generation to television broadcasting, while American governments have generally been content to regulate privately owned businesses in these same industries. And they are much more actively involved in promoting particular cultural values, especially those associated with bilingualism and multiculturalism, than are most governments in the United States. In Canada, the state used to account for a larger share of gross national expenditure than in the United States—and spends more on redistributive social programs and also takes a larger share of citizens' incomes in taxes. But all in all, this adds up to a mixed picture, and certainly not one that would allow us to say confidently that Canada is a more statist society than the United States.

What about the evidence for Canadians' alleged deference to authority and passivity in the face of government actions that they dislike? It was once fairly common to hear Canadian political experts intone that "freedom wears a crown," meaning that the more orderly society and the stability that Canadians experienced through this country's parliamentary system and titular monarchy, compared to the rather chaotic "mobocracy" to the south, provided a sort of protective mantle under which citizens were better able to enjoy their democratic rights and freedoms. "We've always accepted more governmental control over our lives than . . . [Americans] have—and fewer civil liberties," argues Pierre Berton, Canada's foremost popular historian. But, he adds, "the other side of the coin of liberty is license, sometimes anarchy. It seems to us that . . . Americans have been more willing to suffer violence in . . . [their] lives than we have for the sake of individual freedom."[34]

Canadians' apparent greater faith in government, compared to the more skeptical attitudes of Americans, owes a good deal to a collectivist ethos that sets Canadians and their history apart from the United States. It is this ethos that Canadian nationalists are invoking when they argue that Canada's public health-care system and more generous social programs reflect the "soul" of this country, and that their dismemberment would send Canadians down the allegedly mean-spirited path of American individualism. Some of Canada's most prominent thinkers, including George Grant and Charles Taylor, have argued that the collectivist ethos and greater willingness to use the state to achieve community goals are central to the Canadian political tradition.

In *Lament for a Nation*, George Grant argues that the Canadian political tradition is marked by a communitarian spirit that rejects the individualism of American-style liberalism. He traces the roots of this spirit to the influence of conservative ideas and the British connection, which helped to keep alive a benign view of government as an agent for pursuing the common good. This distinctive national character is, Grant believes, doomed to be crushed by the steamroller of American liberalism and technology, which, he maintains in later works, would ultimately flatten national cultures throughout the capitalist world.

Grant's "lament" is in the key of what has been called **Red Toryism**. Red Tories are conservatives who believe that government has a responsibility to act as an agent for the collective good, and that this responsibility goes far beyond maintaining law and order. Grant and others in this tradition favour state support for culture through the Canadian Broadcasting Corporation. They are comfortable with the welfare state and the principle that government should protect the poor and disadvantaged. Critics claim that Red Toryism is a rather paternalistic philosophy of state–citizen relations. Defenders, however, maintain that it is compassionate and a true expression of a collectivist national ethos that distinguishes Canadians from their southern neighbours.

Charles Taylor is not a Red Tory. Canada's most internationally acclaimed living philosopher is firmly on the left of the political spectrum. He agrees with Grant about the importance of collectivism in Canada's political tradition. Taylor has always been extremely critical

Red Tory
a conservative who believes that government has a responsibility to act as an agent for the collective good, and that this responsibility goes far beyond maintaining law and order

Inside Politics

BOX 2.2 | What Architecture Says about a Nation's Politics

Canadians' preference for *neo-Gothic* rather than *Greco-Roman* architecture in their government buildings may also reflect a preference for the ideas of *conservatism* such as tradition and social order over *liberalism* and the ideas of individualism and democratic values. The columns found in the Greco-Roman architecture of many American political buildings suggest a reliance of society and of state on individuals, whereas the keystones and arch architecture found in Canada's Parliament buildings suggests a reliance on institutions such as the monarchy in maintaining the integrity of the state.

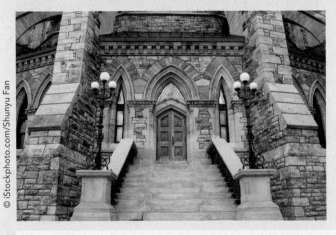

(Top left) United States Capitol Building. (Top right) United States National Archives, column detail. (Bottom left) Doorway to the Canadian Parliamentary Library. (Bottom right) Hallway in the interior of the Canadian Parliament buildings.

of what he calls the "atomism" of American liberalism, a value system that he believes cuts people off from the communal relations that nurture human dignity. Like most Canadian nationalists, he believes implicitly in the moral superiority of Canada's collectivist political tradition. Taylor is one of the leading thinkers in the contemporary movement known as communitarianism, which is based on the belief that real human freedom and dignity are possible only in the context of communal relations and collaboration. Taylor argues that the key to Canadian unity lies in finding constitutional arrangements that enable different groups of Canadians to feel that they belong to Canada and are recognized as constituent elements of Canadian society. "Nations . . . which have a strong sense of their own identity," says Taylor, "and hence a desire to direct in some ways their common affairs, can only be induced to take part willingly in multinational states if they are in some ways recognized within them."[35] He calls this the recognition of "deep diversity." The realization of deep diversity would require, at a minimum, official recognition of Quebec as a distinct society and probably constitutional acknowledgement of an Aboriginal right to self-government. To some this might sound like a recipe for dismantling whatever fragile sense of Canadian community already exists. Taylor insists, however, that one-size-fits-all notions of community do not work in the modern world.

Deference and Changing Canadian Values

The characterization of Canadians as more deferential and less likely to question authority than Americans has been challenged in recent years. In *The Canadian Revolution*, Peter C. Newman argues that the historically elitist tenor of Canadian life collapsed between 1985 and 1995 under the pressure of developments in Canada and in the world at large. Newman speaks of the rise of a "new populism" and of what he calls the "breakdown of trust between the governors and the governed."[36] He attributes this transition to a constellation of factors that includes the arrogance of politicians, the more competitive global economy, the inability of Canadian government to continue financing the system of entitlements that Canadians came to take for granted in the 1960s and 1970s, and the decline in religious faith, among other things.

A more quantitative treatment of the same phenomenon is offered by Neil Nevitte in *The Decline of Deference*.[37] Nevitte agrees that Canadians are less deferential today than in the past. He attributes this change to the post-materialist values of those born following World War II. **Post-materialism** is an ideology that attaches comparatively greater importance to human needs for belonging, self esteem, and personal fulfillment than does **materialism**, which places greater stress on economic security and material well-being. Such issues as employment and incomes matter most to materialists, whereas post-materialists are likely to place higher value on so-called quality-of-life issues such as the environment, human rights, and group equality. Materialists are less likely than post-materialists to have confidence in public institutions and to trust in the judgments of elites.

Nevitte shows that Canadians' confidence in government institutions, including the armed forces, police, Parliament, and public service, declined during the 1980s, and that high levels of

post-materialism an ideology that attaches comparatively greater importance to human needs for belonging, self-esteem, and personal fulfillment

materialism an ideology that places greater stress on economic security and material well-being

Canadian Spotlight

BOX 2.3   Changing Canadian Values

Canadian "baby boomers'" values were influenced by historical events such as

- World War I
- the Great Depression
- World War II

Recent generations of Canadians have had their values shaped by

- the bombing of the World Trade Center on 11 September 2001
- global warming
- self-actualization and better education
- globalization

The "New Left" in Canada is less concerned with traditional moral standards (for example, it is in favour of same-sex marriage) and more concerned with tolerance and the environment. There is less attachment to hierarchies and traditional parties, and, as a result, Canadians are considered by some to be more "difficult to govern."

Source: Neil Nevitte, *The Decline of Deference* (1996), discussed in Robert J. Jackson and Doreen Jackson, *Politics in Canada*, 7th edn (Toronto: Pearson Education Canada, 2009), 67.

confidence are much less likely to be expressed by those between the ages of 25 and 54 than by older citizens. He also finds that Canadians are, if anything, slightly more skeptical of government institutions than are Americans—not the traditional stereotype of deferential Canadians and defiant Americans one would expect to find.

We should not be too quick to conclude, however, that the old characterization of Canadians as more deferential of authority and trusting of government than Americans is no longer accurate. Post-materialist values may indeed be more pervasive in Canada than in the United States. But data from the 2012 AmericasBarometer survey show that only with respect to the armed forces and the president/prime minister do Americans express more confidence than Canadians. Levels of confidence in the police, Parliament/Congress, the public service, and government are not very different in the two countries.[38]

These attitudes are also evident when we examine another way of measuring deference, which involves looking at peoples' defiant actions toward authority. When Canadians and Americans are asked whether they have attended a lawful demonstration, joined an unofficial strike, or occupied a building or factory, or might do any of these, Canadians are somewhat less likely to answer "yes." The differences between the two populations are small—and have decreased from 10 years earlier—but this piece of evidence does not support the claim by some that Canadians, emboldened by the experience of life under the Charter of Rights and Freedoms, have become less deferential than Americans.

Canadians and the Notion of Social Capital

Citizens' expectations of government can also be examined by looking at social capital—the fabric of connections between members of a community. Social capital is made up of both norms, such as trust in one's neighbours, and behaviours, such as voting and participating in community organizations. The roots of this concept can be found in Alexis de Tocqueville's observations on the propensity of mid-nineteenth-century Americans to join voluntary associations in order to achieve communal goals. Tocqueville believed that these voluntary associations were the connective tissue of American democracy. They reminded citizens that they belonged to a community and depended on one another.

Many commentators argue that social capital in American society has been in serious decline for years. While the evidence for this claim is not rock solid, it is clear that Americans continue to be more likely than the citizens of Canada and other rich democracies to belong to and participate in voluntary associations such as religious, youth, sports and recreation, educational, and cultural groups.[39] These activities are more likely to be publicly funded in Canada and the responsibility of state agencies. This difference in social capital between Canadians and Americans is corroborated by the 2012 AmericasBarometer survey. Using a composite measure of civic engagement (attending local meetings, helping solve local problems, following the news daily, participating in demonstrations or protests, signing petitions, sharing political information, and having an interest in politics), it was found that Americans were significantly more likely than Canadians to have high scores in civic engagement.[40] One might conclude that Americans are more likely than Canadians to believe that private citizens and the voluntary associations they create—not the state—should be responsible for meeting many of society's needs.

Canadians and Religious Values

Significant parts of the civic and communal engagement of Americans are due to the far greater strength of traditional religious values in the United States compared to Canada. Canada is simply a more secular society than the United States, though not nearly as secular as some Western European democracies. Secularization involves a decline in the belief that religion and religious authorities should be looked to for guidance about behaviour and an increase in the social, cultural, and political influence of elites whose expertise is not based on religious faith.

For most of their respective histories, Canada and especially French-speaking Canada were generally considered more traditionally religious than the United States. Religious elites certainly appeared to have more influence in Canada, at least until the 1960s. Since then, the process of secularization has advanced more rapidly in Canada and other Western democracies than in the United States. A number of measures have shown that Americans tend to be more traditionally religious than Canadians.

The more secular character of Canada's political culture helps to explain why issues with moral dimensions, such as abortion and embryonic stem cell research, are more controversial in the United States, and why Canadian legislation recognizing same-sex marriage was passed

social capital the fabric of connections between members of a community

secularization a decline in the belief that religion and religious authorities should be looked to for guidance about behaviour and an increase in the social, cultural, and political influence of elites whose expertise is not based on religious faith

in 2005. This particular battle raged on longer in the United States. In 2015, the Supreme Court finally ruled that anti-gay marriage legislation in 14 states was unconstitutional. The more secular nature of Canadian culture also helps to explain why Canadian politicians, unlike their American counterparts, infrequently invoke religious references or even mention God in their public statements. Being perceived as too religious can even be a liability in Canadian politics, as Canadian Alliance leader Stockwell Day discovered in the 2000 federal election, when his born-again Christianity made him a target of the media and rival parties.

Summary

While history and geography may have played a part in shaping Canadian democracy, Canadians and their political leaders have also made choices leading to the development of democratic institutions of government that are distinct from those of other countries. As we saw in this chapter, the choices that a society makes with respect to its governance and the institutions and constitutional arrangements it uses to govern itself stem from its political culture, which includes the values, attitudes, and expectations of its citizens. We also explored the main ideologies in Canadian politics to see how ideological differences drive government policies, political actions, and social change.

Another way of explaining political culture and politics is to use theoretical models such as the fragment theory approach, the role of formative events approach, and/or the class analysis (economic theory) approach. Models such as the left- and right-wing concept and the political compass continue to be useful for those who study politics because they help us differentiate between the main ideologies and political parties in Canadian democracy.

Much of the chapter was dedicated to explaining the role that political culture plays in Canadian democracy, and the similarities and the differences between Canadian and American political culture, particularly around diversity and the different interpretations of equality. In the end, the most significant aspects of the debate over the value differences between Canada and the United States may be that it has gone on for so long and that it continues to generate controversy among those who study Canadian politics. The differences are relatively small, certainly, compared to those between Canada and most other Western democracies.

Review Exercises

1. Using Table 2.1 and the political compass in Figure 2.3, where would you place each party represented in the federal or provincial legislatures? Where would you place yourself and why?

2. Choose any three organizations from the following list. Visit their websites and determine whether each organization advocates mainly collectivist or individualistic ideas.

    Fraser Institute: www.fraserinstitute.ca

    Centre for Social Justice: www.socialjustice.org

    Canadian Centre for Policy Alternatives: www.policyalternatives.ca

    Canadian Labour Congress: www.clc-ctc.ca

    Sierra Club Canada: www.sierraclub.ca

    C.D. Howe Institute: www.cdhowe.org

    National Citizens Coalition: www.morefreedom.org

    Council of Canadians: www.canadians.org

3. What would you say are the formative events of your grandparents' generation? How are these different from the formative events of your parents' generation and of your own generation?

Up for Debate

1. Canadians are essentially Americans living inside a different border. Read the Dominion Institute's five articles published in 2005 on "American Myths" (www.dominion.ca/americanmyths/), which argue that the beliefs that many Canadians hold about Americans and how Canadians differ culturally from their southern neighbours are fundamentally wrong. Are you convinced by the arguments and evidence in this series? Why or why not?
2. Resolved: Canada is/is not a "nation" like the United States is a "nation."

Starting Points for Research

Fierlbeck, Katherine. *Political Thought in Canada: An Intellectual History*. Toronto: University of Toronto Press, 2006.

Grabb, Edward, and James Curtis. *Regions Apart: The Four Societies of Canada and the United States*. Toronto: Oxford University Press, 2010.

Lipset, Seymour Martin. *Continental Divide: The Values and Institutions of the United States and Canada*. Toronto: C.D. Howe Institute, 1989.

Resnick, Philip. *The European Roots of Canadian Identity*. Peterborough, ON: Broadview Press, 2005.

Thomas, David, and David Biette, eds. *Canada and the United States: Differences That Count*, 4th edn. Toronto: University of Toronto Press, 2014.

CBC Archives and TVO's *The Agenda*

Visit the companion website for *Canadian Democracy: A Concise Introduction* to follow links to audio and video footage related to the main themes of the chapter: www.oupcanada.com/BrooksConcise2e.

Relevant Websites

Visit the companion website for *Canadian Democracy: A Concise Introduction* to browse a collection of websites featuring material related to the key themes of the chapter, an excellent starting point for research: www.oupcanada.com/BrooksConcise2e.

3 The Social and Economic Setting

Canadians commonly view the United States as a benchmark against which we compare ourselves and our achievements. Historically, when some Americans have felt politically vulnerable, they have sought refuge in Canada. Examples include the vast numbers of Loyalists who settled in Ontario around the time of the American Revolution, African American slaves escaping to Canada via the Underground Railroad up until the end of the American Civil War, blacklisted Hollywood writers coming to Canada during the 1950s McCarthy era, and draft dodgers fleeing to Canada during the Vietnam War. In fact, even after President George W. Bush's 2004 re-election, many Canadians were gratified to read stories about Americans, including Hollywood celebrities, inquiring into the possibility of moving to Canada. These examples seem to confirm the typical Canadian belief that Canada is superior in important

⬆ While Canada remains one of the wealthiest countries in the world, studies report that the gap between its richest and poorest citizens is growing. Such social and economic settings play a dominant role in defining and establishing Canada's political structure.
Source: Roberto Machado Noa/Getty Images.

ways to the powerhouse to the south. The Canadian self-image is one of compassion, tolerance, and prosperity. Our southern neighbours may be richer, but we tend to believe that our country's prosperity is more equally shared. The resilience of the Canadian banking system compared to the near-collapse of the American banking system during the 2008 economic *meltdown* provided another example of how our economic and political systems might have advantages.

Canadians are indeed fortunate. But politics unfolds against a backdrop of social and economic conditions, and not all Canadians share in that good fortune. A 2015 study of 111 countries by the Pew Research Center shows that between 2001 and 2011 Canada ranked seventh in overall growth of wealth; however, the fastest growth has been among the high-income earners, and our middle class has been shrinking.[1] Moreover, roughly 3 million Canadians have fallen below the "poverty line," the low-income point established by Statistics Canada.[2] Some organizations such as Canada Without Poverty say that the actual number is higher: one in seven, or 4.9 million.[3] In recent years, there have been many criticisms of the conditions in which the poor in Canada live and our government's performance in this regard.

As we discussed in Chapter 1, politics is often about conflict over values and over the allocation of resources. Just as the values of a society and the institutions of the state establish boundaries to political life, so do the social and economic settings. These determine the sorts of problems a society faces, the resources available for coping with these problems, the nature and intensity of divisions within society, and the distribution of valuable resources between societal interests. This chapter focuses on specific socio-economic aspects of Canadian society including material well-being, equality, discrimination, poverty, and quality of life, as well as political and economic sovereignty. After reading this chapter, you should be able to

1. explain the social and economic settings of Canadian politics
2. compare socio-economic regions within Canada or between Canada and other countries
3. discuss poverty, the distribution of income, and socio-economic mobility in Canada
4. discuss how the Canadian democratic political system has been able to overcome socio-political divisions created by scarcity
5. measure the quality of life in Canada and compared to other states
6. identify economic and cultural factors that limit Canada's independence

Material Well-Being

Canada is an affluent society—a simple fact sometimes obscured by bad news such as plant closings, slipping competitiveness, and growing poverty. For most of the last generation, the average real purchasing power of Canadians was the second-highest in the world, topped only by that of Americans. While Canada has slipped several notches in the last decade, it remains among the wealthiest countries in the world.[4]

Degrees of affluence affect both the opportunities and problems faced by policy makers. For example, the problems of poverty in an affluent society like Canada differ from those in a poorer society like Mexico or a destitute one like Sudan. Not only do Canada's poverty problems look enviable compared to these countries, but Canadian governments have far greater means to deal with the problems. The very definition of a "public problem" in need of government attention is also influenced by a society's material conditions. For instance, environmental pollution or animal rights can be prominent issues on the public agendas of affluent societies, but they tend to be a less pressing problem in poorer societies.

Within affluent societies, cultural and institutional differences are probably more important in determining public agenda and government response than differences in material well-being. For example, Western democracies tend to have a high regard for the rule of law and for the role of the judiciary. But the characteristics of a national economy, factors upon which material affluence depends, significantly influence the politics and public policies of any society. These characteristics include the sectoral and regional distribution of economic activity, the level and distribution of employment, the characteristics of its labour force, the profile of its trade with the rest of the world, and so on.

The frequent mention of the issue of employment in the news should indicate just how important it is to Canadians. Despite their high standard of living, Canadians have seldom been complacent about their affluence and they often worry that Canada's material well-being may be fragile. As Canadians grapple with globalization and the meaning of economic restructuring, these fears have become increasingly urgent. Most people want a secure job at a decent rate of pay; it enables one to plan for one's future as well as for one's family. Unemployment can be personally and socially devastating. Governments react with rhetoric, gestures, and policies. These policies may or may not succeed in reducing unemployment or increasing the number of non-precarious jobs, but no government would pass up an opportunity to express its commitment to increasing employment and its sympathy for the unemployed.

What does Canada's employment record look like? Compared to other advanced industrialized democracies, Canada has done fairly well. Over most of the past 30 years the national level of unemployment has averaged between 7 and 9 per cent. This may not impress Americans, whose unemployment rate has typically been a few percentage points below Canada's. This situation changed temporarily, after the 2008 recession. However, as of March 2016, Canada's overall unemployment rate was 7.1 per cent,[5] compared to 5 per cent in the United States[6] for the same period, and averaging 6 per cent over the last three decades. Canadians, however, are used to dismissing the superior employment record of the United States as being bought with lower wages and greater income inequality than most Canadians would tolerate (the claim about lower wages is simply not true, however, if one compares real wages and net after-tax incomes).

When we look beyond the United States for comparisons, we see that Canada's unemployment rate has been close to the average for the more affluent countries belonging to

"When America sneezes, Canada catches a cold." This saying from the world of finance and economics indicates just how closely the two countries' economies are intertwined. Should it make Canadians nervous, then, to look through their binoculars and see the American economy struggling? Even if the Canadian economy is currently outperforming America's, is that performance sustainable over the long term? Why or why not?

the Organisation for Economic Co-operation and Development (OECD). Since the mid-1990s, Canada has had the highest annual growth rate of any G7 economy, which has translated into the best record of job creation in this elite club of affluent democracies.[7]

Moreover, the economy's ability to create new jobs has been among the best—an important point, because Canada's labour force has grown faster than those of most other advanced industrial democracies.

The distribution of employment across sectors of the Canadian economy closely resembles that of the world's other major capitalist economies. More than three-quarters of workers are in service industries (sales, communications, transportation and warehousing, tourism, finance, public administration, etc.). In June 2012 approximately 10 per cent were employed in the manufacturing sector; less than 4 per cent worked in primary industries like farming, fishing, forestry, and mining; and 7 per cent worked in construction.[8] These proportions are

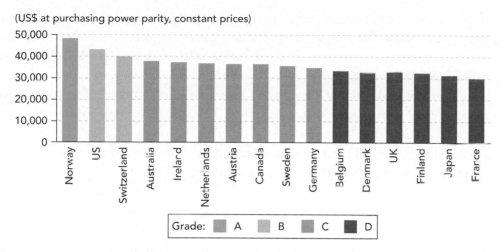

(US$ at purchasing power parity, constant prices)

FIGURE 3.1 Income per Capita, 2012

Source: Jean-Pierre Maynard, The Comparative Level of GDP Per Capita in Canada and the United States: A Decomposition Into Labour Productivity and Work Intensity Differences (Ottawa: Statistics Canada, 2007)

similar to those in our major trading partner, the United States. Over time, the service sector's share of total employment has grown dramatically, from about 40 per cent in the mid-twentieth century to the current level of more than 7 in 10 jobs. The shares in the primary and secondary sectors have obviously declined, more sharply in primary industries than in manufacturing. These employment trends have led many to worry about the "deindustrializing" of the Canadian economy and **precarious employment**—work that is insecure and unskilled, and pays wages that cannot support a household. However, these employment trends are broadly similar to those that have characterized all the world's major capitalist economies over the last several decades.

In the last two decades, a debate has emerged over the relative value to an economy of service versus manufacturing jobs. Some argue that service industries, particularly in generating knowledge and distributing information, also produce value, and so there is no reason to worry about a shrinking manufacturing base. Others argue that the manufacturing sector is especially important and that a point can be reached in Canada and the United States where further decline of the manufacturing base undermines the economy's overall competitiveness and drags down real incomes.[9] Much of this argument hinges on the often-heard claim that new jobs in the burgeoning service sector tend to be unskilled and low-paying—"McJobs." These jobs, it is said, have increasingly replaced better-paying manufacturing jobs that have been exported to low-wage economies. The belief that the new economy primarily creates McJobs, however, is false. The new economy also creates better-paying jobs in information technology, communications, financial services, and other service industries that require education and skills. What have been lost in the new economy are the low-skilled/high-paying manufacturing jobs that characterized the factory economy of the 1950s to the 1970s. Their disappearance has heightened the importance of education and skills as necessary qualifications for well-paying jobs. While instances of PhDs driving taxis or flipping burgers will

precarious employment work that is insecure and unskilled, and pays wages that cannot support a household

always be reported by the media, studies of education and income in developed and developing economies show that education and training generally translate into better incomes and job security. Economists, however, do not agree on the question of whether a shrinking manufacturing sector and greater reliance on service-sector employment is necessarily a bad thing from the standpoint of incomes and general prosperity. Some, including Harvard economist Michael Spence, argue that globalization is directly responsible for a dearth of jobs in the American and other Western economies. Others, including another Harvard economist, Robert Lawrence, and business writer Richard Katz, maintain that a shortage of jobs and flat incomes have much more to do with government policies and internal factors than with the outsourcing of jobs.[10]

Canada's job creation rate has been one of the best in the developed world for over a decade, and projections suggest that as the country's population continues to age, the supply of workers, including those needed to fill high-skilled and well-paying jobs, will not meet the demand.[11] But even if it could be shown that outsourcing has and will continue to result in a hemorrhage of jobs, one could still make the case that sharing employment opportunities with people in less affluent parts of the world is preferable to providing them with foreign aid. If Canadians truly believe, as polls suggest, that the world's wealth should be shared more equally, then they should applaud the redistribution of economic activity from the rich countries to the poorer ones. But most do not.

Media Beat

BOX 3.1 The New Underclass: Choose Your Career Wisely

Before you decide that your choice of a degree in something other than engineering, health sciences, or international copyright law was perhaps not such a good idea, or that maybe you should have paid more attention when your high school guidance counsellor was making the case for a career in welding or heavy machinery operation, consider these facts.

In January of 2013, *Maclean's* magazine featured a cover story on what it called "the new underclass." "Underclass" is a term that came into use in the United States in the 1960s to describe that stratum of American society that was at the very bottom of the socio-economic ladder, with few prospects for a better life. Scholars such as William Julius Wilson argue

that the underclass, predominantly black and usually estimated by sociologists to be not more than 1–2 per cent of the total population, emerged in large part because of economic restructuring and the disappearance of unskilled manufacturing jobs.

However, the Canadian underclass that *Maclean's* had in mind is "a generation of well-educated, ambitious, smart young Canadians that," the article controversially concluded, "has no future." The lives and prospects of those to whom the term was applied bear little resemblance to the destitution, violence, and general hopelessness of the American underclass. What they call the new underclass, many argue, has been created by the dynamics of economic restructuring. "There's been growth at the top—there's more good, white-collar jobs than there used to be," says labour studies professor Wayne Lewchuk, "but we have fewer middle jobs, and more bad jobs. . . . So the problem now is if you get one of those bad jobs, even out of university, there's no middle rung for you to go to. . . . [University graduates are] stuck in that bottom tier and they're just not seeing a path to a better job—ever."[12]

How did this happen? While economic restructuring and corporate cost-cutting—both consequences of globalization—have played a part in the hollowing out of the middle class, the *Maclean's* analysis acknowledged that uninformed labour market choices by many young Canadians have contributed to the problem of underemployment and low incomes for many with post-secondary degrees. Slightly more than one in four Canadians between the ages of 25 and 29 lives with their parents (2011),

compared to 11 per cent in 1981, suggesting that a growing number of young Canadians are having to put their independence and their hopes on hold.

The likelihood of being unemployed drops significantly with formal education. As of 2011 about 16 per cent of those who dropped out of high school were unemployed, compared to 8 per cent for high school graduates and just under 5 per cent for university graduates.[13] The proportion of workers with a university degree who held low-skilled jobs (requiring a high school diploma at most) did not change among workers aged 25–34 between 1997 and 2012.[14] You may wish to take heart from the conclusion of a recent study: "The data show that while the number of post-secondary graduates has grown in recent years, the benefits of a degree in terms of more stable employment and higher earnings have not diminished."[15]

Equality

Canadians are not used to thinking of themselves and their society in terms of class. Pressed to self-identify with a particular rung on the class ladder, the majority of Canadians choose middle class. The 2012 Focus Canada survey found that 56 per cent self-identified as middle class, 19 per cent as lower-middle class, and 18 per cent as upper-middle class. Only 1 per cent called themselves upper class and just 5 per cent, lower class.[16] Canada is, at least in terms of how its citizens perceive themselves, a middle-class society.

Canadians have become increasingly aware of inequalities based on income. Asked who Canadian politicians defend, the rich, the poor, or both equally, 51 per cent said that they defended the rich, 43 per cent said that they defended the rich and the poor equally, and only 6 per cent said that they defended the poor over the rich. Six out of ten said that politicians *should* defend the rich and the poor equally, and one out of three said that they should defend the poor over the rich. Slightly more than half of Canadians (51 per cent) said that the government should implement strong policies to reduce income inequality, and almost one-third said that the way to do this is to increase taxes on the rich.[17]

Wealth is unevenly divided in all societies. Few people believe that the sort of levelling implied by Karl Marx's aphorism, "From each according to his abilities, to each according to his needs," is desirable. But many are disturbed by the jarring contrast between conspicuous luxury and destitution in their society. The gap between rich and poor is smaller in Canada than in some other industrialized democracies. Nevertheless, it is considerable and persistent. Moreover, some groups bear the brunt of poverty much more heavily than others.

> One of the most persistent images that Canadians have of their society is that it has no classes. This image becomes translated into the assertion that Canadians are all relatively equal in their possessions, in the amount of money they earn, and in the opportunities which they and their children have to get on in the world. . . .That there is neither very rich nor very poor in Canada is an important part of the image. There are no barriers to opportunity. Education is free. Therefore, making use of it is largely a question of personal ambition.[18]

This may well have been the image held by most Canadians when sociologist John Porter wrote these words more than fifty years ago. It is doubtful whether Canadians today are as confident that their society is without serious inequalities. Stories about homelessness, food banks, poverty, and growing income inequality have become routine. Moreover, charges of discrimination made by women's groups, Aboriginal Canadians, visible minorities, gays and lesbians, and other marginalized groups are more commonly heard today. The passage of provincial human rights codes and of the Charter of Rights and Freedoms and the proliferation of human rights officers (e.g., ombudspersons and race relations or equity officers) have increased the awareness of inequality. These reforms were inspired by a sense that existing policies and institutions did not adequately protect the equality of citizens and that, in some cases, laws and institutions actually perpetuated social and economic inequality.

The Canada that Porter analyzed existed half a century ago. Nevertheless, many critics argue that structural inequalities of the sort that he described still characterize Canadian society. Canadians are more attuned to the issues of inequality today than they were two generations ago. At the same time, they still believe overwhelmingly that they are middle class and that theirs is a middle-class society. The idea that Canada is a vertical mosaic is no longer a radical and strange notion. But the hammerlock that Canadians of British and French ancestry held on positions of prestige, influence, and high incomes is no longer as tight as it was in Porter's time. Moreover, the explosion in higher education since the 1960s—in 1965 there were about 204,000 students enrolled in Canadian universities compared to about 1,150,000 in 2011—has meant that access to the middle class, while not equal across all ethnic, racial, and other lines in Canada, is certainly greater today than it was in Porter's day.

Wealth is unevenly divided in all societies, but many people are disturbed by the jarring contrast between eye-popping luxury and destitution. The gap between rich and poor is not as great in Canada as in some other industrialized democracies, but it is persistent and, according to recent reports, growing.[19]

Some groups bear the brunt of poverty more than others. According to Statistics Canada, until recently the distribution of income had remained essentially unchanged for decades. According to the census, in 2011 the wealthiest 20 per cent of the population accounted for about 47 per cent of all income, while the poorest one-fifth accounted for slightly less than 5 per cent.[20] If social security benefits are left out of the picture, the inequality gap is much wider: the bottom fifth of Canadians accounts for barely 1 per cent of earned income.

Canada is fairly typical when its income distribution is compared to that of other advanced capitalist societies. Its distribution of income is more equal than in countries such as the United States, but less equal than in others such as Japan and Sweden.

These proportions are not dramatically different from what they were a half-century ago. The change over time looks a bit more dramatic if one focuses on the very wealthiest of Canadians. The top 1 per cent of tax filers accounted for just under 10 per cent of income in 1960 and just over 12 per cent in 2010. Perspective is sometimes everything. Before World War II, the top 1 per cent of income earners in Canada accounted for about 18 per cent of income, a share that declined dramatically during the war and then more gradually in the following decades, reaching a low of about 8 per cent in the late 1970s. All these figures include social transfers such as public pensions, social security payments, and Employment Insurance. State spending narrows the gap between those at the top and bottom of the income ladder from what it would be in the absence of redistributive policies. In 2011 the lowest quintile of income earners received 29.1 per cent of the value of all federal transfers, compared to 11.4 per cent for those in the highest quintile. At the same time, those at the top of the income ladder account for a greater share of government revenue. In 2010 the top 1 per cent of income earners paid 21.2 per cent of federal, provincial, and territorial income taxes, compared to 13.4 per cent in 1982. The share paid by the other 99 per cent of tax filers in 2010 was 78.8 per cent, down from 86.6 per cent in 1982.

Recent news stories and academic studies purporting to show a growing gap between the rich and the poor in Canada contribute to a widespread belief that inequality has worsened. A study by Nicole Fortin and her colleagues show that the distribution of both market and disposable income in Canada has grown more unequal since the late 1970s.[71] Most of the increase in inequality occurred during the 1990s. This trend has flattened in recent years. Both the increase in inequality and the more recent levelling off are due to the share of income going to the very wealthiest Canadians.

An assessment of equality involves analyzing both the extent of poverty and the distribution of income. Poverty is to some degree a relative concept, meaning something different in an advanced industrialized society than in a developing country. According to the United

TABLE 3.1 Measuring Class by Annual Income

In early 2015, *Maclean's* magazine asked: How does your income stand up?

	Unattached Individuals ($)	Families of Two or More ($)
Bottom 20%	0 to 18,717	0 to 38,754
Lower-middle 20%	18,718 to 23,356	38,755 to 61,928
Middle 20%	23,357 to 36,859	61,929 to 88,074
Upper-middle 20%	36,860 to 55,498	88,075 to 125,009
Highest 20%	55,499 and up	125,010 and up

Source: *MoneySense* estimates for 2013 based on Statistics Canada 2011 data reprinted in David Hodges and Mark Brown. (Jan. 27, 2015). "Are you in the middle class?" *Macleans Magazine*.

Gary Clement/ National Post

As this cartoon suggests, annual income can be used as a determinant of economic class. However, other variables may also come into play such as the rate of inflation, one's education, one's neighbourhood, and one's diet. Why might these factors be important in determining economic class? Which other factors be added to the list?

extreme poverty
an international standard definition of income of less than $1 a day

poverty line
Statistics Canada's "low-income-cut-offs" (LICOs); the threshold at which a household spends over 20 per cent more of its annual family income on the basic necessities of life (food, clothing, and shelter) than does the average household

Nations, the international standard of **extreme poverty** is an income of less than $1 a day.[22] Canada does not presently have a definition of poverty; poverty is usually measured using Statistics Canada's definition of an income so low that an individual or household lives in "straitened circumstances." Statistics Canada's low-income cut-offs (LICOs) are generally referred to as the **poverty line**. This is the threshold at which a household spends over 20 per cent more of its annual family income on the basic necessities of life (food, clothing, and shelter) than does the average household. The term "poverty line" has become part of Canada's political vocabulary and for many Canadians evokes images of need and destitution. But some criticize this measure of poverty. The National Council of Welfare[23] describes its limitations:

- Poverty lines are relative and arbitrary.
- Poverty lines measure the incomes of groups of people, not the individual's needs.
- Some poverty line definitions are better than others, but none of them are perfect.

The likelihood of being poor is not, however, evenly distributed across the population. Consider that the groups most at risk are recent immigrants, lone-parent families headed by women, and the roughly half-million Aboriginal people who live on reserves.

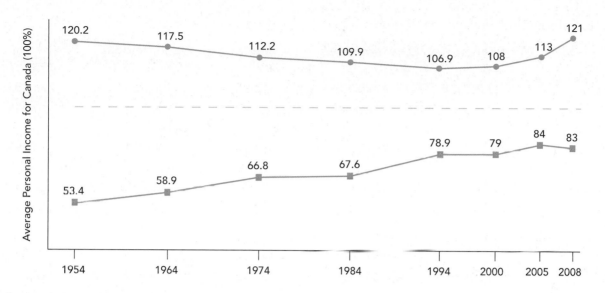

FIGURE 3.2 Low-Income Rates among Working-Age Main Income Recipients, Various Groups, 2010

Source: Employment and Social Development Canada, www4.hrsdc.gc.ca/.3ndic.1t.4r@-eng.jsp?iid=23.

Why are these groups particularly susceptible to poverty? There is no simple answer, but a few contributing causes are clear. In the case of Aboriginal Canadians, discrimination can partly explain the higher jobless rate and lower incomes. Lower levels of education also are a factor for Aboriginals and for non-Aboriginal Canadians. They are particularly low among Aboriginals who live on reserves. Reserves tend to be small and far from major population centres, and employment opportunities are comparatively few. Likewise, educational aspirations and opportunities are much less prevalent than in off-reserve communities.[24]

Regionalism and Inequality

Inequality in Canada also has an important regional dimension. Income levels and employment rates vary dramatically and persistently between provinces, as well as between regions within provinces. Personal incomes in what have traditionally been the poorest provinces (Newfoundland and Labrador, New Brunswick, and Prince Edward Island) are about 85–90 per cent of the Canadian average. These citizens have been more dependent than Canadians in wealthier provinces on transfer payments from government. The inter-regional variation in average personal incomes has narrowed over the last few decades, although it is still quite wide. The narrowing of the gap has been due mainly to government transfers that provide greater income benefits to the residents of the poorer provinces than to those of the richer ones. In the 2012–13 fiscal year, on average Ottawa transferred $3,541 per person to residents of PEI and $3,289 to those of New Brunswick, but only $1,015 to each Albertan and $1,244 per person to Ontarians.[25]

TABLE 3.2 Individual Income by Region

	Poorest 20%	Lower-middle 20%	Middle 20%	Upper-middle 20%	Richest 20%
Canada	17,267	41,707	66,397	100,260	226,792
Newfoundland and Labrador	17,042	40,010	64,769	97,566	207,733
Prince Edward Island	16,135	35,954	56,895	84,381	171,197
Nova Scotia	16,468	37,562	60,001	88,822	175,234
New Brunswick	15,861	36,075	57,298	84,923	168,278
Quebec	15,726	36,023	57,447	87,225	185,155
Ontario	18,745	44,787	72,111	108,928	247,521
Manitoba	16,899	39,070	62,992	93,371	198,223
Saskatchewan	16,802	39,174	64,333	97,388	219,360
Alberta	22,457	51,964	81,663	122,294	291,260
British Columbia	16,769	40,276	64,699	97,511	212,944
Territories	22,384	55,743	90,020	129,492	242,262

Source: Statistics Canada, CANSIM, table 111-0008.

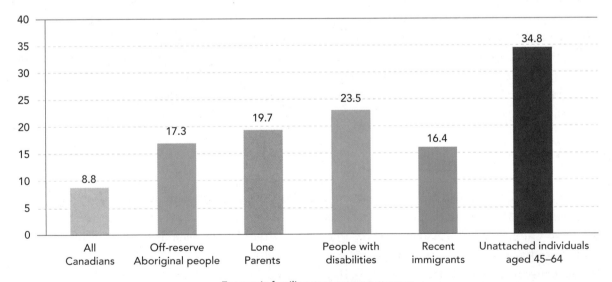

Economic families, two persons or more

FIGURE 3.3 The Gap between the Richest and Poorest Provinces, 1954–2011

Note: Until 2005, the two provinces used in this comparison were Ontario and Newfoundland and Labrador. Newfoundland and Labrador has continued to have the lowest per capita income in most years since then, but Alberta has been the wealthiest provinces most years since 2005.

Source: Statistics Canada, Provincial Economic Accounts.

Socio-Economic Mobility

One of the important dimensions of equality is **socio-economic mobility**. This refers to the ability of individuals, families, and groups to move from one social or economic position to another. Socio-economic mobility implies the existence of hierarchically arranged differences in society, such as those that exist between income groups and occupations. These differences exist to varying extents in all societies. In an *open society*, where socio-economic mobility is high, movement up and down the social ladder is common and the barriers to entry into high-paying occupations, prestigious groups, or elites are low. In a *closed society*, there is relatively little intergenerational movement on the social ladder, and barriers into these privileged groups are high.

Most Canadians believe that theirs is a relatively open society, and compared to many it is. But evidence shows that social stratification in Canada remains high and that socio-economic mobility is lower than many believe.

The *vertical mosaic* that John Porter described over five decades ago has been opened up, but several studies show that gender, ethnicity, race, and family background continue to exert a tremendous downward pull on mobility. Of these factors, family background appears to be the most important. More specifically, the education, occupation, and income of one's parents—these three factors being highly correlated—have a significant impact on the likelihood that a person's income and class position will be better or worse than that of his or her parents. (Mobility is a two-way street and includes the possibility of slipping down the income ladder between generations, not just climbing it.)

Miles Corak has examined how closely sons' rankings on their society's income ladder are related to the earnings of their fathers. He reports that intergenerational mobility in Canada is surpassed by that in only a small number of wealthy democracies, and then just marginally. Corak reports that the probability of a son born to a father whose income is in the lowest 20 per cent of income earners reaching the upper half of all Canadian income earners is 38 per cent.[26]

The good news is that intergenerational social mobility in Canada appears to be higher than in the US, the UK, and some other wealthy democracies.[27] Moreover, Canada does a better job than many other societies in terms of how quickly immigrants and their children are able to climb the socio-economic ladder.[28] Despite the fact that the Canadian economy has needed highly skilled immigrants for decades, smooth integration by immigrants into the labour force is not always immediate. Indeed, evidence shows that their skills are frequently underutilized, at least for a few years after their arrival. A 2003 Statistics Canada study found that 6 in 10 immigrants were working in occupational fields different than those for which they had been trained in their first country. As indicated by Figure 3.4, the employment prospects of immigrants compared to those of the Canadian-born have deteriorated somewhat in recent years, particularly in Ontario.[29]

Immigrants' job prospects do, however, improve over time. The employment rate of those between the ages of 25 and 44 arriving in Canada between 1991 and 1996 was 61 per cent, but increased to 74 per cent by 2001. Although this figure was still several percentage points

socio-economic
mobility
the ability of
individuals, families,
and groups to move
from one social or
economic position
to another

TABLE 3.3 Moving Up and Down the Income Ladder: Income Mobility in Canada, 2005–9 and 1993–7

	2005–9			1993–7		
	Proportion of Persons Who Moved into a Higher Quintile (%)	Proportion of Persons Who Moved into a Lower Quintile (%)	Total Mobility (%)	Proportion of Persons Who Moved into a Higher Quintile (%)	Proportion of Persons Who Moved into a Lower Quintile (%)	Total Mobility (%)
Lowest quintile	43	0	43	41	0	41
Second quintile	41	20	61	38	20	58
Third quintile	34	29	63	33	27	60
Fourth quintile	24	38	62	25	34	59
Highest quintile	0	40	40	0	39	39
Overall average	28	25	53	27	24	51

Source: Statistics Canada. 2011. Income in Canada, 2009. Ottawa, ON: Statistics Canada.

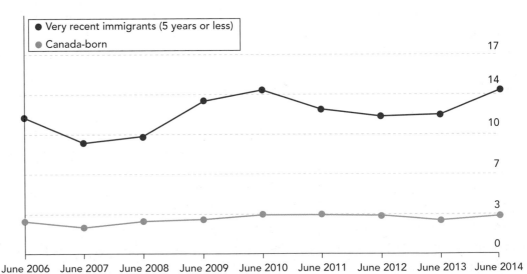

FIGURE 3.4 Canada-Wide Unemployment Rates for University Graduates, 2006–2014

Source: Statistic Canada data published in Anna Mehler Paperny. (July 30, 2014). "Unemployment's up for Canada's most educated immigrants." Global News.

below the employment rate for those born in Canada, it clearly was a significant improvement over a relatively short time. Some immigrants simply need to spend some time in school, upgrading their education, acquiring language skills, or becoming certified in their occupational field. The fact that an increasing number of immigrants in Canada's labour force are of non-European descent and are members of what in Canada are called *visible minorities* raises the issue of whether some barriers that immigrant workers face are due to discrimination.

The problems of assessing foreign credentials, lack of Canadian work experience, and language and cultural barriers may be more significant in explaining the underemployment and underutilization of skilled and educated immigrants. Indeed, in some parts of Canada, foreign-born people are as common as Canadian-born. According to the 2011 census, the foreign-born made up about 46 per cent of the population of the Greater Toronto Area, 40 per cent of the population of the Vancouver metropolitan region, and 23 per cent of the population of Montreal. Visible minorities (which, according to the government's definition, do not include Aboriginal peoples) constitute significant shares of the population in these cities: 47 per cent in Toronto, 45 per cent in Vancouver, and 20 per cent in Montreal. Although few would claim that prejudice has disappeared from their workplaces, cultural diversity is now firmly anchored in these and other major urban centres in Canada. In such countries as France, the United Kingdom, Germany, and the Netherlands, those who have been born in the country to immigrant parents continue to lag far behind the native-born in education and income. This is not true of Canada.[30]

The Canadian Elite and Socio-Economic Mobility

What about the political and economic elite in Canadian society? John Porter argues that these classes were largely self-perpetuating, recruiting new members chiefly from those groups that already dominated them. Does this continue to be true? Canadians were used to thinking about their society as a pluralistic mixture of ethnicities, languages, and religions even before the notion and policy of multiculturalism came into fashion, but academic and journalistic opinion on Canada's *corporate elite* agrees that this group is highly unrepresentative of the general population and that access to it appears to be much easier for those from certain backgrounds than from others. The most systematic studies of the corporate elite's social characteristics were carried out by sociologists John Porter and Wallace Clement. Porter's study was based on 1951 data and Clement's on 1972 data.[31] They both found that of this elite (which they defined as the directors of Canada's dominant corporations),

- most were male
- about a third had attended private schools such as Upper Canada College or Ridley College
- many had upper-class backgrounds (50 per cent in 1951 and 59.4 per cent in 1972)
- those of non-Anglo-Saxon ethnic origin were under-represented (13.8 per cent of Clement's 1972 group, compared to 55.3 per cent of the Canadian population)
- about half (51.1 per cent in 1972) belonged to one or more of the six most prominent private clubs in Canada

The picture they sketched was one of a self-perpetuating group whose social backgrounds and adult activities set them sharply apart from the general population (see Box 3.2).

Access to the political elite is certainly more open today than in the past. Traditionally, the major political parties were dominated by males of either British or French ethnic origins. They still are, but the representation of females and Canadians of non-British, non-French origins has increased sharply over the last couple of decades. Visible minorities constituted only about 6 per cent of MPs elected over the thirty-eighth, thirty-ninth, and fortieth general elections, which was about half their share of the Canadian population. A study by the Public Policy Forum reported that just under 10 per cent of MPs elected in 2011 were members of visible minority groups.[32] By the forty-second general election in 2015, that number had jumped to 14 per cent.[33]

The election of Audrey McLaughlin as NDP leader in 1989 marked the first time a woman had been chosen to lead a national political party, followed by the 1993 selection of Kim

"A ceiling? All this time I thought it was a floor."

The "glass ceiling" is an invisible form of job discrimination that excludes large numbers of women from the higher-paying and more prestigious jobs that have historically been held by men. Do you think that representation quotas—that is, requiring organizations, including political parties, to employ a proportional number of women or other marginalized minority groups—are an effective way for women to break through the glass ceiling? Why or why not?

Campbell as leader of the Progressive Conservative Party and of Alexa McDonough as leader of the NDP in 1994. Women account for just over one in four members of the House of Commons, a figure far below the female share of the population but significantly greater than it was a generation ago. In 2014, there were four female provincial premiers. Several of Canada's major cities have had female mayors. The continuing domination of Canada's political elite by males of British and French ethnic origins, albeit less strikingly than in the past, thus seems to be the result of systemic rather than deliberate discrimination.

The Roots of Inequality

Why do inequalities like those described above exist? And what are the consequences for Canadian politics and society? These are complex questions that cannot be fully dealt with here but several factors seem to contribute to inequality, including deliberate discrimination, systemic discrimination, choice, and politics.

Deliberate Discrimination

The prejudice that one person feels toward the members of some group or groups becomes **deliberate discrimination** when it is acted upon. Deliberate discrimination is characterized by the intent to treat the members of some group in an unequal manner. For example, the landlord who refuses to rent to someone he suspects of being homosexual is discriminating against that person and against all members of that group. While there is no doubt that this sort of discrimination still exists in Canadian society, it is probably much less important in explaining inequality than the following three causes.

deliberate discrimination prejudice that one person feels toward the members of some group or groups

Systemic Discrimination

Systemic discrimination is discrimination without conscious individual intent. It is the discrimination inherent in traditions, customary practices, rules, and institutions that have the effect of favouring the members of one group over another. For example, in 1999 the British Columbia Human Rights Commission ruled that the section of the province's Highway Act requiring motorcyclists to wear helmets unintentionally discriminated against male Sikhs, whose religion requires them to wear a turban. Other examples are the height or weight requirements for certain jobs that discriminate against women, because women are typically smaller than men. Everyone recognizes, however, that some job requirements may be reasonable, even if they discriminate against certain groups.

systemic discrimination the discrimination inherent in traditions, customary practices, rules, and institutions that have the effect of favouring the members of one group over another

Yet another example of how deeply rooted systemic discrimination may be is the way in which our society often assumes that child rearing is primarily a female function. This assumption is deeply embedded in our culture and social practices, and is even reinforced through the law. The result is a situation where the opportunities effectively open to men and women are not equal. It may appear that individual choice entirely determines what opportunities are

Canadian Spotlight

BOX 3.2 Canada's Corporate Elite: Where Everyone Looks the Same

These are the leaders of Canada's biggest companies by market cap [the investment community's assessment of a company's net worth, calculated by multiplying its share price by the number of shares in circulation], ranked from one to 50. . . . With one exception, they're all white, middle-aged males. If corporate Canada was an ice cream, it would be vanilla—make that two scoops. That in itself shouldn't be surprising, but what is rather shocking is the almost complete absence of any kind of diversity. Not one woman heads up a Top 50 company, despite women making up half the workforce. Only one visible minority—John Lau at Husky Energy—found his way to the top, even though at least 13.4 per cent of the population identifies themselves as such. . .

Aside from being white, the men at the top of Canada's corporate food chain are middle-aged, with the typical exec being almost 53, and very well educated. Oddly enough, though, it turns out a business degree isn't the path to fame and fortune: turns out your average Canadian CEO is more likely to have a bachelor of science degree. Roughly a fifth of them reported having an MBA. Roughly half have multiple degrees. . . .

Hard work, and biding your time while rising through the ranks, can also pay off. Telus's Darren Entwistle started out a telephone lineman for Bell Canada; Canadian National Railway's Hunter Harrison's first job was crawling under box cars to oil wheel bearings; and Canadian Pacific Railway's Fred Green has been with the company since 1978. Clearly, this group is bright and hard-working—positive signs of meritocracy at work. Now, the challenge is to get that culture of meritocracy to extend beyond white middle-aged men.

Source: Excerpted from Andy Holloway, "The Big 50: The CEOs of Canada's Largest Companies," *Canadian Business*, 22 May–4 June 2006.

pursued, but these individual choices are shaped by the weight of social practices and cultural values that have the effect of discriminating between males and females.

Choice

Individual *choice* can contribute to inequality. For example, a status Indian who decides to stay on the reserve reduces his or her opportunities of finding a job, and if employment is found, it will probably pay less than a job in the city. First Nation reserves are usually far from centres of population and economic activity, so an economic cost accompanies the choice of life on the reserve. Likewise, persons who move to areas such as Cape Breton or Northern Ontario, or many other regions of Canada, are more likely to be unemployed or earn less than those who move to Toronto or Calgary.

Mobility choices like these are not always easy. A person who grows up in the poverty and deprivation that characterize most First Nation reserves may not perceive the choices or have the resources to make some choices. For example, some First Nation reserves are geographically remote. Therefore, the cost of transportation and lodging can have a significant impact on people's education and career choices. Nevertheless, individual choice affects inequality.

Politics

Although debates over equality generally use the language of civil rights and social justice, they are essentially struggles over *politics*. How much inequality is enough or socially acceptable? Are some forms of discrimination necessary to protect or promote other values? If so, which groups should be targeted for affirmative action schemes?

As values and beliefs change, a society's notions of what is fair may also be transformed. A century ago only a small minority of Canadians regretted the fact that women were without most rights that are taken for granted today. Poverty was once believed to be primarily the fault of those experiencing it—an explanation that absolved society, the economic system, and governments from blame.

Value shifts are almost always accompanied and influenced by political struggles. If Canadians are more conscious today of the discrimination that has been practised against the country's Aboriginal peoples it is because Aboriginal groups have brought these inequalities to the public's attention and influenced government policy. The social policies that redistribute wealth from more affluent to less affluent Canadians were built up over time in response to struggles between conflicting interests and values. Political parties, interest groups, individuals, and various parts of the state all participate in such struggles.

The structure of the state also affects what sorts of inequalities are dealt with by governments, which influences the opportunities and resources available to different interests. The fact that Canadian governments have long targeted more money at regional economic inequalities than have American governments is likely due to the constitutional division of powers between Ottawa and the provinces and the relatively greater leverage of the provincial governments compared to America states. And the entrenchment of the Charter of Rights and Freedoms in the Canadian Constitution has had an impact on the prominence of equality rights issues, the strategies that interest groups use, and the treatment of certain groups. The interplay of interest, ideas, and institutions that is politics plays a key role in determining what inequalities get the attention and how they are dealt with.

Measuring Quality of Life

In spite of its wealth, the United States suffers from a number of social pathologies such as racism, urban blight, a high rate of alcoholism, many thousands of homeless people, and a high level of marriage breakup, which creates numerous single-parent families, usually headed by women, and leads to a high incidence of child poverty. Canadians often take smug pride in

quality of life (QOL)
a measure of social
and economic
prosperity using
a combination
of objective
and subjective
determinants

being less afflicted by these problems. But Canada's high standard of living is also tarnished by problems that undermine the **quality of life (QOL)** experienced by millions. The QOL index measures social and economic prosperity using a combination of objective and subjective determinants. Social problems often become politicized as groups demand government action to deal with them. In some cases, government policies are blamed for causing or contributing to QOL problems. For example, Aboriginal groups and sympathizers argue that the appallingly bad quality of life experienced by many Aboriginal Canadians is due to unjust and discriminatory policies. While the QOL in Canada is comparatively high, the picture is not uniformly bright for all groups.

One way to measure the QOL in a society is to ask people how happy they are. Pollsters have done this for decades. They find that generally Canadians are relatively happy most of the time. However, there is no particular correlation between the happiness of national populations and material well-being. Canadians, Italians, and Finns, for example, are much less likely to say they are happy compared to people in much poorer countries such as Nigeria, Tanzania, or Mexico.[34] There is, however, a clear correlation between material well-being and the level of satisfaction with life expressed by a nation's population. Canadians and the citizens of other wealthy countries are more likely to express a high degree of satisfaction with their lives than to say that they are very happy. The 2012 AmericasBarometer survey found that 25 per cent of Canadians said they were very satisfied with their lives, and another 60 per cent said that they were somewhat satisfied. But a persistent and significant minority of Canada's population is not satisfied. Attitudinal data like these tell one nothing about the causes of dissatisfaction or the sorts of problems that actually undermine the QOL in a society. To get at these one must rely on objective measures that may reasonably be construed as reflections of QOL. We will look at mortality, crime, suicide, alcoholism, and destitution.

Compared to other advanced industrialized societies, Canada does relatively well on these measures. Its overall mortality rate of about 8 per 1000 and the infant mortality rate of just under 5 per 1000 are about average for wealthy democracies. Life expectancy is above average, at about 81 years, 20 years longer than it was in 1961. And Canadians can expect to live in full health for 73 years or 90.5 per cent of their life.[35]

Crime, Suicide, and Drug Abuse

In terms of violent crime, Canada is unexceptional. Although rates vary marginally from year to year, the statistics do not support the popular assumption that murders in Canada have become more common; Canada's homicide rate has actually declined since the mid-1970s.[36]

Statistics on other violent crimes, such as rape, domestic violence, and assault, are difficult to interpret. This is partly because of changes in laws, attitudes, and reporting procedures that can produce statistical changes. For example, the dramatic increase in the number of rape charges and convictions from several decades ago may be due to victims' greater willingness to come forward, resulting from changed social attitudes and reforms to the law on sexual assault. Comparisons between countries are complicated by variations in policing practices, the definition of offences, and the manner in which crime statistics are collected. Interpretation

In late 2011, the leadership of the Attawapiskat First Nation, a Cree community in the Kenora region of Northern Ontario, declared a state of emergency—the third in three years—in response to dropping temperatures and a concern for residents living in inadequate housing. Dilapidated structures like this one are common; they house large families and have substandard insulation, no running water, and no access to sanitation systems. Why do you think the issues of substandard socio-economic conditions on reserves keep resurfacing and command so little of the Canadian public's attention?

problems aside, the data suggest that Canada is not a dangerous place to live. However, the widespread belief that Canada is much less crime-ridden than the United States is not supported by the empirical evidence. A 2004 survey of crime victimization in Western democracies found that, with the exception of homicide, victimization rates for other violent offences and crimes against property were not lower in Canada than in the US. In some cases these rates were even higher in Canada.[37]

Estimating the abuse of alcohol and other substances is difficult, but a high level of drug use in a population carries high personal and social costs. The 2004 Canadian Addiction Survey found that 24 per cent of respondents said they had experienced some form of harm from their own alcohol abuse at some point in their lifetime, and 33 per cent said they had experienced some harm during the previous year, ranging from insults and verbal abuse to physical assault, as a result of someone else's alcohol consumption.[38]

Alcoholism in Canada is about average for Western industrialized countries and is dramatically lower than in such countries as Hungary, Germany, Italy, and France. Abuse of other non-medical drugs generally is not considered to be a major problem in most of Canadian society, although particular cities, including Vancouver and Toronto, and some isolated Aboriginal communities have been well-publicized exceptions. On the whole, the social and economic costs associated with illegal drug use in Canada are probably less than those produced by alcohol and tobacco consumption, although the lack of hard data makes it difficult to reliably assess the costs inflicted on individuals and society by drug abuse.

Homelessness and the Welfare Gap

Advanced industrial societies all have in place a "safety net" of social programs intended to protect individuals and households from destitution. Examples of such programs include social welfare, public housing, employment insurance, public health insurance, and workers' compensation. Nevertheless, some people do not or cannot get the help they need. When the safety net fails those who cannot make ends meet, surely the QOL for some people is falling below acceptable standards. Homelessness and the demands placed on food banks are two indicators of holes in the social safety net.

The extent of homelessness is difficult to pin down accurately because the homeless do not have fixed addresses or telephone numbers. The 2008 Senate report *Poverty, Housing and Homelessness* acknowledges the difficulties and does not even attempt to attach a number to this problem. The Calgary-based Sheldon Chumir Foundation for Ethics in Leadership estimated that in 2005 the number of homeless was somewhere between 200,000 and 300,000, figures widely reported by the media even though their reliability was suspect. Based on various sources of data, a 2013 report of the Canadian Alliance to End Homelessness estimates that about 150,000 persons use homeless shelters each year, which does not include street people who do not use shelters, those who use women's shelters, or the "hidden homeless," who stay with friends or family.[39]

The number of Canadians who rely on food banks also increased. Food Banks Canada estimates that Canada's more than 800 food banks provided food to roughly 900,000 people during a typical month. About half of food bank users live in Ontario; only 12 per cent were employed. Just over half were on social assistance such as welfare or Old Age Security. Aboriginal Canadians and single-parent families are disproportionately represented among food bank users. About 40 per cent of Canada's food banks are run solely by volunteers.[40]

While demands on food banks are largely cyclical, increasing during periods of high unemployment, there appears to be a permanent component. Even when the rate of unemployment has fallen in recent years, demand has grown. This demand, many argue, is created by the **welfare gap**, the gap that exists between the income that social assistance provides and the cost of living. The size of this gap varies across the country, first, because social assistance benefits are determined by the individual provinces and second, because of regional variations in the cost of living. But the gap is wide in all provinces.[41] As social assistance benefits fail to keep

welfare gap
the gap that exists between the income that social assistance provides and the cost of living

pace with increases in the cost of living, the demand on food banks inevitably increases. Given the growth in the "normal" use of food banks, increasing unemployment pushes an already strained system to the breaking point.

Political, Economic, and Cultural Sovereignty

Political Sovereignty

In most contexts, **sovereignty** is understood to mean the ability of a person or entity to act independently without outside interference. A democracy requires sovereignty and self-government. This means that public policies affecting the lives of citizens should be formulated by people elected by and accountable to these same citizens.

As we will see in Chapter 6, The Constitution and Charter of Rights and Freedoms, step by step the Canadian state achieved the full powers of self-government beginning with the adoption of the Westminster model of parliamentary democracy in 1848. With the passage of the Constitution Act in 1982, the last formal impediment to political sovereignty was removed. But political sovereignty has been far less controversial in the modern politics of Canada than economic and cultural sovereignty. The real limitations on Canadian independence, many have argued, are not the vestiges of colonialism but result from *economic dependence* on, first, Great Britain and then the United States, and by the "colonization" of Canada by American cultural industries. Formal political sovereignty, according to Canadian nationalists, is meaningless as long as the country's economic and cultural destinies are controlled by others.

sovereignty the ability of a person or entity to act independently without outside interference

Economic Sovereignty

No self-governing democracy is totally independent of external influences—especially in this era of globalization. Trade, military alliances and animosities, and contemporary mass media are some of the chief factors that have created a web of interdependence between modern societies. Whether the nature and extent of these external influences undermine a country's political independence has become increasingly important to Canadians. There is no denying that Canada has been and continues to be enormously dependent on foreign investment capital, imports, and markets for Canadian exports. Some of the main features of Canada's international economic relations are listed in Box 3.3.

This dependence must, however, be put into perspective. Several advanced industrial democracies like Canada, including the Netherlands, Belgium, Sweden, the United Kingdom, and Germany, rely on trade for much of their national income. These countries are members of the European Union, which imposes considerably greater limitations on the policy makers of its member states than the North American Free Trade Agreement (NAFTA) imposes on the Canadian, American, and Mexican governments. What is unique about Canada is the extent to which our trading relations depend on a single partner—the United States. Among advanced industrialized economies, only Japan comes close to this level of dependence on a single trading partner (close to half of Japan's exports are purchased by the United States).

Canadian Spotlight

BOX 3.3   Canada's Economic Links to the United States and the Rest of the World

Past

- Much of the money used to build the roads, railways, and canals of Canada's early commercial economy was borrowed from foreign, mainly British, investors.
- At Confederation, Canada was already heavily in debt to foreign investors.
- An estimated 450 American companies had established subsidiaries in Canada by 1913.
- By the 1920s, the United States had surpassed the United Kingdom as the major source of foreign investment.
- The level of foreign ownership in Canada peaked in 1971 at 37 per cent of corporate non-financial assets. The level was close to 60 per cent for manufacturing industries.

Present

- The Canada–US trade relationship is the largest in the world, involving $742 billion in goods and services in 2012. (China–US trade is next and closing fast, at about $560 billion in 2012.)

- Foreign investors, mainly American, control about one-fifth of corporate non-financial assets in Canada.
- About one-third of Canada's GDP comes from trade. In 2011, roughly two-thirds of Canadian trade in goods and services was with the United States (about 70 per cent of our export trade and 61 per cent of import trade).
- Canada went from being a net importer of investment capital to a net exporter around 1996. As of 2011, the estimated market value of foreign direct investment in Canada was $607 billion, 54 per cent of which was American investment. The market value of Canadian direct investment abroad was about $684 billion, 40 per cent of which was in the United States. Canada is one of the top 10 sources of foreign investment in the United States economy.
- Since the mid-1990s Canada has negotiated dozens of trade and foreign investment arrangements. The more recent trade agreements include the Canadian–European Trade Agreement (CETA) and the Trans-Pacific Partnership (TPP).[42]

In terms of investment, Canada remains heavily dependent on foreign capital. But this dependence has weakened over the last couple of decades as Canadian investment abroad has increased and the American share of foreign ownership in our economy has declined. Indeed, as a result of the increasing globalization of business and investment, Canada has come to look more like several other advanced industrial economies with respect to foreign ownership. Again, however, Canada is rather unusual in the degree to which it is dependent American foreign investment. This long-time controversial relationship with the United States is discussed in Chapter 12.

Cultural Sovereignty

Culturally, Canada, especially English-speaking Canada, has always lived in the shadow of the United States (see Box 3.5). Physical proximity, a common language, and shared values have facilitated the flow of cultural products such as books, magazines, films, television programs, and music recordings between the two countries, but mostly from the United States to Canada. This largely one-way flow exists because greater domestic audiences and readership are available to American producers, which better enables them to produce high-quality, low-cost, mass-appeal products that are attractive to advertisers. Advertising revenue is the main or sole source of income for most privately owned media businesses (producers of films, compact discs, DVDs, video games, and books are the chief exceptions). It thus makes economic sense for Canadian broadcasters, for example, to buy a program that is demonstrably popular with viewers, at a fraction of the cost of production in Canada.

Predictably, American-made films, television programs, video games, popular music, books, and magazines dominate Canada's English-language market. In spite of their steady decline, newspapers are the main exception to the rule of American dominance, partly due to provisions in Canada's Income Tax Act that heavily favour Canadian-owned newspapers, and partly because, for most people, newspapers are primarily sources of local information.[43]

With respect to sovereignty, questions arise: Is Canada's political independence undermined by its economic dependence on the United States and by the enormous influence of American mass media? How so? And is the Canadian predicament so different from other industrialized democracies in the face of globalization?

The answer to the first question is clearly "yes." Canadian policy makers must be sensitive to the actions and possible reactions of governments in the United States. Moreover, numerous public policy matters, from transboundary pollution to interest rates, are affected by circumstances in the United

Courtesy Magazines Canada, www.magazinescanada.ca

Magazines Canada is the national trade association representing Canadian-owned and Canadian content magazines in English and in French. Would seeing the organization's logo on a publication at the newsstand make you more inclined to buy it? Do you think it is important to distinguish Canadian content in this way? Why or why not?

States—circumstances over which Canadians and their governments can exert little, if any, control. Canada's economic and cultural linkages with the United States affect us in too many ways to be listed here. The fact that roughly 70 per cent of our export trade is with the United States obviously means that our economy is vulnerable to changes in the American economy and to currency exchange rates. The fact that Canadians are raised on a heavy diet of American films, television, magazines, and Internet programming affects the images and ideas in our heads, which, in turn erode Canadian values (whatever these may be or might have been). One may argue that they also erode the cultural basis for a Canadian society and for public policies that are unique to our needs.

Faced with challenges from a larger, more powerful economy and a predatory mass culture, governments typically respond with protectionist policies. They attempt to protect domestic industries or local culture through import restrictions, subsidies to domestic producers, regulations affecting business practices and cultural industries, and so on. Canadian policy makers have resorted to all these measures. To cite but one example, Canadian cultural policy is determined largely by the rules that the Canadian Radio-television and Telecommunications Commission (CRTC) imposes on broadcasters. The CRTC establishes and enforces regulations governing Canadian content on radio and television. The bottom line is simple: to ensure that more Canadian music and television programming reaches the airwaves.

Democracy Watch

BOX 3.4 CRTC: Protector or Punisher?

Since 1999, commercial radio licences in Canada require stations to program 40 per cent Canadian content, defined as meeting at least two of the following criteria:

M (music): composed solely by a Canadian
A (artist): a Canadian performs the music or the lyrics
P (performance): recorded in Canada or performed and broadcast in Canada
L (lyrics): written by a Canadian

While established to promote Canadian arts, these rules raise difficult situations. Home-grown stars such as Avril Lavigne and Drake can be forced to record in Canadian studios, even if they are living elsewhere, in order to meet the Canadian content requirements. In a famous 1991 case, Bryan Adams clashed with the CRTC over his international hit "(Everything I Do) I Do It for You," which was deemed "not Canadian" because it was co-written by a British producer. (It was following this case that the "L" was added to the list of criteria to allow more songs to be considered Canadian.)

Media Beat

BOX 3.5 **The Long Shadow of American Culture**

- About two-thirds of television viewing time in English Canada is spent watching American programs. This proportion rises to 90 per cent of drama and comedy viewing time.
- During a fairly typical week in mid-May 2016, 24 of the 28 most-watched television programs in English Canada were entirely American. The exceptions included the NHL playoffs, the NBA playoffs (in which the Toronto Raptors were playing), *CTV Evening News*, and *Big Brother Canada*. In contrast, only one of the 30 highest-rated programs in the French-language market for that week was American (dubbed in French).
- The Canadian and American cinema markets are, for the most part, treated as one by film producers, distributors, and advertisers.
- Canada's feature film and television production industries depend on a life-support system of government subsidies channelled through the Income Tax Act and Telefilm Canada, and through the production activities of the Canadian Broadcasting Corporation and the National Film Board. Despite this support, few genuinely Canadian films reach the box office.

The growing desire by Canadians to access online and on-demand streaming of movies and television programming by providers such as Netflix, Google, and YouTube appears to be undermining the CRTC's efforts to encourage Canadian content. As noted in a report by Nordicity for the annual Digital Media at the 2016 Crossroads Conference, regulating or subsidizing online content is not without controversy:

> The report is a powerful reminder of the ripples that spread out from the cultural industries: As consumers shift to digital platforms and digital formats, they export not only their media spending but also the ad revenue that follows their viewing, reading and listening. Here's a wake-up call to government: Canada is now bleeding $700-million to $800-million in cultural spending every year—dollars that used to support, whether directly or, more often, indirectly, the creation of Canadian films, TV shows, recordings, books, newspapers and magazines. . . .
>
> [Creating] new levies on digital distributors would be highly controversial while solving the problem of discoverability—there is no point subsidizing Canadian

content online if nobody can find it—will take some clever innovations. First of all, however, there is a need not merely for conferences and panel discussions, but also for a collective sense of urgency before Canada's cultural industries are decimated.[44]

Finally, is the Canadian situation really so different from that of other small and middle-sized democracies? After all, Hollywood's *Transformers: Age of Extinction*; *X-Men: Days of Future Past*; and *Guardians of the Galaxy* were the box office hits of 2014 throughout much of the world, just as they were in North America. McDonald's restaurants span the globe, so much so that the standardized cost of a Big Mac hamburger is used by the respected business newspaper *The Economist* as a measure of the cost of living in different countries. The US-dominated Internet, direct broadcast satellites, cable news networks, international credit cards, and multinational corporations have shrunk the globe, so that no country is free from some other's cultural or economic incursions.

A debate continues on whether Canada should have an industrial strategy to counter the recent loss of sovereignty and Canada's industrial base. In late 2011, many economists and political pundits, including economist Jim Stanford, were wondering why Canada did not have an industrial strategy. Stanford noted that in 1999 finished goods made up almost 60 per cent of our exports; by July 2011, two-thirds of our exports were in unprocessed or semi-processed goods.[45] In a July 2015 report by the labour organization Unifor, looking at 16 economic indicators in the categories of work, production, and distribution and debt, from 1946 to 2014, concluded that the effectiveness of Prime Minister Harper's government in dealing with the economy ranked last among the nine postwar prime ministers.

> In summary, there is no empirical support for the claim that Conservative governments in general—and the Harper government in particular—are the "best economic managers." To the contrary, Canada's economy has never performed worse, since the end of World War II, than under the present Conservative government. Alternative policies (emphasizing job creation, real growth, rising incomes, and equality) will be required to put Canada's economy back onto a more optimistic path.[46]

Other analysts, particularly in the resource-rich West, have argued that imposing an industrial strategy would harm the one area of the economy that had been doing well until recently, namely resource extraction, and hinder trade with other nations.

Summary

The Canadian economy is changing rapidly because of a worldwide rationalization of manufacturing and services and the changing value of the Canadian dollar. We have witnessed job losses in some sectors such as the oil industry and a resurgence in some areas such as tourism and manufacturing, and in the service sector, creating high-paying, skilled jobs. In spite of these economic changes, Canada continues to be a caring and sharing society. When QOL measures are examined and compared with other countries, Canada continues to be a good place to live. Nonetheless, the distribution of income in Canada has changed over the last several decades, with some groups in Canadian society, namely women and Aboriginals, more likely to live in poverty.

Has Canada lived up to its self-image and idealized standards of compassion, tolerance, and prosperity? In this chapter we have tried to explain how Canadian society and its politics are influenced by its socio-economic setting. Canada is an affluent society that arguably has managed, perhaps because of a wealth of resources, government policies, and good fortune, to overcome some of the socio-economic problems that plague governments in other countries. In fact, Canadians have prided themselves on overcoming several of the socio-economic problems that afflict their powerful neighbour to the south.

With respect to cultural and economic sovereignty, Canada is not unique in its struggle with external influences that limit the sovereignty of its elected governments. These influences seem to be felt somewhat more powerfully in Canada because of its proximity to the United States. The debate continues about which economic approach is best for Canada. And questions arise about the kind of society Canada ought to be. How much dependence on another economy is too much? Is a diversified economy preferable? If most Canadians prefer American films, television programs, Internet programming, and magazines, should their governments interfere? Obviously the protectionist measures such as the Canadian content quotas imposed on radio stations are not a response to listener demands. And anyway, which distinctive elements in Canadian culture should be preserved? The answers to these many questions are inevitably coloured by one's own values.

Review Exercises

1. Education is one of the principal ladders for upward socio-economic mobility. Where do the wealthiest Canadians go to school? How accessible is post-secondary education in Canada compared to other wealthy democracies?
2. How many homeless people are in your community? How much food bank use is there?
3. Make a list of the most influential people in your town or city. Are they politicians, business people, journalists, or activists?

Up for Debate

1. Are the CRTC's Canadian content rules outmoded? Do artists deserve air time based on MAPL criteria or on the merits of their work? Should it be part of the government's mandate to promote Canadian culture in this way?

2. Do the economic elite owe their wealth and power to hard work, creativity, and intelligence, or to inherited position, exploitation of workers, deceiving consumers, and manipulating the laws?
3. Resolved: The state has an obligation to provide social programs.
4. Resolved: A guaranteed annual income is a good idea.

Starting Points for Research

Conference Board of Canada. *How Canada Performs*. www.conferenceboard.ca/hcp/default.aspx.

McMullin, Julie. *Understanding Social Inequality: Intersections of Class, Age, Gender, Ethnicity, and Race in Canada*, 3rd edn. Toronto: Oxford University Press, 2014.

Rice, James J., and Michael J. Prince. *Changing Politics of Canadian Social Policy*, 2nd edn. Toronto: University of Toronto Press, 2013.

Sharma, Raghubar D. *Poverty in Canada*. Toronto: Oxford University Press, 2012.

Statistics Canada. www.statcan.gc.ca/start-debut-eng.html.

CBC Archives and TVO's *The Agenda*

Visit the companion website for *Canadian Democracy: A Concise Introduction* to follow links to audio and video footage related to the main themes of the chapter: www.oupcanada.com/BrooksConcise2e.

Relevant Websites

Visit the companion website for *Canadian Democracy: A Concise Introduction* to browse a collection of websites featuring material related to the key themes of the chapter, an excellent starting point for research: www.oupcanada.com/BrooksConcise2e.

4 Regionalism and Canadian Politics

"Canada has too much geography," declared the country's longest-serving prime minister, William Lyon Mackenzie King. By this he meant that the country's vastness and the diversity in natural endowments and interests of its regions produced conflicts that would likely not exist in a more compact country. Canadians have always accepted the truth of King's dictum, believing that the challenges of *regionalism* and inter-regional conflict are central to the Canadian story. Indeed, one of the most astute Canadian political observers, Donald Smiley, identified regionalism as one of the three fundamental axes of Canadian politics—the other two being the rift between English Canadians and French Canadians, and Canada's long-standing relationship with the United States. As Smiley indicated, regionalism has been the source of major political divisions and controversies in Canadian history, and continues to be a defining feature of its political landscape.

↑ Regionalism in Canada has and continues to influence political direction due to vast differences in regions' needs.

Source: zennie/Getty Images.

This chapter looks at several important aspects of regionalism in Canadian politics, including the following topics: predicting the demise of regionalism; the persistence of regionalism; the boundaries of Canada's regions; regional political cultures; regional grievances and Western alienation; and Western versus Central Canadian "visions" of the country. After reading this chapter, you should be able to

1. describe the six different regions in Canada
2. explain how their different economies affect their political aspirations
3. outline the tensions between any two regions of Canada
4. identify three national structures or policies intended to accommodate regional interests
5. discuss the history of Western alienation in Canada and the Western Canadian conception of equality
6. explain how Canada's political institutions deliberately accommodate regional differences

Along with King, most Canadians have viewed regionalism as a problem. Aside from occasional patriotic celebrations of Canada's regional diversity and sheer size, few have argued that size and regional diversity are positive attributes in political life. Students of American politics will know, however, that some founders of the United States believed size and diversity were positive characteristics of a political system that respects freedom. For example, in the *Federalist Papers*, James Madison argued that a larger territory encompassing a greater diversity of regional interests was more likely to provide protection for personal freedoms, group rights, and sectional interests. Madison reasoned that as a country's physical size increased, and the scope of its social, and especially its economic interests, grew, the less likely it was that any particular group or coalition of interests could dominate others. Small countries with comparatively homogeneous populations were, he thought, unable to maintain respect for individual and minority rights, and the majority would inevitably exercise a form of tyranny by using their superior numbers to oppress the rights of others.

Despite some agreement in Western Canada, Madison's argument that vast republics help protect rights has never resonated very positively in Canada. Canada's expansion was seen by most as a necessary pre-emptive action to reduce the possibility that the western territories would be annexed by a United States where the ideas of territorial expansion and **manifest destiny**, a nineteenth-century American belief that the United States was destined to expand to include all North America, were riding high. One of the few Canadians to theorize about regionalism's consequences in the style of Madison was Pierre Trudeau, usually considered a prime minister with a strong preference for centralized federal power. Trudeau's thoughts on the political virtue of regionalism were, however, formulated before he entered federal politics in 1965. Aside from the early Trudeau and some disgruntled Westerners, few Canadians have disagreed with Mackenzie King's assessment that regionalism has been a burden.

manifest destiny a nineteenth-century American belief that the United States was destined to expand to include all North America

The Unexpected Persistence of Regionalism

In the last few decades there has been an upsurge in regionalism in Canada, a trend mirrored in many other parts of the world. The signs of this upsurge can be seen in the *party system*, *Western alienation*, *regional economic disparities*, and *intergovernmental conflict*.

The Party System

For most of Canada's history, the two dominant parties have been the Liberals and Conservatives (called Progressive Conservatives between 1942 and 2003). Although they did not draw equally well from all regional segments of the electorate—the Liberals did much better than the Conservatives in Quebec for most of the twentieth century and the Conservatives tended to be stronger in the West for most of the second half of that century—both were very clearly national political parties with significant support across Canada.

Since the 1993 general election, the character of Canada's party system has appeared to be based more regionally than nationally. This is most obvious in the case of the Bloc Québécois, which runs candidates only in Quebec; it elected more MPs from that province than any other party in the 1993, 1997, 2004, 2006, and 2008 elections before the party's collapse in the 2011 general election. The Canadian Alliance, formerly the *Reform Party*, won almost all its seats west of Ontario and received the greatest share of the popular vote of any party in the four combined Western provinces in the 1993, 1997, and 2000 federal elections. The Progressive Conservative Party, long a truly national party in terms of the regional breadth of its support, elected more of its MPs from the Atlantic provinces in these same three elections than from any other part of the country. The Alliance and the Progressive Conservatives merged into the Conservative Party of Canada in 2003, a union that delivered fewer than a quarter of the seats in Ontario and none from Quebec in the 2004 election. Only the Liberal Party appeared able to claim significant support in all regions of the country over the four national elections between 1993 and 2004, although even its regional support was very uneven.

In the 2006 and 2008 elections, Liberal support continued to be very weak west of Ontario, but Conservative support rebounded in Ontario and even in Quebec. There was an expectation that the trend of fragmentation along regional lines would continue in the 2011 general election, but the election surprised many and may have signalled a political shift. It was an unprecedented disaster for the Liberal Party, which lost support to the Conservatives and NDP in many of its traditional strongholds. The Conservative Party could now claim that it was truly Canada's new "natural governing party"—a label once given to the Liberal Party. In 2011, the Bloc Québécois was all but annihilated in Quebec and the NDP made unprecedented gains there, winning enough seats in that province to become the official opposition. The Bloc's fortunes were not changed in the 2015 election, and the Liberals were able to recover many of their old seats from the NDP and Conservative parties.

Western Alienation

Western grievances against both Ottawa and the Ontario–Quebec axis have dominated the national political scene ever since the Western provinces joined Canada. But in the 1970s there was a sharp upward ratcheting in the rhetoric associated with these grievances, and the term "Western alienation" entered the lexicon of Canadian politics. As always, economics was at the root of this discontent. Spokespersons for the Western provinces argued that Ottawa treated the resources with which the West was well endowed and which formed the basis for Western prosperity differently and less favourably than those located in central provinces. Although Albertans were the most vocal, politicians and industry leaders in British Columbia and Saskatchewan provided a supportive chorus.

Economic Disparities

In terms of real prosperity, the gap between Canada's richest and poorest provinces has not narrowed. Indeed, if the federal government transfers intended to narrow this gap are excluded, the

© Michael de Adder/Artizans

Every province is interested in acquiring the greatest share of resources for its population. One often hears of provincial premiers wanting more power in matters such as natural resources and constitutional jurisdiction or wanting a greater share of federal equalization payments. A province's citizens may consider competing with the federal government as to the right thing to do, but is there a downside to practising this kind of self-interest?

disparity has increased between wealthy provinces like Alberta and Ontario and the less affluent provinces like New Brunswick and Nova Scotia. (Since the 2009–10 fiscal year, however, Ontario has been a "have-not" province, meaning it received equalization payments from the federal government to make up a shortfall in the tax the province was able to collect.) Such a disparity does not necessarily mean greater inter-regional conflict if the central government is able to subsidize incomes and public services in the poorer regions, and if taxpayers in the wealthier regions are willing to pay for this redistribution of wealth. However, these conditions have been eroded in the last two decades as the political will to maintain these redistributive transfers has weakened.

Intergovernmental Conflict

The pendulum of federal–provincial power has swung back and forth between Ottawa to the provinces since Confederation. Sir John A. Macdonald's hope and expectation that the provincial governments would become little more than "glorified municipalities," deferring to Ottawa on all matters of national importance, was stymied from the beginning by provincial politicians who had other ideas and by judges whose interpretation of the division of powers in Canada's Constitution did not accord with Macdonald's. Today, regionalism and intergovernmental conflict in areas such as environmental policy, health care, taxation, cities, and post-secondary education are part of the Canadian political landscape.

Predicting the Demise of Regionalism

The persistence and even resurgence of regionalism in Canada and elsewhere surprised most twentieth-century social and political observers. They had agreed that as the conditions of people's lives became more similar, their values, beliefs, and behaviour would likewise converge. As modern transportation, mass media, public education, and consumer lifestyle habits broke down the barriers that previously separated regional communities and nurtured their distinctiveness, regionalism would become a weaker force in social and political life. Even theorists on the left predicted that region, like religion and ethnicity, would be replaced by class as the main fault line in the politics of modernized societies.

Contrary to these expectations, and despite the undeniable fact that in many important ways the lives of people throughout the world's rich industrialized societies are more alike today than a generation or two ago, regionalism and nationalism continue to be important forces in political life. This certainly is true in Canada, as the signs of regionalism's vitality and the persistence of a nationalist movement in Quebec demonstrate. Three principal factors help to explain the attraction and persistence of regionalism:

1. the continued strength of regionally based elites
2. the failure of national institutions
3. the persistence of differences in regional economic interests and social characteristics

Regionally Based Elites

First, traditional thinking underestimated the degree to which regionally based states and elites may invest in regionalism—and regionally based nationalism, too, as in Quebec—when this investment either serves their own interests or promotes their vision of the regional community that they purport to represent. During the 1970s Canadian political scientists began to use the term **province building** to describe the phenomenon of powerful provincial governments using the constitutional, legal, and taxation levers to increase their control within their provincial borders and, consequently, their stature vis-à-vis Ottawa. Alberta and Quebec were often cited as examples of provincial state elites seeking to extend the scope of their authority.

But the phenomenon of province building has not been limited to Alberta and Quebec. Alan Cairns argues that regionalism's strength in Canada is primarily due to a Constitution that gives Canada's provincial governments considerable law-making and revenue-raising powers, reinforced by the natural tendency of those who control, work for, or depend on provincial governments, or rather "states," to protect and extend their control. We will have more to say about this later.

province building
the phenomenon of powerful provincial governments using the constitutional, legal, and taxation levers to increase their control within their provincial borders and, consequently, their stature vis-à-vis Ottawa

The Failure of National Institutions

A second factor not anticipated by those who predicted the demise of regionalism is the failure of Canadian political, cultural, and economic institutions to produce levels of national

Canadian Spotlight

BOX 4.1   Modernization and Regionalism

The Expectation . . .

In . . . modernizing societies, the general historical record has spelled centralization. . . . the main reasons for this change, the major grounds of centralization and decentralization are to be found not in . . . "ground rules" [the Constitution and court rulings] . . . [or] in the personal, partisan or ideological preferences of officeholders, but in the new forces produced by an advanced modernity.

—Samuel Beer, *The Modernization of American Federalism*, 1973

The Canadian Reality . . .

Modernization had led not to centralization in the Canadian federal system but rather to the power, assertiveness, and competence of the provinces. Furthermore, the provinces where modernization has proceeded most rapidly are insistent about preserving and extending their autonomy.

—Donald Smiley, "Public Sector Politics, Modernization, and Federalism: The Canadian and American Experiences," 1984

integration and identity that would overcome regionally based thinking and acting. Many Canadians, particularly in Quebec and the West, remain unconvinced that the institutions of the national government and its policies have their best interests in mind. Students of federalism make a distinction between *inter-state federalism*, where conflict and co-operation play out between the national and regional governments, and *intra-state federalism*, where these forces are contained within the institutions of the national state. There certainly is no shortage of national structures and policies designed to accommodate regional interests. A short list of these, past and present, includes the following:

Structures

- The Senate incorporates the principle of regional representation: Ontario, Quebec, the four Western provinces, and the three Maritime provinces have the same number of seats.
- The Supreme Court Act requires that at least three of the nine justices be members of the Quebec bar. Moreover, a custom has developed whereby three judges will be from Ontario and at least one from each of Western and Eastern Canada.
- The federal cabinet has always reflected regional representation. Whenever possible a prime minister will include representatives from each region and province.
- Section 36 of the Constitution Act, 1982 commits the federal government to the principle of "making equalization payments to ensure that provincial governments have sufficient revenues to provide reasonably comparable levels of taxation." The spirit of the Constitution clearly involves a federal obligation to assist the less affluent provincial governments.

Policies

- For about two decades, and in response to criticism that the Canadian media system and federal cultural policy has a strong Central Canada bias, Ottawa has attempted to "regionalize" its cultural activities in various ways. One way involves regional programming through the Canadian Broadcasting Corporation (CBC), and another involves the programs and spending activities of the Canadian Heritage department. Both have a mandate to express Canada's diversity.
- Federal support for regional economic development has a long and much-criticized history. These activities were given an organizational focus and a major spending boost through the 1968 creation of the Department of Regional Economic Expansion, which has morphed into departments and agencies by other names over the years. Today, Ottawa's support for the economies of the less affluent provinces is channelled mainly through mainly through five regional development agencies under the Department of Industry.
- Ottawa is always sensitive to the probable reactions of citizens and their spokespersons when making decisions with regional spending and employment implications.

These structures and policies have not been complete and abject failures, and while they have not succeeded in neutralizing regionalism, regional grievances and acrimony might have been worse without these efforts at intra-state federalism.

Regional Economic Interests and Social Characteristics

A third factor to thwart the predicted demise of regionalism is the persistence of differences in the economic interests and social characteristics of regions. In many respects, how people in Ontario and Saskatchewan live, the sorts of jobs they are likely to do, what they watch on television, and the cultural milieu in which they live are more alike today than two generations ago. But differences persist and their political importance, often fanned by politicians or other regional spokespersons, is considerable. For example, about one-quarter of Alberta's GDP derives from the petrochemical industry, a level of dependence on a particular industry that is unrivalled in Canada. Ontario's economy depends on the automobile industry, with automotive vehicles and parts accounting for close to 30 per cent of all provincial exports—about 11 per cent of Ontario's

© Cindy Hopkins/Alamy

Nunavut (which means "Our Land"), with an Aboriginal population of more than 85 per cent, is a unique region of the country. Its distinctive character is visible in the design of its legislative building—called "The Ledge" by locals in Iqaluit—which incorporates Inuit themes in its architecture (for instance, the entrance is shaped like a dog sled) and uses local symbols and resources in its décor (e.g., the assembly's seats and benches are upholstered in sealskin and the ceremonial mace is carved from walrus tusk and adorned with precious metals and stones found in the region). Also noteworthy is the assembly's circular seating area. How might this round configuration, quite different from other government houses in which parties sit opposite each other across aisles, affect the debates, discussions, and negotiations that take place within it?

GDP. Almost all the exported automotive goods go to the United States. British Columbia accounts for over half of all Canadian lumber and wood product exports, most of which go to the United States, China, and Japan. As these examples suggest, the economic issues that capture the attention of politicians and the public differ considerably among the provinces.

Demography

We also find some significant differences in the demography of provinces and regions. On the whole, and with one major exception, these demographic differences tend to have considerably less political impact than do Canada's different regional economic interests. The major exception is Quebec, which is the only majority francophone province, with over 80 per cent of the provincial population claiming French as their mother tongue and a majority having French ancestry. Another region whose ethnic character is dramatically different from the rest of Canada is Nunavut, where about 85 per cent of the population is Aboriginal. This is not to say that there are not enormous differences in the demographic character of provinces like British Columbia, with its large non-European and Asian immigrant population, and Nova Scotia, where people of British Isles ancestry predominate. But the ethnic characters of British Columbia and Nova Scotia do not get expressed in our politics the way that Quebec's francophone character does.

Mapping Regionalism in Canada

How many regions does Canada have? The answer depends on our definition of "region." A map with boundaries drawn along economic lines will look different from one drawn along lines of demography or history. Some argue that the only sensible way to conceive of Canada's regions is along provincial lines, such that each province constitutes a separate region. More commonly, however, political observers tend to combine certain provinces into the same region, particularly the Western and Eastern provinces. But here, too, there are difficulties. The justification for lumping Manitoba and British Columbia into a common region designated "the West" is unclear. Aside from both being west of Ontario they may appear to have no more in common than do Manitoba and Nova Scotia. Difficulties aside, it has been common to speak of five or six main regions in Canada:

- the West (or British Columbia and the Prairies)
- Ontario
- Quebec
- the Atlantic provinces
- the Canadian North

There are three principal ways to determine the boundaries of regions: economics, values, and identity.

 Listen to the "Is It Time to Redraw the Regional Map of Canada?" podcast at www.oupcanada.com/BrooksConcise2e.

Canada's Economic Regions

Common economic interests, often linked to physical geography, may provide a basis for classifying regions. Atlantic Canada's greater dependence on fisheries, Ontario and Quebec's greater manufacturing base, and the West's comparatively greater reliance on grain production and natural resource extraction, are economic interests that provide a basis for considering these parts of Canada as constituting distinctive regions. As Table 4.1 shows, the economic characteristics of Canada's provinces vary considerably.

The regional variation in Canada's industrial structure is often at the root of major political conflicts between regions and between Ottawa and the provinces. The Kyoto Protocol, which requires policies that would reduce the use of carbon-based fuels, pitted Ottawa against Alberta for about a decade. Albertans and their government knew that the environmental gains of the protocol would be achieved at the expense of the industry that is central to their economy. The federal government was able to point to public opinion polls showing that a clear majority of Canadians favoured ratifying the Kyoto agreement. As it turned out, the Conservative Party's victory in the 2006 national election rendered the issue moot, given the party's lack of sympathy for the Kyoto guidelines and its less interventionist approach to global warming.

Ottawa's position climate change was reversed with the election of a Liberal government in 2015. The Liberal government signed the Paris Agreement in 2015, and a more interventionist

social licence
the approval by a community or by an alliance of interests or stakeholders for a proposed project

Canadian Spotlight

BOX 4.2 Alberta's Reliance on Fossil Fuels and Its Economic Predicament

Alberta's economic predicament that began in 2014 presents an unfortunate example of how economic interests vary from one region to the next and of just how complex the accommodations of certain regional, national, and international interests can be. A number of factors have contributed to Alberta's economic picture. Alberta has one of the largest oil reserves in the world, but much of this oil requires additional processing that gives off greenhouse gases. Also, Alberta is landlocked and needs to deliver its oil either by rail or by pipeline through other jurisdictions. Any project proposing pipeline construction for natural gas or oil has been heavily criticized by local groups, Aboriginal groups, and a host of non-governmental organizations. In moves that are seen as pandering to interest groups withholding their **social licence**—the approval by a community or by an alliance of interests or stakeholders for a proposed project—certain governments began to veto the building of pipelines through the lands they controlled:

- In 2015 American president Barack Obama refused to grant approval of the Keystone XL pipeline project, which was designed to take oil from Alberta to refineries in Texas.
- The Kinder-Morgan Trans Mountain pipeline was opposed by the British Columbia government in early 2016.

- The Northern Gateway pipeline projects were approved by the federal government in 2014, but after the Liberals formed the government in 2015, they imposed a ban on oil tanker traffic, which killed the project.
- In January 2016, Montreal-area mayors voiced their opposition to the Energy East natural gas pipeline from Alberta to the east coast, saying it was "too risky."

Alberta's economy was also affected by the falling price of a barrel of oil, which dropped from a high of $136 in 2008 to below $40 in 2016. So, the fight against global climate change and greenhouse gas emissions could not have come at a worse time for Alberta's economy, the cost of which would weigh heavily on the slumping Alberta oil industry. And, as if things were not already bad enough, Alberta's oil industry was almost completely crippled when a wildfire in 2016 forced the evacuation of tens of thousands of Fort McMurray residents, many of whom were working directly or indirectly for the oil industry. This was largest and most expensive wildfire evacuation in Canadian history.

Brian Gable/The Globe and Mail/The Canadian Press

As the cartoon suggests, there are those who believe that projects such as mining, airports, garbage dumps, and so on should never be started without the approval of the surrounding community, the stakeholders, and special interests, even though the project might benefit the society at large. Are there ever circumstances when the withholding of a social licence might go too far?

TABLE 4.1 Selected Economic and Population Characteristics, by Province

Province	Median Family Income (2011)* ($)	Unemployment Rate (average for 2008–12) (%)	Manufacturing Share of GDP (2011)(%)	Key Industries	Population Growth, 2006–11 (%)	Median Government Transfers to Families (2011) ($)
NL	53,000	13.7	3.2	Fishing, mining, oil & gas, newsprint	1.8	12,300
PEI	53,000	11.3	8.7	Agriculture, tourism, fishing	3.2	11,300
NS	60,600	8.8	7.5	Forestry, agriculture, tourism, fishing	0.9	8,400
NB	54,000	9.3	11.3	Forestry, mining, agriculture	2.9	9,700
QC	58,500	7.9	14.2	Manufacturing, mining, hydro-electric power	4.7	7,900
ON	70,600	8.0	12.4	Motor vehicles & parts, manufacturing, finance	5.7	5,900
MB	67,900	5.1	11.5	Manufacturing, agriculture	5.2	4,600
SK	77,700	4.8	6.3	Agriculture, mining	6.7	4,500
AB	91,300	5.4	6.4	Oil & gas, agriculture	10.8	2,300
BC	67,600	6.8	7.2	Forestry, tourism, mining	7.0	5,200
Canada	68,400	7.4	11.5		5.9	6,000

*Households consisting of a couple living together, with or without children. This is market income, not including government transfers or income tax.

Source: Various online publications of Statistics Canada www.statcan.ca.

approach to fighting global carbon emissions was adopted by the federal government and by several provincial governments, including the NDP government in Alberta.

Historically, the federal government's major economic policies have been slanted toward the interests of Central Canada. On occasion, the discrimination against and even exploitation of other regions, particularly the West, have been egregious. Examples include interprovincial tariffs, each province's terms of entry into Confederation, and the National Energy Policy. Given the other examples listed in Box 4.2, it is easy to see why Albertans might feel slighted by their partners in Confederation.

Tariffs

For most of Canada's history, a cornerstone of economic policy was high tariffs on manufactured imports, whose costs and benefits were distributed unequally between regions. The cost for Western farmers to ship grain by rail to Thunder Bay, despite federal subsidies, always seemed greater than it should have been. And the costs of shipping Eastern-manufactured goods to the West made prices higher than they might have been if trade—protected by the high tariffs of the National Policy beginning in 1879—had followed more natural north–south lines with American states and regions. The Canadian Pacific Railway's control over extensive prime lands (part of its original agreement with the federal government in the nineteenth century) also rankled Western sensitivities.

One study of tariff impacts prior to the 1989 Canada–US Free Trade Agreement concluded that the per capita benefits for Ontario were about equal to the per capita costs imposed on the West and Atlantic Canada. Quebecers were also net beneficiaries, but the decline of that province's manufacturing base by the 1980s reduced the level of these benefits from what it had been for most of the previous century.[1]

Terms of Entry into Confederation

Outside Alberta and Saskatchewan, few Canadians know that when these provinces entered Canada in 1905 they did not immediately receive all the law-making powers and control over natural resources that the other provinces enjoyed. This discriminatory treatment was due to Ottawa's desire to retain control over the economic development of the Prairies, then being settled rapidly, and whose expansion was essential to the National Policy goal of building a larger domestic market for Quebec and Ontario manufacturers.

The National Energy Program (1981)

A generation after it was abolished by the Conservative government of Brian Mulroney in 1984, the **National Energy Program** (NEP—a scheme brought in by the Liberal government of Pierre Elliott Trudeau to control the cost of energy to the rest of Canada) remained vivid in the memory of many Albertans who saw the NEP as a thinly disguised subsidy their province was made to pay to Central Canada.

When world oil prices doubled in 2007–8, there was less talk about the rest of Canada getting a slice of Alberta's growing revenue pie. One reason for this change was probably the fact of a federal Conservative government in power, holding all 28 Alberta seats in the House of Commons and led by a prime minister from that province. But another reason was that the issue of energy costs was now framed largely in environmental terms. How to reduce consumer

National Energy Program (NEP) a scheme brought in by the Liberal government of Pierre Elliott Trudeau to control the cost of energy to the rest of Canada

and industry dependence on fossil fuels and reduce CO^2 emissions had become more important than whether some provinces should share their wealth.

Canada's Cultural Regions

In a widely cited and disputed 1974 study of regional political cultures in Canada, Richard Simeon and David Elkins conclude that "there are strong differences among the citizens of Canadian provinces and those of different language groups in some basic orientations to politics."[2] They argue that these regional variations cannot be totally explained by demographic and socio-economic differences between Canada's regions. They maintain that the sources of these differences are unclear, but that their existence is undeniable.

Other researchers have arrived at very different conclusions about regional political cultures in Canada. There is a shaky consensus that regional variations in basic and enduring political values and beliefs are not very great in English-speaking Canada, and that the differences between French-speaking Quebec and the rest of Canada are not enormous. Several surveys appear to support this conclusion:

- *Charter values.* A 2002 survey by Environics Research Group notes the "lack of any significant regional differences of opinion on the Charter's legitimacy or the relationship between Parliament and the courts."[3] Moreover, there does not appear to be any difference in support across Canada's regions for such Charter principles and values as bilingualism and minority-language rights, education rights, multiculturalism, the appropriateness of "reasonable limits" on freedom of expression, and the rights of the accused.
- *Trust.* A 2013 survey by Ekos Politics found that, for the most part, provincial populations differ only slightly in the level of trust they have in various groups and institutions. Respondents were asked to indicate how much trust they had in government, nurses, doctors, teachers, newspapers, journalists, television news, pollsters, social media, and bloggers. If there was any discernible pattern at all, Quebecers appear to be somewhat more trusting than other provincial populations.[4]
- *Faith and religious authority.* Quebec, once thought to be the most traditionally religious province, now appears to be the least. Variations among other provincial populations are small.[5]
- *Diversity.* Once again, Quebecers appear to stand apart from the populations of other Canadian regions. While there is widespread support across Canada for the concept of diversity, Quebecers are more likely than other Canadians to express some doubts.[6]
- *Ideology.* The conventional wisdom, as found in the media, is that Canada's most left-leaning province is Quebec and the most right-leaning is Alberta. The rest fall somewhere in between. A 2012 survey by Ekos provides only tepid confirmation of this claim.[7]

The case for the existence of strong regional political cultures in English-speaking Canada is not helped if one looks at how provincial populations view their attachment to Canada and to their own province and at whether they believe that Canadians generally share the same values. Quebec tends to be the outlier among the provinces when it comes to most of these perceptions. As may be seen in Figure 4.1, the sense of belonging to Canada is very high across the predominantly English-speaking provinces. In Quebec, however, it is comparatively low.

Quebecers are not, as one might expect, more likely than other Canadians to report a strong sense of belonging to their province that compensates for their weaker attachment to Canada. Identities, attachments, and loyalties are not necessarily competitive. This is evident from the fact that citizens in Saskatchewan and in Atlantic Canada tend to have a very strong sense of belonging both to Canada and to their own region. They appear to be even more likely than Quebecers to have a strong attachment to their province. Ontarians are the outliers when it comes to the sense of belonging to one's province. They are considerably less likely than Canadians in other provinces to report a strong provincial attachment.

Canadians in all provinces except Quebec believe that they have much in common with their compatriots in other parts of the country. Significant majorities in all the predominantly English-speaking provinces strongly agree that, despite differences, Canadians have many things that unite them. As may be seen in part C of Figure 4.1, Quebecers are dubious. They are also only half as likely as other Canadians to agree that citizens in all provinces have the same values (see Figure 4.1, part D).

Cross-Border Regions

A more recent method of mapping regions is suggested by Debora VanNijnatten and her colleagues in their work on **cross-border regions** (CBRs). They define a CBR as a distinct grouping of neighbouring and nearby provinces and states whose economic, cultural, and institutional linkages create commonalities between the members of this binational (Canada–US) grouping and set it apart from other regions. Based on an analysis of the density of economic, institutional, and socio-cultural ties between adjacent and nearby provinces and states, VanNijnatten and her colleagues propose a rather different regional map (see Figure 4.2). It includes the following (sometimes overlapping) regions:

cross-border regions (CBRs) a distinct grouping of neighbouring and nearby provinces and states whose economic, cultural, and institutional linkages create commonalities between the members of this binational (Canada–US) grouping and set it apart from other regions

- *The West.* This CBR includes British Columbia, Alberta, and Yukon in Canada, and Alaska, Washington, Idaho, Oregon, and Montana in the United States. It is characterized by a sense of remoteness from each country's central government, a strong regional identity, and similar values. A dense network of private and public institutional linkages spans the Canada–US border, and more emphasis is placed on shared environmental issues than in other regions.
- *The Prairie–Great Plains.* This CBR includes Alberta, Saskatchewan, and Manitoba in Canada, and Montana, Wyoming, North Dakota, South Dakota, and Minnesota in the United States. Although the institutional linkages between these relatively sparsely populated and natural resource–dependent provinces and states are less entrenched than in other CBRs, the region features extensive economic ties and strong linkages based on shared management of common watersheds.

A. Personal sense of belonging to Canada (% saying extremely strong*)

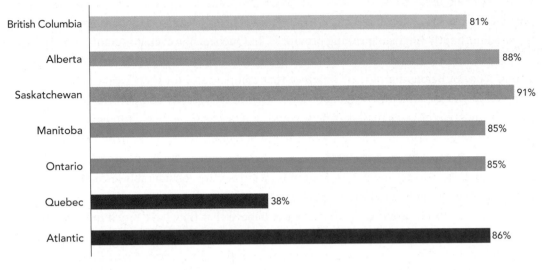

*On a 7-point scale where 7 was the strongest score, respondents who chose 5–7.

B. Personal sense of belonging to your province

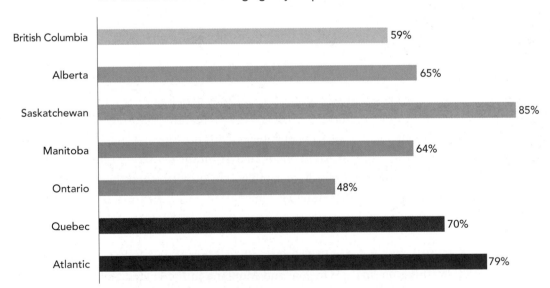

FIGURE 4.1 Regional Perceptions of Belonging and of Shared Canadian Values

Source: Adapted from multiple sources: Ekos Politics.(2014). *Looking Backward, Looking Forward: Five Big Forces Shaping Our Society*, p. 36-36; Environics Institute. (2012). *Focus Canada*, p.21; *Environics Institute. (2012). America's Barometer*, p. 26.

- *The Great Lakes–Heartland.* The shared waters of the Great Lakes and the enormous volume of trade and daily flow of vehicles and people across the Canada–US border are the most obvious features of this CBR. A dense network of cross-border institutions, public and private, link its states—Michigan, Indiana, and Ohio—and province—Ontario. But unlike in the West, there is no strong sense of shared regional identity.

- *The East.* Although Quebec and the Atlantic provinces have some significant trade and institutional linkages, their ties to adjacent and nearby American states are rather different. Quebec is part of a CBR that includes Vermont, Maine, New Hampshire, and New York, while the Atlantic provinces belong to a CBR that includes Maine, New Hampshire, Massachusetts, Rhode Island, and Connecticut. The Quebec–New England CBR is characterized by strong ties of history, trade, transportation, and institutions, but little shared regional identity. The Atlantic–New England grouping is based on ties of history, trade, and environmental and energy co-operation; a rich network of institutional linkages; and a strong sense of regional identity.

Thinking about Canadian regions while taking into account these cross-border linkages is useful. First, we can explain the causes and nature of integration between Canada and the United States and describe the integration between the states and provinces in each of these four CBRs. As VanNijnatten puts it, North American integration is a bottom-up phenomenon.[8] Second, the powers held by provincial or state and local governments on both sides of the border, and the fact that transportation, the environment, security, energy supply and distribution, and many other matters tend to be regional, ensure that these subnational governments

FIGURE 4.2 Cross-Border Regions

Source: Adapted from Debora VanNijnatten, 'Canada-US Relations and the Emergence of Cross-Border Regions', Government of Canada, Policy Research Initiatives, 2006, www.policyresearch.gc.ca.

Democracy Watch

BOX 4.3 Canada: All Things to All People?

Canada will be a strong country when Canadians of all provinces feel at home in all parts of the country, and when they feel that all of Canada belongs to them.

—Pierre Elliott Trudeau

and private regional organizations and institutions are important players in managing cross-border issues.[9]

Regional Identities and Western Alienation

What if, instead of looking for significant and enduring regional differences in fundamental political values and beliefs, we asked whether citizens of Canada's regions view their history differently or hold different aspirations for their country and their region's role in it? We find then compelling evidence for the existence of regional political cultures. In particular, we find that the West has long been characterized by sentiments of resentment toward and alienation from Ottawa and by what Westerners perceive to be the political preoccupations of Central Canada. Roger Gibbins and Sonia Arrison argue that it is reasonable to speak of "national visions" in the West that, in their words, "address not simply the place of the West within the Canadian federal state, but also the nature of *Canada* as a political community."[10] These national visions are more than feelings of being unfairly treated and marginalized—the resentment captured in the Reform Party's slogan, "The West Wants In"—they are deeply rooted in regional histories that have forged a collective consciousness and memories that are different from those of Central and Eastern Canada.

Starting in the 1950s with W.L. Morton, Western Canadian historians began to react against what they saw as a narrative of Canadian history told from a Central Canadian perspective. This perspective, said Morton,

> fails to take account of regional experience and history and makes coherent Canadian history seem an "imperialist creed," an imposition on Maritime, French-Canadian, Western and British Columbian history of an interpretation which distorted local history and confirmed the feeling that union with Canada had been carried out against local sentiment and local interest.[11]

Morton and many others have attempted to counter the centralist bias of Canadian history writing, but the belief lives on that the West's stories are not given fair weight by a Canadian economic, academic, and cultural establishment centred in the Toronto–Ottawa–Montreal triangle (see Box 4.4).

In a similar vein, Barry Cooper, a Calgary-based political scientist, argues that a distinctive history and political tradition exists in Western Canada:

> . . . dualism is not the political issue in the West that it is in central Canada. Moreover, multiculturalism does not mean the same thing to a third or fourth generation non-French, non-British Westerner as it does to someone from the Azores or Calabria living on College Street in Toronto.[12]

What is referred to as Western **alienation**, Cooper argues, is not in fact a psychological, sociological, or economic condition. Rather, it is the awareness that the public realm—whose voices are heard and what counts as legitimate political discourse—belongs to others. These "others" are the citizens of Central Canada and their elites.

alienation the awareness that the public realm—whose voices are heard and what counts as legitimate political discourse—belongs to others

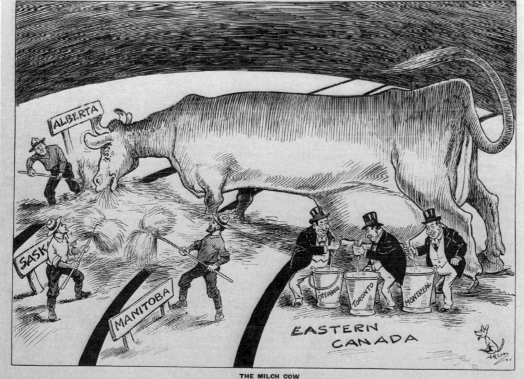

THE MILCH COW

Our artist has here attempted to portray the idea which the Big Interests of Eastern Canada seem to have of the proper function of the Western Provinces. The Bankers, the Railway Corporations and the Manufacturers rejoice to see a big crop in the West because it will increase their own profits, but when the farmers of the West ask for lower rates of interest, lower freight rates and Free Trade, so that they can get the full value of the crops they produce, Big Business, with the aid of the Party Politicians, always succeeds in having their demands refused.

Glenbow Museum Archives (NA-3055-24)

This political cartoon depicts a long-held belief of Western Canadians that there is a Canadian economic, academic, and cultural establishment centred in the Toronto–Ottawa–Montreal triangle.

Canadian Spotlight

BOX 4.4   The West as Canada's Internal Colony

To trace the decreasing sensitivity of the national government to influences which are specifically provincial or regional would be to write the history of Canadian political institutions over more than a century.

—Donald Smiley, *Canada in Question: Federalism in the Seventies*, 1976

Unfortunately, federal policies, the attitudes of Central Canadian governments and the biases of so-called national institutions, such as the Canadian Broadcasting Corporation, have painted regionalism with the brush of divisiveness, disunity and even treason. Influences tending to strengthen regional power are "balkanizing," while those working to increase the central power are "in the national interest."

But this is true only if what is good for Central Canada is also good for Canada.

—David Jay Bercuson, *Canada's Burden of Unity*, 1977

Western Canada has paid for the development of Canadian nationality, and it would appear that it must continue to pay.

—Harold Innis, *History of the C.P.A.*, 1923

The West has never felt in control of its own destiny. None of the wealth of recent years has eased this feeling. In fact, the tremendous wealth of the region merely sharpens the contrast with the political powerlessness that exists on the national level.

—Doug Owram, "Reluctant Hinterland," 1981

Western alienation, however, should not be dismissed as mere history. The sense of regional grievance, with roots reaching back to the nineteenth century, can resurface very quickly and with real political consequences. During the 2012 federal by-election in Calgary Centre, comments by federal Liberals Justin Trudeau and David McGuinty were widely covered and criticized by the local media. In a 2010 interview Trudeau had said that "Canada isn't doing well right now because it's Albertans who control our community and socio-democratic agenda."[13]

Along with McGuinty's comment that Alberta MPs were "shills" for the oil industry and his suggestion that they "go home"—as if somehow Canada is not home to Albertans—these reminders of the East–West divide may well have cost the Liberals their chance to win that election. For a while there seemed to be a nationwide perception that there is an East–West clash over the evidence for global warming and what to do about it. The 2015 decision by Alberta premier Rachel Notley's NDP government to impose a carbon tax may have changed these perceptions.

Of course, the evolution of the West's history and the political traditions are not disconnected from those of the rest of Canada. Likewise, as Gibbins and Arrison observe, "Western visions" of the nature of the Canadian political community and their region's place in it are not restricted to the West. They identify a set of core values that they believe are more solidly anchored in the West than in other regions of Canada; the same values also find support, but to a lesser degree, among Canadians in other regions, including French-speaking Quebec. Western visions of Canada are more likely to embrace the individual equality of all Canadians, the equal status of all provinces, and a populist style of doing political business.

Individual Equality

Concerning the first of these values—*individual equality*—Gibbins and Arrison rightly note that reservations about the official recognition and even constitutionalization of multiculturalism and a group rights concept of Canada have come largely from such popular Western spokespersons as John Diefenbaker and Preston Manning, and, one would add, Stephen Harper. Such visions of Canada are part of what Alberta political scientist Barry Cooper refers to as the "Laurentian Canada" perspective that projects the history, preoccupations, and preferences of Ontario and Quebec onto the rest of the country.[14] The argument that Westerners are more receptive to a so-called classically American conception of equality is corroborated by the election of ideologically conservative provincial governments (for example, those of Ralph Klein and Ed Stelmach, in Alberta and Gordon Campbell in British Columbia), and the impressive support in the West for Reform/Alliance and the Conservative Party in federal elections. These core values include treating all individuals equally regardless of group membership and ensuring formal equality of opportunity. On the other hand, it must be said that there is little data to support the claim that Westerners are significantly different from their compatriots when it comes to equality. The surprise majority win by Rachel Notley and the Alberta NDP in the 2015 provincial election, which saw the toppling of a 40-year Progressive Conservative dynasty, is a good example of why generalization about values is tricky.

Provincial Equality

The second core value of the Western vision that Gibbins and Arrison identify is *provincial equality*. They argue that provincial equality has two components: the sense that Canadian federalism would operate more fairly if the West had more influence on decisions taken by Ottawa, for instance, in an elected Senate with equal representation for each province; and the opposition to any arrangement that appears to treat Quebec differently or more favourably than the Western provinces. Observers of the Western political scene know that Westerners have often felt resentment against Quebec. The notion that Quebec is the "spoiled child" of Confederation is seen, particularly in Western provinces, in the opposition to the Charlottetown Accord and the 1992 referendum, and to the constitutional recognition of Quebec as a *distinct society*.

Populism

The third component of the Western vision involves a *populist style of politics*. **Populism**, which seeks to return power to the common people, arose in the American West and Midwest in the

populism a style of politics that seeks to return power to the common people

late 1800s out of the perception that economic and political elites, often far from where the people affected by their decisions lived, were too powerful and unsympathetic to the people's interests. The Western Canadian version of populism was a combination of imported ideas and homegrown conditions that made the American message resonate in this farm- and resource-based economy, where people were constantly reminded by railroads, banks, tariffs, and grain elevator companies that they did not control their own destiny. It sees elected politicians as delegates of those who elected them and therefore is hostile to party discipline and aspects of parliamentary government. Populists favour recall votes to remove unfaithful public officials from office, plebiscites and referendums to give people a more direct say in the decisions that affect them, short terms of office, and term limits for public officials. At the provincial level, British Columbia has been in the forefront of populist democracy in Canada. It has held four referendums since 1991, including one in 2002 on the highly contentious question of Aboriginal land claims and treaty negotiations in the province. In 1995 it passed a recall and citizen initiative law—the first province to do so. In 2011, this legislation was used to abolish the unpopular Harmonized Sales Tax (HST) in British Columbia. All four Western legislatures have laws requiring that proposed constitutional amendments be submitted to the people in a referendum, although Canada's Constitution does not require this. Thus, there have been strong indications that populist values are more solidly rooted in the West than in the rest of Canada. On the other hand, even though the twenty-first Conservative Party has been shaped and led by Westerners, its commitment to egalitarian populism waned during the time it formed the federal government.

The Atlantic Provinces

As Canada's poorest region, with its own list of grievances toward the federal government and Central Canada, the Atlantic provinces might be expected to generate an eastern version of Western alienation. The easternmost provinces have produced occasional leaders, such as Newfoundland premiers Joey Smallwood (1949–72), Brian Peckford (1979–89), and Danny Williams (2003–2010), who were outspoken critics of what they saw as Ottawa's unjust treatment of their province. However, the dissatisfaction of Atlantic Canadians has never produced the vehicles for expressing alienation such as those found in Western Canada, including the Progressive movement of the 1920s, the Social Credit Party from the 1930s to the 1970s, and the Reform Party in the late 1980s and 1990s. Why not?

The answer is complex, but two elements are crucial. First, the populist values linked to Western alienation have been comparatively weak in the Atlantic provinces due to the demographic and economic differences between the eastern and western regions, as well as the differences in their political histories. Unlike Alberta and Saskatchewan, Nova Scotia and New Brunswick (and soon afterward PEI) were full members of the original Confederation pact. The historically dominant parties of Canada also have deep roots in the Maritimes stretching back to Confederation.

Economically and demographically the Maritimes have been in decline relative to the rest of Canada since the late nineteenth century. The region's population as a share of the national population has plummeted since Confederation; and the economies of the Eastern provinces are among the weakest in Canada. This remains true, despite Newfoundland and Labrador's impressive resource-fuelled growth of recent years. It may be important to note that in spite of ongoing economic and political problems, and strong encouragement by the British government, Newfoundlanders and Labradorians were never enthusiastic about joining Confederation. The promise of improved incomes and government services convinced a small majority to vote for Confederation in a 1949 referendum. Most Eastern provinces depend on money redistributed by Ottawa from more prosperous regions in order to pay for public services. These conditions stand in stark contrast to the prosperity that Saskatchewan, Alberta, and British Columbia have experienced in recent decades. The more assertive attitude of Western Canadians and their greater willingness to reject the traditional political parties is surely linked to some degree to confidence in their region's economic future. "The West Wants In" was not the plea of a weak and supplicant region, but rather the demand that Canada adjust to the reality of the West's economically powerful and growing provinces.

Summary

Regionalism continues to cut deep grooves across Canada's political landscape due to political and bureaucratic rivalries, different economic interests, and inequalities in political and economic clout between the provinces. The importance of these factors has not diminished over time. Regional conflict remains, as Donald Smiley once described, one of the three major axes of Canadian politics. With varying degrees of success there have been attempts at accommodating regional interests and perspectives through national structures and policies. We have discussed the history of Western alienation in Canada and the Western Canadian conception of equality, and how the grievances of the Atlantic provinces have not led to the alienation and political fallout seen in the West. However, in spite of these attempts at accommodation, Western and Atlantic provinces' grievances against Ottawa and the Ontario–Quebec axis—fuelled by the party system, Western alienation, regional economic disparities, and intergovernmental conflict—continue to dominate the political landscape.

Review Exercises

1. Compare media coverage in three different regions of the country. Do this by consulting three daily papers in three different provinces—one from the West, one from Ontario, and one from an Eastern province.
2. Who were Amor de Cosmos, Henry Wise Wood, Louis Robichaud, and Joseph Howe? What is the significance of each for his region of the country?

3. Does the toppling of the right-wing Progressive Conservative political dynasty in the Alberta's 2015 provincial election at the hands the left-leaning Rachel Notley and the NDP represent a shift in Albertan's values, or were these values always there?

Up for Debate

1. Given the distinct regional identities throughout the country, can Canada ever be all things to all its people? Should it be?
2. Should a politician follow his or her conscience or the will of the people?
3. Can the notion of social licence go too far?
4. In his book *Reflections of a Siamese Twin: Canada at the Beginning of the Twenty First Century*, John Ralston Saul argues that Canadians continue to struggle with their identity. Do you believe that Canadians have an identity crisis?

Starting Points for Research

Archer, Keith, and Lisa Young, eds. *Regionalism and Party Politics in Canada.* Toronto: Oxford University Press, 2002.

Dunn, Christopher, ed. *Provinces: Canadian Provincial Politics*, 2nd edn. Toronto: University of Toronto Press, 2006.

Berdahl, Loleen, and Roger Gibbins. *Looking West: Regional Transformation and the Future of Canada.* Toronto: University of Toronto Press, 2014.

Janigan, Mary. *Let the Eastern Bastards Freeze in the Dark: The West Versus the Rest Since Confederation.* Toronto: Random House, 2012.

Wiseman, Nelson. *In Search of Canadian Political Culture.* Vancouver: University of British Columbia Press, 2007.

CBC Archives and TVO's *The Agenda*

Visit the companion website for *Canadian Democracy: A Concise Introduction* to follow links to audio and video footage related to the main themes of the chapter: www.oupcanada.com/BrooksConcise2e.

Relevant Websites

Visit the companion website for *Canadian Democracy: A Concise Introduction* to browse a collection of websites featuring material related to the key themes of the chapter, an excellent starting point for research: www.oupcanada.com/BrooksConcise2e.

5 Diversity and Canadian Politics

Sometimes, the institutions and processes of Canadian democracy are best understood by examining the issues that roil the waters of politics. As Richard Gwyn and others have suggested, it is a marvel that Canada exists at all. Indeed, it could be argued that Canadian political history is replete with issues of diversity that would have destroyed most countries. The Canadian political system has been affected by the relationship between a multiplicity of communities, but the values and the constitutional features and democratic institutions have made it possible for these communities to co-exist in relative peace and prosperity. And the resulting conflicts and subsequent accommodations have shaped our laws, our Constitution, and the processes that influence the relationships that have allowed Canada to endure.

↑ An Indigenous elder represents Canada at the 2015 International Aborigines Festival in Kuala Lumpur, Malaysia. Canada's multicultural society has had a profound impact on the nation's politics.

Source: Mohd Samsul Mohd Said/Getty Images.

This chapter will look at diversity issues that continue to foster change in the Canadian political landscape in areas such as language politics and Quebec, multiculturalism and accommodation, gender politics, and the relationship between Aboriginal Canadians and other citizens and governments in Canada. These are crucial to understanding the Canadian condition.

After reading this chapter on contemporary issues in Canadian political life, you should be able to

1. explain why language and the status of Quebec are such prominent issues in Canada
2. describe the politics of multiculturalism and of gender
3. outline Aboriginal politics and its core issues, such as self-government, land-ownership, and discrimination

Without a common ethnic identity, without much remembered (or imagined) history, without external walls, the Canadian community either exists as a political entity within which all who live here act as citizens, involving themselves with others in "a not too-strict account of how much the [tax] bargain is worth," in Michael Ignatieff's phrase, or there is no particular reason for the Canadian community to exist at all.

—Richard Gwyn, *Nationalism Without Walls*, 1995

Language Politics and French Canada

Lord Durham's words, written some 170 years ago, still ring true today: Canada is "two nations warring in the bosom of a single state." The "Quebec question," with demands for changes to Quebec's constitutional status and for language rights, has surfaced repeatedly in Canadian politics. The "Quebec question" might just as fairly be called the "Canada question." Even if Quebec were to separate from Canada, practical matters related to language and economic relations with the rest of Canada would still have to be addressed. Why are Quebec and language so central to Canadian politics? Why has nationalism always been the key to unlocking the mysteries of Quebec politics? And what does Quebec want from the rest of Canada, and the rest of Canada from Quebec? Answers to these questions have been elusive.

History and the Demographics of Language Politics

When New France was formally placed under British control in 1763, francophones outnumbered anglophones by about eight to one. Forty years later, the two groups were of roughly equal size. The wave of immigrants from the British Isles in the 1800s was such that by the 1871 census, Canadians of French origin made up about one-third of the population.[1] The extraordinarily high birth rate among French-Canadian women enabled francophones to hold their own until the end of the 1950s. The end of *la revanche des berceaux* ("revenge of the cradle")—the high birth rate that for close to a century enabled French Canada to maintain its numerical strength—coupled with the fact that the vast majority of immigrants had chosen to speak English, finally led to a decline in the francophone share of the Canadian population by the early 1960s. The key factor in shifting the linguistic balance of Quebec was immigration. By the 1960s, immigration became the sole reason for provincial population growth; the fertility rate had fallen below the replacement levels.

The francophone share of Canada's population has nudged down to its present all-time low of about 22 per cent.[2] More worrisome to Quebec governments has been the fact that demographers began to predict a fall in the francophone share of that province's population, particularly in Montreal, where most new immigrants chose to establish themselves. Except for the relatively few immigrants whose native tongue was French, all other groups (known as **allophones**—a term used by Canadian demographers for those whose native language is neither English nor French) have overwhelmingly adopted English for themselves and their children. The possibility that francophones would become a minority in Quebec has often been raised by Quebec nationalists[3] and has provided the impetus for provincial language laws intended to stem this tide.

French outside Quebec

Outside Quebec the language picture looks very different. Except in New Brunswick and Ontario, the francophone populations of the other provinces are tiny. In fact, in certain provinces and in all but a handful of Canada's major metropolitan areas outside Quebec, some of the non-official-language communities are considerably larger than the French-speaking minority. In all provinces except Quebec, the French-language communities have been experiencing **assimilation**: the absorption of the minority culture into the majority (English) culture. By contrast, the rate of language retention among native English-speakers is high everywhere in Canada. This is not a recent development.

In *Languages in Conflict*, Richard Joy carefully documented the trend toward the assimilation of francophones outside Quebec.[4] Only in what Joy called the *bilingual belt*, the narrow region running from Moncton, New Brunswick, in the east, to Sault Ste Marie, Ontario, in the west, was the rate of assimilation among all generations significantly lower. Joy's prediction was

la revanche des berceaux ("revenge of the cradle") the high birth rate that for close to a century enabled French Canada to maintain its numerical strength

allophones a term used by Canadian demographers for those whose native language is neither English nor French

assimilation the absorption of the minority culture into the majority (English) culture

Colin McConnell/Toronto Star/Getty Images

In 2008 a new French immersion public elementary school named after former Governor General and Quebec resident Michaëlle Jean opened in Richmond Hill, Ontario. If you had children, would you send them to French immersion so that they could become bilingual? To what extent do you feel it is important for citizens to be fluent in both official languages?

that the failure to retain young francophones would contribute to the steady erosion of the community's base. The reason, of course, was that the francophones were losing the things that keep language alive such as the ability to shop, work, or worship in one's own language. Studies also suggest that a combination of aging populations, low birth rates, and marriage to non-francophones will soon lead to a collapse of many francophone communities outside of Quebec. This explains why René Lévesque once referred to the French-Canadian communities outside of Quebec as "dead ducks."

Immersion education has been heralded by some as a guarantee that bilingualism will survive outside of Quebec. For example, there has been a rapid expansion of French immersion schools since the 1980s, particularly in Ontario, which accounts for over half of all immersion students in Canada. However, many are skeptical. The fact that increasing numbers of those whose mother tongue is English are "functionally fluent" in French does not mean that French will be used more often in the home, in the workplace, or wherever communication takes place. Indeed, there is a good deal of evidence suggesting that four decades of French

receptive bilinguals people who are capable of responding to French communications but do not themselves initiate conversations in French, consume French-language media, or seek out opportunities to live in their acquired second language

immersion education[5] has produced a wave of **receptive bilinguals**—people who are capable of responding to French communications but do not themselves initiate conversations in French, consume French-language media, or seek out opportunities to live in their acquired second language. There is certainly nothing wrong with this and, indeed, much that is good about the expansion of bilingualism, receptive or otherwise! However, we might want to be careful about our conclusion here. In fact, the 2011 census found that the level of bilingualism among anglophones outside Quebec has been declining in recent years. The bottom line is that the social and economic milieux outside Quebec have not become more supportive for francophones.

From French-Canadian to Québécois Nationalism

French-Canadian nationalism, Pierre Trudeau writes, was originally a system of self-defence. Conquered by arms, the French-speaking people of New France found themselves subordinated to an anglophone minority about one-eighth their size. English was the language of the new political and commercial elites. The *Conquest* left French a second-class language within Quebec, and francophones were largely excluded from the colony's structures of power. Three chief factors can explain why French Canadians did not assimilate in Quebec as they did in Louisiana after it too passed from French control.

First, the British colonial authorities in New France, by the terms of the Quebec Act of 1774, granted formal protection to the status of the Roman Catholic religion and the *code civil*, the basis of civil law in New France.[6] The recognition of the French-Canadian rights may have been motivated by the desire to ensure the allegiance of the clerical and civil leaders at a time when the British were facing a rebellion in the Thirteen Colonies, which two years later would successfully declare their independence from Britain. These significant accommodations officially recognized the rights of the francophone Catholic majority and reinforced the leadership role of that community's clerical elite.

Second, French speakers in the southern United States were quickly swamped by a growing anglophone population. Although the immigration of Loyalists from the United States and English-speakers from the British Isles eventually tipped the linguistic balance in Canada toward English by the early nineteenth century, the high fertility rate among French Canadians enabled them to hold their ground at about one-third of Canada's population between Confederation and the 1950s.

Third, the defensive posture of French-Canadian nationalism enabled French Canada to resist assimilation. The clerical elite's leading social role was strengthened when anglophones occupied the political and commercial elites of the colony, and French Canada met the challenge of English domination by remaining loyal to traditional values and institutions.

Traditional French-Canadian nationalism during the nineteenth to the middle of the twentieth century was guided by the idea of *la survivance*—survival against the pressures of a dominant culture that was anglicizing, Protestant, materialistic, liberal-democratic, and business oriented. According to this ideology, the dominant anglophone culture was all the things that French Canada was not and should not become. While liberal voices of dissent were occasionally heard,[7] the chief characteristics of this dominant nationalist ideology were that

> *la survivance*
> survival against the pressures of a dominant culture that was anglicizing, Protestant, materialistic, liberal-democratic, and business oriented

- French Canada formed a distinct nation, whose chief characteristics of Catholicism and the French language were considered inseparable.[8]
- French-Canadian people had a vocation; their mission was to remain faithful to their roots. The democratic belief in secularism, the separation of church and state, was a heresy spawned by the American and French Revolutions.
- The character of the French-Canadian people was most secure in Quebec, but French Canada was not restricted to the boundaries of that province.

> secularism
> the separation of church and state

Traditional nationalism came under mounting pressure during the middle of the twentieth century. The emigration of hundreds of thousands of French-speaking Quebecers to the northeastern United States during the 1800s clearly demonstrated the weakness of the traditional nationalism. There simply was not enough arable land to support the rural parish lifestyle that the ideologues of the traditional nationalism clung to so tenaciously. By the early twentieth century the "typical" Québécois lived in an urban setting and had family members who had left in search of employment opportunities.

Quebec's path of modernization produced a political side effect of enormous importance: the increasing realization that francophones, despite accounting for about four-fifths of the Quebec population, were largely shut out of the economic decision making and control over much of the province's wealth. "Is there any inherent or unavoidable reason why," asked Abbé Lionel Groulx in 1934, "with 2,500,000 French Canadians in Quebec, all big business, all high finance, all the public utilities, all our water rights, forests and mines, should belong to a [mostly English-speaking] minority of 300,000?"[9] Between the 1930s and 1950s, many argued that educated francophones needed to rid themselves of their apparent distaste for careers in industry and finance.[10]

In these decades emerged the first serious challenge to the conservative ideology since the crushed rebellion of 1837. A diverse group of university professors and students, journalists, union activists, liberal politicians, and even elements within the Catholic Church were united in their opposition to the so-called "unholy alliance" of the Catholic Church, anglophone capital, and the Union Nationale party of Maurice Duplessis, and to the conservative nationalism that sought to justify French Canadians' marginal economic status. Their goal, known in Quebec as *rattrapage* ("catching up"), was to recoup lost ground and bring Quebec's society up to date.

The challenge to the conservative establishment and ideology came from Laval University, the intellectual journal *Cité libre*, and the provincial Liberal Party. As the political party attempting to depose Duplessis, the Quebec Liberal Party naturally attracted the energies of those who saw the ideologically conservative Union Nationale under his leadership as one of the main obstacles to reform. The Union Nationale managed to hold on until the 1960s, largely because of the patronage that Duplessis used to keep the party in power between 1945 and his death in 1959. The Liberal Party's election victory in 1960 was likely the result of disorder within the Union Nationale and popular support for change. The time for reform had come.

The Quiet Revolution and Nationalism

Quiet Revolution
a time of many
socio-political
reforms and
changes, and a
turning point in the
history of Quebec

Duplessis's death in 1959 and the election of the provincial Liberals under Jean Lesage in 1960 opened the way to many socio-political reforms and changes, and a turning point in the history of Quebec known as the **Quiet Revolution**. At the heart of these reforms lay an increased role for the Quebec state, which replaced the Catholic Church in social services and education and also acquired a vastly broader range of economic functions. The provincial state was seen as the prime mover of Quebec's break with the past, its attempt to modernize, and the focus of nationalist energies.

Nationalism is always based on some concept of the "nation": who belongs to it and who does not. The traditional nationalism, defined by such people as Abbé Lionel Groulx, went beyond the territory or the powers of the Quebec state. For reasons that had to do with Catholicism and an extended role for the Church, and the *anti-statist* quality of the traditional nationalism, the boundaries of *la nation* extended beyond Quebec to embrace French Canadians throughout Canada. Traditional nationalism was an ideology of *conservation*. It emphasized preservation of the *patrimoine*—the language, the faith, the mores of a community whose roots went back to New France, as well as a leading role for the Church in articulating these values and controlling these structures (i.e., the schools, hospitals, labour unions, etc.). The modern welfare state threatened this dominant social role of the Church.

Instead of defining *la nation* in terms of language and religion, the nationalism of the Quiet Revolution developed an understanding of Quebec's history, economy, and social structure that was based on language and dependency. The *dependency* perspective portrayed Quebec as a society whose evolution had been shaped and distorted by the economic and political domination of English Canadians. This secularized version of French-Canadian history, particularly of francophone Quebec, suggested that if the problem was that *Québécois* were dominated economically and politically by English Canada, then the solution was to take control of their economic and political destiny through the Quebec state. The Quiet Revolution saw state reforms such as the nationalization of hydroelectric companies and the creation of a provincial ministry of education, a Quebec Pension Plan, and Crown corporations like la Caisse de dépôt et placement.

The replacement of the traditional nationalism by the state-centred nationalism of the Quiet Revolution was not uniform or as abrupt as history might suggest. The new nationalism forces shared a common antipathy toward the old order but they were also divided on three main levels.

First, there was a split between the federalists, like Pierre Elliott Trudeau, Jean Marchand, and Gérard Pelletier of the Liberal Party of 1965, who advocated either a special status or independence for Quebec, and those who believed in autonomy, like René Lévesque, who later became the first leader of the Parti Québécois in 1968.

The second division concerned the size and functions of the Quebec state. Even within the reformist Liberal government of Jean Lesage, there were sharp differences over the role of the provincial state in Quebec society and over the extent of the nationalization policies.

And third, Quebec separatists were divided on ideological lines: those who, like René Lévesque, Jacques Parizeau, and Claude Morin, were ideologically liberal; and those for whom Quebec independence was linked to the overthrow of what they saw as a (predominantly English) bourgeois state.

Two developments indicate that a state-centred nationalism emerged out of the Quiet Revolution. First, the identification of French Canada with the territory of Quebec was a view shared by most nationalists. Indeed, the entry of Trudeau and his fellow federalists into national politics was chiefly a reaction to this Quebec-oriented nationalism. The provincial Liberals' 1962 campaign slogan, *Maîtres chez nous* ("Masters of our own house"), captured a nationalist consensus that has been an accepted tenet of Quebec politics. Second, key institutional

patrimoine
the language, the faith, the mores of a community whose roots went back to New France, as well as a leading role for the Church in articulating these values and controlling these structures

reforms of the Quiet Revolution, such as the Caisse de dépôt et placement, Hydro-Québec, and the jurisdictional terrain that the Quebec government wrested from Ottawa in social policy, immigration, and taxation, have left an important mark on Quebec nationalism.

Quebec's Unilingual Approach

The origins of present-day language policy in Canada lie in developments in Quebec during the 1960s. With the election of the Quebec Liberal Party in 1960, the political obstacles to change were removed and the outdated character of the traditional ideology was exposed. It was replaced by an emphasis on catching up with the level of social and economic development elsewhere. The state, traditionally viewed as a second-class institution, became the focus of nationalist energies. The ideology of *rattrapage* and the identification of French Canada with Quebec had important consequences for language policy in that province. In its new role as the instrument for economic and social development, the Quebec state expanded the scope of its economic activities. In doing so it provided career opportunities for the growing number of educated francophones graduating from the province's universities. Certain social and demographic trends shaped Quebec's language policy. For one, access to high-paying managerial and technical jobs in the private sector remained blocked by anglophone domination of the Quebec economy,[11] which ran directly counter to the goals of the Quiet Revolution. For another, immigrants to the province overwhelmingly adopted the English language. This fact, combined with the dramatically lower birth rate among francophones, suggested that francophones might eventually become a minority even within Quebec.

To counter these trends the 1972 Quebec Royal Commission of Inquiry on the Situation of the French Language and on Language Rights in Quebec recommended the passage of provincial laws to promote the use of French in business and education. Following these recommendations the Quebec Liberal government introduced the Official Language Act[12] and the subsequent Parti Québécois government passed the *Charte de la langue française*[13] (Bill 101). Despite some setbacks in the courts, the principles on which Quebec's language policy rests have remained substantially unchanged since the passage of Bill 101. Here are some features:

- In spite of a 1979 decision by the Supreme Court of Canada that a section of Bill 101 violated section 133 of the BNA Act, which guarantees the co-equal status of the French and English languages at the federal level and in the province of Quebec,[14] the principal language of provincial government services and the courts in Quebec is French. Many provincial and local services are not available in English in much of the province.
- Through a requirement that businesses with 50 or more employees receive a *francization* certificate as a condition of doing business in the province, the Quebec government seeks to increase the use of French as a working language of business in the province. Despite some initial resistance from the anglophone business community, this has generally been accepted by employers. More controversial have been the provisions requiring that public signs and advertisements be in French only. Certain

Language laws have stirred up demonstrations in Quebec on both sides of the argument. (Left) A war veteran makes his views known outside the Quebec Language Commission in 1987. (Right) A supporter carries a sign (translation: "In Quebec, everything in French and in French only") in a 2007 march in favour of Bill 101. Do you think Bill 101 is an infringement on civil liberties or a necessary tool for the preservation of the French language?

provisions were relaxed to make exceptions for "ethnic" businesses and because of a 1988 Supreme Court ruling that Bill 101 violated the freedom of expression guaranteed in the Charter.[15]

- The provisions of Bill 101 that initially excited the most controversy were those restricting access to English-language schools in Quebec. Under this law, children could enroll in an English school only if certain conditions were met, and these conditions would not apply to most immigrants. The intent was obviously to reverse the overwhelming preference of immigrants for the English language. The Supreme Court was unwilling to accept the Quebec government's argument that the demographic threat to the position of the French language justified this restriction on language rights. In 1993 the education provisions of Bill 101 were brought into conformity with section 23 of the Charter.

If one looks at its main objectives of increasing French language use in the Quebec economy and stemming the decline in the francophone share of the provincial population, Bill 101 must be judged a success.

In the 2015 general election, the Harper Conservatives tried to gain electoral support by tapping into the "fear of the Other" in both Quebec and the rest of Canada. Like the local government of Hérouxville in its code of behaviour, the Conservatives proposed a law banning those who wear a face veil from voting and promised to fund a telephone hotline that would enable citizens to phone in complaints about neighbours involved in "barbaric practices."

Recently, the debate over immigration in Quebec has shifted somewhat from the impact of immigrants on the French language to the integration of newcomers into its culture and society. Tensions in the province were crystallized in the highly publicized case of Hérouxville, a small town north of Montreal whose local government adopted a declaration of cultural standards that newcomers were expected to respect.[16] This apparently xenophobic resolution from the heart of rural Quebec—the former bastion of traditional Quebec nationalism—targeted, among others, Muslims, Sikhs, and South Asians. Immigrants were unwelcome if they, for example, covered their faces, carried weapons to school, or practised genital mutilation. The Hérouxville story gained worldwide attention, and the furor led the Quebec government to appoint the Bouchard–Taylor consultative commission on "reasonable accommodation."

The commission's report seemed to some to recommend that the Quebec government and Quebec citizens adopt a form of provincial multiculturalism similar to that of the federal government.

> Our deliberations and reflections have firmly convinced us that integration through pluralism, equality and reciprocity is by far the most commendable, reasonable course. Like all democracies in the world, Québec must seek to reach a consensus against a backdrop of growing diversity, renew the social bond, accommodate difference by combating discrimination, and promote an identity, a culture and a memory without creating either exclusion or division.[17]

The report's reception was not enthusiastic. Most French-speaking Quebecers felt that the emphasis in the Bouchard–Taylor report leaned too far toward accommodation on the part of old-stock Québécois—sometimes called *les québécois de souche*—and not enough on the need for newcomers to adapt to the language of the French majority, as well as their culture. Premier Jean Charest's response to the report was to take a middle path:

- reinforce francization prior to the arrival of immigrants
- provide for a signed statement by potential immigrants committing to the common values of our society
- develop a mechanism to help decision makers handle questions of *accommodation* while respecting the secular character of our institutions
- adopting Bill 63, which would amend the Charter of Rights and Freedoms to affirm the equality of men and women[18]

Ottawa's Bilingual Approach

Since the 1960s, and in response to the new assertive nationalism of the Quiet Revolution including the placing of bombs in mailboxes and at public monuments, as well as demands for more taxation powers and less interference by Ottawa, the federal government has pursued a very different approach to language policy—one based on a conception of French and English Canada that cuts across provincial borders. The Liberal government of Lester Pearson established the *Royal Commission on Bilingualism and Biculturalism*. As Eric Waddell writes, "The federal government was facing a legitimacy crisis in the 1960s and 1970s and had the immediate task of proposing a Canadian alternative to Quebec nationalism."[19] The commission was a first step toward adopting a policy of official bilingualism and was partly intended to defuse the *indépendantiste* sentiment in Quebec by opening career opportunities in Ottawa to rival the Quebec public service.

As expressed in the federalist philosophy of Pierre Trudeau, language rights would be guaranteed to the individual and protected by national institutions. This meant changing the overwhelmingly anglophone character of the federal state so that francophones would not feel excluded. These changes have been carried out on two fronts. First, a change in Canadian symbols has been implemented since the 1960s so as not to evoke Canada's colonial past and

British domination, including adopting a new flag, proclaiming "O Canada" as the official national anthem, and renaming federal institutions, documents, and celebrations to make them more language neutral. Second, to redress the under-representation of French Canadians in the federal civil services and increase the level of services to the French-speaking populations, the Official Languages Act (1969) was passed, making bilingualism official policy. The Act established the Office of the Commissioner of Official Languages as a "watchdog" to monitor the three main components of language equality:

1. the public's right to be served by the federal government in the official language of their choice
2. the equitable representation of francophones and anglophones in the federal public service
3. the ability of public servants of either language group to work in the language of their choice

Evidence demonstrates that the linguistic designation of positions has indeed worked to the advantage of francophones. But as the Commissioner of Official Languages regularly observes, increased representation of francophones is not an indication that French and English are approaching greater equality as *languages of work*. Outside of federal departments and agencies located in Quebec, the language of work remains predominantly English. And inside Quebec, the ability of anglophone public servants to work in English is often limited. In short, fluency in French has become a valuable attribute from the standpoint of career advancement, without French becoming a working language on a par with English.[20]

A Distinct Society?

distinct society
a society noticeably different than other provinces

It is a fair bet that few Canadians had heard of "distinct society" before the late 1980s, when the Meech Lake Accord failed over a proposal to recognize Quebec as a distinct society. Does Quebec constitute a **distinct society**—a society noticeably different than other provinces? And is this distinction necessary? In spite of much study and debate, most Canadians are vague about the meaning of "distinct society." What is clear is that the demand for constitutional recognition of Quebec as a distinct society has been a non-negotiable requirement for Quebec's political elite since the late 1980s.

Whether or not Quebec is a distinct society depends on what criteria we use in comparing Quebec to the other provinces. Quebecers' lifestyle choices, how they make a living, which movies they watch, and so on, do not make them remarkably different from other Canadians. However, its social, historic, and regional characteristics, as well as values and belief systems, are traits that distinguish Quebec from other regions. But why all this fuss over distinct society clauses in the failed Meech Lake and Charlottetown constitutional accords? What probably bothers English-speaking Canadians is their gut sense that distinct society status for Quebec undermines their ideas about national unity and of Canada as an egalitarian society. Many English Canadians believe that a "distinct society" recognition would give Quebec legislative powers not possessed by other provinces. And some worry that minority rights—of non-francophones in Quebec and of francophones outside the province—would suffer.

In an unspoken way, English Canadians sense that distinct society recognition for Quebec is a sort of Trojan horse for a *two-nations* conception of Canada: a theory that has been very popular in certain political parties and among anglophone political scientists. For example, the report of the Commission on the Political and Constitutional Future of Quebec made it clear that the "one Canada" and "dual societies" conceptions have become irreconcilable since the passage of the Charter and other constitutional reforms of 1982. According to the commission, from Quebec's point of view, "Canada's federal system was founded . . . on Canadian duality [French/English] and the autonomy of the provinces. Canadian duality, which rests on the relationship between the French-Canadian and English-Canadian peoples . . . is a 'pact' which exists between these two peoples that may only be changed with the consent of each of these parties."[21]

Listen to "The Reasonable Accommodation of Cultural Difference: The Case of Quebec" podcast at www.oupcanada.com/BrooksConcise2e.

Although many of Canada's national political elite have for years denied that the "one Canada" aspirations of most English Canadians conflict with the recognition of Quebec as a distinct society, Québécois political leaders suffer from no illusions on this count. This offends against a particular understanding of equality that—again, while usually unspoken—objects to the idea that there are categories of Canadians instead of Canadians, period.

The commission argued that the Constitution Act, 1982 was based on three principles that are fundamentally opposed to the idea of Quebec as a distinct society:

- the equality of all Canadian citizens, from one ocean to the other, and the unity of the society in which they live
- the equality of all cultures and cultural origins in Canada
- the equality of the 10 provinces of Canada

The fact remains that Quebec is a province *pas comme les autres* ("unlike the others") and one that continues to attract special attention from federal politicians. In 2006, the House of Commons passed a Conservative government resolution affirming that the Québécois are a "nation within the nation of Canada." One of the politically significant ways in which this difference may be seen is in French-speaking Quebecers' weaker attachment to Canada, particularly among younger citizens. A 2006 survey found that young francophones were far less likely than anglophones to believe that independence would harm Quebec's economy (29 versus 72 per cent).[22]

And so, whatever a distinct society constitutional clause might mean in practice, the Quebec elites expect it to make a difference. Distinct society is, in their eyes, a corrective against the centralizing implications of the Charter and, moreover, represents a return to the founding spirit of Canada. For their part, the PQ and the Bloc have been determined to shift the debate away from a federalist framework—the one over distinct society and constitutional vetoes—onto a debate over political independence and economic association.

History has taught us not to be complacent about Quebec's relationship to the rest of Canada, in spite of sudden shifts in the electoral winds such as the failures of the Bloc Québécois in the 2011 and 2015 federal elections, the surge in support for the NDP and Liberal federal parties in

Listen to the "Does Quebec Separatism Have a Future?" podcast at www.oupcanada.com/BrooksConcise2e.

those elections, and the defeat of the PQ in the 2014 provincial election. Foremost among these facts is the growing gap between the vision of the "one Canada," of the equality of the provinces, and of a multicultural country, which dominate outside Quebec, from the vision insisted upon by most Quebec politicians and opinion leaders—federalists and separatists alike—that Quebec must be considered a society whose language, culture, and history make it distinct from the rest of Canada. Canadian national unity involves finding ways to bridge this gap.

Multiculturalism and Politics

Diversity is nothing new in Canada: it has always been a pluralistic society. For example, the official recognition of group rights goes back at least as far as the 1774 Quebec Act, under which the British authorities recognized the religious rights of French Canadians. What is relatively new, however, is the level of awareness of diversity and the idea that it should be recognized, protected, and even nurtured by the state.

multiculturalism the idea that not only is cultural diversity good for society, it should also be encouraged

The group composition of Canadian society has changed significantly over time. Canada has moved away from the concepts of "two nations" or "two founding peoples" to the concept of **multiculturalism**: the idea that not only is cultural diversity good for society, it should also be encouraged. Some might say that diversity has become *the pre-eminent Canadian cultural*

© Ptoone | Dreamstime.com

This illustration from a Canadian blog celebrates diversity and suggests that "Canada is the world."

trait, a quality that more than any other defines what Canada is about and differentiates it from those of other countries, particularly the United States. Canada is, as former prime minister Joe Clark once put it, "a community of communities."

The very idea that there is such a thing as a "Canadian ethos"—that Canada is a democracy built around tolerance, accommodation, respect, the recognition of group rights, and a belief in the equal dignity of different cultures—is comparatively recent. As the multicultural map of Canada suggests, many Canadians see Canada as a pluralistic society par excellence, and a model of cultural coexistence.

This image of Canada is not without its ironies and skeptics. Foremost is the fact that separatist sentiment in Quebec is far from extinguished and challenges this rosy picture of Canada as a model of cultural coexistence. Some skeptics maintain that the diversity-centred image of Canada and its policies and institutions undermines rather than strengthens Canadian unity. Others question whether multicultural democracy can work at all, in Canada or elsewhere, except in special circumstances. They note the resurgence of ethnicity-based nationalism in the modern world and the breakup or instability of many countries that combine different cultures.

From Founding Nations to Multiculturalism

The Canada that we know today was built upon two pillars: the displacement and marginalization of Aboriginal Canadians, and the settlement and development of what would become Canada by European immigrants. The overwhelming majority of the immigrants who settled in Canada during the country's formative years were of French and British Isles origins (although many of the latter came to Canada via the United States in the wave of Loyalists who fled the American War of Independence). The languages were mainly French and English. With very few exceptions their religions were Christian (Roman Catholic or Protestant). They would be referred to as the *founding nations* or *charter groups*: one French and Catholic and the other English and mainly Protestant—an image of Canada as a partnership—albeit an unequal one—of two European charter groups that survived well into the twentieth century.

The two-nations image was not questioned until the 1960s with the work of the Royal Commission on Bilingualism and Biculturalism. Ukrainian spokespersons, among others, were critical of the two-nations, bicultural image. They stopped short of demanding equality of status with English and French for their groups and languages. But what they won was official recognition of Canada as a *multicultural society*, not a bicultural one. This was achieved through the 1971 passage of the Multiculturalism Act and the creation of a ministry responsible for multiculturalism, which today falls under the Ministry of Immigration, Refugees and Citizenship Canada.

The push to replace biculturalism with multiculturalism would not have had much effect were it not for the accelerated changes to Canada's population that were underway by the 1960s. The newer waves of non-Christian, non-French, and non-English ethnic-origin immigration, particularly from Asia and the Middle East, presented newer challenges to the older notions of Canadian pluralism than those first launched by the earlier immigrants from eastern and southern Europe. As Figures 5.1 and 5.2 show, the ethnic composition of Canadian society has changed significantly over the last half-century, particularly in Canada's largest metropolitan

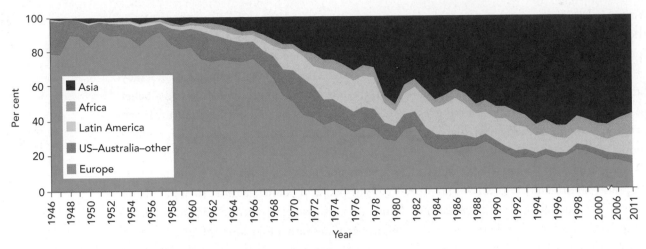

FIGURE 5.1 Place of Birth of Immigrants, 1946–2011

Sources: Statistics Canada, Census of Population; Statistics Canada, Immigration and Ethnocultural Diversity in Canada, National Household Survey, 2011.

areas, where the new Canadians of neither British nor French ethnic origins have clustered, and where the visible minority population has increased significantly in recent years.

Canada remains a predominantly Christian society in spite of the recent waves of immigration from non-European countries. However, Canadian society has become much more secular than it was even a few generations ago, and religion tends not to be an important political factor. People belonging to non-Christian religions constitute a rather small minority, at about 6 per cent of the population. About four out of five Canadians claim an affiliation with either the Catholic Church or a Protestant denomination. This is down from all but a sliver of the population at the time of Confederation, and even represents some small slippage since 1971. This slippage is due to a recent sharp increase in the number of people without a religious affiliation.

The growth of the non-European and non-Christian elements of Canadian society has not been without tensions and unease in some communities. Most people appear to accept the changes taking place in their society, but a 2004 survey of attitudes toward cross-cultural and interracial marriage found that a significant minority of the population is uneasy with the idea of their children mixing with members of certain groups. Tolerance is greater among younger age cohorts.[23]

Other Types of Diversity

Along with greater diversity in the ethnic, religious, and racial composition of Canada, the demographic picture has become more recognizably varied in other ways, too, including family composition, sexual orientation, and disability.

- *Families.* Families tend to be smaller today than they were a generation ago and considerably smaller than they were two generations ago. There are many more single-parent families and many couples choose not to marry. Same-sex couples are also more frequent.
- *Sexuality.* Sexual diversity is much more apparent today. The ratio of heterosexuals to those who are gay or lesbian has probably not changed, but what has

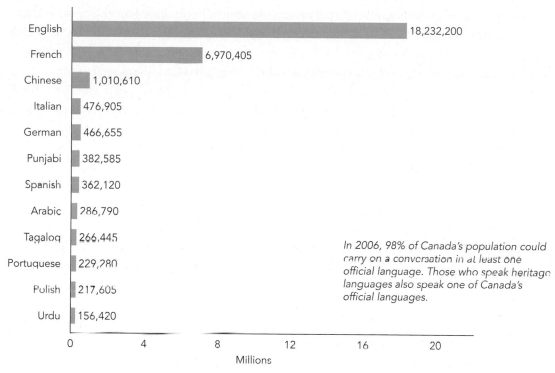

FIGURE 5.2 Breakdown of Canadian Population by First Language, 2006

Source: Canadian Population Census 2006, Statistics Canada

changed is the willingness of non-heterosexuals to proclaim openly their sexuality and the readiness of a growing number of Canadians to accept this in many, if not all, circumstances.

- *Disability.* A greater proportion of the population is disabled today than at any point in Canada's history. Health Canada reports that about one in eight Canadians claims to experience either a mental or a physical disability. It is doubtful whether the incidence of Canadians with a disability is actually greater today, but what has changed is our society's ideas about what constitutes a disability, and its legal definition. The recognition of disability has become one of the diversity criteria used by governments in making public policy, and its definition establishes eligibility for pensions, workers' compensation, social assistance, employment, housing, and other matters.

Official Recognition and Institutionalization of Diversity

In 1972, multiculturalism was given its own minister. But the official recognition of groups according to their group characteristics and the institutionalization of diversity go back much further. We have already mentioned that the Quebec Act of 1774 represented the first official confirmation of the status and rights of a particular group, in this case French-speaking Catholics. But the distinction of "first" probably belongs to the Royal Proclamation of 1763, which recognized the presence and rights of "the several Nations or Tribes of Indians with whom we are connected, and who live under our protection." Aboriginal Canadians were recognized by the Proclamation as distinct rights-bearing peoples under the protection of the British Crown. This relationship continues to the present day with the Canadian state, perpetuated and institutionalized through the Indian Act and section 35 of the Constitution Act, 1982, which embeds the treaty rights of Aboriginal peoples in Canada.

Until the 1960s, the official recognition of groups extended principally to the French- and English-language communities (s. 133 of the Constitution Act, 1867), the Catholic and Protestant religions for schooling purposes (s. 93 of the Constitution Act, 1867), and Aboriginal Canadians. This changed in the 1960s and 1970s as a result of the emergence of feminism and the increasing popularity of multiculturalism and group-oriented thinking about rights.

Leslie Pal argues that the institutionalization of diversity in Canadian public life was leveraged from the late 1960s to the 1980s by the activities of the Citizenship Branch within the Department of Secretary of State (SOS).[24] The grants were disbursed through a variety of programs that helped finance thousands of organizations. The programs and the dollars may have been small, but their enduring significance, Pal argues, was to reshape the structures of groups of citizens and their relationship to the state in ways that institutionalized diversity.[25]

In addition, federal and provincial human rights commissions have expanded the concept of *minorities*. The emphasis on language, religion, and ethnic origins has recently shifted to non-racial and noncultural forms of minority status such as gender, sexual orientation, drug dependency, and social conditions. Human rights commission officials, as R. Brian Howe and David Johnson argue, have actively promoted the recognition of diversity through expanding the number of rights-bearing groups.[26]

At the federal level, the activities of the CBC, the National Film Board, and Telefilm Canada have contributed to the public projection of images of Canadian society as historically and demographically diverse. This is also true of the Department of Canadian Heritage which has inherited the functions pioneered by the Citizenship Branch, providing grants to an enormous array of groups and operating as the leader within government for the promotion of Canadian pluralistic identity.

Diversity and Political Representation

The 1878 cabinet of Sir John A. Macdonald had 14 members. All but one were born in Canada. About 80 per cent (11 of 14) had British Isles ethnic origins and the others were of French ethnic origin. All were either Catholic (4 of 14) or Protestant. As recently as fifty years ago John Porter remarked that Canada's political elite had been slow to change, failing to reflect the increasing ethnic diversity of the country. It was, he said, still an elite dominated by males from the two charter groups. Members of these groups continue to be disproportionately represented, at least in the federal cabinet. The 2010 cabinet of Stephen Harper was not as different from Sir John A.'s government as one might have expected, given the enormous demographic

Canadian Spotlight

BOX 5.1 *Little Mosque on the Prairie*

From 2007 to 2012, *Little Mosque on the Prairie*, a CBC sitcom about a makeshift mosque in a small Canadian Prairie town, was praised by critics for raising the issue of accommodation for cultural minorities. The premise of the show was straightforward: Muslims are different in terms of their religious beliefs and practices, some of which translate to lifestyle differences, but these differences are insignificant compared to the values that they share with other Canadians.

© AP Photo/Christopher Brown

Actors from the cast of *Little Mosque on the Prairie* joke with their director during a rehearsal. What other popular television shows or films can you think of that play on the theme of showcasing different cultures' similarities despite their obvious differences?

shifts that have occurred in Canadian society. Of its 32 members, only a couple were born outside Canada. The vast majority, about 85 per cent, had French or British ethnic origins. The religious affiliation of MPs seems to be far less important today. On the whole, however, the demographic composition of Harper's 2010 cabinet was similar to the Macdonald cabinet of 1878, except in one striking respect; the Harper government included seven women and one Aboriginal Canadian, whereas Macdonald's included none. Feeling that even more gender parity and diversity needed to be reflected in the cabinet, Prime Minister Justin Trudeau made it a point of principle that 50 per cent of the cabinet posts should be held by women and that other groups be represented as well. When asked why gender parity mattered so, he replied: "Because it's 2015."

The level of diversity seen in Trudeau's cabinet may not be common in other economic sectors or in other levels of government, and we are not suggesting that the continuing dominance of these elites by members of the French and British charter groups is evidence of discrimination against other groups. A couple of factors need to be taken into account. First, it takes time for demographic change to work its way through a political system. For example, the decline in the share of Canada's population claiming either French or British Isles ethnic origins has only occurred since the 1970s. We might expect to see more elite representation by non-charter group Canadians as the number of such people with the qualifications and other necessary attributes grows. Second, a growing number of Canadians have mixed ethnic origins, and a considerable share of the population now rejects the traditional ethnic identities, preferring to describe themselves as "Canadian." Consequently, it may be more accurate to say that the elites in Canada are dominated by persons of French, British, and Canadian origins.

The Under-Representation of Women

Women constitute about 52 per cent of the Canadian population and a slightly larger percentage of the electorate. Despite their numerical superiority, few women had been elected to the leadership of political parties in Canada and achieved high public office until recently. The percentage of female candidates nominated by the major political parties has never been as high as it is today.

A similar pattern of under-representation is found in the case of non-elected positions within the state. Notwithstanding significant gains made over the past couple of decades in the number of women elected to public office, their representation in politics continues to be below their share of the population. As of 2012, approximately one in five parliamentarians were women, federally and provincially. About one-third of all candidates in the 2011 and 2015 federal elections were women. Only one party leader, Elizabeth May of the Green Party, was female. About one-quarter of municipal councillors across Canada are female. In 2013, however, five of ten provincial premiers, representing 85 per cent of the country's population, were women, although this number had fallen to three by 2015. Moreover, women are more likely to vote than their male counterparts in every age cohort except the oldest voters, those over the age of 65.

With respect to appointments, about 31 per cent of federally appointed judges are women. Significant inroads also have been made into the senior ranks of the bureaucracy. Federally, women account for about 30 per cent of senior management personnel and about 45 per cent of all executive positions. It is now common for women to be appointed to the boards of directors and leading management roles of Crown corporations, filling approximately one-third of these positions as of 2012.

The reasons behind female under-representation are, however, more easily explained than are its consequences. Let us begin with the relatively uncontroversial part.

Why Aren't More Women Involved in Political Life?

The riddle of women's under-representation in public life appears simple: they have been less interested than men. Female participation in voting and campaigning have been about the same as men's, but much lower for more demanding activities, such as running for office. "The higher, the fewer" is how Sylvia Bashevkin describes the political participation gap between

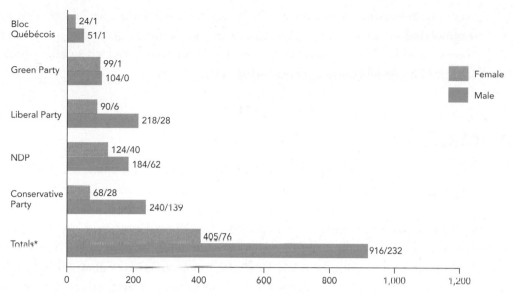

FIGURE 5.3 Gender of Candidates for the Five Main Parties in the 2011 Election

*These totals include only the candidates of these five registered parties in the 2011 election.

Note: The number of male and female candidates for each party is indicated to the right of each bar, followed by the number of male or female candidates actually elected.

Source: Based on data provided in the Report of the Chief Electoral Officer of Canada, 41st General Election (2011).

males and females.[27] This gap has narrowed over time, but continues to exist. What explains different levels of interest? The answer lies in social learning.

Traditionally, females learned from the world around them that politics was a predominantly male occupation. The prime minister/president and cabinet ministers were men, and leadership or active involvement beyond the family and the neighbourhood were associated with masculinity. The influence of social learning was reinforced by the sexual division of labour in society, particularly in the family but also in the workplace. The traditional male breadwinner–female homemaker family and the more contemporary two breadwinner–female homemaker household are universally acknowledged by feminists as important sources of female subordination to males, including their comparatively marginal status in politics. This subordination and marginalization operates on two main levels:

- *Psychological.* Child rearing and housework are necessary activities, but society's attitude toward them is ambivalent, and the traditional roles of mother and homemaker are not likely to generate the motivations, interests, and personal resources for political activism.
- *Status and professional achievements.* Traditionally, women have been underrepresented in those occupations from which political office holders tend to be drawn: law, business, and the liberal professions. Their formal educational attainments and

their representation have tended to be lower in fields like finance, economics, and engineering—important for many senior positions in the public service. Even when women made "non-traditional career choices," they were expected to take primary charge of household duties and nurturing of the children.

Women in Politics

Women were active in politics before being entitled to vote and run for office. Much of this activity was aimed at achieving full citizenship rights for women. But this was far from being the sole concern of women's groups during the pre-suffrage era. They were also active in demanding a long list of social reforms ranging from pensions for widowed mothers to non-militaristic policies in international relations. By contemporary standards, however, the early women's movement was small and politically weak. Moreover, its demands and values—although radical in the context of the times—today appear to have been quite moderate and sometimes even reactionary. The history of women's political involvement in Canada is characterized by social and ideological forces, as well as the issues, organizations, strategies, and accomplishments.

Phase One: Industrialization and Democracy

Feminist writings and occasional incidents of women mobilizing around particular events or issues before the nineteenth century were quite rare. The overthrow of absolute monarchy in Britain (1688) and the American (1776) and the French Revolutions (1789) generated some agitation for the liberal ideals of equality of political rights and democratic rights, but not for women. In matters of law and property, a woman was subsumed under her father and, after marriage, her husband.

The origins of the women's movement usually are located in the mid-nineteenth century. As Sheila Rowbotham writes, "Feminism came, like socialism, out of the tangled, confused response of men and women to capitalism."[28] The progress of capitalism produced both affluence and misery. As more and more people crowded into the cities whose growth was spawned by factory production, the harshness of industrialization and a new set of social problems was revealed: increased poverty due to the low wages of working-class women and children; overcrowded cities with poor sanitation and improperly ventilated housing; low life expectancy and high infant mortality due to improper diet and alcoholism. These were the central issues of the early women's movement because of their perceived impact on the family and on prevailing standards of decency. Organizations such as the Woman's Christian Temperance Union (WCTU) and the Young Women's Christian Association (YWCA), which sprang up across Canada in the late nineteenth century, advocated for social reforms and urged governments to protect women and the family from the perceived corrosive influences of industrial life.

Early feminism was not merely a response to the contradictions that industrialization created for women. Democracy was also full of contradictions. The arguments used to deny political rights for women were intellectually flabby: "nice women do not want the vote" or "my wife doesn't want the vote."[29] But the logic of democratic rights is universal. The early women's

Canadian Spotlight

BOX 5.2 Timeline: Milestones in Women's Legal and Political Equality

1916 Alberta, Saskatchewan, and Manitoba give the vote to women.

1918 Women are given the franchise in federal elections.

1921 Agnes Macphail is the first woman elected to Parliament.

1929 The Judicial Committee of the British Privy Council overturns the Supreme Court decision that women are not "persons" and cannot be appointed to the Senate.

1931 Cairine Wilson is the first woman appointed to the Senate.

1940 Quebec gives the vote to women.

1955 Restrictions on married women in federal public service are removed.

1957 Ellen Fairclough is sworn in as the first female federal cabinet minister.

1967 The Royal Commission on the Status of Women is established.

1971 The Canada Labour Code is amended to allow women 17 weeks' maternity leave.

About one-third of university graduates are female.

1973 The Supreme Court upholds the section of Indian Act depriving Aboriginal women of their rights.

The Supreme Court denies Irene Murdoch the right to share in family property.

1977 The Canadian Human Rights Act is passed, forbidding discrimination on the basis of sex.

1981 Canada ratifies the UN Convention on the Elimination of All Forms of Discrimination against Women.

Just under half of university graduates are female.

1982 Bertha Wilson becomes the first woman appointed to the Supreme Court of Canada.

1983 Affirmative action programs become mandatory in the federal public service.

1984 Twenty-seven women are elected to Parliament and six are appointed to cabinet.

1985 Section 15 of the Charter of Rights and Freedoms comes into effect.

Employment Equity legislation is passed.

1988 The *Morgentaler* decision strikes down Canada's abortion law.

1989 The Indian Act is amended to remove discrimination against Aboriginal women. The *Andrews* decision introduces the concept of "substantive equality" in applying section 15 of the Charter.

Audrey McLaughlin is chosen to lead the national NDP.

1991 Ontario passes a pay equity law that applies to the private sector (repealed in 1995).

1993 Kim Campbell becomes Canada's first female prime minister.

1995 Alexa McDonough is chosen to lead the national NDP.

Continued

1997	Sixty-one women are elected to Parliament and eight are appointed to cabinet.	2011	Seventy-six women are elected to Parliament; 10 of 39 cabinet ministers are women.
2000	The Right Honourable Beverley McLachlin is appointed Chief Justice of the Supreme Court of Canada.	2013	Five of Canada's 10 provincial premiers are female.
2001	Just under 60 per cent of university graduates are female.	2015	Eighty-eight women are elected to Parliament; 15 of 31 cabinet ministers are women.

movement focused mainly on three issues: political rights, legal rights, and social reform. The demands made by organizations like the WCTU and YWCA and by prominent feminists like Nellie McClung were based on the traditional values and middle-class morality of the times and the perceived threats to the security of women and the family.

The dominant middle-class morality could, and eventually did, accommodate itself to political rights for women. "Respectable" feminists were those who consented to play by the rules of the game, and organizations like the WCTU, the YWCA, and the Women's Institutes were politically moderate organizations, fundamentally conservative in their goals and their strategies for attaining them. Even Nellie McClung, who was considered a firebrand, did not in the least suggest that the social roles of "man the provider" and "woman the nurturer" be changed. Instead, most leaders of the early women's movement wanted to put women's role on a more secure material footing. Unlike their sisters in Great Britain and the United States, Canadian *suffragists* did not resort to confrontational methods such as resisting the police or hunger strikes. Instead, they relied on petitions to government and efforts to persuade public opinion.

After decades of campaigning, women achieved the right to vote provincially between 1916 (Manitoba) and 1940 (Quebec), and federally in 1917–18. The right to hold office in the House of Commons was granted in 1918, although women appeared to be barred from the non-elected Senate and other appointed public offices, such as judgeships, as they were not considered "persons" under the law.

Absurd though it may seem, the personhood of women was still dubious in the years following their enfranchisement.[30] After a couple of provincial rulings in their favour, the question was placed before the Supreme Court of Canada in 1927. Feminists were shocked when the Court ruled that the legal meaning of "persons" excluded female. This decision was reversed on appeal by the British Judicial Committee of the Privy Council in 1929.

Phase Two: After the Vote, What?

"Is Women's Suffrage a Fizzle?" asked a 1928 article in *Maclean's*. Little, it seemed, had changed. Men still dominated the political process. The issues that interested women's groups, except for prohibition, were no more prominent than before women's suffrage. And women were still viewed as an oddity in public life. Those who believed that the vote for women would be used to change the world were wrong.

The breakthroughs and accomplishments of a few women running and winning public office stood in sharp contrast to the unchanged status of the many. Among the plausible reasons for this lack of change were the nature of early feminism, the party system, and societal attitudes. Early mainstream feminism was a weak force in Canadian politics, and hard-core feminism barely scratched the surface of public and political discourse.

Why social attitudes were slow in changing is a complex issue. However, the ability of women to better control their reproductive role and to choose to stay in school or participate in the workforce longer was a chief factor contributing to this change. Reproductive choice, which became available to women in the 1960s with the birth control pill, was a crucial material condition for *women's liberation* in other aspects of life. And other factors came to bear, such as sexuality, secularism, and economics.

Sexuality, a topic shrouded in mystery and taboo, was publicly debated in such matters as reproductive rights and women's control of their bodies, pornography's impact on violence against women, and sexual stereotyping. Conventional beliefs about female passivity, maternal instincts, and home-centredness were now deemed to be the structural foundations of women's political subordination.

Secularism was a second factor that contributed to the changed character of second-wave feminism. Traditional religious values regarding the family, procreation, and appropriate behaviour, as well as the patriarchal authority structures of most churches, became targets of feminist criticism.

With respect to *economics*, the two conventional beliefs—that women should only take jobs not held by men and that outside employment was fine for single but not for married women—began to weaken during the 1950s and 1960s. Women's share of the labour force increased. The falling real family incomes and the introduction of labour-saving household appliances might account for some of these trends, but the fact was that women wanted more than a husband, children, and a home.[31] Post–World War II service industries also underwent a remarkable expansion, which increased the supply of low-wage, "female" employment. As their participation in the economy increased, segregation into low-pay, low-prestige occupations[32] became less palatable to women.

Phase Three: The Personal Is Political

The 1950s was like the quiet before the storm. Once women had achieved political rights, it seemed that equality was no longer an issue. Postwar economic growth and the "baby boom" combined to reinforce traditional gender roles and stereotypes. Television, films, and popular magazines mostly portrayed the male breadwinner–female homemaker family as the pinnacle of human happiness. The syrupy bliss of the era, it turned out, was an illusion. By the early 1960s women were challenging the deep-seated beliefs and social structures that limited their participation in the male-dominated world. The "problem" was given a name: **sexism**, a term coined in the 1960s to label behaviour that treated males and females unequally for no

sexism
a term coined in the 1960s to label behaviour that treated males and females unequally for no better reason than their sex

Library and Archives Canada/Credit: Cyril Jessop/Canadian Intellectual Property Office fonds/PA-030212

Nellie McClung was one of the leading figures in advancing the feminist causes of her day. Name a woman in politics whose work you feel has made a contribution to contemporary Canadian society.

better reason than their sex. Sexism became the target of the women's movement. This revival was the result of several factors.

Intellectually, writers like Simone de Beauvoir, Germaine Greer, and Gloria Steinem were developing a powerful analysis that went beyond the earlier feminist concerns of political and legal rights and social reform, and exposed the social, cultural, and economic roots of inequality.

Politically, this was also the era of the civil rights movement in the United States. Student radicalism, anti-war or anti-establishment protest marches, sit-ins, and occasional violence were the visible signs of a reaction against the status quo. While the feminist movement did not spearhead the 1960s protest movements, it profited from the way these movements saw established power relations as unjust. American civil rights advocates argued that **affirmative action** programs—the logic and machinery of targeting groups for preferred treatment—were necessary to provide real equality of opportunity for blacks. Women in many countries borrowed the same arguments and policies.

Although Canada had had no first-hand experience with racially based affirmative action policies before the 1960s, the logic of affirmative action was not foreign to Canada. Language policies, in Quebec and nationally, incorporated elements of such an approach by the mid-1970s. As such, affirmative action was already embedded in the Canadian state.

Organizing for Influence

affirmative action
the logic and machinery of targeting groups for preferred treatment

Women have long been active in Canadian politics, and several important women's organizations date from the pre-suffrage era. But contemporary feminism is different from the first wave of the movement, when suffrage and social reform were the key issues. Today, the organizational network of women's groups is much more developed, and new strategies distinguish it from its predecessor. Moreover, the political parties have provided something of a channel for women's participation in political life. Over time these organizations have been joined by hundreds more. As the organizational network proliferated, new state structures were created to deal with "women's issues."

The women's or feminist movement is not a monolithic bloc; there is an enormous diversity of perspectives within feminism. Perhaps the most prominent and crippling division within the Canadian women's movement has been between the predominantly white middle-class feminists who have led the movement since the 1960s and the non-white feminists of less privileged ethnic groups and classes. This second group emphasizes race and class as central themes of their feminist vision. At the extreme, some segments of the feminist movement like the *National Action Committee* (NAC) have argued that white middle-class feminists are incapable of truly understanding and representing the circumstances and aspirations of women who are black, Aboriginal, or poor, or who belong to some other historically oppressed group. This claim has generated considerable controversy. And this division appears to have made it easier for governments to question whether the NAC truly represented the concerns and values of Canadian women. By 2004, this once influential voice no longer had enough money to staff a permanent office. The organizations that had traditionally been voices for women—the National Council of Women of Canada, women's teacher and nursing associations, and others—were pushed aside by groups such as the Canadian Abortion Rights Action League and the Women's Legal Education and Action Fund (LEAF).

The decline of the NAC is sometimes seen as a decline in the organizational power of women. Indeed, some feminist writers and intellectuals have parted company with their liberal and radical sisters to become what has been called a "third wave," with an emphasis on individual empowerment and on personally claiming the gains of the second wave rather than continuing to repeat what they see as the self-defeating narrative of "victimhood."

Nonetheless, consolidating and extending the achievements of the second wave is the central task of a number of vibrant organizations today including LEAF, la Fédération des femmes du Québec, and the National Association of Women and the Law. But even more significantly, women's issues and representation have been institutionalized in many labour unions, professional associations, and departments and agencies of the state at all levels.

Achievements

The achievements of modern feminists can be grouped into three types of change: legislative reform, changes in the decision-making process, and the material and social conditions of women. Together these add up to a mixed record of success and failure.

Legislative Reform

Some of the most celebrated achievements of the women's movement have been in changes to the law. Sex was not one of the proscribed grounds of discrimination in the 1981 draft Charter until women's groups made vigorous representations before the Special Parliamentary Committee on the Constitution. Lobbying by women's groups also produced the section 28 guarantee of legal equality for men and women.[33] And in perhaps the most publicized of court decisions on the Charter, in 1988 the Supreme Court of Canada struck down the section of the Criminal Code dealing with abortion. Other major legislative changes and judicial rulings include:

Equal Voice Canada

Green Party leader Elizabeth May speaks after accepting an award from Equal Voice (www.equalvoice.ca), a group advocating for the election of more women at all levels of government. Organizations such as Equal Voice strive to break down the barriers to women's participation in politics through such avenues as recruiting and training, working to create family-friendly work environments, advocating for electoral reform, and running public awareness campaigns. Give three reasons why you think there are not more women representatives in municipal, provincial, and federal politics.

- 1970: Maternity leave provisions are written into the Canada Labour Code.
- 1983: Amendments to the Unemployment Insurance Act eliminate discrimination against pregnant women; pay equity laws are passed by Ottawa and the provinces.
- *Blainey* (1986): An Ontario Court of Appeal decision that opened boys' sports leagues to girls
- *Daigle* (1989): A Supreme Court ruling that the father of a fetus cannot veto a woman's decision to have an abortion
- 1998: A Canadian Human Rights Tribunal pay equity decision found that the federal government owed $5 billion in back pay to female public servants.
- *Ewanchuk* (1999): A Supreme Court ruling that no defence of implied consent to sexual assault exists under Canadian law
- *Falkiner v. Ontario* (2002): The Ontario Court of Appeal struck down the "spouse in the house" rule for social assistance recipients on the grounds that it discriminated against women.

- *D.B.S. v. S.R.G.* (2006): The Supreme Court ruled that the payers of child support, predominantly males, are required to pay increased child support when their income has increased.
- *Watson* (2008): The BC Court of Appeal upheld legislation banning protests within a certain distance of abortion clinics.

Human rights codes and commissions to enforce them exist nationally and in all the provinces in part because of the women's movement. They provide opportunities to challenge discriminatory employment and commercial practices that fall outside of the Charter. In spite of these advances, women's groups point to inaction or government's inadequate responses to such issues as day care, affirmative action, female poverty, pay equity, and pornography. And more recently, many feminists argue that a popular backlash has enabled governments to roll back some of the gains made in the past.

Material and Social Conditions

The record of achievement in equality, the material circumstances of women, and social attitudes is mixed. Social attitudes regarding appropriate roles and behaviour for males and females have changed over the last two generations. Most Canadians believe that a woman could run any business as well as a man, and most claim that the sex of a political party leader does not influence their likelihood of voting for that party. On such issues as abortion and equality of job opportunities, there is little evidence of a significant gender gap. Canadians' attitudes toward gender equality are more progressive than those of the populations of most other affluent democracies.[34]

Nevertheless, considerable sexism persists. Signs of it include gender characterizations in commercial advertising and entertainment programming; the child-rearing practices of many, indeed probably most, parents; the unequal division of domestic responsibilities between men and women; and the rarity of women's career choices taking precedence over men's even in this age of two-earner households. The 2001 Canadian census reported that women were twice as likely as men to say that they spent 15 hours or more each week on housework and almost twice as likely as men to say that they spent at least 15 hours per week on unpaid child care.[35]

When one turns to the material conditions of women the record is mixed and shows evidence of a significant class divide. Today more women are lawyers, professors, accountants, and engineers than in the past, and females are more likely than males to attend university. About one-third of Canadian women between the ages of 24 and 35 have at least a bachelor's degree. Indeed, in 2010, *The Atlantic* featured an analysis of gender accomplishments and current trends. "The End of Men: How Women Are Taking Control of Everything" concluded that the gender equality pendulum now swings in favour of females in affluent democracies such as the United States and Canada, which would have been unimaginable 20 years ago. Today, however, such stories are commonplace. Over one-third of Canadian dentists are females, roughly four in ten family and specialized physicians are women, over 40 per cent of lawyers are female, and even in engineering, long a male bastion, women constitute about one in eight engineers.

These percentages are higher, in some cases much higher, if we look only at those aged 25 to 34 within each of these professions.

While their participation in the political elite has been increasing, a glass ceiling remains for women in key business positions. The belief that more women in the corporate elite would make a difference in the decisions made by major corporations may also be mistaken. As economies become internationalized and globalized, domestic politics matters less and business matters more. Increasingly, decisions with major social implications are made by the corporate elite, from which women are still largely excluded. For example, CBC News reported in 2015 that women held only 8.5 per cent of the highest-paid positions in Canada's top 100 companies.[36]

There is a growing realization that the decline in the power of the "state" relative to globalized markets and corporations has reduced the political clout of women's groups.

Materially, women are still less well off than men despite the legal reforms and changed social attitudes that have been produced by the women's movement. Here are a few examples:

- Close to two-thirds of all employed women continue to be found in what traditionally have been predominantly female occupations.
- The average income of a full-time female worker in 2013 was 82.4 per cent of what the average male earned.[37]
- Women are more likely to be poor than men. Approximately 60 per cent of those below the poverty lines established by Statistics Canada are women.

So far as women are concerned, Canadian democracy remains flawed. Poverty and economic dependence undermine individuals' ability to control their lives and to grasp the opportunities promised by formal legal and political equality. Nevertheless, to a significant degree the feminist movement, in Canada as elsewhere, pioneered the modern discourse of diversity politics: that real democracy cannot be achieved without recognizing the different circumstances experienced by members of different groups, and that justice requires laws and institutions that recognize these different group experiences in its treatment of them.

Aboriginal Politics

For most of Canada's history Aboriginal affairs were relegated to the dim corners of public life. Politicians and most Canadians paid them little attention. This has changed. Aboriginal groups have become much more sophisticated in their political strategies and tactics, and the issues that concern them, from landownership to abuse and discrimination, have become part of the political conversation in Canada.

In 2013 and 2014, three human rights groups, including two from the UN, visited Canada to examine living conditions in Aboriginal communities and to investigate whether authorities had been doing enough to deal with the extraordinary number of murdered and missing Aboriginal women. The state of Canada's Aboriginal peoples has also been the subject of critical inquiry: in 1993, when there was a spate of youth suicides among the Innu of Davis Inlet; in

Media Beat

BOX 5.3 Parental Leave: Where Are the Fathers?

In 2016, the Organisation for Economic Cooperation and Development (OECD) compared the paternity benefits offered by its 34 member countries and came to the following conclusions:

- That some 23 OECD countries offer parental leave but the number of fathers who apply for benefits is low.
  - Fathers are more likely to take the benefits when there is a "daddy quota" or bonus months (months specifically dedicated to paternal leave).
  - Fathers who take parental leave to look after newborns are more likely to stay involved as the children grow up. Mothers and fathers report higher levels of life satisfaction and the children do better physically, psychologically, and emotionally.
  - There are limits to what social policy can achieve in light of cultural norms, wage inequality, and gender norms. However, policy can help by reserving specific periods for fathers or other partners; by promoting awareness campaigns; by reducing the financial burden on parents through financial incentives; and by ensuring leave arrangements are flexible.
  - Some countries are more resistant to the idea of paternity or parental leave than others: e.g., Australia, Japan, the US, Poland, and France.

The OECD is hopeful that as more countries implement paternal leave policies, the idea will gain legitimacy.

Source: Organisation for Economic Cooperation and Development, *Parental Leave: Where are the Fathers?* OECD Policy Brief, March 2016 https://www.oecd.org/policy-briefs/parental-leave-where-are-the-fathers.pdf

2004, when there were reports of gas-sniffing by teenagers and young children in the Innu community of Sheshatshiu in Labrador; and in 2011, when there was housing crisis in Attawapiskat First Nation, Ontario. Suicide rates among Inuit youth are about 11 times the national average and among Aboriginal Canadians overall are almost six times the national average.

These stories, which have generated headlines in Canada and abroad, stand in stark contrast with the celebration of Aboriginal symbols and culture in places like the Canadian Museum of History in Gatineau, Quebec. Many Canadians are puzzled that circumstances like those at Sheshatshiu and Attawapiskat exist. After all, government expenditures per Aboriginal person are substantially higher than for non-Aboriginals and have been growing.[38] Canadians are also perplexed by news stories of continuing tensions and occasional outbreaks of violence

This photo was taken at one of the many Idle No More demonstrations across Canada. The movement began in 2012 as a protest against legislation in Bill C-45 that would have weakened protections for development and waterways in First Nations territory.

between some Aboriginal communities and their neighbours or the political authorities. Why, they wonder, after years of treaties, legislation, government programs, inquiries, apologies, and financial settlements, do so many issues remain unresolved?

Aboriginal Demographics: Who and How Many?

Aboriginal Canadians are those who can trace their ancestry back to before the arrival and permanent settlement of Europeans in what would become Canada. The actual size of this population is uncertain and a source of controversy. Estimates range from 1 million to 3 million (5.5 to 9 per cent of the national population).

Statistics Canada defines **Aboriginal** as a person who self-identifies as North American Indian (First Nations), Métis, or Inuit. According to the 2011 census,

Aboriginal
a person who self-identifies as North American Indian, Métis, or Inuit

- 1,836,035 people, 5.5 per cent of the Canadian population, gave as their ethnic origins North American Indian, Métis, Inuit, or a combination of one of these with some other ethnic origin.
- 1,400,685 people, 4.3 per cent of the population, identified with an Aboriginal group—up from 3.3 per cent in 2001.

- 637,660, 2 per cent of the population, are status Indians, i.e., those to whom the Indian Act applies. Just under half live on reserves.

The regional distribution of those who identify themselves as Aboriginal Canadians is shown in Figure 5.4.

As evidenced by the news reports of the stories mentioned above, the social and economic conditions of Aboriginal Canadians tend to be considerably worse than those of the general population. Statistics confirm that Aboriginal Canadians are less well off than their fellow Canadians. Many Aboriginal Canadians live in isolated communities. Aboriginal Canadians earn about one-third less than non-Aboriginal Canadians. Government transfer payments make up about one-fifth of Aboriginal income, compared to about one-tenth for non-Aboriginal Canadians. The likelihood of falling below the Statistics Canada low-income line is twice as great for the non-reserve Aboriginal population as for the non-Aboriginal population, and considerably higher than this for those living on reserves. Over four out of ten Aboriginal Canadians have not completed high school, a figure that rises to about six of ten for those who live on reserves, compared to just over two out of ten for the non-Aboriginal population. Non-Aboriginal Canadians are about three times more likely than Aboriginal Canadians to have graduated from university.

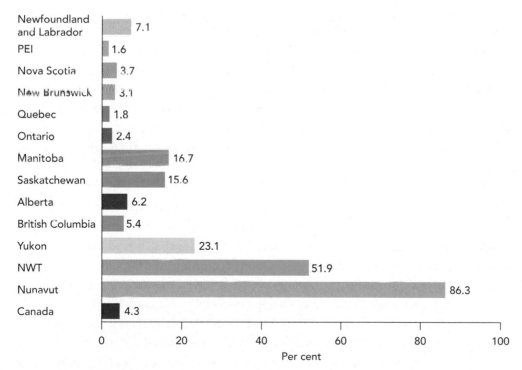

FIGURE 5.4 Aboriginal Identity Population as Percentage of Total Population, Provinces and Territories, 2011

Source: Statistics Canada Aboriginal Peoples, 2006 Census (97-558-X).

The Language of Aboriginal Politics

The words used to describe those whose ancestry pre-dates the arrival of Europeans provide a useful starting point for understanding the politics of Aboriginality. For most of Canada's history these people and their communities were only marginally acknowledged in the official life of the country and were barely visible in mainstream interpretations of Canadian history and society. The terms "Indian," "Métis," and "Eskimo" were used to describe various segments of the Aboriginal population. The legal meanings and implications of these terms were sometimes contested in the courts. Until the 1960s, there was little controversy over the terms used to characterize the Aboriginal population of Canada.

By the 1960s, labels and concepts that had been considered acceptable and appropriate were brought into question because of changing Western thought. The communitarian belief that communities and communal identities are essential to individual dignity and to the health of democratic societies was gaining ground. At the street level, this belief system was embodied in elements of the black civil rights movement, in echoes of Quebec nationalism from books like Pierre Vallières's *Nègres blancs d'Amérique* (*White Niggers of America*), and to René Lévesque's insistence that Quebecers could not have a free and democratic society without an independent state. During these years black, ethnic, and women's studies emerged at universities across North America.

An additional and crucial feature of the communitarian model involved *inequality*. Virtually all calls for greater group self-awareness and demands for official recognition of this collective identity were linked to an analysis and historical narrative of discrimination, exploitation, and unjust treatment, especially in relations between the group and the state. Post–World War II liberal thinking aimed at eradicating poverty, socio-economic inequality, and discrimination. And the path to progress involved the *full and equal integration of all people*, as individuals, into society and the dismantling of laws, norms, and practices that treated people differently on the basis of skin colour, ethnicity, or religion—that officially recognized and institutionalized differences.

For Aboriginal Canadians, the first step was to reject the mid-twentieth-century language of *integration* and *liberal notions of equality*: these ideas were leading to assimilation and cultural genocide. Despite the obvious misnomer applied by the early European explorers to native North Americans, the term "Indian" was not immediately rejected. Indeed, "Indian" continues to be used by community members and their leaders today.

By the late 1970s and 1980s, "Indian," which carried the historical baggage of conquest, displacement, and subordination, was being replaced by "Native," "Aboriginal," and "First Nations." This shift was both intellectual and political. Intellectually, the change reflected a reappropriation of Aboriginals' identities and histories. Politically, the term *First Nations* carried connotations of prior claims as well as communal status and rights. The language of *nationalism* and the *claims of nations*, particularly nations that had been colonized by foreign powers, became familiar and powerful. The dismantling of European colonial empires and the 1960 UN Declaration on the Granting of Independence to Colonial Countries and Peoples reinforced nationalist claims and the idea that "all peoples have the right to self-determination." If the Québécois could make nationalist claims, then why not Aboriginal Canadians as well? Indeed, it is difficult to argue that Aboriginal peoples are somehow less deserving of nation status than the Québécois. They certainly can make a more compelling case for having experienced "alien subjugation" and "domination," terms used in the UN Declaration.

And as with the Québécois, the matter of whether Aboriginal communities are "nations" is also disputed. More important is whether the widespread acceptance of terms like "First Nations" and "Indigenous peoples" can have consequences with respect to legitimacy and a group's claims. Relations between Aboriginal communities and the Canadian state were long about treaty obligations and reserves. Consequently, the language of treaty obligations continues to be important and reserves still exist. Several other terms and associated issues have become part of the conversation on Aboriginal affairs: "sovereignty," "self-government," "self-determination," and "nation to nation." The new vocabulary reflects a recent change in the scope and nature of Aboriginal demands in Canada—demands that rest on an increasingly influential *communitarian ethos*.

Who Is an Indian?

Practically speaking, the word "Indian" must be used in any discussion of government policies toward Aboriginal peoples. Until the Indian Act and the legal status of "Indian" are abolished, we cannot avoid using these terms. Under Canada's Indian Act (1876), a person who qualifies as an Indian under the law has certain entitlements that do not apply to others. In law, an Indian or status Indian is anyone who has been or is entitled to be registered under the Indian Act, including those who belong to communities covered by treaties. The defining characteristics are both biological and social. An Indian was any male person of Indian blood who belonged to a band recognized by the federal government, any child of such a person, or any woman married to such a person. Moreover, Indian bands that live on land referred to in law as Indian *reserves* are subject to special legal provisions such as limits on individual landownership and transfer, a prohibition against mortgages, and numerous economic restrictions.

Prior to the Charter, an Indian woman who married a non-Indian lost her legal status and entitlements as an Indian. This discriminatory section of the Act was changed by the federal government in response to pressure from Aboriginal women and to conform to the UN International Covenant on Civil and Political Rights, and the Charter of Rights and Freedoms.

Ancestry is not the only criterion determining who is an Indian under the law. Indeed, the courts have recognized that a person's "associations, habits, modes of life, and surroundings" may weigh more heavily in the balance than the ethnicity of one's forebears in determining legal status as an Indian.[39] Canadian law also recognizes the Métis and Inuit as two other categories of Aboriginal peoples of Canada. The Inuit and Métis are grouped with the Indian people of Canada by the Constitution Act, 1982, which recognizes and affirms the "existing aboriginal and treaty rights of the aboriginal peoples of Canada."

The Reserve System

There are over 2300 Indian reserves in Canada. They cover about 28,000 square kilometres, an area half the size of Nova Scotia. Some have called Indian reserves Canada's own system of apartheid. Superficially, the apartheid label seems a fair one. The reserve system was created to provide a sort of fixed homeland for Indians, and the vast majority of those residing on reserves today are status Indians.

Canada is an affluent society whose social pathologies are similar to those of other advanced industrial societies. Based on its quality of life (QOL) measures, the United Nations is certainly right in rating Canada as one of the world's best countries in which to live. But the QOL is sharply lower for Aboriginal Canadians. Consider these facts:

- For those on reserves, life expectancy and incomes are significantly lower than the Canadian norms. Life expectancy for Aboriginal Canadians is about seven years less than for the population as a whole.
- Rates of suicide, alcoholism, violent death, unemployment, crowded housing conditions, and infant mortality are all higher, sometimes dramatically higher, than the Canadian average.
- Infant mortality rates are twice as high among Aboriginals as among non-Aboriginals.
- Aboriginal Canadians are three times more likely to die of accidents, violence, or self-inflicted harm than the general population.
- Although less than 4 per cent of the population are Aboriginal Canadians, just under one-quarter of those in prisons are Aboriginal.
- Alcoholism is much more prevalent among Aboriginals than non-Aboriginals.

The enormous disparity between life on reserves and in mainstream society, combined with the racial basis for the physical segregation of Indians, does sound like apartheid. But when the Liberal government's 1969 White Paper proposed the abolition of reserves along with all the other legal and paternalistic structures that treated Indians differently, the Aboriginal community leaders responded with a vehement "no." Why then is this apparent form of apartheid not rejected outright by those who are its "victims"? To understand why, we must look at the origins and operation of Indian reserves in Canada as well as the goals of today's Aboriginal leaders.

The Indian Act of 1876 defines a reserve as ". . . any tract or tracts of land set apart by treaty or otherwise for the use or benefit of or granted to a particular band of Indians, of which the legal title is in the Crown, but which is unsurrendered, and includes all the trees, wood, timber, soil, stone, minerals, metals, or other valuables thereon or therein." Central to this definition and to the reserve system is the *guardianship* relationship between the federal government and Indians living on reserves. Reserve land belongs to the Crown, but the land and its resources must be managed for the "use or benefit" of the band, which meant that virtually all legal or commercial transactions by Indians living on a reserve required the permission of the federal Department of Indian Affairs (now called Indigenous and Northern Affairs).

Restrictions have been eased somewhat recently. When critics speak of the Indian Act's paternalism, they may be referring to the fact that band members may not sell any part of the reserve or use the land as security for loans, and that the federal government has the ultimate authority to grant timber-cutting licences.

Roughly 400,000 Indians live on reserves, but about three-quarters of all reserves are uninhabited, since many bands have leased their reserve land to non-Indians for various economic and recreational uses. A vast majority of reserves are in rural and remote areas, with populations that vary from a handful to just under 20,000. Most reserves have fewer than a thousand inhabitants. This has important social and economic consequences. Job opportunities are fewer, and many who want secondary or post-secondary education must leave home.

Physical isolation impedes the integration of reserve populations into the rest of society. However, as Harvey McCue explains, not everyone considers physical isolation a bad thing:

> To many Indians, reserves represent the last visible evidence that they were the original people of this country. The reserve nurtures a community of "Indianness" and reinforces spiritual unity among Indians. Despite the manifest poverty, ill health, poor housing and lack of services, the life-style on reserves, traditional values, kinship affiliations and the land itself all contribute to an Indian's identity and psychological well-being.[40]

As McCue suggests, the pressure on Aboriginal Canadians to assimilate is powerful. Language loss is one of the key indicators of assimilation. Only three of Canada's roughly 53 Aboriginal languages—Cree, Inuktitut, and Ojibwa—continue to be spoken by significant numbers of Aboriginal Canadians. While there still is cause for concern, however, in the first years of the twenty-first century, fluency in some Aboriginal languages was holding steady, indicating that there is renewed interest and impressive effort in keeping these languages alive.[41]

Assimilation, Integration, and Self-Determination

Although some major components of present-day Aboriginal policy have been in place since before Confederation, the principles underlying federal policy have undergone important transformations.

Under French colonial rule two key principles underlay Aboriginal policy in New France: the non-recognition of any Aboriginal proprietary rights in the lands claimed by France, and assimilation. France laid claim to territory in the New World by right of discovery and conquest. As well, conversion of the Aboriginal population to Christianity was a central objective of French colonial policy. Notably, French policy did not consider the Aboriginal population to be subhuman and beyond redemption. In fact, the 1627 Charter of the Company of One Hundred Associates declared that a converted Aboriginal had the status and rights of a naturalized French citizen.

The transfer of French territories in Canada to the British laid the foundation for Aboriginal policies for the next two centuries. The *Royal Proclamation of 1763* and the treaties between the colonial authorities and Indian tribes were clearly based on the assumption that Aboriginals had fallen under the protective stewardship of the British state. Unlike the French, the British acknowledged a proprietary Aboriginal interest in the land, but within the broader context of British sovereignty and the colonial authorities' expectations that European settlement would continue to expand onto land traditionally occupied by Aboriginal peoples. Moreover, as both the Royal Proclamation and early dealings between the British and Indians show, the British believed that they were required to compensate the Aboriginal population for land through treaties and purchase agreements. And unlike the French, the British were much less concerned with the state of Aboriginals' souls than with ensuring that the Indigenous population did not impede the colonies' growth. To this end, the policy of reserving certain lands for occupation and use by Indians was practised by the British—a policy that was continued after Confederation.

Under the BNA Act (now called the Constitution Act, 1867), Ottawa assumed exclusive legislative authority over Indian affairs. Within a decade, the federal government passed the Indian Act: a sweeping piece of legislation that consolidated the dependency relationship that already had been developing between Aboriginals and the state. Under the Act, Indians living on reserves were placed under the almost total control of the Superintendent-General of Indian Affairs, whose god-like powers would be exercised by federal bureaucrats in Ottawa and by powerful officials in the field, referred to as Indian agents.

The Indian Act made it impossible for Indians living on reserves to assume responsibility and control over their social and economic development. Unlike many Aboriginal traditions of governance that involved traditional and inherited leadership, the Act conferred extremely limited powers of self-government on elected reserve bands.

Until well into the latter half of the twentieth century it was widely believed that Aboriginal Canadians would gradually abandon their language and culture and be absorbed into Euro-Canadian society. The 1884 ban on the potlatch ceremony and on religious ceremonies exemplifies the sanctions used to stamp out Aboriginal traditions. The goal of assimilation is especially apparent in the sections of the Indian Act that set out procedures whereby an Indian could *request* to become a Canadian citizen. While enfranchisement was automatic for Indians who acquired a certain education or social rank, full Canadian citizenship was not granted to all Aboriginal people until the Act was amended in 1960.

Residential Schools

The prohibition against students speaking Aboriginal languages in the federal government's *residential schools* was another attempt at assimilating Aboriginal people into mainstream society. The residential schools issue was examined and reported on in detail by the 2015 Truth and Reconciliation Commission (TRC). Some 150,000 Inuit, Métis, and First Nations children were placed in these residential schools between 1870 and the 1990s. The schools' main purpose appears to have been assimilation. According to the TRC:

> For over a century, the central goals of Canada's Aboriginal policy were to eliminate Aboriginal governments; ignore Aboriginal rights; terminate the Treaties;

and, through a process of assimilation, cause Aboriginal peoples to cease to exist as distinct legal, social, cultural, religious, and racial entities in Canada. The establishment and operation of residential schools were a central element of this policy, which can best be described as "cultural genocide."

Nevertheless, the TRC was hopeful as it offered a "reconciliation framework" as a peaceful solution to these historical wrongs:

> A reconciliation framework is one in which Canada's political and legal systems, educational and religious institutions, the corporate sector and civic society function in ways that are consistent with the principles set out in the *United Nations Declaration on the Rights of Indigenous Peoples*, which Canada has endorsed. Together, Canadians must do more than just talk about reconciliation; we must learn how to practise reconciliation in our everyday lives—within ourselves and our families, and in our communities, governments, places of worship, schools, and workplaces. To do so constructively, Canadians must remain committed to the ongoing work of establishing and maintaining respectful relationships.[42]

The 1969 White Paper

The extension of voting rights to Aboriginals brought their political status closer to that of other Canadians, but their legal and social status, and their civil rights, remained distinct. Moreover, instead of disappearing, as many had hoped, Indian reserves continued to exist as islands of shame within an affluent and democratic society.

The government of Pierre Trudeau set out to change this by introducing the 1969 White Paper (a report for discussion on a major piece of legislation being proposed by government) on Aboriginal reform. It proposed dismantling the Indian Affairs bureaucracy, bringing an end to the reserve system, abolishing different status for Indians under the law, and transferring responsibility for the education, health care, and social needs of Aboriginal citizens, as for other Canadians, to the provinces. These proposed changes were in keeping with the ideas of the civil rights movement of the 1950s and 1960s, which proposed *inclusive integration* as a remedy—barriers to the full economic, social, and political participation of historically disadvantaged minorities would be abolished.

The reaction of Canada's Aboriginal leadership to the 1969 White Paper was swift and overwhelmingly negative. And although its authors certainly did not intend such interpretations, some critics equated its "liberal integrationist" vision with assimilation, "cultural genocide," and "extermination."[43] Nothing galvanized Aboriginal opposition more.

The very concept of a treaty between one part of society and the government of all the people was morally and philosophically repugnant to Pierre Trudeau, who objected to a different status for Quebec and its citizens on the same grounds. The government argued that while it recognized its lawful obligations, treaties should not be expected to define in perpetuity the relationship between Aboriginals and the government of Canada. This vision

White Paper a report for discussion on a major piece of legislation being proposed by government, which is based on research by the bureaucracy or the legislature, and serves as a statement of the government's legislative intentions

© Library and Archives Canada/MIKAN 3191693

The residential school system was an attempt at assimilating Aboriginal communities into mainstream Canadian society, as evidenced by the European-style clothing. Can you name some of the long-lasting negative effects of these kinds of attempts at assimilation?

and its premises survive today in some of Canada's political and intellectual elites but have been refuted by numerous court decisions on treaty rights and Aboriginal land claims. Since the 1969 White Paper, the government appears to have recognized, in the law and in the Constitution, the separate and distinct status of Aboriginal communities within Canadian society—a concept of *self-government* for Aboriginal communities. This status is now endorsed by the Assembly of First Nations (AFN) and accepted as both fair and desirable by many Canadians.

The self-government vision for Aboriginal Canadians was set forth in the 1996 report of the Royal Commission on Aboriginal Peoples (RCAP). The philosophical premises and policy proposals of RCAP were diametrically opposed to those of the 1969 White Paper. Of RCAP's 440 recommendations, the most prominent are

- issue an official admission of the wrongs done to Aboriginal people
- recognize the inherent right of Aboriginal self-government as a right that exists under the Constitution

- provide Aboriginals with dual citizenship, as Canadians and as citizens of Aboriginal communities. The report proposed some 60–80 self-governing groups through a political merger of 1000 or so Aboriginal communities across the country.
- establish an Aboriginal parliament with an advisory role concerning all legislation affecting Aboriginal Canadians
- negotiate with Métis representatives on self-government and the allocation to the Métis people of an adequate land base
- have Aboriginal representatives participate in all future talks on constitutional reform, with a veto over any changes that affect Aboriginal rights
- allocate more money for Aboriginal programs

The problem with previous federal policies is that they had not provided the Aboriginal population with the decision-making autonomy or enough financial resources to escape the cycle of dependency perpetuated by the Indian Act and reserve system.

As discussed below, a number of these recommendations have been acted upon. However, the federal government has been unwilling to concede the division of sovereignty that seemed to be at the heart of RCAP's approach to reform—a notion of self-government premised on the idea that Aboriginal sovereignty is similar to the sovereign constitutional relationship Ottawa has with the provinces.

Landownership and Sovereignty

Disputes over land—who owns it, and who can live on it, benefit from it, and make laws that apply within its boundaries—are among the most intractable. Aboriginal Canadians have come to realize that the crux of their demands involves land. Phrases like "self-government for Canada's Aboriginal peoples" have inoffensive and even positive associations for many Canadians until these claims affect them personally or affect territory they believed was part of Canada. Aboriginal and European-based cultures view the land and their relationship to it very differently. The land was crucial to the traditional lifestyles of Aboriginal peoples: hunting and fishing rights recognized in many treaties were important to the Aboriginal peoples but were often restricted or ignored by governments and private citizens. Somewhat more controversial are claims to control mineral or other resources valued by Europeans cultures but that have little or no relationship to Aboriginal cultures. Canadian courts have addressed this issue in recent years.

Treaties signed by British authorities prior to Confederation and by Ottawa after Confederation—which were intended to extinguish Aboriginal claims to these territories in exchange for reserves, money, and other benefits—do not cover all of Canada. In fact, enormous areas encompassing much of the North and both the western and eastern extremities of the country were not covered by treaties. Many First Nations people are members of bands that have not signed treaties with Ottawa. Having never been vanquished militarily or given up their territorial rights through a treaty, they claim that the land their ancestors inhabited still belongs to them.

Ownership of a particular parcel of land does not exempt a person or group from the obligation to obey the law of the sovereign country in which their land is located. But many leaders within Canada's Aboriginal communities deny the sovereignty of the Canadian state over them and their land. Former AFN national chief Ovide Mercredi's comment is fairly typical: "We will not allow some other society to decide what we can do and determine the limits of our authority."[44] Nonetheless, while virtually all Aboriginal spokespersons express support for the principles of *Aboriginal self-government* and Aboriginal rights, most advocate some form of self-determination that would be realized within the context of the Canadian state.

Indeed, those who make the case for Aboriginal sovereignty often begin with the Royal Proclamation of 1763. The Proclamation included detailed provisions regarding relations between the British and the Aboriginal inhabitants, who generally view the Royal Proclamation as an affirmation of their existing right to the lands they occupied. It is not entirely clear, however, that the Proclamation—which was formally incorporated into the Constitution through section 25 of the Charter of Rights and Freedoms—recognizes Aboriginal sovereignty. What is clear, however, is that the Proclamation speaks of the "Sovereignty, Protection, and Dominion" of the Crown in relation to the Aboriginal inhabitants who "live under our protection."

That the Royal Proclamation recognizes Aboriginal rights is indisputable. However, a ruling by the British Judicial Committee of the Privy Council in 1888 stated that the Proclamation did not explicitly recognize Indian sovereignty. Perhaps there is an implicit recognition of Aboriginal sovereignty which seems to support those who characterize it as a *nation-to-nation* agreement. The restriction on the use of "Lands of the Indians" might be interpreted as an acknowledgement of Aboriginal sovereignty. It seems to establish an Indian right to compensation for land transferred by them to the Crown.

A number of land issue cases, including *St Catherine's Milling and Lumber Company v. the Queen* (1888), *Calder et al. v. Attorney General of British Columbia* (1973), *Hamlet of Baker Lake et al. v. Minister of Indian Affairs* (1980), and *Regina v. Sparrow* (1990), set the stage for *Delgamuukw v. Attorney General of British Columbia*, which worked its way through the courts from 1987 to 1997. In *Delgamuukw*, the issue of Aboriginal title was addressed head-on. A group of Gitksan and Wet'suwet'en chiefs argued that they owned an area in British Columbia roughly the size of Nova Scotia. The stakes were high. Following rejection of the claim by the British Columbia Supreme Court in 1991, and an upholding of this judgment on appeal, the Supreme Court of Canada in 1997 ruled that the Gitksan and Wet'suwet'en are the owners of the land to which they lay historical claim.

The *Delgamuukw* decision generated many questions, but what is clear is that Court's interpretation of Aboriginal title means that Aboriginal communities have a right to compensation for land determined to be theirs by historical right. Aboriginal groups can now say that they have a constitutionally protected right of ownership that can be extinguished only through the terms of a treaty with the Crown.

The Supreme Court's 2014 ruling in *Tsilhqot'in Nation v. British Columbia* provides the clearest statement yet of the meaning of Aboriginal title and has a great deal of relevance for mineral exploitation, pipelines, electrical transmission corridors, and other infrastructure.

What form that Aboriginal self-determination takes has yet to be determined and there are many questions—some of them potentially sensitive for both Aboriginal and non-Aboriginal Canadians. How much Aboriginal sovereignty can be accommodated without challenging the integrity of the Canadian state? Can the Aboriginal peoples truly be sovereign when many of them are dependent on the Canadian state? Will the arrangements between Aboriginal Canadians and the Canadian government result in different types of Canadian citizens, with some having more rights and privileges than others? Similar questions were being asked when Quebecers were asking for a special status within the Canadian constitutional arrangement.

Do Land Rights Convey Sovereignty?

While some have argued that the treaties and other agreements are tantamount to international treaties, the Supreme Court's 1997 decision did not establish a constitutional right to self-government for Aboriginal communities. If this is so, then it would follow that these Aboriginal peoples have been recognized as sovereign nations capable of entering into agreements with other nations on a basis of legal equality. But even in their generally sympathetic treatment of Aboriginal rights, Peter A. Cumming and Neil H. Mickenberg say that historically and legally there is little basis for interpreting treaties as international treaties. They note that the Supreme Court of Canada has rejected this view. Moreover, they note that "the Government did not consider the Indians to be independent nations at the time the treaties were made . . . and both the Government representatives and the Indian negotiators indicate that they considered the Indian peoples to be subjects of the Queen."[45]

On the issue of treaties with European powers, Georges Erasmus and Joe Sanders write, "Our people understood what the non-native people were after when they came amongst our people and wanted to treaty with them, because they had done that many times amongst themselves."[46]

According to Cumming and Mickenberg, however treaties were viewed by the Aboriginal people, there is little doubt that colonial officials and subsequent Canadian authorities used the "language of real property law" and interpreted the treaties as a way of ". . . extinguishing Indian title in order that lands could be opened to white settlement. The treaties, therefore, can be best understood . . . when considered as agreements of a very special nature in which the Indians gave up their rights in the land in exchange for certain promises made by the Government."[47]

The question of how treaties were negotiated centuries ago often arises; treaties were negotiated by parties who spoke different languages, written in the language of only one party, and operated from very different cultural premises. For instance, in *R v. Marshall* (1999), the Supreme Court made two controversial rulings. In the first ruling, the Court stated that according to 1760s treaties with Britain, the Mi'kmaq Indians had the right to catch and sell fish, and that federal fisheries regulations infringed on those rights. In the second ruling, the Court indicated that Aboriginal treaty rights were still subject to treatment under Canadian law.

The Institutionalization of Aboriginal Affairs

The treaties and the federal Indian bureaucracy that has existed since and even before the Indian Act (1876) would ensure that Aboriginal affairs were embedded in the activities of the Canadian state. Government transfers to Aboriginal communities under the terms of treaties, which were administered through Indian agents, and transfers to individual Aboriginals through welfare spending (Aboriginal Canadians living off-reserve are about three times more likely than other Canadians to receive social assistance) created a web of financial dependency on the state that continues to exist. The institutionalization of Aboriginal affairs into the structure and activities of the Canadian state has also created and perpetuated dependency relations. Dependency continues in spite of some important reforms designed to break the cycle.

The web of dependency relations and institutionalization of relations has come about in three ways. The first, as mentioned above, has come in the form of transfer payments and social assistance. The second has come about in the form of initiatives for Aboriginal affairs, identity, and language in areas such as television and radio programming and broadcasting through the Canadian state. Several initiatives were launched between 1960 and the mid-1990s, but the consensus is that the major impact of broadcasting to the North, where most viewers and listeners were Aboriginal Canadians, was to "accelerate the process of cultural and language loss, particularly among the young."[48] The airwaves in Aboriginal communities continue to be dominated by English programming, and the use of Aboriginal languages continues to decline.

And finally, another way in which Aboriginal concerns and issues have been institutionalized through the Canadian state involves employment. For instance, Aboriginal representation in the federal public service, negligible for most of Canada's history, today is about proportional to the size of the Aboriginal identity population of the country. Aboriginal Canadians make up about 4.5 per cent of the federal public service and 2.5 per cent of all those in the executive category of the bureaucracy. In the National Capital Region the figure is about 3 per cent, but Aboriginal employees represent closer to one-quarter of federal bureaucrats in the combined territories of Yukon, the Northwest Territories, and Nunavut.

Some, like former Liberal minister of Indian Affairs Hugh Faulkner, have argued that the motive behind his government's deliberate policy of funding selected interest groups, including Aboriginal organizations, was progressive and intended to strengthen the political voice of such groups.[49] Others, like Noel Starblanket of the National Indian Brotherhood, accused Ottawa of using money as part of a divide-and-conquer strategy for dealing with Aboriginal groups.[50] Roger Gibbins and Rick Ponting agree that the potential for the co-optation and control of Aboriginal organizations certainly existed as Ottawa became increasingly involved in the funding of these groups.[51]

The leading organizational voices for Aboriginal Canadians continue to depend on public funding mainly from Indigenous and Northern Affairs. However, there is little evidence that this dependence has muted their criticisms. For example, money spent on legal proceedings against the Canadian state, and for lobbying and advertising campaigns to influence public opinion on policy, has come, at least in part, from the state. Attempts to renegotiate treaty obligations between the federal government and the AFN, for example at the 2013 National Treaty Gathering at Onion Lake, Saskatchewan, have created divisions between Aboriginal leaders. Some criticized the Conservative government for orchestrating the division, but others have observed that different groups have different views on what needs to be reformed and on the future of relations between the Canadian state and their communities.

A Way Forward

In January 2013, when the Idle No More protests were front-page news across Canada, the *National Post*'s letters editor asked readers to "solve Canada's Native issue, in 75 words or less." One reader's comment seems apt: "We will have to stop using inane, simplified, and misleading phrases like 'the native issue.'"[52] There is, as we have seen, no single issue when it comes to the conditions and demands of Aboriginal communities. These communities are quite diverse. They are represented by many different organizations, and their perspectives on and preferences in their relationship with the Canadian state and the rest of Canadian society vary quite significantly.

The Idle No More protests, as was also true of the Oka crisis in 1990, the Ipperwash stand-off in 1995, the occupation of a housing project at Caledonia, Ontario, in 2006 (which is still unresolved as of 2016), and lesser confrontations between Aboriginal protesters and state authorities, give the impression that little progress has been made in resolving the many and complex issues that lead to conflict.

Conflict, rancour, stalemate, and dire living conditions capture the headlines, but relations between Aboriginal communities and the state are not entirely devoid of progress. Among these positive developments are

- the creation of Nunavut in 1999
- the formal apology in 2008 and compensation for the victims of abuse in residential schools
- the recent land transfer agreements between the Cree and the government of Quebec
- steps taken toward the reform and perhaps dismantling of the Indian Act
- the 1997 *Delgamuukw* decision of the Supreme Court granting Gitksan and Wet'su-wet'en historic rights to their traditional lands
- the Court's 2014 *Tsilhqot'in Nation* decision, which determined that Aboriginal communities have a legal right to veto any development on land to which they hold Aboriginal title, which provided a much firmer basis for claims of Aboriginal landownership than previously existed

Much of the recent progress involved agreements between Aboriginal communities and private-sector companies, which have provided employment and economic opportunities. Examples include the 2012 agreement between Pinehouse First Nation and uranium companies Cameco and Areva in northern Saskatchewan, agreements in the Alberta oil sands between Syncrude and Suncor and Aboriginal groups, and the Inuit participation in the Baffinland (Mary River) iron ore mine, which has been cited as a model for further business–Aboriginal co-operation.

More relevant to the lives of Canada's reserve and off-reserve Indian populations is reform of the Indian Act, which virtually everyone now agrees must be reformed or even abolished.

In 2012 the Conservative government announced its support for Bill C-428, the Indian Act Amendment and Replacement Act. The bill quite rightly describes the Indian Act, which has gone largely unreformed since its passage in 1876, as "an outdated colonial statute." As journalist and writer Wab Kinew puts it, "The Indian Act, as it exists right now, is an affront to these Indigenous systems of law, culture and governance. The Indian Act asserts the supremacy of western law and implies that Indigenous laws and cultures do not have value."[53] Unlike the White Paper proposals of 1969, Bill C-428 did not repeal the Indian Act but instead was an attempt at cleaning up many of the provisions that were seldom used or considered archaic.

Many, like Kinew, worried that the bill was yet another attempt to impose a solution onto Aboriginal people: a paternalistic approach that had not worked so well in the past. The AFN was supportive of most of the bill's changes; however, not all Aboriginal groups were. Manitoba grand chief Derek Nepinak spoke for many Aboriginals leaders in arguing that

> [i]mposing legislation on first nations people pursuant to the Indian Act in this manner perpetuates the federal government's unilateral interpretation of first nations self-government. This approach is inconsistent with our inherent rights, international law, and declarations endorsed by Canada. . . . [Bill C-428] is another piece of federal government-owned legislation that perpetuates Canada's self-proclaimed authority over indigenous people.[54]

It is not surprising that reform of the Indian Act raises a red flag for so many people. Despite the fact that virtually everyone believes the Act is paternalistic and archaic, the shadow of the 1969 White Paper remains, as do fears that the Act's abolition might result in cultural genocide. By the time the TRC released its report on the residential schools in 2015, Bill C-428 had already removed provisions of the Indian Act that had made the residential schools policy and other abuses possible.

The way forward, it turns out, is likely to look like neither the integrationist vision of the 1969 White Paper nor the grand "People to people, nation to nation" vision expressed in the RCAP report in 1996. It is, however, likely to include some elements of both of these visions and, moreover, to emphasize ways of breaking down the ties of paternalism and dependency that

Democracy Watch

BOX 5.4 Speak Up for Your Most Important Contemporary Issue

This chapter explores several prominent issues in contemporary Canadian political life. These are not the only contemporary issues of importance to Canadians. However, some people in this country are very concerned about the erosion of ethics in government, particularly after events like the Liberal sponsorship scandal, the two prorogations of Parliament by the Conservatives, the robo-call scandal, and the Senate spending scandal. Others point to under-spending on infrastructure or a lack of action on climate change and global warming. Still others worry about youth and their employment prospects and the precariousness of Canada's place in a globalized economy.

Canadian Spotlight

BOX 5.5   Timeline: Major Violent Confrontations between French Canadians and English Canadians

Disagreements and disputes both between French- and English-speaking Canadians and between Aboriginals and non-Aboriginals represent significant challenges to the notion of a single Canadian political community. As indicated below, animosities that have existed between French and English Canadians have crystallized around violent events on several occasions.

1885   The francophone Métis leader Louis Riel is hanged after the defeat of the Northwest Rebellion. The government's unwillingness to commute the death sentence is seen by the francophones as anti-French prejudice.

1917   Anti-conscription riots take place during World War I in Quebec. French Canadians believe Canada's participation is motivated by colonial attachments.

1955   Riots occur in Montreal following Maurice "Le Rocket" Richard's suspension by Clarence Campbell, the president of the National Hockey League. French-Canadian supporters see the suspension as motivated by discrimination on the part of *les maudits anglais* ("the damned English").

1960s   A spate of bombings and vandalism in the 1960s is directed at symbols of the federal government's authority and anglophone domination in Quebec.

1970 October   The FLQ kidnap British trade commissioner James Cross and kidnap and assassinate Quebec cabinet minister Pierre Laporte. The federal government reacts by invoking the War Measures Act, under which normal civil liberties are suspended.

(Left) Montrealers take to Victoria Square on 24 May 1917 to protest compulsory service enacted by Prime Minister Sir Robert Borden, an anglophone, during World War I. (Right) A man is arrested by two Montreal policemen during the 1955 riot over the suspension of Maurice Richard at the Montreal Forum.

have been the hallmarks of relations between Aboriginal communities and the Canadian state. As has been true over the past four decades, there will not be one path toward reform. It will take place through the courts, Parliament, and the impact and benefit agreements that private resource companies make with Aboriginal communities.

Political Violence and Challenges to the Political Community

Canadians are not accustomed to the violent resolution of political disputes. Until the violent terrorist attacks and deaths of Warrant Officer Patrice Vincent and Corporal Nathan Cirillo in October 2014, there had only been two political assassinations since Confederation. The first came in 1868 when D'Arcy McGee was shot down in Ottawa, and the second in 1970 when Quebec's minister of labour, Pierre Laporte, was kidnapped and strangled to death by members of the FLQ. *The World Handbook of Social and Political Indicators* ranks Canada well down the list of countries in terms of political violence. This is why the murders of Vincent and Cirillo came as such a shock to many Canadians. And even though non-violent protest is more common in Canadian politics than violence (as one would expect in any genuine democracy), protest demonstrations historically have been much rarer in Canada than in most other advanced industrialized democracies.

Violence, however, has been neither absent nor unimportant in Canadian politics. Much of that violence has involved labour disputes or workers' protests where the police or military were called in to protect the interests of employers and the capitalist social order. Examples include the violent suppression of the Winnipeg General Strike in 1919 and the use of the Royal Canadian Mounted Police in Regina in 1935 to break up the "On to Ottawa Trek" of unemployed workers during the depth of the *Great Depression*. The forcible detention of many Japanese, German, and Italian Canadians during World War II is another instance of state political violence. Indeed, in most of these cases it was the state that decided to use violence to settle some conflict or deal with some perceived menace. The most significant instances of political violence instigated by groups or individuals against the state have been related to the French–English conflict and, more recently, the status of Canada's Aboriginal population.

Violence in Canadian–Aboriginal History

In recent years political violence has been linked most often to unresolved disputes between groups of Aboriginal Canadians and public authorities. During the summer and autumn of 1990—a time now known as the "Indian summer of 1990"—a group of Mohawk Warriors protested the planned expansion of a golf course on land they claimed as their own near Oka, Quebec, by barricading a road leading to the golf course. The confrontation eventually escalated, resulting in the death of one Quebec police officer, a sympathy blockade by Mohawks at

Canadian Spotlight

BOX 5.6 Major Violent Confrontations between Aboriginals and Non-Aboriginals and/or Political Authorities

1700s Many Beothuk Aboriginals are killed by European settlers to Newfoundland.

1763 Led by Odawa war chief Pontiac, a confederation of tribes (Seneca, Ojibwa, and other tribes in the Detroit area) rebel against British rule in several bloody confrontations.

***circa* 1794** Shawnee and other tribes in the Ohio River Valley, led by war chief Tecumseh, attempt unsuccessfully to resist non-Aboriginal settlement.

1869–70 In the Red River Rebellion, Manitoban Métis fight for provincial status and guaranteed land and cultural rights.

1885 In the Northwest Rebellions, a series of battles take place between Métis and First Nations forces on one side and non-Aboriginal militia volunteers and soldiers on the other.

1990 An armed confrontation at Oka, Quebec, results in the death of a police officer and riots against Aboriginals protesting the expansion of a golf course on land that Mohawks claim is theirs by historical right.

1995 Armed confrontations take place at Gustafsen Lake, British Columbia, and Ipperwash Provincial Park in Ontario. In both cases a small group of Aboriginals (Shuswap in BC and Chippewa in Ontario) occupy land they claim is sacred. An Aboriginal protester is killed at Ipperwash.

(Left) In a now-famous image, Canadian soldier Patrick Cloutier and Saskatchewan Aboriginal Brad Larocque come face to face in the tense standoff at the Kanesatake Reserve in Oka, Quebec, on 1 September 1990. (Right) Aboriginal protesters stand their ground on a blockade erected near Caledonia, Ontario, on 22 May 2006.

© The Canadian Press/Shaney Komulainen

© CP Photo/Hamilton Spectator—Sheryl Nadler

Continued

2000	Conflict between Aboriginal Mi'kmaq and non-Aboriginals erupts at Burnt Church, New Brunswick, over fishing rights.
2004	Anti-police riots take place when 67 Aboriginal officers of Kanesatake, Quebec, who were authorized by the local band council and financed by the federal government, are trapped in the police station for three days by armed

protesters from the local Mohawk community.

2006–8 At Caledonia in Southern Ontario, police arrest 16 Aboriginal protesters who claim that land being developed for houses rightfully belongs to them, dating back to the Haldimand Grant of 1784, although an Ontario court had ruled otherwise. Other protesters respond to the arrests by setting fires and blockading a major highway.

Kahnawake of the Mercier Bridge leading into Montreal, and similar blockades by other First Nations bands in communities across the country. Eventually, the standoff at Oka led to riots involving the non-Aboriginal townspeople and members of the local Mohawk band of Kanesatake, the intervention of thousands of Canadian troops, and even visits by United Nations observers.[55]

Fears of another Oka were raised in 1995 when small groups of Aboriginals occupied land that they claimed was sacred at Gustafsen Lake, British Columbia, and at Ipperwash Provincial Park in Ontario. Violence broke out in both cases, and an Aboriginal was shot dead at Ipperwash. Since then a number of violent episodes, but no deaths, have occurred in New Brunswick, Ontario, and Quebec (see Box 5.6). Although the circumstances of each case were unique, they all had one element in common: resistance by Aboriginal Canadians against laws, policies, or property claims that violated what they maintained to be their distinct status and rights. In the standoff at Caledonia, Ontario, from 2006 to 2008, some spokespersons for the Six Nations Reserve stated bluntly that the rulings of Canadian courts do not apply to their people. Some non-Aboriginal Canadians agree.

Summary

In his study of democracy in America, Alexis de Tocqueville paid close attention to the tyranny of the majority and how democratic majorities could lead to the oppression of minorities. And while the residential schools abuses and the internment of Japanese Canadians during World War II are certainly examples of such oppression, there are substantially more instances of accommodation in Canadian history. From our discussion of the contemporary diversity issues of language, multiculturalism, gender relations, and Aboriginal politics, a number of observations can be made about the nature and the evolution of Canadian democracy. The total of the achievements in all of these areas should not lead to satisfied complacency, but neither should they be dismissed as inconsequential.

This is true about Quebec's relationship with Canada. One of the most enduring facts of this situation is the gap between the vision of one Canada (the dominant view outside of Quebec that insists on the equality of the provinces and on multiculturalism) and the insistence by Quebec's politicians and opinion leaders (federalists and separatists alike) that Quebec must be considered a province *pas comme les autres*. The art of national unity involves finding ways to bridge gaps such as this one.

And while multiculturalism has become one of the central values associated with Canadian democracy, there is no corresponding community belief system or pan-Canadian nationalism—as in the United States—that supersedes ethnicity, religion, and culture. Some Canadians worry that this is a recipe for division, resentment, and preferential treatment. Others believe that the Canadian model of equality should be tried in other parts of the world to reduce conflict.

The impact of the politics of diversity has been most profound in gender relations. In a little more than a generation, the Canadian political, social, and economic scenes now provide women with many more choices and opportunities than existed previously. Today, the same ideas form the basis for political demands of groups that include Aboriginal Canadians, visible minorities, gays and lesbians, and the disabled.

And finally, as we saw in the discussion on Aboriginal politics, the relationships between these groups and the Canadian state are continually being redefined. A number of issues appear to have been resolved, but the central question seems to be how much Aboriginal sovereignty can be achieved within the parameters of the Canadian state.

One could argue that an important precedent was set in Canadian politics when French-Canadian Catholics were accommodated after the Battle of the Plains of Abraham in 1759. And some have argued that the practice of inclusion and accommodating the "other" pre-dates the arrival of the Europeans. Whatever the theory, the fact remains that Canadians have tended to accommodate diversity rather than fight against it, and this may well explain why we have enjoyed a relatively peaceful history.

Review Exercises

1. What circumstances do you think would have to exist for a referendum on Quebec independence to succeed?
2. How bilingual is your community? Make an inventory of the indications that French (or English, if you are in Quebec) language rights are protected and the French language promoted.

3. How many women or members of visible minorities hold public office on your municipal council or as your provincial or federal representative?
4. Research how the status and conditions of Aboriginal Canadians compare with their counterparts in the United States or Australia.

Up for Debate

1. In your opinion, what is the most important contemporary issue in Canadian politics? Why is it important to you? And should it be important to everyone else?
2. Statistics Canada has sometimes asked Canadians to declare their sexual orientation in a national survey. Do you think this information should be collected?
3. Do you believe on balance that the Canadian political system has been effective at accommodating minority groups?
4. Should the Charter of Rights and Freedoms apply to all Aboriginal communities in all respects and at all times? Or should Aboriginal rights and the concept of self-government be construed so that they take precedence over the Charter in some circumstances?

Starting Points for Research

Language

Cook, Ramsay, ed. *French Canadian Nationalism: An Anthology.* Toronto: Macmillan, 1969.

Gagnon, Alain-G., ed. *Quebec: State and Society*, 3rd edn. Toronto: University of Toronto Press, 2004.

Iacovino, Raffaele. *Federalism, Citizenship, and Quebec.* Toronto: University of Toronto Press, 2007.

McRoberts, Kenneth. *Quebec: Social Change and Political Crisis*, 3rd edn. Toronto: Oxford University Press, 1999.

Stevenson, Garth. *Community Besieged: The Anglophone Minority and the Politics of Quebec.* Montreal and Kingston: McGill–Queen's University Press, 1999.

Taylor, Charles. *Reconciling the Solitudes: Essays on Canadian Federalism and Nationalism.* Montreal and Kingston: McGill–Queen's University Press, 1993.

Diversity

Abu-Laban, Yasmeen, and Christina Gabriel, eds. *Selling Diversity: Immigration, Multiculturalism, Employment Equity and Globalization.* Peterborough, ON: Broadview Press, 2002.

Bissoondath, Neil. *Selling Illusions: The Cult of Multiculturalism in Canada.* Toronto: Penguin, 2002.

Breton, Raymond, and Jeffrey Reitz. *The Illusion of Difference: Realities of Ethnicity in Canada and the United States.* Toronto: C.D. Howe Institute, 1994.

Kymlicka, Will. *Multicultural Odysseys: Navigating the New International Politics of Diversity.* Toronto: Oxford University Press, 2007.

Newman, Jacquetta, and Linda White. *Women, Politics, and Public Policy: The Political Struggles of Canadian Women.* Toronto: Oxford University Press, 2006.

Tremblay, Manon, and Linda Trimble, eds., *Women and Electoral Politics in Canada.* Toronto: Oxford University Press, 2003.

Aboriginal Politics

Belanger, Yale D. *Aboriginal Self-Government in Canada: Current Trends and Issues,* 3rd edn. Saskatoon: Purich Publishing, 2008.

Dickason, Olive Patricia, with David T. McNab. *Canada's First Nations: A History of Founding Peoples from Earliest Times,* 4th edn. Toronto: Oxford University Press, 2009.

Magocsi, Paul Robert, ed. *Aboriginal Peoples of Canada: A Short Introduction.* Toronto: University of Toronto Press, 2002.

Sawchuck, Joe. *The Dynamics of Native Politics.* Saskatoon: Purich Publishing, 1998.

CBC Archives and TVO'S *The Agenda*

Visit the companion website for *Canadian Democracy: A Concise Introduction* to follow links to audio and video footage related to the main themes of the chapter: www.oupcanada.com/BrooksConcise2e.

Relevant Websites

Visit the companion website for *Canadian Democracy: A Concise Introduction* to browse a collection of websites featuring material related to the key themes of the chapter, an excellent starting point for research:www.oupcanada.com/BrooksConcise2e.

PART II
The Structures of Governance

The root of the word "government" is the Latin verb "gubernaro," meaning "to guide or direct." Indeed, government does provide direction for a society through the management of the public's business. This general function is performed through a number of specialized institutions, including a legislature, a head of state and head of government (executive), a bureaucracy, and a court system (judiciary). The authority and roles of these institutions within a country's governmental structure depend in large part on its constitution. Laws are made, implemented, and enforced, and redress is provided to aggrieved citizens, on the basis of written and unwritten rules embodied in a country's constitution. This is the ideal of democratic governance.

Constitutions and structures of government reflect the societies in which they are embedded. In the case of Canada, the Constitution adopted in 1867 and the country's parliamentary system of government may be understood as responses to particular societal and historical circumstances. The same is true for the revisions in the Constitution Act, 1982. But once in place, constitutions and government institutions tend to have what political scientists call an *independent effect* on political outcomes. In other words, the issues that get onto the political agenda, how they are framed, what voices are listened to, and what ultimately happens is to some degree influenced by the structures of government. Societal factors are important—the environment of ideas and interests that press on those who exercise public authority—but political outcomes depend to some degree on the nature of the constitutional and governmental systems through which they are processed.

One of the most difficult challenges in political analysis is to distinguish between the influence of *societal factors* and that of *structural factors* (constitutions and institutions) on politics and policy. The balance between structural and societal factors depends on the issue in question; however, governmental structures almost always play a role in determining political outcomes.

← The Senate Chamber on Parliament Hill in Ottawa. The structure of Canadian politics is a reflection of the historical and societal circumstances in which it is embedded.
Source: Gail Mooney/Masterfile.

6 The Constitution and Charter of Rights and Freedoms

Constitutions are at the heart of democratic politics. A constitution is a set of fundamental rules that govern political life in a particular territory. It is an essential ingredient of democratic politics. A constitution is no guarantee that human rights will be respected, that group rights will be protected, or that political opposition to those who govern will be tolerated. South Africa, for example, for decades had a constitution that denied its black majority equal rights. Closer to home, a well-established constitutional government deprived thousands of Japanese Canadians of their rights as citizens during World War II. And in Alberta in the 1950s, the provincial government allowed the forced sterilization of people deemed to be mentally retarded.

↑ Canada's constitution, written in a series of documents ranging from 1867 to 1982, outlines the country's system of government and the rights of citizens. This stamp was released in 1982, the same year the Charter of Rights and Freedoms was imbedded in the Constitution.

Source: © Canada Post Corporation 1982. Reproduced with Permission.

Without a constitution, however, the concepts of rights and limited government have no secure protection. It is "fundamental" because all other laws must conform to the constitution in terms of both how they are made and their substance. A constitution is a necessary condition for democratic politics. Without it there is no civilized way to resolve conflicts and no way to predict either the powers of government or the rights of citizens.

After reading this chapter, you should be able to

1. outline the major functions performed by a constitution
2. explain the relationship, rights, and obligations that a constitution sets up between the citizen and the state
3. explain the role ascribed by a constitution to the branches of government as well as their relationship to each other
4. identify the categories of rights and freedoms protected by the Canadian Charter of Rights and Freedoms
5. compare the pre-Charter era (1867–1981) with the Charter era
6. outline the ways of amending the Canadian Constitution

Constitutions and Constitutionality

A constitution is expected to establish order, allowing for the peaceful settlement of differences. Early liberal thinkers like Thomas Hobbes, John Locke, and Jean-Jacques Rousseau all used the concept of the "state of nature" to illustrate the impulse behind constitutional government. The state of nature, wrote Hobbes, was one of chaos in which no one feels secure about their property or their life. *Insecurity* leads people to accept the necessity of a constitution and demand that it provide greater security, even if agreement on its precise components is difficult.

In modern societies the alternatives to constitutional government are anarchy or totalitarianism. Where **anarchy** reigns, such as the chaos and civil strife that broke out in Iraq in 2003 and Libya in 2011 after despots Saddam Hussein and Moammar Gadhafi were removed from power, there are no generally accepted rules for resolving the differences between factions of the population. The state ceases to exist.

anarchy chaos and civil strife

Under **totalitarianism**, in which all dissent is suppressed in the name of some supreme goal, as in the current North Korea, the state exists, but because its powers are unlimited, and all realms of social and economic life are subordinate to it, it makes no sense to talk of a constitution. The constitution ceases to be one when the rules of the political game can be changed for convenience or if its terms are purely arbitrary.

totalitarianism a system of government that suppresses all dissent in the name of some supreme goal

The rules that make up a constitution deal with two sets of relations. The first involves the relationship between citizens and the state. A constitution empowers the state to act—to pass laws on the community's behalf—but it also limits the state's power by identifying those individual and group rights that the state cannot infringe. The second set of relations involves the distribution of functions and powers between different parts or branches of the state: the *legislature* (making the law); the *executive* (implementing the law); and the *judiciary* (interpreting the law). But the reality of the modern state is more complicated than this tripartite division of powers suggests.

In a **federal system** of government like Canada's, there is also a third set of relations: a constitutional division of law-making powers between a national government and regional governments. This third aspect of the Constitution has overshadowed the other two for most of Canada's history. Indeed, before 1982, when the Charter of Rights and Freedoms was entrenched in the Constitution, the relations between individuals and the state in Canada were defined by the courts mainly in terms of federal and provincial legislative powers.

A constitution's rules may take three forms: written documents (e.g., the BNA Act of 1867), the decisions of courts (called the *common law*), or unwritten conventions.

Constitutional conventions are those practices that emerge over time and are generally accepted as binding rules of the political system. An example of the "unwritten" aspect of a constitutional convention is the convention that the leader of the party that captures the most seats in a House of Commons election is called on to form a government: nowhere is this actually written. In Canada the first two components of the Constitution—written documents and the common law—together make up *constitutional law*. Conventions, while part of the Constitution, do not have the status of constitutional law, at least not in Canada. This distinction was made by the Supreme Court of Canada in a 1981 ruling (*Attorney General of Manitoba et al. v. Attorney General of Canada et al.*). It should not be interpreted to mean that constitutional law is more important than constitutional conventions. What it does mean, however, is that the rules of constitutional law are enforceable by the courts, whereas constitutional conventions are not.

Constitutional Functions

A constitution does more than provide a basis for non-violent politics. As discussed below, it also performs several specific functions that involve representation, power sharing, rights, community identity, and national purpose.

Representation

All modern democracies are *representative democracies*, in which politicians make decisions on behalf of those who elect them. But this still leaves enormous room for variation in how the population is represented, who is represented, and how representatives are selected.

A constitution describes both the basis of political representation and the method by which representatives are chosen. The basis of democratic representation may be by population, by territory, or by group. **Representation by population** is based on the principle of "one person—one vote," where all elected members of the legislature should represent approximately the same number of voters. This arrangement is most likely to allow the preferences of a simple majority of the population to be translated into law. Although virtually all modern democracies incorporate some form of "rep by pop" in their constitutions, many temper majority rule by requiring regional representation as well. For example, the American Constitution gives

federal system a system of government in which there is a constitutional division of law-making powers between a national government and regional governments

constitutional conventions practices that emerge over time and are generally accepted as binding rules of the political system

representation by population the principle of "one person—one vote," where all elected members of the legislature should represent approximately the same number of voters

each state the right to two senators. Representation in Canada's Senate is also by region: Ontario, Quebec, the West, and the Maritimes each have 24 seats, Newfoundland and Labrador has six, and the northern territories one each. Federalism (discussed in detail in Chapter 7) is a form of government that embodies the principle of territorial representation. It does so by giving regional governments the exclusive right to pass laws on particular subjects.

A constitution may also accord representation to groups. Suggestions for Senate reform in Canada have included proposals to guarantee seats for women and for Aboriginal Canadians. The defeated 1992 Charlottetown Accord would have ensured that Quebec, whose share of Canada's population has been falling, would maintain one-quarter of all seats in the House of Commons, which is about its current share. This was, one might argue, a thinly disguised guarantee of francophone group representation.

A constitution also establishes how public office holders are selected. Election and appointment are the two basic methods, but each allows for a wide variety of procedures that affect who is represented and their responsiveness to the popular will. For example, members of the judiciary are typically appointed for life, a practice that is expected to insulate them from popular passions and the influence of elected governments. An elected legislature is a standard feature of democratic political systems and, for that matter, of non-democratic ones. But many constitutions divide the legislative power between an elected chamber and an appointed one, as in Canada, the United Kingdom, and Germany.

Finally, the electoral process itself has a crucial influence on representation. The **single-member constituency** system used in Canada, in which each constituency (riding) gets one representative in the House of Commons and provincial legislature, discourages political parties from directing their appeals at a narrow segment of the national electorate. Unless that segment happens to be concentrated in a particular region, such a strategy will not pay off in elected members. A case in point is the Green Party's failure to win a seat in the 2008 federal election despite gaining 6.8 per cent of the popular vote. A system of **proportional representation**, whereby a party's percentage of the popular vote translates into a corresponding share of seats in the legislature, has a very different effect. It promotes a splintering of the party system and allows for the direct representation of much narrower interests, as is sometimes seen in countries like Germany, Israel, and Belgium. In a system like Canada's, groups with narrower interests must often rely on whatever influence they can achieve within one of the larger political parties or turn to non-electoral political strategies.

single-member constituency an electoral system in which each constituency (riding) gets one representative in the House of Commons and/or provincial legislature

proportional representation an electoral system in which a party's percentage of the popular vote translates into a corresponding share of seats in the legislature

Power

Constitutional government means that the state is empowered to act and that its actions may be backed up by the full weight of public authority. A constitution, therefore, provides the basis for the management and the legitimate exercise of power by the state including coercion and use of force. But a democratic constitution also limits and divides power. For example, a requirement that elections be held periodically restrains state power by making politicians accountable to, and removable by, the electorate. The fact that Canada has had peaceful changes of government since 1848, one of the longest such periods in the history of modern democracies, is proof that constitutional restraints and time limits on who can wield government power do provide peaceful, stable changes of government. The existence of separate branches of government, or of two levels of government as in the case of federalism, divides state power between different groups of public officials. How power is divided among the various parts of the state, or between the national and regional governments, is not determined solely by the constitution. But constitutional law and conventions affect the extent and distribution of state power.

Rights

right something that a person is entitled to

Constitutions vary in the particular rights that they assign to individuals or to groups. A **right** is something that a person is entitled to, like the right to vote or the right not to be arrested without a reason. At a minimum, a democratic constitution establishes the basic right of citizens to choose their government. But most constitutions also guarantee—although not without limit—such rights as the individual's right to *free speech*, *freedom of association*, and *freedom of religion and conscience*, as well as legal rights such as *freedom from arbitrary detention and illegal search and seizure*. These rights limit the state's power vis-à-vis the individual, either by making that power dependent on popular consent (democratic rights) or by establishing an individual's right not to be interfered with by the state (personal liberty).

Rights may also empower individuals by requiring the state to either protect or promote their interests. For example, a right to equal treatment under the law provides a constitutional remedy for individuals who have been discriminated against because of their sex, race, ethnic background, or whatever other basis prohibited by the constitution. The state is obliged to protect their interests. This may involve judicial decisions that remedy a private wrong (for example, requiring a minor hockey association to permit females to play in the same league with males). But the protection of equality may also entail the state being involved in broader activities like affirmative action or racial desegregation.

codified constitution a formal, written constitution found in a unified document

uncodified constitution the powers of government, as well as the limits to government power, are unwritten or based on precedents, or embedded in the country's laws, conventions, and traditions

Constitutions may also recognize the special status of particular groups, giving special rights to their members that are not enjoyed by others. For example, Canada's Constitution declares that both French and English are *official languages* with "equality of status and equal rights and privileges as to their use in all institutions of the Parliament and government of Canada."[1] This is a positive right, in the sense that it obliges the state to assume particular linguistic characteristics and to protect the rights of both French- and English-speakers in matters that fall under Ottawa's jurisdiction. A constitution that recognizes the special status of particular religious groups, as the Israeli constitution recognizes the Jewish religion; the Iranian, the religion of Islam; or the British, the Church of England, empowers certain groups and gives them state-protected rights that are not held by others.

It may be helpful to note that some constitutions, such as Iran's, are **codified**, meaning that Iran has a formal, written, unified document, whereas some countries, such as Britain and Israel, do not. Canada has both a codified and an **uncodified constitution**. Many of the powers of government, as well as the limits to government power, are unwritten or based on precedents, or embedded in the country's laws, conventions, and traditions—many of them borrowed from the system of government in the United Kingdom.

Community, Identity, and Citizenship

When Pierre Trudeau wrote that "A nation is no more and no less than the entire population of a sovereign state,"[2] he was arguing that a constitution establishes a community. And in an obvious sense it does. A constitution establishes rules within a given territory and establishes a shared condition—a constitutional community and legal membership—for those who live in that territory. Individuals in Rimouski, Quebec, and in Kitimat, British Columbia, are part of the same constitutional system and share a formal political status as Canadians.

Carrying the same national passport and being eligible to vote in the same elections may, however, seem a rather weak basis for a *sense of community*. The fact of being citizens of the Soviet Union, for example, did not erase the strongly nationalist sentiments of Ukrainians, Estonians, and other ethnic communities; for these groups the Soviet constitution and the political community it created were things to regret. Likewise in Canada, a significant minority of the population—Quebec separatists—rejects the Canadian political community and would prefer to live under a different constitution creating an independent Quebec.

A constitution, therefore, may inspire negative, positive, or indifferent feelings among the members of a political community. These feelings may be associated with the political community that a constitution creates, or with the particular institutions, values, and symbols embedded in a constitution. The monarchy and other institutions and symbols of Canada's colonial past have historically been aspects of our Constitution that have divided Canadians of French origin from those of British origin.

In general, a constitution may generate a shared identity and unity among a country's citizens, and sometimes people have positive feelings toward the political community it creates and the values it embodies. On these counts, Canada's Constitution has had a mixed record of successes and failures. On the one hand, there has been overwhelming support in all regions and social groups for the Charter of Rights and Freedoms. However, official bilingualism and constitutional proposals to recognize Quebec as a "distinct society" within Canada have been two of the most divisive constitutional issues in recent years.

National Purpose

The Constitution Act, 1867 not only created Canada but also included provisions that embodied a national purpose. This purpose was building a new country and an integrated economy stretching from the Atlantic to the Pacific.

A communal goal—a constitutional sense of purpose and direction for society—is not so rare. When the first permanent non-Aboriginal settlement was established at what today is Quebec City in the early seventeenth century, it operated under a royal charter that proclaimed the Catholic mission of the French colony. The colony was an outpost of a political and economic empire, but it was also a beachhead from which Catholicism would spread to the rest of the continent. Many constitutions have a national purpose. The Constitution of the People's Republic of China refers to building a socialist society. And those of the Islamic Republics of Iran and of Pakistan declare that society should conform to Muslim religious teachings.

"I think Trudeau's proposed new constitution is a credit to our profession . . . devious, full of loopholes, escape clauses, obscurities. . . ."

Most Canadians have not read our country's Constitution, assuming it is written largely in legal jargon, which can sometimes be difficult for the average person to interpret. Is it? Visit the companion website (www.oupcanada.com/BrooksConcise2e) to read the Constitution Act, 1867 and the Constitution Act, 1982 for yourself. Do you find the documents easy to understand? If not, which parts are most difficult to grasp? Should these Constitution documents be "translated" into everyday language so that all Canadians can consider them carefully?

Meech Lake Accord a 1987 attempt by the federal government and some provincial governments to reform Canada's Constitution such that, among other things, it would recognize Quebec as a "distinct society."

Canada's nation-building goal in 1867 is evident in the anticipation that other parts of British North America would eventually join it[3] in the prohibition of barriers to trade between provinces,[4] and in the commitment to build the Intercolonial Railway—a project described as "essential to the Consolidation of the Union of British North America."[5] The Constitution Act, 1982 commits Ottawa and the provinces to promoting equal opportunities for all Canadians and reducing regional economic disparities.[6]

The most controversial part of the failed **Meech Lake Accord** of 1987, an attempt to reform Canada's Constitution, was the recognition of Quebec as a "distinct society." This would have transformed Quebec nationalism from a political movement to a constitutionally entrenched fact. The Quebec legislature and government would have been constitutionally required to "preserve and promote" the distinct French-speaking character of the province.

Features of the Canadian Constitution

As constitutional documents go, Canada's is fairly long. In fact, it is not one document but a series of laws passed between 1867 and 1982, which form a body of law both longer and more detailed than the American Constitution. Even so, these documents provide a fragmentary and even misleading picture of how the Constitution actually works. In fact, many of the Constitution's most basic features—including the democratic accountability of government to the people—are not in these documents. On the other hand, some of what is included in the written Constitution would, if acted upon, probably result in a constitutional crisis! For instance, the Queen is formally the head of state in Canada and has the authority to make decisions such as when an election will take place and who will be appointed to cabinet. No one expects our head of state to actually make such decisions, but they are constitutionally plausible.

Canada's Constitution embodies values and principles that are central to the political life of the country. In its 1998 decision on the constitutionality of Quebec separation, the Supreme Court of Canada referred to these values and principles as the "internal architecture" of the Constitution.[7] Although not necessarily part of the *written* Constitution, these principles, which include federalism, democracy, constitutionalism and the rule of law, and respect for minority rights, "form the very foundation of the Constitution of Canada."[8]

Federalism

"The principle of federalism," declares the Supreme Court, "recognizes the diversity of the component parts of Confederation, and the autonomy of provincial governments to develop their societies within their respective spheres of jurisdiction."[9] In other words, provinces are not subordinate to the federal government, nor is Ottawa dependent on the provinces for the exercise of those powers assigned to it by the Constitution. The written Constitution distributes law-making and revenue-raising authority between the central and regional governments. The underlying federal principle is that some matters properly belong to the provinces, while others are national in scope and are decided by the federal government.

Democracy

Democracy has always been one of the fundamental, if unwritten, "givens" of Canada's constitutional system. In fact, aside from a written requirement for periodic elections under the Constitution Act, 1867, there were few other explicit indications that the Constitution adopted by the founders was democratic. And while the authority of governments was detailed painstakingly, the Constitution was remarkably silent on the rights of citizens. Why was this?

Before the 1982 Charter, the Supreme Court noted that to have declared explicitly that Canada was a democracy would have seemed to the founders redundant and even silly: "The representative and democratic nature of our political institutions was simply assumed."[10] In the preamble to the Constitution Act, 1867, the framers wrote that Canada had adopted "a constitution similar in Principle to that of the United Kingdom." Our government would operate according to democratic principles.

As we saw in Chapter 1, the meaning of the democracy principle is not obvious and has evolved over time. For example, women did not have the vote for more than 50 years after

Canadian Spotlight

BOX 6.1   Timeline—Canada's Constitutional History

1867   The British North America (BNA) Act (Constitution Act, 1867) is passed in Britain and creates Canadian Confederation by joining Ontario and Quebec (the province of Canada) with Nova Scotia and New Brunswick.

1870   The province of Manitoba is established.

1871   British Columbia joins Canada.

1873   Prince Edward Island joins Canada.

1905   The provinces of Saskatchewan and Alberta are established.

1926   The Imperial Conference: the colony of Canada is proclaimed "autonomous."

1927   The process of finding ways of amending the Constitution begins.

1931   The Statute of Westminster proclaims that Canada is a sovereign country.

1949   Most of the Constitution can now be interpreted and amended in Canada. The Supreme Court of Canada replaces the Judicial Committee of the British Privy Council as the final court of appeal for Canada. Newfoundland joins Canada.

1960–6   Quebec seeks to change the Constitution.

1967–71   Negotiations to amend the Constitution fail.

1976   The Parti Québécois is elected as Quebec's government.

1980   The Quebec government loses a referendum on sovereignty-association.

1982   The BNA Act is patriated to Canada, and the Constitution Act, 1982, along with the Charter of Rights and Freedoms, is adopted. All parts of the Constitution can now be amended in Canada.

1987   The prime minister and premiers agree to make constitutional changes through the Meech Lake Accord.

1990   The Meech Lake Accord fails to pass in the Newfoundland and Manitoba legislatures.

1992   The prime minister, premiers, and Aboriginal leaders reach agreement with the Charlottetown Accord. The Accord fails to pass in a national referendum.

1995   A Quebec referendum on sovereignty is narrowly defeated.

2000   The conditions for a province to achieve sovereignty are laid out in the federal Clarity Act.

Confederation. Even when the meaning of democracy is written and defined, as it was in the United States Constitution, expectations and understandings change over time. What meaning do we attribute to the democratic principle of Canada's Constitution today?

The Supreme Court's 1998 decision on separation answers this question by distinguishing between process and outcomes. On the process side, the Court observed that majority rule is a basic premise of constitutional democracy in Canada. The fact that Canada has a federal Constitution means, however, that "there may be different and equally legitimate majorities in different provinces and territories and at the federal level."[11] In other words, a nationwide majority does not trump a provincial majority if the matter in question (e.g., most constitutional amendments) belongs constitutionally to the provinces or requires the approval of some number of provincial legislatures.

In a 1986 Charter decision,[12] the Supreme Court had expressed the view that the democratic principle underlying the Charter and the rest of Canada's Constitution is also linked to substantive goals: respect for the inherent dignity of every person; commitment to equality and social justice; and social and cultural diversity, including respect for the identities of minority groups' social and political institutions that enhance the opportunities for individuals and groups to participate in society. This view was echoed in the Supreme Court's 1998 ruling in

Brent Lynch/© Simon Fraser University

The crafting of a constitution and implementation of constitutional reforms are processes that require participation, co-operation, and compromise among many stakeholders. Can you think of any unique challenges that Canada might face if it wanted to undertake any changes to its current Constitution?

words that were directly relevant to the issue of Quebec separation. The Court said, "The consent of the governed is a value that is basic to our understanding of a free and democratic society."[13] Democratic government derives its necessary legitimacy from this consent. Moreover, the legitimacy of laws passed and actions taken by a democratic government rests on "moral values, many of which are imbedded in our constitutional structure."[14] The Supreme Court did not expand upon these moral values.

The Principles of the Rule of Law and of Constitutionalism

"At its most basic level," declares the Supreme Court, "the rule of law vouchsafes to the citizens and residents of the country a stable, predictable and ordered society in which to conduct their affairs."[15] The **rule of law** guarantees that all public authority must be exercised in accordance with the law and that there will be one law for all persons. We are often offended when we hear that a public official has overstepped the bounds of his or her office, regardless of his or her intentions, or that someone has been accorded preferred treatment because of personal connections. We see these actions as violating the rule of law: ours is a government of laws, not of individuals, and everyone is entitled to equal treatment under the law.

The **constitutionalism** principle involves predictable governance that has its source in written rules rather than the arbitrary wills of individuals. For example, section 52(1) of the Constitution Act, 1982 states that the Constitution is the supreme law of the land and that all government action must conform to the Constitution. Until the constitutionalism principle was expressly stated and the Charter entrenched in 1982, the final authority of the Constitution was less certain. The pre-Charter era was one of **parliamentary supremacy**: Parliament's authority was considered superior to that of all other institutions of government. Constitutionalism, by contrast, places certain matters (rights and guarantees) beyond the reach of government.

Constitutionalism and the rule of law temper and modify the principle of majority rule in a democracy. Together, they constitute a sort of bulwark against what Tocqueville called the "tyranny of the majority"; even if an overwhelming majority supports a particular government action, the action can be carried out only if it is either lawful or constitutional.

Protection of Minorities and Group Rights

Canada's history of *accommodation* and of recognizing group rights goes back to early British colonial rule. The Royal Proclamation of 1763 included details on the rights of the "several Nations or Tribes of Indians . . . who live under our protection." The Quebec Act of 1774 recognized the rights of Catholics in Quebec and guaranteed the overwhelmingly French-speaking population the enjoyment of their "Property and Possessions, together with all Customs and Usage's relative thereto, and all other their Civil Rights." Most historians agree that these concessions were intended to ensure the support of the Catholic Church in Quebec at a time when rebellion was simmering in the American colonies. Group rights were recognized again through the "double majority principle" that operated when Canada East (Quebec) and Canada

rule of law the guarantee that all public authority must be exercised in accordance with the law and that there will be one law for all persons

constitutionalism a principle that involves predictable governance that has its source in written rules rather than the arbitrary wills of individuals

parliamentary supremacy a principle that Parliament's authority was considered superior to that of all other institutions of government

West (Ontario) were united through a common legislature from 1841 to 1867. Under this principle any bill touching on language or religion in either Canada East or Canada West had to be approved by majorities of legislators from both Canada East—mainly French and Catholic—and Canada West—mainly English and Protestant. This gave a veto to each ethnolinguistic community on legislation affecting minority rights.

The Constitution Act, 1867 entrenched the principle of minority rights through the section 93 guarantee of minority religious education rights and the section 133 declaration that French and English were to have official status in the Parliament of Canada, the legislature of Quebec, and courts created by either of those bodies. "The protection of minority rights," declares the Supreme Court, "was clearly an essential consideration in the design of our constitutional structure even at the time of Confederation."[16] The principle acquired a new level of prominence as a result of the Charter of Rights and Freedoms. The Charter enlarges the scope of official-language minority rights, explicitly recognizes Aboriginal rights, opens the door to a multitude of group rights claims through its equality section (s. 15), and provides a basis for a variety of minority rights claims through other sections, including its legal rights and democratic rights provisions. A recent example was the 2016 Supreme Court decision to extend rights of status Indians to Métis and non-status Indians.

Understanding the Relationships in the Constitution

A useful way of analyzing a constitution is to approach it from the relationships governed by constitutional rules:

a. rules between individuals and the state (the Charter of Rights and Freedoms)
b. rules between the various institutions of government (the machinery and process of parliamentary government)
c. rules that establish procedures for constitutional change
d. rules between the national and regional governments (federalism)

The first three constitutional relationships are dealt with in this chapter. The federal relationship will be dealt with in Chapter 7.

A. The Charter of Rights and Freedoms

In modern democracies political demands are often expressed in the language of rights and freedoms. Like the Ten Commandments, rights and freedoms are usually expressed in uncompromising language. Those who argue the case for a woman's right to control her body, or a fetus's right to life, or an individual's right not to be discriminated against on the basis of race or gender typically advance their claims as moral absolutes. Moral absolutes, like Biblical injunctions, are non-negotiable. Either a right or freedom exists or it does not. And if it exists, it must be respected in all cases and not simply when governments or the majority find it convenient to do so. The politics of rights tends to reduce the space for and possibility of negotiation and compromise.

In reality, however, no right or freedom is absolute. There are two reasons for this. One is that rights and freedoms may collide, necessitating some compromise. Does freedom of expression, for example, protect the right of an individual to falsely shout "Fire!" in a crowded theatre? Obviously, there must be limits. To guarantee an individual's freedom of expression in such circumstances could jeopardize the right of other individuals to be protected from unreasonable danger. Many other complex issues arise. Should freedom of expression protect people who "willfully promote hatred"[17] against some group? When do national security considerations trump the individual's right to privacy? Is affirmative action a legitimate means for promoting social equality, or is it **reverse discrimination**—policies that shift the burden of injustice onto the shoulders of the qualified members of advantaged groups who are not personally responsible for the injustices suffered by minority groups? Who should determine these issues: the courts or the people's elected representatives?

A second reason why no right or freedom can be treated as an absolute is that this is often impractical. If, for example, a constitution guarantees the right of official-language minorities, does that mean that all government services in the whole country should be available in each of the official languages? Common sense suggests that there are *limits* to how far, and in what circumstances, the principles of linguistic equality and minority rights should apply.

In another example that occurred in 1990, an Ontario Superior Court judge decided to dismiss hundreds of cases that had been on the docket for months, because the time spent by many accused persons in jail or on bail while waiting for their trial date violated section 11(b) of the Charter—the right "to be tried within a reasonable time." Can the bureaucratic procedures and budget constraints that led to these delays and inflicted real hardship on individuals be justified as "practical limitations" on rights? Or are they matters of mere administrative convenience or policy that should not take precedence over individual rights? Dilemmas like this await us at every turn.

Despite such controversies, and despite the passions they usually unleash, rights and freedoms have had a low profile in Canadian politics for most of this country's history. The courts were reluctant to question the authority of elected legislatures to pass laws, except to decide whether the matter in question constitutionally belonged to Ottawa or to the provinces. As a result, civil liberties issues were transformed into squabbles over the federal–provincial division of powers. This situation changed, however, with the passage of the Charter of Rights and Freedoms in 1982. The Charter entrenched various rights and freedoms in the Constitution and placed these rights more or less beyond the interference of governments, essentially establishing a principle of *constitutional supremacy* over that of *parliamentary supremacy*.

During the first couple of decades after the Charter's passage, the Supreme Court of Canada handed down several hundred Charter rulings at a rate of about 20–30 per year, including many that had major effects on public policy. And while the pace of judicial interventions seems to have slowed recently, the Charter has decisively changed the face of Canadian politics. The authority of elected legislatures has receded before the authority of the Constitution and the courts, and the venues and the language of Canadian politics have changed. The discourse of

reverse discrimination policies that shift the burden of injustice onto the shoulders of the qualified members of advantaged groups who are not personally responsible for the injustices suffered by minority groups

"rights," always a part of the political scene, has assumed much greater prominence since passage of the Charter. Individuals, organized interests, and even governments have turned increasingly to litigation as a means of influencing public policy. But what are the consequences of what Michael Mandel has called the "legalizing of politics"? Is Canada in the era of the Charter more or less democratic? And aside from lawyers, which groups have gained from these changes?

TABLE 6.1 Human Rights and the Charter

Rights Category	Pre-Charter Protections	Charter Protections	Examples of Charter Cases (See Table 6.5 for a brief explanation of each case.)
1. Political rights/ fundamental freedoms	Common-law protections implied in the preamble of the Constitution Act, 1867	s.2	R. v. Oakes
2. Democratic rights	Constitution Act, 1867, ss. 41, 50, 84, 85	ss. 3–5	Reference Re Provincial Electoral Boundaries
3. Legal rights	Common law; Criminal Code	ss. 7–14	R. v. Morgentaler Re BC Motor Vehicle Act Hunter v. Southam Inc. Andrews v. Law Society of British Columbia R. v. Collins R. v. Stinchcombe R. v. Askov
4. Economic rights	Common-law rights re contracts, property, mobility, etc.	s. 6 (and implied under some other sections)	
5. Equality rights	Common law, s. 93 of Constitution Act, 1867, guaranteeing educational rights of religious denominations	ss. 15, 28	Law v. Canada Vriend v. Alberta
6. Language rights	Constitution Act, 1867, s. 133	ss. 18–23	
7. Aboriginal rights	Treaties	ss. 25, 35	R. v. Sparrow
8. Social rights	None	Although not mentioned directly, some court rulings suggest that some social rights are implied	

Since 1982, the Charter of Rights and Freedoms has included formal distinctions between fundamental political freedoms, democratic rights, mobility rights, legal rights, equality rights, language rights, and Aboriginal rights. Most categories of rights and freedoms set down in the Charter were already part of Canada's Constitution before 1982. Some can be found in the Constitution Act, 1867. Others were established principles of the common law. The setting down of rights and freedoms in a Charter, however, has made an important difference in Canadian politics.

Fundamental Freedoms

fundamental freedoms basic individual political rights (or liberties) that include freedom of religion, belief, expression, the media, assembly, and association

The **fundamental freedoms** guaranteed in section 2 of the Charter are basic individual political rights (or liberties) that include freedom of religion, belief, expression, the media, assembly, and association. In the pre-Charter era these freedoms were part of the common law and of Canada's British parliamentary tradition. Individual freedoms were part of the British constitution, and thus became part of Canada's. However, before the Charter the protection of political freedoms by the courts was rather tenuous. Except in a few instances, the courts were unwilling to rule that a freedom was beyond the interference of government. Instead, political liberties were defended using the federal division of legislative powers as the basis for striking down a particular government's interference with individual freedom.

Democratic Rights

democratic rights the right of citizens to vote in periodically held elections and to stand for public office

Democratic rights include the right of citizens to vote in periodically held elections and to stand for public office. This right to vote pre-dated Confederation and was embodied in the Constitution Act, 1867 through those sections that establish the elective basis of representation in the House of Commons and in provincial legislatures (ss. 37 and 40), through the requirement that the legislature meet at least once a year (ss. 20 and 86), through the right of citizens to vote (s. 41), and through the five-year limit on each term of both the House of Commons and provincial legislatures, thereby guaranteeing regular elections (ss. 50 and 85). All these sections are now superseded by sections 3–5 of the Charter.

Mobility Rights

mobility rights the rights of citizens to move freely within a country's borders

Mobility rights, which are the rights of citizens to move freely within a country's borders, were not explicitly mentioned in Canadian constitutional law before 1982, nor was there any mention of restrictions on people's movement. However, Ottawa feared that some provincial governments were undermining Canadian citizenship by discriminating in favour of their own permanent residents in some occupational sectors and by imposing residency requirements as a condition for receiving some social services. Therefore mobility restrictions were prohibited by section 6 of the Charter. But the Charter does allow "reasonable residency requirements as a qualification for the receipt of publicly provided social services"[18] and permits affirmative action programs favouring a province's residents "if the rate of employment in that province is below the rate of employment in Canada."[19]

Legal Rights

legal rights procedural rights intended to ensure the fair and equal treatment of individuals under the law

Legal rights are mostly procedural rights intended to ensure the fair and equal treatment of individuals under the law. These include the right to a fair trial, the right not to be held without a charge being laid, and the right to legal counsel. Before these rights were entrenched in the Constitution through the Charter, they were recognized principles of the common law and constitutional convention. For example, the field of administrative law was based largely on the principles of *natural justice:* both sides of a case must be heard, and no one should be a judge in his own case. These were accepted parts of Canada's democratic tradition and Constitution even before they were entrenched in section 7 of the Charter. And along with other freedoms and rights, legal rights were included in the 1960 Canadian Bill of Rights. In addition, the rights of accused parties were set forth in Canada's Criminal Code. The constitutional entrenchment of legal rights, however, has expanded the legal rights of the accused, convicted criminals, and immigrants.

In the Charter era, the courts have been much bolder in striking down parts of laws and in overturning administrative and police procedures. For example, successful legal challenges to Canada's abortion law in 1988 and prostitution laws in 2013 only became possible when the right to "security of the person" was explicitly recognized in section 7 of the Charter.[20]

Equality Rights

Equality rights embody the rule of law principle that everyone should be treated equally under the law. These are now entrenched in the Constitution through section 15 of the Charter. But the Charter extends this principle to expressly prohibit discrimination based on race, national or ethnic origin, colour, religion, sex, age, or mental or physical disability.[21]

The terms in this list are important, given that Canadian courts historically have preferred to base their rulings on the precise text of laws and the Constitution. Women's groups and those representing the disabled fought successfully to have the original wording of section 15 changed. The 1960 Canadian Bill of Rights, which applied only in areas of federal jurisdiction, did not include age or disability as prohibited grounds of discrimination. The equality rights section of the Constitution cuts two ways: the Charter explicitly declares that affirmative action is constitutional,[22] and it provides individuals with grounds for redress. Moreover, since 1975 every province has had a bill of rights that is administered and enforced by its human rights commission.

equality rights rights that embody the rule of law principle that everyone should be treated equally under the law

Language Rights

Language or **linguistic rights** are guarantees by the state that an individual or a group has the right to choose a particular language for use in private or in public, and to use that language in a given jurisdiction, such as in the educational system, in the government, or in the courts of a given territory. At Confederation, the Constitution Act, 1867 dealt with language rights in three ways. First, section 133 declared that both English and French were official languages in the Parliament of Canada and in the Quebec legislature, and in any court established by either the national or the Quebec government. Second, section 93 declared that rights held by denominational schools when a province joined Canada could not be taken away. Third, section 92 puts forth the most important language rights provision and assigns provincial jurisdiction over "all Matters of a merely local or private Nature in the Province" (s. 92.16). When combined with provincial jurisdiction over education (s. 93), the provincial governments have the power to promote or deny the language rights of their anglophone or francophone minorities.

language (linguistic) rights guarantees by the state that an individual or a group has the right to choose a particular language for use in private or in public, and to use that language in a given jurisdiction, such as in the educational system, in the government, or in the courts of a given territory

The Constitution Act, 1982 extends language rights in four ways. First, section 133 of the Constitution Act, 1867 declares English and French as officially equal and is also broadened to encompass "their use in all institutions of the Parliament and government of Canada" (s. 16.1) and services to the public (s. 20). Second, the New Brunswick legislature's earlier decision to become officially bilingual was entrenched in 1982. Third, the official status of English in the legislature and courts of Quebec and Manitoba is reaffirmed (s. 21). And finally, where demand warrants, anglophones and francophones have the entrenched right to educate their children in their mother tongue (s. 23).

Aboriginal Rights

Aboriginal rights a recognition and a set of guarantees by the state that Indigenous peoples have certain rights such as civil rights and the rights to land, to preservation of culture, and to self-government

In very general terms, **Aboriginal rights** refers to a recognition and a set of guarantees by the state that Indigenous peoples have certain rights such as civil rights and the rights to land, to preservation of culture, and to self-government. The recognition of Aboriginal rights in the Constitution dates from the Charter in 1982. Section 25 declares that the rights and freedoms set forth in the Charter shall not be construed so as to "abrogate or derogate" from whatever rights or freedoms the Aboriginal peoples of Canada have as a result of any treaty or land claim settlement. It also entrenches in the Constitution "any rights or freedoms that have been recognized by the Royal Proclamation [of 1763]." Section 35(1) appears to limit Aboriginal rights to the status quo that existed in 1982, stating that "[t]he *existing* aboriginal and treaty rights of the aboriginal peoples of Canada are hereby recognized and affirmed" [emphasis added]. However, this clause has been less a limit than a boost for Aboriginal rights, which were effectively constitutionalized by the 1982 Constitution Act. We examined this in greater detail in Chapter 5.

B. The Machinery of Parliamentary Government

Listen to the "Perspectives on Proroguing" podcast at www.oupcanada.com/BrooksConcise2e.

British parliamentary government was exported to Canada during the colonial period. Its main features have remained largely unchanged since the middle of the nineteenth century, when the British North American colonies achieved the right to self-government in their domestic affairs. While the declaration that Canada has adopted "a Constitution similar in Principle to that of the United Kingdom" might appear vague, Canada's founders understood exactly what it meant. The constitution of the United Kingdom was, and remains today, a set of political traditions rather than a series of constitutional documents. Our founders took these traditions as their starting point and grafted onto them certain institutions and procedures—particularly federalism—that were not part of the original British parliamentary model (see Table 6.2).

The most fundamental principles of democracy and practices essential to the functioning of government are not written in the Canadian Constitution. These include

- the selection of the prime minister
- which party has the right to form a government
- the relationships between the Crown and the government and between the government and the legislature
- the rights of the political opposition and the role of the judicial branch of government

TABLE 6.2 Canada's Hybrid Political System

Political System	Federation	Unitary State
Parliamentary	Canada	United Kingdom
Republic	United States	France

This table illustrates the hybrid nature of the Canadian political system. The founders of the Canadian Constitution adopted the British parliamentary democracy model and an American-style federal arrangement.

Nevertheless, in all these matters certain rules are generally agreed upon and are vital parts of the Constitution—so vital, in fact, that when they are challenged the political system faces a crisis, such as in the parliamentary impasse and resulting prorogation, or suspension of Parliament, that occurred over the government's budget update shortly after the October 2008 general election.

Parliament

The distinguishing feature of British-style parliamentary government is the relationship between the various institutions that together make up Parliament. Parliament comprises the monarch and the legislature. The monarch, currently Queen Elizabeth II, is Canada's head of state. While the role is primarily a ceremonial one, and almost entirely symbolic, according to the Constitution the monarch wields formidable powers in these areas:

- choosing which party will be called upon to form the government
- dissolving Parliament and calling for a new election
- signing all federal and provincial legislation, into law (giving royal assent)

When the monarch is not in Canada (which is most of the time), her powers are exercised by the Governor General, and at the provincial level, the lieutenant-governors.

The power that resides formally in the monarchy is in practice held by the Crown's advisers, the **Privy Council**, which includes all members of the present and past cabinets. However, only present members of cabinet exercise the powers of the Privy Council, and these people are usually elected members of the legislature. At the head of the cabinet is the prime minister. The structure of Canada's Parliament is shown in Figure 6.1.

Parliament comprises, then, both the *executive* and *legislative* branches of government. Those who actually exercise the executive power are drawn from the legislature. In deciding who among those elected members of Parliament (MPs) and appointed senators will become members of the government, the rule is quite simple. The leader of the political party with the most seats in the elected House of Commons has the right to try to form a government that will be supported by a majority of MPs.

Responsible Government

If at any time the government loses its majority support (confidence) in the House, tradition requires that it resign. At this point, and in most cases, a fresh election would be called.

Privy Council that part of the executive, made up of the Crown's advisers, in which the power of the monarch resides; it formally includes all members of the present and past cabinets

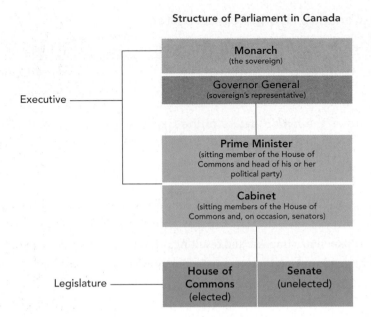

FIGURE 6.1 The Structure of Parliament in Canada

responsible government
the constitutional principle that the prime minister and cabinet require the confidence of the elected House of Commons in order to govern

party discipline
a tradition of British parliamentary government, according to which a party's MPs generally vote as a unified block in the legislature

minority government
a government that depends on the support of another party's MPs in order to win votes in the legislature

However, if another party can put together a government that would be supported by a majority of MPs, the Governor General may call on the leader of that party to try to form a government.

The constitutional principle that the prime minister and cabinet require the confidence of the elected House of Commons in order to govern is called **responsible government**. If a government loses the *confidence* of the House—through either a defeat on an important piece of legislation (i.e., the annual budget or legislation related to government spending) or on a motion of non-confidence proposed by an opposition party—it loses the right to govern. This may appear to place enormous power in the hands of MPs, but it does not. The reason why responsible government does not translate into fearful governments is **party discipline**: another tradition of British parliamentary government, according to which a party's MPs generally vote as a unified block in the legislature.

In Canada, however, party discipline is more rigidly practised than in the British Parliament. Of the 38 Canadian governments that were elected between 1867 and 2006 only six fell because of a defeat in the legislature. All six were **minority governments**: those that depended on the support of another party's MPs in order to win votes in the legislature. But even in these circumstances, it is usually the government that finally determines when an election occurs.

On only one occasion has a government been defeated in the Commons and then had its request for *dissolution* of Parliament and an election denied by the Governor General. This was the 1926 "King–Byng affair," and the denial provoked a constitutional crisis over the appropriate role of the Governor General. There was at least the chance of history repeating itself when the Progressive Conservative government's budget was defeated in 1979. The government had been in place a mere nine months, and the possibility of a minority Liberal government supported by the NDP was not totally outrageous. As it happened, however, Governor General Ed Schreyer granted

Prime Minister Joe Clark's request for a new election, although Schreyer claimed afterward that he seriously considered asking the leader of the official opposition to try to form a government. In December 2008, when Prime Minister Stephen Harper faced a non-confidence vote in the House of Commons over a mini-budget, he asked the Governor General, Michaëlle Jean, for a prorogation of Parliament even though there had been a general election less than two months earlier.

Responsible government, then, is part of the living Constitution. It operates today, but not in the narrow sense of legislatures making and defeating cabinets. While disciplined political parties and dominant prime ministers ensure that cabinets seldom are defeated at the hands of uncooperative legislatures, the practice of cabinet government that is accountable to the elected legislature remains a central feature of Canadian democracy. *Responsible government* combines the *rights of the legislature* and the corresponding *obligations of the government* into a parliamentary process.

The legislature

- has the right to scrutinize, to debate, and to vote on policies proposed by the government
- has the general right to question the government and to demand explanations for its actions and for those of bureaucratic officials who act in the government's name

The government has a constitutional obligation

- to provide opportunities for legislative scrutiny of its policies
- to account for its actions before Parliament

These rights and obligations are largely codified in the *standing orders*—the rules that govern parliamentary procedure.

Ministerial Responsibility

Two fundamental principles of British parliamentary government, strong executive authority and democratic accountability, come together in the concept of ministerial responsibility.

Strong executive authority is a tradition that dates from an era when the monarch wielded real power, and the principle that these powers depended on the consent of the legislature was not yet established. When the legislature finally gained the upper hand in the seventeenth century, the tradition of strong executive power was not rejected. Instead, it was tamed and adapted to the democratic principle that government is based on the *consent of the governed*. Since then, individual ministers and cabinet as a whole have exercised the powers that, symbolically, continue to be vested in the Crown. But they do so in ways that enable the people's elected representatives to vote on their proposals and to call them to account for their policies (see Figure 6.2).

Democratic accountability of the government to the legislature is the reason behind the **ministerial responsibility** principle of British parliamentary government. It entails the obligation of a cabinet minister to explain and defend policies and actions carried out in her or his name. This individual accountability of cabinet ministers rests on a combination of constitutional

ministerial responsibility
the obligation of a cabinet minister to explain and defend policies and actions carried out in her or his name

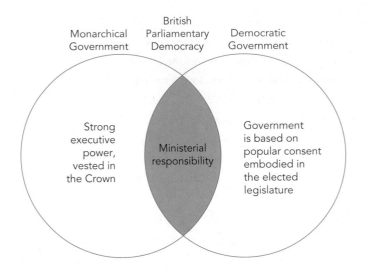

Monarchical Government

British Parliamentary Democracy

Democratic Government

Strong executive power, vested in the Crown

Ministerial responsibility

Government is based on popular consent embodied in the elected legislature

FIGURE 6.2 The Constitutional Roots of Ministerial Responsibility

law and parliamentary tradition. Section 54 of the Constitution Act, 1867 gives to cabinet the exclusive right to put before the legislature measures that involve the raising or spending of public revenue. The Constitution also requires that any legislation that involves raising or spending public money must originate in the elected House of Commons. In practice, such measures are introduced by particular members of the government. For example, changes to the tax system are proposed by the minister of finance. This reflects the liberal-democratic principle of no taxation without representation, whereby only the people's elected representatives should have the right to propose laws that affect voters' pocketbooks. The accountability of ministers is, therefore, to the people's elected representatives.

In recent times the constitutional principle of ministerial responsibility has come under increasing pressure because of the enormous volume of decisions taken in a minister's name, and a vital link in the chain of accountability that joins the people to those who govern them is lost. In fact, no minister can be well informed about all the policies and actions undertaken in his or her name. Much decision-making power has passed into the hands of unelected officials. Some have suggested that accountability should be located where decision-making power really lies but that elected members of the government remain directly accountable for the general lines of policy and for major decisions.

Parliamentary Supremacy versus Constitutional Supremacy

Behind the principle of parliamentary supremacy are the notions that the courts will not second-guess the right of Parliament to pass laws, that Parliament embodies the popular will, and that unpopular laws can always be changed by changing the government at the next election. In our federal system, the division of law-making powers between the national and provincial governments complicates matters by giving some citizens and provincial political elites a sense that local or regional matters should be given a priority. But as long as Ottawa and the provinces act within their own spheres of authority, both the federal and provincial parliaments are supreme.

This was the situation in Canada until 1982. When called on to determine whether a law was constitutional or not, the courts almost always referred to the federal division of powers set down in the Constitution Act, 1867. Certain procedural rules of the common law could be challenged, but the substance of laws would not be questioned.

Michael de Adder/Artizans

In the Charter era, an increased number of rights issues are being handled by the courts rather than the legislatures. In fact, in several landmark cases federal laws were struck down by the courts because of rights entrenched in the Constitution since 1982. These included laws governing prostitution, physician-assisted suicide, and mandatory sentencing for certain offences. Which losses is the cartoonist alluding to in this cartoon?

Those who opposed the Charter argued that entrenching rights and freedoms would result in a transfer of power from legislatures to the courts. This is indeed what has happened since 1982. The Supreme Court has struck down numerous federal and provincial laws on the grounds that they violated the Charter guarantees. Parliamentary supremacists claim that court-protected rights and freedoms are fundamentally undemocratic. Their reasoning is that it substitutes the decisions of non-elected judges for those of elected representatives.

What is beyond doubt is that parliamentary supremacy has been replaced by **constitutional supremacy**. Section 32 declares that the Charter applies to both the federal and provincial governments and to all matters under their authority. Section 52(1) of the Charter is even more categorical: "The Constitution of Canada is the supreme law of Canada, and any law that is inconsistent with the provisions of the Constitution is, to the extent of the inconsistency, of no force or effect." A vestige of Parliament's former superiority is retained, however, through section 33 of the Charter: the so-called "**notwithstanding clause**," which enables either Parliament

constitutional supremacy the concept that the constitution (the law of laws) is above all else, even the Parliament

notwithstanding clause a feature of the Charter of Rights and Freedoms that enables either Parliament or a provincial legislature to declare that a law shall operate even if it violates the fundamental freedoms, legal rights, or equality rights sections of the Charter. Such a declaration must be renewed after five years; otherwise the Constitution reasserts its supremacy.

or a provincial legislature to declare that a law shall operate even if it violates the fundamental freedoms, legal rights, or equality rights sections of the Charter. Such a declaration must be renewed after five years; otherwise the Constitution reasserts its supremacy.

Judicial Independence and the Separation of Powers

The role of the judicial branch of government is based on constitutional convention rather than law. The fundamental principles that underlie that role are *judicial independence* and *separation of powers*. The Constitution Act, 1867 includes several sections that deal with the system of provincial courts, including the selection and removal of judges, the retirement of provincial Superior Court judges (at age 75), and judicial salaries.[23] However, Canadian constitutional law is silent on the powers and the existence and composition of the highest court of appeal, the Supreme Court of Canada. Unlike the American Constitution that provides lengthy descriptions of the powers and separate roles of the legislative, executive, and judicial branches, the relationship between the judicial and other branches of government is not described in detail. Instead, section 101 authorizes Parliament to establish a "General Court of Appeal for Canada," which it did in 1875 with the Supreme Court of Canada and again in 1970 with the Federal Court of Canada.

> **judicial independence** the principle that judges are to be free from any and all interference in their decision making

It is essential that judges be protected from interference by the government. **Judicial independence** means that judges are to be free from any and all interference in their decision making. According to former Supreme Court Chief Justice Brian Dickson, this principle involves "the complete liberty of individual judges to hear and decide the cases that come before them."[24] The principle of judicial independence is deeply embedded in Canada's political culture and enshrined in laws on contempt of court and in guidelines for ministerial conduct. However, doubts have been raised over whether these protections are adequate when, for example, court budgets are determined by governments.[25] One important example of the judiciary expressing its independence occurred in 2014, when Justice Marc Nadon of Quebec was rejected as the Harper government's appointee to the Supreme Court because he did not have the required experience of practising law in Quebec. The principle of *separation of powers* guarantees the special role of the judiciary, which is to interpret the law and the Constitution when disputes arise. As does judicial independence, this principle relies more on cultural norms, statute law, and constitutional convention than it does on constitutional law. There is at least one important reference to the role of the judicial branch in section 24 of the Constitution Act, 1982, which declares that the Charter shall be enforced through the courts.

The perception, since the passage of the 1982 Charter, that the courts represent a check on the powers of Parliament and the provincial legislatures reflects an *Americanizing* trend in Canadian politics. However, the concept of checks and balances, which is basic to the American Constitution, is not part of British parliamentary democracy.

The ability of the federal and provincial governments to refer a resolution or draft legislation to the courts for a decision on its constitutionality does not, strictly speaking, respect the principle of separation of powers. Constitutional reference cases enable governments to use the provincial and Canadian supreme courts to receive advisory opinions before acting or thrusting politically volatile issues into the courts. The separation of powers may also be breached when

TABLE 6.3 The Canadian System of Checks and Balances

The Features	Checks and Balances
Constitutional monarchy	The Crown (the monarch or his or her representative) has these powers to keep the government and the Parliament in check: • choosing which party will be called upon to form the government • dissolving Parliament and calling for a new election • signing all federal and provincial legislation, into law (giving royal assent) • commanding the service of the military and the bureaucracy (these do not serve the politicians)
Judicial review and independence	• The courts serve as arbitrators in the cases of disputes between the citizen(s) and the state and disputes between the federal and provincial governments. • The judiciary are the gatekeepers of the Constitution and can strike down legislation deemed unconstitutional.
Rule of law	A constitutional guarantee ensures that all public authority is exercised in accordance with the law and that there is one law for all persons.
Representative democracy	Periodic elections ensure that legislators and government are accountable for their actions and can be peacefully replaced when the values of the electorate are no longer reflected in their government.
Responsible government	Without majority support of the members of Parliament (the confidence of the House of Commons), the government (the prime minister and the cabinet) must resign and either be replaced or face an election.
Federalism	• The Canadian federal system of government is a sharing of sovereign power between two levels of government. • The Constitution cannot be changed without the permission of the federal government and the provinces—in some cases all the parties must agree. • The system distributes law-making and revenue-raising authority.

Canadians are reminded, particularly in times of crisis or political scandal, that our political system offers many protections against abuses of power by the state or by politicians. The six features listed below may not be as elegantly divided or symmetrical as those outlined in the American Constitution, but they have proven to be very effective at managing power for the greater good.

judges step outside their role as interpreters of the laws and become advocates for reform. Since the mid-1980s, Supreme Court justices, in public speeches and interviews, have occasionally weighed in on matters of public controversy, including the funding of bilingualism, multiculturalism, gender bias in the law and the justice system, and the role of the judicial branch in Canada's parliamentary system. For example in 2004, Chief Justice Beverley McLachlin spoke out on the matter of Canadian identity in a speech called "Globalization, Citizenship and Identity":

> We have achieved a common national space, a space that reflects our history and our shared values. But it has not been easy. Our shared history is not one of continuous bliss and harmonious interaction between diverse groups. Viewed from the perspective of Aboriginal peoples, ethnic minorities, disabled people or women, it is a history marked by profound mistakes. Despite the dark

chapters of our history, an ethic of respect and inclusion has been part of Canada's fabric from its beginnings. Canadian history is replete with the efforts of men and women who sought to define their identity in terms that included the other.

I believe that this distinctively Canadian ethic of inclusion and tolerance, this distinctively Canadian definition of self and of citizenship is what continues to help us overcome the feelings of loss and alienation that can readily emerge in communities transformed by immigration. . . .

This recognition of the intrinsic diversity of all Canadians provides an avenue for sustainable public discourse within a political community marked by cultural pluralism. In terms of governance, in terms that matter to you as public servants, the task is to uphold communities and institutions where the overlapping commitments of participants are fostered. In a country of diversity, successful communities are those that serve both as refuge and as springboard—those communities that are the "anchor for self-identification and the safety of effortless secure belonging," but also the catalyst

© CP Photo/Jonathan Hayward

After a judicial career in city and provincial courts in British Columbia, Beverley McLachlin was appointed Chief Justice of the Supreme Court of Canada in 2000, the first woman to hold that position. Her reputation for reaching out and actively engaging Canadians with their highest court can be seen in her speech "Globalization, Citizenship and Identity." Why might it be appropriate for a judge to start such a conversation with the public about an issue so central as Canadian identity?

of broader civic duties to larger communities. Much like a family, successful communities and institutions should push us to encounter the world, while remaining shelters of comfort and warmth.[26]

Relations between the House of Commons and the Senate

When the founders designed Canada's Parliament, they took the **bicameral legislature** structure of the British model. Accordingly, the legislative branch comprised two bodies: an elected House of Commons (the lower house) and an appointed Senate (the upper house). A literal reading of the Constitution suggests that their powers are roughly equal, the major difference being that money bills must be introduced in the House of Commons. However, the superiority of an elected House of Commons has always been clear. The unelected nature of the Senate, along with the brazen patronage of most senators by the government, has significantly undermined its legitimacy.

The superiority of the House of Commons over the Senate is reinforced by several constitutional conventions. The prime minister and other members of the government, for example, are almost always drawn from the House of Commons. And it is unthinkable that a prime minister and most cabinet ministers not be elected MPs. Occasionally, a senator or two are appointed to cabinet. This usually occurs when the party in power has few (or no) MPs from a particular region of the country. And occasionally the prime minister will appoint to cabinet someone who is neither an MP nor a senator. By tradition, however, this person will very soon afterward seek election to the House of Commons. The system of democratic accountability would crumble if the prime minister and members of the government were not elected and removable by the electorate.

Another convention that reinforces the House of Commons' superiority is that all bills must pass both the Senate and the House of Commons before they become law. Moreover, the stages through which a bill must pass are identical in both houses of Parliament. While the Senate might occasionally suggest minor revisions to legislation, it was generally accepted that the Senate did not have the right to obstruct or reject the will of the House of Commons. This thinking has changed recently, however. After the 1984 election of the Progressive Conservative government, the Senate, which was dominated by Liberal-appointed senators, became more recalcitrant. The Senate delayed and in some cases rejected bills on such matters as drug patents, unemployment insurance, the goods and services tax, and the Canada–United States Free Trade Agreement. Constitutional law gives senators this right; constitutional convention suggests that they should not try to exercise it. In 2010, Prime Minister Harper broke an election promise on Senate reform and engineered a Conservative majority in the Senate by filling several vacant seats with Conservative appointees. With the express desire of making the Senate less partisan, Liberal leader Justin Trudeau ejected all the Liberal senators from the party's caucus in 2014, thereby creating much speculation about what the Senate might look like without a government side and an opposition.

The Biases of British Parliamentary Government

In discussing ministerial responsibility, we noted that the pre-democratic tradition of strong executive authority was never abandoned under British parliamentary government (Westminster

bicameral legislature a legislature comprising two bodies: in Canada, an elected House of Commons (the lower house) and an appointed Senate (the upper house)

model). Instead, it was adapted to the democratic principle that government is based on the consent of the people, a principle embodied in the powers of an elected legislature and in the doctrine of responsible government. However, this was not especially democratic; the legislature was elected by, and accountable to, only a fraction of the people, i.e., property-owning males. Universal male suffrage did not arrive until the late 1800s, and females were enfranchised early in the twentieth century. And while these changes extended *participatory rights* to all the people, it did not fundamentally alter the *non-participatory* biases of the Westminster model.

statism
a political tradition characterized by a relatively strong political executive and by a population that tends to be deferential toward those in power

In *Parliament vs. People*, Philip Resnick argues that these biases are a form of statism—a political tradition characterized by a relatively strong political executive and by a population that tends to be deferential toward those in power. The adoption of the Westminster model in Canada mainly reaffirmed the tradition of centralized executive authority that had existed before the elected legislature's approval was needed to pass laws. Resnick argues that the strong executive power is apparent throughout Canada's founding Constitution Act. "What our Founding Fathers were doing was consolidating an orderly . . . move from direct colonial rule to House Rule. . . . They had a particular kind of [political] order in mind, the parliamentary system as it had evolved in Britain, combining the interests of monarchs, lords and commoners." Today's executive may be more responsive to the electorate, but it has not become a servant of the electorate.[27]

Resnick makes the point that the more *deferential political culture* of Canada has been generated to some degree by parliamentary institutions that discouraged popular participation in politics beyond voting. It enshrined a sort of top-down philosophy of governance.[28] Parliament was sovereign, yes, but Parliament was not merely the people. It also included the Crown, the traditional seat of state authority, whose powers came to be exercised by a prime minister and cabinet with few serious checks from the legislature.

The evidence suggests that Resnick is right. There may have been some influential currents of participatory politics in Canadian history, particularly coming out of Western Canada, but these populist urges have struggled against a parliamentary tradition that concentrates political power in the hands of the prime minister (or premiers) and cabinet.

As we indicated above, the Charter of Rights and Freedoms may have modified the British parliamentary government in Canada by replacing parliamentary supremacy with constitutional supremacy. The Charter has no doubt generated a greater consciousness of rights among members of the public and shifted Canadian politics away from its elitist past toward a more participatory model. Nevertheless, the British parliamentary system that operates in Canada does not appear to be challenged by the fact that many groups are now bypassing electoral and legislative politics in favour of resolving political issues in the courts. The prime minister and cabinet are still powerful, and many agree that politics waged in the courts is not necessarily more democratic.

C. Amending the Constitution

Constitutions are meant to last a very long time, but they seldom do. Forty-seven countries were independent prior to 1900; only about a third of them were independent by 1950.

Canada's Constitution Act, 1867 is one of the oldest and most durable. Only the United States (1789), Sweden (1809), the Netherlands (1814), and the United Kingdom (1832) have older constitutions.

A **coup d'état**, the illegal overthrow of a government by violence or threat of violence, is one way of changing a constitution or re-writing the *social contract*. Peaceful means may also accomplish change, including the replacement of one constitution by a different one. But radical alteration of the fundamental rules and structures of government is much less common than constitutional reform. Reforms, or **constitutional amendments**, aim to change some aspect(s) of the existing constitution, leaving the basic constitutional structure intact. Amendments are generally accomplished through formal procedures set down in the constitution.

It is difficult to pinpoint when constitutional reform becomes constitutional upheaval. The line has certainly been crossed when a constitution is no longer recognizably what it was before. For example, the 1982 Constitution Act did three main things:

- transformed Canada's written Constitution from a set of British laws into Canadian constitutional law
- entrenched the Charter of Rights and Freedoms in the Constitution
- established formal mechanisms for changing the Constitution

These important changes did not amount to a new Constitution because most features of parliamentary government and of federalism remained the same. Examples of radical change to the Canadian Constitution would be the replacement of parliamentary government by American-style congressional government, the elimination of federalism, or the political independence of Quebec.

Constitutional change may also come about through the gradual evolution of principles and practices. For example, the principle that the Governor General should accept the advice of the prime minister on the matters of calling elections and on the prorogation of Parliament is one that emerged gradually as Canada shook off the vestiges of colonialism. This principle was breached by Governor General Lord Byng in 1926 when he denied Prime Minister Mackenzie King's request to dissolve Parliament and call an election; it only then became clear that this relationship between the prime minister and the Governor General was part of the Constitution.

The superiority of the House of Commons over the Senate on matters of legislation is another constitutional convention that became clearer with the passage of time. Those appointed to the Senate in 1867 were largely prominent politicians from the new provinces. It was during this early period that the Senate became known as the chamber of "sober second thought." Over time, however, the practice of patronage appointments, the emergence of assertive provincial governments as spokespersons for regional interests, and changing ideas about democracy and representation all contributed to the Senate's decline vis-à-vis the Commons. The idea that senators should be elected in the province that they represent is a relatively recent notion, which we will discuss in Chapter 8.

coup d'état the illegal overthrow of a government by violence or threat of violence

constitutional amendment a change in some aspect(s) of the existing constitution, leaving the basic constitutional structure intact

Canadian Spotlight

BOX 6.2 Evolution from Colony to Sovereign State

1848 The principle of responsible government is introduced in the colonies of Nova Scotia and United Canada (Ontario and Quebec).

1867 Full self-government was almost achieved with Confederation and the British North America Act of 1867. It created one country out of Nova Scotia, New Brunswick, and United Canada, and transferred to its federal and provincial legislatures the right to make laws for Canada and its provinces. Certain powers were withheld from Canadian governments and its voters.

1926 The Imperial Conference: the colony of Canada is proclaimed "autonomous."

1931 The Statute of Westminster proclaims that Canada is a sovereign country and the *power to enter into foreign treaties* is transferred from the United Kingdom.

1947 Until the passage of the Canadian Citizenship Act in 1947, there was no Canadian citizenship status that did not involve being a British subject.

1949 The Constitution can now be interpreted and amended in Canada and the Supreme Court of Canada replaces the Judicial Committee of the British Privy Council.

1982 The BNA Act is patriated to Canada, and becomes the Constitution Act, 1982. All parts of the Constitution can now be amended in Canada.

Amending the Constitution before 1982

The Constitution Act, 1867 gave Ottawa a very modest power to amend Canada's Constitution regarding matters that concerned only the federal government.[29] In practical terms, this power amounted only to the ability to change electoral districts and boundary lines. The provinces were given a similar power.[30] Canada's founders, however, provided very limited amendment powers in sections 91(1) and 92(1) of the Constitution Act, 1867; these did not allow for changing the division of powers and other important matters. The Canadian Constitution was in fact a British law, and constitutional change had to be requested from the British Parliament.

Many questions were left unanswered, however. Who here in Canada would have to agree before a resolution could be sent to London? Would all provincial governments have to agree? Just how much provincial consent was needed? Could any one province veto amendments? What if all 10 provincial legislatures and the House of Commons agreed to an amendment, but the Senate rejected it?

The issue was finally decided by the Supreme Court of Canada in 1981, when a stalemate in constitutional negotiations had developed between Ottawa and the provinces. The Liberal government of Pierre Elliott Trudeau wanted to patriate the Constitution, entrench in it a Charter of Rights and Freedoms, and establish a formal procedure for future amendments. Only the governments of Ontario and New Brunswick supported Ottawa's proposal. The conflict ended up in the courts when Manitoba, Newfoundland, and Quebec each asked their provincial supreme courts whether Ottawa's actions were constitutional. The provinces asked: (1) whether Ottawa's proposed amendments affected provincial powers; and (2) if provincial consent was constitutionally required in order to make such changes. Quebec also asked if it had a special veto over amendments. These decisions were then appealed to the Supreme Court of Canada. In its *Reference on the Constitution*[31] the Court ruled that

- Some level of provincial consent was required for changes affecting provincial powers. This requirement was a constitutional convention, not constitutional law, and could not, therefore, be enforced by the courts.
- The level of required provincial consent was not at all clear. A majority of the provinces had to agree, but unanimous consent was not necessary.
- In constitutional law, no province had a veto over constitutional change. The Court did not opine on whether such a right existed as a matter of constitutional convention.
- Ottawa did not need provincial consent to ask the British Parliament to change Canada's Constitution in ways affecting provincial powers. If the federal government chose to act unilaterally or with the support of only a few provinces, this would be legal, but at the same time unconstitutional!

Not surprisingly, both Ottawa and the dissenting provinces claimed victory. Legally, the way was clear for Ottawa to act with or without the consent of the provinces. Politically, unilateral action remained a very risky option, particularly in light of the Court's acknowledgement that some level of provincial consent was required by constitutional convention. All 11 governments returned to the bargaining table, and in

© McCord Museum/Aislin (alias Terry Mosher)

By telling the provinces that the federal government would patriate the constitution from Britain with or without the provinces, Prime Minister Trudeau forced the 10 premiers to participate in a constitutional conference to discuss the terms of patriation, the entrenchment of the Charter of Rights and Freedoms, and a constitutional amending formula. He is depicted here putting the provincial premiers' toes to the proverbial constitutional fire.

November 1981, 10 of them were able to reach agreement on a compromise document that became the Constitution Act, 1982. Only the Parti Québécois rejected the proposed changes. Despite Quebec's refusal to sign the 1981 agreement, the Constitution Act, 1982 is constitutional law in that province just as it is elsewhere in Canada. A 1982 Supreme Court decision confirmed this.[32]

Amending the Constitution since 1982

The uncertainties surrounding constitutional amendment have been largely dispelled by the Constitution Act, 1982. Part V of the Act establishes four different procedures, each of which applies to certain types of constitutional change. These procedures and when they are used are explained in Table 6.4.

Any of the four amendment procedures may be set in motion by either Ottawa or a provincial government (s. 46(1)). But because intergovernmental agreement is crucial to the success of most amendments, the most likely scenario is that the prime minister and the provincial premiers will first reach an agreement, which will then be submitted to their respective legislatures. This was the procedure that led to the Meech Lake Accord, the first proposal for constitutional amendment under the 1982 rules. The new procedures have not formally expanded the opportunities for public participation, nor have they enlarged the legislature's role in the process.

In addition to the four different procedures for amending the Constitution, the 10 governments also agreed that the 1982 Constitution Act should include an "opting-out" clause. Under section 40, a provincial government that does not agree to an amendment that transfers powers relating to education or other cultural matters from the provinces to Ottawa is not obliged to give up this power. Moreover, Ottawa is required to provide "reasonable compensation" to any dissenting province.

The Failure of the Meech Lake Accord

The first effort at amending the Constitution, using the 1982 rules, ended in acrimonious failure. The proposed amendment was in fact a group of changes collectively known as the Meech Lake Accord. The accord was a 1987 agreement between Prime Minister Brian Mulroney and the 10 provincial premiers. It was a response to five demands that the Quebec Liberal government of Robert Bourassa wanted met before signing the 1981 agreement that produced the Constitution Act, 1982. The main changes proposed by the accord included

- recognition of Quebec as a *distinct society*
- constitutional recognition of a province's right to control its own immigration policy (something Quebec had had since 1978)
- provincial power to nominate justices for the Supreme Court of Canada
- constitutional entrenchment of a province's right to opt out of federal–provincial shared-cost programs and to be reimbursed for running parallel programs of its own
- certain changes to constitutional amendment procedures and categories (see Table 6.4)

TABLE 6.4 Amending the Constitution

Procedure	Requirement	Application
1. General (ss. 38, 42)	• Resolution passed by the House of Commons and the Senate* • Two-thirds of the legislatures of the provinces that together make up at least half the population of all the provinces	• Reduction or elimination of powers, rights, or privileges of provincial governments or legislatures • Proportionate representation of the provinces in the House of Commons • Senate • Supreme Court of Canada (except its composition) • Extension of existing provinces into the territories • Creation of new provinces
2. Unanimous consent (s. 41)	• Resolution passed by the House of Commons and the Senate* • Resolution passed by every provincial legislature	• Queen • Governor General • Lieutenant-governors • Right of each province to at least as many seats in the House of Commons as it has in the Senate • Use of the English or French language (except changes that apply only to a single province) • Composition of the Supreme Court • Changing the amending procedures of the Constitution
3. Ottawa and one or more provinces (s. 43)	• Resolution passed by the House of Commons and the Senate* • Resolution passed by the legislature of each province where the amendment applies	• Alteration of boundaries between provinces • Use of French or English in a particular province or provinces
4. Ottawa or a province acting alone (ss. 44, 45)	• If Ottawa, a resolution passed by the House of Commons and the Senate* • If a province, a resolution passed by its legislature	• Executive government of Canada, the Senate, and the House of Commons, subject to the limits established by ss. 41 and 42 of the Constitution Act, 1982

*If after 180 days the Senate has not passed a resolution already passed by the House of Commons, Senate approval is not necessary.

After three years of wrangling marked by an anti-French backlash in parts of English Canada and a revival of separatist nationalism in Quebec, the accord expired when the legislatures of Manitoba and Newfoundland failed to ratify it by the constitutionally imposed deadline of 23 June 1990.

Both the birth and the death of the Meech Lake Accord indicated the amendment process, though formalized, is still difficult. The accord represented a deal struck by 11 heads of government with no public participation or legislative debate and which could not be altered. It was submitted to their legislatures for ratification, not for modification. Many denounced the process as undemocratic

...IF IT IS SO HARD TO AGREE ON MEECH LAKE WHY DON'T THEY TRY ANOTHER LAKE?....

NEWS MEECH IN MESS

Bob Bierman/© Simon Fraser University

The failure of the Meech Lake Accord is a testament to the difficulty of amending the Constitution.

because public participation was not solicited until the accord seemed destined for defeat.

Meech Lake came to grief because of the same obstacle that had blocked previous efforts at constitutional change. The final months leading up to the ratification deadline were marked by acrimonious debate and some ad hoc efforts to salvage the accord, and finally ended with Quebec being isolated from the other provinces. There was a sense of déjà vu. Quebec had been similarly isolated in 1971 when the first Bourassa government suddenly withdrew its acceptance of the Victoria Charter amendments, and then again in 1981 when René Lévesque claimed to have been betrayed by a last-minute deal between the other provinces and Ottawa. In each case, agreement ran aground because the Quebec government and some governments of English Canada were unable to settle their differences on Quebec's status within Canada.

The Failure of the Charlottetown Accord

Charlottetown Accord a second round of reforms from 1990 to 1992, called the "Canada round," attempted by the federal government after the Meech Accord failed in 1987; this second attempt also failed

The **Charlottetown Accord** of 1992 was a second attempt at constitutional reform and was the culmination of what the federal government rather misleadingly called the "Canada round" of constitutional negotiations (the period leading up to Meech Lake having been labelled the "Quebec round"). However, there were two chief reasons why the constitutional issue dominated Canadian politics between 1990 and 1992: the desire to get the Quebec government's agreement to the constitutional changes of 1982, and the worry over the post–Meech Lake resurgence of separatism. The deal struck at Charlottetown in August 1992 bore a striking resemblance to the Meech Lake Accord in some important respects. There were certain carry-overs from Meech, such as Quebec's "distinct society" status, Supreme Court nominations, and provinces' ability to opt out of shared-cost programs without penalty. The main features included

- a "Canada Clause" listing the fundamental characteristics of Canadian society
- entrenchment of the right to Aboriginal self-government
- an elected Senate with equal representation from the provinces and, eventually, special seats for Aboriginal representatives
- a francophone veto in the Senate regarding bills affecting the French language or culture
- a guarantee to Quebec of at least 25 per cent of the seats in the House of Commons

- confirmation of the provinces' exclusive jurisdiction in several policy areas
- some decentralization of powers to the provinces in immigration and labour policy

To avoid the charges of elitist deal making that had been levelled at the Meech Lake process, over the next two years there were dozens of government-organized public hearings on the Constitution and hundreds of conferences and forums organized by academics, political parties, and interest groups. But the Charlottetown Accord also failed.

Although there were opportunities for citizens and groups to express their views, the proposals presented to Canadians in the 26 October 1992 referendum were widely viewed as yet another instance of the elites cutting a deal and trying to foist it on the public. The potentially far-reaching changes proposed in the Charlottetown Accord are reflected in the Canada Clause. Its provisions sought to express the fundamental values of Canadians. Had the accord been passed, the Canada Clause would have been included as section 2 of the Constitution Act, 1867 and would have given the courts guidance in their interpretation of the entire Constitution. It is impossible to know how judges would have interpreted the provisions of the Canada Clause. However, it certainly would have given to the courts new opportunities beyond the Charter to involve themselves in the policy-making process. One could predict that subsection (1)(f) of the proposed Canada Clause, committing Canadians to "respect for individual and collective human rights and freedoms of all people," could become the legal basis for challenges to social spending cuts, or that subsection (1)(b) on the Aboriginal peoples of Canada could become the basis for legal claims on tax resources and legal rights for Aboriginal Canadians.

In the national referendum on the Charlottetown Accord, a majority of Canadians (54.5 per cent) rejected the proposed reforms. During the impassioned referendum campaign it was clear that many English Canadians said "no" to the Charlottetown Accord because they thought it gave Quebec too much. A further decentralization of powers to the provinces and special status for Quebec proved to be more than most English Canadians could stomach.

Conversely, many francophone Quebecers rejected the deal because they believed it gave them too little! Indeed, the only serious question asked by the Quebec media and politicians during the campaign was "Did Quebec get enough in the Charlottetown Accord?" Although it provided the Quebec government with more than the Meech Lake Accord, this was not enough given the nationalist political climate. The failure of the Meech Lake and Charlottetown Accords confirmed that a wide gap existed between the aspirations of francophone Quebecers and those of their compatriots in the rest of the country.

Citizen Participation in Constitutional Reform

For most of Canada's history the only direct actors in constitutional reform were governments. This changed during the negotiations and debates that led to the Constitution Act, 1982, when a number of citizens' interest groups played an active role through lobbying government and attempting to influence public opinion. These groups, and many others inspired by the opportunities created by the Charter, were instrumental in bringing about the death of the 1987 Meech Lake Accord, which had been agreed to by the 11 first ministers in the old pre-1982 style. During the two years of consultation and negotiation that preceded the signing of the 1992 Charlottetown Accord these citizens' interest groups were very much part of the process. Informally at least, Ottawa and the provincial governments appeared to have conceded the legitimacy of a more inclusive style of constitution making.

What they did not concede, however, was a direct role for public participation and consent. Under the old *elitist policy-making style*, popular consent was mediated by the heads of government. Under the more *inclusive policy-making style* that emerged in the early 1980s, popular consent was mediated by these heads of government plus certain citizens' interest groups claiming to speak on behalf of women, ethnic and racial minorities, Aboriginal Canadians, the disabled, official-language minorities, and so on. But it was not until the decision was made in the late summer of 1992 to submit the Charlottetown reforms to the people in a national referendum that popular consent was unmediated and the public was given a direct role in the constitutional amendment process. This change represented a remarkable break from Canada's elitist tradition of constitution making.

However, the idea of holding referendums, while initially considered alien to Canadian political tradition, has gradually emerged in the last 40 years as a means of dealing with contentious matters of provincial or national importance. The flood of condemnation that followed the death of the Meech Lake Accord and the Quebec government's commitment to holding a provincial referendum on whatever agreement it reached with Ottawa promoted the view of referendums as an alternative to elitist-style traditional decision making. The decision to hold a national referendum (a legally non-binding popular vote) on the Charlottetown Accord appeared to mark the beginning of a new era in Canadian constitution making. Most commentators believed that governments in the future would find it difficult to ignore the 1992 precedent of a popular ratification vote. In British Columbia and Alberta, which have more of a populist tradition, the political pressure for constitutional referendums may be irresistible. It remains to be seen whether governments will feel obliged to submit future agreements to the electorate for ratification or whether the Charlottetown experience was an aberration that has left no mark on Canada's political culture.

The Right to Secede

On 20 August 1998 the Supreme Court of Canada handed down its much-awaited decision on the constitutionality of Quebec separation. To some, the most remarkable aspect of the ruling was that it was made at all. The separation of Quebec, if and when it comes about, is a political matter that will be determined by politicians and the people, not by nine appointed judges in Ottawa. This was certainly the view of most Quebec nationalists and of Quebec's Parti

Democracy Watch

BOX 6.3 Referendums: Should the Constitution Be Open to Populist Decision Making?

Shouldn't all Canadians have a say in the Constitution that determines how their country should be governed?

In a representative democracy like Canada, power is transferred from the people to elected representatives who form the government and who are entrusted with making decisions related to governing the country. However, declining levels of trust in politicians in recent years have made populist political tools such as the referendum attractive to voters.

One theory suggests that Canadians should be consulted via referendum when an issue is of "transcending national importance."[33] But do all Canadians agree on what is a matter of national importance? For instance, is a movement to include environmental rights in the Canadian Constitution (approximately 90 other countries have done so in the last 40 years) as important nationally as, say, a movement to change the number of regional representatives in the House of Commons? Moreover, do all Canadians feel confident casting a vote on matters grounded in legal, rather than social, terms?

Québécois government, whose disdain for the process was such that it refused to send lawyers to argue the case for the constitutionality of Quebec secession. Indeed, the Supreme Court's involvement in this matter was widely viewed by francophone Quebecers as unwarranted meddling in the internal affairs of the province.

In 1996, Ottawa had decided to refer the issue of the constitutionality of unilateral secession by Quebec to the Supreme Court. There were political risks associated with Ottawa's involvement in a court challenge to Quebec secession. The Liberal government's decision to push forward, despite these risks, was consistent with what had come to be known as the "Plan B" approach to Quebec separatism. Whereas "Plan A" had involved efforts to satisfy moderate Quebec nationalists with promises of distinct society status for Quebec and some decentralization of powers to the provinces, "Plan B" was a hard-line approach that relied on convincing Quebecers that separation would carry significant economic costs and that some parts of Quebec's lands might not fall under the authority of an independent Quebec state (this was the partition threat, made by predominantly anglophone communities and Aboriginal groups in Quebec, and occasionally expressed by Stéphane Dion, the Liberal minister of intergovernmental affairs). The court challenge to Quebec secession became a major component of the "Plan B" strategy.

Ottawa submitted three questions to the Supreme Court:

1. Under the Constitution of Canada, can the National Assembly or government of Quebec effect the secession of Quebec from Canada unilaterally?
2. Does international law give the National Assembly or government of Quebec the right to effect the secession of Quebec from Canada unilaterally? In other words, is there a right to self-determination in international law that applies to Quebec?
3. If there is a conflict between international law and the Canadian Constitution on the secession of Quebec, which takes precedence?

The Court decided that there was no conflict as in question 3, and so only the first two questions were addressed.

The Court's answer to the first question was a model of ambiguity that provided both federalists and separatists with arguments. In strictly legal terms, said the Court, the secession of Quebec involves a major change to the Constitution of Canada that "requires an amendment to the Constitution, which perforce requires negotiation."[34] However, the Constitution of Canada consists of more than the Constitution Acts passed between 1867 and 1982. "Underlying constitutional principles," said the Court, "may in certain circumstances give rise to substantive legal obligations . . . which constitute substantive limitation upon government action."[35] These underlying constitutional principles provided the basis for the Court's argument that if a clear majority of Quebecers voted "yes" to an unambiguous question on Quebec separation, this would "confer legitimacy on the efforts of the government of Quebec to initiate the Constitution's amendment process in order to secede by constitutional means."[36] These underlying constitutional principles also impose on Ottawa and the provincial governments outside of Quebec an obligation to negotiate the terms of secession, if and when Quebecers and their provincial government express the democratic will to separate.

So who wins on the first question? Both federalists and separatists found enough in the Supreme Court's ruling to allow them to claim victory. Federalists emphasized that, legally speaking, Quebec has no constitutional right to secede unilaterally, and that even if separatists were to win a referendum the Court had specified that a "clear majority" on an "unambiguous" question would be required before such a vote could be considered an expression of the democratic will of Quebecers on so weighty a matter. Separatists—or at least those who were even willing to acknowledge the Court's ruling— emphasized that the Court had agreed that the democratically expressed will of Quebecers had to be taken into account in determining whether unilateral secession was constitutional, and that if Quebecers were to express their clear support for separation the rest of Canada would be constitutionally bound to respect this decision and negotiate the terms of secession.

The Court's answer to the second question—whether international law gives Quebec the right to secede—was both shorter and less ambiguous. The Court said "no." While acknowledging that the right of self-determination of peoples exists in international law, the Supreme Court held that this right did not apply to Quebec.

The Court did not answer the contentious question of whether the Quebec population or a part of it constitutes a "people" as understood in international law. It argued that such a determination was unnecessary because, however the Quebec people might be defined, it is clear that Quebecers are neither denied the ability to pursue their "political, economic, social and cultural development within the framework of an existing state,"[37] nor do they constitute a colonial or oppressed people (a claim that is a staple of contemporary Quebec historiography). The Court's pronouncements on these matters are found in Box 6.4.

Does the Supreme Court ruling make a difference? Probably not, or at least not much of one, as the Court seemed to acknowledge at various points in its decision. On the issue of what would constitute a "clear majority" and an "unambiguous question" in a referendum on Quebec independence, the Court admitted that "it will be for the political actors to determine what constitutes a 'clear majority on a clear question.'"[38] Likewise, the practical meaning of the Court's ruling is that the constitutional obligation of the rest of Canada to negotiate the terms of separation with Quebec, if Quebecers express the democratic will to secede, would be for political actors to settle. Finally, in response to the argument that a unilateral declaration of independence by Quebec would be effective whether or not the Court's test of a clear majority on a clear question was met, the judges could say only that this might well be true, but the action would be unconstitutional nonetheless. One suspects that separatists would not lose much sleep over the constitutionality of such a declaration, particularly if, as seems possible, France and certain other countries were to immediately recognize the new Quebec state.

The Clarity Act

Ottawa's response to the 1998 Supreme Court ruling was to pass the Clarity Act in 2000. The Act empowers Parliament (1) to review the wording of any future referendum question to determine whether it is "unambiguously worded" and (2) to determine whether the margin of victory for the separatism option constitutes a "clear majority"—both requirements of the Supreme Court ruling. Under this law the Parliament of Canada could, conceivably, refuse to enter into negotiations on separatism with Quebec if it determined that one or both of these conditions were not met. "Conceivably" is the key word here. There are strong reasons to think that Ottawa's rejection of a referendum question designed by a sovereignist Quebec government, or of even a fairly narrow margin of victory for those in favour of independence, could well backfire, playing into the hands of separatists who would be quick to accuse the federal government and the rest of Canada of meddling in Quebec's affairs. The aim of the Clarity Act was doubtless to strengthen the federalists' hand in a future Quebec referendum, but the actual result could prove to be quite the opposite.

© CP Photo/Fred Chartrand

Surrounded by his Liberal MPs, Prime Minister Jean Chrétien stands in the House to cast his vote for the Clarity Act (Bill C-20) in 2000. The Act outlines conditions under which the government of Canada would enter into negotiations with a province attempting to secede. Although the Clarity Act would apply to any province orchestrating a separation from the rest of the country, many Quebecers interpreted the Act as a means to squelch any further forays down the path of separation.

civil liberties or **civil rights** the rights of citizens to equality and to social and political freedoms

Universal Declaration of Human Rights A declaration passed by the UN in 1948 that provides the basis for various international covenants to which Canada is a signatory.

human rights all the basic rights and freedoms of citizens

Civil Liberties and Civil Rights

Civil liberties or **civil rights** are terms sometimes used to refer to all the basic rights and freedoms of citizens. Under the influence of the United Nations' **Universal Declaration of Human Rights** (1948), the term **human rights** has become more commonly used to refer to this bundle of rights and freedoms. They include fundamental/political rights and freedoms, democratic rights, legal rights, economic rights, and equality rights.

These five categories are not exhaustive. Other rights could such as *language rights* or *group rights* (e.g., religious minorities or Aboriginal peoples) are discussed earlier in the chapter. Some have argued that *social rights* or *entitlements*, including the right to a job, economic security, housing, and health care, should be entrenched in the Constitution. *Environmental rights* have also been advocated. In Canada, many of the main categories of human rights are entrenched in the Charter, which means that they are firmly established in the Constitution, and that changing or removing them is difficult and unlikely.

Equality rights are the most recent and probably the most controversial category of rights. The American Constitution, the first modern constitution to include an entrenched guarantee of equality rights, refers only to every person's right to "equal protection of the laws."[39] The more recent tendency, however, has been to enumerate the proscribed bases of legal discrimination, such as race, religion, ethnicity, gender, and age. Canada's Charter includes mental or physical disability in this list, and has been interpreted by the courts to prohibit discrimination based on sexual orientation.

The Pre-Charter Era

In the pre-Charter era, 1867–1981, rights had a low profile. A couple of factors were responsible for this; the most important was federalism. The Constitution Act, 1867 contains very few references to the rights and freedoms of Canadians. It does, however, include a very detailed catalogue of the "rights" of governments, i.e., the legislative and fiscal powers of Ottawa and the provinces. Faithful to the principle of parliamentary supremacy, the courts were unwilling to overrule the authority of elected legislatures. What appeared to be rights issues were often decided as matters of federalism, that is, of which level of government had jurisdiction. To have a chance at success, therefore, rights claims had to be packaged in the constitutional categories of federalism. The resulting jurisprudence was bizarre, to say the least. Very few court decisions were based on a clear-cut rights argument.

A second factor was responsible for the relatively low profile of rights issues until well into the twentieth century. Most Canadians probably felt that rights were best protected by legislatures, the common law, and a vigilant public: the system that Canada had inherited from the United Kingdom. But increasingly, doubts about the adequacy of these guarantees were being expressed during the 1940s and 1950s by apparent rights violations like Quebec's infamous "Padlock Law" (1937), the Alberta government's attempt to censor the press (1937), the threatened deportation of Japanese Canadians in 1945–6, and the arbitrary measures taken during the Igor Gouzenko spy affair of 1946.

The growing concern over civil liberties was shared by influential groups such as the Canadian Bar Association. They argued that a bill of rights—one that reflected the human rights commitments entered into through the UN—should be entrenched in the Constitution. When the Progressive Conservative Party came to power in 1957 under the leadership of John Diefenbaker, an outspoken advocate of entrenched rights, the timing for a Bill of Rights seemed propitious. The **Canadian Bill of Rights** was a statutory declaration of rights passed by the Canadian Parliament on 10 August 1960. These rights were not entrenched as those in the 1982 Charter of Rights and Freedoms would be and therefore did not carry the same constitutional and legal weight and influence. It proved to be a major disappointment for civil libertarians. As several court cases would show, the bill seemed to apply only to the federal government. For almost a decade afterward, the Supreme Court decisions on its application were very conservative and merely reaffirmed the status quo of rights and freedoms prior to 1960.

One particular case, though, seemed to buck the trend. Under the Indian Act, it was illegal for an Indian[40] to be intoxicated off a reserve. In the 1970 *R v. Drybones* case, the

Canadian Bill of Rights a statutory declaration of rights passed by the Canadian Parliament on 10 August 1960

Court agreed that the charge of intoxication against Joseph Drybones conflicted with the Canadian Bill of Rights guarantee of "equality before the law," by subjecting Indians to criminal sanctions that other people were not exposed to. By a five-to-three vote, the Supreme Court used the Bill of Rights to strike down section 94 of the Indian Act.[41] The *Drybones* case proved to be an aberration, however. In subsequent rulings, the Supreme Court retreated from this interpretation of the Bill of Rights. The glimmer of hope that the *Drybones* decision had sparked was extinguished during the 1970s, producing renewed calls for constitutionally entrenched rights.

But there was a major snag. Constitutionally entrenching a Bill of Rights that would affect the powers of both Ottawa and the provinces seemed to require the consent of the provinces. It was clear that some provinces would oppose entrenchment; this was the reason the Conservative government had chosen to introduce the Bill of Rights as a statute, requiring only the approval of the House of Commons and the Senate.

Before passage of the Charter, the only rights entrenched in Canada's Constitution were associated with religion, language, and elections. However, even on those matters the courts tended to defer to governments and the laws they made. In the Constitution Act, 1867, neither section 93, dealing with education as it related to religion, nor section 133, establishing the equal standing of French and English in Parliament and in federal courts, and in Quebec's legislature and courts, proved to be very effective in protecting minority rights.

Despite the provisions of section 93, the Manitoba Public Schools Act was passed in 1890, which eliminated the Catholic and Protestant schools that had existed in the province and replaced them with a single public school system. In two other cases involving section 93, the courts refused to accept the argument that this section also protected the educational rights of language minorities. The argument had at least a ring of plausibility because, historically, the Roman Catholic schools in Manitoba were predominantly francophone, in Ontario they were often francophone, and Quebec's Protestant schools were anglophone. Thus, when in 1913 the Ontario government banned the use of French as a language of instruction in both public and separate (Catholic) schools, this had a negligible impact on public schools but dealt a major blow to the mostly francophone Catholic schools of eastern Ontario. The issue arose again in the 1970s when the Quebec government passed Bill 22, restricting access to the province's English-language schools, most of which were under the control of Protestant school boards. In both instances the courts rejected outright the claim that section 93 should be read as a protection for linguistic rights in addition to denominational ones.[42]

From the standpoint of promoting bilingualism outside of Quebec, the courts' unwillingness to read language rights into section 93 represented a real setback. On the other hand, the "victories" for language rights in a pair of Supreme Court decisions handed down in 1978 and 1979 produced few practical consequences. Both of these decisions involved the limited guarantee of bilingualism established by section 133 of the Constitution Act, 1867. In both cases the Court declared that this guarantee was beyond the interference of governments, thus repudiating the idea that no action lay outside the competence of Parliament or a provincial

Canadian Spotlight

BOX 6.4   International Law and the Self-Determination of Quebec

There is no necessary incompatibility between the maintenance of the territorial integrity of existing states, including Canada, and the right of a "people" to achieve a full measure of self-determination. A state whose government represents the whole of the people or peoples resident within its territory, on a basis of equality and without discrimination, and respects the principles of self-determination in its own internal arrangements, is entitled to the protection under international law of its territorial integrity.

The Quebec people is not the victim of attacks on its physical existence or integrity, or of a massive violation of its fundamental rights. The Quebec people is manifestly not, in the opinion of the *amicus curiae*, an oppressed people.

For close to 40 of the last 50 years, the Prime Minister of Canada has been a Quebecer. During this period, Quebecers have held from time to time all the most important positions in the federal cabinet. During the 8 years prior to June 1997, the Prime Minister and the Leader of the Official Opposition in the House of Commons were both Quebecers. At present, the Prime Minister of Canada, the Right Honourable Chief Justice and two other members of the Court, the Chief of Staff of the Canadian Armed Forces and the Canadian ambassador to the United States,

not to mention the Deputy Secretary-General of the United Nations, are all Quebecers. The international achievements of Quebecers in most fields of human endeavour are too numerous to list. Since the dynamism of the Quebec people has been directed toward the business sector, it has been clearly successful in Quebec, the rest of Canada and abroad.

The population of Quebec cannot plausibly be said to be denied access to government. Quebecers occupy prominent positions within the government of Canada. Residents of the province freely make political choices and pursue economic, social, and cultural development within Quebec, across Canada, and throughout the world. The population of Quebec is equitably represented in legislative, executive, and judicial institutions. In short, to reflect the phraseology of the international documents that address the right to self-determination of peoples, Canada is a "sovereign and independent state conducting itself in compliance with the principle of equal rights and self-determination of peoples and thus possessed of a government representing the whole people belonging to the territory without distinction."

—Excerpt from the Supreme Court of Canada, *Reference re the Secession of Quebec (1998)*.

legislature as long as it did not encroach on the constitutional powers of the other level of government.

In *Attorney General of Quebec v. Blaikie*,[43] the Supreme Court upheld a Quebec Superior Court decision that had ruled unconstitutional those sections of Quebec's Bill 101

Some critics have suggested that if judges are going to play an increased political role in our democracy, there should be a public review of the candidates for the Supreme Court, as there is in the United States. In 2016, the Trudeau government proposed an appointment process with a non-partisan advisory board. The hope was that this process would see more openness, transparency, and accountability, and a reduction in prime ministerial influence. How engaged do you anticipate Canadians might be in a discussion around candidates' eligibility for positions as judges on the Supreme Court of Canada?

that attempted to make French the sole official language in that province. While Bill 101 did not ban the use of English from the legislature and the province's courts, and the Quebec government continued to print and publish laws and legislative documents in both languages, the law's clear intent was to make French the only official language for all government activities and the dominant language in the province's courts. This, the courts decided, violated the spirit—if not the strict letter—of section 133.

The Charter Era and the Emergence of Rights Issues

Rights issues emerge out of political struggles, and this struggle is a necessary condition for rights claims. What may appear to be obvious and uncontroversial rights claims in Canadian society—for example, the right to vote or the right to express one's personal beliefs—are denied in many societies. Only some political conflicts acquire the character of rights issues. For a rights issue to be considered legitimate, a rights claim must be anchored in one or more of a society's core values/beliefs. These fundamental values operate as limits on rights discourse. And a claim made by an individual or a group will be expressed as a right only when it is denied or placed in jeopardy by the words or actions of another group.

Consider the familiar issue of abortion. Those who argue for a woman's right to abort her pregnancy have often linked this rights claim to individual freedom of choice, a fundamental value in liberal-democratic society. Those who oppose abortion, or who favour restrictions on access to it, often argue that the human fetus has a right to life, the most fundamental of rights in any civilized society. Those who favour access to abortion would, of course, object to the imputation that they do not value human life, just as those who oppose abortion would deny that they undervalue individual freedom. Behind these rights, as with all the rights recognized in democratic political systems, rest fundamental values, such as the equality of human beings, the autonomy of the individual, and, most important, the nature of the good society. The abortion issue illustrates well the way in which rights claims tend to be squeezed into existing ideological and legal categories, and how unconventional political discourses are discouraged by legalized politics. The success of individual women, women's organizations, and abortionists like Dr Henry Morgentaler in challenging legal restrictions on access to abortion has been due to their case being framed in legal arguments and moral claims that fall within the dominant ideology.

The passage of the Charter opened up new legal avenues to abortion advocates. Canada's abortion law was eventually ruled unconstitutional by a 1987 Supreme Court decision in which the majority ruled that the law violated security of the person. But the same majority agreed that the state has an interest in protecting the fetus, although the Court did not specify the circumstances or stage of fetal development in which abortion would be unacceptable. This acknowledgement of fetal rights provided some encouragement to the anti-abortion coalition, whose political strategy focused increasingly on claiming the personhood of the unborn.

The Americanization of Canadian Politics

During the 1980–81 debate on constitutional reform, critics of an entrenched charter of rights warned that entrenchment would lead to the "Americanization" of Canadian politics, and to the regret of many, the prediction has come true. This Americanization has two main aspects. One involves a more prominent policy role for unelected judges and a related decline in the status of elected legislatures. The other has been an explosion in the number of rights cases brought before the courts, with an accompanying shift to the courts solving political disputes. In short, parliamentary supremacy has been replaced by constitutional supremacy and an increased importance of judges in the governmental process.

Those who advocate the American model of entrenched rights prefer to put their faith in the Constitution and the judges who interpret it. Those who prefer the *British model of parliamentary supremacy* are more dubious about judge-made law and more inclined to place their trust in the prudence and democratic responsiveness of elected governments.

Does the record of rights enforcement in different countries permit us to draw conclusions about whether the American or the British model is "best"? And has the Charter improved how rights are protected in Canada? There are no easy answers to these questions. Rights activists are themselves divided in their assessment. But if definitive answers are elusive, we can at least attempt to understand how rights have been argued and enforced in Canadian politics. From any perspective, the Charter represents an important watershed.

In terms of "quality," the change produced by the Charter has been no less pronounced. The previous pattern of deciding rights issues as federalism cases, asking only whether a government was trespassing on the jurisdictional turf of the other level of government, has been abandoned. Rights issues are now dealt with head-on, argued by litigants and decided by judges on the basis of the Charter. Moreover, the courts have shed most of their traditional reluctance to question the substance of duly enacted laws and regulations. Emboldened by the Charter's unambiguous declarations that the "Constitution is the supreme law of Canada" and that the courts have exclusive authority to interpret and enforce the Charter's guarantees, judges have struck down provisions in dozens of federal and provincial statutes. Judges are quite aware of the expanded role they play in the political process, but most insist that there is nothing undemocratic in this. Table 6.5 gives a sense of the many important Charter cases that have come before the Supreme Court since 1982.

Has the Charter Americanized Canadian politics? Early critics of the Charter said that it would by doing three things. First, it would elevate the importance of unelected judges and the courts, giving them a much more prominent role in determining important policy matters. Second, it would undermine the operation of parliamentary government in Canada and make legislatures accountable to the courts rather than to the people. Third, it would generate a more litigious society in which individuals and groups are more likely to base their claims and political arguments on rights, making compromise more difficult and bypassing such political processes as elections and lobbying in preference for the courts.

Judges are indeed far more prominent in policy making than they were in the pre-Charter era. Parliamentary supremacy has been replaced by constitutional supremacy, with the Supreme Court as chief arbiter, and important issues are often decided in the courts or as a result of court decisions pushing governments in a particular direction. Yet, in spite of these important changes, the Charter has not resulted in a wholesale Americanization of Canadian politics. Judges in Canada have tended to interpret the Charter's guarantees in distinctively Canadian ways, anchored in aspects of Canada's political culture that are different from those of the United States.

Reasonable Limits and the Charter

judicial restraint a legal concept expressed in the Charter that judges should defer to the legislature when exercising their judicial power

reasonable limits legislative limits that can be placed on human rights if it can be established that they are in the best interest of a free and democratic society

The courts are "invited" to exercise self-restraint, commonly called **judicial restraint**, by the opening words of the Charter. This is a legal concept expressed in the Charter that judges should defer to the legislature when exercising their judicial power. Section 1 declares that the guarantees set forth in the Charter shall be "subject only to such reasonable limits prescribed by law as can be demonstrably justified in a free and democratic society." What are these **reasonable limits**? In the case of *R v. Oakes* (1986)[44] the Supreme Court establishes a standard known as the *Oakes* test on what legislative limits can be placed on human rights if it can be established that they are in the best interest of a free and democratic society. The first part of this test asks whether a government's objective in limiting a right is sufficiently important to warrant such an encroachment. The second part asks whether the extent of the limitation is proportionate to the importance of the

TABLE 6.5 Classic Charter Cases

Landmark Case	Charter Issue
R. v. Oakes	The "Oakes test" of "reasonable limits" on civil rights
R. v. Sparrow	Aboriginal rights
Law v. Canada	Equality rights
R. v. Morgentaler	Women's rights
Re BC Motor Vehicle Act	The right to not be arbitrarily detained
Vriend v. Alberta	Gay rights
Hunter v. Southam Inc.	Government use of search warrants
Andrews v. Law Society of British Columbia	Government use of search warrants
R. v. Collins	The "Collins test" on admissibility of evidence
R. v. Stinchcombe	Burden of truth
R. v. Askov	Trial in a timely manner
Reference Re Provincial Electoral Boundaries	Clarifying the right to vote

government's objective. In order to satisfy this second criterion, a limitation must meet three conditions:

1. It must be rationally connected to the government's objective.
2. It should impair the right in question as little as is necessary to meet the government's objective.
3. The harm done to rights by a limitation must not exceed the good that it accomplishes.

Some might cite the *Oakes* test as a case of judges interfering with parliamentary authority. But why shouldn't judges give legislators an idea of how the law needs to be changed to bring it into line with their interpretation of the Constitution? The point is, however, that means and ends are not neatly separable in the real world of politics. And who should determine how much or little is enough? Is proportionality an appropriate matter for unelected judges to decide, or should this be determined by elected legislatures?

These questions resurfaced with a vengeance when the Supreme Court ruled on 21 September 1995 that the federal ban on tobacco advertising violated the Charter's guarantee of freedom of expression. Many staunch Charter boosters became skeptics overnight. They were awakened by the tobacco advertising decision to a basic truth of constitutionally entrenched rights: the price of entrenchment is that judges assume a more important role in political life.

The Notwithstanding Clause: Section 33

"What the Charter gives, the legislature may take away." This appears to be the meaning of section 33 of the Charter, the notwithstanding clause. The clause was inserted at the insistence of

© CP Photo/Peter McCabe

"Don't touch Bill 101." In the case of Bill 101, which protects the French language in Quebec, not using the notwithstanding clause would have been more costly to the Quebec government.

several provinces. The constitutional deal that produced the Charter would have died without this concession.[45]

Although the notwithstanding clause appears to provide governments with a constitutional escape hatch from much of the Charter, it is not clear that it actually has this effect. It has been resorted to on only a handful of occasions. Why have governments generally been reluctant to use section 33 to avoid or reverse court decisions declaring their laws to be in violation of the Charter? In the words of civil libertarian Alan Borovoy, an outspoken critic of the notwithstanding clause, "The mere introduction of a bill to oust the application of the Charter would likely spark an enormous controversy. . . . Without solid support in the legislature and the community, a government would be very reluctant to take the heat that such action would invariably generate."[46] Some civil libertarians have argued that a legislature's decision to invoke section 33 should itself be subject to review by the courts and therefore possibly be overturned. In a 1985 ruling, the Quebec Court of Appeal agreed. This decision was, however, overruled by the Supreme Court of Canada in *Ford v. Attorney General of Quebec* (1988). The Court pronounced in favour of a literal interpretation of section 33—which also happens to correspond to the intentions of those provincial governments that insisted on the notwithstanding clause—requiring only that a legislature expressly declare its intention to override the Charter.

Democracy Watch

BOX 6.5 To Keep or Not to Keep the Notwithstanding Clause

Those in favour of section 33 say

- In exceptional circumstances, the notwithstanding clause allows elected governments to make policy decisions independent of unelected judges.
- This override mechanism is subject to public debate at the time it is enacted and at the time of any re-enactment.
- The clause acts as a "safety valve" to preserve certain social values and goals if they are threatened by the Charter.

Those opposed to section 33 say

- The clause is inconsistent with the firm establishment of human rights and freedoms guaranteed by the Charter.
- The clause may be used in a situation where a principle is only perceived as being, and is not actually, under threat (in other words, it can be used solely as a political tool, perhaps for winning favour with particular special-interest groups).
- The clause can be invoked against those rights and freedoms most in need of protection.

While it appears that there are no serious legal obstacles to a government using section 33 to circumvent the Charter, governments do not want to give the appearance of denying rights to their citizens. In fact, if one does not take into account the PQ's symbolic policy, between 1982 and 1985, of inserting the notwithstanding clause into all laws passed by the Quebec legislature and retroactively into all existing provincial statutes, section 33 has been invoked on only a couple of occasions.

There are, however, circumstances where the denial of rights inflicts little political damage on government and may even produce political dividends. This was certainly true of the Quebec Liberal government's decision to use the notwithstanding clause to re-pass, with some modifications, the provisions of Bill 101 (legislative restrictions on the use of languages other than French) that had been ruled unconstitutional by the Supreme Court. While the government's move precipitated the resignation of three anglophone cabinet ministers and alienated many English-speaking voters, there is no doubt that the political costs of not overriding the Charter would have alienated the much larger French-speaking population and media. The political costs were also negligible when Saskatchewan's

Progressive Conservative government inserted section 33 in a 1986 law to force striking public servants back to work.

Do public opinion and vigilant media provide adequate protection against legislative abuses of the notwithstanding clause? This may depend on our expectations for democracy. For some, a law that denies rights to some persons is not a legitimate basis for invoking section 33. They would argue that if the Charter does not protect rights when they are vulnerable, then it fails the real test of its worth: rights are either entrenched against popular passions, the "tyranny of the majority," and legislative assault, or they are not.

But for others, the notwithstanding clause is a mechanism for asserting the *popular will* in exceptional circumstances. For example, some conservative critics of the Charter have argued that governments should be prepared to use the notwithstanding clause more often to reassert the will of the public, particularly on matters like same-sex marriage. The only other way of overcoming an unpopular court decision on the Charter would be to amend the Constitution, a difficult and time-consuming process. The controversy over section 33 is, in the final analysis, nothing less than the familiar debate over parliamentary versus constitutional supremacy.

Applying the Charter

News stories on attempts to use the Charter to challenge some law or administrative procedure have become routine. Only a small fraction of the hundreds of trial court rulings on the Charter ultimately reach the provincial superior courts, and fewer still are appealed to the Supreme Court of Canada. Even so, these cases represent a large share of the courts' workload. More than two decades after its passage, it is possible to identify the main tendencies in judicial interpretation of the Charter.

Scope and Authority

With respect to how far the Court would be willing to go in using the Charter to strike down laws passed by elected legislatures, rulings in cases such as *Law Society of Upper Canada v. Skapinker* (1984) indicate that although the Constitution must be considered the supreme law of the land, judges should interpret it in ways that "enable [the legislature] to perform the high duties assigned to it, in the manner most beneficial to the people."[47] In other words, judges should not be too quick to second-guess elected lawmakers.

An additional feature of the Court's approach to the Charter's scope deserves mention. This involves its insistence that the Charter applies only to relationships between the state and citizens, not to private-sector relationships. Thus, the Charter cannot be used by someone who believes that he has been denied a job or an apartment because of his race, or whose private-sector employer requires that she retire at the age of 65. Forms of discrimination like these are pervasive throughout society, but they are not inequalities that can be overcome using the Charter. The Supreme Court has on several occasions articulated this distinction between public (covered by the Charter) and private, as in *Dolphin Delivery* (1986):[48] "[The Charter] was set up to regulate the relationship between the individual and the government. It was intended to restrain government action and to protect the individual."[49] This position is, in fact, faithful to the intentions of those who framed and agreed to the Charter.

This is true in the case of hate speech targeting a particular group, where approaches have been significantly different. The difference boils down to this. In the United States, just because you say something demonstrably false and odious about the members of a group does not mean that you lose the Constitution's protection to speak your mind. If, however, this speech becomes what lawyers call "fighting words," liable to incite violence, then it loses the protection of the First Amendment. But in Canada, some speech is considered to be so nasty that, by its very nature, it promotes hatred and is undeserving of constitutional protection, as is demonstrated by the majority opinion in *R v. Keegstra*, the case of a public school teacher who was deemed guilty of promoting hate by teaching a social studies course where students were told that the World War II Holocaust was a fraud and that Jews were "power-hungry," "money-loving," "sadistic," and "child killers" (see Box 6.7). Moreover, the greater willingness of Canadian courts and legislatures to restrict hate speech on the grounds that some ideas and their expression contribute nothing to democratic life, and therefore can be restricted without doing any harm to freedom, is consistent with a cultural difference between these countries that pre-dates the Charter era.

Democracy Watch

BOX 6.6 Bill C-51, the Anti-terrorism Act

The Anti-terrorism Act, which passed into law in June 2015, has attracted criticism for its curtailing of civil rights and may result in more court challenges. Here are some of the changes:

- Promoting terrorism is now a jailable offence.
- It cracks down on the dissemination and sharing of deemed terrorist propaganda.
- More arrests may be made without warrants.
- Personal information can now be shared across departments.
- The Canadian Security Intelligence Service may now disrupt terrorist plots.

Source: Hayden Watters, "C-51, Controversial Anti-Terrorism Bill, Is Now Law. So, What Changes?" CBC News, 18 June 2015, http://www.cbc.ca/news/politics/c-51-controversial-anti-terrorism-bill-is-now-law-so-what-changes-1.3108608.

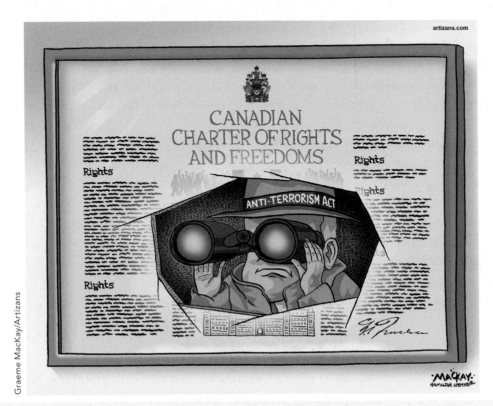

Graeme MacKay/Artizans

This editorial cartoon refers to the anti-terrorism legislation, Bill C-51, that was passed following two instances of homegrown terrorism in the fall of 2014. Just how far should the state be allowed to go in its obligation to protect society against crime and terrorism? For example, can it curtail civil liberties and spy on its citizens? This is a perpetual dilemma in all democratic societies.

Inside Politics

BOX 6.7 | Is Hate Speech Protected by Free Speech?

In Canada

Hate propaganda contributes little to the aspirations of Canadians or Canada in either the quest for truth, the promotion of individual self-development or the protection and fostering of a vibrant democracy where the participation of all individuals is accepted and encouraged. . . . Consequently, the suppression of hate propaganda represents impairment of the individual's freedom of expression which is not of a most serious nature. . . .

Indeed, one may quite plausibly contend that it is through rejecting hate propaganda that the state can best encourage the protection of values central to freedom of expression, while simultaneously demonstrating dislike for the vision forwarded by hate-mongers. In this regard, the reaction to various types of expression by a democratic government [and the criminalization of certain forms of speech] may be perceived as meaningful expression on behalf of the vast majority of citizens.

Source: *R v. Keegstra*, [1990] 3 S.C.R. 697.

In the United States

The First Amendment generally prevents government from proscribing speech, or even expressive conduct, because of disapproval of the ideas expressed. Content-based regulations are presumptively invalid. From 1791 to the present, however, our society, like other free but civilized societies, has permitted restrictions upon the content of speech in a few limited areas, which are "of such slight social value as a step to truth that any benefit that may be derived from them is clearly outweighed by the social interest in order and morality."

. . . One must wholeheartedly agree . . . that "it is the responsibility, even the obligation, of diverse communities to confront [hateful] notions in whatever form they appear," but the manner of that confrontation cannot consist of selective limitations upon speech. . . . The point of the First Amendment is that majority preferences must be expressed in some fashion other than silencing speech on the basis of its content.

. . . [T]he reason why fighting words are categorically excluded from the protection of the First Amendment is not that their content communicates any particular idea, but that their content embodies a particularly intolerable (and socially unnecessary) mode of expressing whatever idea the speaker wishes to convey.

Source: *R.A.V. v. St Paul*, 505 U.S. 377 (1992).

The Charter's Legacy

By 2012, some pundits such as John Ibbitson of *The Globe and Mail* were calling the Charter on its thirtieth anniversary "Canada's gift to the world."[50] Yet others wondered, in the same edition of *The Globe and Mail*, whether 2012 would see the Conservative government colliding with the judiciary and the Charter in areas such as mandatory minimum sentencing, prostitution, assisted suicide, electronic surveillance, the power to appoint judges, and enhanced police powers.[51]

It is probably fair to say that the changes generated by the Charter have far exceeded the expectations of all but a few of the politicians and experts who presided at its birth. There has been an explosion in the number of rights cases brought before the courts, as well as a shift in the venue of some political conflicts. For the moment, parliamentary supremacy appears to have been replaced by constitutional supremacy, which has increased the importance of judges in the governmental process.

It is true, of course that every major Supreme Court ruling on the Charter serves to clarify the scope and authority of judicial review. We have focused on several early Charter decisions in order to demonstrate that the Court very quickly assumed the mantle of judicial activism. How far judges go in using the Charter to strike down laws and administrative practices is largely up to them. There are, however, two provisions of the Charter that were intended to rein in the courts' authority: the reasonable limits clause (s. 1) and the notwithstanding clause (s. 33). In practice, however, neither of these has been very effective in limiting the scope of judicial activism.

Is there an identifiable pattern in the Court's interpretation of the individual rights guaranteed by the Charter? In essence, and aside from what most commentators characterize as a moderately activist approach, the Court has shown few sharply pronounced tendencies.

Summary

What should we remember about the Canadian Constitution? First, our Constitution has both written and unwritten components and is an agglomeration of traditions, conventions, statutes, and documents. Second, our constitutional founders borrowed the British parliamentary model of democracy as well as the American federal model for sharing power between the central and provincial governments. Third, our Constitution establishes a set of important relationships: between the individuals and the state (fundamental rights and freedoms, guarantees for individuals and groups); between the different institutions of the state (executive, legislature, and judiciary); and between central and regional governments (federalism). And finally, our Constitution embodies certain key principles and concepts (many of them derived from our British parliamentary heritage) that are essential to the proper functioning of our democracy:

- constitutional monarchy
- rule of law
- judicial review
- representative government
- responsible government
- ministerial responsibility
- federalism

We should also remember that our Constitution has continuously evolved since it was first written in 1867. Failure to achieve constitutional changes in the 1970s led to the first Quebec referendum on separation in 1980 and a promise by Prime Minister Pierre Trudeau to patriate and amend the Constitution. One of the most important changes to the Constitution when it was patriated in 1982 was the constitutional entrenchment of the Charter of Rights and Freedoms. The entrenchment of certain rights and guarantees has resulted in a significant shift away from parliamentary supremacy and given our judiciary a greater role in matters that affect ordinary Canadians, and a shift toward what some critics call "the Americanization of Canadian politics." The procedures used to amend the Constitution also changed after 1982 and made it possible to amend the Constitution here in Canada. Since 1982 there have been two attempts at amending the Constitution: the Meech Lake Accord and the Charlottetown Accord. Both ended in failure. These failures led to a second Quebec referendum in 1995.

With respect to a province's right to secede from Confederation, our own Supreme Court and international law both suggest that secession is possible, but that certain conditions would have to be met for the act of secession to be considered legitimate.

Review Exercises

1. How do you think our constitutional system would change if all votes in the House of Commons were free votes?

2. What conditions would have to be met for a province to be allowed to secede from Confederation? And which matters would have to be negotiated for this province to leave Confederation?

3. Find a story in the media that deals with the Charter and answer the following:

   a. What are the circumstances?
   b. Who are the people or organizations involved?
   c. What law/regulation/action/practice is being challenged?
   d. At what stage is the challenge?
   e. Are lawyers or other experts interviewed? Who are they?
   f. What right or freedom of the Charter is at stake in this story?

Up for Debate

1. Is the average Canadian qualified to vote on all constitutional matters? Should changes to the Constitution be made via mandatory referendum? What alternatives can you think of to involve the citizenry in constitutional reform?

2. Examine the model of the Nunavut Legislative Assembly, where the 19 members sit in a circle, and the parliamentary model used in Ottawa where the government and the opposition parties sit across a centre aisle from each other. Which model works best?

3. Since 2014, Justin Trudeau—first as Liberal leader & now as PM—has insisted that senators should be non-partisan and has ejected Liberal senators from the Liberal caucus. Would the Westminster parliamentary system of government be better without partisanship?

4. Does free speech include the right to tell others to "shut up"?

Starting Points for Research

Cairns, Alan. *Constitution, Government, and Society in Canada: Selected Essays.* Toronto: McClelland & Stewart, 1988.

Cairns, Alan. *Disruptions: Constitutional Struggles, from the Charter to Meech Lake.* Toronto: McClelland & Stewart, 1991.

Hogg, Peter W. *Constitutional Law of Canada.* Scarborough, ON: Carswell, 2007.

Kelly, James B., and Christopher P. Manfredi, eds. *Contested Constitutionalism: Reflections on the Canadian Charter of Rights and Freedoms.* Vancouver: University of British Columbia Press, 2009.

Leuprecht, Christian, and Peter H. Russell, eds. *Essential Readings in Canadian Constitutional Politics.* Toronto: University of Toronto Press, 2011.

Manfredi, Christopher. *Judicial Power and the Charter: Canada and the Paradox of Liberal Constitutionalism,* 2nd edn. Toronto: Oxford University Press, 2001.

Roach, Kent, and Robert J. Sharpe. *The Charter of Rights and Freedoms,* 5th edn. Toronto: Irwin Law, 2013.

Russell, Peter. *Constitutional Odyssey: Can Canadians Become a Sovereign People?,* 3rd edn. Toronto: University of Toronto Press, 2004.

Scott, F.R. *Essays on the Constitution.* Toronto: University of Toronto Press, 1977.

CBC Archives and TVO's *The Agenda*

Visit the companion website for *Canadian Democracy: A Concise Introduction* to follow links to audio and video footage related to the main themes of the chapter: www.oupcanada.com/BrooksConcise2e.

Relevant Websites

Visit the companion website for *Canadian Democracy: A Concise Introduction* to browse a collection of websites featuring material related to the key themes of the chapter, an excellent starting point for research:www.oupcanada.com/BrooksConcise2e.

7 Federalism

Canada's Constitution establishes two levels of government—national and provincial—both with important law-making and taxation powers. This system of divided jurisdiction is known as federalism. When the proposal to create an independent Canada was discussed at Charlottetown (1864) and Quebec (1867), the main subject of debate was the relationship between the new national and regional governments. Two decades of self-government and the constitutional traditions imported from Britain provided the colonies with ready guideposts for most other features of the Constitution. Federalism, by contrast, was uncharted territory. Most of the founders' practical knowledge of the principles and operation of federalism was based on their observation of the federal system in the United States, which did not inspire much confidence following the secession of the Confederacy and the bloody Civil War of 1861–5. Despite all this, Canada's founders opted for a federal system of government.

After reading this chapter you should be able to

1. define and differentiate the federal and unitary systems of government
2. discuss the origins and the maintenance of Canadian federalism
3. list the federal division of powers in the Constitution

↑ The Centennial Flame, located on Parliament Hill, commemorates Canada's 100th year anniversary as a Confederation. Canadian Confederation symbolizes the foundation of Canadian federalism—the division of law-making and taxation powers between national and provincial governments.

Source: Peter Pesta Photography/Getty Images.

4. outline the courts' role in the evolution of Canadian federalism
5. discuss Quebec's impact on federalism
6. explain how federalism is financed

What Is Federalism?

federal system
a form of
government with
a constitutional
authority to make
laws and to tax,
divided between a
national government
and some number
of regional
governments

In a **federal system** of government the constitutional authority to make laws and to tax is divided between a national government and some number of regional governments. Neither the national government acting alone nor the regional governments acting together have the authority to alter the powers of the other level of government. They are coordinate and independent in their separate constitutional spheres. Citizens in a federal state are members of two political communities, one national and the other within the boundaries of a regional unit called a province, district, state, or canton, depending on the country.

"Federalism" is a legal term, and its existence is based on a constitution. If a single government controls all legislative and taxation powers in a country, then no amount of administrative decentralization or variation in the economic, social, or cultural characteristics of its regions will make it a federal state. Federalism divides political authority along territorial lines, but it is not the only form of government to do so. Important policy-making and administrative powers may be exercised at the regional level even in a **unitary state** where sovereignty or competence resides exclusively with the central government and regional or local governments are legally and politically subordinate to it. The extent to which the activities are *decentralized*, that is, placed in the hands of regional officials, or remain *centralized* at the national level, is determined by a country's particular social, geographic, and political conditions. This is also true of a federal state, where the constitution provides only a partial and sometimes very misleading guide to the real division of powers between governments. Political authority is also linked to territory in *confederations* and *economic communities*. These are formal groupings of independent states that have agreed to assign certain legislative and administrative functions to a common institution or set of institutions. All member states have a say—though not necessarily an equal say—in the decision making of such a body, while retaining their ultimate sovereignty (see Table 7.1).

**unitary state
system** a form of
government where
sovereignty or
competence resides
exclusively with the
central government,
and regional or
local governments
are legally
and politically
subordinate to it

The Origins, Maintenance, and Demise of Federal States

Only about two dozen of the 192 member countries of the United Nations have a federal system of government. This is an estimate of the actual number of federal states, because the determination of whether a political system is federal is not an exact science. For example, Mexico,

TABLE 7.1 Territory and Political Authority

Model	Arrangements, Responsibilities, and Relationships	Example
Unitary state	A form of government where sovereignty or competence resides exclusively with the central government, and regional or local governments are legally and politically subordinate to it	France
Federation	A voluntary, power-sharing arrangement where sovereignty or competence is distributed between central and provincial (or state) governments so that, within a single political system, neither order of government is legally or politically subordinate to the other, and each order of government is elected and exercises authority on the electorate	Canada
Confederation	A voluntary arrangement where there is a considerable allocation of responsibilities to central institutions or agencies. Sovereignty is retained by the member-state governments, and the central government is legally and politically subordinate to them. Furthermore, the members of the major central institutions are delegates of the constituent state governments, and changes to the constitution require unanimity.	Switzerland
Economic association	A voluntary political arrangement, with a confederal type of government with common organizing institutions. The functions assigned by the participating states to the common institutions are limited mainly to economic co-operation and coordination.	European Union

Source: Adapted from Canada, Task Force on Canadian Unity, *Coming to Terms: The Words of the Debate* (Hull, QC: Supply and Services Canada, 1979): 21–2.

Argentina, and Russia generally are included in the club of federal states, but the central governments of these countries have sometimes interfered with the autonomy of state governments. Although the *federalism club* is small, it does include some of the world's largest and most important countries. Unitary government is far more popular, even in countries where regional political conflicts are strong.

What circumstances lead to the adoption of a federal political system? There is no simple answer. But it is possible to identify a general condition that is present at the birth of all federal states and vital to their continued health: an agreement among the regional components that the benefits of a union exceed the costs of membership. A federal state is essentially a *consensus of regions*. Students of international law and federalism may disagree over the legal right of any part of a federal state to separate from the union, but the political fact is that when a region no longer shares the national consensus upon which federalism is based, its separation becomes a real possibility.

"Federalism," declared Pierre Trudeau, "has all along been a product of reason in politics. . . . It is an attempt to find a rational compromise between the divergent interest groups which history has thrown together; but it is a compromise based on the will of the people."[1] This is why federal unions are often referred to as "pacts," "contracts," or "bargains." The key role of consent may be seen in the case of the Soviet Union, when, as part of the post–World War II deal between the Soviet Union and the United States–led Western democracies, the countries of Estonia, Latvia, and Lithuania were made members of the Soviet "federal" state against their will. Moscow dominated the regional republics through a Communist party monopoly until the fall of the Soviet Union in 1991.

Trudeau's argument that federalism is the product of reason will not convince Quebec separatists, who view 1867 as a sellout by an elite of "cannibal kings"[2] willing to collaborate with the Anglo-Saxon oppressor. Nor does reason appear to be the chief factor explaining why disgruntled regions remain part of a federal union when their politicians and their people clearly believe that they are treated unfairly and exploited for the benefit of other regions—a century-old view in Western Canada. Some argue that it is the rationale and self-interest of only some groups that lead to federal union, and that federalism may not be reasonable from the standpoint of other groups' self-interest.

compromise a coming to terms with concessions on two or more sides and a joint decision to abide by an agreement

Nevertheless, the origins of federal democracies lie in **compromise**—a coming to terms with concessions on two or more sides and a joint decision to abide by an agreement. Some regions may be enthusiastic, while others enter a federal compromise out of despair at the lack of viable alternatives. This does not diminish the fact that the voluntary consent of the regions forms the basis of a federal union. Once established, however, a federal state may achieve a new dynamic. The existence of a national government and the idea of national citizenship can be centralizing factors that offset the decentralizing pull of regional interests. Thus, federalism is sustained by a *sense of political nationality* rather than purely rational calculations on the part of regional populations and politicians.

Federalism and Political Nationality

According to Donald Smiley, an expert on Canadian federalism, *political nationality* "means that Canadians as such have reciprocal moral and legal claims upon one another that have no precise counterparts in their relations with others, and that Canadians as such have a continuing determination to carry out a significant number of important common activities together."[3] While this sense of political community may not replace the other identities that citizens have of themselves, it does transcend regional, ethnic, and linguistic identifications.

Federalism is ultimately sustained by the sense of political nationality—or community—that develops around the national state. By the same token, the breakup of a federal state is sure to be presaged by the deterioration of this sense of community. Sometimes a sense of political nationality is never solidly established in the first place. A fragile political nationality may be destroyed by a particularly divisive regional conflict, as American federalism was split asunder by slavery. The most stable federal systems are those where regional communities share in a sense of political nationality that dampens the decentralizing tendencies produced by regional differences. Switzerland, the contemporary United States, and Austria are good examples of how regional divisions need not prevent the development of a durable political nationality.

What determines the strength of political nationality? And why do regional divisions become independence movements in some federal states but not in others? Several factors come into play, but the most basic is *regional inequality*. If the citizens of a region feel strongly that existing federal structures discriminate against their interests economically and politically, this places a strain on the sense of political nationality. Sentiments like these are very common. For example, a 2005 survey by the Centre for Research and Information Canada found that Ontarians were almost twice as likely as Canadians in most other provinces to believe that their province was treated with the respect it deserved.[4] Studies show, however, no direct correlation between perception of respect for the province and the level of affection and loyalty of provincial populations toward Canada. Nor does a strong provincial identity appear to prevent its people from also identifying with Canada. As Roger Gibbins has observed, with the exception of Quebec, it is probably a mistake to think of national and provincial loyalties as competitive.[5]

Regional grievances are more likely to threaten the stability of federalism when they are linked to a nationalist movement. Nationalism becomes a political force when the values and beliefs shared by the people of a territory or a community are translated into a public policy or agenda. Nationalist values and beliefs are usually accompanied by territorial claims. Nationalism is distinguished from regionalism by its demands on behalf of both a territory and a community within that territory that shares some ethnic, linguistic, or other cultural traits. These claims can range from demands for outright independence to more moderate calls for greater autonomy for regions where members of the national community are concentrated. Nationalism is far more difficult to accommodate within a federal state than is a region's complaints of unfair treatment. Indeed, nationalism is fundamentally at odds with the concept of political nationality on which a viable federal state depends.

nationalism the translation of values and beliefs shared by the people of a territory or a community into a public policy or agenda

TABLE 7.2 Factors Contributing to the Choice of Federalism

Common Interests	External and/or Internal Threats
• Shared political values • Expectations of stronger economic ties and associated benefits • A multiplicity of ranges of communications and transactions • The desire for political independence • Prior political association • Strategic (territorial) considerations • Geographical proximity • Common cultural and ideological factors, such as nationalism, religion, and inherited traditions and customs • Political leadership and a broadening of the political elite • Similarity of social and political institutions • The appeal of federal models • The culmination of historical processes that were founded upon prior political commitments	• A sense of military insecurity, real or imagined • A sense of economic insecurity, real or imagined • A sense of cultural insecurity, real or imagined • A perceived threat to the stability of the existing political order

Source: Michael Burgess, *Comparative Federalism: Theory and Practice.* (New York: Routledge, 2006), p. 100.

Inside Politics

BOX 7.1 | A Tale of Two Countries: Language, Nationalism, and Federalism

This country has two major language communities that have coexisted on sometimes uneasy terms since the country achieved independence in the nineteenth century. One of these communities has a significant nationalist movement that includes a couple of political parties committed to independence for their national community. Many of this country's citizens believe that their language community and region has subsidized public services and incomes in the other community for decades, and they feel resentful. This resentment is deepened by long historical memories of social and political inequality between the two communities. As of 2010, the prospects for their continued cohabitation seemed rather bleak.

The country described here is Belgium. It has often been compared to Canada, facing similar challenges and attempting to manage conflict between its two main language communities, French and Flemish, through a federal constitution. Unlike that in Canada, however, the nationalist movement aspiring to break up Belgium is associated with the wealthier majority community—the Flemish-speaking northern region of the country. In the national election of 2010 the most popular political party in that region was the Flemish Nationalist Party, a party committed to independence and led by a multilingual historian whose victory speech began with the words "Nil volentibus arduum" ("For those who have the will, nothing is impossible").

Comparisons between Belgium and Canada can be misleading. Nevertheless, political scientists and constitutionalists from each country have often looked to the other to find answers about managing inter-community relations in a federal state. If developments in Belgium hold any lessons for Canada, the main one is probably this: When the ties of identity and shared cultural values between communities are weak, and when one group believes that existing state institutions treat it unfairly, federalism is in trouble. The compromise at the heart of federalism's viability ultimately depends on the sentiment of the people or, more precisely, the peoples who live together under a federal constitution. This is what the French historian Ernest Renan meant when he said that federalism is a daily referendum of the popular will.[6]

The Origins of Canadian Federalism

Canada's federal Constitution was a compromise. Most of the anglophone Fathers of Confederation favoured a unitary system of government similar to Britain's under which all power would be in the hands of a new national Parliament. They were opposed, however, by two groups. The strongest opposition came from the French-Canadian representatives of Canada

East (now Quebec) who believed that a federal union with constitutional protections and exclusive provincial jurisdiction over linguistic and cultural matters would protect their interests. Federalism was also preferred by Maritime politicians. Maritimers had developed strong local identities that they were unwilling to see submerged under unitary government. Besides, in this era politics and patronage were virtually synonymous; it was reasonable that provincial politicians would want to retain control over public contracts and political appointments.

Some anglophone politicians of Ontario and Quebec also saw the merits of federalism. For example, Grit politician George Brown expressed the view that conflict between the English Protestant and French Catholic communities—conflict that had produced government instability and political deadlock in the legislature of United Canada and that was one of the reasons behind the Confederation movement—would be reduced by assigning local matters to the provincial legislatures.[7] Ottawa would deal with matters of national interest, such as trade and commerce, immigration, defence, and transportation. The presumption that sectional rivalries and local interests would not enter into deliberations on these national issues was naive, to say the least.

Federalism was a necessary compromise between two contradictory tendencies. The forces that were pushing the British North American colonies toward a political union wanted a strong national government. A larger union, with a wider revenue base and an integrated national economy, was crucial to the railroad promoters' interests and to the Canadian financial institutions linked to them. Likewise, a strong central government was needed if British North America was to assume the burden of its own military defence and to expand into the sparsely populated region between Ontario and British Columbia. Tugging in the opposite direction were the forces of cultural dualism as well as the colonial administrations and regional societies that were unwilling to be submerged in a unitary state dominated by Ontario and Quebec.

What sort of federal union did the founders envisage? Expectations varied greatly. Some, such as Canada's first prime minister, John A. Macdonald, anticipated that the provincial governments would be little more than glorified municipalities, subordinate to Ottawa. Others, like Ontario's third premier, Oliver Mowat, did not share this centralist vision and he led the movement for provincial rights during the 1870s and 1880s.[8]

The agreement the founders reached gave to the federal government what then were the most important legislative powers and sources of public revenue. (For a complete list of federal, provincial, and shared responsibilities, refer to Table 7.3.) When we consider that promoting economic growth and military defence (also a federal responsibility) were two of the chief functions of the nineteenth-century state—maintaining public order was the third, and responsibility for this was divided between Ottawa and the provinces—there is little doubt that Ottawa was assigned the major legislative powers of that era. The federal government was also assigned the duty to build an intercolonial railway connecting Montreal to Halifax. Responsibility for immigration and agriculture was divided between the federal and provincial governments, but in the event of a conflict Ottawa's legislation would prevail.

Ottawa's superiority was also clear on the taxation front. Donald Smiley notes that customs and excise taxes—indirect forms of taxation—accounted for about three-quarters of colonial revenues prior to Confederation. The provinces were restricted to the less developed field of "direct taxation" (e.g., sales tax), as well as royalties on provincially owned natural resources.

George P. Roberts/Library and Archives Canada/C-000733

The Fathers of Confederation at Charlottetown. Canada's adoption of federalism was far from a unanimous decision; rather, the system of divided jurisdiction was a compromise that made Ottawa the seat of national power to control certain issues while leaving the provinces to oversee others.

These were meagre revenues compared to those of the federal government. The Confederation agreement also established the practice of federal money transfers to the provinces. The dependence of the economically weaker provinces on federal subsidies began in 1867 and continues to this day. Together, the powers and tax revenues appeared to establish Ottawa's clear superiority over the provinces in economic matters (see "Financing Federalism" later in this chapter).

In addition to all this, the Confederation agreement included several provisions that have been described as *quasi-federal*. They appear to establish a nearly colonial relationship between Ottawa and the provinces by permitting the federal government to intervene in a provincial economy on matters of "public works" in the national interest, to disallow laws passed by provincial legislatures, and to pass laws protecting rights held by denominational minorities at the time of a province's entry into Confederation. While the disallowance of laws pertaining to the protection of minority rights in education was never used, the other powers were used widely during the first few decades after Confederation and periodically during the first half of the twentieth century. In most instances, Ottawa was reacting to provincial economic policies that challenged its own priorities and jurisdiction.

Do the founders' intentions really matter? Legally, no. In interpreting the federal division of powers the courts have been unreceptive to arguments about what the Fathers of Confederation had in mind.[9] Indeed, the Supreme Court of Canada's ruling in the 1981 Patriation Reference, *Re Resolution to amend the Constitution*, declared that "arguments from history do not lead to any consistent view or any single view of the nature of the British North America Act. So, too, with pronouncements by political figures or persons in other branches of public life. There is little profit in parading them."[10]

The Compact and Contract Theories of Canadian Federalism

Politically, however, arguments about intentions can matter. There are two arguments most frequently made about Canadian federalism:

- it represents a *compact* between French and English Canada

or

- it is a *contract* by the provinces to give up certain powers to a new national government of their creation

Both the compact and contract theories of federalism maintain that the federal "bargain" cannot be changed without the mutual consent of those who agreed to it.

The *compact theory* suggests that Quebec—the province in which most francophones reside and the only province in which they are in the majority—should have a veto over any constitutional change that affects either the federal distribution of powers or the relative weight of Quebec in Parliament and on the Supreme Court (where three of the nine justices must be members of the Quebec bar). This argument was rejected by the Supreme Court of Canada in the 1981 Patriation Reference.

The proponents of *contract theory* claim that each province has the right to veto constitutional change that affects provincial powers or national representation. In fact, there are three variants of contract theory. One would restrict the right of veto to the original signatories (Nova Scotia, New Brunswick, Quebec, and Ontario). A second extends it to all provinces, regardless of when they joined Canada. The third maintains that the unanimous consent of the provinces is not required to change the federal distribution of powers, but that "substantial provincial agreement" is necessary. Like compact theory, none of these variants of contract theory has any legal foundation.

The political importance of both compact and contract theories may be seen in the fact that Canadian governments were for nearly 50 years (1935 to 1982) unable to agree on a formula for amending the Constitution. Unanimous provincial consent appeared to be a political requirement for enacting an amendment formula. Moreover, many experts assumed wrongly, it turned out, that unanimity or something close to it was also a legal requirement.

The compact interpretation of Canadian federalism continues to carry political weight. The Quebec government's refusal to agree to the Constitution Act, 1982 was widely viewed as a serious blow to the Constitution's legitimacy. Prime Minister Brian Mulroney regularly, if misleadingly, spoke of bringing Quebec into the Constitution. Legally, of course, the 1982 reforms applied right across Canada. But politically the prime minister had a point. The government of Quebec, representing about 90 per cent of Canadian francophones, did not consent to far-reaching constitutional changes. Both the Parti Québécois and the Quebec Liberal Party insist that Canadian federalism must be viewed as a compact between founding nations, a view that enjoys diminishing support in the rest of Canada. Claude Ryan, as leader of the Quebec Liberal Party, claimed that diminished support for the idea of Canada as a binational compact is precisely the problem:

> If the movement in favour of sovereignty was able to put down its roots and develop itself in Quebec, it is precisely because more and more Quebecers came to the conclusion that this equality, which had been the dream of many generations, will never be realized with the Canadian federation.[11]

The contract theory of Canada lives on politically in the idea of the formal equality of the provinces. Section 2 of the 1997 Calgary Declaration, an agreement among all the provinces except Quebec on the parameters for future constitutional negotiations, states, "All provinces, while diverse in their characteristics, have equality of status." The declaration also states that any constitutional amendment that confers powers on one province must make these powers available to all provinces. This involves a fundamentally different view from that of the compact theory. For example, the contract theory idea that provinces are and ought to remain formally equal is not easily squared with the compact theory notion of Quebec as a "distinct society."

The Federal Division of Powers

Whatever may have been the intentions of the founders in 1867, it is clear today that both levels of government exercise wide-ranging legislative and taxation powers. Canada's founders took exceptional pains to specify the responsibilities of each level of government. But a literal reading of the division of powers drafted in the 1867 Constitution, as well as the formal changes that have been made since, provides a misleading guide to Canadian federalism. Some policy areas, such as electronic communications, air transportation, and environmental protection, were unimagined when the federal division of powers was framed, and so are not explicitly assigned. In other cases, what were minor responsibilities in the nineteenth and early twentieth centuries, such as health, education, and welfare, have assumed greater importance as a result of economic and societal changes, and of changes to the state itself.

The heart of the federal division of powers is found in sections 91 and 92 of the Constitution Act, 1867. These sections contain a detailed list of enumerated powers that belong exclusively to Parliament (s. 91) or the provincial legislatures (s. 92). Combined with other sections that also deal with the division of powers, this is the constitutional foundation of Canadian federalism. An examination of powers reveals that both Ottawa and the provinces have the capacity to act in most of the major policy fields (see Table 7.3).

Some of the constitutional powers listed in Table 7.3 could have been placed under more than one policy heading. The authority to tax, for example, has been used to promote economic

TABLE 7.3 The Federal Division of Powers and Responsibilities

Federal	Provincial	Shared
• Any mode of taxation • National defence • Aboriginal Canadians • Banking and monetary standards • Criminal laws and penitentiaries • Judicial appointments • Interprovincial transportation and communications • Official bilingualism in federal institutions • Protection of denominational education rights • Equalization of provincial public revenues • Treaties • Laws for the "peace, order, and good government" of the country • Matters not enumerated in powers of the provinces	• Direct taxation within province • Natural resources • Hospitals and health care • Education • Property and civil rights • Administration of justice and organization of courts • Municipalities • Public lands	• Immigration • Old-age pensions • Agriculture

growth, redistribute income, and subsidize special interests. Unemployment insurance is both an economic policy tied to retraining and job finding and a social policy that redistributes income to less affluent regions. Immigration policy has always been harnessed to the needs of the Canadian economy and has also been tied to cultural policy through citizenship services and language training for immigrants.

At the same time, governments have sometimes found the authority to legislate through powers that are implied rather than stated in the Constitution. The most important example is the federal government's spending power. Ottawa spends billions of dollars annually on programs that fall under the jurisdiction of provincial and municipal governments. These include federal monies given to universities for research and student scholarships, to school boards for language instruction, and to individuals for purposes that might appear to fall under provincial jurisdiction (e.g., tax benefits for child care). Ottawa's constitutional "right" to spend money for any purpose has never been definitely established in the courts.[12] Nevertheless, the spending power today provides the constitutional basis for such major federal grants to the provinces as the Canada Health Transfer (CHT), the Canada Social Transfer (CST), and equalization payments.

The Courts and Federalism

Laypersons might expect constitutional terms such as "trade and commerce," "property and civil rights," and "direct taxation" to have straightforward meanings. For constitutional lawyers, governments, and private interests, however, the federal division of powers is a dense thicket of contradictory and contested meanings and opportunities and is often a matter to haggle over in the courts. The judicial decisions that have resulted from these disputes have played an important role in shaping the evolution of Canadian federalism. Among the many contentious sections of the Constitution, the courts' interpretation of Ottawa's authority to "make laws for the peace, order, and good government of Canada" and the federal government's "trade and commerce" power have had the greatest impact on the division of powers. We will look briefly at each of these.

Peace, Order, and Good Government

The courts have tended to place a narrow interpretation on the federal Parliament's general authority to make laws for the "**peace, order, and good government of Canada**" (POGG). This has been reduced over time to an emergency power that can provide the constitutional basis for federal actions in special circumstances, but that cannot be used to justify federal laws during "normal" times. The narrow interpretation of POGG began with the *Local Prohibition* case (1896). The Judicial Committee of the Privy Council (JCPC) ruled that Ottawa could not use POGG to override the enumerated powers of the provinces. The decision also marked the introduction into Canadian constitutional law of the "national dimensions" test. Lord Watson wrote:

> Their Lordships do not doubt that some matters, in their origin local or provincial, might attain such dimensions as to affect the body politic of the Dominion, and to justify the Canadian Parliament in passing laws for their regulation or abolition in the interest of the Dominion.[13]

When does a matter acquire "national dimensions"? This question was addressed in a series of three decisions handed down in 1922, 1923, and 1925. In *Re Board of Commerce Act, 1919*, and the *Combines and Fair Prices Act, 1919* (1922), the JCPC struck down two federal laws introduced after World War I to prevent business monopoly and hoarding of essential commodities. For the first time the "emergency doctrine" was articulated, according to which Parliament could pass laws under the authority of POGG only in the case of a national emergency. Writing for the majority, Viscount Haldane declared:

> Circumstances are conceivable, such as those of war or famine, when the peace, order and good Government of the Dominion might be imperilled under conditions so exceptional that they require legislation of a character in reality beyond anything provided for by the enumerated heads in either s. 92 or s. 91.[14]

In these and other cases the JCPC essentially ruled that some national crisis, specifically a wartime emergency, had to exist before federal laws could be based on POGG.

In the 1970s the Supreme Court of Canada found that POGG could be used to justify federal laws during peacetime. The Court was asked to rule on the constitutionality of Ottawa's Anti-Inflation Act, 1975. A majority of the Court accepted the federal government's argument that mounting inflationary pressures constituted an emergency justifying legislation that encroached on provincial jurisdiction. Not only was the "emergency doctrine" liberated from

peace, order, and good government of Canada (POGG) an important constitutional principle and emergency power that can provide the constitutional basis for federal actions in special circumstances, but that cannot be used to justify federal laws during "normal" times

war-related circumstances, the Court also indicated its reluctance to challenge Parliament's judgment on when emergency circumstances exist. The result, according to constitutionalists such as Peter Russell, is that Ottawa now appears to have fairly easy access to emergency powers under this doctrine.[15] Constitutionally, this may be so. Politically, however, any federal government would think twice before legislating under this contentious power. In the three decades since Ottawa won this constitutional victory there has not been a single instance where the federal government has relied on POGG as the basis for an alleged intrusion into provincial jurisdiction.

Trade and Commerce

On the face of it, Ottawa's authority over the regulation of trade and commerce in section 91(2)[16] of the Constitution Act, 1867, appears rather sweeping. However, court decisions have construed the trade and commerce power to be much narrower, limited largely to interprovincial and international trade. At the same time, provincial jurisdiction over property and civil rights in the province (s. 92(13))[17] has been interpreted as the provinces' own "trade and commerce" power. In the *Parsons* decision of 1881, the JCPC felt that a literal interpretation of section 91(2) would leave the provinces powerless to affect business. They interpreted "regulation of trade and commerce" to include "political arrangements in regard to trade requiring the sanction of parliament, regulation of trade in matters of interprovincial concern, and it may be that they would include general regulation of trade affecting the whole Dominion."[18] To construe Ottawa's trade and commerce power otherwise would be to deny the "fair and ordinary meaning" of section 92(13) of the Constitution Act, 1867, which assigns property and civil rights in the province to the provincial governments.

The legacy of *Parsons* has been that Ottawa's authority to regulate trade and commerce has been limited to interprovincial trade, international trade, and general trade affecting the whole of Canada. But even this definition of federal jurisdiction has presented problems of interpretation. A series of Supreme Court decisions signified a broader interpretation of Ottawa's power to regulate interprovincial trade.[19] Ottawa's authority was given an additional boost by a 1971 reference decision of the Supreme Court. In *Attorney General for Manitoba v. Manitoba Egg and Poultry Association et al.* (1971), the *"Chicken and Egg" Reference*—no kidding—the Court ruled unconstitutional a provincial egg marketing scheme that restricted imports from other provinces, on the grounds that it encroached on Ottawa's trade and commerce power. In *General Motors of Canada Ltd. v. City National Leasing* (1989), the Supreme Court laid down five criteria that must be met before Ottawa may regulate commerce under the "general trade" provision of section 91(2) of the Constitution. They are

(1) the impugned legislation must be part of a general regulatory scheme;
(2) the scheme must be monitored by the continuing oversight of a regulatory agency;
(3) the legislation must be concerned with trade as a whole rather than with a particular industry;

(4) the legislation should be of a nature that the provinces jointly or severally would be constitutionally incapable of enacting; and

(5) the failure to include one or more provinces or localities in a legislative scheme would jeopardize the successful operation of the scheme in other parts of the country.[20]

The Evolution of Canadian Federalism

Court rulings seldom put an end to conflicts between Ottawa and the provinces. Instead, they typically become part of the bargaining process between governments. Consider examples such as the *Employment and Social Insurance Act Reference* (1937). The JCPC struck down a federal statute establishing a program to deal with national unemployment, which was followed by negotiations that led to a 1940 constitutional amendment that gave Ottawa authority over unemployment insurance. In *Public Service Board v. Dionne* (1978), the Supreme Court confirmed Ottawa's exclusive jurisdiction over television broadcasting. Immediately afterward, the federal minister of communications announced Ottawa's willingness to negotiate some division of authority with the provinces. Other cases such as *CIGOL v. Government of Saskatchewan* (1978) resulted in further negotiations and new arrangements. Or, as in *Reference re Secession of Quebec* (1998), which dealt with Quebec's right to secede from Canada unilaterally, the Court provided all sides in this ongoing political struggle with ammunition for future sniping.

Judicial review may have shaped the evolution of federalism in a way that the Fathers of Confederation had not planned, but, as Pierre Trudeau observed,

> . . . it has long been the custom in English Canada to denounce the [Judicial Committee of the] Privy Council for its provincial bias; but it should perhaps be considered that if the law lords had not leaned in that direction, Quebec separatism might not be a threat today: it might be an accomplished fact.[21]

Legal disputes over the division of powers are symptomatic of other underlying tensions. These tensions have three main sources:

1. the status of Quebec and the powers of the Quebec state
2. relations between the more heavily industrialized and populous centre of the country and the outlying western and eastern regions (centre–periphery relations)
3. the political and administrative needs of governments

Quebec's Role in Federalism

"What does Quebec want?" The question has been asked countless times over the years by English Canadians. Some genuinely want to know; others ask it out of exasperation. In order to understand what Quebec wants from Canada it is also necessary to consider what the rest of Canada expects from, and is willing to concede to, Quebec.

Quebec's unique role in Canadian federalism derives from two factors. One is its predominantly French-speaking character. Over 80 per cent of the provincial population claims French as their mother tongue, and about 90 per cent of all Canadian francophones reside in Quebec. The second factor is Quebec's size. In 1867, it was the second-most populous province, and Montreal was the hub of Canada's commercial and financial industries. Today, Quebec is still Canada's second-most populous province, accounting for approximately one-quarter of Canada's population. Economically, Quebec's gross provincial product is surpassed only by Ontario.

Quebec's distinctive social and cultural fabric explains why it has made special demands on Canadian federalism. Because of its size, Quebec has the second-largest bloc of seats in the federal Parliament, and because francophones have always been able to control Quebec's provincial legislature, its demands have had a significant impact on the evolution of federalism in two areas: the Constitution and the financial and administrative practices of federalism. We will examine Quebec's impact on the financial and administrative arrangements later in this chapter.

Quebec and the Constitution

Quebec's influence on the Constitution pre-dates Confederation. Between 1848 and 1867 Ontario and Quebec formed United Canada, governed by a single legislature in which the two colonies held equal representation. To become law, a bill had to be approved by a majority of members on both the Ontario and Quebec sides of the legislature, also known as a *double majority*. This was Canada's first experience with the federal principle of regional representation, and it turned out to be a failure because of the many tied votes in the legislature.

Quebec's influence on the Constitution of 1867 is strongly evident. Its representatives insisted on a federal constitution where the provincial government would have authority over matters vital to the preservation of the language, religion, and social institutions of Quebec. Indeed, for decades the clerical and political leaders of French Canada viewed Canadian federalism as a *pact* between two peoples. "Canadian Confederation," declared Henri Bourassa, "is the result of a contract between the two races in Canada, French and English, based on equality and recognizing equal rights and reciprocal duties. Canadian Confederation will last only as long as this equality of rights is recognized as the basis of the public right in Canada, from Halifax to Vancouver."[22]

The equality Bourassa had in mind did not last very long. It was violated in Manitoba where the status of French in the provincial legislature and the educational rights of francophone Catholics were swept away soon after that province entered Confederation. It was also violated in Ontario, where Regulation 17 (1913) banned French instruction from the province's public schools. As a result, French Canada began to identify with Quebec as the only province in which the francophone majority could defend its rights and culture.

The consequences of limiting French Canada to the boundaries of Quebec became apparent by the middle of the twentieth century. As Ottawa became increasingly involved in areas

Co-operative federalism revolves around the idea that federalism can be a decentralized and possibly an unequal sharing of power and financial resources. What does this editorial cartoon seem to be saying about the co-operative federalism that existed from the 1930s to the 1970s?

of provincial jurisdiction, particularly through its spending power and control of direct taxation between 1947 and 1954, the Quebec government became more protective of provincial powers. Indeed, the Quebec government of Maurice Duplessis was the first to reject Ottawa's monopoly over the personal income tax field, imposing its own provincial income tax in 1954. But not until the Quiet Revolution of the 1960s was Quebec's resentment of Ottawa's encroachment onto provincial territory matched by aggressive constitutional demands. The first instance occurred during the negotiations on a public old-age pension scheme (1963–5). Premier Jean Lesage stated that his government would agree to a constitutional amendment giving Ottawa the authority to pass pension legislation only if Quebec were able to opt out of the plan. Ottawa agreed, and so began the practice of provinces being able to opt out of a federal shared-cost program without any financial loss.

Quebec's constitutional demands appeared to become even more ambitious a few years later. In the 1966 provincial election, the Union Nationale party ran on the slogan "Québec d'abord!" ("Quebec first!") The party's leader, Daniel Johnson, called for major constitutional reform that included the transfer of most social and cultural matters to the province, constitutional recognition of Canada's binational character, and exclusive provincial control over the major tax fields then shared with Ottawa. With the exception of international representation for Quebec, however, these demands were not pursued with much vigour during the five years that the Union Nationale was in power (1966–70). As Kenneth McRoberts observed,

> In purely symbolic terms Quebec's demands seemed very significant; Quebec was seeking to assume what many regarded as the trappings of sovereignty. Yet . . . these demands did not directly attack the real distribution of power and responsibilities to the extent that various Lesage demands, such as a separate Quebec Pension Plan, had.[23]

Despite the lack of substantive change in Quebec's constitutional status and powers during this period, the province's nationalist undercurrent was gaining momentum. The creation of the Parti Québécois (PQ) in 1968, under the leadership of René Lévesque, brought under one roof most of the major groups committed to the eventual political independence of Quebec. The Liberal Party of Quebec (LPQ) remained federalist but advocated what amounted to special status for Quebec within Canadian federalism. "Un fédéralisme rentable" ("profitable federalism") was the passionless way in which Liberal leader Robert Bourassa explained Quebec's commitment to Canada.

Constitutional negotiations between Ottawa and the provinces had been ongoing since 1968. The 1970 election of a Liberal government in Quebec appeared to provide an opportunity for successful talks. But when the 11 heads of government met in Victoria in 1971, Quebec's price for agreeing to a constitutional amendment formula and a charter of rights was higher than Ottawa was willing to pay.[74] Quebec demanded constitutional supremacy, as well as the fiscal means to pay for programs in social policy areas that Ottawa controlled such as family allowances, unemployment insurance, employment training, and old-age pensions. Ottawa went

Canadian Spotlight

BOX 7.2   Important Examples of Federal–Provincial Co-operation

1931   Progressive Conservative prime minister R.B. Bennett hosts a "dominion–provincial conference" on the Statute of Westminster.

1963   Liberal prime minister Lester Pearson brings together the 10 premiers to discuss a Canada Pension Plan.

1981   Liberal prime minister Pierre Trudeau hosts a federal–provincial conference on the patriation on the Constitution in 1982. Quebec premier René Lévesque accuses the other premiers of betraying Quebec after they had agreed to patriation. He dubs their duplicitous meeting the "night of the long knives." Quebec has yet to sign the agreement.

1987   Progressive Conservative prime minister Brian Mulroney convenes the premiers to agree to the Meech Lake Accord, which was designed to recognize Quebec as a "distinct society," give the provinces more power, and get Quebec to sign the Constitution. The accord failed to pass in every provincial legislature.

2004   Liberal prime minister Paul Martin meets the premiers and concludes a $41-billion, 10-year health-care funding agreement.

Source: Robert Benzie, "When Feds and Provinces Co-operate," *Toronto Star*, 1 September 2015, A4.

some way toward meeting these demands. But the Trudeau government refused to concede the principle of provincial supremacy over social policy and would not provide a constitutional guarantee that provinces would receive financial compensation for operating their own programs in these areas. The federal–provincial compromise reached in Victoria fell apart days later in Quebec, where the deal was seen as constitutional entrenchment of the status quo.

After Quebec's rejection of the Victoria Charter, the Bourassa government adopted a piecemeal strategy for changing federalism, negotiating with Ottawa on single issues. It was unsuccessful, however, in extracting any major concessions from a federal government that believed provincial powers were too great and opposed to special status for Quebec.

A different strategy was followed by the PQ government of René Lévesque after it came to power in 1976. The PQ was committed to holding a provincial referendum on its option of political sovereignty for Quebec, combined with an economic association with the rest of Canada. Instead of confrontation with Ottawa, the Lévesque government pursued a gradualist strategy of providing "good government." This required some degree of co-operation with Ottawa, given the intricate network of intergovernmental programs and agreements, while attempting to convince the Quebec population of the merits of sovereignty-association—a term generally understood to mean a politically sovereign Quebec that would be linked to Canada through some sort of commercial union or free trade agreement. The two governments co-operated on many new capital spending projects, on management of the economy, and on immigration policy. The PQ government even participated in federal–provincial talks on constitutional reform in 1978–9. All this occurred against the background of the looming referendum on the PQ's separatist option.

Sovereignty-association was rejected by Quebec voters in May 1980. But they re-elected the PQ to office in 1981. It was thus a PQ government that participated in the constitutional negotiations on "renewed federalism" that the federal Liberal government had initiated after the Quebec referendum. But it was also a PQ government that refused to sign the 1981 constitutional accord that became the Constitution Act, 1982. The PQ's refusal was hardly surprising given that none of the demands that Quebec governments had made since the 1960s were included in the accord. Even Quebec Liberals rejected it. Although the legality of the Constitution Act, 1982 was not in doubt, its political legitimacy was. The government of the country's second-largest province, and home to 90 per cent of Canada's francophones, had not agreed to the most significant changes to the Constitution since 1867.

The return of Robert Bourassa and the Liberals in the 1985 provincial election appeared to reflect the muted tenor of Quebec nationalism in the post-referendum era. Change had also taken place in Ottawa. Prime Minister Brian Mulroney, who was elected in 1984, did not share Pierre Trudeau's view that the provinces were too powerful and that Quebec needed some form of special status. Conditions seemed propitious, according to Mulroney, for "bringing Quebec into the constitutional family."

It was not to be. The Quebec government put forward a package of five demands that had to be met before it would agree to the 1982 constitutional reforms. These proposals, agreed to by Ottawa and all the provincial premiers on 30 April 1987, formed the basis of the Meech Lake Accord. As we saw in Chapter 6, these constitutional proposals died on the drawing board

sovereignty-association
a term generally understood to mean a politically sovereign Quebec that would be linked to Canada through some sort of commercial union or free trade agreement

The Canadian "night of the long knives," 5 November, 1981, when "a radiant Trudeau announced the deal that had been reached with the nine provinces" and a "fuming Lévesque looked on."[25]

in 1990, and two years later, in 1992, the Charlottetown proposals for constitutional reform, which offered Quebec even more and also brought Aboriginal Canadians to the table, were defeated in a national referendum.

In the wake of the Charlottetown Accord's rejection, politicians of all stripes fled from the constitutional issue. It was not an issue in the 1993 federal election campaign, at least not outside Quebec. In Quebec, however, these matters were kept before the voters by the Bloc Québécois, led by Lucien Bouchard. The Bloc's raison d'être was, of course, to achieve political independence for Quebec. Their success in capturing 54 of Quebec's 75 seats in the House of Commons may not have been a vote for separation, but it demonstrated the depth of Quebec voters' dissatisfaction with federalism.

Despite their obvious wish to avoid the constitutional quagmire, the federal Liberal government elected in 1993 was forced to confront the issue of separation following the 1994 election of the PQ in Quebec. The PQ were committed to holding a referendum on Quebec independence within a year of their election. When the referendum campaign began in September 1995, there appeared to be little enthusiasm among Québécois for the PQ's separatist vision. The federalist campaign relied on messages intended to convince Quebecers that they would suffer economically if the province voted "yes." About halfway through the campaign, however, leadership of the "yes" side passed from Quebec premier Jacques Parizeau to Bloc Québécois leader Lucien Bouchard. Support for independence took off, due largely to Bouchard's charismatic style and

"Oui" supporters rally on the floor of the Palais de congrès in Montreal as they wait for the results of the 1995 referendum vote (left); "Non" supporters react to poll results as the pro-Canada vote inches up to 50 per cent en route to a slim victory in the 1995 sovereignty referendum (right).

emotional connection with francophone Quebecers, but also due to an uninspired federalist campaign. Prime Minister Jean Chrétien stayed on the sidelines until polls showed the "yes" side to be leading. His initial refusal to make any offer to Quebec wavered when he suggested that he supported constitutional recognition of Quebec as a "distinct society" and a Quebec veto over constitutional reform. On 30 October 1995, the "no" side emerged with the narrowest of victories: 49.6 per cent against independence, 48.5 per cent for it.

The federal Liberals' uncertain performance in the referendum campaign and their reluctance to deal with Quebec's demands and constitutional reform may have been due to Canadians' reactions to constitutional issues, which ranged from indifference to deep hostility. But it may also have been due to their inability to formulate a positive response to the sovereignty option proposed by Quebec nationalists. This inability can be traced to the Liberal model of federalism that took shape during the Trudeau era. Although not a centralist model, it assumes that a strong central government is essential to Canadian unity. Moreover, this model is generally opposed to what is called **asymmetrical federalism**, the constitutional recognition of differences in the status and powers of provincial governments; in particular, it is against a constitutional entrenchment of special status for Quebec. The Constitution Act, 1982, particularly in the Charter and the denial of a right of constitutional veto to any single province, embodies this vision of federalism.

This model is hotly contested not only by the separatists but also by Quebec's nationalist-federalists such as the Liberal Party of Quebec. They argue that to keep Quebecers interested in federalism, constitutional reforms should include a recognition of Quebec's special responsibility for the survival of the French language in Canada and a veto over constitutional change. Since Trudeau stepped down as party leader in 1984, the federal Liberals have shown a willingness to concede many of those demands. However, their enthusiasm for constitutional reforms has been tempered by mixed feelings among voters in Ontario and downright

asymmetrical federalism the constitutional recognition of differences in the status and powers of provincial governments

hostility in Western Canada, and by a loyalty among some Liberals to Trudeau's brand of no-special-status-for-Quebec federalism.

In the wake of the close call for federalists in the 1995 Quebec referendum, when a clear majority of francophones voted for the sovereignty option, the federal Liberal Party visibly distanced itself from the Trudeau era. Only weeks after the referendum the Liberal government introduced a motion

1. recognizing Quebec as a distinct society
2. assigning the province a veto over constitutional change (Ontario and British Columbia were also assigned veto power, as were the Prairie and Atlantic regions if at least two provinces representing more than 50 per cent of the regional population opposed a proposed amendment)
3. transferring to Quebec some authority for job training

The first two of this trio of reforms have clear constitutional implications. While this motion did not change the written Constitution, it did change the Constitution in an informal way. Likewise, the resolution introduced by the Conservative government and passed by the House of Commons in 2006, recognizing Quebec as "a nation within a united Canada," does not change the constitutional status of Quebec in any formal way. But it arguably conferred a sort of de facto special status on Quebec in matters of constitutional reform. In fact, these measures marked a return to a tradition of flexibility in Canadian federalism that pre-dates Pierre Trudeau's entry into federal politics. It is a tradition familiar to students of the British Constitution and of Canadian federalism alike, whereby constitutional change is the result not of formal amendments to the written Constitution but of developments in policy and practice whose status is greater than that of ordinary laws but not quite "written in stone."

Centre–Periphery Relations

Geography is a central feature of Canadian life. Canada spans five and a half time zones and occupies the second-largest land mass of any country, and yet the narrow belt that runs between Windsor and Montreal—the "industrial heartland" of Canada—is home to over 55 per cent of Canada's population and generates about 60 per cent (2007) of national income and production. Ontario and Quebec together account for just under 60 per cent of the 338 seats in the House of Commons. Despite significant population and economic growth in Western Canada, no national political party can hope to form a government without substantial support from the voters of at least one, and usually both, of these provinces. They form Canada's *centre*, in terms of both their political and economic power.

Predictably, the governments of Ontario and Quebec carry greater weight in Canadian federalism than those of the other provinces. The other eight provincial governments preside over regions whose interests have usually been subordinated by Ottawa to those of Central Canada. In this sense these other provinces constitute Canada's *peripheries*, situated on the edge of national politics. As we discussed elsewhere, resentment toward Central Canada and the federal government has deep roots in these provinces, particularly in the West. A short list of their historical grievances includes a tariff policy that for a century protected manufacturing jobs and corporate profits in Ontario and Quebec; the perceived insensitivity of the country's Toronto- and Montreal-based financial institutions to Western interests; until recently, Ottawa's treatment of the petroleum resources concentrated in the West; investment and spending decisions by the federal government; official bilingualism; and the perception of Ottawa's favouritism toward Quebec's interests. As Donald Smiley has written, "there are dangers that Canadian problems will be resolved almost entirely within the framework of the heartland of the country with the progressive alienation from national affairs of those who live on the peripheries."[26]

The federal principle of regional representation is embodied in the Canadian Senate and is practised by prime ministers in selecting cabinet ministers and in other federal appointments. And yet, this federal deference to regionalism has not provided these regions with what they believe to be adequate influence in Ottawa. **Intra-state federalism**—the representation and accommodation of regional interests within national political institutions—has been an abysmal failure. Deprived of this influence, the peripheral regions have tended to rely on their provincial governments to promote their interests.

intra-state federalism
the representation and accommodation of regional interests within national political institutions

The fact that more MPs are elected from Ontario and Quebec than from all other provinces combined has been the root cause of Ottawa's tendency to favour Central Canada. This tendency has been reinforced by the ideological bias of Canadian politics to interpret Canadian history and identity in terms of experiences that are more germane to Central Canada than to the peripheral regions. The Central Canadian identity is based on a concept of "Canada" that has two sources: a *counter-revolutionary/Loyalist tradition*, which rejected the values and political institutions of the United States; and a *cultural dualism*, which is so important to its political history. Neither of these experiences is central to the identity and political consciousness of Western Canadians.[27] In the Maritimes, too, the national myths, symbols, and identities associated with "Canada" often have had little relationship to their experience.[28]

The subordinate interests and cultural values of the peripheral regions of the country have often been reflected in relations between Ottawa and the provincial governments of the peripheries. For example, Ottawa has exercised its constitutional power to disallow provincial laws 112 times, but only a few of these were Ontario or Quebec laws.[29] When Manitoba joined Confederation in 1870, and again when Saskatchewan and Alberta became provinces in 1905, they did so without control of their public lands. For some time, Ottawa retained control to promote its own nation-building strategy relating to railway construction, Western settlement,[30] and control over natural resources.[31] Of course, these provinces received subsidies from Ottawa as compensation for the revenue they were deprived of. However, they never considered the compensation adequate for the quasi-colonial status imposed on them by Ottawa.

There is nothing subtle about the disallowance or denial of provincial constitutional powers. Today, grievances against Ottawa are about less blatant forms of policy discrimination against the interests of the peripheries. Among the items perennially on this list are claims that Ottawa does too little to support Prairie grain farmers or the east coast fishing industry, and that the federal government's spending decisions unfairly favour Ontario and Quebec.

Even in provinces like Alberta, British Columbia, and Saskatchewan, which are wealthy by Canadian standards, a sense of powerlessness is a major component of their provincial politics. "The West," observes Alberta historian Doug Owram, "has never felt in control of its own destiny. None of the wealth of recent years has eased this feeling. In fact, the tremendous wealth of the region merely sharpens the contrast with the political powerlessness that exists on the national level."[32] Having an Albertan, Stephen Harper, as prime minister from 2006 to 2015 had taken the edge off this sentiment, but it has not disappeared entirely. The outraged reaction of Albertans, when, several weeks after the 2008 federal election, the opposition parties attempted to dislodge the Conservatives from power and replace them with a coalition government supported by the Bloc Québécois, showed that the region is still very conscious of the long decades when

Newfoundland discusses alienation with other provinces. Given Canada's large geographic size, to what extent do you believe it is possible for the country to practise federalism and not have certain regions feel some degree of alienation?

it was on the outside of federal politics, looking in. After the election of a Conservative majority government in May 2011, and its growing population and economic strength, the West seemed to have become less resentful of what it perceives to be the domination of national politics by Ontario and Quebec. Nonetheless, in a study commissioned by the Canada West Foundation, Loleen Berdahl argued that although Western dissatisfaction with Ottawa had declined under the Conservative government, long-standing sentiments of resentment and mistrust could be reawakened by a change in political circumstances.[33] In fact, not two days after the Conservative majority was replaced by a Liberal majority in the 2015 general election, some Western Canadians were calling for an "Independent Republic of Western Canada."[34]

State Interests and Intergovernmental Conflict

The fact that Quebec is overwhelmingly francophone gives it a special set of interests that any Quebec government feels bound to defend. Likewise, grain farming and resource extraction in Saskatchewan, petroleum in Alberta, the automotive industry in Ontario, and forestry in

British Columbia shape the policies of these provincial governments on taxation, trade, and other policies affecting these interests. Each province comprises a set of economic, social, and cultural interests that influence the demands each government makes on federalism. Intergovernmental conflict, then, is essentially a clash of conflicting regional interests.

Governments do not simply reflect societal interests, however. They actively shape these interests through their policies, sometimes deliberately and other times inadvertently. Moreover, governments have their own political and administrative interests, the pursuit of which may have nothing to do with the interests of those they represent. "Canadian federalism," Alan Cairns has argued, "is about governments, governments that are possessed of massive human and financial resources, that are driven by purposes fashioned by elites, and that accord high priority to their own long-term institutional self-interest."[35] The *state-centred* interpretation of federalism maintains that conflicts between governments are likely to be generated or influenced by the "institutional self-interest" of politicians and bureaucrats.

The evidence for this view is overwhelming. Intergovernmental turf wars over taxation and jurisdictions often seem remote from the concerns of Canadian citizens. For example, in its 2013 budget, Ottawa proposed the creation of a Canada Job Grant program for the unemployed. The provincial governments reacted with a solid wall of opposition, demanding both that their own job training programs not be replaced by this new shared-cost program and that they have the right to opt out of the Canada Job Grant program with compensation to pay for their own provincial programs.[36]

From the unemployed person's perspective, this provincial grievance was totally irrelevant. But from the state's point of view, the ability to control revenue sources and legislative competence affects the ability of both federal and provincial politicians to pursue their respective interests in re-election, in career advancement, and in personal prestige, as well as their own conception of the "public interest." The same may be said of the personal careers, ambitions, and fortunes of bureaucratic officials who have a vested interest in their organizations and programs.

A concept that has often been associated with the provincial governments of Alberta and Quebec[37] is **province building**. As the term suggests, it occurs when the political administrative needs of governments are reinforced by the demands of province-oriented economic interests. This is the opposite of the **nation-building** orientation of Sir John A. Macdonald's post-Confederation government, and has been defined as the "recent evolution of more powerful and competent provincial administrations which aim to manage socioeconomic change in their territories and which are in essential conflict with the central government."[38] But the Ontario government is as "powerful and competent" as these other provincial states, and no one would accuse Ontario of "province building." Ontario's pivotal status in Canadian politics, however, based on its large population and economic importance, has meant that it generally has been able to count on a sympathetic hearing in Ottawa. Aside from a few recent instances of complaining about fiscal imbalances in the federal equalization payments to the provinces, aggressive and persistent "fed-bashing" by Ontario provincial politicians has not been a popular tactic because it has not been necessary for the achievement of their goals. In other respects, however, Ontario governments have not lagged behind their more aggressive counterparts.

province building
the reinforcing of political administrative needs of governments by the demands of province-oriented economic interests

nation building
the recent evolution of more powerful and competent provincial administrations which aim to manage socio-economic change in their territories and which are in essential conflict with the central government

Intergovernmental Relations

The Constitution, as we have seen, does not establish a neat division of legislative and taxation powers between Ottawa and the provinces. The chief sources of public revenue are shared between the two levels of government. The same is true of their involvement in most major policy fields. Defence and monetary policy come closest to being exclusive federal terrain, although provincial governments do not hesitate to express their views on such issues as the location of armed forces bases, major defence purchases, and interest rates. On the provincial side, local functions such as snow removal, garbage collection, and sidewalk maintenance are typically free of federal involvement—but not entirely, because the money that Ottawa transfers annually to the provinces affects how much they in turn transfer to their municipalities, thereby affecting the municipalities' ability to carry out these local functions.

Divided jurisdiction has given rise to a sprawling and complicated network of federal–provincial relations. This network has often been compared to an iceberg, only a small part of which is visible to the eye. The "visible" tip of intergovernmental relations involves the much publicized meetings of the prime minister and provincial premiers (first ministers' conferences) as well as meetings of provincial premiers. Less publicized, but far more frequent, are hundreds of annual meetings between federal and provincial cabinet ministers and bureaucrats. Many of these meetings take place in the context of ongoing federal–provincial structures like the Continuing Committee on Fiscal and Economic Matters, established in 1955, and the Economic and Regional Development Agreements negotiated between Ottawa and the less affluent provinces. Others are generated by the wide range of shared-cost activities that link the two levels of government, from major spending programs such as the Canada Health Transfer to smaller federal subsidies such as those for official minority-language education. In 2013, 79 federal–provincial meetings took place at the level of ministers, deputy ministers, and other senior officials.[39]

Executive federalism is a term sometimes used to describe the relations between cabinet ministers and officials of the two levels of government. The lack of input from the public or the legislatures, the lack of distinction between provincial and federal responsibilities, and the secrecy that generally cloaks the negotiations and the decision-making process, have generated accusations that executive federalism is undemocratic, for several reasons. First, it undermines the role of elected legislatures, whose role is usually limited to ratifying *faits accomplis*. Second, an agreement to jointly finance a program or to share responsibilities in a particular field makes it difficult for citizens to determine which level of government should be responsible for specific policies. Third, executive federalism provides no meaningful opportunities for public debate (including political parties, interest groups, and individual Canadians) of important intergovernmental issues that directly affect citizens, such as health-care services, welfare, and post-secondary education.

Donald Smiley lists three other concerns about executive federalism:[40]

- *It distorts the political agenda.* Executive federalism has a territorial bias. It reinforces the significance of territorially concentrated interests and of the provincial governments that represent them, at the same time as it undervalues the importance of other interests.

executive federalism a term sometimes used to describe the relations between cabinet ministers and officials of the two levels of government

- *It fuels government expansion.* Competitive relations between Ottawa and the provinces have produced inefficient duplication, as each level of government has its own bureaucracy to pursue similar goals.
- *It perpetuates intergovernmental conflict.* The increasing sophistication of executive federalism, conducted through specialized bureaus staffed by intergovernmental affairs specialists, reduces the likelihood of resolving federal–provincial disputes. This happens because specialized intergovernmental affairs bureaus, which exist in all provinces and at the federal level, and the experts who staff them tend to perceive issues in terms of the powers and jurisdiction of their particular government. Intergovernmental conflict is in a sense institutionalized by the fact that what is perceived to be at stake are the power, resources, and prestige of one's government.

The practitioners of executive federalism argue that policy making carried out in a closed fashion, dominated by cabinet ministers and bureaucratic elites, is an unavoidable fact of life under a federal constitution with "overlapping powers." Is it realistic to imagine that complex administrative and financial agreements can be negotiated in public forums? Why condemn executive federalism for traits that are deeply embedded in Canadian policy making generally? The fact is that the characteristics of executive federalism are out of sync with the less deferential political culture that has evolved in Canada over the last generation. Governments continue to negotiate behind closed doors, and the constitutional overlap, competition, and ambiguity persist, but public acceptance of executive federalism and elitist policy making is much weaker today than in decades past.

The fact that a meeting between Prime Minister Harper and the premiers did not occur between 2009 and the 2015 general election warrants some comment. Prime Minister Harper's critics charged that he avoided these meetings because of a decision-making style averse to circumstances he was unable to control. His spokespersons argued that Harper had more than 250 face-to-face meetings and telephone conversations with premiers between his election in 2006 and the summer of 2013. Other supporters argued that this standoffish approach reflected Mr. Harper's personal preference for a one-on-one style as well as the Conservative Party's belief that the provinces should be left to manage their own affairs without federal interference. And, after all, had history not shown that first ministers' meetings too often resulted in a wall of provincial demands for more money from Ottawa?[41]

The Justin Trudeau government, on the other hand, made federal–provincial collaboration on a broad range of matters a cornerstone of their policy initiatives. Trudeau and the premiers had their first meeting within five months of his coming to office, and by July 2016, with the encouragement of the federal government, the provinces and territories had agreed to what was called an "unprecedented Canadian free trade deal."[42]

Financing Federalism

From the very beginning, money has been at the centre of intergovernmental relations. The Confederation agreement included an annual per capita subsidy that Ottawa would pay to all

Jonathan Hayward/Canadian Press

Until the July 2016 trade deal between the territories and the provinces, the general consensus in business was that trade between Canada, the US, and Mexico was less restricted than that between the provinces.

provincial governments.[43] Moreover, the new federal government agreed to assume liability for the debts of the provinces as they stood in 1867.[44] Taxation powers were divided between the two levels of government, with Ottawa receiving what were at the time the major sources of public revenue.

These financial arrangements have never been adequate. The root of the problem is that the provinces' legislative responsibilities proved to be much more extensive and expensive than the founders had anticipated. This has been referred to as the *fiscal gap*. Provincial governments attempted to fill this gap between their revenues and their expenditures through an array of provincial taxes such as licence fees, succession duties, and personal and corporate income taxes. In addition, the provinces pressed Ottawa for more money. Indeed, two years after Confederation the federal subsidy paid to Nova Scotia was increased, setting an important precedent: federal–provincial financial relations are determined by governments, not by the Constitution.

As Ottawa conceded *tax room*—in particular, revenue sources like the personal income tax—the provinces' revenues improved steadily between the 1950s and the 1970s (see Figure 7.1). Today, combined provincial and local revenues exceed those of the federal government. But at the same time, provincial dependence on subsidies from Ottawa remains high in several provinces. In the case of the poorest provinces, money from Ottawa currently accounts for about half of their total revenue. Part of this dependence has been encouraged by Ottawa through **shared-cost programs**, provincially administered programs where Ottawa's financial contribution is geared to what a province spends. Until 1995 the major shared-cost program was the Canada Assistance Plan (CAP), which financed welfare and other provincial social services. That year, CAP was replaced with the Canada Health and Social Transfer, which was not geared

shared-cost program
a provincially administered program where Ottawa's financial contribution is geared to what the province spends

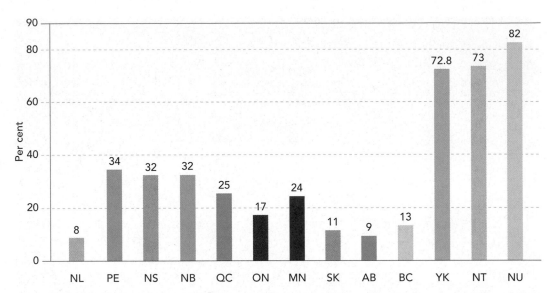

FIGURE 7.1 Federal Cash Transfers as Percentage of Provincial/Territorial Government Revenues, 2012–2013

Source: Canada, Department of Finance, Federal Support to Provinces and Territories, 2016-17. http://www.fin.gc.ca/fedprov/mtp-eng.asp.

block funding
Ottawa's financial contribution geared to the previous year's subsidy plus an amount calculated on the basis of growth in the recipient province's gross product

to provincial spending. Federal grants for health care and post-secondary education also were launched on a shared-cost basis, but were converted by Ottawa into **block funding** programs where Ottawa's financial contribution is geared to the previous year's subsidy plus an amount calculated on the basis of growth in the recipient province's gross product. The federal government argued that the shared-cost formula did not encourage the provinces to control program costs. Under block funding, Ottawa is not obliged to match provincial spending, and indeed the effect of the switch to block funding has been to transfer an increasing share of the burden of health care and post-secondary education costs onto the provinces.

Not surprisingly, provincial governments have made several criticisms about the shift in financial burden. First, they claim that it is unfair for Ottawa to encourage them to spend more on social services by offering to share program costs on a matching basis and then backing out of the financial arrangement. Second, the provinces' ability to increase their own sources of revenue to compensate for reduced federal transfer payments is limited by the fact that they share all the major tax fields with Ottawa. Unless the federal government is willing to give up some tax room to the provinces, provincial governments face the hard choice of increasing the total tax burden on their citizens. Third, any reduction in Ottawa's commitment to financing provincial social services hurts the poorer provinces more than it does the wealthier ones. As Figure 7.1 shows, the Maritime provinces in particular depend on federal transfers for maintaining the level of social services at comparable levels to other provinces.

Some of the money that Ottawa transfers to the provinces carries conditions as to how it must be spent. These are called conditional grants. Transfers with no strings attached are called unconditional grants. Important examples of both include the following:

- The block transfer that Ottawa makes to the provinces under the CHT and the CST must be spent on health care, post-secondary education, and social services previously covered under CAP. Previous residency in the province should not be a condition for receiving benefits from provincial social assistance programs: need should be the only requirement.
- The Canada Health Act, 1984 allows Ottawa to reduce its payment to provincial governments that permit physicians to extra-bill their patients. The terms of the CHT and CST also specify that provinces must respect the principles of the Canada Health Act, 1965 (portability of coverage between provinces, comprehensiveness of provincial plans, universality, public funding, and public administration).

According to a complex negotiated formula, **equalization payments** are paid to provincial governments whose per capita tax revenues fall below the average of the two most affluent provinces. Equalization accounts for about one-quarter of all federal cash transfers to the provinces and about one-fifth of the total revenue of the poorest provincial governments. There are no spending conditions. Table 7.4 provides a breakdown of federal transfers to the provinces.

equalization payment funds paid to a provincial government whose per capita tax revenues fall below the average of the two most affluent provinces

TABLE 7.4 Federal Transfers to Provinces and Territories, 2005–2015

Major Transfers	(millions of dollars)									
	2005–6	2006–7	2007–8	2008–9	2009–10	2010–11	2011–12	2012–13	2013–14	2014–15
Canada Health Transfer	20,310	20,140	21,729	22,768	24,476	25,672	26,952	28,569	30,283	32,114
Canada Social Transfer	8,415	8,500	9,607	10,552	10,857	11,179	11,514	11,859	12,215	12,582
Equalization	10,907	10,907	11,535	12,925	13,462	14,372	14,659	15,423	16,105	16,669
Offshore accounts	219	386	563	663	645	869	787	443	350	203
Territorial formula financing	2,058	2,118	2,279	2,313	2,498	2,664	2,876	3,111	3,288	3,469
Other payments					74	525	952	680	56	
Total federal support	41,909	42,680	47,102	49,758	52,736	55,281	57,539	60,085	62,297	65,037
Change from 2005–6		+.771	+5,193	+7,849	+10,827	+13,372	+15,830	+18,176	+20,389	+23,128
Per capita allocation (dollars)	1,301	1,312	1,434	1,499	1,570	1,628	1,683	1,731	1,774	1,831

Source: Canada, Department of Finance, Federal Support to Provinces and Territories, 2016-17. http://www.fin.gc.ca/fedprov/mtp-eng.asp.

The adequacy of federal transfers is not the only issue that has set Ottawa against the provincial governments. The provinces have complained that shared-cost programs distort provincial spending priorities because of the enticement of matching federal grants, and that Ottawa's spending power also permits undue federal interference in provincial jurisdictions. The government of Quebec has been most insistent about this. Indeed, there are several instances since the 1950s of Quebec governments declining monies or declining participation in shared-cost programs. Both the Meech Lake and Charlottetown Accords included a provision for Ottawa to provide "reasonable compensation" to provinces choosing not to participate in a new national shared-cost program, as long as their own program was "compatible with the national objectives." Critics argued that this eroded the **national standards** in social policy, which linked federal monies to Canada-wide standards in the delivery of social programs, through which the federal government hoped to have uniformity of service for all Canadians and create a "national social union." Defenders claimed that this particular section merely constitutionalized a long-standing practice in Canadian federalism.

national standards
Canada-wide standards in the delivery of social programs to ensure uniformity of service for all Canadians and create a "national social union"

Democracy Watch

BOX 7.3 Making a Case for Federalism

Pros of Federalism

- *Promotes loyalty.* Residents of provinces become attached to their regional identities, and giving these regions power fosters a sense of belonging.
- *Makes running the country easier.* Canada is a large geographic region, and its population is diverse; giving power to regional authorities makes the federal government's job easier.
- *Fosters pluralism.* By giving provincial and municipal governments power, the federal government allows the diverse populations in each region to interact with their local officials and tackle issues unique to each area.
- *Prevents tyranny.* With provinces responsible for specific programs and services, there is protection against the federal government dictating how things should be run.

Cons of Federalism

- *Inhibits national cohesion.* Allowance for provincial independence can make it difficult for various regions to see eye-to-eye.
- *Inhibits accountability.* A blurring of the boundaries between provincial and federal jurisdiction can make it difficult to sort out what went wrong when policies and/or programs fail.

The Federal Spending Power, National Standards, and the Social Union

In the 1990s it became popular to vilify certain provincial governments, such as the Progressive Conservative governments of Ralph Klein in Alberta and Mike Harris in Ontario, for having undermined national standards in social programs. One of the major threats to national standards, however, came from Ottawa's shrinking financial commitment to provincially administered social programs. Federal transfers as a share of provincial program spending fell from 21 per cent in 1986–7 to 16 per cent in 1996–7.[45] Wealthier provinces, including Ontario, Alberta, and British Columbia, faced the largest burden of these cuts.

Ottawa's retreat from financing provincial social programs became unmistakable in the 1995 federal budget. Liberal finance minister Paul Martin's "new vision of Confederation" replaced the shared-cost programs that paid for welfare and social services, as well as the funding for health and post-secondary education, with a single block transfer called the Canada Health and Social Transfer (CHST). The CHST institutionalized the ad hoc freezes and caps on transfers that had been imposed from the early 1980s. It did so, in Ottawa's words, by ensuring that "the amounts transferred will not be determined by provincial spending decisions (as under cost-sharing)."[46] The transition to block funding under the CHST was argued to have the following beneficial effects:

- Provinces will no longer be subject to rules stipulating which expenditures are eligible for cost-sharing or not.
- Provinces will be free to pursue their own . . . approaches to social security reform.
- The expense of administering cost-sharing will be eliminated.
- Federal expenditures will no longer be driven by provincial decisions on how, and to whom, to provide social assistance and social services.[47]

Provinces would not be free to do whatever they pleased under the new fiscal arrangements: health care and social assistance were two areas where national standards would be maintained. Critics noted that even if Ottawa were able to enforce national standards, the lumping together of Ottawa's transfer for health care, social assistance, and post-secondary education under the CHST would permit provinces to shift spending from politically unpopular welfare programs to more popular health care and education.

The CHST appeared to end the notion of shared-cost programs and thus mark a retreat from Ottawa's commitment to maintaining national standards in social policy: a commitment that has always depended on the federal spending power. In 2004 the CHST was divided into the Canada Health Transfer and the Canada Social Transfer, a change that provided greater transparency in identifying how much money was being transferred for specific provincial purposes.

Inside Politics

BOX 7.4 | Two Former Premiers and Two Views on Federal Transfers

For

No Canadian should have his or her life chances determined solely by geography. Canadians enjoy a political culture much like a family; we are all responsible for each other. These principles, enshrined in our Constitution, differentiate us from our friends in the United States where no such program exists. The vehicle for leveling the national playing field is the country's equalization program. Because of equalization, the gap between richer and poorer provinces has been reduced. The Canadian people understand the principle. [Polls demonstrate] that overwhelming majorities in each province support equalization.

Still, ideological opponents of equalization argue that such a program is wrong; they claim that it interferes with the operation of market forces and perpetuates poverty in some regions of the country. These claims are demonstrably wrong. Equalization has never prevented provinces from developing their own natural resources. Saskatchewan's oil and natural gas industries were developed even though that province's equalization payments declined as a result. Equalization did not obstruct the mining of potash in Saskatchewan, nickel in Manitoba, and hydroelectric development in Quebec, Manitoba, and Newfoundland and Labrador. There is no reason for it to be otherwise in the future. Furthermore, Ontario has always supported equalization, recognizing as it does that a strong Canada also strengthens that province.

—Howard Pawley, former premier of Manitoba (1981–8) and adjunct professor, University of Windsor, in *Opinion Canada* 7, 10 (17 March 2005). Reprinted with permission of the author.

Against

I think it was Karl Marx who once said that religion is the opiate of the masses. Well, I can tell you that federal dependency is the opiate of this region, Atlantic Canada. Dependency—unemployment insurance, welfare cheques, transfer payments—have all become a narcotic to us to which we have become addicted. And there is not a person in this room that can tell you and me that we have not been influenced and affected, and had our behaviour modified by being part of that culture, because it shaped everything that we are. We know it to be true. We know it better than anybody else in Canada.

Looking at experience from all over the world, I can tell you that those jurisdictions which establish low and predictable corporate tax regimes end up resulting in much better growth, and long-term growth, and a much better environment for business to prosper.

What we need to do is get rid of all of the make-work projects and the money we spend transferring people to federal unemployment. We need to get rid of all those programs and either get rid of the taxes low-income people pay or offer income supplementation so they are always better off working in a job. If we do that, if we change that incentive system, it will have a powerful impact on Atlantic Canada.

I despise the people who whine and snivel about their lot in life within this country. People who tell us that, unless they get their lighthouses saved, they're going to separate from Canada, have no time in my book. We may not like base closures in Atlantic Canada, and we certainly don't like transfer payment cuts . . . but we will not—we will not—consider that an act of alienation or humiliation.

—Frank McKenna, former premier of New Brunswick (1987–97), in a speech to the Atlantic Vision Conference of Atlantic Canadian Premiers in Moncton, NB, 9 October 1997. Reprinted by permission.

Appearances may deceive, however. The Liberals' determination to rein in federal transfers to the provinces was not matched by corresponding decentralization. On the contrary, the Liberal government refused to make concessions on national standards, particularly in regard to the health-care system. Essentially, their message was this: "We will give you fewer and fewer dollars to pay for your health care services, but we will continue to set conditions on how those services must operate."

The Liberals' resolve was put to the test by the Progressive Conservative government of Alberta, which allowed the establishment of private clinics for certain health services like cataract operations, where patients, for a price, could jump the queue of the publicly funded system. In the end, all Ottawa could do was withhold some of the health-care dollars that Alberta would normally receive—not much of a penalty for a wealthy province like Alberta.

Ottawa's retreat from its financial commitment to provincially administered social programs was not well received by provincial governments. Ottawa's success in transforming budget deficits into surpluses in the 1990s was largely due to cuts in transfers to

It seems to have grown since your health care deal with the provinces.

Not to worry, we professionals call it 'asymmetrical federalism'...

CANADA

© Roy Peterson/Artizans

In a 2004 initiative on health care struck between Liberal prime minister Paul Martin and the provincial premiers, Quebec negotiated a separate deal in acknowledgement of its unique health-care system. Some Canadians felt this "special treatment" was unfair, especially since attempts by Alberta to introduce new elements into its system, such as limited private care, had previously been opposed by the federal government. Is allowing each province to strike its own deals with the federal government an advantage or disadvantage of federalism?

the provinces, the use of Employment Insurance fund surpluses as general revenue, and increased federal tax revenues, and had very little to do with cuts to Ottawa's own program spending. From the provinces' point of view, Ottawa's deficit-cutting strategy left them to deal with the politically difficult choices of raising taxes, cutting services, or both. Moreover, the Liberal government's insistence that national standards for health care and welfare would have to be respected was particularly galling.

This was the background to the idea of a Canadian *social union*, a concept that emerged in the wake of the transfer cuts announced in Ottawa's 1995 budget. The social union involves some new set of arrangements for funding and determining program standards in health, welfare, and post-secondary education. Provinces like Alberta and Ontario, who receive the lowest per capita payments under the CHT and CST, tend to see the social union as a commitment to national standards that are negotiated with Ottawa. This is a decentralized version of the social union, under which the control and funding over social programs would shift to the provinces. Ottawa and some transfer-dependent provinces insist on a central role for the feds in financing and maintaining the uniformity of social program standards. Quebec governments have avoided social union negotiations and have insisted that no one has the constitutional authority to interfere with Quebec's autonomy.

Until the 2008 recession the federal government experienced large annual budget surpluses for several years, totalling over $61 billion between 1997 and 2005. But anyone who expected that this would lead to a return to the older model of fiscal federalism, whereby Ottawa

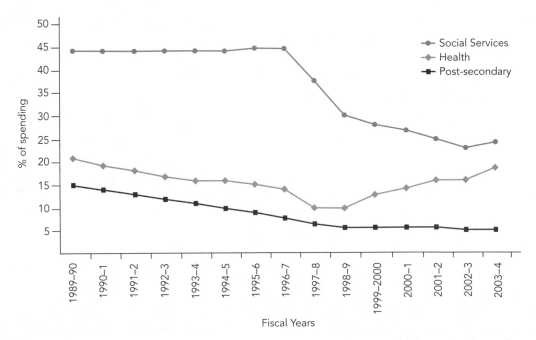

FIGURE 7.2 Federal Social Transfers as a Percentage of Provincial Program Spending, 1989–2003

Source: Department of Finance Canada, Fiscal Reference Tables, October 2004; Statistics Canada, Cansim, table 385–001.

helped the provinces to achieve their social policy objectives, was disappointed. The exception has been health care. As Figure 7.2 shows, the federal share of provincial spending on health care rebounded after the trough experienced in the late 1990s. This rebound continued under the Conservative government from 2006 until 2015. The 2002 report of the Romanow Commission on the Future of Health Care suggested that in order to retain certain standards in health-care delivery, Ottawa's contribution would have to be at least 25 per cent, and in 2005, Parliament legislated an automatic escalator of 6 per cent per year—an increase that was slated to continue until 2014. In 2012 the Parliamentary Budget Officer, Kevin Page, indicated that Ottawa's contributions to health care would keep pace with provincial spending until 2016–17, after which they would be tied to the rate of growth in economy.[48]

Kevin Page and other analysts predicted that increases in health-care spending would continue to outstrip the rate of increase in the economy, but that Ottawa's share of total health-care spending would begin to fall. By the spring of 2016 analysts were reporting that health transfers under the Liberals would be increasing by $1 billion, or 2.8 per cent in 2017–18, to $37.1 billion; however, this would be below the 3 per cent minimum increase promised by the Harper government. The fact is that given the low GDP growth of Canada's economy, Ottawa will be transferring about $5 billion less a year in health-care cash to the provinces by 2020 than it would have under the 6 per cent escalator rate.[49]

Summary

The Canadian federal arrangement is essentially a great compromise of power sharing between competing regional interests and values. It is an agreement by regional governments to give up some of their sovereignty to a central governing authority with a constitutional purpose: economic, political, or both. We have outlined the origins of Canadian federalism and discussed the initial division of powers, which has regularly caused disputes between Ottawa and provincial governments. And the federalism we see in Canada today is likely different from what the Fathers of Confederation envisioned because the power-sharing arrangement has evolved through precedents, through negotiations between Ottawa and the provinces, and through the courts' interpretation of the Constitution in jurisdictional disputes.

Many Canadians may feel a genuine sense of political nationality; however, regional differences continue to exercise significant political influence on provincial and federal issues. Particularly in Quebec, nationalism has sometimes been a competing force and influence within the federation. For instance, many Canadians do not accept Ottawa as a dominant partner in the relationship. There seem to be two interpretations of the nature of federalism in Canada: some, particularly those in French Canada, see federalism as a *compact* between English and French Canada, while others see federalism as an equal-partner *contract* in which the provinces agree to give up some powers to Ottawa. The compact/contract approach is certainly helpful in appreciating the stance that some provinces have taken in their relationship with Ottawa.

Much of the relationship between Ottawa and the provinces has had to do with money. Under the Constitution, the provinces have certain responsibilities, such as health care, education, and social services, that have increased in importance and costs since 1867. And for mostly political reasons, the federal government has gradually agreed to take on a sizable share of the fiscal burden through cost-sharing agreements and equalization payments to the poorest provinces. These are designed to ensure that Canadians receive a minimum standard of care and service across the country.

In post-secondary education and social services, Ottawa has been able to create and administer its own programs. Health care has been an exception; in order to maintain some leverage, Ottawa has had to increase its financial contribution to provincial health-care programs. Nonetheless, because of financial constraints, the scale of federal transfers has to decrease over time from a 50/50 financing formula to closer to 20 per cent. If there is a federalism lesson to be learned from the last 30 years of intergovernmental conflict over health care it is this: sharing the costs of an expensive policy area is a prescription for political and bureaucratic rivalry, muddied accountability, and mutual recriminations.

Review Exercises

1. What are the intergovernmental issues that exist in the province or territory that you live in? Are these issues related to geography, economics, history, or constitutional matters?
2. Draw up a list of issues that would have to be resolved if Quebec were to separate from the rest of Canada. Attach a level of difficulty to each, ranging from 1 (easily resolved) to 10 (impossible to resolve).
3. Does it matter which level of government pays for what share of health-care costs and which level or levels set the rules for health policy? In answering this question be sure to address the issues of constitutionality, political accountability, Canadian values, and taxpayer interests.

Up for Debate

1. Given these pros and cons of federalism, what would be your recommendation and rationale to a government of a currently non-federalist country that is contemplating this style of governance?
2. Resolved: Unitary political systems, such as those of France and Britain, have fewer political problems than those with federal systems, such as those of Canada and the US.
3. Resolved: The federal government does not have an obligation to pay for social services and infrastructure projects that are under the jurisdiction of the provinces and the municipalities.

Starting Points for Research

Bakvis, Herman, and Grace Skogstad, eds. *Canadian Federalism: Performance, Effectiveness, and Legitimacy*, 3rd edn. Toronto: Oxford University Press, 2012.

Cairns, Alan. *Charter versus Federalism: The Dilemmas of Constitutional Reform.* Montreal and Kingston: McGill–Queen's University Press, 1992.

Simeon, Richard. *Political Science and Federalism: Seven Decades of Scholarly Engagement.* Kingston, ON: Institute of Intergovernmental Relations, Queen's University, 2002.

Smith, David E.. *Federalism and the Constitution of Canada.* Toronto: University of Toronto Press, 2010.

Trudeau, Pierre Elliott. *Federalism and the French Canadians.* Toronto: Macmillan, 1968.

CBC Archives and TVO's *The Agenda*

Visit the companion website for *Canadian Democracy: A Concise Introduction* to follow links to audio and video footage related to the main themes of the chapter: www.oupcanada.com/BrooksConcise2e.

Relevant Websites

Visit the companion website for *Canadian Democracy: A Concise Introduction* to browse a collection of websites featuring material related to the key themes of the chapter, an excellent starting point for research: www.oupcanada.com/BrooksConcise2e.

8 How Parliamentary Government Works in Canada

Modern government is a complicated affair. Many of its parts seem to perform no useful function, and it appears to have been assembled without much planning or replacing old parts with new ones. The politics of democracies is not pretty to look at and the purpose of the machinery of government is easily lost. But for all its inelegance and appearance of muddling, parliamentary government does produce results. Laws are passed, regulations are applied, applications are dealt with, cheques are issued, and the innumerable other tasks of governing are carried out. How well these tasks are done, or whether they are done at all, are important questions. But before we

↑ Former US President Barack Obama addresses the House of Commons. The structure and procedures of Canada's parliamentary government are founded on a set of principles, constitutional conventions, and institutional devices that prevent the abuse of power.

Source: BRENDAN SMIALOWSKI/Getty Images.

can answer them, we need an understanding of the machinery itself—the individual parts, the functions they perform, and the relations between them.

This chapter focuses on state institutions at the national level; but Canadians also encounter the machinery of government at the provincial and municipal levels, where the state's activities affect their lives in ways that often seem more direct and significant. Hospitals, schools, police, garbage collection, transit, roads, and water treatment: these are primarily the responsibilities of provincial and local governments. Together, provincial and local governments out-spend and out-tax the federal government.

After reading this chapter on the key components of the machinery of government, you should be able to

1. analyze the working relationships between the three branches of Canadian government to determine how each branch contributes to the management of power and of conflict in Canadian society
2. outline the role and residual powers of the Crown in parliamentary democracy
3. explain the concentration of power in the office of the prime minister and the cabinet
4. discuss the role of central agencies, the bureaucracy, and the regulatory agencies
5. compare the parliamentary and presidential political systems to examine governance in liberal democracies
6. describe the role, influence, and activities of the average member of Parliament (MP)

The Organization of Government

The formal organization of the government of Canada, as portrayed in Figure 8.1, seems deceptively simple. The three branches of government coincide with three major functions of democratic governance: the legislature makes the laws, the executive implements the laws, and the judiciary interprets the laws.

Unlike the American system of government, where the three branches of government are clearly demarcated and constitutionally separated, the Canadian parliamentary government does not have a clear *separation of powers* or a clear system of *checks and balances* to prevent any one branch of government from abusing power. There are many examples. For instance, legislative and executive functions are fused in the office of the prime minister (PM), who is both the head of the legislature and, informally, the head of the executive. The legislature, in fact, is dominated by a small group of its members—the prime minister and the cabinet—who oversee the executive branch. Laws may be debated and passed in the legislature, but these laws typically originate in the executive branch as bills that are seldom expected to change

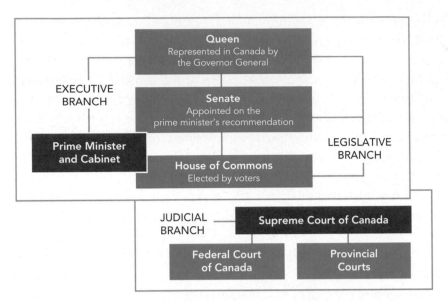

FIGURE 8.1 The Formal Organization of the Canadian Parliamentary System of Government

In this system of government, which is based on the Westminster model from the United Kingdom, there is no clear separation of the branches of government as there is in the republican model, shown in Figure 8.2.

Source: "At Work in the House of Commons," House of Commons, (2008). *The House of Commons Report to Canadians,* http://www.parl.gc.ca/About/House/ReportToCanadians/2008/rtc2008_05-e.html.

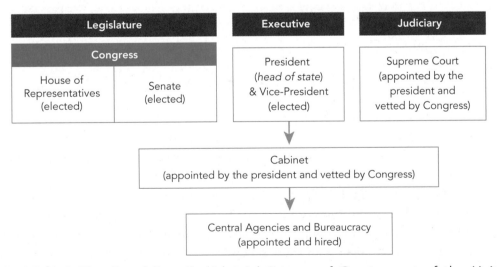

FIGURE 8.2 The Republican-Presidential System of Government of the United States

Note the clear separation of power between the main branches of government, which allows for a system of checks and balances against potential abuses of power.

much. In the case of the judicial branch of government, the courts do not, strictly speaking, involve themselves in the making of laws. In recent times, however, Canadian courts have played a major role in the determination of policy on important matters such as Sunday shopping, abortion, Aboriginal landownership, collective bargaining rights, prostitution, same-sex pension benefits, and the legal definition of marriage. And finally, the bureaucrats whose job it is to implement the laws passed by their political masters in the executive branch often have enormous discretion in determining the actual meaning of laws.

Nevertheless, it would be a mistake to think that there are no checks and balances in the parliamentary system of government. The respective roles of the legislative, executive, and judicial branches are significantly different, and their differences are rooted in our expectations of democratic government that power is not abused and that conflicts are resolved according to the rule of law as outlined in the Constitution:

The legislative branch shall

- represent the people
- be accountable to people through periodic elections
- debate public issues
- provide a forum for competition between political parties
- approve government spending
- make laws

The executive branch shall

- implement the laws
- ensure that the public's business is carried out efficiently, accountably, and in accordance with the law
- be non-partisan at the bureaucratic level, such that non-elected officials faithfully carry out the policies of whatever party forms the government of the day on behalf of the Crown

The judicial branch shall

- be non-partisan and free from interference by the government
- interpret the law's meaning
- not substitute its preferences for those of elected public officials in matters of public policy, as distinct from legal and constitutional interpretation

These democratic expectations are not immutable. Today, many people expect that the bureaucracy should be representative of the population it serves, which may affect bureaucratic recruitment and promotion policies. Some argue that it is neither realistic nor desirable to expect non-elected officials to be politically neutral, and that accountability for policy (as distinct from its implementation) should be shared between politicians and bureaucrats. The elevated status of Canadian courts in the political process since the 1982 Charter of Rights and Freedoms has been welcomed by those who see judges as more likely than politicians to

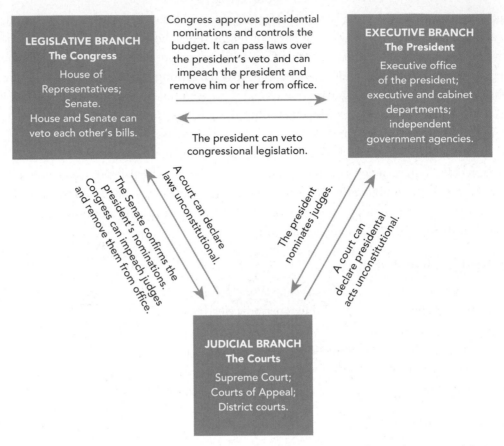

FIGURE 8.3 How the System of Checks and Balances Works in the United States

Source: The Social Studies Help Centre, http://www.socialstudieshelp.com/Images/ChksBalnces.gif

protect rights and promote democracy. Others with more traditional expectations complain the courts are trespassing on turf that properly belongs to the people's elected and accountable representatives. The courts are also expected by many to be representative of Canada's diversity, interests, and values.

In this chapter we discuss the main characteristics and roles of the institutions of Canadian government.

The Executive Branch

The Monarch and the Governor General

constitutional monarchy a system of government with a monarch as a formal head of state that operates within a constitutional framework

Canada is a **constitutional monarchy**: a system of government with a monarch as a formal head of state that operates within a constitutional framework. The monarch, currently Queen Elizabeth II, embodies the authority of the Canadian state. Any action of the government of Canada is taken in the Queen's name,[1] also known as the *Crown*. The monarch has a number of very important duties including

- giving royal assent to new legislation
- the prorogation of Parliament
- the appointing of the prime minister
- deciding when Parliament will be dissolved and a new election held

When she is not in Canada, which is of course most of the time, her duties are carried out by the Governor General, currently His Excellency the Right Honourable David Johnston. Although the Constitution suggests that the role of the monarch is formidable, most Canadians realize that the Queen and Governor General perform mainly symbolic functions. The real decision-making powers of the executive are exercised by the prime minister, who is the head of government and of cabinet.

Constitutional convention is far more important than the discretion of the monarch in matters such as the selection of the prime minister and the dissolution of Parliament. For example, the party that wins a majority of seats in an election gets to form the government, and the choice of prime minister is automatic. Even when no party has a majority, it is understood that the leader of the *party with the most seats* gets the first opportunity to form a government that has the support of a majority in the legislature. If, however, it is clear that the members of the other parties will not support a government led by this person, the Governor General may turn to the leader of another party. A Governor General cannot simply decide that there is no point in convening the legislature and that a new election should be held; a newly elected legislature must be given the opportunity to meet.

Likewise in the case of dissolving Parliament, the monarch's discretion is limited by constitutional conventions. The prime minister's request that Parliament be dissolved and a new election held is usually granted automatically. It is conceivable, though improbable, that in circumstances of minority government the Governor General could refuse such a request and instead ask the leader of another party to try to form a government. The last time this happened was 1926, when Governor General Lord Byng refused Prime Minister Mackenzie King's request for a new election. This refusal provoked a minor constitutional crisis. Since then, the view of most constitutional experts has been that the monarch's representative is required to accept the "advice" of the prime minister. In 2015, Prime Minster Harper asked Governor General David Johnston to extend his appointment for two years because he felt that His Excellency's experience in constitutional matters might prove valuable if the 2015 general election were to result in a hung Parliament with no clear winner.

The Byng precedent suddenly and rather unexpectedly became relevant several weeks after the federal election of 2008, which had produced a Conservative minority government. Although the factors that precipitated the affair are disputed, the opposition parties agreed to bring down the government on a motion of non-confidence in the House of Commons, based on the government's financial statement ("mini-budget"). They also agreed to a coalition pact whereby the Liberals and NDP would form a **coalition government** (a temporary agreement

Listen to the "Who Is Canada's Head of State (and Does It Matter)?" podcast at www.oupcanada.com/BrooksConcise2e.

coalition government a temporary agreement between two or more political parties to form a government

Canadian Spotlight

BOX 8.1   How Responsible Government/The Westminster Model Works in Canada

Named for the Palace of Westminster, the seat of Parliament in the United Kingdom, the Westminster system of government has these key features:

- a sovereign head of state (in Canada, the Queen's representative, the Governor General)
- a head of government (in Canada, the prime minister)
- the executive branch of government (in Canada, the ruling party's cabinet)

- the opposition (in Canada, formed by the multiple parties that do not win a majority government)
- the legislature (in Canada, the elected House of Commons and the appointed Senate)
- a record of the legislature's activity (in Canada, these minutes take the traditional name of *Hansard*)

The operation of government in this model looks something like Figure 8.4.

The government (prime minister and the cabinet) is responsible to the House of Commons, and needs the support of a majority (50% plus one) of the duly elected members of Parliament for all of its activities, legislation, and expenditures.

As occurred in April of 2011, the opposition parties can ask for a "vote of confidence" in the government.

If the government does not get the required majority, then it is deemed to lack the "Confidence of the House of Commons" and the government must offer its resignation to the head of state or their representative (in Canada, the Governor General). The prime minister must then visit the Governor General and offer his or her government's resignation. The prime minister can recommend that Parliament be dissolved and that an election be held. The Governor General does not have to accept this advice.

The Governor General has one of two options:

Option 1: Accept the prime minister's resignation, dissolve Parliament, and sign the writs of election;

or

Option 2: Ask one of the other party leaders, usually the leader of the loyal opposition, to form a new government if they enjoy the confidence of the House of Commons.

FIGURE 8.4 How Responsible Government/The Westminster System Works in Canada

between two or more political parties to form a government) for a period of at least two years, supported by the Bloc Québécois. But before this coalition could replace the Conservatives as the government, the Governor General would have to refuse Prime Minister Harper's request for a new election and then call on Liberal leader Stéphane Dion to form a government. Constitutional experts were divided on the question of whether the Governor General would be breaking an unwritten rule of the Constitution in turning down such a request. In the end, the question became moot when Prime Minister Harper decided instead to request a **prorogation**, a postponement of parliamentary activities without a dissolution of Parliament, until late January 2009, when the government planned to introduce a new budget.

The monarch and Governor General play no significant role in setting the government's policy agenda or in the decision-making process. Royal assent to legislation is virtually automatic—it has never been withheld from a law passed by Parliament. The disallowance and reservation powers have been used by the monarch's provincial representatives, the lieutenant-governors, but this was almost always at the behest of the elected government in Ottawa.[7]

While the monarch's role today is primarily symbolic, the functions performed by the Queen, Governor General, and lieutenant-governors are important. The ceremonial duties of government must be performed by someone, and assigning them to an *impartial* head of state may reduce the association between the political system itself—the state—and the leadership of particular political factions within it. As James Mallory argues, "[the

> **prorogation** a postponement of parliamentary activities without a dissolution of Parliament

Canadian Spotlight

BOX 8.2 Minority Governments in Canada

There have been 13 federal minority governments in Canada since 1867 and many more at the provincial level. The governing party in a minority Parliament must be sensitive to the needs of the other parties or risk being defeated in the House of Commons.

1921–25	William Lyon Mackenzie King, Liberal
1925–26	William Lyon Mackenzie King, Liberal
1926	Arthur Meighen, Conservative
1957–58	John Diefenbaker, Conservative
1962–63	John Diefenbaker, Conservative
1963–65	Lester B. Pearson, Liberal
1965–68	Lester B. Pearson, Liberal
1972–74	Pierre Trudeau, Liberal
1979–80	Joe Clark, Conservative
2004–06	Paul Martin, Liberal
2006–08	Stephen Harper, Conservative
2008–11	Stephen Harper, Conservative

According to *The Canadian Encyclopedia*, of the six Conservative minority governments, only two have endured for more than a few months (2006–8 and 2008–11) and only two (1957–8 and 2006–8) did not fall on confidence votes. Of the six Liberal minority governments, two were defeated in the House (1972–4 and 2004–6) and three were able to govern with the support of the third parties until they could call elections at a time of their choosing (1921–5, 1963–5, and 1965–8). One government, under William Lyon Mackenzie King (1925–6), left office following the Governor General's refusal to dissolve Parliament and call an election.

Source: Courtesy of *The Canadian Encyclopedia*, Historica Canada, "Minority Government," http://www.thecanadian encyclopedia.com/en/article/minority-government/.

monarchy] denies to political leaders the full splendor of their power and the excessive aggrandizement of their persons which come from the undisturbed occupancy of the centre of the stage."[3] While there is no clear evidence that democracies are imperilled when these state functions are performed by an elected president, as is the case in the United States and France, both the American and French political systems have *legislative checks* on executive power that do not exist in a British-style parliamentary system. Mallory may be correct: having a non-elected head of state may contribute to the protection of Canada's democratic social order.

Nonetheless, the monarchy has not always been an uncontroversial pillar of stability in Canadian politics. The monarch's status in Canada's system of government is *King* or *Queen of Canada*, not of the United Kingdom. But some perceive the institution as an irritating reminder of Canada's colonial ties to Britain and of the dominance of Anglo-Canadians in our politics. Despite occasional imbroglios over royal visits, however, we should not exaggerate the institution's contribution to national disunity.

A new sort of controversy was associated with the position of Governor General during the tenures of Adrienne Clarkson (1999–2005). Clarkson's spouse, John Ralston Saul, a well-known philosopher-historian and author, made a number of pronouncements on contemporary issues that focused attention on the question of whether his relationship to the Governor General ought to have limited his forays into political matters. Whether he ought to have limited his participation in the more controversial side of public life was a matter of disagreement.

Listen to the "Who Should Represent Canada and Why?" podcast at www.oupcanada.com/Brooks Concise2e.

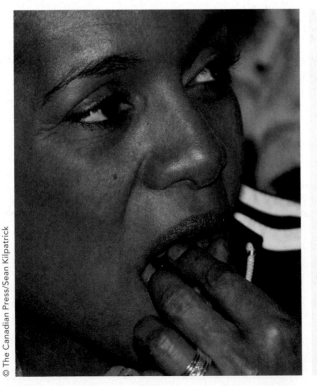

© The Canadian Press/Sean Kilpatrick

During her term as Governor General, Michaëlle Jean did not shy away from controversy. In an official visit to Nunavut in the Canadian North, Jean joined with community members in eating raw heart as part of the ancient and cultural tradition of the seal hunt. Animal activists labelled the act "barbaric," but Jean said her detractors were "completely missing the reality of life here." After reading both sides of the story in the article at the link below, how would you either defend or condemn the Queen's representative and her actions?

"Governor General Has a Heart—Raw Seal, That Is": http://www.thestar.com/news/canada/article/640335.

Perhaps more important, Governor General Clarkson occasionally showed signs of wanting to reshape the boundaries of the office's role in public life. When, in 2001, she sent a message of congratulations to a newlywed gay couple in in Toronto at a time when there was much public controversy over the legal definition of marriage, critics charged a non-elected and non-partisan head of state should not have expressed views that might be construed as critical of existing law and therefore as politically divisive. Michaëlle Jean, Clarkson's successor, was also not averse to potential controversy. For example, in a speech to Alberta's legislature in May 2006, Governor General Jean urged it to share the province's wealth with the rest of Canada. And in 2007, Jean's speech on the twenty-fifth anniversary of the Charter drew criticism because it was perceived to be critical of a cabinet decision to end the Court Challenges Program.

The Prime Minister and Cabinet

Unlike the monarchy in its passive and principally symbolic roles, the prime minister (PM) and cabinet are at the centre of the policy-making process. The PM is the head of government in Canada. By convention, the PM is the leader of the dominant party in the House of Commons. One of the PM's first duties is to select the cabinet ministers. In the British parliamentary tradition, cabinet members are always drawn from the PM's political party. Cabinet ministers are almost always elected members of the House of Commons, but occasionally, a senator or two are appointed when there is little or no representation from a particular region or because of their special abilities. In recent years, the size of the federal cabinet has ranged from a low of 20 to a high of almost 40 members. Provincial cabinets tend to be smaller.

The cabinet, also called the Privy Council, is under the leadership of the PM. The power of the PM and cabinet rests on a combination of factors, including section 11 of the Constitution Act, 1867, which states "There shall be a Council to aid and advise in the Government of Canada, to be styled the Queen's Privy Council for Canada." Section 13 goes even further to specify that the actions of the monarch's representative in Canada, the Governor General, shall be undertaken "by and with the Advice of the Queen's Privy Council for Canada." Although, formally, anyone who has ever been a member of cabinet retains the title of privy councillor after leaving government, only those who are active members of the government exercise the constitutional powers.

Cabinet dominates the entire legislative agenda of Parliament, including control over the budget. Section 54 of the Constitution Act, 1867 requires that legislation or other measures that involve the raising or spending of public revenue be introduced by cabinet. MPs who are not members of the cabinet do have the right to introduce private members' bills; however, party discipline and the meagre time allocated to considering these bills combine to kill the prospects of most of these initiatives.

Although the position of prime minister is not written in the Constitution, the leader of the dominant party in the House of Commons has many powers:

- appointing and removing cabinet ministers
- determining when a new election will be held

- setting out the administrative structure and decision-making process of government
- making appointments to many positions including deputy ministers, judges of all federal and provincial courts, senators, members of federal regulatory agencies and of the boards of directors of federal Crown corporations, ambassadors, etc.

This list explains why the PM is the pre-eminent figure in Canadian government: a pre-eminence that is reinforced by constitutional conventions on accountability. Although individual cabinet ministers are separately accountable to Parliament for the actions of their departments, the entire cabinet is collectively accountable for government policy. The PM cannot avoid personal accountability for policies and overall government performance. The opposition parties and the media ensure that the PM is held to account.

Responsible government is another constitutional convention that strengthens the power of the PM and cabinet. As we noted in Chapter 6, responsible government encourages party discipline because the government will fall if the members of the governing party break ranks. Consequently, the elected members of a party tend to act and vote as a unified bloc on most matters, like budget measures and important government legislation. Party discipline ensures that members of the governing party are normally docile in their support of the government's policies. When the government has a majority in both the House of Commons and the Senate the automatic support of the government party's **backbenchers** (MPs who are not cabinet ministers) enables the PM and cabinet to move their legislative agenda through Parliament without serious impediment.

backbencher an MP who is not a cabinet minister

The weakness of Canada's political party organizations also reinforces the dominance of the PM and cabinet. Parties, particularly Liberals and Conservatives, are geared primarily toward fighting election campaigns and are much more concerned with raising money, selecting candidates, and contesting elections than with formulating policy. Neither the Conservative Party nor the Liberal Party is considered a social movement party with extensive ties to organizations and groups in civil society. A party usually has little influence on the policies adopted by its leadership when it forms the government, for two main reasons. First, the parties try to attract a broad base of support, which requires that the party's leadership be allowed a large margin of manoeuvrability in communicating to different groups. Second, except for the NDP, which has some affiliation to labour organizations, parties tend not to have formal affiliations with organized interests. Formal affiliations usually narrow a party's electoral appeal and increase the organizations' influence in a party's internal affairs. But history shows that when in power, provincial NDP governments have been unwilling to tie themselves rigidly to the party's platform.

The constitutional and statutory foundations of prime ministerial and cabinet powers are reinforced by the relationship between the political executive and the media. This relationship is close and mutually dependent. The PM and members of cabinet regularly speak "directly" to the people or to targeted publics via the media. Even when presenting or defending the government's policies in the House of Commons, they are aware of the wider audience. For their part, journalists typically turn first to the PM and the responsible ministers when reporting on politics. In doing so, the media contribute to the personalization of politics and to the popular identification of government with the PM and cabinet.

Direct communication between the PM and cabinet and the public has undermined the role of the legislature and political parties. When public sentiment can be gauged through public opinion polls, and when the PM and cabinet ministers can speak to the general public or targeted groups via the media and personal appearances, there is less need to communicate through government MPs and the party organization. This trend appeared to deepen following the election in 2006 of the Harper government, which gradually restricted the media's access to the prime minister, government ministers, members of Parliament, and the civil service. Parliament often seemed to be little more than a procedural sideshow, which infuriated some constitutional purists, for whom Parliament is the proper conduit between the state and society. The Trudeau government reversed this trend as soon as it was elected in 2015. The fact remains that, in spite of the Liberals' new openness to the public, responsible government continues to be attenuated by party discipline.

The communications role of the PM and cabinet is related to their representative functions. From the beginnings of self-government in Canada, cabinet formation has been guided by the principle that politically important interests should be "represented" by particular

Prime Minister Trudeau and his cabinet ministers at the swearing-in ceremony at the Governor General's residence, Rideau Hall, on 4 November 2015. When Trudeau was asked why he had made it a point to appoint an equal number of males and females to the cabinet, he famously replied, "Because it's 2015."

cabinet ministers. Representation of different regions and particular provinces has always been considered important, as has representation of francophones. The numerical dominance of anglophones has always ensured that they would be well represented in any government. Representation from the business community—the minister of Finance often has professional connections to either the Toronto or the Montreal corporate elite—and of spokespersons for particular economic interests, particularly agriculture and occasionally labour, have significantly influenced appointments to particular cabinet positions. Some representational concerns, such as the inclusion of various religious denominations, have diminished in importance while others, such as the representation of women and non-French, non-British Canadians, have become significant.

Representational concerns also surface in the case of the PM, particularly when a party chooses its leader. Party members and the media look at candidates in terms of their likely ability to draw support from politically important regions and groups. An aspiring leader of a national political party cannot be associated too closely with the interests of a single region of the country. Given the numerical superiority of anglophone voters, it goes without saying that any serious leadership candidate must be able to communicate well in English. But he or she must be at least competent in French. For example, one of the hindrances faced by Green Party leader Elizabeth May in her bid to have her party seen as a national alternative in the 2015 general election was her weak grasp of the French language.

Being the leader of a national political party or even PM does not automatically elevate a politician above the factional strife of politics and accusations of regional favouritism. Despite holding a majority of that province's seats in the House of Commons between 1958 and 1962, Conservative prime minister John Diefenbaker (1957–63) was never perceived as being particularly sensitive to Quebec's interests. Similarly, Liberal prime minister Pierre Elliott Trudeau (1968–79, 1980–4) was never able to convince Western Canada—not that he always tried very hard—that he shared their perspectives. For Westerners, the Trudeau Liberals represented the dominance of "the East" and favouritism toward Quebec. Conservative prime minister Brian Mulroney (1984–93) may have been more successful than Trudeau in drawing support from all regions. But he, too, came under attack for allegedly neglecting Western interests in favour of those of Central Canada, especially Quebec. Liberal prime minister Jean Chrétien was widely perceived as more successful than his predecessors in attracting the support of both French and English Canadians. However, under Chrétien's leadership the Liberal Party did less well in Quebec than during the Trudeau years.

A prime minister whose party's representation in the House of Commons from a key region is relatively weak can attempt to convey a message of inclusion by appointing a high-profile cabinet minister from that region. This is precisely what Conservative prime minister Stephen Harper did after the 2006 election. His party won only 10 of Quebec's 75 seats, but he moved immediately to appoint to the Senate and to cabinet Quebec's Michael Fortier, and he appointed four newly elected Quebec MPs to his cabinet. On the other hand, when the Liberals won a majority government in the 2015 general election, with support from across Canada, many pundits felt that Trudeau would not have difficulty finding cabinet appointments from every region of the country.

Bruce MacKinnon/Artizans

It was widely believed on the eve of the 19 October 2015 general election that the Liberals under the leadership of Justin Trudeau would gain enough seats to form a minority government. The Liberal gains that night broke a record, and the Liberals went from 34 seats to 185. Many saw the election as an overwhelming rejection of Stephen Harper's style of governance.

Democracy Watch

BOX 8.3 Prime Minister–Designate Justin Trudeau Receives Advice from Former Conservative Chief of Staff David MacLaughlin

Dear prime-minister-designate Trudeau:
Congratulations on your historic win! Now, on to government! But first, you need to form a cabinet.

You, like me, may be wondering who the heck are all these new people just elected. Any prime minister would rightly note that this is a sunny problem to have; after all, it means you are in government. And, boy, are you in government! With a strong, stable majority government, or so the saying goes.

But please remember, majority governments may provide an embarrassment of riches in forming a cabinet, but a richness of embarrassment can lie just underneath if not done right.

Continued

. . . [H]ere's a handy guide to follow:

First, match your best performers with your most important files. Voters will forgive second-rate ministers but will always remember second-rate results. Not every platform commitment matters equally. The most important ones are typically the most difficult ones. . . .

Second, attach an agenda to your cabinet. Don't wait for the Throne Speech to tell Canadians what you plan to do. Transition is not simply about taking office; it is about exercising office in the critical early days while securing momentum to take on issues. . . .

Third, adapt the machinery of government to your agenda, not the other way around. Four years is an awfully short time, in reality, to make progress on thorny issues such as climate change or democratic reform. . . . How to get things done is what bedevils officials now, not what needs to be done.

Fourth, remember where you came from. Under Stephen Harper, Alberta and Ontario had pride of place in the cabinet, holding most of the senior portfolios commensurate with most of the Conservative seats. This time, having given every seat to your party, Atlantic Canada will be vying for recognition along with Ontario, Toronto, and (once again) Quebec. As for everywhere else, you won seats in every province so the perennial regional representation matter for cabinet doesn't matter that much.

Fifth, re-establish cabinet government and make Parliament relevant again. Frankly, none of the above matters much if, as prime minister, you do not allow your cabinet to exercise influence and authority. It is what responsible government and parliamentary accountability is meant to be. . . .

Finally, dear PM-D, here's a novel idea for communicating about your new cabinet. Instead of announcing it the old way at Rideau Hall or on Twitter, why not just put their names and portfolios on a decks of cards?

When that obligatory cabinet reshuffling of the deck comes along mid-term, those cards might come in handy.

Source: David McLaughlin, "Cabinet-Making Tips for the Novice PM," *The Globe and Mail*, 27 Oct. 2015, http://www.theglobeandmail.com/globe-debate/cabinet-making-tips-for-the-novice-pm/article26995524/.

Setting the Agenda

Representation is about power. The PM and cabinet wield considerable power over the machinery of government, which is why representation in the inner circle of government is valued by regional and other interests. This power is based on the agenda-setting role of the PM and cabinet and on their authority within the decision-making process of the state. Setting the agenda is part of the decision-making process in government. It is a crucial part, the early stage during which public issues are defined and policy responses are proposed.

Each parliamentary session begins with the Speech from the Throne, in which the Governor General reads a statement explaining the government's legislative priorities. This formal procedure is required by the Constitution.[4] Although a typical throne speech is packed with generalities, it also contains some specific indications of Parliament's upcoming agenda.

Budgets are a second way for the PM and cabinet to define the policy agenda. Every winter, usually in late February, the minister of Finance tables the Estimates in the House of Commons—also known as the *expenditure budget*. It represents the government's spending plans for the forthcoming fiscal year (1 April–31 March; see Figure 8.5). Given that most public policies involve spending, changes in the allocation of public money indicate shifts in the government's priorities. The government can also use the expenditure budget to signal its overall fiscal stance: increased spending may indicate an expansionary fiscal policy, while restraint and cutbacks may signal a concern that public spending is damaging the economy.

Usually every two years, the minister of Finance presents in Parliament either a **revenue budget** or a major **economic statement**. The former outlines the government's plans to change the tax system. The latter provides the government's analysis of the state of the economy and where the government plans to steer it. Both are major opportunities for the government to shape the economic policy agenda.

The government influences the policy agenda by deciding which initiatives are placed before Parliament and the strategies for manoeuvring policies through the legislature and communicating them to the public. As Figure 8.5 shows, cabinet and cabinet committees such as the Treasury Board are central players in the budget-making process.

The roles of the PM and cabinet in the policy process are institutionalized through the formal structure of cabinet decision making. But this formal structure and cabinet's committee structure have never been more than an imperfect guide to who has influence over what within the current government. The one reliable rule of thumb is this: ministers are influential to the degree that the prime minister allows them to be. A minister who has the PM's ear and is part of the PM's favoured circle can be influential and get support for his or her favoured projects and initiatives.

No organization chart can capture the informal but crucial aspect of ministerial influence. Nor can it convey the extent to which the prime minister dominates this decision-making process. Political observers have long characterized the PM's status in cabinet as *primus inter pares*—first among equals. But as Donald Savoie notes, there is no longer any *inter* or *pares*. There is only *primus*, the PM, when it comes to setting the government's agenda and making major decisions.[5]

Ministerial control over the bureaucracy is another dimension of cabinet's decision-making authority, but the word "control" should be used carefully. Ministers are virtually never involved in the day-to-day running of the departments under their nominal control. Moreover, policy initiatives are more likely to be generated within the bureaucracy than from the responsible minister. There are, of course, exceptions. Stéphane Dion, when he was the federal minister of intergovernmental affairs, was the principal author of the 2000 Clarity Act, an idea that he had championed from the time of the 1995 Quebec referendum. Under the Conservative government of Stephen Harper, unelected advisers in and around the Prime Minister's Office seemed to play a greater role in shaping the government's policy agenda. At the time this book was written, Prime Minister Trudeau appeared to have a much looser approach to shaping the policy agenda. Generally, however, most ministers act as cabinet advocates for the

revenue budget a document that outlines the government's plans to change the tax system

economic statement a document that provides the government's analysis of the state of the economy and where the government plans to steer it

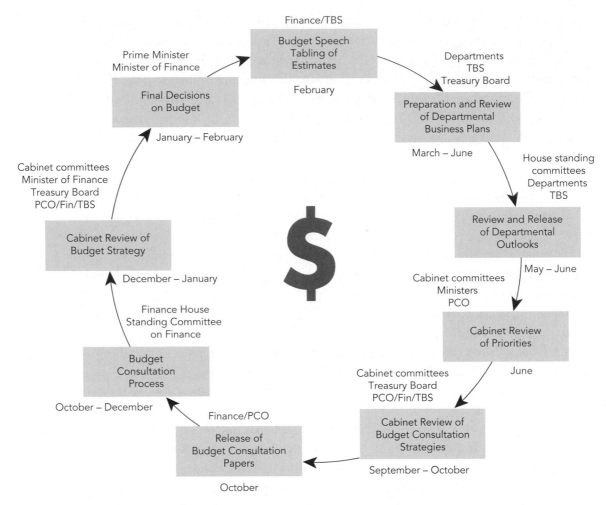

FIGURE 8.5 The Expenditure Management System

Source: The Expenditure Management System, Treasury Board of Canada 2010. Reproduced with the permission of the Minister of Public Works and Government Services, 2012. http://www.tbssct.gc.ca/Pubs_pol/opepubs/TB_H/images/figure1e.gif.

interests of their department and the groups that depend on them. But we should not succumb to the caricature of wily, powerful bureaucrats manipulating their hapless political "masters." Departments and other parts of the bureaucracy are created and restructured as a result of cabinet initiatives, and changes to their budgets and programs are often undertaken in spite of bureaucratic opposition.

Central Agencies

Cabinet has always been a decision-making body. But when John A. Macdonald and the first cabinet met in 1867, they dealt with a workload that was only a fraction of that which faces government today. In order to deal with the sheer volume of information and decision making that comes before cabinet, the cabinet needs help. This help is provided by central agencies.

Central agencies are areas of the bureaucracy whose main or only purpose is to support the decision-making activities of cabinet. They provide cabinet with information, apply cabinet decisions, and communicate cabinet decisions and their implications to the public, provincial governments, or other organizations within the federal state. The general character of their policy role, their direct involvement in cabinet decision making, and their ability to intervene in the affairs of departments led political scientists Colin Campbell and George Szablowski to refer to the senior officials of central agencies as "superbureaucrats."[6] The main organizations usually considered to have central agency status are the Department of Finance, the Privy Council Office (PCO), the Treasury Board Secretariat, the Prime Minister's Office, and, within the PCO, Intergovernmental Affairs.

central agency an area of the bureaucracy whose main or only purpose is to support the decision-making activities of cabinet

Department of Finance

The Department of Finance plays the leading role in formulating economic policy. Its formal authority is found in the Department of Finance Act, 1869 and in the Financial Administration Act. The authority that the law confers on Finance is reinforced by the department's informal reputation within the state. Although comparatively small (about 750 people in 2012), Finance has always been a magnet for "the best and the brightest" within the public service because of its unrivalled status in all aspects of economic policy making.

Finance officials can influence the entire spectrum of government policy through their role in the annual formulation of the expenditure budget. The Finance department has what amounts to almost exclusive authority over the preparation of the revenue budget, budget speeches, and economic statements delivered in Parliament by the Finance minister. Whatever input other parts of the bureaucracy and interests outside of government have is at the discretion of the minister of Finance and the department.[7] New initiatives in taxation and trade policy and in managing the level of government spending and debt will often be generated within Finance. Even when a new policy idea originates elsewhere, it is unlikely to reach the legislation stage if Finance is steadfastly opposed.

The unrivalled status of Finance within the federal bureaucracy is one factor that effectively reinforces the power of the PM, who, along with his or her minister of Finance, is the only member of the government to be intimately involved in the process that leads up to tabling a budget or economic statement in the House of Commons. As Donald Savoie observed,

> . . . the budget has come to dominate policy and decision-making in Ottawa as never before. This holds significant advantages for the centre of government. It enables the prime minister and the minister of finance to introduce new measures and policies under the cover of budget secrecy and avoid debate in Cabinet—and perhaps, more importantly, long interdepartmental consultations and attempts to define a consensus.[8]

Finance is directly responsible for only a handful of programs, but they are important, big-ticket ones. One of these is *fiscal equalization*, under which unconditional payments are made to the poorer provincial governments.

THE CANADIAN PRESS/Galit Rodan

Minister of Finance Bill Morneau tries on new shoes prior to delivering the March 2016 budget. The reading of a new budget is a ceremonial affair in Ottawa, and though no one knows its origin, it is a long-standing tradition for the Finance minister to purchase and wear a new pair of shoes for the occasion.

The Privy Council Office

The Privy Council Office (PCO) is the cabinet's secretariat and a principal source of policy advice to the prime minister. Donald Savoie characterizes it as "the nerve centre of the federal public service."[9] The PCO was formally created by order-in-council in 1940. In 2012 it employed about 800 people, but its influence cannot be gauged by its size. In the first comprehensive study of central agencies, Campbell and Szablowski argue that the PCO is the lead agency for "strategic planning and formulation of substantive policy."[10] The PCO's role is strategic because it is situated at the confluence of all the various policy issues and decisions that come before cabinet. If the government of Canada is a railway, the PCO is Grand Central Station.

The PCO is organized into a number of secretariats that provide support services for the various committees of cabinet. These services range from scheduling and keeping the minutes of committee meetings to activities that carry the potential for real influence, such as providing policy advice and dealing directly with government departments. Perhaps more than any other single component of the bureaucracy, the PCO can see "the big picture" of government policy, which embraces both policy and political concerns. A former head of the PCO, Gordon Robertson, has summarized the different roles of the PCO and the Prime Minister's Office in this way: "The Prime Minister's Office is partisan, politically oriented, yet operationally sensitive. The Privy Council Office is non-partisan, operationally oriented, yet politically sensitive."[11]

The position of Chief Clerk of the Privy Council (CCPC) was made statutory in 1974, without any specification of the duties associated with this position. The authority of this person, who is the head of the public service, and the influence of the PCO derive mainly from their intimate and continuous involvement in cabinet decision making. The CCPC is a sort of deputy minister who reports directly and daily to the prime minster, and is one of the most influential people in the federal government.

The Treasury Board Secretariat

The Treasury Board Secretariat (TBS) is an administrative adjunct to the Treasury Board, which in turn is the only cabinet committee that has a statutory basis, going back to 1869. The Treasury Board is, in a sense, guardian of the purse strings, but it performs this function in more of a micro fashion compared to Finance's macro authority in relation to spending matters. The Treasury Board is also the government's voice on employment and personnel matters and on administrative policy within the federal government. Its authority is, in a word, extensive. But although the responsibilities of the TBS are wide-ranging and important, it occupies the shadows of the policy-making and agenda-setting process compared to Finance and the PCO. Donald Savoie quotes a senior federal official who compares the roles of the three central agencies: "PCO looks after the broad picture and resolves conflicts between ministers and departments. Finance looks after the big economic and budgeting decisions. The Treasury Board looks after the little decisions."[12]

"Little" does not mean "unimportant." The TBS functions include conducting departmental audits, establishing and enforcing accounting standards in government, and evaluating particular programs. As government employer, the Treasury Board negotiates with federal public-sector unions, establishes the rules for recruitment and promotion, implements the terms of the Official Languages Act, and is responsible for setting rules for increasing the representation of women, visible minorities, disabled persons, and Aboriginals in the Canadian public service.

TBS officials formulate the expenditure outlook that, along with the economic outlook and fiscal framework developed by Finance, is the starting point in the annual expenditure budget exercise. These forecasts are used by cabinet in allocating financial resources between competing programs. Preparation of the main **Estimates**, the detailed spending plans that the government tables in the House of Commons each winter, is the responsibility of the TBS. The PCO and Finance often consult it for information and advice because the TBS has the deepest knowledge of government spending programs.[13]

Estimates the detailed spending plans that the government tables in the House of Commons each winter

The Prime Minister's Office

Unlike the other central agencies, the Prime Minister's Office (PMO) is staffed chiefly by partisan appointees rather than by career public servants. These officials are the prime minister's personal staff, performing functions that include handling the PM's correspondence and schedule; speech writing; media relations; liaison with ministers, caucus, and the party; and providing advice on appointments and policy. Gordon Robertson observes that the PMO is "partisan, politically oriented, yet operationally sensitive."[14] It serves as the PM's political eyes and ears, and can speak on behalf of the PM. The PMO is headed by the PM's chief of staff. No other non-elected official is in such regular contact with the PM.

Since the expansion in the PMO that took place under Pierre Trudeau nearly five decades ago, the size of the prime minister's staff has varied from about 80 to 200 people. Today it is around 100. Why so many? The demands on the prime minister's time are enormous, and co-ordinating the PM's activities, providing him or her with briefing and advice, and dealing with the large volume of communications are daunting tasks. The goal for all PMO staff, according to one former PMO staffer, is clear: "Our job is quite simple really, we make the PM look good."[15] "Senior PMO staff," says Savoie, "will get involved in whatever issue they and the prime minister think they should."[16]

Consider, for example, how PMO officials help the PM prepare for *question period* in the House of Commons every day that the House is sitting. When the PM is in Ottawa, he or she is expected to attend to answer questions about the activities and policies of his or her government. Question period can be a political minefield, and it is well attended by journalists. Given the stakes, preparation of the PM and cabinet ministers is crucial. The PMO staff crafts responses to anticipated questions, a process that involves considerable partisan and tactical thinking. The most successful responses are those that turn the tables and put the opposition on the defensive.

Prime Ministerial Government

Many have asked whether Canadian prime ministers have become more "presidential" in their stature and power. This question is based on the false premise that an American president is more powerful than a prime minister in relation to the country's legislation and his own party. In fact, there are fewer checks on the power of a Canadian prime minister than on that of an American president, and it is now widely recognized that the prime minister has far more clout in the Canadian system of government than the president has in the American system. Indeed, that power has become increasingly centralized in the hands of the PM and those around him or her. There are more counterweights to the PM's power in the courts, the media, and in some provincial capitals than in Parliament. Many political commentators now characterize Canada's system of government as *prime ministerial* rather than *parliamentary*.[17] Donald Savoie and Jeffrey Simpson are among those who argue that not only has the influence of Parliament been effectively eclipsed by the growth of **prime ministerial government**—government where the executive is essentially dominated by the prime minister and the PMO—but cabinet, too, has been marginalized; Jeffrey Simpson calls cabinet a "mini-sounding board"[18] where decisions already approved by the PM and his advisers are rubber-stamped. As Savoie writes,

prime ministerial government government where the executive is essentially dominated by the prime minister and the PMO

> Cabinet has now joined Parliament as an institution being bypassed. Real political debate and decision-making are increasingly elsewhere—in federal–provincial meetings of first ministers, on Team Canada flights, where first ministers can hold

informal meetings, in the Prime Minister's Office, in the Privy Council Office, in the Department of Finance, and in international organizations and international summits. . . . The Canadian prime minister has little in the way of institutional check, at least inside government, to inhibit his ability to have his way.[19]

The greater influence of a Canadian prime minister compared to an American president is partly due to structural differences between these two governmental systems. But the high degree of centralization of power that commentators such as Savoie and Simpson argue has occurred under recent prime ministers—a trend that was not reversed when Stephen Harper came to power—may be explained by a combination of personal style and the political incentives to choose more rather than less centralization. Some prime ministers have preferred a more participatory process, such as Lester Pearson (1963–8) and Pierre Trudeau (1968–79, 1980–4). Marc Lalonde, one of the most influential ministers during the Trudeau era, described cabinet meetings under Trudeau as resembling university seminars. Prime Minister Justin Trudeau has indicated that he would like to return to a more collegial and collaborative style in cabinet. This is the decision-making style in which the prime minister has been depicted as *primus inter pares*, or "first among equals." The historical evidence suggests that this style has been relatively rare. More common, certainly in recent times, has been a more centralized decision-making style in which priorities are effectively set and decisions are made by the prime minister and a relatively small group of advisers, only some of whom may be cabinet ministers.

The risks that a prime minister would take by adopting a more collegial approach are fairly easy to identify:

- The decisions or publicly expressed views of individual cabinet ministers might be perceived to conflict with other government actions.
- It is also well known that ministers often see their role at the cabinet table as that of defender of "their" department, programs, budget allocation, etc. The collegial approach to cabinet decision making probably has a built-in bias toward protecting the status quo and against change that might threaten their portfolios.

A collegial approach is more likely to allow the emergence of powerful, high-profile cabinet ministers and possible rivals to the prime minister. Out of concern for the pre-eminence of a Canadian prime minister and a corresponding decline of parliamentary democracy and the role of members of Parliament, Conservative member of Parliament Michael Chong pushed for legislative reform. In the final days of the forty-first Parliament, his private member's bill called the Reform Act, 2014 was passed. The MPs, not the leadership, would determine who gets to sit in caucus and when a caucus member should be expelled. It would also prevent the leadership from having the only say on who gets to run for the party. And, finally, the Reform Act gives MPs the power to call for a leadership review to remove an abusive leader. The legislation was intended to restore Parliament as the source of democratic power by making it easier for a party's caucus to remove a caucus member, a caucus chair, or a caucus leader (including the PM). A leadership review or expulsion vote can take place when 20 per cent of the caucus members call for one. If the 20 per cent threshold is achieved, then a secret ballot takes place where

A 21 May 2011 *Globe and Mail* editorial cartoon depicts Prime Minster Stephen Harper and his newly appointed cabinet ministers marching in step. What do you think cartoonist Brian Gable is saying about nature of this prime minister's leadership style?

a 50 per cent plus one majority decides whether to keep, replace, or expel the caucus leader, the party leader, or a caucus member.

The Bureaucracy

bureaucracy the political rule by unelected government officials

The original meaning of the word **bureaucracy** (*bureaucracie*, coined by the French writer Vincent de Gournay in the mid-1700s) is derived from the French word for "desk" (*bureau*), and was used to describe the political rule by unelected government officials. Ever since, the study of bureaucracy has revolved around the study of the political power of unelected officials.

For policies to have an impact, they must be implemented. The Employment Insurance (EI) program, for example, depends on the administrative efforts of thousands of public servants employed in Canada Employment Centres across the country, to administer the EI benefits, deal with EI appeals, and applying regulations under the Employment Insurance Act. Similarly, educational policy is implemented through bureaucratic structures at the federal (student loans, support for research), provincial (ministries of education), and local (school boards) levels.

Policy implementation is the role of the bureaucracy. Implementation is not, however, an automatic process of converting legislative decisions into action. Unelected officials often wield enormous discretion in applying laws and administering programs. Moreover, their influence is not restricted to the implementation stage of policy making. It begins at the agenda-setting stage, when problems and possible responses are being defined. Bureaucratic influence is felt at numerous points in the decision-making process that precedes the actual introduction of a bill in Parliament. Often, the decision-making process has little or no parliamentary involvement.

The Structure of Canadian Bureaucracy

In 2015, the federal public sector employed roughly 453,000 people working in close to 400 different organizations—down from 486,000 in 2007.[20] Just over 60 per cent of them work directly for government departments and agencies. They are "public servants" in the narrow legal sense of this term. Their employer is the Treasury Board, and the organizations they work for fall directly under the authority of a cabinet minister. Close to 20 per cent are employed by federally owned Crown corporations and the remainder (another 20 per cent) work in the Canadian Forces; while these organizations receive all or part of their funding from the federal government, and are subject to its rules, there is some degree of autonomy.

Public-sector employment is even greater at the provincial, territorial, and local levels. Roughly one-tenth of Canada's population, or 3.6 million people, worked for an organization related to or sponsored by government in 2011.[21] If we define the **public sector** broadly to include those organizations that receive all or a major part of their operating revenues from one or more levels of government, then 20–25 per cent of Canadian workers fall within this sector. It includes nurses, teachers, firefighters, police officers, workers for Children's Aid Societies and at some women's shelters, and so on. According to an interprovincial comparative analysis prepared by the Quebec Secretariat of Intergovernmental Affairs, the general trend for most governments in 2011 was to downsize the public service.[22] Nonetheless, the public sector remains quite extensive.

public sector the part of the economy that includes those organizations that receive all or a major part of their operating revenues from one or more levels of government

What we often label the "bureaucracy" may be divided into three main components: the public service (chiefly departments); independent and semi-independent agencies and tribunals; and Crown corporations.

- *Public service*. Comprising about half the federal public sector, it includes all statutory departments and other organizations whose members are appointed by the Public Service Commission (PSC) and are employees of the Treasury Board. This is the part of the bureaucracy most directly under the authority of cabinet.
- *Agencies and tribunals*. These organizations perform a variety of regulatory, research, and advisory functions, and often have almost total independence from government. With few exceptions their members are not appointed by the PSC, nor are they employees of the Treasury Board. Among the most widely known federal regulatory agencies are the Canadian Radio-television and Telecommunications Commission (CRTC, which regulates communications and broadcasting), the National Transportation Agency

(regulates air, water, and rail transportation), and the National Energy Board (regulates energy when it crosses provincial and international boundaries). Many important areas of regulation, including trucking, public utilities within provincial boundaries, and most labour relations, are controlled by provincial governments.

- *Crown corporations.* These are organizations such as Canada Post that generally perform commercial functions and typically operate at "arm's length" from the government. They hire their own employees, determine their internal administrative structures, and often behave like privately owned businesses. Over the last couple of decades some of the largest of these corporations, notably Air Canada, Canadian National Railway, and Petro-Canada, have been privatized.

These three categories do not cover the entire federal bureaucracy. Some small but important parts of that bureaucracy, including the Auditor General's Office and the Commissioner of Official Languages, are independent of cabinet, reporting directly to Parliament. The Royal Canadian Mounted Police also has a distinct legal status, as does the Canadian Forces.

This vast administrative apparatus has responsibility for implementing public policy, but it is not a uniform structure. The bureaucracy has several different functions:

- provision and administration of services to the public, often to narrow economic, social, or cultural clientele groups

Inside Politics

BOX 8.4 | The Role of the Deputy Minister

The deputy minister acts as the senior adviser to the minister concerning all the responsibilities exercised by him. His mission is to serve the minister in non-partisan fashion, competently, impartially, diligently and loyally. So as to optimize the management of the minister's time and to inform him in his decisions and projects, the deputy minister provides professional, non-partisan advice concerning the development and implementation of policies, provides interministerial consultations, drafts policies and prepares the tools that will enable the minister to take a discerning stand in public, and manages the compliance of the decisions he makes. On a daily basis, he ensures the sound operational management of the department, but is also there to help government look good and offer timely cautions to keep it from getting into trouble.

Adapted from *Restoring Accountability*, Research Studies: Volume 1, *Parliament, Ministers and Deputy Ministers* (Privy Council Office, 2006), 258, 259. http://publications.gc.ca/site/eng/286124/publication.html. Reproduced with the permission of the Minister of Public Works and Government Services, 2012.

- provision of services to other parts of the bureaucracy
- integration of policy in a particular field, or the generation of policy advice
- adjudication of applications and/or interpretation of regulations, such as product safety standards, or the determination of what constitutes morally offensive scenes of sex or violence in films
- disbursement of funds to groups or individuals, as with the grants to artists and cultural organizations administered by the Canada Council
- production of a good or the operation of a service that is sold to buyers, such as permits or passports

And these functions are not mutually exclusive. A large and organizationally complex department such as Transport Canada delivers services, regulates transport standards, and develops policy. Almost all government departments, regardless of their primary orientation, have a policy development capacity. The turnover rate for deputy ministers and other senior bureaucrats has increased since the era of the "Ottawa mandarins," from the 1940s to the 1960s. (The term "mandarin" usually refers to powerful senior civil servants.) The more recent emphasis has been on senior officials as managers, whose management skills are transferable across policy fields. In fact, it would be more accurate to say that this power has become more diffuse. The days when a mere handful of key deputy ministers could dominate the policy-making process are gone. Today, bureaucratic influence is distributed more widely, largely because of the increased importance of central agencies like the Privy Council Office and the Treasury Board Secretariat, but also because a deputy minister rarely remains in charge of a particular department for more than a few years. Nevertheless, there is little doubt that senior bureaucrats continue to be key players in policy making.

The passing of the era of the Ottawa mandarins and the emergence of central agencies as an alternative source of expert policy advice to cabinet have not undermined the fundamental basis of bureaucratic influence on policy. This influence rests on the following factors:

- Ministers invariably depend on the permanent bureaucracy for advice on policy and programs (current and past) and their day-to-day operations.
- A department has a relationship with the social or economic interests that benefit from the programs it administers, and departments are an important target for professional lobbyists and interest group representatives who wish to influence policy.
- Given the competing pressures on a minister's time, "Ministers," observes Savoie, "do not manage."[23] Their deputy ministers perform this job, and often have the chief responsibility for policy direction.
- Most laws contain provisions delegating to bureaucrats the authority to interpret the general terms of the law in its application to actual cases. This is also true of other statutory instruments such as **orders-in-council**, which are administrative orders (appointments, regulations, or legislative orders authorized by an existing act of Parliament) issued by cabinet and approved by the Governor General.

order-in-council an administrative order (appointment, regulation, or legislative order authorized by an existing act of Parliament) issued by cabinet and approved by the Governor General

representative bureaucracy a concept and an expectation that the bureaucracy should "represent" the population and reflect in fair proportion certain demographic characteristics of society

On top of all the other expectations about bureaucracy, democratic societies also expect **representative bureaucracy**: a concept and an expectation that the bureaucracy should "represent" the population and reflect in fair proportion certain demographic characteristics of society. Affirmative action programs and quota hiring are the tools used in pursuit of this goal. The basic reasoning behind arguments for representative bureaucracy is threefold: first, it will have greater popular legitimacy; second, the services it provides will be sensitive to the values and aspirations of the governed, and third, it will help ensure that the advice bureaucrats give to politicians reflects these values and aspirations.

The idea and implementation of representative bureaucracy can be problematic. Which groups should be represented? What constitutes "fair proportion"? Is government efficiency compromised by equal representation? Can representative bureaucracy be politically neutral?

Problems aside, it is clear that a grossly unrepresentative bureaucracy can pose problems. Governments that have instituted policies of affirmative action and quota hiring have done so chiefly for political reasons such as national unity. The fact that comparatively few French Canadians were found at the senior levels of the federal bureaucracy was already controversial in the 1940s, 1950s, and 1960s, and led to major public service reforms and Canada's first policy of representative bureaucracy under Lester Pearson and Pierre Trudeau. As the ethnic composition of Canadian society has changed—people of non-British, non-French ancestry now constitute over one-quarter of the population—and especially as the discourse of collective rights and group identities has achieved greater prominence, the old concern with "fair" linguistic representation has been joined by efforts to recruit and promote women, visible minorities, Aboriginal Canadians, and the disabled.

The Legislature

The legislature is a study in contrasts. Its physical setting is soberly impressive, yet the behaviour of its members is frequently the object of derision. Its constitutional powers appear to be formidable, yet its actual influence on policy is often much less than that of the cabinet and the bureaucracy. All major policies, including all laws, must be approved by the legislature, but in Canadian politics the legislature's approval often seems a foregone conclusion and a mere formality—especially when the governing party holds a majority in the House of Commons and in the Senate.

The contradictions of the legislature have their source in the tension between traditional ideas about political democracy and the character of the modern state. *Representation, accountability to the people*, and *choice* are the cornerstones of liberal-democratic theory. An elected legislature that represents the population either on the basis of population or by region, or both, and party competition are the means by which these democratic goals are accomplished. But the modern state, we have seen, is characterized by a vast bureaucratic apparatus that is not easily controlled by elected politicians. Moreover, while the prime minister's power has always been vastly greater than that of other members of Parliament, the concentration of power in and around the office of the prime minister appears to have reached unprecedented levels. As the scale and influence of the non-elected parts of the state have grown and prime ministerial government has been consolidated, the inadequacies of traditional democratic theory—centred on the role of the legislature—have become increasingly apparent.

There have been calls for reforms, such as a more representative and democratically responsive bureaucracy, to alleviate the problem of power without accountability. (Recall MP Michael Chong's 2014 private member's bill to curtail the power of the prime minister in the party caucus.) Reforms, however, cannot substitute for elections. If one begins from the premise that the free election must be the cornerstone of political democracy, the role of the legislature is crucial.

One way of ensuring that the legislature better performs its democratic functions is to improve its representative character. Possible ways include reforming the political parties' candidate selection process, instituting a proportional representation electoral system, or reforming the Senate. Another option is tightening the legislature's control over the political executive and the non-elected parts of the state. This may be done by increasing the legislature's access to information about the intentions and performance of the government and bureaucracy, providing opportunities for legislative scrutiny and debate of executive action, and enabling legislators to influence the priorities and agenda of government.

Canada has a **bicameral legislature**: a legislature with two chambers—the House of Commons, which is democratically elected, and the Senate, with appointed senators. Representation in the elected House of Commons is roughly according to population—roughly, because some MPs represent as few as 20,000 constituents, while others represent close to 200,000. Each of the 338 members of the House of Commons is the sole representative for a constituency, also known as a "riding."

Senators are appointed by the government of the day when a vacancy occurs. They hold their seats until age 85. As we see in Table 8.1, representation in the Senate is based on Canada's regions. In recent years there have been suggestions that senators be elected, and some have proposed that a certain number of Senate seats be reserved for women and Aboriginal Canadians.

In law, the powers of the House of Commons and Senate are roughly equal. There are, however, a couple of important exceptions. Legislation involving the spending or raising of

bicameral legislature a legislature with two chambers

TABLE 8.1 Regional Representation in the Senate

Region	Number of Senate Seats
Ontario	24
Quebec	24
Western provinces: Manitoba, Saskatchewan, Alberta, British Columbia	24
Maritimes: Prince Edward Island, New Brunswick, Nova Scotia	24
Newfoundland and Labrador	6
Yukon, Northwest Territories, and Nunavut	3
Total	105

public money must, under the Constitution, be introduced in the House of Commons. And when it comes to amending the Constitution, the Senate can only delay passage of a resolution already approved by the Commons. But all bills must pass through identical stages in both bodies before becoming law (see Box 8.7 later in this chapter).

Despite the similarity of their formal powers, the superiority of the elected House of Commons is well established. For most of its history, the Senate has deferred to the will of the Commons. This changed, however, after the 1984 election of a Progressive Conservative majority in Parliament. On several occasions the Liberal-dominated Senate obstructed bills that had already been passed by the Commons. When the Senate balked at passage of the politically unpopular goods and services tax (GST), the Mulroney government used an obscure constitutional power and appointed eight new Conservative senators, thereby giving the Conservatives a slender Senate majority. Under the Chrétien government the partisan balance in the Senate shifted back to a Liberal majority. The squabbles that often occurred after 1984, when the House of Commons was controlled by one party and the Senate by another, became increasingly rare from 1993 to 2006, when the Liberals formed the government and re-established a Liberal majority in the Senate through the filling of vacancies. When this Liberal Senate majority posed a problem for the minority Conservatives government of Stephen Harper, blocking and delaying legislation sent to it from the House of Commons, Prime Minister Harper allowed vacancies to accumulate and then appointed 18 new senators in December 2008. This was done in spite of Conservative election promises to turn the Senate into an elected body. The Conservative government had been unable to win enough support in the House of Commons for such reform and, in any case, it was not clear that direct election and term limits for senators could be accomplished without changing the Constitution.

In 2014, after stories broke about inappropriate spending by a number of senators, Liberal Party leader Justin Trudeau ejected the Liberal senators from the caucus, thereby turning them into independent senators overnight. After winning the October 2015 election, Prime Minister Trudeau created an independent, non-partisan panel to select future appointments to the Senate. It remains to be seen whether the Senate can function effectively without the traditional party discipline and partisanship typical of our parliamentary system.

If you listen closely you can hear the sound of your money being squandered

Bruce MacKinnon/Artizans

The Senate continues to stir emotions in Canadian politics. This editorial cartoon portrays the feelings of voters after several news stories broke in 2013 and 2014 about inappropriate spending by Canadian senators. Even after attempts to clean up the Senate and to prosecute senators who may have broken the law, the impression that the Senate is a "waste of money" persists among a majority of Canadians.

Democracy Watch

BOX 8.5 An Elected Senate?

The Senate currently has a few key roles in Canada's system of government: (1) Revising legislation, and (2) protecting linguistic and other minority groups—essentially acting as a "second sober thought" to all legislation moving through the system.

Some Arguments for an Elected Senate

- If elected, this body would acquire democratic legitimacy by being accountable to constituents.
- Elected senators could champion the issues most important to their regions.
- The public would have an opportunity not to re-elect a senator tied to any scandal or misconduct.

Some Arguments against an Elected Senate

- Debate about whether or not the Constitution Act, 1982 would allow Parliament to reform the main functioning of the Senate is unresolved, and therefore current reform discussion are irrelevant.
- Using current demographics of the elected House of Commons as a guide, opening up Senate positions to election may result in fewer women and minorities serving in the Senate.
- It is the House of Commons' role to channel public opinion and table legislation; it is the Senate's role to scrutinize that legislation. Making senators beholden to constituents might interfere with their ability to look critically at legislation moving through the system.

Functions of the Legislature

The legislature performs a number of functions that are basic to political democracy: the passage of laws by elected representatives, which includes the approval of budget proposals and new policy initiatives. The operation of party discipline ensures that bills tabled in the legislature are seldom modified in major ways during the law-passing process. However, Parliament's approval of the government's legislative agenda is not an empty formality. The opposition parties have opportunities to debate and criticize the government's proposals.

Robert Jackson and Michael Atkinson argue that those involved in the pre-parliamentary stages of policy making anticipate the reactions of the legislature and of the government party caucus before a bill or budget is tabled in Parliament.[24] Recent evidence suggests, however, that the PM and those who actually make policy decisions and draft legislation pay closer attention to the results of surveys and focus groups and less attention to how backbench MPs will react.

caucus the body
of elected MPs
belonging to a
particular party

On the influence of **caucus**, the body of elected MPs belonging to a particular party, Donald Savoie states that "[government party MPs] report that they are rarely, if ever, in a position to launch a new initiative, and worse, that they are rarely effective in getting the government to change course. They also do not consider themselves to be an effective check on prime ministerial power."[25] As one government party MP remarked, "We simply respond to what Cabinet does, and there are limits to what you can do when you are always reacting."[26] This being said, the legislature is far from being irrelevant in making policy. The legislature's functions include scrutiny of government performance, constituency representation, debate of issues, and legitimation of the political system.

Scrutinizing Government Performance

Various regular opportunities exist for the legislature to prod, question, and criticize the government. These include the daily question period in the House of Commons, the debates that follow the Speech from the Throne and the budget, and opposition days when the opposition parties determine the topics of debate. Committee hearings and special parliamentary task forces also provide legislative scrutiny of government actions and performance, although the subjects that they deal with are mainly determined by the government. Party discipline is a key factor that limits the critical tendencies of parliamentary committees, particularly under a majority government.

While many have criticized the behaviour of MPs during question period, for better or for worse, it has become the centrepiece of Parliament's day and the chief activity shaping most Canadians' ideas of what goes on in Parliament. The introduction of television cameras into the legislature in the late 1970s reinforced the stature of question period as the primary way that the opposition can hold the government to account. Question period is the opposition parties' main chance to influence which issues are discussed in the media and how they are portrayed. In fact, journalists often react—although not always in the way that opposition parties may like—to the questions and lines of attack that opposition parties launch against the government. Critical scrutiny of the government clearly serves the interests both of the opposition parties, who wish to see the government embarrassed and its popular support drop, and of the media, who know that controversy and the scent of wrongdoing tends to attract more readers and viewers.

Students of American politics know that the real action in Congress takes place in congressional committees, and that what enters the committee process may not resemble what emerges from it. In Canada's Parliament, however, committees (whose membership is generally about 20 MPs) usually only marginally modify and virtually never derail any government bill. The committees may appear to be a forum for backbench MPs to acquire some expertise in areas that will enable them to assess the merits of legislation in a more informed and less partisan manner. However, evidence suggests otherwise. In his study of MPs' behaviour and perceptions of their jobs, David Docherty states that "several rookie Liberals indicated that the failure of their own executive to treat committee work and reports seriously was the single most frustrating (and unexpected) aspect of their job as an MP."[27] Docherty found that frustration with House committees was not limited to government party members. Opposition MPs also expressed disappointment with the inability of committees to make a significant difference.

Party discipline seems to be at the root of this dissatisfaction. Despite some attempts at reform over the last couple of decades, party discipline continues to operate in committees, just as it does on the floor of the House of Commons. It is too soon to tell whether the Trudeau government's 2015 promises of more openness, transparency, and collaboration with the opposition parties will reduce MP dissatisfaction and increase participation in policy initiatives and committee work.

Senators argue that life is different in the Senate, also known as the Red Chamber. They point to the Senate's long string of committee and task force studies on topics ranging from corporate concentration in Canada's media industries to the decriminalization of marijuana possession. Many senators point to the product of their committees as their proudest accomplishments, doing the same work as think tanks, academics, and government commissions. Being appointed to serve until the age of 75 and not having to face an electorate or the approval of the party leadership, most of them argue, loosens the constraint of party discipline. Senators can behave far more independently than their House of Commons colleagues. While Senate

Democracy Watch

BOX 8.6 Edmund Burke and the Role of Members of the Legislature

Edmund Burke was a member of the British House of Commons in the late 1700s. In his famous "Letter to the Sheriffs of Bristol," Burke explained why a member of the legislature—even one elected by the people—should not be overly concerned to ascertain and reflect the ideas and preferences of his constituents. Lawmakers should see themselves as trustees, he argued, not as the mere servants of public opinion. "Your representative owes you, not his industry only, but his judgment," said Burke, "and he betrays, instead of serving you, if he sacrifices it to your opinion."

Burke's comments raises the dilemma of whether representatives in a democracy should follow the will of their constituents, the will of their party, or their own conscience.

A number of questions arise about the ability of the parliamentary system to function when obligations to the party or the electorate are removed. One wonders, for example, whether Canadian senators are more likely to act according to their conscience because they are appointed and not beholden to an electorate. Liberal leader Justin Trudeau seemed to be saying that senators should follow their own conscience when in 2013 he declared that Liberal senators would no longer be part of the Liberal caucus. But do you believe that the House of Commons or the Senate can function effectively without a corresponding party system and MPs that must support their party? What happens to the principle of responsible government without partisanship? Do you agree with Trudeau that senators should sit as independents?

committee reports have often influenced the public debate on an issue, there is no reason to believe that House of Commons committees could not make this same contribution to scrutinizing government policy, investigating important issues, and proposing legislative change. But how many Canadians know or care about Senate committee work? The truth is that, until spending scandals erupted in late 2012 around the spending habits of high-profile senators like Mike Duffy and Pamela Wallin, the media seldom reported this side of the Senate.

Representation

The House of Commons is both symbolically and practically important as a contact point between citizens and government. Symbolically, the elected House embodies the principle of government by popular consent. The partisan divisions within it, between government and opposition parties, have the additional effect of affirming for most citizens their belief in *pluralism* and the competitive character of politics. At a practical level, citizens often turn to their elected representatives when they experience problems with bureaucracy or when they want to express their views on government policy.

 Listen to the "Political Parties and the Parliamentary System" podcast at www.oupcanada.com/Brooks Concise2e.

Despite the fact that senators are appointed to represent the various provinces and regions of Canada, the Senate does not perform a significant representational role in Canadian politics. The unelected character of Canada's upper house and the crassly partisan criteria that prime ministers have usually relied on in filling Senate vacancies have undermined whatever legitimacy senators might have achieved as spokespersons for the regions. Provincial governments, regional spokespersons in the federal cabinet, and regional blocs of MPs within the party caucuses are more significant in representing regional interests.

Debate

The image that most Canadians have of Parliament is of the heated exchanges that take place across the aisle that separates the government and opposition parties. Parliamentary procedure and the physical layout of the legislature are based on the adversarial principle of "them versus us." At their best, debates in Parliament can provide a public forum for discussing national issues, as well as highlighting the policy differences between the parties. Unfortunately, the quality of parliamentary debate in Canada is often dragged down by the wooden reading of prepared remarks, heckling and personal invective, and occasional blatant abuses of either the government's majority or the opposition's opportunities to hold up the business of Parliament. In December 2015, the new speaker of the House of Commons, Geoff Regan, promised a friendlier tone in the proceedings: "My role as your Speaker is to be fair, and I want to assure you I intend to be fair and I intend to be firm. I will not tolerate heckling. We don't need it."[28]

Generally, MPs' minds are made up when a measure is first tabled in Parliament. So why spend long hours criticizing and defending legislative proposals and the government's record? There are two reasons. First, outcomes are not always predictable. Even when the government party holds a commanding majority in Parliament, or when the policy differences between government and opposition are not significant, the trajectory of a debate on an issue may be diverted by media coverage, opinion polls, opinions by respected experts, or the interventions by organized interests.

Parliamentary debate is also important because it reinforces the popular belief in the open and competitive qualities of Canadian democracy. The stylized conflict of the British parliamentary system often produces an exaggerated impression of the open and competitive qualities of Canadian politics. The fact is that these partisan disagreements take place within a fairly narrow band of consensus on basic values, and consequently parliamentary debates provide valuable support and legitimization for the existing political system and hide many non-mainstream interests and concerns from getting views onto the public agenda.

Legitimation

As suggested above, Parliament is both a *legislative* and a *legitimizing* institution. Parliament represents the people. Laws must pass through the parliamentary mill before being approved, and the legitimizing mechanisms of democratic scrutiny and accountability are embodied in the structure and procedures of Parliament. Along with elections and judicial review of the Constitution, Parliament appears to be a check against the abuse of power by a government.

If most Canadians saw the legislature as a farce, then the legitimacy of the government would be undermined. This is not the case, however. Canadians may be cynical about the integrity of their politicians, but they appear to have faith in their parliamentary institutions. In the minds of many Canadians, the structures and procedures of the legislature are built around the ideas of open government and popular consent and the constitutional requirement that the actions of government must be approved by Parliament.

Although the concentration of power in and around the prime minister has reached unprecedented levels, the legislature is not the helpless pawn of the executive. Witness the sanctioning of the Conservative government and the vote of non-confidence against it that precipitated the May 2011 federal election. Using the rules of parliamentary procedure, opposition parties can prod, question, and castigate the government in front of the parliamentary press gallery and the television cameras in the House of Commons. The opposition's behaviour is usually reactive, responding to the government's proposals and policies. Nevertheless, the legislature's function as a talking shop—the *parler* in "parliament"—enables it to draw attention to controversial aspects of the government's performance. MPs are not quite "nobodies," as Pierre Trudeau once labelled them. But they are far from having the policy influence of their American counterparts, who, because of loose party discipline and very different rules governing the law-making process, are often assiduously courted by interest groups and the president.

Earlier, we said that caucus, the body of elected MPs belonging to a particular party, generally has little influence on the party leadership, at least in the government party. When Parliament is in session, a party's caucus usually meets at least weekly. When they are in Ottawa, the prime minister and cabinet members regularly attend the government caucus. These meetings often amount to little more than what one MP describes as "bitching sessions," but almost never do MPs challenge the prime minister behind the closed doors of the party's weekly

a)

1 Speaker

2 Pages

3 Government Members*

4 Opposition Members*

5 Prime Minister

6 Leader of the Official Opposition

7 Leader of the Second Largest Party in Opposition

8 Clerk and Table Officers

9 Mace

10 Hansard Reporters

11 Sergeant-at-Arms

12 The Bar

13 Interpreters

14 Press Gallery

15 Public Gallery

16 Official Gallery

17 Leader of the Opposition's Gallery

18 Members' Gallery

19 Members' Gallery

20 Members' Gallery

21 Speaker's Gallery

22 Senate Gallery

23 T.T. Cameras

*Depending on the number of MPs elected from each political party, government Members may be seated on the opposite side of the Chamber with opposition Members (or vice versa).

b)

FIGURE 8.6 Layouts of the Canadian House of Commons and the American House of Representatives

As this figure shows, the Canadian House of Commons (and the Senate) is designed for debate between opposing sides and is similar to parliaments around the world that use the Westminster model of parliamentary democracy (a). The semicircular design of the American House of Representatives in Washington, DC, suggests that representatives are gathered to listen, discuss and achieve a consensus (b).

Sources: (a) "House of Commons," *The House of Commons Report to Canadians 2008*, p. 4 http://www.parl.gc.ca/About/House/ReportToCanadians/2008/HOC_RTC2008_E.pdf; (b) © iStockphoto.com/GYI NSEA

meeting.[29] Some insiders have argued that the government caucus provides a real opportunity for backbenchers to influence government policy away from the peering eyes and listening ears of the media and the opposition. This may occasionally be true, and may be more common with the passing of the Reform Act, 2014, but the limits on the influence of caucus are readily apparent from two facts. First, extremely unpopular policies or government priorities, such as the GST, have traditionally not been affected by caucus opposition. The same has been true of policies that create sharp divisions in a party's caucus, such as the Liberal government's 1995 gun control law. If the policy is a high priority, the prospect of a caucus revolt is extremely remote. Members who fail to toe the line are likely to experience the fate of those Liberal MPs who voted against the government's gun law in 1995: the loss of committee assignments. Expulsion from caucus is another sanction that may be used to punish recalcitrant backbenchers. Second, the caucus of the governing party—like the legislature as a whole—usually enters the policy-making process late, after study, consultation, and negotiation have taken place. The government caucus is thus asked to vote for a complex fabric of compromises and accommodations between government, interest groups, agencies of government, or even the provinces. It is unlikely that the government would allow this fabric to unravel because of caucus opposition.

What Does an MP Do?

It is almost certainly true that most Canadians believe that their MPs are overpaid and underworked. Stories of "gold-clad" MPs' pensions and of senators who slurp at the public trough while living abroad help to fuel this widespread but generally unfair charge. Most backbench MPs work very long hours, whether in Ottawa or at home in their constituencies. The demands are even greater for members of the government and party leaders who are required to travel extensively in carrying out their jobs. But what does a typical MP do? For most MPs, the single largest block of their working day is devoted to taking care of constituency business. David Docherty reports that the MPs he surveyed from the thirty-fourth (1988–93) and thirty-fifth (1993–7) Parliaments claimed to spend just over 40 per cent of their working time on constituency affairs. The second-largest block of time was spent on legislative work, such as committee assignments and attending question period and debates. These activities run a fairly distant second, however, to constituency work, as shown in Figure 8.7.

In performing their functions, all MPs are provided with a budget for hiring staff in Ottawa and in their riding office. They choose how these resources are allocated; however, most MPs opt to have two staffers in Ottawa and two in the constituency office. MPs are also provided with public funds to maintain their constituency office and are allowed an unlimited regular mail budget and four mass mailings to constituents—known as "householders"—per year. Although these resources are paltry compared to those at the disposal of US congressional representatives and senators, they are superior to those of legislators in many other democracies. And while they are adequate to enable an MP to carry out his or her constituency duties, they are not sufficient to pay for policy analysts and other research staff.

Docherty found that MPs who were new to Parliament tended to spend more time on constituency work than those who had been in the legislature longer. "[T]he longer members serve

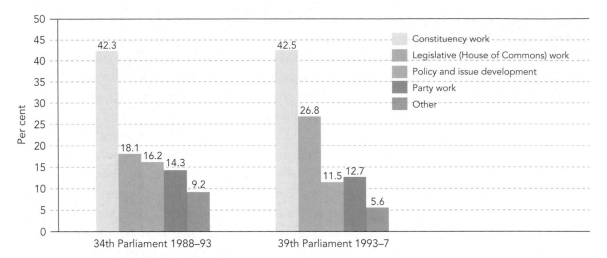

FIGURE 8.7 How an MP Spends the Day (percentage of working time devoted to different tasks)

Source: This figure is reprinted from *Mr. Smith Goes to Ottawa: Life in the House of Commons*, by David Docherty © University of British Columbia Press 1997. All rights reserved by the Publisher.

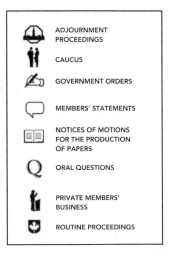

FIGURE 8.8 A Typical Week in the House of Commons

Source: Parliament of Canada, http://www.parl.gc.ca/About/Parliament/WeekInHouse/index-e.asp.

in office," he observes, "the less time they will devote to constituency work."[30] This shift from constituency to policy-oriented work does not, however, mean that a veteran MP's constituents are less well served than those of an MP who is new to Parliament. Docherty found that the Ottawa staffs of veteran MPs tended to make up the difference, spending more of their time on constituency business as their MPs' focus shifted to policy concerns. "No matter what stage of their career," Docherty states, "members of parliament see helping individuals as their most crucial duty."[31]

Is There a Democratic Deficit in Canada?

During the 1990s it became increasingly popular to speak about a **democratic deficit** in Canadian politics, resulting from what critics believed to be the excessive centralization of power in and around the prime minister and cabinet and the marginalization of the legislature. In his book *The Friendly Dictatorship*, Jeffrey Simpson made the case for significant reform of the way in which Parliament conducts its business, as have many other political commentators.

Prime Minister Harper's prorogation of Parliament in November 2008 and December 2009, each time in circumstances where it appeared likely that the government was on the brink of being defeated in the House, fuelled charges that the democratic deficit was deeper than ever.

Those who think that the prime minister should have a relatively unfettered hand in shaping and passing legislation do not think there is a democratic deficit. Jeffrey Simpson, Donald Savoie, and others insist that the deficit is large and perhaps growing larger.

A recent book on the democratic deficit in Canada and the United States, edited by Patti Tamara Lenard and Richard Simeon, suggests several factors that may have contributed to a growing disconnect between the people and those who govern them and to what is believed to be an unhealthy concentration of political power. The impotence of the Canadian legislature and the emergence of prime ministerial government are only part of the picture they describe.[32]

As indicated above, to counter the undemocratic consequences of the party leadership's control over what happens in Parliament and restore respect for the institution, Conservative MP Michael Chong was able to pass a private member's bill through Parliament, the Reform Act, 2014. The solution to the democratic deficit and to the dysfunctionality of Parliament, Chong argued, would start with the reform of question period. He has described it as "an anger-filled screaming match, characterized by aggressive body language and by those who can yell the loudest and yell the biggest insults."[33] Changes would also have to occur in how the party caucuses operate and in a shift of power from the leadership to the MPs.

There is little doubt that "democratic deficit" may be merely a slogan when used by some critics who do not like the ideological coloration or policy direction of a particular government or the sort of outcomes produced by the electoral or legislative system. At the same time,

democratic deficit the excessive centralization of power in and around the prime minister and cabinet and the marginalization of the legislature

however, the term performs the very useful function of causing us to think about how well our political institutions achieve the goals we associate with democracy. And if we find they do not provide the transparency, accountability, and responsiveness to the popular will that we expect, then this indeed is a democratic deficit.

The Judiciary

Courts apply and interpret the law. They perform their role in matters ranging from contested driving offences to disputes over the most fundamental principles of the Constitution. As we have seen in previous chapters, judges' decisions often have profound implications for the rights and status of individuals and groups, for the balance of social and economic power, and for the federal division of powers. The socio-political significance of the judicial process and the methods of interpretation typically used by the courts cannot be overstated.

Responsibility for Canada's judicial system is divided between Ottawa and the provinces. While the Constitution gives the federal government the exclusive right to make criminal law, it assigns responsibility for the administration of justice and for law enforcement to the provinces. Consequently, all provinces have established their own systems of courts that interpret and apply both federal and provincial laws.

The Constitution also gives Ottawa the authority to create courts. This authority was used in 1875 to create the Supreme Court of Canada, and since 1949, the Supreme Court has been Canada's highest court of appeal. Ottawa again used this constitutional power in 1971 to create the Federal Court of Canada. It has jurisdiction over civil claims involving the federal governments, cases arising from the decisions of federally appointed administrative bodies such as the Immigration Appeal Board, and matters relating to federal income tax, copyrights, and maritime law—all of which fall under the legislative authority of Ottawa. The structure of Canada's court system is shown in Figure 8.10.

The independence of judges is the cornerstone of the Canadian judicial system. Judges are appointed by governments. But once appointed they hold their office "during good behaviour"[34]—or to age 75. What constitutes a lapse from "good behaviour"? A criminal or a serious moral offence could provide grounds for removal, as could decisions of such incompetence that they undermine public respect for the law and the judiciary. In such circumstances the appointing government may launch removal proceedings against a judge. In fact, formal proceedings have rarely been initiated and have never been prosecuted to the point of the actual removal of a judge by resolution of Parliament or a provincial legislature. Judicial independence is also protected by the fact that judges' salaries and conditions of service are established by law. Consequently, governments cannot single out any individual judge for special reward or punishment.

But as Ralph Miliband puts it, to say that judges are "independent" raises the question, "Independent of what?" Judges, observes Miliband, "are by no means, and cannot be, independent of the multitude of influences, notably of class origin, education, class situation and professional tendency, which contribute as much to the formation of their view of the world as they

Royal Commission a task force or some other consultative body created by the government to study and make recommendations on an issue

Canadian Spotlight

BOX 8.7   How a Law Is Passed

The law takes various forms. A statute passed by the House of Commons and the Senate, and given royal assent by the Governor General, is clearly a law. But decisions taken by cabinet that have not been approved in the legislature also have the force of law. These are called orders-in-council. Thousands of them are issued each year, and they are published in the *Canada Gazette*. The decisions of agencies, boards, and commissions that receive their regulatory powers from a statute also have the force of law. Finally, there are the regulations and guidelines issued and enforced by the departmental bureaucracy in accordance with the discretionary powers delegated to them under a statute. These also have the force of law.

In a strictly numerical sense the statutes passed annually by Parliament represent only a few of the laws promulgated each year. Nevertheless, virtually all major policy decisions—including budget measures and the laws that assign discretionary power to the bureaucracy—come before the legislature. The only exceptions have occurred when the normal process of government was suspended under the War Measures Act. This happened during World War I, again during World War II, and briefly in 1970 when Ottawa invoked the War Measures Act after two political kidnappings in Quebec by the Front de libération du Québec. The War Measures Act was replaced by the Emergencies Act in 1988.

During normal times the law-making process involves several stages and opportunities for debate and amendment. The steps from the introduction of a bill in Parliament to the final proclamation of a statute are set out in Figure 8.9.

There are two types of bills: private members' bills and government bills. Private members' bills originate from any individual MP, but unless they get the backing of government they have little chance of passing. Government bills dominate Parliament's legislative agenda. When major legislation is being proposed, a bill is sometimes preceded by a White Paper—a report for discussion on proposed legislation. Major legislation may also follow from the recommendations of a **Royal Commission**, a task force, or some other consultative body that has been created by the government to study and make recommendations on an issue.

Once a bill has been drafted by government, it may be introduced in the Senate, but is usually introduced in the House of Commons. Here, it is given *first reading*, which is just a formality and involves no debate. Then the bill goes to *second reading*, when the main principles of the bill are debated and a vote is taken. If the bill passes second reading it is sent to a smaller legislative committee, where the details of the bill are considered clause by clause. At this *committee stage*, amendments can be made but the principle of the bill cannot be altered. The bill is then reported back to the House, where all aspects, including any amendments, are debated. At this *report stage* new amendments also can be introduced. If a bill passes this hurdle it then goes to *third reading* when a final vote is taken, sometimes after further debate. Once a bill has

Continued

been passed in the House, it is sent to the Senate where a virtually identical process takes place. If a bill was first introduced in the Senate, then it would now be sent to the House. Finally, a bill that is passed in both the House and the Senate can be given royal assent and become law.

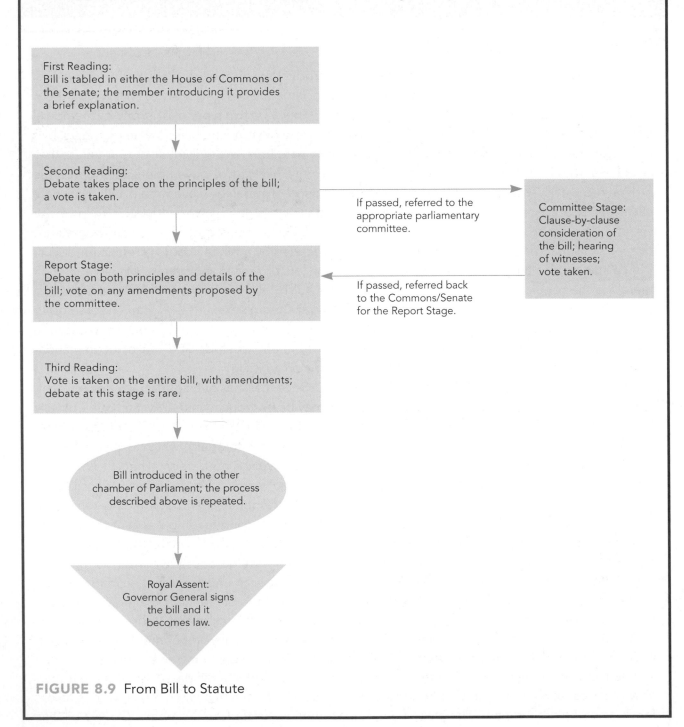

FIGURE 8.9 From Bill to Statute

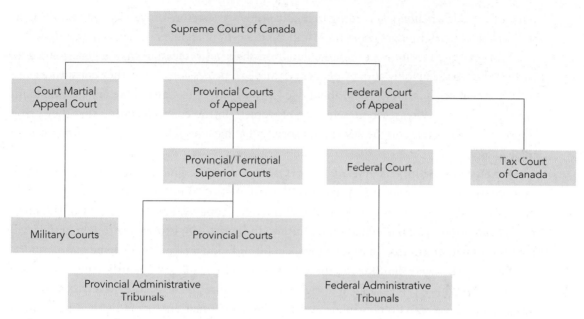

FIGURE 8.10 The Structure of Canada's Court System

Source: Canada's Court System 2011 http://www.justice.gc.ca/eng/dept-min/pub/ccs-ajc/page3.html Dept. of Justice Canada, 2011. Reproduced with the permission of the Minister of Public Works and Government Services, 2012.

do in the case of other men."[35] Thus, to say that the judiciary is "independent" is to describe its formal separation from the executive and legislative branches of the state. When it comes to the dominant value system of their society, judges are no more independent than are the members of any other part of the state elite. Leaving aside the socio-economically unrepresentative character of the legal profession and the effects of formal training in the law, in British-style parliamentary systems all judges are appointed by governments.[36] One would hardly expect these governments to appoint radical critics of society, even supposing that many such individuals could be found within the more respected ranks of the legal profession. The fact that governments control promotion within the court system may also deter unconventional judicial behaviour.

Some argue that the socio-economic background of judges and the process of selection have introduced conservative tendencies into the judiciary. But these are not the only factors that may incline the courts toward protection of the status quo. The law itself is often a powerful conservative force. We are used to thinking of the law as simply "the rules made by governments" that "apply to everybody in society,"[37] but the law also represents values that have accumulated over a long time. The concepts, meanings, precedents, and interpretive rules that shape judicial decision making tend to inhibit sharp breaks with the past.

The socio-economic background of judges and the process by which they are selected have been argued by some to introduce certain biases into the judiciary. In recent years the legal profession from which judges are selected has become more representative than it was through most of Canada's history. According to a 2012 study by Ryerson University's Diversity Institute, visible minority judges constituted under 3 per cent of all federally appointed judges.[38]

Women have much greater representation in the legal profession than a generation ago. In 1971 they made up only about 5 per cent of the legal profession. Today they constitute close to 40 per cent of all lawyers. Also, about one-third of judges in Canada are female. The main argument for the increased representation of women on the courts has been that they bring important perspectives on the law and on society that have been less likely to be embraced by male judges.[39]

Judges work within the embedded premises of the law. Among the most important of these premises, in terms of their impact on the distribution of power in society, are the rights of the individual, the rights associated with private property, and the concept of the business corporation as an individual under the law. Individualism is woven throughout the legal fabric of Canadian society. In practice, respect for individual rights tends to be more important for the privileged than for the disadvantaged. While this is obviously true in the case of property rights—protecting these rights matters more to those who have something to lose than to those who do not—it also tends to be true in matters like individual freedom of expression. The powerful tug of *liberal individualism* on judicial reasoning was clearly demonstrated in a 1987 Supreme Court of Canada decision on the right to strike. A majority of the justices decided that "The constitutional guarantee of freedom of association . . . does not include, in the case of a trade union, a guarantee of the right to bargain collectively and the right to strike."[40] To put it very simply, economic rights were viewed as subordinate to political ones. The Court said as much: ". . . the overwhelming preoccupation of the Charter is with individual, political, and democratic rights with conspicuous inattention to economic and property rights."[41] But in practical terms "conspicuous inattention" meant that the existing balance of power and rights between employers and workers was considered to be correct, and that workers and unions could not count on the courts to defend their rights against governments intent on diminishing them.

On the other hand, judges are generally quite aware of the socio-economic and political consequences of their decisions. In his dissent from the majority decision in the 1987 right-to-strike case, Chief Justice Brian Dickson observed, "Throughout history, workers have associated to overcome their vulnerability as individuals to the strength of their employers. The capacity to bargain collectively has long been recognized as one of the integral and primary functions of associations of working people."[42] Collective bargaining, according to Dickson, requires that workers have the right to strike. Moreover, in a 1989 decision the Supreme Court rejected the traditional liberal notion of equality as *identical treatment before the law* in favour of what is sometimes called **substantive equality**, which means that individuals should be looked at in terms of their group characteristics and the possible advantages or disadvantages they may have experienced as a result of these attributes.

Aspects of liberal individualism are also embedded in the judicial process. All judicial systems are adversarial: the plaintiff in civil cases or the prosecution in criminal cases brings an action against the defendant. Common-law systems like Canada's represent the most extreme form of this adversarial process. In civil cases the onus is placed on the individual

substantive equality the principle that individuals should be looked at in terms of their group characteristics and the possible advantages or disadvantages they may have experienced as a result of these attributes

parties—plaintiff and defendant—to make their respective cases before the court. In criminal proceedings the state is responsible for prosecuting the case against an individual or organization, but that individual or organization is responsible for the defence. In both civil and criminal proceedings, the role of the court is to hear and weigh the evidence, and the court does not participate in the development of either side of the action.

It is up to a plaintiff or defendant to make his or her most persuasive case. The ability of each to do so depends, in part, on his or her access to competent legal counsel. In criminal proceedings, the state pays for legal counsel for defendants who cannot afford to hire a lawyer. Legal aid is available in all provinces for those who cannot afford the legal costs of a civil action. But these forms of subsidized legal assistance by no means equalize access to effective legal counsel. High-priced legal professionals, whose assistance is beyond the means of most people, are backed up by the resources of a large law firm.

Although the judicial system is hardly a level playing field, it would be wrong to suggest that it serves only the interests of the wealthy and powerful. Indeed, particularly since the addition of the Charter of Rights and Freedoms to Canada's Constitution, groups representing women, Aboriginal Canadians, the disabled, gays and lesbians, and other interests that could hardly be described as being near the epicentre of power in Canadian society have frequently achieved successes in the courts that were not possible in legislative and electoral forums.

The era of judges deferring to the will of elected officials is over. The Charter was the catalyst for what both critics and supporters see as an enormous increase in the policy role of the courts. However, as Chief Justice Beverley McLachlin has argued (see Box 8.8), criticism of the courts in the Charter era too often has confused *outcome* (determination of social policy) with *process* (the impartiality of the courts as opposed to the partisan nature of the process by which governments and legislatures seek to establish social policy). Of course, some critics would challenge the chief justice's claim regarding the impartiality of judges and the judicial system.

The Charter has been a decisive factor in this matter of judges being more willing to depart from legal precedents. In one of the earliest Charter decisions, *R v. Big M Drug Mart Ltd* (1985), the Supreme Court stated that the Charter "does not simply 'recognize and declare' existing rights as they were circumscribed by legislation current at the time of the Charter's entrenchment." The Charter has enabled Canadian judges to look at familiar issues through a different lens and arrive at very different rulings, thus weakening the conservative tug of **stare decisis**— the legal principle of determining the points in litigation according to precedent. Those who argue that the courts should play a transformative role were deeply disappointed in September 2013 when the Ontario Superior Court refused to hear a case involving homelessness. Advocates for the homeless argued that sections 7 and 15 of the Charter should be interpreted as providing a right to housing and that the existence of homelessness is a Charter violation. The governments of Ontario and Canada opposed this interpretation, insisting that the courts had no authority to decide such matters. The Ontario Superior Court agreed.

Some argue that recourse to the courts to achieve ends that cannot be accomplished through the political process is fundamentally undemocratic and has weakened *parliamentary*

stare decisis the legal principle of determining the points in litigation according to precedent

Inside Politics

BOX 8.8 | Chief Justice McLachlin Defends the Court's Involvement with Questions of Social Policy

The fact that judges rule on social questions that affect large numbers of people does not, however, mean that judges are political. There is much confusion on this point in the popular press. Judges are said to be acting politically, to have descended (or perhaps ascended) into the political arena. Judges, on this view, are simply politicians who do not need to stand for election and can never be removed.

This misapprehension confuses outcome with process. Many judicial decisions on important social issues—say affirmative action, or abortion, or gay rights—will be political in the sense that they will satisfy some political factions at the expense of others. But the term "political" is used in the context to describe an outcome, not a process. While the outcomes of cases are inevitably political in some broad sense of the term, it is important—critical, even—that the process be impartial. It is inescapable that judges' decisions will have political ramifications. But it is essential that they not be partisan. In their final form, judgments on social policy questions are often not all that different from legislation. It is the process by which the judgments are arrived at that distinguishes them. Legislation is often the product of compromise or conflict between various political factions, each faction pushing its own agenda. The judicial arena does not, and should not, provide simply another forum for the same kind of contests. Judges must *maintain the appearance and reality of impartiality*. It is impartiality that distinguishes us from the other branches of government, and impartiality that gives us our legitimacy.

—Remarks of the Right Honourable Beverley McLachlin, PC, Chief Justice of Canada, on "The Role of Judges in Modern Society," given at the 4th Worldwide Common Law Judiciary Conference in Vancouver, BC, on 5 May 2001. Supreme Court of Canada, 2001, www.scc-csc.gc.ca/court-cour/ju/spe-dis/bm01-05-05-eng.asp. Reproduced with the permission of the Minister of Public Works and Government Services, 2012.

supremacy in Canada. It is simply wrong, however, to conceive of the courts as being outside the political process. Even before the Charter, the courts were very much a part of politics and policy making in Canada. Their rulings on the federal–provincial division of powers and on all manner of policy questions have always been part of Canadian politics. Quebec nationalists have long complained that the Supreme Court of Canada has a pro-federal bias, a claim that—true or not—reflects the inescapable involvement of the Court in the politics of federalism. The fact that by law three of the Supreme Court's nine judges must be members of the Quebec bar, and that by tradition three should be from Ontario, two from the West, and one from Atlantic Canada, shows that the essentially political issue of regional representation has been considered important for the judicial branch, just as it is important in the executive and legislative branches of government.

In recent years the issue of representation on the bench, particularly on the Supreme Court, has become even more politically charged. The death of Justice John Sopinka in 1997 and the retirement of Justice Peter Cory in 1999 unleashed flurries of behind-the-scenes lobbying and public advocacy on behalf of particular candidates for the vacancies on Canada's highest court. Gender and judicial ideology appear to have become more prominent criteria in the Supreme Court selection process, at least in the eyes of many advocacy and rights-oriented groups.[43] Many critics have argued that the judicial selection process is mired in partisanship and a lack of transparency and should be reformed, including a public review of judicial appointees. The Liberal government was criticized in 2016 for not coming up with a plan to fill the many judicial vacancies that had been left behind in the wake of the Conservative government. Shortly after appointing 15 new judges in June 2016, the Trudeau government outlined a Supreme Court appointment process and the creation of an advisory board headed by former Conservative prime minister Kim Campbell. The process allows any qualified lawyer or judge to submit their name to the board. The advisory board will draft a list of three to five candidates to be reviewed by among others, the Chief Justice of Canada, the opposition parties' justice critics, and provincial attorney generals.

If we accept, then, that the courts are unavoidably part of the political process, is there any basis for the claim that recourse to the courts may be undemocratic? The short answer is "yes." Several decades before the Charter, James Mallory argued that business interests cynically exploited the federal division of powers in the British North America Act to oppose increased state interference in their affairs, regardless of which level of government was doing the interfering.[44] Respect for democratic principles and the Constitution was the cloak behind which business attempted to conceal its self-interest.

In the Charter era similar criticisms have been expressed. Charter critics like Rainer Knopff and Ted Morton argue that recourse to the courts by abortion rights advocates, gay and lesbian rights groups, and Aboriginals, among others, has produced rulings that often elevate the preferences of special interests over more broadly held values. These critics agree with Michael Mandel's argument that the Charter era has witnessed the "legalization" of Canadian politics.[45] Emboldened by the entrenchment of rights in the Constitution and the declaration of constitutional supremacy in section 52 of the Constitution Act, 1982, judges have been less deferential to governments and legislatures than in the past. Moreover, a network of rights-oriented advocacy groups, law professors, lawyers, journalists, and bureaucrats working within the rights apparatus of the state (from human rights commissions to the ubiquitous equity officers found throughout the public sector) has emerged; in the words of Morton and Knopff, it "prefers the policy-making power of the less obviously democratic governmental institutions."[46] The institutions they are referring to are the courts and quasi-judicial rights commissions and tribunals.

Whatever disagreements Canadians may have with specific decisions of the Supreme Court, such as same-sex marriage, assisted suicide, and rights for Métis and non-status Indians, a survey published in 2015 by the Angus Reid Institute indicated that most Canadians

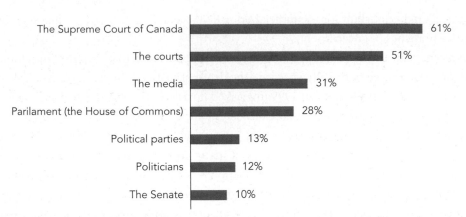

FIGURE 8.11 Canadians' Confidence in Political Institutions and Media

An Angus Reid survey asked Canadians how much confidence they had in several institutions. The chart shows the combined results for the responses "a great deal" and "quite a lot."

Source: Angus Reid Institute, "Canadians Have a More Favourable View of Their Supreme Court than Americans Have of Their Own," http://angusreid.org/supreme-court/

continue to respect the courts. In fact, Canadians had a more favourable opinion of their Supreme Court than Americans had of their own. Canadians also seemed to trust the courts far more than they do their political and media institutions. As Figure 8.11 indicates, 61 per cent of Canadians expressed "a great deal" or "quite a lot" of confidence in the Supreme Court opposed to levels of confidence in Parliament at 28 per cent.

Summary

Those who teach and study Canadian parliamentary democracy often remark on its complexity. Yet our system of government has managed to work in Canada, in spite of its complexity and many societal cleavages, for 150 years—longer than any other Commonwealth country, except the United Kingdom. The roles and the working relationships of the branches of government— the executive (including the bureaucracy), the legislature, and the judiciary—are based on the Westminster model, which was introduced in the British North American colonies in 1848. Unlike the republican-presidential model, the Westminster model provides no clear separation of powers between the branches of government. Nor is there a codified or formal system of legislative checks and balances to protect democracy. Instead, there is a set of principles, constitutional conventions, and institutional devices that have evolved over several hundred years to prevent our political elites or any one person or a branch of government from abusing power. These principles, conventions, and devices are at the heart of our democracy. They are embedded in institutional features such as *constitutional monarchy*, *representative government* and *responsible government*, the *rule of law*, and *independent judicial review* (see Table 6.3, The Canadian System of Checks and Balances).

Our system of government makes the monarch, and, in her absence, her representative, the Governor General, the formal head of state and the impartial head of the executive. The position has become mostly symbolic over the centuries, but it has retained some significant powers such as prorogation and dissolution of Parliament and legislative assent. Some experts have suggested that these powers could be used to protect Canadian democracy.

In practice, however, it is the prime minister who is the head of the executive and simultaneously the head of the legislature. This makes the office of prime minister very powerful. In fact, the PM and cabinet essentially dominate the legislative agenda of Parliament. The leader of the party winning the most seats in a general election is given the first opportunity to form the government. In some ways, responsible government, which has evolved over centuries to prevent abuses of power by the prime minister and the cabinet, may in fact strengthen the PM's position, by requiring MPs to act as a disciplined bloc along party lines to keep the government from falling. Party discipline has diminished the role of the backbench MPs to the point where they tend to spend much of their time dealing with constituency matters, and less time with policy and legislative matters. Some pundits now wonder whether the office of prime minister has evolved to a point in Canada where the institutional and democratic checks against abuses of power no longer work effectively.

Cabinet ministers have a much greater say than backbenchers in policy matters and legislation. This is why cabinet positions are so desirable, and why it is important to a government's success that various regional interests and other special interests at least appear to be well represented in the cabinet. While ministers are also involved in the running of their departments, they rely heavily on public servants to manage day-to-day matters. The bureaucracy enters the policy process both early and late. Bureaucrats are the people who actually administer the programs established by law. In doing so they regularly exercise considerable discretion in policy and fiscal matters—a fact that often leads special-interest groups to focus at least part of their attention on the bureaucracy.

The judiciary has certainly played an important role in arbitrating disputes between Ottawa and the provinces, but the courts have also ensured, especially with the entrenchment of the 1982 Charter of Human Rights and Freedoms, that legislation and government policies are in keeping with the Constitution. Some critics have said that the Canadian courts have been the keepers of a proper balance between the powers of the state and the rights of the individual, while others have observed that unelected officials (judges) have become "political" and have supplanted the notion of parliamentary supremacy.

Review Exercises

1. Visit the government of Canada website (https://www.canada.ca/en/government/system.html) and answer these questions:
   a. What major government programs and services can be identified from this website?
   b. According to the website, how does the government ensure accountability?
   c. What does the government list as its major priorities?
2. Develop a list of the checks on a prime minister's power and compare them to those of an American president.
3. List the various governmental organizations (federal, provincial, municipal) you have ever been in contact with and the reasons for the contact(s).
4. Most Canadians believe that public-sector organizations are less efficient than those in the private sector. Define "efficiency" and develop criteria you would use to measure the efficiency of private and public organizations. Can the same criteria be used for both?

Up for Debate

1. Resolved: Members of Parliament should always follow the will of their party.
2. Resolved: Canadian senators should be independent of the party that appointed them.
3. Could the Canadian parliamentary system function without a corresponding party system?
4. Resolved: Judges should be elected.

Starting Points For Research

Aucoin, Peter, Mark Jarvis, and Lori Turnbull. *Democratizing the Constitution: Reforming Responsible Government.* Toronto: Emond Montgomery, 2010.

Miljan, Lydia. *Public Policy in Canada*, 6th edn. Toronto: Oxford University Press, 2012.

Savoie Donald. *Governing from the Centre: The Concentration of Power in Canadian Politics.* Toronto: University of Toronto Press, 1999.

CBC Archives and TVO's *The Agenda*

Visit the companion website for *Canadian Democracy: A Concise Introduction* to follow links to audio and video footage related to the main themes of the chapter: www.oupcanada.com/BrooksConcise2e.

Relevant Websites

Visit the companion website for *Canadian Democracy: A Concise Introduction* to browse a collection of websites featuring material related to the key themes of the chapter, an excellent starting point for research: www.oupcanada.com/BrooksConcise2e.

PART III
Participation in Politics

Politics does not stop at the doors of Parliament. It spills out onto the streets and into community halls and corporate boardrooms, involving citizens, organized interests, and the media. What is sometimes referred to as *civil society* both acts on and is itself acted on by the institutions of the state, making demands, organizing resistance, and providing support in various ways.

The participation of groups in civil society assumes many forms. Citizens play a role individually as voters and collectively through what is described as public opinion. Some are involved in more active ways, belonging to and working for political parties or groups that attempt to shape the political conversation and government policy. Organized interests often attempt to influence the actions of government, through a range of techniques that include lobbying, legal action, and attempting to shape public opinion. The media's specialized function involves reporting and framing the political conversation. Most of what we know about the political world is mediated by those whose job involves selecting information (i.e., news) for print and broadcast and then interpreting it.

In the following three chapters we will examine some of the most important forms of participation in Canadian politics.

← Students protest rising university tuition in Montreal. Politics extends far beyond the doors of Parliament; civil society participates in politics by making demands, organizing resistance, and providing support.
Source: ROGERIO BARBOSA/Getty Images.

9 Parties and Elections

Political parties and elections are essential features of modern democracy. After reading this chapter, you should be able to

1. define "political party" and explain the function of political parties in Canadian democracy
2. explain the origins and the evolution of the party system in Canada
3. outline the role of brokerage politics in Canadian political parties
4. compare the Canadian first-past-the-post electoral system with the electoral systems of other democracies
5. discuss how political parties are financed and the potential for undue influence by special interests
6. explain voting behaviour in Canada

↑ An essential feature of modern democracy, elections allow citizens to play a political role both individually and collectively.

Source: Bloomberg/Getty Images.

Elections, and the political parties that contest them, represent the main contact points between most citizens and their political system. Most adult citizens vote at least some of the time, although perhaps not in every election and probably more often federally than provincially or locally. This may be the extent of their participation in politics: short bursts of attention to candidates and their messages and occasional visits to the polls, interspersed around lengthier periods of inattention and political inactivity. Until the 2015 general election, when almost 69 per cent of voters cast a ballot, the last few federal elections had seen only about 6 of 10 eligible voters do so. We can assume that even of those who did not vote, most were aware that an election was taking place.

Elections remind us that we live in a democracy in which those who wish to govern must win the support of a considerable number of the governed. Elections are the corner-stone of democratic governance, yet many believe they have become meaningless and even farcical affairs orchestrated by the same people who put together marketing campaigns for cars and deodorants. Treating voters as taxpayers who shop for the political party that will give them the most "bang for their buck" is something explored by Susan Delacourt in her book *Shopping for Votes: How Politicians Choose Us and We Choose Them*. She writes, "In a nation of consumer-citizens, the customer is always right. It is not the politician's job to change people's minds or prejudices, but to confirm them or play to them, to seal the deal of support . . . . Speeches are not made to educate or inform the audience but to serve up market-ing slogans. Political parties become 'brands' and political announcements become product launches."[1] Political parties and candidates have also been criticized for avoiding important issues and framing electoral discourse in ways that deflect attention from major divisions in society, and for trivializing politics by replacing substance with style and image. Some have argued that the "dumbing down" of public life has been facilitated by the fact that modern elec-tions are fought largely through the medium of television, which elevates images over ideas. Is it any wonder that political parties have for years ranked among the lowest of social institutions in public esteem? Democracy's cornerstone appears to have developed some worrisome cracks.

Doubts about the democratic integrity of elections are not new. One of the oldest fears is that those with money are more likely to influence voter behaviour. For example, Hugh Allan essen-tially bankrolled the Conservative Party in the 1873 federal election in exchange for a promise from John A. Macdonald that Allan would be made president of the company chartered to build a trans-continental railroad. Over a century ago Liberal cabinet minister Joseph-Israël Tarte remarked that "Elections are not won with prayers," a fact of political life that has become even truer in the age of television campaigning. But fact of life or not, if parties and votes can be purchased by those with deep pockets, this surely undermines the democratic credibility of the electoral process.

Canadians are not used to comparing their democratic institutions and processes to those of undemocratic or failed regimes. The problems of one-party states—ballot fraud, voter in-timidation, and bribery—are routine in many countries. And when compared to the electoral systems of Zimbabwe, Côte d'Ivoire, or Russia, these criticisms of parties and elections in Canada seem petty. We place the bar higher and measure the performance of our political par-ties and our electoral system against ideas of *equality* and *participation* that have evolved out of our liberal-democratic tradition. Critics may differ over the nature and extent of its shortcom-ings, but judged against these values, the Canadian experience is not perfect.

Canadian Spotlight

BOX 9.1   What Do Canadians Get Worked Up About?
Single-Issue Elections in Canadian History

As the 1891 general election poster below suggests, the issue of free trade has figured prominently in several Canadian general elections, and it has been the single-most important issue in three general elections since Confederation. In fact, free trade was an important issue before Confederation. One of the arguments used by the Fathers of Confederation in 1867 was that the trade created by Confederation would help replace the international trade lost when, in the 1850s and 1860s, Britain moved away from preferential trade with its colonies, and when, in 1866, the US cancelled the Reciprocity Treaty with the British North American colonies.

A number of single-issue elections have been fought since Confederation, in which one issue, including free trade, has dominated the debate:

1891	Free trade with the United States
1896	The Manitoba schools question
1898	Free trade with the United States
1917	Conscription during World War I
1926	The role of the monarchy in Canadian politics
1945	Social programs and the welfare state
1957	One-party rule
1963	Foreign policy and nuclear weapons
1979	Central government power
1981	Central government power
1988	Free trade with the United States (NAFTA)

Free trade also became a prominent campaign issue in the 2015 general election following the negotiation of the Trans-Pacific Partnership (TPP) trade agreement.

What does a review of our media headlines tell us about current issues in Canadian politics? If a general election were held tomorrow, which issue(s) would be most likely to capture the Canadian public's attention? Is there one particular issue that stands out?

Library and Archives Canada, Acc. No. 1983-33-1102

THE WAY HE WOULD LIKE IT.
CANADA FOR SALE.

PUBLISHED BY THE INDUSTRIAL LEAGUE. FREDERIC NICHOLLS HON. SEC.

In this 1891 campaign poster, John A. Macdonald and his Conservative Party were trying to persuade voters that *Reciprocity*—a policy of free trade with the United States proposed by the Liberals during the election—was tantamount to selling off Canada, and would eventually lead to the United States annexing Canada. Similar arguments were made by the Liberals and the NDP when Brian Mulroney's Progressive Conservatives made a free trade deal with the US the main issue of the 1988 general election.

The Definition and Functions of Political Parties

A **political party** may be defined as an organization that offers slates of candidates to voters at election time. To this end, parties

- recruit and select party candidates
- raise money for their campaigns
- develop policies that express the ideas and goals their candidates stand for
- attempt to persuade citizens to vote for their candidates

political party
an organization that offers a slate of candidates to voters at election time

In a democracy, parties are not created by nor are they agents of the state. They are, in Eugene Forsey's words, "voluntary associations of people who hold broadly similar opinions on public questions."[2]

It would be misleading to characterize political parties as organizations focused simply on the election of "governmental office holders."[3] While most parties do hope to elect candidates to office, and perhaps enough candidates to form a government, some parties may contest elections as a means of making their ideas public. This is true of the Marijuana Party, whose stated mission is the decriminalization of cannabis, and the Marxist-Leninist Party, whose quixotic advocacy of global revolution by the proletariat has remained largely unchanged since the *Communist Manifesto* of 1848. The now defunct Rhinoceros Party, one that injected some welcome humour into elections—it stood for the repeal of the law of gravity, among other things—ran candidates in many Canadian ridings during the 1970s and 1980s, without any serious expectation of electing candidates.

John Meisel, one of Canada's foremost experts on parties and elections, identifies seven functions that political parties serve in a democracy.[4]

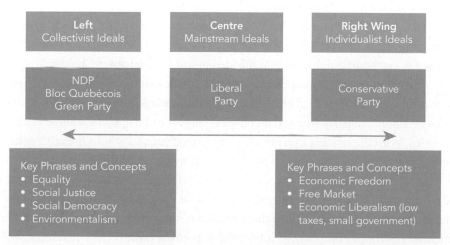

FIGURE 9.1 Socio-Economic Values as Reflected by Canadian Political Parties

1. *Integrating citizens into the political system.* Through voting for parties and thinking about public affairs in terms of the policies and ideologies represented by parties, citizens develop attachments to the political system more generally. This connection, Meisel argues, has weakened recently as political parties are often perceived as yet another distant and unaccountable institution.

2. *Developing policy.* In many democracies, political parties represent clear ideological and policy options. Moreover, the deliberations of the party membership are important sources of policies that a party will seek to implement once in power.

3. *Elite recruitment.* With rare exceptions, those who run for and are elected to federal and provincial office in Canada do so as the official candidates of their parties. Parties choose their candidates and their leaders, and in doing so they determine the pool of persons from whom elected public officials, including members of the government, will be drawn. While the bar for selection of members, of electoral candidates, and of party leadership is set fairly low in most democracies, those with more formal education, higher incomes, and jobs of greater social status tend to participate more in the selection of party candidates and leaders, as well as being candidates themselves.

4. *Organization of government.* Governing parties propose; opposition parties oppose. This somewhat oversimplified formula expresses the fact that political parties play an important role in how governance occurs in democracies. Parties provide a partisan structure to the process of law-making and the debate of public affairs. Under the parliamentary system that exists in Canada, this partisan structure is by design an adversarial one, from the physical layout of the legislature to the traditions and procedures observed in conducting the business of Parliament.

5. *Structuring the vote.* Just as parties lend structure to the activities of the legislature and allow for the identification of the government with a particular party (or coalition of parties in some democratic systems), they also serve to structure the vote in elections. The fact that only a handful of political parties are serious contenders for citizens' votes simplifies the information-gathering task facing voters. Each party represents, in a sense, a particular selection on a limited menu.

6. *Organizing public opinion.* Parties are often characterized as right wing, left wing, or centrist; as liberal, conservative, or socialist; or by some other set of labels signifying that they occupy particular places on the ideological map (also see Chapter 2). Parties reflect, but may also help create or at least reinforce, divisions within society. Canada's two historically dominant political parties have used **brokerage politics**, which is a strategic choice by a political party to avoid ideological appeals in favour of a flexible centrist style of politics. With the notable exceptions of the Conservative Party in the 2015 general election, Canadian political parties have generally avoided speaking the language of class politics and have attempted to accommodate the preferences of major interests, regions, and communities through their flexible policy style.

7. *Interest aggregation.* Organizations that represent secondary school teachers, gays, or wetlands conservationists may be influential in politics; however, the narrowness of their respective agendas and their population base mean that they could not hope to elect a

brokerage politics a strategic choice by a political party to avoid ideological appeals in favour of a flexible centrist style of politics

Teachers' Party, Gay Rights Party, or Save-the-Ducks Party to power. Parties, especially those that hope to form a government, must bring together a coalition of different interests sufficiently broad to win election. It is not always possible to satisfy all interests, and paradoxically, the practice of interest aggregation may reinforce regional division. In fact, history shows that it is seldom possible to avoid playing off one region against another in Canadian politics. The Liberal Party, the most successful of our national parties, has often formed a government with little representation from Western Canada.

The Origins and Evolution of Canada's Party System[5]

The Nature of Brokerage Politics

The origins of Canada's two major political parties—the Conservatives and the Liberals—can be traced back to the shifting coalitions and alignments in the United Province of Canada in the 1840s and 1850s. Although these groups were much more amorphous and unstable than modern political parties, and would not really coalesce into cohesive organizations until the 1880s, they did represent distinct political tendencies. On the one hand was the governing coalition of Liberal–Conservatives (which would eventually drop the "Liberal" from its official name) under the leadership of Sir John A. Macdonald in Canada West and his French-Canadian counterpart, George-Étienne Cartier, in Canada East. It was a disparate organization encompassing a number of distinct groups. Many of these groups had potentially conflicting interests (Catholics and Protestants, French and English, urban and rural dwellers), but the organization was held together largely by the political dexterity of Macdonald and by the gradual development of a unifying vision, one based on the nation-building program eventually enshrined in the *National Policy* of 1878–9. The key elements of this program were the implementation of a protective tariff designed to promote the growth of domestic manufacturing in Ontario and Quebec, the encouragement of Western settlement to open up a market for the products of Central Canadian industry and to protect this territory from American encroachment, and the creation of a transcontinental railroad to ship the manufactured goods of the centre to the newly opened Western territories.[6]

On the other side was an even looser opposition coalition, comprising the Clear Grits of Canada West and the *Rouges* of Canada East. Both groups shared a common admiration for the republican and individualist ideas of the United States and both advocated free trade with the Americans. They also shared an unrelenting hostility to the commercial and banking interests linked to Macdonald's governing party. But the two groups were an uneasy partnership and there was considerable ethnic and religious tension. It was only when Wilfrid Laurier assumed the leadership of the Liberal Party in 1887 that these diverse elements were moulded into a relatively cohesive political organization.

We should not make too much of the doctrinal differences between Liberals and Conservatives during these formative years of the party system (roughly 1880 to 1920). Admittedly, the Liberals were identified with free trade and provincial rights, and after 1885 (when Louis Riel was hanged for treason following the failed Northwest Rebellion) they appeared to be "more sensitive to the interests of French Canada" than the Tories.[7] They were also more sympathetic to the plight of the farmer than were the Conservatives. The latter, meanwhile, were generally thought of as the party of the British connection, the party of privilege—in the sense that its leading spokesmen claimed that all healthy and stable societies are ruled by a "natural governing" elite—the party of centralization and economic protection. But these ideological differences were almost always subordinate to the central preoccupation of Canadian politics: **patronage**, which is the distribution of favours by a governing politician (e.g., political appointments or government contracts) in exchange for political support.

The scramble to control the distribution of government patronage was the dominant feature of Canadian politics during the 1860s and 1870s. A number of provisions in our electoral law have shaped our political life. For example, the use of the **open ballot**, an electoral system whereby voters simply declared their choice publicly at the polls in the presence of a government official (and anybody else who happened to be in the room at the time!), provided numerous opportunities for bribery, coercion, and intimidation. This made it difficult for anybody whose livelihood depended on government contracts to vote against candidates supported by the ruling cabinet. And the non-simultaneous, or staggered, elections permitted the government to call elections in safe ridings and forced candidates in many ridings to be *ministerialists*, so called because their "politics were not to support a party but a ministry and any ministry would do."[8] This non-partisan stance ensured a steady flow of government patronage into the successful candidate's constituency.

The open ballot and staggered elections were eliminated by the late 1870s, and elections were gradually standardized across the provinces. However, this did not reduce the importance of patronage. In fact, the federal parties continued to operate without civil service reform (the merit principle) and with a highly restricted franchise and a weak working class (from an organizational and numerical standpoint). It has been suggested that these factors predisposed political parties to appeal to potential supporters through networks of *patron–client relations* (where votes are exchanged for certain "favours") rather than on the basis of *collectivist* or *solidaristic* appeals (class-based ideologies).[9] This is the situation described by the French political sociologist André Siegfried when he visited Canada just over 100 years ago. Siegfried complained that the preoccupation with questions of "material interest" and "public works" tended to "lower the general level of political life" in Canada. He also noted that Canadian politics was hardly lacking in substantive issues—rivalries between Catholics and Protestants, French and English, for example—that could have been addressed by the two major parties, but that the party leaders "prefer that they should not be talked about. The subjects which remain available for discussion are not numerous. In addition, the parties borrow one another's policies periodically, displaying a coolness in this process that would disconcert us Europeans."[10]

Siegfried's comments on the nature of party competition in Canada are still remarkably relevant. If Siegfried were somehow transported to present-day Canada, he would probably

patronage
|the distribution of favours by a governing politician (e.g., political appointments or government contracts) in exchange for political support

open ballot
an electoral system whereby voters simply declared their choice publicly at the polls in the presence of a government official

conclude that there have been few substantive changes in our party system since he published his work in 1906. The emphasis on accommodating the diverse interests—regional, linguistic, ethnic, class, religious—of the electorate through the prudent employment of "public works" and individual material incentives is still a characteristic feature of federal and provincial politics. Elections are usually preceded by many new government programs and spending initiatives—ill-disguised attempts by the party in power to purchase electoral support in key ridings. As well, the borrowing of elements of one party's program by another party is still going on today. These features of Canadian politics, as well as the many flip-flops by the older parties on key issues such as the GST only serve to fuel the electorate's cynicism about politics and their distrust of politicians.

The electoral opportunism exhibited by the Liberals and the Tories in recent decades does not mean that the two older parties have no principles or ideological commitments whatsoever. In recent times Canada's oldest parties have represented distinct traditions, particularly on matters concerning federalism and Canada–US relations. With the accession of Pierre Trudeau to the party leadership in 1968, the Liberals became identified in the minds of most Canadian voters with a strong central state (hence the ongoing battles between Ottawa and the provinces over control of natural resource revenues), with economic nationalism (Petro-Canada, the National Energy Program, the Foreign Investment Review Agency), and with "French power." The Tories, meanwhile, came increasingly to be associated with political decentralization: Joe Clark, when he was leader of the party and briefly prime minister in the late 1970s, described Canadian federalism as a "community of communities," which Trudeau sarcastically rejected as "shopping-mall" federalism. As prime minister, Stephen Harper refused to meet with the provinces and continued to increase the equalization payments to the provinces without any of the controls that Liberal governments might have imposed. The Conservatives also came to embrace the notion of free trade with the United States; this represented a reversal of the party positions on the subject in the late nineteenth and early twentieth centuries, when the Liberals strongly advocated continentalist economic policies. Stephen Harper made free trade a central feature of his government, signing more than a dozen free trade deals since 2006. Finally, the neo-conservatism of the 1980s, spearheaded by British prime minister Margaret Thatcher and US president Ronald Reagan, found its most receptive audience among the Conservatives during the Mulroney years. In recent years the federal Liberal Party has been associated with a somewhat more centralist vision of federal–provincial relations and a brand of mild to occasionally hotter anti-Americanism, while the Conservatives have branded themselves as more decentralist and more sympathetic to Washington.

Despite these apparent differences in the recent policy orientations of the two older parties, Siegfried's central contention about the Canadian party system remains accurate. Our historically dominant parties have always been much more flexible, more opportunistic, more wary of ideological appeals to the electorate than those in most European nations, and, as Siegfried wrote, dominated by their leaders:

> . . . it is of the first importance to the success of a party that it should be led by someone who inspires confidence, and whose mere name is a program in itself.

As long as the Conservatives had Macdonald for their leader, they voted for him rather than for the party. So it is with Laurier and the Liberals of today. If Laurier disappeared, the Liberals would perhaps find that they had lost the real secret of their victories. . . . Canadians attach themselves rather to the concrete reality than to the abstract principle. They vote as much for the man who symbolizes the policy as for the policy itself.[11]

The nature of our electoral system and the norms that govern its party competition are such that the Liberals and Conservatives can usually fight elections without having to worry about keeping their principles intact or consistent. Many observers of Canada's party system have called this type of mainstream or flexible, non-ideological party system a *brokerage party system*. That is, the two older parties at the federal level act as "brokers of ideas . . . middlemen who select from all the ideas pressing for recognition as public policy those they think can be shaped to have the widest appeal."[12] Each of the parties attempts to cobble together a winning coalition of voters at election time; the voting support for the two major parties, therefore, does not come from stable, well-defined social groups, as is the case in many Western European countries. Most importantly, politics in Canada lacks an obvious *class* dimension. Conflicts between the working class and capitalists over the political and economic rights of workers, and over the distribution of national wealth, take a back seat to other issues—those arising out of religious, ethnic, and regional rivalries, for instance.

This peculiarity of Canadian politics has led some observers to describe the Canadian party system as less developed or less modern than those of most other industrial nations. Robert Alford, for example, declared in his classic study of voting behaviour in four Anglo-American democracies (the United States, Canada, Great Britain, and Australia) that Canada had the lowest level of class voting among the nations he examined.[13] Alford's explanation of this situation echoed the one advanced by Siegfried almost 60 years earlier: "Class voting is low in Canada because the political parties are identified as representatives of regional, religious, and ethnic groupings rather than as representatives of national class interests, and this, in turn, is due to a relative lack of national integration."[14] Class divisions and antagonisms are certainly not absent in Canada, Alford observed, and he predicted that once the issue of national unity had been resolved, class voting would increase and Canada would come to resemble other modern democracies—Great Britain, for instance. Fifty years later, Alford's prediction has simply not come true: the questions of national unity and regional or ethnic grievances are still more important than class. The two older parties do not normally appeal to specific class constituencies and still evade class issues when possible. Moreover, the self-described left-wing party in Canada, the NDP, receives nowhere near a majority of the votes of blue-collar workers.

Brokerage theory, then, makes two fundamental claims about Canada's two historically dominant political parties: first, they do not appeal to specific socio-economic groupings and they lack cohesive ideological visions, especially those based on class interests and identity; second, the parties are flexible and opportunistic because this sort of behaviour is necessary to preserve the fragile unity of the nation. This brings to mind Siegfried's observation that the prudent and cautious leaders do not want to discuss some of the pressing issues to be discussed for fear of inflaming group jealousies and thereby jeopardizing the stability of the country.

An alternative explanation of the absence of class politics in Canada is advanced by Janine Brodie and Jane Jenson in *Crisis, Challenge, and Change*.[15] They argue that brokerage theory tends to view political parties as more or less passive transmission belts for societal demands. The more important role of political parties in liberal democracies, however, is to create a *definition of politics*

> through which people make sense of their daily lives. Because issues are raised and choices provided in particular ways, this cultural construction defines the content and sets the limits of partisan politics. Social problems never included within the bounds of partisan political debate remain invisible and confined to the private sector or private life for resolution. From a myriad of social tensions the definition of politics identifies and selects those susceptible to "political" solutions. Political parties, in other words, by defining the political, contribute to the organization and disorganization of groups in the electorate.[16]

Brodie and Jenson argue that in the period immediately following Confederation, class, religion, language, and other social differences competed with each other as potential support bases for the two federal parties. Since both of these parties drew the bulk of their support from the same social group—the bourgeoisie—they tended to avoid the issue of class in their competition for votes.

Brodie and Jenson's explanation of the non-class nature of the Canadian party system is an important contribution. Nevertheless, it does seem somewhat overdrawn, since it appears to downplay or minimize the pre-eminence of religious and ethnic divisions in Canadian society in the late nineteenth century and to exaggerate the extent to which the parties have been able to play up the issues of language and culture for their own advantage. A large part of the explanation of the relative unimportance of class issues in Canadian politics must be found in the social organization of the working class itself and not simply attributed to the major parties' manipulation of the definition of politics.

The Role of Minor Parties in the Brokerage System

By the summer of 1991, almost three years into its second mandate, the Progressive Conservative government of Prime Minister Brian Mulroney had sunk to historic lows in public opinion polls. In fact, the Conservatives were being rivalled in voter popularity by a fledgling organization that was beginning to capture a great deal of voter and media attention: the Reform Party of Canada. Under the leadership of Preston Manning, the son of the former Social Credit premier of Alberta Ernest Manning, the Reform Party was founded in late 1987 primarily as a vehicle for Western discontent (its original slogan was "The West Wants In"). The Reform Party, which became the Canadian Alliance Party in 2000, was the latest in a string of Western protest movements that have tapped into the powerful feelings of economic and political alienation in the Western provinces. The two major parties have been seen as co-conspirators in this vicious circle of exploitation, since they are beholden to the powerful economic interests in the metropolitan areas and are compelled to enact policies that favour those regions where the bulk of the seats are to be won in a federal election.

This deep-seated suspicion among Westerners had been briefly dispelled by the 1984 federal election. Although the new prime minister, Brian Mulroney, was himself a bilingual Quebecer, for the first time since the Diefenbaker interlude of the 1950s, a large number of Westerners were placed in key cabinet positions. Western voters seemed to be saying that they were getting a government that would understand and respond to their concerns. Gradually, however, the guarded optimism gave way to disillusionment, as the Conservative government made a number of policy decisions that were viewed as detrimental to Western interests. The most publicized instance of "biased" government decision making was Ottawa's awarding of a multi-million dollar maintenance contract for the CF-18 fighter aircraft to a Quebec-based firm, despite the fact that Bristol Aerospace of Winnipeg had presented what federal officials acknowledged was a technically superior bid. Many Westerners concluded that the system itself—especially the "national" parties—was biased against the West. A new voice—a regionally based protest party like the Reform Party—was necessary to extract favourable policies from Central Canada.

Although the Reform Party began its life as a strictly regional organization, it quickly capitalized on the public's growing disenchantment with so-called "traditional" political parties to make inroads into Ontario, the bastion of Central Canadian power. The percentage of Canadians expressing "a great deal" or "quite a lot" of confidence in political parties had dropped from 30 per cent in 1979 to only 7 per cent in 1991.[17] Reform attacked existing political institutions as being unresponsive, unaccountable, and elitist, and attempted to portray itself as a *populist* movement rather than a political party. Rigid party discipline—which various governments had promised to relax, without much noticeable effect—was singled out by voters and the Reform Party alike as one of the biggest culprits in driving a wedge between the individual citizen and the political system. Under the Mulroney Conservatives, two Tory backbenchers who were publicly critical of the GST found themselves expelled from the party's caucus. Likewise, and despite Jean Chrétien's promise to relax party discipline, those Liberal MPs who opposed the government's 1995 gun control law were stripped of their parliamentary committee assignments. Such incidents remind voters that elected MPs are expected to vote as the party brass decides, even if this collides with the desires of their constituents.

There is also a generalized suspicion, fuelled by occasional sordid conflict-of-interest scandals at the federal and provincial levels, that politicians have become overly concerned with furthering their own careers or lining their pockets, at the expense of their constituents. The issue of MPs' pensions is a lightning rod for this popular sentiment. The Reform Party made much of its commitment to opt out of what it considered to be the unfairly generous terms of MPs' pensions, and in 1995 all but one of the party's MPs chose not to participate in the pension plan. Finally, there was a declining tolerance among voters for the kind of closed-door, elitist decision making that traditionally has characterized Canadian politics under Liberal and Conservative governments.

Responding to the widely held demands among the electorate for greater accountability and a more democratic political structure, the Reform Party and then the Canadian Alliance followed in the path of their populist predecessors, the Progressives of the 1920s and Social Credit of the 1930s and 1940s, and called for a number of institutional reforms that would increase the individual citizen's control over his or her representatives. The Alliance advocated greater use of referendums and citizen initiatives, the right of constituents to recall their MPs, and relaxation of party discipline and more "free votes" in Parliament. The Reform/Alliance ideology was conservative, and it regularly found itself the sole political party advocating radical change to the policy status quo. For example, during the 1993 election campaign it was the only party to advocate a major reduction in Canada's annual intake of immigrants during times when the economy was weak. It was also the only party to insist that deficit reduction, to be achieved mainly through spending cuts, should be Ottawa's top priority (a policy that the Liberal government subsequently embraced). Reform Party MPs were the main critics in Parliament of the 1995 gun control law requiring the registration of all firearms. The party also stood alone in its opposition to official multiculturalism and bilingualism.

Preston Manning, who founded the Reform Party of Canada and led it from 1987 to 2000, helped to "fan the flames" on Western regional and social conservative issues, forcing the country's dominant parties into ideological debates that would not have surfaced otherwise.

Although the Conservatives, Liberals, and NDP all initially tried to ignore or downplay the significance of the Reform Party, by the summer of 1991—when the report of the Spicer Commission was released, documenting the deep dissatisfaction of many Canadians with the functioning of their traditional democratic institutions, especially the political parties—this protest movement was simply too powerful to be casually dismissed.

"Minor" parties such as Reform/Alliance perform an important function in our brokerage party system: they provide a much-needed source of policy innovation, goading the major parties into acting on the concerns of regions, classes, or significant social groups that they have traditionally ignored or underestimated. This is exactly what happened during previous cycles of regional protest: the major parties were eventually compelled to head off the electoral challenge of a nascent protest movement (whether it was the Progressives, the Co-operative Commonwealth Federation [CCF], or Social Credit) by endorsing policies that appealed to the new party's supporters. Walter Young, in his history of the national CCF, described the contribution of third parties to the Canadian political system:

> By providing . . . the kind of ideological confrontation which is typically absent in contests between the two major parties, [minor parties] have served to stimulate the older parties and reactivate their previously dormant philosophies. . . . Two parties alone cannot successfully represent all the interests or act as a broker—honest or otherwise. Attempts to represent a national consensus have been usually based on the assessment of a few with limited access to the attitudes of the whole. The result has been that the national consensus has in fact been the view of the most dominant voices in the old parties. And these are the voices at the centre; historically, the voices of the elite or the establishment.[18]

The 1993 and 1997 Elections: The End of Brokerage Politics in Canada?

Before the 1993 election it was common to speak of Canada's "two and one-half" party system. The Liberals and Progressive Conservatives were the parties that had a realistic chance of forming a government, while the NDP was a stable minority party on the federal scene, regularly winning 15–20 per cent of the popular vote and occasionally holding the balance of power during a period of minority government.

The old certainties were shattered by the 1993 election results. The Liberals won a solid majority, taking 177 of the 295 seats in the House of Commons, with 41.3 per cent of the popular vote. Neither the Conservatives nor the NDP elected enough MPs to qualify for official party status, which guarantees the opportunity to speak in the House during question period as well as automatic funding for research staff. On the other hand, the Reform Party jumped from one seat to 52 seats. And the Bloc Québécois, created in 1990 by the defections of several Tory and Liberal MPs, went from seven to 54 seats. Not since 1921, when the Progressives came second to the Liberals, had the national party system received such a jolt from voters.

Neither the Reform Party nor the Bloc gave signs of being interested in brokerage-style politics. Many interpreted the 1993 election results as a political realignment of voters as well as a display of voters' dissatisfaction with brokerage-style politics. This interpretation was greeted with some skepticism. Critics of the realignment argument pointed to such factors as the monumental unpopularity of former Conservative prime minister Brian Mulroney, the erosion of NDP support in Ontario where an unpopular NDP government was in power, a wave of Western disaffection with the major parties, and the unusual and presumably passing phenomenon of the Bloc Québécois, spawned in the bitter wake of the 1990 defeat of the Meech Lake Accord.

The elements for a durable party realignment seemed to exist. One of these elements involved the low esteem in which parties and politicians were held by voters. The Royal Commission on Electoral Reform and Party Financing noted

Canadians appear to distrust their political leaders, the political process and political institutions. Parties themselves may be contributing to the malaise of voters. . . . Whatever the cause, there is little doubt that Canadian political parties are held in low public esteem, and that their standing has declined steadily over the past decade. They are under attack from citizens for failing to achieve a variety of goals deemed important by significant groups within society.[19]

As may be seen in the summary of federal election results in Table 9.1, the wave of cynicism that has been building in the Canadian electorate has weakened attachments to the traditional parties.

A second element in the party realignment seemed to come from a so-called *shrinking centre* in Canadian politics. The traditional dominance of the Liberal and Progressive

TABLE 9.1 Comparison of Election Results, 1993–2015

Party	1993	1997	2000	2004	2006	2008	2011	2015
Liberal	41.3%	38.5%	40.8%	36.7%	30.2%	26.2%	18.9%	39.5%
	177	155	172	135	103	77	34	184
Progressive Conservative/ Conservative*	16.0%	18.8%	12.2%	29.6%	36.3%	37.6%	39.6%	31.9%
	2	20	12	99	124	143	166	99
NDP	6.9%	11.0%	8.5%	15.7%	17.5%	18.2%	30.6%	19.7%
	9	21	13	19	29	37	103	44
Bloc Québécois	13.5%	10.7%	10.7%	12.4%	10.5%	10.0%	6.0%	4.7%
	54	44	38	54	51	49	4	10
Reform/ Alliance	18.7%	19.4%	25.5%	—	—	—	—	—
	52	60	66	—	—	—	—	—
Green Party	—	—	—	4.3%	4.5%	6.8%	3.9%	3.4%
	—	—	—	0	0	0	1	1
Others	3.6%	1.6%	2.2%	0.3%	1.0%	1.1%	1.0%	0.8%
	1	1	0	1	1	2	0	0
Total valid votes	13,667,671	12,95,964	12,857,774	13,489,559	14,815,680	13,832,972	14,720,580	17,559,353
Total seats	295	301	301	308	308	308	308	338

Even a cursory examination of these numbers shows why there are ongoing calls for electoral reform and moving away from the first-past-the-post (FPTP) system of elections. As we saw in the 1997, 2011, and 2015 elections, it is possible to win a majority of seats with less than 40 per cent of the popular vote. One of the most blatant examples of the unfairness of FPTP was seen in 2008 when the Green Party obtained 6.8 per cent of the popular vote but had no elected MPs. The Green Party managed to elect only one MP in 2011 and 2015, with less than 4 per cent of the national vote, by focusing their efforts and resources on fewer ridings.

Notes:

Columns may not add up to 100 per cent due to rounding.

*In 2003 the Progressive Conservative and Canadian Alliance parties merged to form the Conservative Party. The election results for 2004 onward for this party are reported at this line.

Conservative centrist parties, which differed very little from one another in terms of their principles and policies, depended on a broad popular consensus within the familiar confines of language, regionalism, and leadership. This popular consensus—in areas such as the welfare state, active economic management by the government, and official bilingualism—had become frayed, and the traditionally dominant parties' ability to keep political conflict within "safe" boundaries was diminished.

Only the Liberal Party succeeded in continuing to practise the old brokerage-style politics. It emerged from the 1993 election as the only truly national party, electing members from every province and territory and receiving no less than one-quarter of the votes cast in any province. It became increasingly evident that the Progressive Conservative Party would have to reposition itself ideologically if it wanted to regain the votes that Reform/Canadian Alliance had siphoned off in the 1993, 1997, and 2000 elections. It could not afford to remain a near-clone of the Liberal Party, especially since the Liberals in power created some distance between themselves and the Keynesian welfare state that they had been instrumental in building. The electoral success of right-leaning Conservatives in Alberta and Ontario suggested that the future of the national party lay in this direction. There is much proof that brokerage-style politics continues to be alive and well in Canadian politics. For example, the continued success of the Conservatives, culminating in a majority government in the 2011 general election, seemed to prove that the Liberals could be replaced by the Conservatives as the only true national party by using brokerage-style politics. And the Liberals under Justin Trudeau were able to win a majority government with substantial representation from every region of the country by appealing to a broad range of elements of Canadian society that were dissatisfied with the Harper government's approach to governance—more brokerage politics.

A Divided Electorate: The 2004, 2006, and 2008 Elections

The 2004 Election

The 2003 merger of the Canadian Alliance and Progressive Conservative Party eliminated what many considered to be the conditions for permanent Liberal government in Canada. A united right, where right-wing voters would have only one rather than two choices, could now make inroads in the Liberal stronghold of Ontario. There were reasons for opposition parties to feel optimistic when the 2004 election was called. In her annual report, the federal Auditor General, Sheila Fraser, had focused attention on the sponsorship scandal, which appeared to be inappropriate and probably unlawful misallocation of public dollars on advertising in Quebec. This affair and subsequent investigation resulted in a sharp drop in Liberal support in Quebec and a corresponding boost in the popularity of the Bloc. The recently chosen Liberal leader, Prime Minister Paul Martin, attempted to distance himself from the scandal, but it cast a shadow and prevented the Liberals from achieving another majority government.

The new Conservative Party and the NDP also went into the 2004 election with new leaders. The stakes were different for these parties. In the case of the Conservatives, a breakthrough in Ontario was the goal. For the NDP, emergence from the near irrelevance that the party had experienced federally since the 1993 election was the objective. Both parties achieved their goals, but neither to the degree hoped for. The election produced Canada's first minority government in a quarter of a century. At one point, with opinion polls showing a steady deterioration in Liberal support in English Canada, it appeared that the Conservatives were on the cusp of sweeping into power with a minority government. However, a barrage of attack ads by the Liberals, which spoke of the Conservative "hidden agenda" to privatize health care, join American-led military ventures, and chip away at abortion rights, reinforced fears many voters held about the Conservatives.

The 2006 Election

Going into the 2006 campaign the polls placed the Liberals comfortably ahead of the Conservatives, but many voters were still undecided, ensuring that this, too, would be a campaign that would matter. The Liberals used a familiar strategy of relying on attack ads and tried to portray the Conservatives and their leaders as having a "hidden agenda" as they had done in 2004. The Conservatives countered with a disciplined campaign and a strategy of introducing a new policy promise each day. This placed the Liberals on the defensive, and the Conservatives were able to dominate the issue agenda and avoid the sorts of embarrassing and potentially damaging statements from candidates that had been used against them in previous campaigns. The Liberals saw their lead slip away. With significant gains in Ontario and a surprising breakthrough in Quebec, the Conservatives achieved a minority government.

The Conservative victory in 2006 was widely interpreted as a rightward shift in Canadian politics. However, several things suggest otherwise: the shift was not very large, as only 36 per cent of the electorate voted for Conservatives; Stephen Harper and his party were careful not to rely on ideologically polarizing language or messages; and the Liberals were handicapped by scandal and a widespread perception that they had become arrogant in power. The NDP increased both its share of the popular vote and its number of MPs back to levels that it had typically enjoyed before the party's collapse in the 1993 election.

The 2008 Election

The 2008 election failed to confirm this rightward shift. The Conservatives managed to increase their share of the popular vote by a couple of percentage points, mainly at the expense of sagging national support for the Liberal Party under the uncertain leadership of Stéphane Dion. The Bloc Québécois remained the dominant party in Quebec, denying the Liberals seats they had long counted on and preventing the Conservatives from capturing the seats that they needed to form a majority government. The centre-left of Canadian politics continued to be strong. But unlike the years before the 1993 election, the votes on the centre-left were distributed between the Liberals, NDP, the Bloc, and the Green Party. The Conservative Party controlled the centre-right of the political spectrum, but there did not appear to be enough votes in this electoral space to deliver the party a majority government.

Realignments and the 2011 Election

realignment
a situation that occurs when an election or series of elections produces a durable change in the parties' bases of support

A **realignment** in a country's politics occurs when an election or series of elections produces a durable change in the parties' bases of support. In Canada, the 1896 election comes closest to deserving the realignment label, as French-Canadian Catholics, a voting bloc that had leaned toward the Conservative Party, shifted to the Liberals after the execution of the Métis leader Louis Riel and the selection of the francophone Wilfrid Laurier as the Liberal leader. The huge vote swings that occurred in 1958, when Quebecers shifted their support to the Conservative Party, and again in 1984, proved not to be durable, and were not realignments.

Canadian elections often produce changes in government, but only occasionally do they redraw the party map. The election of 1921 was one such case, when the Progressive Party, which had no seats in the House of Commons prior to the election, became the official opposition. By the 1926 election things were back to normal and the Liberal–Conservative duopoly in Canadian party politics had been re-established. The election of 1993, when the Conservative Party's support collapsed and the Bloc Québécois and Reform Party surged into second and third place respectively, was another case where the party map was dramatically redrawn.

No such surprises were expected when, on 26 March 2011, the fortieth Parliament was dissolved and an election was called. The conventional wisdom was that not very much was likely to change in the party standings. Most speculation involved whether the governing Conservative Party would manage to eke out a narrow majority this time. There were no clear issues dividing the parties and galvanizing voters, and another Conservative minority government was anticipated. Many thought that if this were to happen, the opposition parties would take the first opportunity to defeat the Conservatives in the House and install a coalition government.

And then, the unexpected happened. The election of 2 May 2011 was a jolting reminder that campaigns matter. No one predicted at the outset that the once mighty Liberal Party, Canada's "natural governing party," would fall to third place with the support of fewer than one out of five voters. Nor did anyone imagine that the NDP would vault into second place, winning more than twice as many seats as its previous election high of 43 in 1988 and doubling its share of the popular vote. There were other surprises, including the startling, almost total collapse of the Bloc in Quebec and the emergence of NDP as Quebec's leading party, capturing 58 of the province's 75 seats.

Explanations for these seismic changes focused on two major factors: leadership and the Quebecers' apparent fatigue with the sovereignists and their goal of Quebec independence. The NDP leader, Jack Layton, was said to have caught the imagination of Canadians, including Quebecers, appearing confident, compassionate, and articulate—qualities some voters thought

Listen to "The 60/40 Country?" podcast at www.oupcanada.com/BrooksConcise2e.

that he already showed in 2004, 2006, and 2008. But in 2011, his rivals for the centre-left vote, the Liberals' Michael Ignatieff and the Bloc's Gilles Duceppe, failed to connect with their usual supporters. The Conservatives won a clear majority nationally, and the possibility of an NDP-led coalition melted away along with the last snow in the province of Quebec.

The 2011 election appeared to be all about change, but buried underneath the focus on the NDP surge, the Bloc collapse, and the Liberals' worst showing ever, there were two important elements of continuity. First, political issues appeared to take a back seat to the issues of leadership. As we saw earlier in this chapter, André Siegfried remarked upon this over 100 years ago—the tendency for Canadian elections to be contests between the parties' leaders rather than struggles between rival ideas and ideologies. It is not that ideas do not matter in Canadian elections, but rather that they become associated with and absorbed into voters' images of the party leaders.

Second, the election results demonstrated once again that Canada is a 60/40 country. In Canada, the balance of the electorate has tended to lean toward the centre-left of the Canadian political spectrum. The Conservative Party, the only party with a centre-right platform, won

The public's perception of a political leader can be very difficult to change. Take a moment to think about the leaders of Canada's main political parties during the 2015 election campaign. What three characteristics would you say were most strongly associated with each, and how did those characteristics influence how you felt about the party each leader represented?

with about 40 per cent of the popular vote. The four centre-left parties, the Liberals being the most centrist of this group, together accounted for about 60 per cent of the vote. With the exception of the 1984 election, when the Conservatives won 50 per cent of the popular vote, this has been the pattern for the past three decades. In the eight elections from 1988 to 2011 the percentage of the vote received by centre-right parties has ranged between 29.6 per cent (2004) and 43 per cent (1988), averaging just over 37 per cent.

After the 2011 election, many analysts wondered whether the Conservative majority, the decline in Liberal fortunes, and the surge of the NDP was an actual realignment in the party system or a one-off affair. Some believed that victory for the left would require that the centre-left parties unite, as the right had united in the 2003 merger of the Canadian Alliance and the Progressive Conservative Party. Many prominent members of both the Liberal Party and the NDP talked openly about a merger that would capitalize on the clustering of voters around the centre-left of the ideological spectrum, while others felt that they would be more comfortable under the Conservative Party banner than in a centre-left party that might be dominated by activists and supporters of the NDP. The 2015 election settled the matter convincingly by proving that 2011 was indeed a one-off affair and not a political realignment. The Liberal Party was not breathing its last breath; Liberals could win large, nationally based majorities; and the NDP would foreseeably remain the third party.

2015 Election: A Change of Tone

The realignment pundits believed they saw in the 2011 election seemed to reverse itself with the strong performance of the Liberals under the effective leadership of Justin Trudeau. The Liberals set a Canadian record when they moved from third-party status with 34 seats to a majority government with 184 seats. The primary issue in this, the longest election campaign in Canadian history, seemed to be that of leadership and whether Canadians could accept another four years of Stephen Harper's approach to governance. The follow-up to this question was whether they would choose Justin Trudeau (referred to in Conservative attack ads as "just not ready") or the leader of the NDP, Thomas Mulcair. Trudeau's performance in the debates seemed to show Canadians that he was in fact ready and that he could think on his feet. The Liberals promised a "sunny ways" approach to governance as opposed to the closed and confrontational approach of the Conservatives. Trudeau also outmanoeuvred the NDP on the left side of the political spectrum with promises to run a deficit in order to invest in infrastructure and bolster the economy, and to reduce taxes on the middle class and raise them on the rich.

The Conservatives came to be seen by many as anti-immigrant and anti-refugee, intolerant, and even un-Canadian by raising the issue of whether Muslim women should be allowed to wear a niqab (face covering) in citizenship ceremonies and offering to create a "barbaric cultural practices hotline." The Conservatives also lost support for their approach on climate change, free trade, and civil rights. In the end, close to 70 per cent of voters chose not to vote Conservative.

Michael de Adder/Artizans

Conventional political thinking at the time seemed to be that promising to run a deficit was a sure way of losing an election. This political cartoon depicts Liberal leader Justin Trudeau to the left of NDP leader Thomas Mulcair and Conservative leader Stephen Harper on the 2015 election issue of running a deficit.

Selecting Party Leaders in Canada

When Wilfrid Laurier was chosen as the first French-Canadian leader of the Liberal Party in 1887, about 80 Liberal MPs in Canada's sixth Parliament did the choosing. The rules for this leadership selection process were not written down in any formal document. It was simply understood that, following the British parliamentary tradition, it was the prerogative of caucus to choose who among its members would be the party leader.

When the Liberal Party of Canada chose Stéphane Dion as its new leader on 3 December 2006, 4605 delegates cast ballots. About 850 of them were *ex officio delegates*, men and women who because of their positions in the Liberal Party—including elected MPs and provincial legislators, senators, and party officials—automatically had the right to attend and vote at the party's leadership convention. All of these delegates cast their ballots on the final day of a five-day party convention that was covered on live television, choosing among a field of eight candidates. It took four ballots to select the party's new leader, following formal rules laid down in the 23-page Rules of Procedure for the 2006 Leadership and Biennial Convention.

Inside Politics

BOX 9.2 | Unite the Left?

When former Ontario NDP leader and then–Liberal MP Bob Rae was asked in June 2010 about rumours of high-level talks concerning a possible merger of the national NDP and Liberal Party, his categorical dismissal of such rumours sounded like exaggeration—prompting some to say, as the Queen in Shakespeare's *Hamlet* "The lady doth protest too much, methinks." Whether or not party heavyweights had sat down in the same room to discuss the idea of a unite-the-left merger of the national Liberal Party and the NDP, the idea of such a marriage had been circulating since the 2006 election of the Conservative minority government. Former Liberal cabinet minister Lloyd Axworthy publicly advocated such a merger after the 2008 election, arguing that it was necessary to defeat the Conservative Party led by Stephen Harper. Several former NDP politicians, including Roy Romanow, Ed Broadbent, and Lorne Calvert had spoken in support of the merger concept. No less a figure than former Liberal prime minister Jean Chrétien admitted in June 2010 to having had informal discussions with former NDP leader Ed Broadbent about ways of uniting the centre-left vote in order to defeat the Conservatives. And then there is the fact that the Liberals and the NDP, with the support of the Bloc, signed a formal agreement in 2008

to bring down the Conservative government on a confidence vote and support a Liberal government for an agreed period of time. Such an agreement was far from a merger, but it showed how desperate the parties were to find a way to dislodge the Conservatives from power, something that neither the Liberals nor the NDP appeared capable of doing on their own at the polls. In fact, there was much talk of a coalition leading up to the 2015 general election, prompting Andrew Coyne to suggest in the *National Post* that "Given the doubts about Mr. Trudeau's abilities, and the aura of competence around Mr. Mulcair, a coalition might not sound like such a scary proposition to cautious centrists any more. It might even be a plus."[20]

On the face of it, a united left may appear to make sense. Axworthy, Broadbent, and others tirelessly pointed out that the Conservatives had governed since 2006, even though about 6 in 10 voters cast their ballots for candidates of parties further to the left. The bold and unpredicted decision of the British Conservative and Liberal-Democratic parties to form a coalition government after that country's May 2010 election seemed to make an inter-party merger in Canada a bit more credible, at least in the eyes of some.

Not everyone, including some in the Liberal and NDP camps, is enthusiastic about the idea of a merger on the left. What do you see as the arguments for and against the Liberals and NDP uniting as a strategy for forming a federal government?

So why do the parties not just merge? There are many significant obstacles:

- Some supporters of both parties hate the idea. Many NDP activists argue that it would pull their party away from its proper left-wing agenda. From the Liberal side, not all activists and voters are left of centre.
- A merger of the parties cannot be achieved just because some leaders want it to happen. The party's constitutions require that their memberships have a say in the matter, as happened in 2003 when the Canadian Alliance and Progressive Conservative parties merged to form the Conservative Party of Canada.
- Egos are at stake. Who would risk losing their careers, their power, and their influence in their own party for a possibility at leading a new party?

None of this means that a merger of the NDP and Liberal Party would not be possible in some future election. But the Liberal election victory in October 2015 is unlikely to encourage the talk of coalition, at least from the Liberal side.

Shortly before the Liberals' 2006 leadership convention *Globe and Mail* columnist Jeffrey Simpson wrote a piece entitled "It's tough to be ahead."[21] And, indeed, in the wake of Michael Ignatieff's defeat at that convention and Stéphane Dion's unpredicted victory, conventional wisdom quickly concluded that there are serious drawbacks to being the front-runner. The scrutiny is more intense, the analysis and criticism of every word and action more unforgiving. Being an underdog, on the other hand, has the advantage of freeing a candidate from the media spotlight and, potentially, enabling him or her to profit from an "anybody-but-front-runner-X" movement.

As plausible as all this sounds, it is also incorrect. If one looks at all the Conservative, Liberal, and NDP leadership conventions that required more than one ballot to choose the leader—16 in total—13 were won by the candidate who led on the first ballot. If there is a lesson to be drawn from the history of leadership conventions in Canada it is that there is a huge advantage to being the front-runner heading into the convention vote.

While the trend to elect front-runners has continued, there are exceptions. Thomas Mulcair won the bruising 2012 leadership race on the fourth ballot, but both Michael Ignatieff in 2009 and Justin Trudeau in 2013 won the Liberal leadership on the first ballot.

Three Models for Selecting Party Leaders

The 2006 Liberal leadership convention involved a method for choosing party leaders that began in Canada in 1919. That year marked the transition from the **caucus model**, in which party leaders are chosen by other elected MPs of their party, to the convention model (see Table 9.2). In some ways this transition was a simple product of circumstances. Wilfrid Laurier had called a national convention of the Liberal Party in 1919 to discuss policy at a time when the party was reduced to mainly Quebec representation in the House of Commons. Laurier died soon after the convention was called, and the party's national executive decided to use the Ottawa meeting as an opportunity to choose his successor. In doing so they were breaking new ground. In no other British-style parliamentary democracy were party leaders chosen in this manner. Presidential candidates in the United States were, of course, selected at conventions that brought together state delegations. In adopting the convention model for their party—a model eventually followed by other Canadian parties—Liberals were aware of the American practice. But the Canadian convention model has always been different from the American one in important ways, from the process used to choose convention delegates to procedures on the convention floor.

Criticisms that the convention model was elitist and too easily dominated by money and backroom deal making were heard with increasing frequency after the 1960s. When the Reform Party began to choose its leaders through a direct vote of all party members, the pressure on other parties to follow suit was difficult to resist. In 1997 the Bloc Québécois chose Gilles Duceppe as its leader using the *one member–one vote* (OMOV) model. The Progressive Conservative Party followed in 1998, choosing Joe Clark as its leader using the OMOV model, and today all parties use some variant of the OMOV model.

Whether the OMOV model produces better results than the caucus or convention is up for debate. The argument for OMOV is that it reduced the influence of elites within the party. Combined with limitations that all the parties place on leadership campaign spending and the contribution limits and reporting requirements that have existed under Canadian law since 2004, this is expected to make leadership races more open.

caucus model
a system in which party leaders are chosen by other elected MPs of their party

Listen to the "Who Is Michael Ignatieff? What Our Leaders' Stories Say about Canadian Politics" podcast at www.oupcanada.com/Brooks Concise2e.

TABLE 9.2 Three Models of Leadership Selection

Model	Participants	Procedures	Most Recent Federal Party Examples
1. Caucus model	Elected members (MPs)	Selection takes place behind closed doors without open competition between rival candidates.	Liberals—Ignatieff in 2008 Conservatives—Meighen in 1941 Bloc Québécois—Bouchard in 1990
2. Convention model (narrow)	Party activists (narrow): Delegates to the leadership convention, elected by party members in their riding associations	Selection takes place at a party leadership convention, after several months of campaigning by candidates.	Liberals—Dion 2006 Conservatives—Mulroney in 1983 NDP—McDonough in 2001 Bloc Québécois—Bouchard in 1991
3. One member–one vote model	Party activists (broad) Party members	Selection takes place by votes cast by party members. Some votes may take place at a fixed convention, but most votes are cast electronically elsewhere. In 2013, the Liberals members' votes were adjusted so that each riding had an equal weight in the result.	Liberals—Trudeau in 2013 Conservatives—Harper in 2004 NDP—Layton in 2003 Bloc Québécois—Duceppe in 1997

The Electoral System and Its Consequences

Many Canadians were shocked when George W. Bush was elected president of the United States in 2000, even though he received about half a million fewer votes than Al Gore. What they did not realize is that this outcome can happen and has happened in Canada. In 1979 the Liberal Party received about 4 per cent more of the popular vote than the Conservatives, but the Conservatives won 22 more seats and formed the government. In fact, Bush won a larger share of the eligible electorate than did Jean Chrétien's Liberal Party in the Canadian election of that same year. But no one seriously contested the legitimacy of Chrétien's victory.

There are many similar examples in Canadian federal and provincial elections of the electoral system not rewarding parties in *proportion* to their share of the popular vote. The Conservative Party garnered 39.6 per cent of the popular vote in the 2011 election and won

54 per cent of all seats in the House of Commons. Conversely, in the same election, the Bloc, with almost 6 per cent of the popular vote obtained in one province, Quebec, received less than 1 per cent of the seats. In the same vein, the prize for apparent injustice was taken by the Green Party in the 2008 election when 6.8 per cent of the popular vote produced no seats in the House of Commons. Similar discrepancies can be found in the 2015 election where the Liberals won 54 per cent of the seats with 39.5 per cent of the popular vote.

To understand what has happened in these elections, we must first describe the Canadian electoral system, whose principal features are the same at both the federal and provincial levels. It is based on the **single-member constituency**: a system of electing representatives to legislatures in which each constituency (riding) gets one representative in the House of Commons (or provincial legislature). Canada has what some call a **plurality system** or a **first-past-the-post system**, where the candidate who receives the most votes in a constituency election becomes the member of Parliament (or provincial legislature) for that constituency. In other words, a majority of votes is not necessary for election and, given the fragmentation of votes between the three main parties, is the exception rather than the rule.

A political party's representation in the House of Commons depends, therefore, on how well its candidates fare in the 338 constituency races that make up a general election today. It regularly happens that the leading party's candidates may account for only about 40 per cent of the popular vote across the country and yet capture a majority of the seats in the Commons. Indeed, the advocates of the single-member, simple plurality electoral system point to this as the system's chief virtue. It manages, they claim, to transform something less than a majority of votes for a party into a majority of seats, thereby delivering stable majority government. However, the *winner-take-all* system's performance on this count has been rather mediocre: nine of the 18 general elections from 1957 to 2008 produced minority governments.

Canada's "winner-take-all" electoral system has its critics as well. In a classic analysis, Alan Cairns identifies several consequences that flow from the single-member, simple plurality system:[22]

- It tends to produce more seats than votes for the strongest major party and for minor parties whose support is regionally concentrated.
- It gives the impression that some parties have no or little support in certain regions, when in fact their candidates may regularly account for 15–30 per cent of the popular vote.
- The parliamentary composition of a party will be less representative of the different regions of the country than is that party's electoral support.
- Minor parties that appeal to interests distributed widely across the country will receive a smaller percentage of seats than votes.

Cairns concludes that the overall impact of Canada's electoral system has been negative. The system has, he argues, exacerbated regional and ethnolinguistic divisions in Canadian

single-member constituency a system of electing representatives to legislatures in which each constituency (riding) gets one representative in the House of Commons (or provincial legislature)

plurality system or **first-past-the-post system** an electoral system in which the candidate who receives the most votes in a constituency election becomes the member of Parliament (or provincial legislature) for that constituency

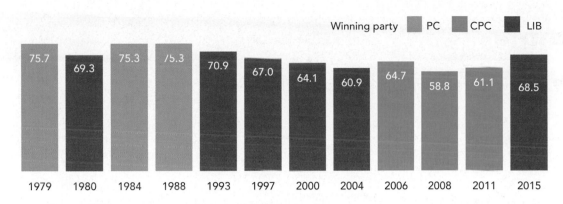

FIGURE 9.2 Federal Election Voter Turnout, 1979–2015
Source: Elections Canada

political life. There are many examples. For instance, the Conservative Party has been shut out in Quebec for most of the last century, which gives the impression that the Liberal Party was the only national party with support in French Canada. Cairns's article on the electoral system's effects was written in the late 1960s. If it were written today it would also mention distortions such as the gross under-representation of the Liberals in Western Canada over the last couple of decades despite their receiving between one-quarter and one-third of Western votes in most elections. As William Irvine observes, "the electoral system confers a spurious image of unanimity on provinces. By magnifying the success of the provincial vote leader, the electoral system ensures that party caucuses will over-represent any party's 'best' province."[23]

Along with the distortions that Canada's electoral system produces, another argument for reform is that the present system leaves many voters feeling disempowered and contributes to low levels of voter turnout. This view has become popular in recent years, and is reflected in what has become known as "strategic voting," whereby voters who do not support the front-runner in their riding will cast their ballots not for the party or candidate of their choice but for the party or candidate most able to defeat the front-runner. This might be a compelling argument for reform of the electoral system, but those who study voting behaviour have been unable to find evidence that any significant number of Canadians vote strategically. On the contrary, there appear to be many cases where labour groups have advocated such voting, without any indication that it works. As Figure 9.2 indicates, voter turnout in federal elections has been declining since the 1970s. It reached a low of 58.8 per cent in the 2008 election. The 2011 and 2015 elections results, with 61.1 and 68.5 per cent respectively, seem to indicate renewed interest and new approaches, such as social media, in attracting voters to the polls. A survey conducted by Elections Canada in 2015 and discussed in Box 9.3 gives stronger evidence that voter disillusionment with the choices on offer can cause some to stay home on election day.

Democracy Watch

BOX 9.3 Low Voter Turnout in Recent Elections

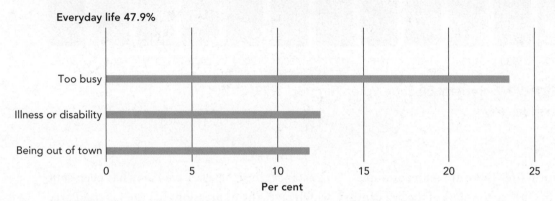

FIGURE 9.3 Reasons for Not Voting in October 2015 Federal Election
Source: Elections Canada

Some might say that the voter turnout of more than 68 per cent during the October 2015 general election was an anomaly, and that the increase was mostly due to Justin Trudeau's youth and his "sunny ways" approach to electioneering. In January 2013, the Conference Board of Canada reported that fewer Canadians were voting than in the past. Voter turnout had declined to its second-lowest rate—53.8 per cent—in Canada during the 2011 federal election. This was only slightly higher than the 53.6 per cent turnout in 2008.[24]

Elections Canada indicated that 23 per cent of eligible voters, or approximately 6 million Canadians, did not vote in the October 2015 election. What reasons did voters have for not voting?

The matter of voter decline has preoccupied politicians, pundits, and Elections Canada for some time now because it speaks to the health of the democratic system of governance. A 2003 report commissioned by Elections Canada indicated that the decline in voter turnout in was mainly due to lower participation of young people, a trend that was likely to continue.[25] The trend was confirmed in subsequent elections. By 2011, only 38.8 per cent of the population aged 18 to 24 voted.[26] The voter participation increases of the forty-second election, in 2015, seemed to buck the trend.

So, what can be done to increase voter turnout? According to Jon Pammett, a political scientist from Carleton University who studies electoral participation, aside from coercing voters through penalties and compulsory voting, there are ways of increasing voter turnout that include

THE ONLY RECKLESS COALITION THAT THREATENS CANADA

© Greg Perry

This cartoonist suggests that one of the greatest threats to Canadian democracy is low voter turnout. What strategies could improve voter turnout at the next federal election? What changes can you suggest to the way election campaigns are run to better engage voters, particularly young people?

- information campaigns that teach people how to vote
- advertising campaigns that explain why voting matters
- grassroots movements that target specific groups such as youth or specific nationalities
- educational programs such as "Canada's Students Vote"[27]

Like Canada, most of its peer countries have also experienced a decline in voter turnout. The 2015 election seemed to buck the trend with a general increase in voter turnout to 66.1 and a substantial increase in all age groups with a significant increase of 18.3 per cent for voters aged 18 to 24, raising voting in this group to 57.9 per cent.[28] Liberals vowed during the 2015 campaign to find ways of increasing voter turnout including electoral reform.

Alternatives to FTPT

Proportional Representation

proportional
representation a
method of electing
government
representatives
whereby a party's
percentage of
the popular votes
translates into a
corresponding
share of seats in the
legislature

The **proportional representation** (PR) electoral system is the chief alternative to the single-member, plurality electoral system. PR is a method of electing government representatives whereby a party's percentage of the popular votes translates into a corresponding share of seats in the legislature. PR may sound eminently fair, but there are three significant criticisms:

- PR promotes a splintering of the party system, by encouraging the creation of minor parties with narrow interests and by undermining the development of broad-based parties capable of bridging rivalries and differences.
- PR is said to produce unstable government. The chances that any party will have a majority of seats is reduced, which necessitates the cobbling together and the maintaining of coalition governments. Inter-party deals may paralyze cabinet decision making, and elections, as illustrated in post–World War II Italy and Belgium, can be frequent. But the opposite is also true, as seen in the Netherlands and Germany.
- PR electoral systems do tend to have more political parties than those with plurality systems, and the ideological distance between the extreme ends of the party spectrum will inevitably be greater than in plurality electoral systems such as Canada and the United States. As a result, PR systems can sometimes encourage ideological polarity and enable extremist parties to achieve representation in the legislature.

Ranked Ballot—Instant Run-Off with a Single Transferable Vote

preferential
voting a ranked
voting system
where voters rank
candidates in order
of preference

In early 2016, the Liberal government began exploring a **preferential voting**—a ranked voting system where voters rank candidates in order of preference—which is an *instant run-off system* with a *single transferable vote* that is said to confer a greater amount of legitimacy to each elected representative and to the elected government. Majority governments would be able to say that they have achieved support from more than 50 per cent of the voting population. This system is similar to the one being used in Australia; each voter gets the opportunity to identify a second candidate who is to receive their transferable vote if their first candidate finishes in last place. The vote stays with the voter's first choice until they are dropped from the ballot. If no candidate wins a majority of votes in the riding, then a recount takes place where the candidate with the fewest votes is dropped and the transferable votes are added to the totals of the remaining candidates. The run-off continues until a candidate achieves a majority (50 per cent plus one vote) and is declared the winner. Criticisms of ranked ballot systems include:

- Some voters might find this level of choice confusing.
- It adds a measure of complexity to counting the votes and election results might be significantly delayed.
- Ranked ballots might favour one particular party over other parties. This was certainly the criticism that was levelled by the Conservative and the NDP when the Liberals proposed the idea of a ranked voting system in 2015.

Hybrid Electoral Systems

Combining anyone of the electoral systems into a hybrid has been proposed on several occasions, especially at the provincial levels. For instance, in two referendums (2005 and 2009) British Columbians rejected an electoral commission's recommendation to replace their single-member constituencies with multiple-member constituencies. In the proposed system, each riding would elect between two to seven representatives to be selected using a ranked ballot system.

And in two referendums, in PEI in 2005 and in 2007 in Ontario, voters rejected a proposal to replace single-member constituencies with "mixed-member proportional" (MMP) constituencies. As the name suggests, 70 per cent of the seats in the provincial legislature would be based on the single-member constituency model and 30 per cent of the seats would be based on proportional representation.

Democracy Watch

BOX 9.4 First-Past-the-Post versus Proportional Representation

Pundits often warn us to be careful what we wish for when pushing for electoral reform. Is it fair that a political party can form a majority government without winning the popular vote in an election? How efficient and productive is a government made up of many minority parties elected by proportion of their share of the popular vote?

These are two of the questions that arise when debating the pros and cons of the electoral systems a country can choose to implement. In Canada there is much debate about whether the first-past-the-post system is still the best way to form government, or if proportional representation is a better contemporary alternative. Let's recap the pros of each.

Pros of the First-Past-the-Post System

- provides a clear choice for voters between major political parties
- produces a single-party-rule government that is able to enact policy and legislation
- produces a strong opposition to scrutinize the party in power (the official opposition)
- prevents parties with narrow focus (and sometimes extreme views) from being represented in the legislature
- encourages relationships between constituents and representatives based on geographical regions

Pros of Proportional Representation (Party Lists)

- encourages governments to compromise and build consensus, as the legislature is composed of voices from many parties instead of a single majority party
- encourages diversity via the election of more minority and women representatives
- makes it more likely that minority parties and independent candidates are represented

Continued

- reduces the effects of "vote-splitting": a vote for a minority party in an area controlled by a majority party is not a "lost" vote
- taps into a worldwide trend in democratic rule: most of the world's democracies use some form of proportional representation

First Past the Post

RESULT: **LIBERAL MAJORITY GOVERNMENT**

LIBERAL	CON	NDP	BLOC	GREEN
184	99	44	10	1

(a)

Instant Runoff

RESULT: **LIBERAL MAJORITY GOVERNMENT**

LIBERAL	CON	NDP	BLOC	GREEN
202	83	46	6	1

BALLOT EXAMPLE:

CANDIDATE A Party A	1	CANDIDATE B Party B	3	CANDIDATE C Party C	2

(b)

FIGURE 9.4 2015 Election: FPTP, Instant Run-Off, and Proportional Representation

The results of the 2015 election under the FPTP system, and hypothetical results under an instant run-off system and a proportional representation (party list) system. Note that each system creates winners and losers, with one system favouring each party differently. How do you see party electoral strategies changing with each electoral system? What effects might we see on the parliamentary system?

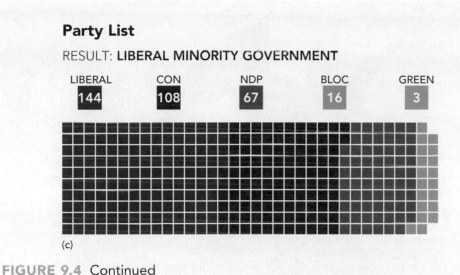

FIGURE 9.4 Continued

Irvine's point, quoted above, that the electoral system tends to magnify the success of a province's most popular party and punish those parties whose share of the vote does not achieve some critical mass, has certainly been borne out by recent election results.

Canadians probably will just have to live with the regionally divisive effects of the existing electoral system. The best hope for overcoming the negative consequences that Cairns, Irvine, and many others have pointed to may be reform of the Canadian Senate. An elected Senate whose members would be chosen according to some system of proportional representation within each province—so that a party's provincial share of Senate seats would be determined by its share of the popular vote in that province—could go some way toward compensating for the regional imbalance of parties' caucuses in the House of Commons. A Senate with greater legitimacy in the eyes of Canadians, and in which members felt free to vote on the basis of regional and other interests, free of the tight leash of party discipline, could be a step toward the better representation of the regions within the institutions of the national government. And although many suggest that major reforms to the Senate are imminent, there are important obstacles to Senate reform in Canada; these include the reluctance of the major federal parties to encourage a serious institutional rival to the powers of the prime minister and the House of Commons. On the other hand, Mr. Trudeau's desire to see a partisan free Senate and to implement an appointment process that reduces the prime minister's influence in the Senate may restore a measure of independence and integrity that will improve its image.

Voting Behaviour

When it comes to the voting behaviour of Canadians, few generalizations withstand the test of time. During the first couple of decades after Confederation, the Conservative Party did

David Parkins

This cartoon, by David Parker of the *Globe and Mail,* was published shortly after the 2015 General Election. It illustrates how difficult it is for a prime minister like Justin Trudeau to live up to electoral reform promises, when the FPTP system that is said to need reform allowed his party to achieve a sizable majority of the seats in Parliament and political power with just under 40 per cent of the popular vote.

better than the Liberals among Catholics and French Canadians, but this changed after the 1885 execution of the Métis leader Louis Riel under a Conservative government and the 1887 selection of Wilfrid Laurier—a Catholic francophone from Quebec—as leader of the Liberal Party. For most of the following century the Liberal Party fared better than the Conservatives among francophones and Catholics, although their support among these groups temporarily weakened in the 1958 election and again in the 1984 and 1988 elections.

The West

Regionally, the Conservative Party began its long association with Western voters in 1957 with the election of the Diefenbaker government. Conservative candidates outpolled Liberals in the West in most elections after 1957. This tendency was accentuated after the 1972 election, when the Liberal Party's Western fortunes sank dramatically under the leadership of Pierre Trudeau and the region began to be regarded as mainly Conservative and NDP turf. The Reform Party, we have seen, became the vehicle for anti-Liberal resentment after many Western voters became disappointed with the Conservative government of Brian Mulroney.

Quebec

Quebec was an electoral stronghold for the Liberal Party over most of the last century. But this association has weakened since the emergence of the Bloc Québécois. The two-party competition between the Liberals and the Bloc between 1993 and 2004, and the continuing strong presence of the Bloc in subsequent elections, differentiated Quebec's situation from that of the rest of Canada. The Bloc has outpolled the Liberals in five of the six general elections since 1993, and in 2006 a resurgent Conservative Party received more votes in Quebec than the Liberals and only two percentage points fewer in 2008, although winning fewer seats in both elections. The Quebec voting pattern was disrupted once again with the NDP winning most of the Quebec seats in the 2011 election and the Bloc losing all but two of its 47 seats. The 2015 election saw many Quebec voters return their support to the Liberals.

Class

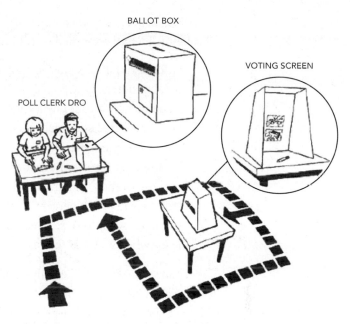

FIGURE 9.5 Map for Voters on Election Day

The tongue-in-cheek term "electile dysfunction" hints at the lack of excitement or engagement by the public on election day, leading many to stay away from the polls. Others believe that fear of the unknown could be another factor in low voter participation rates. One possible remedy for low voter turnout is a straightforward diagram, like this one, showing what a voter can expect on election day. Were you nervous the first time you voted? Would a diagram like this, showing exactly how the process unfolds, have helped you overcome your fears?

Source: Canada.com blog network: http://blogs.canada.com/2011/05/05/electile-dysfunction/

In regard to social class, differences between voters for the Liberal and Conservative parties have never been very great and certainly have been less important than regional and ethnolinguistic differences. The NDP's formal affiliation with organized labour might have been expected to reflect a preference among working-class Canadians for that party. But class has never been a particularly strong political identity for most Canadians. Electoral studies carried out since the 1960s have shown that NDP support generally is stronger among voters who belong to unions than among most other segments of the electorate.

Gender and Rural/Urban Split

Two of the most widely accepted claims about the differences between Liberal and Conservative supporters are (1) women are less likely than men to prefer the Conservative Party, and (2) urban Canadians prefer the Liberals while rural voters tend to favour the Conservatives.

With respect to women and the Conservative brand, McGill University political scientist, Elisabeth Gidengil remarked in 2010 that

> "[t]he search for an elusive "women's vote" misses the point: sex differences in political preferences and vote choices don't have to be dramatically different to have a significant impact on election outcomes, especially in tight races. The Conservatives have had some success in attracting women to the right. They fare particularly well among women who are more religious and women who are have more traditional views about gender roles and sexual orientation. There are not enough of these women, though, to guarantee the party a majority. The Conservatives are still dogged by the perception that they have a "hidden agenda" and are a threat to Canada's social programmes. Shaking that perception may be their biggest challenge when it comes to winning more votes from women."[29]

The female vote was fairly evenly divided between the Liberals and Conservatives in 2006 (as it also was in 2004), but male voters were significantly more likely to have voted Conservative. Table 9.3 shows that there was a significant shift to the left in how Canadian women voted in 2008, as much fewer than half of them intended to vote Conservative.

With respect to urban voters, their votes were evenly divided between the Liberals and Conservatives in 2006, with slightly more voting Liberal in 2004, but rural voters were much more likely to have voted Conservative, particularly in 2008. This claim about the supposed rural/urban divide in Canadian politics seemed to hold true in the 2006 and 2008 elections.

During the 2011 election, there was a perception that the Conservatives had benefited from the differences in perception between the rural and urban voters on specific national priorities such as crime and justice, and on issues such as Charter rights, property rights, and gun registration. In fact, NDP leader Jack Layton accused Prime Minister Harper of driving a wedge between the rural and urban electorate by raising these priorities and issues.[30] As proof, pundits pointed out that in 2008 the Liberals did well in Toronto, Montreal, and Vancouver, while the Conservatives did not win a single seat from these three cities and received slightly fewer than half the number of votes cast for their Liberal rivals.[31]

However, this theory seemed to be turned on its head in the 2011 general election. In an April 2011 *National Post* article, journalist Kevin Libin proposed that the urban/rural divide was a myth and that the divide was regionally based.[32] In their rush to be interesting and insightful, pollsters, pundits, and political scientists sometimes allow sloppiness to creep into

TABLE 9.3 How Women Were Likely to Vote in 2008

	Women versus Men
Likely to vote on the right (Conservative)	Ipsos-Reid Poll 26% versus 48% Ekos Poll 28% versus 46% Strategic Counsel 34% versus 40%

Source: Andrew Heard, "Elections: Women and Elections," Simon Fraser University, 2011, https://www.sfu.ca/~aheard/elections/women.html.

A. Age

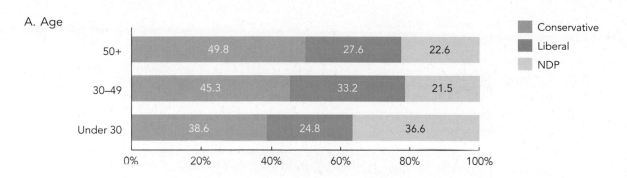

B. Religion

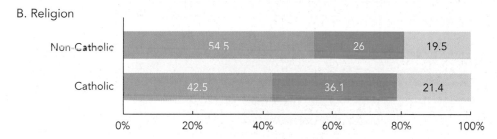

C. Sex

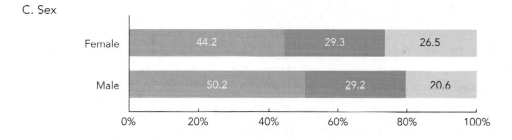

D. Country of Birth

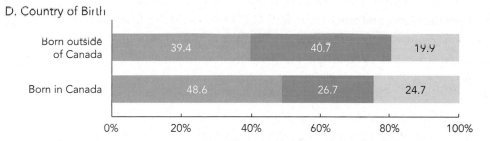

E. Importance of Religion

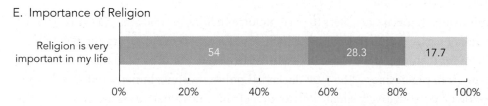

FIGURE 9.6 Voting Behaviour outside Quebec, 2008 Election

Source: Data compiled from Elections Canada. Many thanks to Professor Lydia Miljan for generating these cross-tabulations.

Continued

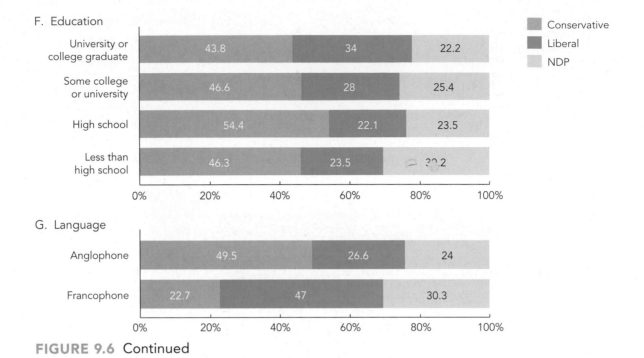

FIGURE 9.6 Continued

their analysis. It is not true that Canada's largest urban centres were unsympathetic to the Conservative Party in 2006. For example, Halifax, Calgary, Edmonton, Winnipeg, Ottawa, Hamilton–Burlington, and Waterloo–Kitchener–Cambridge all elected Conservative MPs. And of the three cities cited as proof of urban Canada's hostility to the Conservatives, the case of Montreal, arguably, had far more to do with language and a decades-old history of voting Liberal than it did with the urban condition. The idea that the conditions and demographics of big cities cause the values and partisan preferences of their residents to be significantly different from those who live in less urbanized settings seems reasonable and is certainly interesting, but the 2008 and 2011 elections put an end to this argument about urban hostility to the Conservative Party.

Party Finances and Special Interests

It is difficult to attach precise numbers to party finances before 1974, for the simple reason that parties were not legally required to disclose their sources of revenue. Prior to the Election Expenses Act, 1974, there appears to have been little transparency, and most of the major parties' money came from big business. The NDP depended on union contributions and was the only party to receive many relatively small contributions from individuals. Passage of the Election Expenses Act, 1974 signalled a watershed in Canadian party finance. The Act included spending limits for individual candidates and political parties during election campaigns, changes to the Broadcasting Act requiring radio and television stations to make available to the parties represented in the House of Commons both paid and free broadcast time during election campaigns,[33] and a system of reimbursement for part of their expenses for candidates who receive at least 15 per cent of the popular vote. This last reform had the effect of subsidizing the three main parties at taxpayer expense, a consequence that can only be defended on the grounds that this public subsidy helps to weaken parties' financial dependence on special interests.

In the 2004 reforms to the Election Expenses Act, *public subsidies* were given to all the parties based on the results of the previous election, and private donations were strictly limited. There were also limits on spending by "third parties," groups that are not registered political parties, during election campaigns and limits on contributions to the contestants in party leadership campaigns. Paid-access opportunities to party leaders continue to be a source of income for parties, and raise the ethical question of whether wealth provides better access to politicians and governments. But from the standpoint of the parties' sources of income, the most important reforms of the Election Expenses Act involved tax credits for political contributions and public disclosure requirements for candidates and political parties. On the first count, changes to the Income Tax Act allow individuals or organizations to deduct from their taxable income a percentage of their donation to a registered political party or candidate. And second, since 2004 the law requires much more transparency in the parties' reporting of their annual and election campaign expenditures: parties and candidates are required to provide the chief electoral officer with a list of all donors who have contributed $200 or more in money or services in kind, as well as an itemized account of their expenditures.

Corporate contributions continue to be important in many ways. In addition to helping finance a party system that is generally congenial to business interests, it was long understood that donations helped buy access. In the words of former Conservative politician and political adviser Dalton Camp: "Toronto money merely maintains access to the parties, keeping open essential lines of communication, corporate hotlines, so to speak, to the right ears at appropriate times."[34] In any given year about half of the largest 100 industrial firms in Canada did not even contribute to either of the two older parties. It would be ridiculous to conclude that their lack of generosity cut them off from direct access to political decision makers. But all things being equal, contributions probably opened the door a bit wider.

The link between party contributions and access became more controversial with the increasing prominence of *paid-access opportunities*: fundraising events such as dinners and cocktail parties, and special clubs where, for an admission price up to several thousand dollars, donors could rub shoulders with party leaders and possibly also members of the government. Money and the invitation list obviously act as filters in determining who can participate in such events.

Donations buy the privilege of invitations to exclusive meetings with party leaders, opportunities that are particularly valuable when that party forms the government and the party leader is the prime minister. It must be said that since the entry bar was set much lower with the 2004 reforms to the Canada Elections Act, these special donor clubs are now less exclusive than they were.

Of course, paid-access opportunities raise ethical questions. At what point does the ability to pay for access to political decision makers subvert the democratic process, by favouring those with the money? Parties need funds to carry out their activities. Even with a tax credit for political contributions, only a small portion of all Canadian taxpayers contribute to parties or candidates. Paid-access opportunities represent the parties' search for stable sources of funds.

One alternative would be to impose severe restrictions on how much money parties can spend, so that individual contributions and the subsidies that candidates receive from the re-imbursement provision of the Election Expenses Act would be sufficient.

Another alternative, one widely used in Western European democracies, is to increase the public subsidies that parties receive, which frees them from dependence on contributions from special interests. This model was adopted in 2004. The major elements of the post-2004 model for party and campaign financing in Canada include the following:

- Donations by special interests, including corporations and trade unions, are banned.
- Individuals may donate up to $1,100 per year to a registered political party or candidate.
- Parties receive an annual public subsidy of $2 (in 2011) for every vote that they receive.
- Third parties—organizations and individuals other than registered political parties and their candidates—may spend no more than $172,050 in total, and no more than $3,441 in any single electoral district, on political advertising during an election.
- Candidates for the leadership of registered political parties must identify those who donate to their campaigns and, as of April 2006, no individual may contribute more than $5,400 in total to the contestants in any party leadership campaign. Corporate or union donations are not permitted. The amount that leadership candidates may spend on their campaigns is set by the parties, not by Canadian law.

Shortly after its re-election in 2008, the minority Conservative government rather imprudently proposed the abolition of this public subsidy system—"imprudently" because this proposal helped unite the opposition parties into a coalition that would have brought down the government at the first possible opportunity. Only the Conservative Party's finances were in good shape at the time, owing to its superior ability to raise private contributions. The Conservative government discovered the truth of the old adage that it is unwise to kick a dog that is already down. But after the 2011 federal elections, the majority Conservative government finally abolished the public subsidy system and it was phased out beginning in 2012.

Regardless of one's views on the rights of ordinary citizens to access political parties and participate in the political process equally, the fact remains that wealthier parties, candidates, private organizations, and individuals are able to purchase better-quality media advertising, and more of it. Given this potential for unequal access to the media, some believe that governments need to regulate who may purchase political advertising, when they may do so, and how much they may spend.

Some European democracies, such as France and Germany, ban paid political advertising on television and radio. Conversely, in the United States, efforts to introduce laws that would limit campaign spending on advertising are seen as a violation of the First Amendment's guarantee of free speech. Canada falls between these positions. Since the mid-1970s Canadian law has empowered the CRTC, Canada's telecommunications regulator, to require television and radio broadcasters to provide a certain amount of air time to registered political parties for their ads during election campaigns. As explained above, campaign spending by so-called "third parties" is sharply limited by Canadian election law. Federal law also limits the amount of money that registered political parties and their candidates may spend during campaigns, thus placing a ceiling on the amount of advertising a party can purchase. The communication activities of political parties via the Internet remain, so far, unregulated.

Summary

Whether or not one lives in a democracy, political parties allow for the aggregation and the articulation of certain interests within the political system. And as we have seen, political parties offer voters a slate of candidates to choose from at election time. However, to paraphrase Eugene Forsey, in a democracy, people voluntarily join these political associations and participate in their activities because they share similar values and hold similar views about the role of government.

The origins of Canada's two major political parties—the Conservatives and the Liberals—can be traced back to the shifting coalitions and alignments in the United Province of Canada in the 1840s and 1850s. During this time, patronage appears to have played an important role in party politics. Mainstream political parties in Canada have traditionally avoided ideological and inflexible policy positions in favour of an adaptable, centrist style of politics. Our historically dominant parties have displayed certain characteristics that are not typical of other democracies: they are flexible and opportunistic, they tend to be dominated by their leaders, and they are wary of ideological appeals to the electorate.

For more than three generations Canada has often been referred to as a two and one-half party system: two dominant brokerage parties competing to form a government and parties like the NDP or the Bloc Québécois steadily winning enough votes and enough seats in the House of Commons to occasionally hold the balance of power during minority governments and even official opposition status. Some pundits saw a "realignment" of the two and one-half party model with the 1993 election and the emergence of the Bloc Québécois as the official opposition, and, in the 2011 federal election, the NDP replacing the Liberal Party as the official opposition. However, the 2015 general election seemed to reaffirm the Liberal and Conservative parties as the historically dominant parties.

Critics argue that our *single-member, simple plurality* electoral system has distorted political representation in our legislatures. It rewards the single-most popular party, as well as parties with regionally concentrated support, and it does not reward minor parties whose support is wide but not deep. Defenders of the system argue that it tends to produce stable majority governments. They also point to what they see as the faults of the alternative models such as proportional representation and ranked ballot systems.

The 7 per cent increase in voter turnout in Canada's 2015 election was heartening for many political watchers who believe that the steady decline of voter participation in democracies around the world, particularly with young voters, is a threat to the health of democracies. Whether this increase was due to dissatisfaction with the Harper government, Justin Trudeau's "sunny ways" approach to campaigning, or the broad range of social media tools now available for contacting voters remains to be seen. But it is clear that social media is changing the way citizens participate in political life, especially for the newer generations. After he was elected in October 2015, Prime Minister Trudeau promised that this would be Canada's last first-past-the-post election. In May 2016, the Liberal government started the process of electoral reform by appointing a multi-party panel of MPs tasked with studying alternatives to FPTP and improving voter turnout.

Review Exercises

1. Using data available at the website of Elections Canada (www.elections.ca) for the last general election, look up the number of votes and percentage of the vote received by each political party across the country. Then calculate the number of seats each party would have received under a straight proportional representation system. Compare these results to the outcome in our first-past-the-post electoral system and draw some conclusions.
2. Visit the websites of two political parties represented in the House of Commons and compare the depth and breadth of information provided about each party's history, current leader, and present policies.

Up for Debate

1. Which model shown in Table 9.2 is best for choosing a party leader?
2. Resolved: Eligible voters who do not exercise their franchise should be imprisoned or fined.
3. Resolved: In the Canadian context, the first-past-the-post system is superior to all other electoral systems.

Starting Points for Research

Anderson, Cameron D., and Laura B. Stephenson, eds. *Voting Behaviour in Canada*. Vancouver: University of British Columbia Press, 2010.

Canadian Election Study. ces-eec.org/pagesE/home.html.

Carty, R. Kenneth, and Munroe Eagles. *Politics Is Local: National Politics at the Grassroots*. Toronto: Oxford University Press, 2005.

Susan Delacourt. *Shopping for Votes: How Politicians Choose Us and We Choose Them*. Toronto: Douglas and McIntyre, 2013.

Gidengil, Elisabeth, Neil Nevitte, André Blais, Joanna Everitt, and Patrick Fournier. *Dominance and Decline: Making Sense of Recent Canadian Elections*. Toronto: University of Toronto Press, 2012.

Young, Lisa, and Harold J. Jansen, eds. *Money, Politics and Democracy: Canada's Party Finance Reforms*. Vancouver: University of British Columbia Press, 2012.

CBC Archives and TVO's *The Agenda*

Visit the companion website for *Canadian Democracy: A Concise Introduction* to follow links to audio and video footage related to the main themes of the chapter: www.oupcanada.com/BrooksConcise2e.

Relevant Websites

Visit the companion website for *Canadian Democracy: A Concise Introduction* to browse a collection of websites featuring material related to the key themes of the chapter, an excellent starting point for research: www.oupcanada.com/BrooksConcise2e.

10 Interest Groups

Politics does not stop between elections; much of the effort to influence the actions of government is channelled through interest groups. In this chapter we examine their characteristics and the role they play in Canadian politics. After reading this chapter, you should be able to

1. define "interest group," "lobbying," and "lobbyist"
2. identify interest groups
3. explain the role of interest groups in a democracy
4. examine the perspectives and biases of interest groups as well as the biases of the interest group system
5. analyze the impact of federalism on interest groups
6. outline strategies for interest group success

⬆ Thousands gather to mark International Women's Day in Toronto. Interest groups have the ability to influence the actions of government through a range of techniques that include lobbying, taking legal action, and holding demonstrations.

Source: Roberto Machado Noa/Getty Images.

While elections are democracy's showpiece, the influence of elections on government is usually blunt and indirect. Policies are more likely to be determined by forces within the state, and by organized groups outside of it, than by elections. Indeed, special interests often seem to dominate the policy-making process in democracies. Their attempts to influence government are unremitting; their resources are impressive; and their access to policy makers is sometimes privileged. The influence of voters seems feeble in comparison.

Interest groups (or **pressure groups**) are private organizations that promote their interests by trying to influence government rather than seeking the election of candidates to manage it.[1] They arise from a basic fact of social life, the diversity in the interests and values of human beings. This diversity, in turn, gives rise to what James Madison called **political factions**: groups of citizens whose goals and behaviour are contrary to those of other groups or to the interests of the community as a whole.[2] If these factions or special interests appear to overshadow the public interest in democracies, there is a simple explanation: the tug of one's *personal interests*—as a teacher, farmer, or postal worker—tends to be felt more keenly than the nebulous concept of *public interest*. Arguments that appeal to interests such as consumer benefits or economic efficiency are unlikely to convince the farmer whose income is protected by the quotas and prices set by a marketing board. But economic interests are not the only factionalism in politics. Group characteristics like gender, ethnicity, and language may also provide the basis for the political organization of interests.

Economically based or not, interest groups are distinguished by the fact that they seek to promote goals that are not shared by all members of society. Paradoxically, however, their success in achieving these goals often depends on their ability to associate their efforts with the broader public interest.

Interest group (or **pressure group**) a private organization that promotes its interest by trying to influence government rather than seeking the election of candidates to manage it

political faction a group of citizens whose goals and behaviour are contrary to those of other groups or to the interests of the community as a whole

Charting the Territory

The world of interest groups is characterized by vastness and variety. Although no unified reliable list of interest groups exists for Canada or any other democracy, the directory *Associations Canada* gives us some idea of the sheer number.[3] In its 2013 edition, it lists some 20,000 organizations, some of which would not meet the criteria of "attempting to influence government." While many groups focus on non-political activities, several thousand regularly or occasionally perform political functions for their members.

Almost every imaginable interest is represented by an organization. There are several hundred women's associations across Canada, close to 1000 environmental groups, over 2000 business associations, perhaps 500 organizations representing agricultural interests, about 200 that focus on Aboriginal issues[4]—the range of organized interests and the number of groups within each general category of interests are enormous. These figures do not include transitory groups that emerge briefly around a single issue. Nor do they include international organizations that may attempt to influence Canadian governments.

While it is impossible to say exactly which associations qualify as interest groups, no doubt many of them are politically active. One way to get a sense of this activity is to look at

THE CANADIAN PRESS/Fred Chartrand

Interest Groups attempt to influence governments in many different ways, both formal and informal. Here, protesters frustrated by the federal government's response to precarious working conditions and other economic issues turn their backs on Prime Minister Justin Trudeau at a summit organized by the Canadian Labour Congress, which is made up of over 1000 interest groups.

the list of groups that make representations to a legislative body or a government-sponsored commission. For example, well over 1000 groups made representations and submitted briefs to the Royal Commission on Aboriginal Peoples in six months of public hearings (1993). And the Commission on the Future of Health Care in Canada received submissions from 429 groups and associations during its public consultation phase (2001). The 2012 Cohen Commission on the decline of sockeye salmon stocks in the Fraser River granted intervenor status to two governments, one government agency, one union, four corporations and business associations, seven conservation groups, six organizations representing fishers, and about 20 Aboriginal groups.

The amount of representation and activity in a single sector can be remarkable. For example, the Canadian Labour Congress is the umbrella organization for hundreds of unions, including provincial and federal federations of labour and 137 district labour councils that together represent about 3 million workers. The Canadian Chamber of Commerce, one of whose main functions is to influence government policies, represents over 500 community and provincial chambers of commerce and boards of trade, as well as close to 100 trade and professional associations and many international organizations.

The Bias of the Interest Group System

Obviously, some interest groups are more influential than others, but which are the most powerful, and why? Is the interest group system biased "in favour of a fraction of a minority"? Some, such as E.E. Schattschneider, claim that the interest group system (the "pressure system") has a business and upper-class bias. "The notion that the pressure system is automatically representative of the whole community is a myth. . . . The system is skewed, loaded and unbalanced in favor of a fraction of a minority."[5]

Schattschneider observed about American politics in the early 1960s that business associations made up the single largest group of organized interests in American society; they were more likely to lobby and spend money on attempting to influence policy makers than other interest groups. Moreover, Schattschneider's research demonstrated that "even non-business organizations reflect an upper-class tendency."[6] Persons with higher incomes or education were more likely to belong to organized groups than those lower down the socio-economic ladder. The business and upper-class bias of interest group politics is a product of superior resources and of the relatively limited size and exclusive character of these special interests. "Special-interest organizations," he argued, "are most easily formed when they deal with small numbers of individuals [or corporations] who are acutely aware of their exclusive interests."[7] This awareness of special interests that are vital to one's material well-being or the well-being of one's organization is characteristic of trade associations like the Canadian Association of Petroleum Producers, or a more broadly based business organization like the Canadian Manufacturers & Exporters. It also characterizes producer and occupational groups like the Quebec Dairy Council and the Ontario Medical Association, but is less likely to characterize organizations that represent more general interests.

Most pundits agree with Schattschneider. Charles Lindblom argues that business occupies a "privileged position" in the politics of capitalist societies. In his book *Politics and Markets*,[8] Lindblom attributes this pre-eminence to business's superior financial resources and lobbying organization, greater access than other groups to government officials, and, most important, propagandistic activities that—directly through political advertising and indirectly through commercial advertising—reinforce the ideological dominance of business values in society.

One of the reasons most cited for the political superiority of business interests is the *mobility of capital*. Investors enjoy a significant amount of freedom to shift their capital between economic sectors and from one national economy to another. Transnational corporations, for instance, are organizations that span a number of national economies and often use their ability to move capital internationally as a lever in dealing with governments. Governments and politicians in capitalist societies tend to be aware of the levels of *business confidence* and are reluctant to take actions that might cause reduced investment or flight of capital, unemployment, falling incomes, and, in turn, popular dissatisfaction.[9]

Another factor that concerns governments is the state's financial dependence on business. A decline in the levels of investment profit is often felt as a drop in government revenues from corporate taxes, employment income taxes, payroll taxes, and consumption taxes. The problem of falling revenues is likely to be compounded by increased state expenditures on social programs, whose costs are sensitive to the levels of economic activity. Borrowing on the public credit is only a temporary solution. This can be both costly and subject to the confidence of international investors, who also influence the cost of borrowing.

No one would argue that business interests "win" all the time. Nevertheless, theorists note that there has been a tendency to favour business interests over others because of the characteristics of capitalist societies. This is one of the few propositions about politics that cuts across the ideological spectrum. There are, however, dissenters. Some are likely to view business interests as being simply one set of interests in a sea of competing interest group claims on government.[10]

Business historian Michael Bliss argues that whatever privileged access business people may have enjoyed in the corridors of political power had largely disappeared by the 1980s. "Groups with powerful vested interests," he writes, "including trade unions, civil servants, tenured academics, and courtesanal cultural producers, perpetuated a hostility toward business enterprise rooted in their own fear of competition on open markets."[11]

David Vogel argues that, on balance, "business is more affected by broad political and economic trends than it is able to affect them."[12] Although Vogel focuses on the United States, he develops a more general argument about the political power of business interests in capitalist democracies. Vogel says that popular opinion and the sophistication of interest groups are the key to understanding the political successes and failures of interest groups. He argues that business's ability to influence public policy is greatest when the public is worried about the economy.

The political organization of business interests is the second key to understanding the ebb and flow of business influence. Vogel maintains that the victories of environmental, consumer, and other public interest groups in the 1960s and 1970s were largely due to their ability to read the Washington map and work the levers of congressional and media politics. Business interests, by comparison, were poorly organized and amateurish. Today, in spite of very effective mobilization by business, divisions within the business community have generally checked its influence.

Another factor that has prevented business interests from dominating politics is what James Q. Wilson has called "entrepreneurial politics."[13] This involves the ability of politicians and interest groups to identify issues around which popular support can be mobilized in opposition to business interests. The opportunities for entrepreneurial politics are fewer in Canada than in the United States because of the tighter party discipline in Canada's legislature. Entrepreneurial politics is, however, practised by interest groups such as People for the Ethical Treatment of Animals (PETA) and Equality for Gays and Lesbians Everywhere (EGALE). Astute use of the media and adept packaging of a group's message so as to generate public awareness and support for its goals are essential to entrepreneurial politics.

Do business groups have greater success in capitalist societies compared to other interest groups? The conclusion reached by recent work on Canadian interest groups, what Paul Pross calls the *post-pluralism* (also called the *neo-institutionalist*) approach, suggests that this is not the case.

This approach is based on the observation that policy making generally involves the participation of a limited set of state and societal actors, a **policy community** that is centred on a sub-government; i.e., that set of state institutions and interest groups usually involved in making and implementing policy in some field. Whether or not a group is part of the policy community and its level of influence depend on the particular policy field and on the configuration of interests in that community. Moreover, neo-institutionalists tend to emphasize the capacity of state actors to act independently of the pressures and demands placed on them by societal interests. This capacity will vary across policy sectors. But the bottom line of the neo-institutionalist approach is that state actors in some policy communities may be well able to resist the societal pressures as well as those from highly organized, well-financed business interests.

policy community a limited set of state and societal actors that is centred on a sub-government; i.e., that set of state institutions and interest groups usually involved in making and implementing policy in some field

PETA is known for evocative protests designed to mobilize popular public support. In this July 2010 protest, a participant is covered in red body paint to represent the blood shed during the annual seal cull in the Arctic. Have your opinions on a controversial issue ever been swayed by an interest group's message?

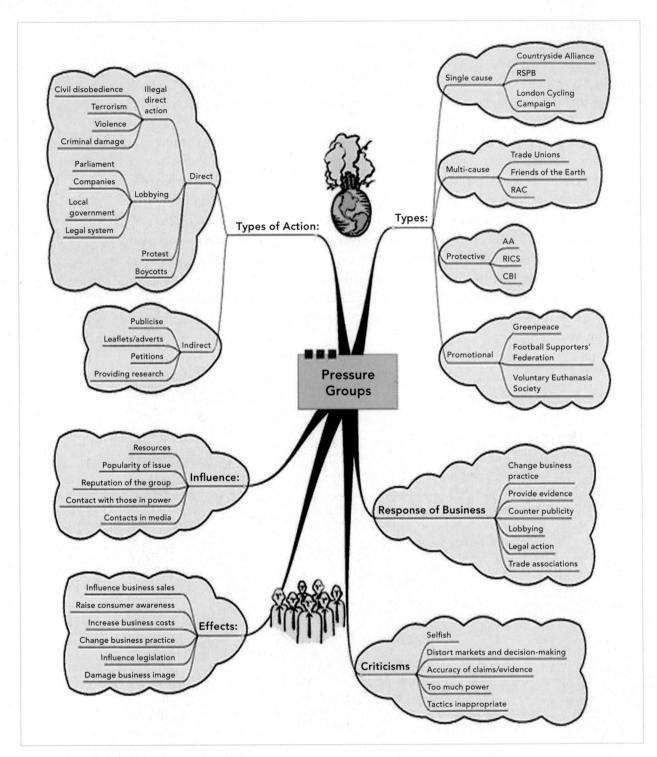

FIGURE 10.1 Interest Group Mind Map

This mind map helps us understand just how complicated interest groups' activities and their consequences can be.

Source: Biz/Ed: http://www.bized.co.uk/educators/16-19/business/external/presentation/pressure1_map.htm.

Analytical Perspectives on Interest Groups

Pluralism Approach

In the pluralism approach, or group theory, organized interests are seen as the central fact of political life; this approach explains politics chiefly in terms of the activities of groups. It is a societal explanation of politics in that it locates the main causes of government action in the activities of voluntary associations, such as trade associations, labour unions, and churches, outside the state. Pluralist theory draws two conclusions about the role and character of the state in democracies. First, the state itself is a sort of group interest—an assortment of different interests associated with various components of the state. Second, in spite of its own interests, the state's main function is to ratify the balance of group interests in a society and to enforce the policies that embody this balance of power. As Earl Latham puts it: "The legislature referees the group struggle, ratifies the victories of the successful coalition, and records the terms of the surrenders, compromises, and conquests in the form of statutes."[14]

Pluralists are sometimes accused of misunderstanding the true character of political power. By focusing on group competition, their critics argue, pluralists are inclined to see political life as relatively open and competitive because they observe struggles between groups and the decisions of governments. But as Bachrach and Baratz suggest, "power may be, and often is, exercised by confining the scope of decision-making to relatively 'safe' issues."[15] Choosing not to make decisions, and to keep issues unformulated and off the public agenda, is a form of power. From this angle, the interest group system appears much less competitive.

Class Analysis Approach

Interest groups are discussed in the class analysis approach, but they are not as important as the class interests these groups are argued to represent. Some of the major works of contemporary Marxist

If special interests are, as pluralism theory suggests, a basic fact of political life, what does this cartoonist seem to be saying about the public's appetite for a system built to serve such groups?

scholarship do not even mention interest groups.[16] In Canada, in the class analysis approach, which is generally referred to as "political economy,"[17] interest groups are sometimes ignored entirely in preference for such categories as class fractions within subordinate and dominant classes. This is not to say that organized interests are denied or ignored entirely. Ralph Miliband's *The State in Capitalist Society* attempts to refute the pluralist model. He observes,

> Democratic and pluralist theory could not have achieved the degree of ascendancy which it enjoys in advanced capitalist society had it not at least been based on one plainly accurate observation about them, namely that they permit and even encourage a multitude of groups and associations to organize openly and freely and to compete with each other for the advancement of such purposes as their members may wish.[18]

From the perspective of class analysis, classes are the basic units of society and political life, whereas organized groups are seen as the bearers of class interests and ideologies. This enables one to acknowledge the uniqueness of individual groups and associations while focusing on larger collective interests represented by individual groups. An association like the Canadian Council of Chief Executives, which represents 150 of the largest private-sector corporations in Canada, would be seen as a representative of "monopoly capital." And the Canadian Manufacturers & Exporters, representing over 3000 corporations in the manufacturing sector, is viewed as a voice for the manufacturing faction of the capitalist class. On the other hand, groups such as labour unions, and groups representing women, Aboriginals, or racial minorities, are viewed as representative of subordinate class interests and ideologies.

Corporatism Model Approach

corporatism a political structure characterized by the direct participation of organizations representing business and labour in public policy making

Corporatism is a political structure characterized by the direct participation of organizations representing business and labour in public policy making. "In its core," states Jurg Steiner, "corporatism in a modern democracy deals with the interactions among organized business, organized labor, and the state bureaucracy. These three actors co-operate at the national level in the pursuit of the public good."[19] Such structures are associated with several of the capitalist democracies of Western Europe.

Compared to pluralism, which is characterized by an intensely competitive interest group system that stands outside the state, a corporatist system is more consensus oriented. It obliterates the barriers between the state and the societal interests represented through corporatist decision-making structures. The distinctiveness of corporatism as an interest group system is based on three characteristics:

- the existence of *peak associations* for business and labour, which are organizations that can claim to represent all significant interests within specific communities and have the ability to negotiate on their behalf

- a tripartite relationship with the formal integration of business and labour into the structures of state authority
- an ideology of social partnership between business and labour

How does the corporatist model apply to interest groups in Canada? The peak associations of business and labour, necessary to make corporatism work, do not exist in Canada. The most inclusive of Canadian business associations, the Canadian Chamber of Commerce (CCC), is simply a loose federation of provincial and local chambers, individual corporations, and trade associations. The national organization exercises no control over its members, and the sheer range of interests represented within the CCC obliges it to focus on very general, broad consensus issues such as lower corporate taxation, cutting government spending, and reducing government regulation of business.[20] On the labour side, the ability of any association to claim to represent Canadian workers is weakened by the fact that fewer than four out of ten members of the labour force belong to a union.

The two other requirements for corporatism—tripartite decision-making structures bringing together the state, business, and labour, and an ideology of social partnership between business and labour—are also absent from the Canadian scene. Indeed, Gerhard Lehmbruch, one of the leading students of corporatism, places Canada in the group of countries having the fewest characteristics of corporatism.[21] Political scientist William Coleman agrees with this assessment, but he notes that corporatist policy-making networks are found in the agricultural sector of the Canadian economy.[22]

Neo-Institutionalism Approach

New institutionalism, or **neo-institutionalism**, is a perspective on policy making that emphasizes the impact of structures and rules, formal and informal, on political outcomes. It is less a model of politics and policy making than a theoretical premise shared by a diverse group of perspectives. The premise is, quite simply, that institutions—their structural characteristics, formal rules, and informal norms—play a central role in shaping the actions of both individuals and the organizations to which they belong. This "insight" is neither new nor very surprising. The founders of modern sociology knew very well the importance of institutions in determining behaviour, a relationship that is most pithily expressed in Robert Michels's aphorism, "He who says organization, says oligarchy."[23] How does this approach help us understand the behaviour and influence of interest groups? Let us begin by examining the diverse roots of the neo-institutionalist approach: economics, organization theory, and society-centred analysis.

> **neo-institutionalism**
> a perspective on policy making that emphasizes the impact of structures and rules, formal and informal, on political outcomes

Economics

Rational choice theory forms the bedrock of modern economics. In the 1950s and 1960s, economists began to systematically apply the concepts of individual (limited) rationality and market behaviour to the study of elections, political parties, interest groups, bureaucracy, and other political phenomena.[24] The economic theory of politics that has developed from this work emphasizes the role played by rules, formal and informal, in shaping individual choices and policy outcomes. In this perspective, "institutions are bundles of rules that make collective action possible."[25]

Organization Theory

organization theory the study of how people act within an organization

Organization theory, the study of how people act within an organization, has been an important source of inspiration for the neo-institutionalist approach. One of the first to apply the behavioural insights of organizations theory to Canadian politics was Alan Cairns. In a 1977 speech to the Political Science Association, he relied heavily on organization theory in arguing that Canadian federalism is influenced mainly by state actors, the "needs" of the organizations they belong to, and the constitutional rules within which they operate.[26]

Society-Centred Analysis

The rising popularity of neo-institutional analysis can be attributed in part to a reaction against explanations of politics that emphasize the role of societal factors like interest groups, voters, and social classes. This reaction produced an outpouring of work on the autonomy of the state (i.e., the ability of state actors to shape societal demands and interest configurations rather than simply responding to and mediating societal interests). Neo-institutionalism is not just a state-centred explanation of politics, but it takes seriously the structural characteristics of the state: the institutions, their structures, and their rules.

Neo-institutionalism deals intensively with the "interior lives" of interest groups: the factors responsible for their creation, maintenance, and capacity for concerted political action. James Q. Wilson identifies four categories of incentives that underlie these interior dynamics:[27]

- *Material incentives.* Money or other material benefits with monetary value
- *Specific solidarity incentives.* Intangible rewards like honours and recognition
- *Collective solidarity incentives.* Intangible rewards created by the act of associating in an organized group; a collective sense of group esteem or affirmation
- *Purposive incentives.* Intangible rewards derived from the satisfaction of a job well done

Economists have also tried to explain what Mancur Olson called the logic of collective action, including how the interior character of a group affects its capacity for political influence.

policy network the nature of the relationships between the key actors in a policy community

The relative importance of *societal* and *state* forces as determinants of political outcomes is often debated in neo-institutionalism. The concepts of policy communities—the constellation of actors in a particular policy field—and **policy networks**[28]—the nature of the relationships between the key actors in a policy community—are the building blocks of the neo-institutional approach. Embedded in them is the irrefutable claim that "the state" is in fact a fragmented structure when it comes to actual policy making. So, too, is society. The interests that are active and influential on the issue of abortion, for example, are very different from those that are part of the official-language policy community. Paul Pross's visual depiction of a policy community

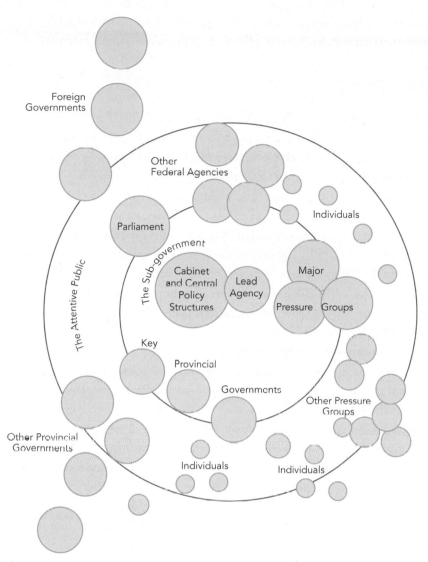

FIGURE 10.2 Policy Community "Bubble Diagram"

Source: From Whittington, M.S. & Williams, G. *Canadian Politics in the 1990s*, 4E. © 1995 Nelson Education Ltd.

conveys a good sense of the complexity and potential for fluidity in the relations between interest groups and the state (see Figure 10.2).

The Ingredients of Interest Group Success

There is no magic recipe for group influence, but it is possible to generalize. Successful strategies and appropriate targets depend on the issues, the resources, and other factors such as public opinion and the political system. Business groups in their dealings with government seem to have these characteristics more than any other set of societal interests.

Organization

Organized interests are usually more influential than unorganized ones, probably because they are able to apply sustained pressure on policy makers. Writing to the prime minister, even a person of national stature is unlikely to have much of an impact. But tens of thousands of people writing or taking to the streets are more likely to get the prime minister's attention. This impact is unlikely to be sustained unless an organization can credibly claim to speak on behalf of thousands and is skilled at media and government relations.

Paul Pross, a distinguished Canadian expert on interest groups, points to the character of modern government and the policy-making process in explaining why organization is crucial. Prior to the 1960s, government was smaller and policies and programs were fewer; power was concentrated in the hands of a small group of senior bureaucrats and cabinet. Groups did not need sophisticated organizational structures to deal with government. This was the era of the "mandarins," when a tightly knit group of deputy ministers dominated the process.[29] Modern government, he observes, is a sprawling, highly bureaucratized affair where power to influence policy is diffused. As the scope of state involvement in economic and social matters deepened, it became desirable for groups to have the capacity to monitor and deal with those levels where the power resided. The result is a veritable explosion of associations representing business interests, environmental concerns, consumer interests, women, Aboriginal interests and so on. Interest groups acquired prominence later in Canada than in the United States, due largely to a defensive reaction against a state that was becoming impenetrable and mysterious—not to mention hostile from the standpoint of those in the business community.

The increasing size and complexity of the public sector has spawned organized interests in another way. Government has also actively promoted the creation of associations that would represent and articulate specific interests. This self-serving phenomenon appears to have begun in World War I, when the federal Department of Trade and Commerce encouraged the creation of trade associations to represent corporations in the same industry.[30] Similarly, in the 1960s and 1970s, the Department of the Secretary of State was instrumental in creating a large number of organizations representing women, ethnic groups, and official-language minorities, particularly through providing core funding to finance their activities.[31] The practice continues today, although it was scaled back considerably during the years of Conservative government. Government agencies have helped organize the interests that depended on their programs and budgets, thereby creating constituencies whose support could be useful to the bureaucracy in protecting its policy and budgetary turf.[32] For example, the Multiculturalism Program, most recently administered by Citizenship and Immigration Canada, involves a wide array of ethnic, racial, religious, and cultural organizations in Canada, many of which continue to lobby and attempt to influence public opinion on matters of concern to them. This program now focuses on integrating groups into Canadian society.[33]

Many Aboriginal and human rights groups receive a significant part of their funding from the Canadian government. And the Court Challenges Program provided funding for almost 25 years to organizations representing "members of historically disadvantaged groups" or official-language minorities. The Women's Legal Education and Action Fund (LEAF), for example, a regular and prominent intervener in Charter cases involving sexual discrimination, often received funding of between $35,000 and $50,000 per case.[34]

Sophisticated organization has become essential for maintaining influence. Paul Pross uses the term "institutional groups" to describe interests that possess the highest level of organization. Institutional groups have the following characteristics:

- organizational continuity and cohesion
- extensive knowledge and easy communication with sectors of government that affect their clients
- stable memberships
- concrete and immediate objectives
- overall goals that are more important than any particular objective[35]

While many groups claim to have these characteristics, business associations are more likely to meet Pross's criteria for institutionalized groups. Indeed, the most organizationally sophisticated interest groups in Canada include associations such as the Canadian Council of Chief Executives, Canadian Manufacturers & Exporters, the Canadian Chamber of Commerce, and the Conseil du Patronat du Québec.

Resources

Money is no guarantee of success, but it doesn't hurt. The most organizationally sophisticated groups and most successful, tend to be well financed. Money pays for the services that are vital for success. A permanent staff costs money; it may include lawyers, economists, accountants, researchers, public relations specialists, and others whose services are needed to monitor government activity and communicate both with the group's membership and with policy makers. And the services of public relations firms, polling companies, or professional lobbyists are usually too expensive for many interest groups.

Business groups tend to have more affluent and stable financial footings than other groups. Their closest rivals are major labour associations; some occupational groups, such as physicians, dentists, lawyers, university professors, and teachers; and some agricultural producer groups. As Table 10.1 illustrates, budgets and personnel of some non-economic groups may also appear to be considerable; however, the size of the budget or the size of an association's staff is not a reliable indicator of its influence. There are three important differences between the monetary resources of major business interest groups and those of other organized interests:

1. The members of business interest groups tend not to rely on their collective associations for political influence to the extent that the members of other interest groups do.

TABLE 10.1 Interest Groups, Their Funding, and Their Staff

Interest Group	Interest Focus	Budget	Approximate Staff Size in 2016	Advocacy in Their Words
Canadian Bankers' Association	60 domestic banks, foreign bank subsidiaries, and foreign banks	Over $25 million (2010)	75	The CBA " . . . works on behalf of 60 domestic banks, foreign bank subsidiaries and foreign bank branches operating in Canada and their 280,000 employees and it continues to provide governments and others with a centralized contact to all banks on matters relating to banking in Canada."
Canadian Council of Chief Executives	Chief executive officers of 150 major Canadian corporations	No data	16	"The CCCE . . . is a not-for-profit, non-partisan organization composed of the CEOs of Canada's leading enterprises. Member CEOs and entrepreneurs represent all sectors of the Canadian economy. The companies they lead collectively administer $7.5 trillion in assets."
Canadian Federation of Independent Business	More than 109,000 small and medium-sized businesses	Over $25 million (2012)	–	". . . [T]he CFIB is the big voice for small businesses . . . [at] all three levels of government in their fight for tax fairness, reasonable labour laws and reduction of regulatory paper burden."
Canadian Medical Association	Approximately 80,000 medical doctors	Over $50 million (2013)	165	"The CMA is a national, voluntary association of physicians that advocates on behalf of its members and the public for access to high-quality health care."
Ecojustice (formerly Sierra Legal Defence Fund)	Environment	$5 million (2011)	75	"Ecojustice is leading the legal fight for a brighter environmental future. We are Canada's only national environmental law charity. We are 100% donor-funded and have a 25-year track record of winning legal victories for people and the planet."
Inuit Tapiriit Kanatami	60,000 Inuit living in 53 communities in Canada	$5.3 million (2015)	28	"ITK represents and promotes the interests of on a wide variety of environmental, social, cultural, and political, issues and challenges facing Inuit on the national level. organization."

This table shows us that funding and staff size of interest groups may not be reliable indicators of their influence and effectiveness. Some groups, especially those backed by corporations, have corporate staff dedicated to working directly with the interest group.

Source: Compiled from Stephen Brooks, *Canadian Democracy*, 7/e (Toronto, OUP: 2012), pp. 354–56 and various organizations' websites.

Large corporations usually have their own public affairs departments to manage the organization's relations with government, and often act on their own in employing the services of a professional lobbying firm or other services to help them influence policy makers. Corporations, more so than business associations, have traditionally been major contributors to the Liberal and Conservative parties. Prior to changes to the Election Act covered in Chapter 9, "purchasing access" was another tactic seldom used by members of other types of interest groups.

2. The monetary resources of business and non-business associations relates to stability. Simply put, business groups rest on more secure financial footing, while many groups rely on the imminently less reliable financial support from government, donations from supporters, or both.

3. A third difference involves the ability of business and non-business groups to raise money to deal with a "crisis" issue. The federal election campaign of 1988 was largely fought over free trade; business associations in favour of the Canada–US Free Trade Agreement outspent their opponents by a wide margin in an attempt to influence public opinion on the deal and to ensure the election of the Conservatives.

Inside Politics

BOX 10.1 | Regulating Cellphone Communications—Money Doesn't Guarantee Success

According to Dr Michael Geist of the University of Ottawa, "Canada ranks among the ten most expensive countries within the OECD in virtually every category and among the three most expensive countries for several standard data only plans."[36] He made this observation in reaction to the 2013 OECD report on telecommunications rates in 34 member countries.[37] The study was published at the same time that the federal government was the target of a no-holds-barred public relations campaign called "Fair for Canada," financed by Rogers, Telus, and Bell Canada Enterprises, which together controlled about 90 per cent of the Canadian wireless communications industry. In full-page newspaper ads and radio spots across the country, these three players claimed that reforms favoured by Ottawa would result in lost jobs and a foreign takeover of the industry and infrastructure they had built and paid for.

When corporations in an oligopolistic industry go public in this way, it is a sure sign that their traditional methods of influencing policy have failed. They generally prefer lobbying over court battles and PR campaigns. That they had to take their argument public did not mean, however, that they had given up on their traditional approaches. *Mclean's* magazine reported that by August 2013, telecommunications giants had dedicated substantial resources to communicating with the PMO and Industry

Continued

Canada, and influencing government policy: Rogers had registered 13 of its board members as lobbyists, Telus had registered 17, and BCE had registered 19.[38]

It is not often that a Canadian government locks horns with corporations as dominant as these three have been in the Canadian wireless industry. It appears that the federal government had hoped that a large American carrier, Verizon, would enter the Canadian industry and in doing so create more competition that would put downward pressure on rates. Verizon declined the opportunity to enter the Canadian market. Ottawa did not, however, give up on its goal of reducing rates. The 2013 Speech from the Throne included what was called a "Consumer First Agenda," targeting the pricing practices of mobile phone service providers and also in the airline and credit card industries. For a Conservative government generally thought of as pro-business and anti-regulation, such measures might appear odd. But even pro-business governments need voters' support at election time.

John Kingdon identifies several resources other than money that enable a group to influence the policy agenda and the options considered by policy makers. These include electoral influence, economic coercion, and group cohesion.[39]

Electoral Influence

The perceived ability to swing a significant bloc of votes is an important group resource, as is the status or wealth of its members and their geographic distribution. Some groups in claiming to speak on behalf of their membership are more credible than others. The distributional factor can cut two ways. With Canada's single-member constituency electoral system, the concentration of a group's members in a particular region may increase the political influence of that group. On the other hand, geographic dispersion of a group's membership may also be advantageous.

Economic Coercion

The ability to harm the economy or public finances in some way can be a powerful resource, one usually associated with business groups. Unions and occupation groups such as physicians and agricultural producers have a more difficult time using "economic blackmail" to influence policy makers for two reasons.

First, when nurses, teachers, or postal workers attempt to tie up the economy or a public service by withholding their labour (striking or working to rule), their behaviour and its socio-economic consequences are extremely visible and likely to be perceived by the public as a *special* interest working against the *public* interest. Public opinion may even be hostile. In fact, surveys regularly show that Canadians hold unions in very low esteem.

Second, business interests have a cultural advantage over other economic interest groups in successfully using the threat of economic damage to pursue their objectives. In capitalist

© John Larter / Artizans

As this illustration shows, Canadians were not amused with the idea that a government program such as the Temporary Foreign Workers program might be encouraging Canadian companies to hire foreign workers over Canadian citizens.

societies, the fundamental values that underpin business interests such as the belief in private property, profits, and the ability of markets to generate and distribute wealth lend legitimacy to the actions of businesses. A union strike is often seen as irresponsible: but if a business refuses to invest in new machinery, lays off workers, or relocates offshore, this is often seen by policy makers and the public as a failure of business confidence. Businesses are less likely to be accused of being irresponsible, because they are just acting in accordance with the rules of a system that most of us accept. There are, however, exceptions. When, in 2014, the C.D. Howe Institute reported that many employers, including banks, were abusing the Temporary Foreign Workers' Program (TFWP), a program designed to help fill Canadian labour shortages, and had in fact increased the unemployment rates in British Columbia and Alberta,[40] many felt that the profit motives of some Canadian businesses had gone too far.

Group Cohesion

"United we stand, divided we fall" has been a sound rule of interest group influence. An association's hand appears stronger to policy makers if it speaks with a single voice and genuinely represents its membership's views. This is not always easy. As we have seen, both labour and business interests are highly fragmented in Canada. There are numerous associations, and not one can credibly claim to speak on behalf of all labour or all business interests.

This is true for many other collective interests in Canadian society such as agricultural producers, Aboriginals, and women. Aboriginals, for instance, are represented by many associations, the largest of which is the Assembly of First Nations. Its ability to speak on behalf of all Aboriginal groups is limited by the fact that it does not speak for Métis, non-status Indians, or Inuit, who are represented by their own associations. Cohesion once appeared to be greatest in the women's movement. In 1972, the National Action Committee (NAC) on the Status of Women was created by, and mainly financed by, the federal government. For many years, the NAC acted as a major umbrella association that represented about 700 smaller women's organizations. However, by the late 1980s, the NAC was increasingly beset by internal divisions, and some women's groups did not agree with the confrontational style that its leadership favoured. By 2004, the NAC was insolvent, and any claim that it was a voice for Canadian women's groups was no longer credible.

Group cohesion typically is less a problem in a small organization of similar members. But this cohesion may, of course, be offset by the perception that an association represents a very narrow special interest. As well, it is easier to present a united front when an association is speaking on behalf of just one group. Alliances with other groups may be politically useful. The downside may be the submerging of group differences when forming a common front.

A rather different problem of cohesion involves the relationship between a group's leaders and its membership. A gap between the goals of leaders and those they purport to represent will undermine an association's credibility in the eyes of policy makers. For example, women's groups like the NAC have sometimes been accused of not expressing the views of a large part of Canada's female population. Labour unions' claims to speak on behalf of Canadian workers are weakened, in the eyes of some, by the fact that they represent fewer than four out of every ten workers.

The Interest Group System

If we turn now to the actual interest group system, we find that business groups tend to be smaller than other interest associations. Indeed, some are quite small, particularly those that represent companies in oligopolistic industries—those that control the size of the market and the prices of goods and services. For example, the Canadian Vehicle Manufacturers Association represents only three companies, the Forest Products Association of Canada has only 15 members, and the Canadian Bankers' Association has 60 member organizations. Some business associations, such as chambers of commerce, the Canadian Federation of Independent Business, and Canadian Manufacturers & Exporters, have much larger memberships. But it is also true that these organizations represent general interests of the business community, while the specific interests of corporations are represented through trade associations that have smaller memberships.

Business groups are not the only ones to rely on exclusive benefits and material incentives to attract, maintain, and motivate members. Labour unions, agricultural producer groups, and professional associations do as well. But one needs to remember that cohesion is only one group resource. Farmers' groups or labour unions may be as cohesive as business associations but still inferior to business in terms of the other resources at their disposal.

Safety in the Shadows

The Canadian public regularly sees the outward signs of interest group activities such as demonstrations, full-page newspaper ads, or well-dressed spokespersons being interviewed outside of Parliament. These approaches may not be the most influential. Often, it is the absence of visible signs of interest group activity that tells us most about the strength of organized interests. In the interest group system, some seek safety in the shadows.

Society's most powerful interests sometimes prefer to avoid the public arena where they have to justify themselves and respond to those who advocate changes that would affect their interests. They are safe in the shadows, and that tells us about their power. As E.E. Schattschneider writes, "The very expression 'pressure politics' invites us to misconceive the role of special-interest groups in politics."[41] "Private conflicts," he argues, "are taken into the public arena precisely because someone wants to make certain that the power ratio among the private interests most immediately involved shall not prevail."[42] But in the light of public debate they become prey to attacks from other groups. Conflict, Schattschneider notes, always includes an element of unpredictability. Indeed, when previously unquestioned interests reach the public agenda and are recognized as group interests, a loss of influence can result.

Federalism and the Interest Group System

Hardly a corner of Canadian political life is unaffected by federalism, the interest group system included. Because the Constitution divides political authority between two levels of government, an interest group must determine where jurisdiction lies or, as is often the case, how it is divided between the national and provincial governments. We will examine three of the more general propositions that emerge from the extensive work on federalism and interest groups in Canada.[43]

The first has been labelled the *multiple crack hypothesis*.[44] According to this interpretation, the existence of two levels of government, each of which is equipped with a range of taxing, spending, and regulatory powers, enables interest groups to seek from one government what they cannot get from the other. Business groups have been the ones most likely to exploit the constitutional division of powers, and have been the most successful.[45]

A second interpretation of federalism's impact on interest groups argues that a federal constitution tends to weaken group influence by reducing the internal cohesion of organized interests. According to this argument, divided authority on matters that affect a group's interests will encourage it to adopt a federal form of organization.[46] Federalism may reduce a group's ability to speak with a single voice and to persuade governments that its member organizations are capable of collective action. A group's influence may be weakened when the two levels of

Democracy Watch

BOX 10.2 Having an Impact: Politician or Special Interest?

It is common wisdom that politicians will at some point need to compromise on their strongly held convictions in order to make policy that is accepted by the mainstream. Members of special-interest groups, on the other hand, can devote their careers to further a cause they are passionate about—though they may never be successful in convincing politicians to translate that cause into actual political policy. Those choosing a career in public service will eventually decide to work either from within the system for incremental change or from outside the system for significant change.

government are in conflict, a situation that may create division within the group itself (for example, along regional lines) and between its representative associations.[47]

A third proposition, which might be called the *statist* interpretation, sees federalism as a constraint on, rather than an opportunity for, the influence of interest groups. According to this view, governments and their sprawling bureaucracies increasingly dominate the policy-making scene, particularly when jurisdictional issues are involved. Even societal groups with considerable resources may be frozen out of the process of intergovernmental relations. Leslie Pal drew this conclusion from his study of the historical development of Canada's Unemployment Insurance program. He found that the impact of societal groups on the original form of UI and on subsequent changes was minor compared to the role played by bureaucratic and intergovernmental factors.[48]

Interest Group Strategies

There are three basic strategies open to interest groups. One is to target policy makers directly (e.g., through personal meetings, briefs, and exchanges of information). This is the *lobbying* option. Another strategy is to target *public opinion* in the expectation that policy makers will be swayed by popular support for a group's position. The media play a crucial role here in communicating a group's message to the wider public. A variation on this strategy involves alliance building. By building visible bridges with other groups on some issue, a group may convince policy makers that its position has broad support. A third strategy involves *judicial action*. This confrontational strategy involves a very public court challenge and an outcome that is likely to leave one a winner or a loser. For some groups, this tends to be an option of last resort. But for other groups, such as the Women's Legal Education and Action Fund (LEAF); EGALE, which advocates for lesbian, gay, bisexual, and transgender issues; Ecojustice; and the Canadian Civil Liberties Association, litigation is a basic weapon in their arsenal of pressure tactics.

A few generalizations are possible about which strategies are effective and when they are used:

- One of the keys to influence is early involvement in the policy-making process through lobbying, which is the generally preferred strategy when policies are just being considered. When confrontation and visibility are low, thorough preparation and credible technical become important.
- Well-established groups that are part of a policy community tend to prefer a lobbying strategy. Public and confrontational strategies have an element of risk and unpredictability and will be used only as measures of last resort.
- Less-established groups within a policy community are more likely to rely on confrontation, media campaigns, and other public strategies.
- Where a group's interests are affected by regulation, lobbying strategies that supply research and technical information to the officials who do the regulating will be most successful.
- Even groups who enjoy regular access to policy makers now often find that lobbying is not enough.
- A successful influence strategy (e.g., hiring public relations or polling experts, or going to court) is usually quite expensive, and business groups tend to have deeper pockets.

These strategies are not mutually exclusive. A group may use more than one at once or switch from one strategy to another.

Just what is the price of influence? It varies, but a legal challenge that makes its way to the Supreme Court can certainly cost millions of dollars in legal bills. If much of the legal work has been contributed on a pro bono basis, as it often is in sexual equality or same-sex discrimination cases, the costs may be considerably less. Large business corporations and industry associations have the financial means to defend their interests in court. For other groups, it is often necessary that a litigation-oriented advocacy group like Ecojustice or LEAF take on the burden of their representation.

A campaign directed at influencing public opinion can also be costly. For instance, the pro-FTA Canadian Alliance for Trade and Job Opportunities probably spent over $2 million even before the final blitz during the 1988 federal election campaign. This case may be a quarter of a century old, and the amount of money may sound paltry by today's standards, but it was in fact a catalyst for reform of the law on third-party spending during election campaigns. But groups outside of business interests also spend lavishly to shape public opinion. Quebec's Cree First Nations spent an estimated $500,000 on paid advertisements and the services of a New York public relations firm in an effort to stop the construction of the Great Whale hydroelectric project in Quebec. In 2013, an American billionaire investor, Tom Steyer, announced that he planned to spend $1 million on ads opposing construction of the Keystone XL pipeline that would transport oil from Alberta to refineries on the Gulf of Mexico.[49]

These sums, however, pale alongside the tens of millions of dollars the Alberta and Canadian governments have spent in recent years to tell Canadians, Americans, and others their side of the oil sands story. It is usually difficult to pinpoint the resources devoted to an advertising campaign to influence public opinion. Walmart is one of many companies that invest a significant amount of money in television and other ads intended to convey an image of a socially responsible company and valued member of the community where its stores are located. The beer and liquor industries likewise invest large amounts of money in advertising that aims to create a favourable public image, and to preclude the sort of regulation and product advertising limits that have been imposed on the tobacco industry. None of this spending is related to election campaigns, and therefore does not fall under the rules set by the Canada Elections Act.

Advocacy Advertising

The purchase of newspaper/magazine space or broadcast time to convey a political message is called **advocacy advertising**. As indicated above, business interest groups are not the only ones to buy advertising to influence public opinion on an issue. However, business groups use advocacy advertising most extensively. The crucial question raised by any form of advertising that carries a political message is whether the ability to pay for media time/space should determine what views get expressed. The critics of advocacy advertising were quick to denounce the blitz of pro–free trade advertising by business during the 1988 election campaign. They argued that the deep pockets of the corporate interests ranged behind free trade made a sham of the democratic political process and totally undermined the intention of the statutory limits on election spending by political parties. The Royal Commission on Elections agreed. Its 1992 report recommended that spending by organizations other than registered political parties be limited during elections. Such restrictions were passed by the federal government in 2000 and their constitutionality was upheld by the Supreme Court of Canada in 2004.

The defenders of advocacy advertising claim that it is a way for business to overcome the anti-business bias of the media and to bridge the "credibility gap" that has developed between business and the public. Mobil Oil, one of the pioneers of this advertising technique, has called it a "new form of public disclosure,"[50] thereby associating it with freedom of information. Business and economic issues are complex, and advocacy advertising—most of which is done through the print media—provides an opportunity for business to explain its actions and to counter public misconceptions. And in any case, argue corporate spokespersons, the biggest spender on advocacy advertising is government, whose justification for this spending is essentially the same as that of business![51] There is no doubt that strategies aimed at influencing public opinion have become increasingly important to interest groups. In fact, in discussing advocacy advertising we have only scratched the surface of these strategies.[52] Important as they are, however, strategies that target public opinion usually take a backseat to those that target policy makers directly. These are lobbying strategies.

Lobbying

Lobbying may be defined as any form of direct or indirect communication with government that is designed to influence public policy.[53] Although the term conjures up images of "old boy

advocacy advertising the purchase of newspaper/ magazine space or broadcast time to convey a political message

lobbying any form of direct or indirect communication with government that is designed to influence public policy

networks" and sleazy deal making, this is a somewhat unfair caricature of lobbying on two counts. First, lobbying is a basic democratic right. When citizens organize to demand a traffic light at a dangerous neighbourhood corner and meet with their ward councillor to express their concerns, this is lobbying. When the president of a powerful business association arranges a lunch with a PMO official with whom he went to law school, this, too, is lobbying. The fact that lobbying is often associated with unfair privilege, and even corruption, should not obscure the fact that it is not limited to organizations representing the powerful. Second, in principle, there is nothing undemocratic about lobbying.

A second way in which the "sleaze" caricature of lobbying conveys a wrong impression is by associating it with practices such as direct meetings with influential public officials, which is only a small part of what lobbyists actually do. Likewise, there is no shortage of evidence that ethically dubious, sometimes illegal relations exist between lobbyists and policy makers. But lobbying is much more than meetings with public officials. Most professional lobbyists spend a lot of their time collecting and communicating information on behalf of their interests. They monitor the political scene as it affects their client's interests. An effective lobbyist does not simply react, but instead acts like an early warning system, providing information about policy when it is still in its formative stages and tracking public opinion on the issues that are vital to their interests. They may also provide advice and professional assistance in putting together briefs, press releases or speeches, as well as public relations services such as identifying and targeting segments of public opinion that influence policy makers on some issue (see Boxes 10.4 and 10.5). Helping to build strategic coalitions with other groups is another function of lobbyists.

President Obama,
You'll never guess who's standing between us and our new energy economy...

Canada's Tar Sands: the dirtiest oil on earth.

President Obama travels to Canada on February 19. We hope he'll discuss his vision for a new energy future with leaders there. The US and Canada can revive our economies, create green jobs, and build a better future for our children.

This is the best path forward.

Right now, Canada is not on that path. Producing oil from Canada's Tar Sands releases massive greenhouse gas emissions, consumes huge amounts of energy, contaminates fresh water and fish, produces toxic waste and destroys vast forests along with their birds and wildlife. And now, downstream indigenous communities are suffering higher than normal rates of cancer.

Prime Minister Harper and the government of Alberta continue to turn a blind eye to these problems.

Your voice counts. Please let President Obama know that he should ask Canada to clean up the Tar Sands.

Take action online today.
Visit ForestEthics.org

FORESTETHICS
VANCOUVER • TORONTO • SAN FRANCISCO • BELLINGHAM

MIKISEW CREE
FIRST NATION

ATHABASCA CHIPEWYAN
FIRST NATION

© ForestEthics, www.forestethics.org

ForestEthics teamed up with the Mikisew Cree and Athabasca Chipewyan First Nations to place this full-page ad in *USA Today*.

David Cooper/Toronto Star via Getty Images

Lobbying in action: an overflowing town hall meeting at the Direct Energy Centre, Exhibition Place in September 2013. Lobbyists often get a bad rap from the media and other quarters for their alleged "sleazy" tactics. But if anyone communicates directly or indirectly with government at any level, with the express purpose of influencing public policy, then they are, by definition, a lobbyist. It is every citizen's democratic right to lobby, and the information that is gathered and provided to government institutions by lobbyists is often vital for making good policy decisions.

Most interest groups lobby government on their own. But for those who can afford it, the services of a professional lobbying firm are also available. There are many such businesses. The *Hill Times* 2013 list of Canada's top 100 lobbyists includes individuals representing 18 government consultant lobbying firms. Some of these businesses employ dozens of professional staff and have annual billings in the tens of millions of dollars; others are small operations that employ a handful of persons (see Box 10.5). In addition, many law firms and accounting companies, including such prominent ones as Osler, Hoskin & Harcourt; Dentons; McMillan LLP; and Stikeman Elliott, do lobbying work. The line between legal representation and lobbying is often nonexistent, a fact attested to by the presence of many law firms on the public registry of lobbyists.

Since 1989, those who are paid to lobby federal public office holders have been required to register with a federal agency. The Lobbyists Registration Act provides for three categories of lobbyists:

- fee-based *consultant lobbyists* who work for various clients
- *corporate in-house lobbyists* who work for a single corporation and lobby federal officials as a significant part of their duties

- *organization in-house lobbyists* who are senior paid officers and other employees of organizations whose activities include lobbying federal officials

The majority of active lobbyists represent corporations and business associations. The clientele lists of Canada's leading government relations firms include major players in the Canadian and international corporate world. Earnscliffe Strategy Group, for example, boasts that it represents such clients as Microsoft, DeBeers, Novartis Pharmaceutical, Chevron, General Motors Canada, and McDonald's Canada.[54]

Democracy Watch

BOX 10.3 Ethical Fundraising

Is it ethical for political parties to raise money by hosting fundraising events that allow those who can pay to have access to the prime minister, provincial premiers, cabinet ministers, or other party leaders? Controversies over corruption and access to politicians for cash regularly show up in the news. Part of the problem come from regulations and contribution limits that have changed frequently and also vary from one jurisdiction to the next. Some political

Canadian Press/ Chris Young

Continued

parties may be unduly affected by the limits and regulations depending on their demographic support. Some citizens may also feel that their democratic rights are being infringed upon simply because they have more money.

The most important federal reforms to political contributions were introduced by the Liberal government in 2004 with a $5000 limit and a per-vote subsidy based on elections results. Elections Canada currently limits individual contributions to $1525 per year with a $25 per year increase.[55]

Provincially, the stories vary. In 2015, the Alberta government moved to eliminate corporate and union donations and limited contributions to $15,000 annually. In 2016, the *National Post* reported that Ontario Liberals raised $2.5 million at a $1600-a-plate dinner in March of that year. The premiers of both Ontario, Kathleen Wynne, and BC, Christy Clark, had to explain why such practices were necessary. Premier Clark has continued to resist changes to BC's electoral act. However, by April 2016, after her party was roundly criticized in the press for receiving donations from corporations and unions in exchange for access to politicians, Wynne decided to follow the federal and Quebec government's lead and introduced new provincial regulations restricting donations by individuals, corporations, and unions and controlling lobbyist access to government officials,

Sources: Allison Jones, "Ont. Liberals Raised $2.5M at $1,600-a-Plate Fundraising Dinner as Premier Promises to Tighten Donation Rules," *National Post*, 31 March 2016, http://news.nationalpost.com/news/canada/canadian-politics/ont-liberals-raised-2-5m-at-1600-a-plate-fundraising-dinner-as-premier-promises-to-tighten-donation-rules; Vaughn Palmer, "Legislature Seethes over Premier's Salary Supplement," *Vancouver Sun*, 28 April 2016, http://vancouversun.com/opinion/columnists/vaughn-palmer-legislature-seethes-over-premiers-salary-supplement; Keith Leslie, "Kathleen Wynne Comes Clean on Fundraising Quotas for Cabinet Ministers," *National Post*, 1 April 2016, http://news.nationalpost.com/news/canada/kathleen-wynne-admits-ontarios-liberal-cabinet-ministers-have-fundraising-quotas.

Box 10.5 lists some of Canada's most prominent consultant lobbyists and some of the clients they work for.

As the scope and process of governance have changed, so too, has the character of lobbying. The old model of lobbying as personal communications by a privileged individual to a high-ranking politician or bureaucrat on behalf of a client is now an activity more akin to Sherpas guiding their climbers toward a destination. Key personal contacts continue to be a large part of what lobbying firms sell, but today, this is reinforced by extensive knowledge and intensive analysis of the policy matters in question. Allan Gregg of Decima Research played an important role in this transformation. Decima offered clients analysis of the public opinion environment in which their activities were situated and that affected the achievement of their goals. The *Decima Quarterly* provided clients with confidential and up-to-date information on public opinion. When Hill & Knowlton, a world leader in the lobbying industry, acquired Decima in 1989, a sort of one-stop-shopping model of public affairs advice and strategic communications was created. The new model fused public opinion expertise, marketing skills,

Inside Politics

BOX 10.4 | What Does a Government Relations Firm Sell?

Stikeman Elliott is one of Canada's best-known and most influential business law firms. Its work often involves activities that, under Canada's Lobbyist Registration Act, fall under the definition of lobbying. Here is what the firm promises its clients.

> Stikeman Elliott is the only Canadian firm that can clearly and strategically integrate government relations and public relations on behalf of our clients. From our involvement in the recent takeover defence of PotashCorp and acting for and opposite governmental authorities in infrastructure, corporate governance and legislative initiatives, to our representation of clients before governmental commissions, securities, competition and telecommunications regulators, and other administrative bodies, Stikeman Elliott has established itself among Canada's leading law firms in the realm of government relations and public policy. Ranked as the 2013 Government Regulations law firm of the year by Corporate INTL, we offer considerable advantage to our clients through our knowledge of and access to the players in multiple sectors and our ability to review a situation to assemble the right resources, including outside government relations and media consultants.
>
> The historical and continuing connection of a number of our partners with governmental and regulatory agencies, and in the Canadian legislative process, adds an important additional dimension to the services we offer. We have access to decision makers at various levels of federal, provincial and municipal government and are consistently able to secure the appropriate audience for our clients. We count several former high level bureaucrats within our ranks.

Source: Stikeman Elliott website, "Government Relations," www.stikeman.com/cps/rde/xchg/se-en/hs.xsl/1279.htm.

and policy analysis with personal access to government officials. This remains the model in Canada, as practised by the heavyweights of the lobbying establishment.

The Lobbyists Registration Act requires that lobbyists identify the general subject matter of their activities as well as the government departments and agencies that they contact on behalf of those they represent. "Industry," "international trade," and "taxation and finance" have, from the beginning of the registration system, been the most frequent subjects on which lobbyists have plied their trade.

"Environment" has moved steadily up the list and was ranked fourth in 2013, reflecting the increasing importance of environmental laws and regulations for corporations and business associations. Matters relating to health policy also have been among the most frequent

Inside Politics

BOX 10.5 | Who Do Government Relations Firms Represent?

Lobbyist	Company	Clients
André Albinati	Earnscliffe Strategy Group	CIBC Eli Lilly Canada Nexen Hoffman-La Roche
David Angus	Capital Hill Group	Police Association of Ontario Molson Canada Hewlett Packard Canada CHC Helicopters MBDA Missile Systems Nishnawbe Aski Nation
Peter Clark	Grey, Clark, Shih	Chicken Farmers of Canada Dairy Farmers of Canada US Lumber Coalition Methanex (multinational methanol producer)
Michael Coates	Hill+Knowlton	Bell Canada Enterprises Blackberry CNOOC (Hong Kong-based petroleum company) SNC-Lavalin

Note: These four lobbyists were selected from the *Hill Times* 2013 list of Canada's 100 top lobbyists.

Source: Industry Canada, Lobbyists Registration System, online public registry, www.ocl-cal.gc.ca.

subjects of lobbying in recent years. Lobbyists are required to indicate the government institutions they contact or expect to contact and, since 2006, the particular public officials they lobby. The departments of Finance, Industry, and Foreign Affairs and International Trade, as well as the PCO and the PMO, are perennially among the most targeted institutions. MPs and senators, who were seldom targeted by lobbyists a decade ago, have become among the most frequently contacted public officials.[56]

Today's lobbyists are sometimes yesterday's politicians and bureaucrats. According to the Lobbyists Registration Act, 1989, individuals who are consultant lobbyists, corporate in-house lobbyists, or organization in-house lobbyists must register and keep records of contacts. The Federal Accountability Act of 2006 also sets some limits on the ability of public officials to lobby the government after leaving the public sector.

Summary

Interest groups are a very important feature of Canadian democracy. There are thousands of organized groups in Canada. Many of these try to influence public policy or public opinion, while others will mobilize as a result of a specific issue or set of circumstances. Research has shown that the interest group system is not representative of the whole community. Experts have noted that business interests occupy a "privileged position" within this interest group competition and these tend to be biased in favour of the wealthy, the educated, and the organized.

Public officials and policy makers do worry that their actions will affect business confidence mainly because corporations and the wealthy can stop investing in the economy or move capital out of the country. This is perhaps one of the greatest sources of influence for groups representing business interests. But interest groups also rely on other means of influence such as advertising, boycotts and other militant behaviour covered by the media, producing studies and disseminating their results and recommendations, celebrity endorsements of a position, and so on.

We have used certain analytical perspectives to explain the behaviour and the effects of interest groups on society. And we noted that a group's influence within a policy community will depend on its internal characteristics and on its external relationships to the larger political system and the state. Successful interest groups have a sophisticated organization that keeps pace with growing and increasingly complex governments, routine access to policy makers, access to resources (especially money), electoral influence, the capacity to affect the economy, and group cohesion. Some experts have argued that federalism tends to strengthen interest groups by increasing the access to policy makers and by making it possible to play one level of government against the other. But others say that federalism can weaken the internal cohesion of organized interests.

Lobbying, litigation, targeting public opinion, or taking to the streets are just some of the strategic options available to groups, and their use will depend on many factors. Some organizations, including business associations and labour unions, engage in direct lobbying. Others hire the services of government consulting/relations firms. It is every Canadian citizen's right to lobby in an attempt to influence government policy, but the ability to lobby effectively and to pay for the services of specialized firms that lobby on behalf of clients is very unevenly distributed in the universe of interest groups.

Review Exercises

1. Find a newspaper story that discusses an interest group and identify its name, the interests or associations it represents, the reason for its being in the news, and the group's demands or values.

2. Make a list of organized groups you have belonged to or contributed to in some way. If you are having trouble coming up with a list, think about jobs that you may have had (were they unionized?); churches, clubs, or associations that you may have belonged to; causes you might have donated money to; petitions you may have signed; and so on. Which of these do you think attempt to influence public opinion or policy?

3. Identify various political activities engaged in by various interest groups. Which activities do you consider to be strongly democratic, somewhat democratic, and undemocratic?

4. Visit https://lobbycanada.gc.ca/eic/site/012.nsf/eng/00403.html. Examine the rules that apply to politicians or civil servants who leave government to work for lobbying firms or interest groups. Discuss the potential for unethical conduct and whether the regulations go far enough.

Up for Debate

1. Can democracies function without interest groups?
2. Resolved: Interest groups only serve to protect elites.
3. Resolved: Lobbyists have greater access to government than citizens.
4. To have maximum effect in making changes that will benefit society, is it better to be a politician belonging to a party or a member of a special-interest group? Defend your choice with three examples.

Starting Points for Research

Campbell, Robert, Michael Howlett, and Leslie Pal. *The Real Worlds of Canadian Politics*, 4th edn. Peterborough, ON: Broadview Press, 2004.

Coleman, William. *Business and Politics: A Study of Collective Action*. Montreal and Kingston: McGill–Queen's University Press, 1988.

Hale, Geoffrey. *Uneasy Partnership: The Politics of Business and Government*. Toronto: University of Toronto Press, 2006.

Pal, Leslie A. *Interests of State: The Politics of Language, Multiculturalism and Feminism in Canada*. Montreal and Kingston: McGill–Queen's University Press, 1993.

Studlar, Donley T. *Tobacco Control: Comparative Politics in the United States and Canada*. Toronto: University of Toronto Press, 2002.

CBC Archives and TVO's *The Agenda*

Visit the companion website for *Canadian Democracy: A Concise Introduction* to follow links to audio and video footage related to the main themes of the chapter: www.oupcanada.com/BrooksConcise2e.

Relevant Websites

Visit the companion website for *Canadian Democracy: A Concise Introduction* to browse a collection of websites featuring material related to the key themes of the chapter, an excellent starting point for research: www.oupcanada.com/BrooksConcise2e.

11 The Media

Media impact on modern political life is profound. After reading this chapter, you should be able to

1. explain how the media shape the political agenda in Canadian democracy
2. describe what the media produce
3. determine what a mass media product is
4. explain the many ways in which the media acts as a filter for much our information

Although most of us have never met the prime minister of Canada or the president of the United States, virtually all of us have ideas about their character, abilities, and performance. The facts upon which we form our judgments concerning these leaders, as well as our beliefs about the world, are based on the edited images and information offered on television screens, in newspapers, over the radio waves, and through other electronic media.

↑ Member of Parliament Laurie Hawn speaks to the media in the hallway outside the House of Commons. Most of what we know about the political world is mediated by those who select and interpret information for print and broadcast media.

Source: Andrew Burton/Getty Images.

If our ideas are based largely on third-hand information, then we should pay careful attention to who communicates this information. For instance, a typical political story on the evening television news may involve about 60–90 seconds of images of the prime minister, cabinet ministers, opposition leaders, or critics, probably in the House of Commons during question period or in the foyer near the entrance to the Commons, where journalists and camera operators await their daily feeding by exiting politicians. The story may include brief segments featuring politicians, experts, and interest group spokespersons commenting on the prime minister's remarks. Some portion of the story will consist of the reporter's own narration of what is happening and what it means. In short, the entire news clip may be described as "third-hand information" because it is the product of many choices by those who assign stories to reporters and those who edit and package the story in the television network's newsroom. Consequently, what the viewer ultimately sees has been influenced by a number of people whose choices contribute to what we call "the news."

Citizens' dependence on the media for much of their ideas and information is not new. What is more recent is our awareness of the role of selection, distortion, and manipulation in the process of reporting the news. Long-standing fears that media might have a partisan bias or that propaganda might subvert democratic politics have been joined lately by worries that the biases are more deeply rooted and insidious than ever before. The "seductions of language," says media expert Neil Postman, are trivial compared to the seductions and manipulative powers of the image-based media.[1]

The ability of those in the media to freely report on public affairs as they see fit is crucial for democracies, but this must be within the limits of defamation laws, public disclosure laws, and national security and policy-making interests. If broadcasters, blogs, or journalists can be shut down, censored, or punished because public officials do not like the information they convey, then open discussion of public issues is diminished, and democracy suffers. The founders of the American republic knew this, which is why freedom of the press, along with freedom of speech, religion, and assembly, was specifically mentioned in the United States Constitution and those of several states. Canada's founders devoted little attention to freedom of the press or other freedoms. They assumed that these would be adequately respected under the system of parliamentary government and that a democratic society had no need to explicitly state the principles that it lived by.

At the same time, all countries regulate the media system in some way. This is particularly true of broadcasting, where the airwaves have been defined as public property throughout the world and where there have been technological reasons for restricting the number of broadcasters and to protect the quality of the television or radio signals reaching consumers. But this traditional argument for regulation has been challenged by newer technologies. The proliferation of websites and blogs has resulted in the kind of explosion of information and a diversity of perspectives never before seen in human history, which makes state regulation of information increasingly difficult.

The state regulation of the media may not be the only threat to freedom of the press and to democracy. A more serious threat, some critics argue, is the economic censorship that may result from the increasing monopolization of media ownership—when too few owners control

Cartoon by Peter Nicholson from "The Australian" newspaper: www.nicholsoncartoons.com.au

What a great thing media diversity is.

Nicholson 16 Mar 06

This cartoon is Australian, but its criticism about the media is commonly heard in most democracies, where fewer and fewer corporations own the radio, television, and print media. Is this criticism fair?

too many media outlets. Critics also claim that most mass media outlets' dependence on advertising results in a filtering out of certain forms of controversial, critical, and non-mainstream coverage of public affairs.

Before we attempt to make sense of the controversial relationship between the media and politics, let us examine the mass media's role in social learning and the chief characteristics of Canada's media system.

"The Pictures in Our Heads"

social learning
the process of acquiring knowledge, values, and beliefs about the world and ourselves

As creators and purveyors of images and information, the media play a role in **social learning**—the process of acquiring knowledge, values, and beliefs about the world and ourselves. Other agents of social learning include the family, schools, peer groups, and organizations that one belongs to. Studies have shown that the family is the most important agent of social learning because of its influence on the development of one's self-esteem, trust, and disposition toward authority, which are generally linked to political attitudes and behaviours. As well, the family typically impacts one's acquisition of communication skills, class identification, and social attitudes (e.g., gender roles). Although none of this learning is about politics per se, it has important political consequences.

While the family and other agents of social learning contribute to what Walter Lippmann called "the pictures in our heads," none of them rival the media in their impact on the political agenda. "The only feeling that anyone can have about an event that he does not experience is the feeling aroused by his mental image of that event."[2] Much of our modern political discourse is determined by the mass media as they process and report on "reality." Moreover, in matters remote from one's daily life—political turmoil in the Middle East, global pollution, or the latest Canadian federal budget—the media are the only source of images and information about the events, issues, and personalities. Politicians and generals recognize the media's importance; this is why the first steps in any coup d'état are to seize control of broadcasting and to shut down or muzzle newspapers not sympathetic to the new regime.

It has been said that the media do not determine what we think so much as what we think about. This formidable power shapes the public consciousness by conveying certain images and interpretations and excluding others. The responsibility that accompanies such power is enormous. A "free press" has been viewed as a necessary ingredient of democratic politics since the American Revolution. The reasoning here is that because all groups and individuals are self-interested, they cannot be counted on to objectively assess their goals and actions. Too often their interests will be best served through concealment, deception, and manipulation, and by propaganda—the dissemination of selected information or misinformation to the public as a means of spreading a particular ideology or doctrine. Many have argued that only the media have an interest in presenting the facts. They may perform their function imperfectly, and particular media outlets may have political biases, which reflect the values and prejudices of their journalists, editors, and readers, but competition ensures that significant points of view reach the public.

Is this an accurate picture of the media's role in a democracy? How well do the media cover all points of view? And what are the consequences of their behaviour on politics? First, let us consider the "products" of the mass media.

> **propaganda**
> the dissemination of selected information or misinformation to the public as a means of spreading a particular ideology or doctrine

What Do the Media Produce?

Television and Radio

Most programming aims to entertain rather than inform. Consequently, only a small portion of our television and radio time is devoted to public affairs. The rest of our time is spent watching drama, comedy, game and talk shows, and sports, or listening to music. The English segment of Canada's television market has always been overwhelmingly dominated by American programming (see Table 11.1) as evidenced by the top-ranked programs for any given week as recorded by the Bureau of Broadcast Measurement.[3]

A 2010 survey found that television was still the medium relied on by more Canadians than any other as their main source of news (46.6 per cent), with radio second (21.6 per cent), the Internet third (17.5 per cent), and newspapers last (14.3 per cent).[4]

Private radio broadcasters account for about 90 per cent of the market, and most of what they offer is music. Although the Canadian Radio-television and Telecommunications

TABLE 11.1 Prime-Time TV Viewing in English Canada, 2013–2014

Rank	Program	Audience (millions)
1	*The Big Bang Theory* (CTV)	3.6
2	*NCIS* (Global)	2.6
3	*The Amazing Race 23 & 24* (CTV)	2.5
4	*Survivor: Blood vs. Water & Brawn vs. Brains* (Global)	2.3
5	*NCIS: Los Angeles* (Global)	2.3
6	*Grey's Anatomy* (CTV)	2.3
7	*C.S.I.* (CTV)	2.2
8	*Criminal Minds* (CTV)	2.1
9	*Marvel's Agents of S.H.I.E.L.D.* (CTV)	2.0
10	*Hockey Night in Canada* (East) (CBC)	2.0

The television programs watched by Canadians are overwhelmingly American. Only one of the top 10 television programs watched by Canadians in the 2013–14 viewing season was Canadian, *Hockey Night in Canada* on CBC. *Master Chef Canada*, a Canadian-produced knock-off of the American version, came in fourteenth.

Source: BBM Canada, Sept 23, 2013 - May 18, 2014 (Weeks 5-38, final data) vs. equivalent weeks in previous years. Audiences prior to August 31, 2009 are based on BBM Nielsen Media Research Mark II meters.

Commission (CRTC), the industry's regulatory watchdog, requires all radio stations to carry news, only the largest privately owned stations generate any significant amount of news themselves. Most rely on information supplied by wire services, newspapers, and local sports and weather to meet their news quota. Only the state-owned Canadian Broadcasting Corporation and Radio-Canada, its French-language counterpart, generate and broadcast a significant amount of national and international public affairs programming.

Like most radio stations, newspapers are geared primarily to the local market. Although all dailies carry national and international news, studies suggest that newspapers are considered to be better than either television or radio as a source of community information, while television is believed to be the best source of information for international, national, and even provincial news. Television is also judged to be most up to date, fair and unbiased, believable, influential, and essential to the country. A 2007 survey conducted for the Information Technology Association of Canada found that this preference for television as the most important and trustworthy medium continues.[5] Newspapers are relied on by most readers chiefly as a source of local information. A few Canadian dailies, including the Toronto-based *Globe and Mail* and the *National Post*, do not conform to this community paper model, and they have the greatest national circulations among Canadian newspapers. Other dailies such as the *Toronto Star, Montreal Gazette, Ottawa Citizen,* and *Vancouver Sun* also include more coverage of national and international news than is typical of most dailies. The *Globe's* long-standing

© ZUMA Wire Service/Alamy

Anchors we watch on a daily basis (pictured here is Lisa LaFlamme of CTV *National News*) become a trusted source of news. After that relationship of trust has been formed, do we become less critical of content? When you watch a nightly newscast, do you think about the perspective from which the story is being told? Do you seek out other perspectives on that story? What might you discover if you watched reports from different broadcasters on the same news item?

reputation as English Canada's "national" newspaper—which the *Post* has challenged since it began in 1998—has been acquired in part because of high-calibre journalism. The political columnists and editorial writers of both the *Globe* and the *National Post* are influential players in defining the country's political agenda. Montreal-based *Le Devoir* plays a similar role in Quebec.

Print Media

Critics of Canadian newspapers have focused on a number of specific concerns relating to industry structure.

First, concentrated ownership is seen as limiting the range of ideas and information that reach the public. However, the need to make a profit and the organizational structure of news gathering and reporting seem to have more impact than competition within the industry.

Second, newspapers that are part of larger corporate networks that include non-media interests may be reluctant to cover stories and interpret events in ways that put their owners' other interests in a bad light. However, the empirical proof for this claim is weak. Incidents of owner interference or media self-censorship based on a sensitivity to an owner's interests occasionally happen.[6] But as Edward Herman and Noam Chomsky argue, it is too simplistic to look for direct correlations between ownership and the handling of particular issues or stories; instead, owners exercise their influence more diffusely through "establishing the general aims of the company and choosing its top management."[7]

Third, ownership is said to produce a certain uniformity in the partisan orientations of newspapers within the chain. This claim is not supported by the evidence either. Studies carried out by researchers at the University of Windsor found no proof that chain ownership is associated with either the patterns of news reporting or editorial policy.[8] Differences between newspapers may have far more to do with readership characteristics than with ownership.

And finally, an increasing number of readers prefer to read online, and many expect to be able to do so without having to pay for what they read. Almost all Canadian journalists now use social media, and blogs have become a significant means of verifying stories. A 2013 study found that over 90 per cent of them used Twitter, over half maintained a personal blog, and about one-quarter had a personal Google Plus page.[9]

This is a worry for those who believe that a healthy democracy depends on a strong news media to hold those in power to account. Lawrence Martin of *The Globe and Mail* noted in early 2015 that since 2008 thousands of journalists had lost their jobs and called for a public inquiry into the state of the journalism in Canada.[10] Andrew Coyne of the *National Post* wrote:

> But however successful my colleagues and I may have been at persuading ourselves of the indispensability of the business we are in—to the point, in some cases, of calling for public subsidy—there is one group that has proved rather less easily persuaded: everyone else.
>
> Alas, that is the more salient fact as far as public policy is concerned.
>
> Newspapers are not failing because the market has failed. Rather, the market is quite accurately reflecting a harsh but inescapable truth: people do not value the thing we are selling at a price sufficient to cover its costs.[11]

Magazines have faced the same challenges confronted by newspapers in recent years. Subscriptions have been falling in an industry that only a couple of decades ago included dozens of magazines that had monthly subscriptions of 100,000 or more. Today only about 10 in the English-language market have paid circulations above this mark. Most of the bestselling magazines, including *Chatelaine, Canadian Living, Reader's Digest*, and *Canadian Geographic*, do not cover much in the way of public affairs and much of the coverage is American based. The

one exception is *Maclean's*. As is also true of newspapers, *Maclean's* has been forced to adapt to the reality of consumers who expect to receive their news immediately, and not just once a week, and on the screen of their smartphone or computer, through a digital edition that features constantly updated content and journalists who blog and tweet.

Film

Compared to the media we have discussed so far, film may appear relatively insignificant. As is true of people throughout the world, Canadians usually turn to films for diversion and entertainment, rather than to be informed about public affairs. The average Canadian goes to the cinema only four or five times per year (city-dwellers more often). Fibre optic television, satellite broadcasting, video-on-demand such as Netflix or Crave TV, Blu-ray players, and smartphones have all increased the market penetration of films, allowing the film industry to bring its product directly to people's home TVs, tablets, and cellphones. New technology has thus enabled the film industry to recapture some of the prominence it held between the 1930s and the 1950s, before the advent of television.

Film seems to excite the modern imagination. If a person has not read the book, they have probably seen its film or television series adaptation. Indeed, we have seen in recent years the power of this visual medium to turn books into motion picture blockbusters like the *Lord of the Rings* trilogy, the Hunger Games series, and the Harry Potter films, and popular television series like *True Blood*, *The Walking Dead*, or *Game of Thrones*. The stories they tell, the characters they portray, and the stereotypes they convey shape and reflect our popular culture. The archetypes and icons of popular culture are more likely to be associated with movies than with any other mass medium. An argument could be made that Leonardo DiCaprio, Brad Pitt, and Jennifer Lawrence have had a greater impact on how North Americans (and Europeans to a lesser extent) view the world and react to it—and have affected it—than has any political leader in the Western world over the last half-century.

What does the film industry offer the viewing public? Hundreds of new releases every year from Hollywood studios, and thousands more from independents in the United States, Canada, and elsewhere, might lead one to assume that the industry produces a richly varied product. It does. But only a narrow band of the entire range of film production is backed up with the marketing resources of the studios that produce *commercial feature films*. The genre may vary, but what distinguishes such a film is the fact that it must appeal to a large mass audience to recoup the millions of dollars—sometimes hundreds of millions of dollars—spent on its production and marketing. Documentary and artistic films by contrast usually cost much less to make and generate smaller revenues. They usually are made by small independent film companies or by state-owned filmmakers like Canada's National Film Board. Little is spent on marketing them, and public access to non-commercial films until recently was limited because distributors did not want to show them. However, technological advancements and the advent of video-on-demand services like YouTube and Netflix is revolutionizing what is being consumed by the viewers and how they view it. Today, films and television productions that might never have been seen in movie theatres or on commercial television under the old model are now being viewed by millions. Viewers now can watch every possible type of video production wherever and whenever they want, and much of it is commercial free. David DiSalvo of forbes.com describes the transformation of the industry this way:

> Netflix films an entire season of the show and then—against every convention inscribed onto the holy tablets of television—releases the entire season . . . *all at once*. When season two of *Orange is the New Black* aired on Friday, June 6, the whole season aired, front to back.
>
> Hundreds of thousands if not millions of fans waiting for the new season were free to binge on every episode—and I'm willing to bet that by now a hefty percentage of those fans have re-binged, with many warming up for a third gorging.
>
> Before Netflix introduced this format, we were still in the mode of weekly allotments of entertainment. HBO long ago christened Sunday nights as the time to receive our weekly dose of quality, commercial-free shows of choice, whether it's *The Sopranos, Six Feet Under, Sex in the City*, or more recently *Game of Thrones* (to name just a few of many legendary shows). All of the major cable and traditional networks offer something similar, but only the premium channels can offer the premium prize of hour-long, commercial free entertainment.
>
> . . . So what happens when Netflix releases an entire season of shows every bit as good as anything on premium cable channels? It's as if all of the disincentives

enforcing delayed gratification in our hypothetical lab rats have suddenly disappeared. The boundaries are cast to oblivion. The tasty treat is right there for the taking, and in a quantity that hardly any rat can resist.[13]

In short, consumers are far less beholden to movie theatre distributors or television program schedulers, who have had to rethink and restructure their entire industries, and are far less subject to the whims of marketers and television advertisers. In addition, as discussed below, programs streamed through the Internet cannot easily be regulated for Canadian content.

The images and stories purveyed by the commercial film industry are often disturbing and occasionally critical of "the system." Indeed, one of the most popular motifs of popular film has long been the lone good man versus the bad system. Bruce Willis, Denzel Washington, and Leonardo DiCaprio have been among the more successful in portraying this character. *It's a Wonderful Life* and *To Kill a Mockingbird* are classic examples of this simple theme, as are the archetypal

Kevin Van Paassen/The Canadian Press

Film tends to reinforce dominant values and institutions, but a recent trend in news satire shows does the opposite. Canada's Rick Mercer, host of the award-winning *Rick Mercer Report*, offers a weekly take on current events that skewers and critiques mainstream politics. In the United States, similar shows such as *The Daily Show* and *Last Week Tonight with John Oliver* offer this alternative view while also poking fun at the "infotainment" formats found on many news channels.

westerns *Shane* and *High Noon*. More recent examples include *Erin Brockovich*, *The Revenant*, and *Hell or High Water*. But on balance, commercial film reinforces dominant values and institutions rather than challenging them. The economics of the industry make this inevitable.

Advertisement

Advertisements are another important part of the media product. Most people are exposed to hundreds of ads each day. Television and radio are heavily laced with them. Newspapers and magazines are bursting with them. Even films have become vehicles for advertising, with companies willing to pay thousands of dollars for *product placement*. Billboards, storefront signs, pamphlets, flyers, cinema advertising, Internet banners, mobile ads, and pop-ups . . . there is no escape. The estimated amount spent on mass media advertising worldwide exceeds the value of Canada's GNP. The advertising assault is so massive and unremitting that the vast majority of it fails to pierce our consciousness. Advertisers have long been aware of this and search continually for ways to target and capture the attention of the public to whom they want to sell something.

While most advertising aims to affect our behaviour as consumers, some advertising aims to persuade people to vote or think in particular ways, or simply provides them with useful information. Much public service advertising by governments falls into this last category. But there is much more to commercial advertising than the message "buy product X." We are urged to buy because a high-consumption capitalist economy is sustained by frenetic materialism, which is reinforced by the mass media through advertising and entertainment programming. The cumulative impact of the "buy this" message being hurled at us hundreds of times a day is to instill and sustain a high-consumption mindset.

Another incidental but pervasive message of commercial advertising is gender stereotyping and the use of sexual imagery and innuendo. The youthful, the slender, the muscular, the large-breasted, the extroverted, the materially successful, and the "cool" are far more likely to appear in mass media ads than the poor, visible minorities, or men and women who do not conform to traditional stereotypes or those defined by the marketers of popular culture. In general, advertisers find it more profitable to appeal to conventional beliefs and prejudices and to very basic emotional needs and insecurities. This aspect of commercial advertising has not changed since its birth on Madison Avenue, New York City, in the mid-1800s (see Box 11.1).

What Determines the Mass Media Product?

No one really believes that the mass media simply mirror reality. "The facts of modern life do not spontaneously take a shape in which they can be known. They must be given a shape by somebody."[14] Confronted with more information than can be conveyed, those who produce the media product must choose what stories, images, and "facts" to communicate to the public.

Media Beat

BOX 11.1 The Art of Selling

The principles underlying advertising are extremely simple. Find some common desire, some widespread unconscious fear or anxiety; find a way to relate this wish or fear to the product; then build a bridge of words or images over which your customer can pass from the dream to the illusion that this product will make the dream come true. "We no longer buy oranges, we buy vitality. We do not buy just an auto, we buy prestige.". . . In toothpaste, . . . we buy, not a mere cleanser and antiseptic, but release from the fear of being sexually repulsive. . . . In every case the motivation analyst has found some deep-seated wish or fear, whose energy can be used to move the consumer to part with cash and so, indirectly, to turn the wheels of industry. Stored in the minds and bodies of countless individuals, this potential energy is released by, and transmitted along, a line of symbols carefully laid out so as to bypass rationality and obscure the real issue.

Source: *Brave New World*, by Aldous Huxley. Copyright © 1932, 1946, by Aldous Huxley. Reprinted by permission of Georges Borchardt, Inc., on behalf of the Aldous and Laura Huxley Trust. All rights reserved. Excerpted from *Brave New World* by Aldous Huxley. Copyright © 1932, 1960 Aldous Huxley. Reprinted by permission of Random House Canada. Reprinted by permission of HarperCollins Publishers.

What ultimately is offered to the consumer is a somewhat distorted version of a "reality" that is constructed by those who contribute to the product. Several factors influence how reality is processed and how news is reported by the media. They are a series of *filters* that let through

Democracy Watch

BOX 11.2 The Future of News Media

In our networked world, the way many people connect with news is changing rapidly. These changes will, in turn, reshape the way people engage with politics. As more and more people come to rely for their news about the country and the world from social media like Facebook, Twitter, and blogs, the dominant role of traditional news organizations will continue to be under pressure. According to the Pew Center's 2015 report *State of the News Media*, in 2014 nearly half of Web-using adults report were getting news about politics and government in

Continued

the previous week on Facebook.[15] Another challenge comes from what the Pew Center says is a continuing decline in news reporting resources at newspapers, magazines, and television broadcasters. "For news organizations," concluded the Pew Center in 2013, "distinguishing between high-quality information of public value and agenda-driven news has become an increasingly complicated task."[16] The Pew Center, again in their 2015 report, continued to stress the importance of the changing news media to the society that it serves. "Americans' [and one assumes Canadians'] changing news habits have a tremendous impact on how and to what extent our country functions within an informed society. So too does the state of the organizations producing the news and making it available to citizens day in and day out."[17]

certain information and images and not others. In short, information and images that threaten the privileges of dominant socio-economic groups are less likely to make it through these filters than those that are orthodox and non-menacing. Most of us are conditioned to believe that the media are independent and frequently critical of the powerful. However, the media's role in politics is essentially conservative: they tend to support rather than erode the status quo.

As we see below, economic pressures, regulatory requirements, the legal system, and cultural norms have an important impact on what the mass media produce.

The Economic Filter

Most media outlets are privately owned, and are subject to the law of the marketplace: they must be able to sell a product that will attract enough subscribers, advertisers, buyers, or patrons to cover production costs and to make a profit. While no single media product needs to appeal to everyone, the high costs of producing a daily newspaper, magazine, television series, or movie requires a mass market. And when a marketplace is competitive, there is a tendency to avoid programming or content that has a limited appeal. The economic filter operates mainly through the influence of advertising and industry structure on the media product. Without advertising dollars, privately owned and even (although to a lesser degree) publicly owned media companies are not economically viable. The media tend to avoid reporting or programming that reduces their attractiveness in the eyes of advertisers.

State ownership alters, but does not eliminate, the economic pressures to which the mass media are exposed. Publicly owned broadcasters must be sensitive to charges of elitism. This is particularly true of television broadcasting, where the costs of producing high-quality entertainment programming are great. Few politicians would risk losing votes over subsidies for programs that attract tiny audiences. Market influences are even greater when a public broadcaster such as the Canadian Broadcasting Corporation (CBC) or TVOntario (TVO) must rely to some extent on revenues from advertising or viewer/corporate support.

How is this relevant to politics? First, dependence on advertising may reduce the likelihood that powerful economic interests will be portrayed negatively. Second, most television broadcasting and viewing time are devoted to lucrative entertainment programming. Consequently, ad-dependent broadcasters tend to schedule high-audience-appeal programming during prime-time hours and leave public affairs programming to off-peak times or to state-owned or viewer-supported broadcasters; they may also adopt an entertainment format, also called "infotainment" or "soft news"—news that is packaged using an entertainment, celebrity-journalist format. As in the United States, the economics of broadcasting in Canada works against the viability of programming that does not attract a mass audience, and so the pressures to adopt the infotainment/celebrity newsreader format are great.

The increase in the availability of electronic media and the merging of information and entertainment makes many wonder how well the media keep us informed about politics. What is your main source of news? Does the information in this chapter make you want to consider alternative sources?

State-owned media outlets like the CBC, TVO, and Télé-Québec in Canada and the viewer-supported Public Broadcasting System (PBS) in the United States are not immune from the influence of advertising. Both the CBC and Télé-Québec rely on advertising for part of their revenue. Viewer-supported broadcasters like TVO and the American PBS rely on government subsidies (directly and through the tax system) and corporate sponsorship of programs for part of their revenue needs. Some critics have argued that corporate sponsorship, like advertising, tends to filter out socially divisive and controversial programming.

Dependence on state subsidies does not necessarily remove all constraints on media content. Public broadcasters must constantly be sensitive to charges of bias and ideological favouritism. Over the years CBC television programs such as *the fifth estate*, *Marketplace*, *The Passionate Eye*, and the various programs hosted by environmentalist David Suzuki, notably *The Nature of Things*, have been accused of having a leftist political bias and of being anti-business. The in-house monitoring of CBC broadcasting for "fairness" has reached unprecedented levels of sophistication. Much of this scrutiny, as during election campaigns, is intended to ensure that the CBC is even-handed in its treatment of the major political parties and their leaders. In the world of public broadcasting, "culturecrats" and politicians' aversion to controversy may substitute for the check that dependence on advertising imposes on private broadcasters.

The CBC, through its English- and French-language divisions, has done far more to Canadianize the airwaves than any other broadcaster, particularly when it comes to dramatic programming and during prime viewing hours. Federal government budget cuts have threatened the CBC's ability to fulfill its mandate. The CBC has responded by increasing its dependence on advertising, which has placed it between a rock and a hard place: the CBC is required to rely on Canadian programming, but it is increasingly dependent on advertising revenues and ever-higher audience ratings. Most of the CBC's advertising revenue is generated during its sports and news programs. Unfortunately, the exclusive rights to *Hockey Night in Canada*, which alone accounted for 40 per cent of this revenue, were lost to Rogers Communications in 2013. And although a deal was struck to allow the CBC to continue broadcasting some NHL games for another four years, the CBC could no longer collect advertising revenue from those broadcasts.

Industry structure is the second component of the economic filter. As the costs associated with producing a newspaper have increased, competition has suffered. Public and private advertising dollars have been steadily shifting from print to the Internet putting pressure on the newspaper industry to concentrate ownership to reduce costs and maintain profitability.[18] The daily newspaper industry in Canada (as in the United States) is characterized by local monopoly, and chain ownership is a feature of both the English- and French-language markets. Prior to 2014, only nine Canadian cities (Halifax, Quebec City, Montreal, Ottawa, Toronto, Winnipeg, Calgary, Edmonton, and Vancouver) had competition between same-language, mass-circulation dailies that have different owners. This number was reduced in 2014 when Postmedia purchased Sun Media. Critics lamented the loss of diversity and of the quality in the news coverage. Postmedia assured readers that no dailies would be shut down and referred to Vancouver as an example of a city being well served by two newspapers with the same owner. Critics noted that Vancouver's two dailies are both centre-right, and while this was better than having only one paper, they pointed to Toronto as an example of a city with three separately owned newspapers where the industry is "scrappier" and better for democracy.[19]

Television and radio markets, to say nothing of the Internet, are much more fragmented than the newspaper market. Cable and satellite technology and the development of the Internet have created unprecedented opportunities for niche programming targeted at smaller audiences than was required previously to ensure profitability. The economics of electronic media are different from those of print media, such that concentrated ownership is not as prominent an issue in broadcasting as in newspaper markets.

Instead, the ownership issue in broadcasting and new media like the Internet is framed chiefly as an issue of American penetration into Canadian markets. There may indeed be hundreds of television stations that Canadian viewers have access to through direct broadcast satellite (DBS), cable technology, or the Internet, but the fact remains that the most popular ones either originate in the United States or rely extensively on American-produced programming. Issues of ownership in the United States and abroad are thereby imported into Canada.

One of these issues involves the new corporate convergence in mass media, particularly in electronic media industries. As the nationalist Friends of Canadian Broadcasting puts it, "large media multinationals are getting larger, concentrating their market power, crossing over into new lines of [media] business and crossing national borders with unprecedented ease."[22] Critics argue

Media Beat

BOX 11.3 Media Ownership

Seventy per cent of Canada's media is owned by two corporations: *CTV-Globe Media* and *Bell Media*.[20] In a 2012 report, *Media Ownership and Convergence in Canada*, Dillan Theckedath and Terrence J. Thomas of the Industry, Infrastructure and Resources Division of the Parliamentary Information and Research Service write,

> Of the eight media conglomerates listed here, three—Rogers, Bell and TELUS—are dominant players in the wireless market. Furthermore, these three companies, along with Shaw and Videotron, dominate the Internet market. The dominance by a small number of firms in these markets becomes a greater concern as the Internet becomes more important to Canadians, with a handful of firms having potential gatekeeping power over the content Canadians wish to access.[21]

© Graeme MacKay/Artizans

that multi-media convergence and the growth of giants like Time Warner, Sony, and Disney (corporate empires that span every kind of media including books, music, magazines, television, films, and pay-per-view TV) will accelerate the erosion of national cultures like that of Canada.

The trend toward the monopolization of media production and distribution is not likely to provide much opportunity for the expression of distinctively Canadian values, perspectives, and stories. Or is it? Homegrown consumption notwithstanding, there is little doubt that more Canadian programming is produced and available today than ever before. This has been largely due to government regulation and subsidies, to which we now turn.

The Legal/Regulatory Filter

Unlike radio and television broadcasters and cable system companies, the print media in Canada and in most other democracies are basically free from direct regulation by government. They essentially regulate themselves through industry-operated press councils. These councils receive and investigate complaints but do not monitor performance. Calls for greater state regulation invariably provoke cries of censorship from those in the newspaper and magazine business.

Nonetheless, indirect forms of regulation may affect the content of print media. Most of these measures aim to promote Canadian values through newspapers and magazines. For example, the federal Income Tax Act permits advertisers to deduct from their taxable income only the cost of ads placed in newspapers or magazines that are at least 75 per cent Canadian owned. This explains why foreign ownership of Canadian newspapers has never been an issue. But has not had much of an impact on the newspaper content. As indicated previously, with the exceptions of *The Globe and Mail*, the *National Post*, and *Le Devoir*, newspapers are geared mainly to local markets. Therefore, the content and their profitability depend on a large local readership, and this has been on the decline.

One might argue that the owner's nationality could influence a newspaper's coverage of national and international news, or of sports and comics, but even Canadian-owned papers, for economic reasons, depend on news purchased from foreign news agencies like the Associated Press. Most important purveyors of values such as comic strips and cartoons are produced by American cartoonists. In the end, the Income Tax Act almost certainly does more to promote Canadian ownership than Canadian culture.

The Canadian ownership provisions of the Income Tax Act also apply to magazines, but the English-Canadian market is dominated by American magazines and split-run publications: magazines that incur most of their editorial and other production costs outside of Canada and have a mostly non-Canadian readership. Split-run editions could be produced at a lower cost by electronically importing the American version and then qualifying for the lower Canadian advertising rates by adding a few pages of Canadian content. This was done in 1993 by Time Warner's immensely popular *Sports Illustrated*, which triggered changes in Canadian tax law to halt the practice.

In 1997, the World Trade Organization, responding to an American complaint, ruled that laws subsidizing Canadian magazines and treating foreign periodicals differently violated Canada's international trade obligations. The federal government responded with Bill C-55, which proposed heavy fines for any magazine publisher selling ads in Canadian editions of foreign magazines, a measure that was clearly targeted at the highly profitable split-run issues of US magazines. When American publishers protested loudly, Canadian advertisers and the American government reached a compromise in 1999 requiring that split-run editions include a majority of Canadian content in order to sell advertising space at the lower Canadian rate.

The split-run issue encapsulates the regulatory dilemma for Canadian policy makers about preserving and promoting Canadian cultural industries: the much larger American market enables US magazine publishers to benefit from economies of scale and produce a glossier product while paying lower rates for content. Moreover, Canadians essentially like what American magazines offer. An estimated 80 per cent of the magazines on Canadian newsstands are American. But with few language or cultural barriers between English Canada and the United States, American magazines do not seem to be foreign in the way that British or other English-language ones do.

State regulation is much more intrusive in the case of the electronic media. The original reason for treating broadcasting differently from print media was the need to prevent chaos on overcrowded airwaves. Controlling and licensing of broadcasters seemed the only practical solution to this potential problem. However, broadcasting policy has always assumed that only extensive state intervention can prevent complete American domination of the Canadian market.[23]

The content regulations for both radio and television constitute one of the pillars of Canadian broadcasting policy. The CRTC establishes and enforces a complicated set of content guidelines that all licensed broadcasters must observe with the aim of ensuring that more Canadian content reaches the airwaves (see Box 11.4).

As in the television industry, the economics of the music recording industry encourages products that are marketable outside of Canada. Radio stations typically deal with Canadian content requirements by relying heavily on recordings by performers like Drake, Michael Bublé, Justin Bieber, the Barenaked Ladies, and the Tragically Hip. One might think that the advent of Internet and satellite radio has presented Canadian regulators with the same old challenge of increasing Canadian appetite for American products.

Governments also affect the content of Canadian film and television productions through subsidies and participation in the industry as broadcasters and filmmakers. The Canadian content quotas are, in the case of television, met largely through sports, news, and public affairs programming. However, most viewing time is spent watching entertainment programs, few of which are Canadian, because American-made products are made at a fraction of the production costs. In English-speaking Canada only the CBC broadcasts a significant amount of Canadian-made entertainment programming. To compensate for the unfavourable economics of domestic production, Ottawa offers subsidies, mostly through Telefilm Canada for Canadian-made feature films, television programs, documentary films, and animation, and also for international co-productions.

Media Beat

BOX 11.4 **What Is Canadian Content?**

Media CRTC Canadian Content Requirements

Radio Musical selections qualify if they meet any two of the following criteria:
- The music is composed entirely by a Canadian.
- The lyrics are written entirely by a Canadian.
- The music is or lyrics are performed principally by a Canadian.
- The live performance is performed wholly in Canada and broadcast live in Canada or recorded wholly in Canada.
- The musical selection was performed live or recorded after 7 September 1991, and a Canadian who has collaborated with a non-Canadian receives at least 50 per cent of the credit as composer and lyricist.

At least 35 per cent of all music aired must meet the above definition. Other factors include:

- In recognition of FM radio's diversity of formats, the CRTC allows different levels of required Canadian music content.
- The quota is as low as 7 per cent for ethnic radio stations.
- At least 65 per cent of the music played on French-language radio stations must have French vocals—a quota that drops to 55 per cent between 6:00 a.m. and 6:00 p.m.

Television The following apply to television:
- To be considered Canadian, a TV program must have a Canadian producer and must earn a minimum six of a possible ten points. Points are awarded when the duties of certain positions are performed by Canadians.
- There are additional criteria regarding financial and creative control for programs involving foreign production partners.
- Canadian programs must be used to fill at least 60 per cent of the overall schedules of both public and private television broadcasters.
- Canadian content must fill at least 50 per cent of evening programming hours for private broadcasters and 60 per cent for public broadcasters.

While the publicly owned CBC, Radio-Canada, TVO, and Télé-Québec have been among the major recipients of money provided through Telefilm Canada over the years, private television and film producers have also drawn on this source of public money. Fears have long been expressed that private producers typically use these subsidies to produce films and television programs that are as far as possible unrecognizable as Canadian productions so as not to alienate potential American audiences. Over two decades ago the report of the Task Force on Broadcasting (1986) characterized the content system applied to television broadcasters as "regulatory tokenism." Many of the programs that qualify as Canadian content, it observed, "could be mistaken for American productions and seem to have been made on the assumption that references to their Canadian origin would hurt their appeal to audiences outside Canada, particularly in the United States."[24] This may be true in many instances such as the partly or wholly produced Canadian television series such as *Hannibal, The 100,* and *Orphan Black,* which have international appeal but may not be recognized as "Canadian." However, the popularity over the years of such recognizably Canadian programs as *Corner Gas, Little Mosque on the Prairie,* and *Rookie Blue* shows that the American clone programming format complained of by the task force has not always been the recipe for success in Canadian television. There are economic pressures to turn out an exportable product in order to recoup costs through foreign (usually American) sales. In the case of feature films, the problem is largely that the sole major distribution chain, Cineplex Galaxy, does little to promote Canadian-made films. And the companies producing films do not have the resources to advertise widely to generate audience interest.

In spite of the unfavourable economics and a system of subsidies that appears to have a limited impact, recognizably Canadian programs and films do get produced. In the end, it falls to public broadcasters and the National Film Board to show Canadians what is distinctive about their society and culture. Under the Broadcasting Act, the CBC is required to be "a balanced service of information, enlightenment and entertainment for people of different ages, interests and tastes covering the whole range of programming in fair proportion." The CBC, as mentioned above, is the primary broadcaster for Canadianizing the airwaves. Its ability to do so, however, is threatened by budget cuts that began in the late 1970s. The CBC has responded by increasing its dependence on advertising, which presents it with a dilemma: continuing to rely on Canadian programming while at the same time increasing its dependence advertising, which requires more popular programming to achieve the viewership that will attract advertisers.

The NFB's mandate is to "interpret Canada to Canadians and the rest of the world" (Film Act). For 70 years the NFB has done this to critical and international acclaim, turning out documentaries and serious drama that the private sector has been unwilling to invest in, produce, distribute, or show.

The pressures to produce programming whose "Canadian-ness" is not apparent have never been greater. Streamed video through Netflix and its competitors is not subject to Canadian content requirements. "Netflix is not a part of the Canadian broadcast ecosystem," complains Scott Moore, CEO of Rogers Media. "They have no Canadian-content requirements. They don't have to spend money on Canadian producers."[25] Short of imposing the sort of Internet censorship practised by such governments as those of China and Iran, it seems certain that new media will undermine whatever effectiveness remains for Canadian television content guidelines. An indicator that regulators like the CRTC are challenged by the arrival of Internet providers was seen in 2015 when the CRTC announced that it would not be taxing Internet services like Netflix and YouTube, and that it would be relaxing the content regulations for traditional TV networks in order to put them on an even footing with the Internet providers.[26]

Media content is also affected through federal and provincial laws dealing with obscenity, pornography, and what is called *hate literature*. None of these terms is defined very precisely in Canadian law, but the federal Criminal Code and the Customs Act, as well as provincial statutes dealing with hate literature, restrict the sorts of printed matter and films that may enter Canada or be distributed here, as well as the media products that individuals may possess.

The issue of when and how to restrict media content raises issues of censorship, individual privacy, freedom of expression, public morality, and the safety of certain groups, such as the children who become fodder for pornographic films, magazines, and Internet sites. These issues have become increasingly complex, and traditional methods used to regulate media content have been challenged by the newer media of satellite communications and the Internet. To this point, however, regulation of the Internet remains relatively slight in Canada and other democracies. Nonetheless, websites and those who communicate via cyberspace, and who fall under the jurisdiction of Canadian governments, are subject to the provisions of the Criminal Code and federal and provincial human rights laws, just as those who communicate through traditional media are.

The Technological Filter

Few things date more quickly than news. The technology of broadcasting is instantaneous and that of newspapers involves a matter of hours. Indeed, we expect that the media will communicate what is happening right now. However, the practical problem is that stories must be edited down to a length suitable for inclusion in a 30-minute news program or the pages of a newspaper.

It is often said that one picture is worth a thousand words. But the moving images on the screen sometimes only capture the surface of events and miss an explanation that is more complicated than the medium can deal with. The visual character of television lends itself to the personalization of reality—an emphasis on individuals and personalities at the expense of broad social forces that are not captured by the camera. Reality becomes a constantly shifting pastiche of images, as though the producers of news and entertainment assume that the viewers have an attention span of a minute or two at best. According to Morris Wolfe, this is due to what he calls the First Law of Commercial Television: "Thou shalt give them enough jolts per minute (JPMs) or thou shalt lose them."[27] Too few JPMs equals fewer viewers lower ratings and fewer advertising dollars. He also argues that "a steady diet of nothing but high JPM television tends to condition viewers' nervous systems to respond only to certain kinds of stimulation.

Their boredom thresholds are frequently so low that TV viewers find it difficult to enjoy anything that isn't fast-paced."[28]

Like entertainers, politicians have long understood the biases of the visual medium. Photo opportunities and structured, controllable events are ways of using television's need for the immediate, the personal, and the visual to their advantage. Social media such as Instagram, Facebook, and Twitter are being used in the same way. Television and social media have had an enormous impact on how elections are fought, how special interests attempt to influence public policy, and how public officials communicate with the people.

The visual character of television introduces two significant biases. First, there is a dependence on what Walter Lippmann called a "repertory of stereotypes." He argued that newspaper reporting consisted largely of fitting current news to these stereotypes for cultural reasons. In the case of a visual medium, there are also technological reasons for this dependence. "Viewers' interest," observes

Television spot ads—usually only 20–30 seconds long—are one of the main vehicles for political communication during election campaigns. Some worry that the medium debases the message, dumbing down the political conversation. Do you take the accusations in attack ads seriously, or do you dismiss them?

Edward Jay Epstein, "is most likely to be maintained through easily recognizable and palpable images, and conversely, most likely to be distracted by unfamiliar or confusing images."[29]

And second, there is an *emphasis on confrontation*. From the standpoint of a visual medium, confrontation has two virtues: it involves *action*, which is a requirement of most television news and public affairs coverage, and it involves *conflict*, which helps present a story in a way that viewers can easily grasp. Epstein notes that "Situations are thus sought out in network news in which there is a high potential for violence, but a low potential for audience confusion."[30]

The Organizational Filter

News gathering and reporting are carried out by organizations. The needs and routine procedures of these organizations influence the content of the news, both what is reported and how it is covered. The organization's difficulty is that news developments are often not predictable, and no organization can be everywhere or cover all stories equally well. News organizations rely on various strategies to deal with this problem. In the case of television, several criteria help make the news credible to the public.

Newsworthiness

Those who have a reputation for being influential or who occupy official positions are more likely to make the news than those who do not. Much depends on the eyes of the news gatherers who automatically confer on them a mantle of credibility. The newsworthy include prime ministers, premiers, and the leaders of opposition parties; mayors and leading councillors when the news is local; and spokespersons for what are considered to be important organizations (e.g., the Canadian Council of Chief Executives, the Canadian Labour Congress, EGALE, or the Catholic Church).

Government officials and powerful private interests understand the routines and operational requirements of news organizations. One may not able to control the news agenda, but there are opportunities to influence news reporting through what is called *news management*. For instance, film footage for the evening news needs to be ready by a certain hour to allow time for editing. And if one wants to influence public opinion, then one should accommodate the media's needs through what Daniel Boorstin has called "pseudo-events," for example well-timed press conferences, photo opportunities, or news releases.

What else is considered newsworthy? The media is unlikely to ignore any pronouncement by publicly acknowledged experts with a specialty or an affiliation with a respectable institution such as the C.D. Howe Institute, the Canadian Centre for Policy Alternatives, or a university. The mass media's demand for the ideas and information generated by experts is based on a combination of factors:

- The media has a self-image as dispenser of the news, reporter of the facts.
- The media needs low-cost information and instant analysis. Conducting their own analysis is expensive and time-consuming, and most journalists are not professionally trained as economists, physicians, or scientists.
- To protect themselves against charges of bias and lawsuits, media organizations and reporters need information "that can be portrayed as presumptively accurate."[31]

In the end, expert opinion and information helps confer a social respectability that in many instances serves to reinforce the political status quo.

Predictability

Predictability is important in determining what becomes "news." Any news organization operates within the framework of a budget and limited resources. Other things being equal, it makes sense to concentrate organizational resources (e.g., researchers, camera crews, and journalists) where news is most likely to happen: at Parliament Hill, the provincial capitals, and internationally as resources permit and at scheduled events. The unplanned and unexpected happenings are less likely to be covered. As Epstein puts it, "The more predictable the event, the more likely it will be covered."[32]

Visual Appeal

Television obviously needs pictures. But some subjects are more telegenic than others. Epstein writes:

> . . . priority is naturally given to the story in a given category that promises to yield the most dramatic or visual film footage, other things being equal. This means, in effect, that political institutions with rules that restrict television cameras from filming the more dramatic parts of their proceedings are not routinely assigned coverage.[33]

Canadians see much more of what is happening in the House of Commons, particularly question period, than they do of the Supreme Court. Yet the Court's decisions have an enormous impact on public policy and in many instances more so than the fairly predictable antics of parliamentarians. Likewise, closed meetings of first ministers or of the institutions of the bureaucracy generally are either inaccessible to cameras or lack the sort of *visual spice* considered crucial to televised news. The result, therefore, is to overemphasize the importance of those actors and individuals who can be filmed in action and to underemphasize the significance of those who are more reclusive, and less confrontational or visually sensational.

The Ideological Filter

Those who report the news are often accused by conservatives and business people of having liberal-left and anti-business biases. They are more likely, it is argued, to favour stories and groups that challenge established authority. The CBC in general and some of its programs in particular have occasionally been accused of ideological bias against conservatism and big business (especially American business). Similar charges have been heard in the United States, where Republicans, conservatives, fundamentalist Christians, and business interests have often accused the major networks, and journalists generally, of having liberal biases.

Studies seem to confirm these claims. An early American study that looked at the social backgrounds, personality traits, ideologies, and world views of business and media elites found that media respondents typically gave more liberal responses to such statements as "Government should substantially reduce the income gap between rich and poor."[34] The researchers concluded that "leading journalists seem to inhabit a symbolic universe which is quite different from that of businessmen, with implications for the manner in which they report the news to the general public."[35] Several American studies have confirmed that those in the media, particularly the electronic media, tend to be more liberal than members of the general population. A study of CBC radio, directed by Barry Cooper, concluded that "on the whole, [the CBC] adopted a left-wing, rather than right-wing critical stance."[36]

This conclusion is reinforced by what is probably the most systematic study of Canadian journalists' values and beliefs to date.[37] Based on a survey of electronic and print journalists and a sample of the general public, Barry Cooper and Lydia Miljan draw two main conclusions. First, English-Canadian journalists tend to be more left of centre than the general public. Second, the left-leaning tendencies of journalists affect the way news stories are reported, which challenges the media's credo of objectivity. The media differ from their audiences and readerships in the following ways:

- Journalists are less religious than the public.
- Although private-sector journalists tend to agree with the general public's ideas on the desirability of capitalism, free markets, and private property, the views of the public-sector CBC journalists are significantly to the left.
- The public is more conservative on social issues than are those in the media.
- Journalists are considerably more likely than the general public to vote for the NDP.

Cooper and Miljan also note that French-Canadian journalists are closer to their audience/readership in their political and social views than are English-Canadian journalists to theirs, which may reflect a more secularized, libertarian, and left-leaning society in Quebec. On the other hand, recent studies by researchers at McGill University found no evidence of a left-leaning partisan bias in the case of Canadian newspapers. Based on their analysis of campaign coverage in 2004 and 2006 in seven major dailies (*The Globe and Mail*, *National Post*, *Calgary Herald*, *Vancouver Sun*, *Toronto Star*, *La Presse*, and *Le Devoir*), they found that reporting tended to be quite neutral between the parties and, on the whole, negative toward all of them. Editorial coverage, however, was characterized by partisan favouritism. The party most likely to be on the receiving end of positive editorial coverage was the Conservative Party, hardly the result one would expect to find if those in the media have a left-of-centre bias. In 2006 and 2008 all the country's leading newspapers, with the exception of the *Toronto Star*, endorsed the Conservative Party.[38] A scandal occurred during the 2015 general election when several newspapers were accused of bias or of bowing to their owners' preferences when their editors endorsed the Conservatives. Many *Globe and Mail* readers were especially irritated when the editors endorsed "the Harper government but not Harper."[39]

When Aboriginal protests associated with the Idle No More movement dominated the Canadian media landscape in early 2013, many opinion leaders in the Aboriginal community and critics on the left charged that the Canadian media, including major newspapers and several of the country's most prominent journalists, were guilty of conservative, anti-Aboriginal biases. Clearly, not everyone agrees with the claim that the sympathies of Canada's media system are on the left.

The ideological gap between the media's left-of-centre views and Canadian society needs to be understood in the context of what "left" and "right" mean in Canadian society. "Left" does not mean fundamental opposition to the basic institutions of the capitalist economy. On the contrary, in the predominantly liberal societies of Canada and the United States, left has always implied ambivalence about business: distrust of excessive concentrations of economic power and the belief that business must be regulated, while accepting the superiority (in most circumstances) of private property and the market economy.

News and public affairs reporting often focuses on conflict and controversy that involves government officials and powerful private interests. This may give the impression that those in the media are anti-establishment critics. However, only a minority of those in the mass media have strong left-wing or right-wing commitments. This is certainly true in Canada. Those on the right, such as David Frum, Ezra Levant, and Mark Steyn, and those on the left, such as Linda McQuaig, David Suzuki, and Naomi Klein, are the exceptions rather than the rule. Most Canadian journalists are in the middle of the ideological spectrum and generally accommodate themselves to the needs of the organization they work for. "They mostly 'say what they like,'" says Ralph Miliband, "but this is mainly because their employers mostly like what they say, or at least find little in what they say which is objectionable."[40]

It should not be assumed that the entertainment and information products of the media industry carry no political messages or ideological biases. They do, both through the images, themes, and interpretations they communicate and through their silences. If the mass media are "more important in confirming or reinforcing existing opinions than they are in changing opinions,"[41] as studies generally suggest, this is partly due to the ideological orthodoxy of most writers, producers, editors, and others who have an influence on the media product.

The Media and Democracy

In regard to propaganda the early advocates of universal literacy and a free press envisaged only two possibilities: the propaganda might be true, or it might be false. They did not foresee what in fact has happened, above all in our Western capitalist democracies—the development of a vast mass communications industry, concerned in the main neither with the true nor the false, but with the unreal, the more or less totally irrelevant. In a word, they failed to take into account man's almost infinite appetite for distractions.[42]

The media often appear to have few friends except themselves. Politicians, business people, and those on the political right regularly accuse the media of irresponsible scandal-mongering, of being inherently and unfairly opposed to established authority, and of having liberal-left biases. The political left are no less critical of the media. They are apt to view the media as the handmaidens of powerful interests. Critics on both the right and the left accuse the media of having anti-democratic tendencies. Conservatives argue that those in the media tend to be more liberal-left than society as a whole, but that they foist their interests and perspectives on the public behind a smokescreen of journalistic integrity. Left-wing critics claim that the media help to "manufacture consent"[43] for a social system that operates mainly in the interests of a privileged minority: that is, they perpetuate a *false consciousness* of the dominant ideology.

On balance, the media do an uneven job of providing Canadians with the information they need to make informed judgments about their society and its political issues. The biases of the mass media are toward familiar images and stories—what Lippmann called a "repertory of stereotypes"—oversimplified conflict; the personalization of events, drama and action; and reliance on established opinion leaders. As we have seen, even media products that are not explicitly political may nonetheless include images, ideas, and messages that have social and political significance. These biases support much more than threaten the status quo.

Summary

In this chapter we have argued that the behaviour of the mass media is shaped by a number of filters. These filters cumulatively determine the sort of "product" that is likely to reach the consuming public. Our conclusion is that the products of the mass media generally support established values and institutions whose interests are best served by the status quo. And while it would be ludicrous to claim that the media avoid all criticism of powerful interests, it is easy to prove that the bulk of what appears in the media conforms to mainstream values.

A news organization's need for stories that are newsworthy, predictable, and visually appealing produces a situation where "the news selected is the news expected."[44] Along with the other filters that we have discussed, the organizational one creates biases that affect media content. Simple dramatized confrontation, familiar players and issues, and a relatively narrow range of locales where most news happens are among these biases. Many older sources of news and public affairs, such as radio stations, television stations, and daily newspapers are finding out the hard way that, because of the Internet and social media, today's public has almost unlimited choices. At the same time, citizens cannot avoid shouldering some of the responsibility for whatever information deficit they experience and ill-founded views they hold. For all the problems surrounding the quality of information that beset the Internet, there is no doubt that it has put an enormous range of information and interpretation within the reach of almost everyone.

The gains made in recent years by socially marginal, politically weak interests, such as women, Aboriginal Canadians, the LGBT community, and environmental activists, have been largely due to media coverage of their demands and spokespersons. The media have helped raise public consciousness of the issues and discourse such as "equal pay for work of equal value," "Aboriginal self-government," and "sustainable development." Moreover, it can hardly be denied that the media usually do a better job of scrutinizing and criticizing government actions, to say nothing of those of powerful societal groups, than do the opposition parties. Indeed, it is precisely the critical and even irreverent tone of much public affairs journalism that contributes to the widespread belief in the mass media's independent and anti-establishment character.

Most of what the mass media offer does not have this character. Frank Lloyd Wright's aesthetic description of television as "chewing gum for the eyes"[45] is a fairly apt characterization of much of the electronic and print media. Aldous Huxley's argument that the "mass communications industry is concerned in the main neither with the true nor the false, but with the unreal, the more or less totally irrelevant,"[46] suggests that the media—particularly their entertainment and advertising components—help foster a false consciousness among the public, the sort of pacified somnolence that characterizes the masses in his *Brave New World*. This may seem harsh, but Huxley is certainly right that news and public affairs reporting has political consequences.

Review Exercises

1. Keep a two-day record of your typical media consumption (e.g., television, films, radio, newspapers, magazines, books, and the Internet), then answer the following:

   a. Which categories does your daily media consumption fall under: entertainment, news and public affairs, or other?
   b. Which medium do you rely upon most for news?
   c. If you pick up a newspaper, which section do you read first? What else do you look at in the newspaper?
   d. Do you read news on the Internet? How often do you click on news stories? Do you rely on blogs or particular websites to keep you informed? Are they Canadian?

2. Watch the late-evening television news broadcast of one of the main Canadian broadcasters (CBC, CTV, or Global). Make a list of those stories where experts are interviewed, and record the positions and affiliations of the experts. Are there other sorts of experts or organizations that could have been contacted for these stories?

3. Find an example of poll results in the media.

   a. Who published the poll?
   b. Who paid for the poll to be conducted?
   c. Was the poll shaped by a political party or a group sympathetic to it or a news outlet sympathetic to its policies?
   d. What is the poll intended to tell the public? Is this information, manipulation, or both?

Up for Debate

1. Given the Pew Center's findings discussed above, news consumed over the Internet may replace traditional media such as newspapers, radio shows, and nightly newscasts as citizens' primary source of political information. Is this good or bad for democracy?

2. Resolved: The government needs to subsidize Canadian culture.

3. Should the Internet be regulated?
4. Resolved: It is entirely acceptable for newspaper editors to endorse politicians or political parties during an election campaign.

Starting Points for Research

Botton, Alain de. *The News: A User's Manual*. New York: McClelland & Stewart, 2014.
Miljan, Lydia, and Barry Cooper. *Hidden Agendas: How Journalists Influence the News*. Vancouver: University of British Columbia Press, 2003.
Nesbitt-Larking, Paul. *Politics, Society, and the Media: Canadian Perspectives*, 2nd edn. Toronto: University of Toronto Press, 2007.
Sauvageau, Florian, David Taras, and David Schneiderman. *The Last Word: Media Coverage of the Supreme Court of Canada*. Vancouver: University of British Columbia Press, 2005.
Soroka, Stuart. *Agenda-Setting Dynamics in Canada*. Vancouver: University of British Columbia Press, 2002.

CBC Archives and TVO's *The Agenda*

Visit the companion website for *Canadian Democracy: A Concise Introduction* to follow links to audio and video footage related to the main themes of the chapter: www.oupcanada.com/BrooksConcise2e.

Relevant Websites

Visit the companion website for *Canadian Democracy: A Concise Introduction* to browse a collection of websites featuring material related to the key themes of the chapter, an excellent starting point for research: www.oupcanada.com/BrooksConcise2e.

12 Conclusion: Canada in the World

Nation-states do not exist in a vacuum. By most accounts there are some 196 nation-states, including Canada, each one seeking to influence or being influenced by other nation-states. This is why a proper understanding of Canada's domestic politics is incomplete without looking at its place on the world scene. The reverse is also true: Canada's foreign affairs have their roots in its domestic affairs.

The study of **international relations**—a branch of political science that studies the relationships between states and the international system of governance—requires a multidisciplinary approach that draws on many areas of knowledge other than politics, including geography, psychology, and history. A multidisciplinary approach is especially important in an era when so many aspects of each nation-state's social, political, economic, and cultural life has become integrated with those of other

international relations
a branch of political science that studies the relationships between states and the international system of governance

↑ Gold medalist Rosannagh MacLennan wins the Trampoline Gymnastics Women's Final at the Rio 2016 Olympic Games in Brazil. In order to fully understand Canada's domestic politics, it is essential to consider Canada in relation to other nation-states around the world.
Source: David Ramos/Getty Images.

countries, and when the globalized environment has made it increasingly difficult for governments around the world to control their domestic affairs.

While our discussion of Canada on the world scene is by necessity too brief to be comprehensive, after reading this chapter you should be able to

1. explain how Canadians view themselves and how these perceptions have often affected Canada's behaviour internationally
2. describe the evolution of Canadian foreign policy
3. identify historical trends in Canada's relations with our most important neighbour, the United States, and other countries
4. develop a sense of Canada's place in a globalized and always-changing world scene

Canada's Century: The Twentieth or The Twenty-First?

"The twentieth century will belong to Canada." This was the bold prediction of Sir Wilfrid Laurier, Liberal prime minister of Canada from 1896 to 1911. Laurier made his forecast of greatness for Canada against the backdrop of the enormous growth that had occurred in the United States over the previous century. In the heady and globally oriented years of the early 1900s, the nation-building strategy launched by Sir John A. Macdonald in 1879 appeared to be fulfilling its promise and about 200,000 immigrants arrived in Canada each year; Laurier's prediction appeared possible.

Over 100 years later, it is clear that the twentieth century did not "belong" to Canada. Both the friends and foes of the United States would probably agree that it was the American century, for better or worse. The sheer economic, cultural, and military dominance of the United States was unprecedented. Its global influence was such that the term "hyperpower" entered the modern lexicon. Notwithstanding the United States' one-time status as the world's only superpower, some Canadians believe that their country has achieved the greatness predicted by Laurier, though not the way he imagined. Canada is, according to many of its opinion leaders, the cosmopolitan, multicultural, equality-oriented, internationalist face of the future. "For generations," says philosopher Mark Kingwell, "we have been busy creating, in [the shadow of the United States], a model of citizenship that is inclusive, diverse, open-ended and transnational. It is dedicated to far-reaching social justice and the rule of international law. And we're successfully exporting it around the world . . . by seeing [the UN] for the flawed but necessary agency it is."[1] Is the "Canadian model" the real achievement of the last century? And is it the one most likely to shape the direction of history in the twenty-first century?

Perhaps so, although Canadians might be surprised to learn that the world does not think of the Canadian model when it thinks of the future of democracy. John Ralston Saul, a prominent Canadian intellectual, argues that "Canada is above all an idea of what a country could be, a place of the imagination . . . it is very much its own invention."[2] Canada is, he has argued, a successful model of accommodation and flexible ways of thinking about citizenship. Indeed, not only our American neighbours, but other national populations as well, appear to know hardly anything about us (except that we are like the Americans in some ways).

Most Canadians view themselves, and their country, as having the following characteristics:

- We are a peace-loving people.
- We are respected, listened to, and admired abroad.
- We stand for multilateralism and reliance on the UN to solve global conflicts.
- We "punch above our weight" in international affairs.

In addition to these national characteristics, most Canadians probably would agree that their idea of citizenship is quite dramatically different from that of our southern neighbours. And as definers of the Canadian identity and interpreters of Canada's role in the world such as

Democracy Watch

BOX 12.1 Our Vision of Ourselves as Canadians

As the text points out, many Canadians would say that as a people we are peace oriented, respected and admired abroad, supporters of co-operative global relationships, and major players in international affairs. Is this description accurate, or could it be argued that Canadians are exactly the opposite?

Material republished with the express permission of: National Post, a division of Postmedia Network Inc.

John Ralston Saul and Mark Kingwell argue, this Canadian idea of citizenship is perhaps our greatest contribution to world history.

For the most part, Canadians tend to be complacent. We feel good about ourselves, our lives, and the state of the country. Complacency and self-congratulations may be appropriate in some circumstances, but when thinking about the hard realities of Canada's relations with and influence in the world, Canadians have a flawed understanding in many important ways. In 2003, an Environics poll showed that three-quarters of Canadians expressed satisfaction with their country's role in the world (30 per cent very satisfied; 46 per cent somewhat satisfied). A decade later, more than four out of five expressed satisfaction (30 per cent satisfied; 52 per cent somewhat satisfied). Over this same period, however, there was a decline in the importance of peacekeeping and economic development projects as part of Canadians' self-image in the world.

Globalization and Canada

globalization
the political, economic, and social integration that comes from the increased international flow of goods, people, capital, and ideas

Globalization is the political, economic, and social integration that comes from the increased international flow of goods, people, capital, and ideas. Canada's economy has always been integrated into greater patterns of trade and shaped by forces beyond its borders. From the arrival more than 500 years ago of European fishermen off the coast of Newfoundland until the middle of the twentieth century, Canada's economic prosperity depended on the exploitation and export of a succession of natural resources to markets abroad, and on the import of people, capital, and finished goods.[3]

At some point, however, there developed a hope and an expectation that Canada would shake off this dependence and become the master of its economic destiny. One sees this in Sir John A. Macdonald's ambitious National Policy of 1879; the first and only coherent and explicit economic development strategy that Canada had known before the decision in the late 1980s to embrace free trade, and therefore dependence, as the Canadian fate. One sees it also in Sir Wilfrid Laurier's optimism and in the rise of economic nationalism in Canada, particularly from the 1950s to the early 1980s, the path of which was marked by a series of policies and institutions designed to limit American influence in the Canadian economy and promote indigenous capital.

Some nationalistic hopes still survive today, but they seem increasingly out of step in a world with unprecedented levels of economic, political, and social interconnectedness. The current debate is not about whether the forces of globalization can be rolled back, but how to control them. In Canada, the question of globalization is inseparable from that of its relationship to the United States. For Canada, at least, globalization has meant an enormous intensification in economic and other ties to the United States. Whether this is a good thing is one of the leading issues in Canadian public life.

Globalization and Anti-Globalization in Canada

The consequences of globalization have been the subject of enormous debate. In some ways, globalization may appear to be a very old phenomenon, one that is millennia old, like the

Silk Road that increased the flow of goods across the eastern Mediterranean, the Middle East, and Asia 2000 years ago. A characteristic of today's globalized world is the unprecedented volume and speed of economic exchanges. According to economist Jeffrey Sachs, in 1980 about one-quarter of the world's population and half of global production was linked by trade. Two decades later, almost 90 per cent of the world's population was so linked.[4]

Economists point to two chief factors that have driven globalization in recent decades. One factor is new transportation, telecommunications, and manufacturing technologies. The other factor—now made possible and profitable by the first—is the integration of global production and sale of goods and services. Witness the increased transnational flows of investment capital, leading to greater integration of financial markets as banks, investment funds, and companies spill across national borders.

It is also important to note that politicians and business leaders around the world have encouraged this integration through international agreements like the European Union and the North American Free Trade Agreement (NAFTA). These deals were designed to reduce trade barriers and open up markets to stimulate political co-operation and economic growth. A more comprehensive agreement, the World Trade Organization (WTO), has now formalized and institutionalized trade liberalization. National subsidies and various forms of protectionism are still practised by all governments, but the overall thrust of Canada's trade policy, as elsewhere, has been toward export-led industrialization and more open markets. The dismantling of the Canadian Wheat Board in 2011 and the proposed dismantling of the dairy and egg marketing boards in anticipation of the Trans-Pacific Partnership trade deal are examples of the push by governments to open markets to international trade.

Globalization is a complex phenomenon involving numerous trends that may or may not be new: the unprecedented global movement of people; the ease with which capital flows from one country to the next; the exchange of ideas and cultural values; the rapid and widespread diffusion of diseases; and the emergence of the virtual global village via telecommunications. And not all aspects of globalization are seen as positive. While liberalized trade may have become the fashion among many elites in developing and developed countries, there has been dissent. Note the violent clashes between protesters and police that accompanied negotiations such as the 1999 Seattle meeting of the WTO; the 2001 G8 meetings in Genoa and in Rostock, Germany; and the 2010 G20 protests in Toronto. Protests in the streets have been joined by other forms of anti-globalization activism. These range from intellectual attacks, to the formation of political parties, to social movements and interest groups for whom the critique of globalization is a central, or the only, ideological principle. Indeed, the chief characteristic of the 2011 *Occupy movement*, in which protesters occupied public spaces in cities around the world, was that participants saw their concerns as "global." The successful 2016 referendum vote for the UK to exit the European Union, also known as Brexit, was seen by many analysts as a vote against globalization and the loss of sovereignty that comes from integration.

In Canada, the anti-globalization message may come from diverse sources: many who teach in the social sciences, a significant part of the country's media elite, much of the leadership of the labour movement, the NDP (as exemplified in the *Leap Manifesto*), many religious organizations, environmental groups, and nationalist groups like the Council of Canadians.

In many ways the anti-globalization movement and its analysis have tended to be ideological and go back to the critique of capitalism developed by Karl Marx in the middle of the nineteenth century. Marx made several claims that sound familiar today. Globalization is blamed for exacerbating the income gap between the rich and the poor, for widening the economic divide between the developed and underdeveloped world, for undermining Indigenous cultures, for weakening the ability of governments to regulate business in the public interest, and for reducing governments' willingness and ability to finance social programs. Degradation of ecosystems, child labour, and international conflict (such as the 1991 Gulf War and the Iraq War begun in 2003, the Syrian civil war that started in 2011, and the rise of global terrorism by organizations like ISIS) can be added to this list.

Their criticisms of globalization receive considerable media and classroom coverage, and are, indeed, widely known to most Canadians. Following are a few examples:

- Transnational corporations are avoiding laws and taxation merely by moving their capital to other countries that have become tax havens.
- Free-market capitalism is creating the conditions whereby one or a few corporations dictate prices.
- Refugees and immigrants are creating cross-border security concerns.
- Invasive or detrimental animal and plant species are being introduced into our ecosystems.
- Dominant cultures are destroying smaller cultures.

Many, if not all, of these claims are difficult to prove with certainty. For instance, while globalization may explain some aspects of income inequality, other causes may be at play, such as government policies, shifting demographic patterns, or economic restructuring. The pros and cons of globalization cannot be detailed or resolved here, but these issues are hotly debated in Canadian politics, and the broader consequences of globalization do affect many Canadians as well as the international system of which Canada is a part.

Globalization and the Canadian Economy

Few would disagree, however, that the worldwide recession triggered by the 2008 "subprime crisis" in American financial markets revealed important weaknesses of globalization. The new post-industrial model spawned by globalization is all about outsourcing. At the extreme, huge companies like communications equipment manufacturer Cisco Systems and computer manufacturer Dell "exert a sort of post-industrial 'Command Control' over a vast network of outsourced production,"[5] depending on minimal parts inventories to keep costs down. Cisco Systems and Dell are not particularly exceptional, differing from such important companies operating in Canada as BlackBerry, Bombardier, Chrysler, and Magna only in the extent of their dependence on a complex chain of outsourcing that extends across the world.

The problem with this model, argues Barry Lynn, is that it introduces *vulnerability* into the economies of rich countries that could be far more significant than dependence on foreign

© Rick Eglinton/Ge-stock

Protesters march along Queen Street in downtown Toronto during the 2011 Occupy movement. Do you agree with the demonstrators' message, that capitalism—the dominant system of private ownership of businesses that create goods or services for profit—is at the root of many of the problems attributed to globalization? Why or why not?

sources of oil. A disruption at a crucial link in the supply and distribution network of a globalized economy, argues Lynn, could bring entire industries to a screeching halt because of the high degree of *specialization* in the globalized supply chain. Lynn's argument is that our exposure to disruptions and the amplitude of their consequences are greater these days than in the past. Canadians had a glimpse of the scenarios that Lynn argues have become increasingly possible after the terrorist attacks of 11 September 2001.

Globalization and Canada–US Relations

Globalized production, sourcing, and investment have forced us to rethink what were, until fairly recently, firmly established ideas about what is "Canadian." Products exported from companies operating in Canada routinely include foreign content, and vice versa. Remarkably, until an interprovincial trade agreement was finally agreed to in 2016, every Canadian provincial economy, with the exception of PEI, had been doing more business with economies outside of Canada than it did with the rest of Canada. Thus, the very notion of a Canadian economy, let alone the concept of "Made in Canada," seems outdated.

Canadian Spotlight

BOX 12.2 The Pros and Cons of Integration for Canada

A **supranational organization** is an international institution with a purpose that transcends national boundaries and that has acquired some legal authority and decision-making power from its member states in order to achieve that purpose.

Economic vulnerability is not the only outcome of the integration that comes with globalization. Through the increased integration that comes with trade deals, improved communication technology, and other pacts achieved through supranational organizations, nation-states around the world are experiencing an unprecedented loss of sovereignty in many areas of domestic affairs such as culture, health care, and trade.

As Table 12.1 indicates, joining a supranational organization represents a trade-off for the country that joins it: in exchange for a loss of sovereignty in a given area, the country may gain benefits in others.

Can you think of other supranational organizations and outline the pros and cons of belonging to them? Will U.S. President Donald Trump's new approach to American foreign policy result in any changes to international institutions and agreements such as those in Table 12.1?

TABLE 12.1 Supranational Organizations

Supranational Organization	Description and Purpose	Pros for Canada	Cons for Canada
United Nations (UN)	An international organization founded in 1945. It is currently made up of 193 member states. The mission and work of the United Nations is multifaceted and includes • promoting peace and security • promoting sustainable development • providing humanitarian aid • protecting human rights • establishing and enforcing international law	• achieves a great deal in advancing Canadian policy positions • helps to preserve Canada's sovereignty, protect key interests, and defend its values • increased collaboration on international matters • helps reduce conflict and resolves differences between countries	• a contribution of approximately $80 million in 2015 • a push to have countries contribute 0.7% of their GDP • harsh criticism from the UN on Canada's human rights record and treatment of Indigenous peoples and missing women • a push to recognize water as a basic human right, which might put pressure on Canada to give some of its water resources to water-starved regions such as the southwestern US
Trade agreements such as the North	Canada has bilateral and multilateral trade agreements with	• The best Canadian companies	• Every trade deal involves a loss of sovereignty and protection for entire sectors of the

Supranational Organization	Description and Purpose	Pros for Canada	Cons for Canada
American Free Trade Agreement (NAFTA), Canada European Trade Agreement (CETA) and the World Trade Organization (WTO)	many countries. The largest of these is the WTO, which administers a trade deal involving 162 member countries.	get to compete internationally. • unrestricted access to other markets (in theory) • lower prices for better-quality consumer goods and services • Competition forces Canadian companies to improve their productivity and improve the quality of their goods and services. • greater incentive for trade partners to collaborate on common problems such as invasive species, climate change, border security, and refugees	economy (e.g. manufacturing, agriculture, and culture). • Canadian companies become vulnerable to greater competition at home and abroad. • Decisions by democratically elected governments can be reversed because of complaints to trade panels or lawsuits by corporations and other countries. • Laws, policies, and government programs must be changed to conform to the agreement and to avoid lawsuits or complaints by corporations and other governments. • Increased pressure to specialize causes less diversity in the national and the global economy; encourages cartels and monopolies. • Local Canadian companies compete with foreign companies for local contracts.
North Atlantic Treaty Organization (NATO)	An alliance created in 1949 to safeguard the freedom and security of its members through political and military means	• economic and political collaboration with allies to address common security issues • Canada can rely on its allies to identify and address internal and external threats to security.	• Financial costs: In 2016–17 Canada is expected to contribute 6.6% of NATO's funding, compared to 22% for the US. • Canada must contribute supplies and personnel when called upon. • puts Canadians in harm's way. (Canadians killed in NATO missions: Afghanistan—152; Korean War—516; Balkans—23) • loss of sovereignty as Canada conforms to its treaty obligations

supranational organization
an international institution with a purpose that transcends national boundaries and that has acquired some legal authority and decision-making power from its member states in order to achieve that purpose

In fact, Canada's economic globalization has really meant greater integration with and dependence on the American economy. With the FTA in 1989 and NAFTA in 1994, the trading relationship has reached unprecedented levels of intimacy. The total value of Canada–US trade in merchandise, services, and investment was, until most recently the largest bilateral trading relationship in the world. In 2015, China was the US's largest supplier of trade goods, whereas Canada was the US's largest export market.[6] Canada has been the major export market for American goods for over half a century and is today the leading export market for about three-quarters of all state economies. The United States has long been the largest source of foreign investment in Canada, currently accounting for 49.4 per cent of all foreign investment,[7] and is the location for about half of all Canadian direct investment abroad (42.2 per cent in 2015).[8]

The trading relationship is both huge and hugely asymmetrical, affecting Canada's vital interests far more than those of the United States. For example, when the Canadian media were full of stories about American duties on Canadian softwood lumber imports in 2005 (an issue that seems to be re-emerging in 2016), there was barely any mention in the American media. But still, Canada has some leverage in this relationship. After all, Canada—not Saudi Arabia!—has been the largest source of energy imports to the United States, and is the destination for over half the value of all US automotive exports. The Canadian economy is extremely important, even strategically important, to the United States. But the influence that this might give Canadians in trade disputes with Washington is diluted by Canada's far broader dependence on the American economy.

The enormous imbalance in the Canada–US trade relationship was one of the chief arguments put forward by Canadian advocates of free trade in the 1980s. Major manufacturers, and also important exporters of natural resources such as wood products, oil and gas, and hydro-electricity, recognized that their growth prospects depended on access to the American market. A growing wave of protectionist sentiment in the American Congress during the 1980s seemed to lend urgency to Canadian free traders' case. Even among many of those who were dubious about some of the economic claims made for free trade, the political argument that this would help shield Canadian industries from Congress's protectionist moods was persuasive.

TABLE 12.2 An Asymmetrical Economic Relationship, 2014

	Canada (%)	United States (%)
1. Exports to the other country as a share of total GDP	20	16
2. Investment from the other country as a share of total stock of foreign investment	49 (1st)	10 (4th)
3. Share of total exports going to the other country	76	41
4. Share of total imports coming from the other country	67	14

Sources: Compiled from CIA Fact Books on Canada and the U.S: https://www.cia.gov/library/publications/the-world-factbook/geos/us.html;https://www.cia.gov/library/publications/the-world-factbook/geos/ca.html.

The Canada–US Free Trade Agreement (FTA) (1989) and NAFTA (1994) created an architecture of dispute settlement rules, agencies, and monitoring requirements that have not taken the politics out of trade disputes, but provided forums for their resolution. The older forums and channels still matter, as does the World Trade Organization. But on the whole, the rules and the dispute settlement mechanisms created under the FTA and NAFTA make it more difficult for member governments to pursue protectionist trade policies.

The asymmetry in the Canada–US economic relationship is not helped by the fact that most Americans are simply unaware of, and (perhaps worse) harbour certain misconceptions about, Canada's economic importance to the United States. When Americans were asked which two countries were the most important markets for American exports, a 2013 poll found that Canada came in fourth, after China, Japan, and Mexico.[9]

Ignorance may sometimes be benign. In this case, however, it may be a liability for Canada. As Allan Gotlieb, Canada's ambassador to the United States from 1981 to 1989, observed, part of Canada's problem in its trade relations with the United States is getting the attention of those who matter in Washington.[10] "Like it or not," Gotlieb said, "in the US political system a foreign country is just another special interest. And not a very special one at that. It lacks the clout of a domestic special interest because it cannot contribute to political campaigns or deliver votes." Gotlieb suggested two approaches: first, a good rapport with the highest level of the American administration (the president and top advisers); and second, a tighter formal integration across the Canada–US border. He advocated a "grand bargain" with the United States, establishing a North American community of law.[11] Canada's 2011 seamless cross-border agreement, with tighter security measures and sharing of information between security agencies in both countries, is proof that this second strategy has now been adopted by the Canadian government. American lack of attention to Canada continues to be a central theme of the relationship. In a 2016 interview on the popular American public affairs program *60 Minutes*, Prime Minister Trudeau stated that he wanted the United States to "pay more attention to Canada."[12]

Canada–US Relations and the Trump Presidency

"Oh my God!" This was the headline on the front page of *Le Journal de Québec* the day after Donald Trump was rather surprisingly elected as the 45th president of the United States. Similar reactions were common around the world and the reaction to the unexpected results was overwhelmingly negative. Much of this negativity was generated by Trump's words: his promise to build a wall along the US–Mexico border; his musings about barring Muslims from entering the United States; his description of NATO as obsolete; his statement that several allies, including Japan would be paying for more of their own defense; and his promise to "tear up NAFTA" and walk away from the Trans-Pacific Partnership trade agreement. Some of the world's jittery and even fearful reactions to Trump's unorthodox political style. "Diplomatic," "conciliatory," and "statesman-like" were words conspicuously absent from virtually all commentary on Trump's style, with the exception of his 9 November 2016 victory speech and his meeting with President Obama a day later.

More than most populations around the world, Canadians appeared to have reason to worry about a Trump presidency. During the campaign, Trump characterized NAFTA as "the worst trade deal in history." Trump promised that, once sworn in as president, he would immediately begin the process of renegotiating better terms for the United States. If renegotiating did not quickly produce a better deal for the United States, Trump declared, he would "kill NAFTA" by invoking the article that enables a party to withdraw after six months notice. Experts were divided on whether President Trump would be able to withdraw without congressional approval. The consequences of an end to NAFTA would be enormous for Canada. Every provincial economy has important trade ties to the United States and would experience both employment and public revenue consequences if the largely tariff-free regime that NAFTA created were to end.

It was not just trade agreements that caused some Canadians to lose sleep. Trump's fossil fuel-friendly policies guaranteed that the Keystone-XL pipeline, blocked by the Obama administration, would be back on the table. Some Canadians looked forward to this while others saw it as a step backward. President Trump's promise to cancel US participation in the Paris Agreement on climate change was sharply at odds with the position of the Trudeau government and the views of most Canadians.

Policy differences aside, there was also the question of whether the general values and style of the Trump administration would damage Canada–US relations. Most Canadians did not expect the same chemistry to exist between Prime Minister Trudeau and President Trump than had existed between Prime Minster Trudeau and President Obama. "I'd be curious to know," said New Democratic Party MP Nathan Cullen in a 9 November 2016 interview, "what values President Trump and Prime Minister Trudeau share." Cullen added, "This is not anyone we've seen before in Canada–US relations....He's a bully." When Prime Minister Trudeau was asked how he would deal with a president who the questioner described as "racist, misogynist, and a bigot," Trudeau deftly avoided responding to this characterization of the man who received the votes of almost 60 million Americans by noting that the Canada–US relationship is much bigger and more longstanding than any person on either side of the border.

Trudeau was certainly right about this. Moreover, when candidate Trump railed against trade deals that were bad for America, he almost always mentioned China, Mexico, and Japan, in that order. Nevertheless, Canada was caught up in the wave of anti-trade sentiment that swept across the United States during the 2016 election cycle. Trump was not the only candidate to ride this wave. Bernie Sanders' remarkable run for the Democratic nomination for president made opposition to free trade one of the centrepieces of his campaign, and even Hillary Clinton felt compelled to distance herself from trade deals that she had supported before Sanders' unexpectedly vigorous challenge for the Democratic Party's presidential nomination. Protectionism was in fashion on both the right and the left during the 2016 US election campaign.

This was not unprecedented. **Protectionism**–the *theory and practice of protecting domestic industries (the opposite of free trade theory and practice)*—was running strong in the United States in the early 1980s, which was a key factor behind the decision of the Conservative government of Brian Mulroney to seek a free trade deal with the United States. During the 2008 primary campaign, both Hillary Clinton and Barack Obama promised to end NAFTA if it could not be renegotiated to better serve the interests of American workers and companies. "I think we should use the hammer of a potential opt-out as leverage," said then Senator Obama, "to ensure that we actually get labor and environmental standards that are enforced."

Threats to walk away from NAFTA, or at least to insist on major reforms, have also come from the Canadian side of the border. In the 1993 federal election campaign, the Liberal Party leader Jean Chrétien promised that, under his government, NAFTA, which had not yet been ratified, would be renegotiated to better serve Canadian interests. As was true of Clinton and Obama's threats and promises in 2008, nothing came of this campaign rhetoric.

"America First" was the campaign slogan that Donald Trump embraced when he laid out his foreign policy goals in April 2016. Whether the wave of protectionism that he encouraged and endorsed during his successful presidential campaign will result in a major reversal of the tide of trade liberalization—a hallmark of globalization—is doubtful. There are too many powerful economic interests in the United States and abroad that depend on a world in which national barriers to the movement of capital and jobs have come down. At the same time, however, national governments and political leaders ignore at their peril the votes of those who have been left behind by free trade. These votes help to explain Donald Trump's 2016 victory, Britain's decision to leave the European Union, and the rise of populist resentment toward political elites across much of the democratic world.

Canadians are not mere bystanders to these developments. A 2016 Angus Reid poll found that about only one-quarter of Canadians agreed that NAFTA is good for the country and about one-third supported its renegotiation. Prime Minister Trudeau appears to recognize that Canadians are ambivalent about free trade, which may explain why, only two days after Donald Trump's election, Trudeau stated, "If Americans want to talk about NAFTA, I'm happy to talk about it." It is hard to imagine that the results of such talks would lead to less economic integration between the world's two most integrated economies.

The Canadian Dilemma in Foreign Affairs

The Canadian dilemma boils down to a choice between maintaining foreign policy independence and maintaining a good relationship with an economic, cultural, and military giant. This dilemma has occupied centre stage in debates over Canadian foreign policy since the end of World War II, and since the emergence of the United States as the unchallenged leader of the Western world. Former Canadian prime minister and Nobel Peace Prize winner Lester B. Pearson, one of the chief architects of Canadian foreign policy, acknowledged Canada's particular dependence on the United States "brought us anxiety as well as assurance." The policy implications of this dilemma on Canada's participation in world affairs can hardly be overstated. The asymmetrical relationship between Canada and the United States, overlain by structures of policy integration that operate through agreements such as NORAD (North American Aerospace Defense Command) and NAFTA, leave Canada with little room to manoeuvre in conflicts with its American neighbour. "One of the great foreign policy challenges facing Canada," observes Michael Ignatieff, "is staying independent in an age of [American] empire."[13]

For several decades successive Canadian governments—the Progressive Conservative government of Brian Mulroney (1984–93) excluded—have searched for and supported counterweights to American dominance. Chief among these have been the United Nations and multilateralism more generally. **Multilateralism** involves the resolution of international differences and conflicts through structures and processes that represent many states. The United Nations has been the most prominent structure for multilateralism in the post–World War II era. There are, however, many other international organizations to which Canada belongs, including the North Atlantic Treaty Organization (NATO), the World Bank, the World Trade Organization, the Commonwealth, la Francophonie, and so on.

Some of these multilateral organizations are dominated by the United States, and therefore can hardly be said to serve as counterweights to its might. NATO, for example, has almost never blocked or modified the military objectives of American administrations. Influence in the International Monetary Fund's decision making is weighted, based on the size of member state contributions, and the United States is its major contributor. In fact, multilateralism may not always dilute American influence: it may actually provide greater political legitimacy to American goals by including other countries in the decision-making process.

Multilateralism is not always a convenient cover for the ambitions and interests of a single member state. States must be willing to accept some limitations on their national sovereignty. Canada's governing elites and opinion leaders "have a vision of a multilateral world in which . . . sovereignty is not unconditional, but limited and bound by human rights agreements, or multilateral engagements which limit and constrain the sovereignty of states in the name of collective social goods."[14] There are many examples of Canada's support of multilateralism and its leadership role: the creation of the International Criminal Court; the Ottawa Process, which led to the international treaty banning landmines; and its ratification of the Kyoto Protocol. Canada has often supported the

multilateralism
the resolution of international differences and conflicts through structures and processes that represent many states

Mike Baldwin/Artizans

Mike Baldwin / artizans.com

One editorial cartoonist's elephant-and-mouse interpretation of the asymmetrical relationship between Canada and the United States. Do you think there are more pros or more cons to Canada's tight policy integration with its neighbour to the south?

UN as the proper forum for the discussion of issues of war and peace and the authorization of the use of force. Not all Canadians accept this multilateral vision of the world—note the 2011 withdrawal of Canada from the Kyoto Protocol by the Conservative government—but recent history suggests that it has broad popular support. As with many other allies of the United States, Canada has also experienced the United States' lack of enthusiasm for multilateralism. This has occasionally produced outcomes that set Canada seriously at odds with its southern neighbour.

One of the great ironies of Canadian politics in recent times is that Canada's greater economic integration with the United States, under the FTA and NAFTA, may well have created the political space for Canada to pursue a more independent foreign policy than was available before. Critics of NAFTA have suggested that Canadian sovereignty would be vaporized by tighter economic integration. However, there are several instances of Canada being at loggerheads with the United States over global warming, landmines, an International Criminal Court, continental missile defence, and, most important, the formal refusal of the Canadian government to join the American-led coalition in the 2003 invasion of Iraq without approval from the UN. Free trade may have loosened the leash somewhat, because some forms of retaliation are no longer available to Congress and the White House or could be challenged under the terms of the free trade agreements.

Of course, the 2006 Canadian federal election brought to office a minority Conservative government intent on improving relations and influence with the United States. This is exemplified by the new government's aim to boost military spending and bolster the image of the Canadian military in Washington, DC. The successful negotiation of a resolution to the two-decades-old softwood lumber dispute in April 2006 was hailed by the Conservative government and its supporters as proof that its new approach was paying off. These celebrations were toned down in 2011 when American claims of unfair lumber subsidies were upheld by an international court.

There have long been limits to how far and in what circumstances Canadian foreign policy can depart from that of the United States. Canada's refusal to support the war on Iraq did not damage the security interests and military goals of the United States. Canada's absence virtually went unnoticed when other countries, including the United Kingdom, Japan, and Australia, joined in the Iraq military action. Canada was less able to avoid the "war on terrorism" launched after the terrorist attacks of 11 September 2001. The policy actions taken by the American government involved matters that directly affected Canada, like border security, air travel, and immigration. Given the amount of trade and the enormous number of jobs and investments that depend on the smooth flow of goods and people across the border, the Canadian government has had little choice but to coordinate its policies with those of the American government. By late 2011, this coordination had evolved into the creation of a common security perimeter around Canada and the United States—a concept that required that Canadian immigration policy be in line with American policy.

From 1993 to 2006, during the years of the Chrétien and Martin Liberal governments, the dominant paradigm for Canadian foreign policy was what is known as **soft power**: a term

soft power
international influence based on intangible or indirect factors that include culture, values, and a sense of legitimacy ascribed to a nation's international aims

Canadian Spotlight

BOX 12.3 Global Media and the Power of Pictures

A tragic picture of the body of a Syrian refugee, toddler Alan Kurdi, washed up on a Turkish beach in September 2015, changed the conversation about the refugee crisis around the world, including in Canada. It also changed the prospects for thousands of refugees. Quite suddenly, more Canadians began to see refugees as desperate people rather than terrorist threats. In the middle the general election, politicians began to make promises to do more. The soon-to-be-elected Liberals, for instance, spoke of Canadian values and promised to re-settle 25,000 refugees by the end of 2015. Some of the goodwill was fleeting, however. The Liberal government's timeline was unrealistic, and by February 2016, 70 per cent of Canadians were concerned that the 25,000 target was too high,16 and there were also calls by some to "stop resettling 25,000 refugees in our peaceful land."17

Canada would eventually meet the target and many Canadians could feel that they were indeed "global citizens." Here Prime Minister Trudeau welcomes one of the 25,000 Syrian refugees.

Nathan Denette/The Canadian Press

coined by Harvard's Joseph Nye, which refers to international influence based on intangible or indirect factors that include culture, values, and a sense of legitimacy ascribed to a nation's international aims. Soft power operates through "the complex machinery of interdependence, rather than . . . expensive new weapons systems."[15] Nye identified Canada and the Scandinavian countries as examples of countries whose governments have successfully exercised soft power, "punching above their weight," as a former Canadian minister of Foreign Affairs, Lloyd Axworthy, liked to say.

It is easy to see the appeal of the doctrine of soft power for many Canadians. It suggests that their country could make a difference internationally and maintain its values and its reputation as a good global citizen, without having to spend much on the latest military technology or to be combat ready. Indeed, despite significant increases over the last several years, Canada spends less on defence, at about 1.2 per cent of GDP, than most of the countries in NATO.

Some have argued, however, that this self-image is an illusion. Although Canadians never hear this from those who govern them, by 2003 Canada had fallen to thirty-fourth in the world in terms of countries' contributions to UN peacekeeping. Bangladesh and India were first and second, and the United States was ahead of Canada. Michael Ignatieff, writing in 2003 as a Harvard professor, before he was leader of the federal Liberal Party from 2008 to 2011, argued that Canadians' belief in multilateralism is laudable, but that international influence requires three national attributes: moral authority as a good global citizen, a military capacity, and an international assistance capability. Canadians' image of themselves as "honest brokers" and good global citizens are not false. But, Ignatieff argues, "The disagreeable reality for those who believe in human rights is that there are some occasions when war is the only real remedy for regimes that live by terror. This does not mean that the choice is morally unproblematic."[18]

What Now with the United States?

More than virtually any other country, Canada is caught in a dilemma: support our most important ally and trading partner, or chart an independent course. Events since 9/11 have brought home to Canadians and people throughout the world the remarkable lopsidedness of the world's power structure, dominated by the United States, and have forced them to think hard about what this means. American decisions relating to "homeland security" and in the name of combatting terrorism—for example, requiring passports for Canadians entering the United States since June 2009, the elimination of regimes deemed to pose a threat to American security, and the creation of a Canada–US security zone in 2011—carry costs. These costs affect individual liberties, such as personal privacy and equality rights, that may be jeopardized by practices like ethnic profiling.

Yet another dilemma arises for Canada about whether to support multilateralism and UN-sanctioned policies and missions to deal with threats to human rights and peace, or to support the Americans as "globo-cops." The presidency of Barack Obama was greeted by many Canadians and others with high expectations. The emphasis on diplomacy and multilateralism, and the intention to shift American troops and resources from Iraq to Afghanistan were viewed positively by most Canadians and their leaders. The announcement that the new president, unlike his predecessor, would resume the long-standing practice of making Canada his first foreign visit was greeted with enthusiasm by Canadians.

 Listen to the "Who Owns the Arctic?" podcast at www.oupcanada.com/ BrooksConcise2e.

Canadian Spotlight

BOX 12.4 Timeline: Canada in the World

Late 1400s–early 1500s
Fishing by Basque, English, Portuguese, French, and Spanish ships on the Grand Banks off the east coast of Newfoundland, and whaling off the Labrador coast and in the Strait of Belle Isle are the first economic exploitation of Canadian resources by Europeans.

Late 1500s
Trade in beaver pelts and other furs begins, providing the basis for the eventual extension of trading routes from Quebec all the way to the north of Saskatchewan and Alberta.

1603–8
Samuel de Champlain makes two visits to Canada, establishing the city of Quebec in 1608 on his second voyage; European colonization of Canada begins.

1759–63
The war between Britain and France spills over into a rivalry in the New World, and British troops defeat French forces at Quebec in 1759. The formal transfer of New France to Britain takes place in 1763 under the Treaty of Paris.

Early 1800s
Canada becomes a major supplier of white pine for British ships.

1812–14
The War of 1812 between Britain and the United States produces many battles on Canadian territory and the shared waters of the Great Lakes.

1820s
In an effort to dilute the influence of American-born residents of Canada, the colonial authorities encourage immigration from the British Isles. The arrival of tens of thousands of Irish immigrants during the potato famine of the 1840s marks the beginning of ethnic pluralism that went beyond the French and English communities.

1854
The first Reciprocity Treaty with the United States is signed, abrogated by the US government in 1865.

1867
The creation of Canada as a sovereign state is prompted by fears that the United States might have designs on parts of British North America and by Britain's unwillingness to continue to pay for the defence of Canadian territory.

1870–1
The vast territories controlled by the Hudson's Bay Company are transferred by Britain to Canada in 1870. British Columbia becomes the fifth province, after which Canada stretches from the Atlantic to the Pacific Oceans.

1879
The National Policy adopted by the Conservative government means increased tariffs on manufactured goods to protect fledgling Canadian producers from American competition. It also encourages US-based companies to operate in Canada. This leads to high levels of foreign ownership and lower levels of productivity as a result of foreign-owned corporations that produce only for the small Canadian market.

1909 The International Boundary Waters Treaty between the United States and Canada takes effect, creating the International Joint Commission (IJC) (see 2009, below).

1911 The Canadian general election is fought largely on the issue of reciprocity in trade with the United States. The pro-reciprocity government of Wilfrid Laurier is defeated.

1914–18 World War I: Canada is a junior partner in the alliance against Germany; Canadian troops fall under the command of British officers.

1919 Canada becomes a founding member of the League of Nations.

1920 Canada passes from the economic orbit of Great Britain into that of the United States; American investment now officially exceeds the value of British investment.

1921 Canada's prime minister, Mackenzie King, sees multilateralism as a way to assert Canada's independence from Great Britain in international affairs.

1931 Under the Statute of Westminster, Canada acquires the authority to negotiate and sign foreign treaties in its own right.

1939–45 Canada participates in World War II, but no longer as a subordinate of Great Britain. Canada emerges from the war as one of the world's leading economies.

1945 Canada becomes a founding member of the United Nations. The UN and multilateralism are seen as counterweights to the influence of the United States on Canadian foreign policy.

1947 Canada is a founding member of the General Agreement on Tariffs and Trade (GATT) and the North Atlantic Treaty Organization (NATO).

1950–3 Canada participates in the Korean War under a UN Security Council resolution.

1956 Suez Crisis: Canada sides with the United States against the Franco–British invasion of Egypt, and Canadian foreign minister Lester Pearson, who brokers a settlement to end the crisis, is awarded the Nobel Peace Prize.

1957 The North American Air Defense Command (NORAD) is created, a partnership of Canada and the United States against the possibility of a Soviet missile attack. Early warning radar stations are established on Canadian territory.

1960s Even though Canadian companies profit from the production of defence-related exports, the Pearson government becomes critical of US involvement in the Vietnam War, and Quebec's premier demands more representation and an independent voice abroad. Canadian dependence on the United States becomes a prominent political issue as American ownership in resources and manufacturing reaches unprecedented levels.

1962 The Kennedy administration requests that the Canadian government permit, under the NORAD and NATO agreements, nuclear warheads on missiles in Canadian territory. The Diefenbaker government denies the request,

Continued

1973 Pierre Trudeau's Liberal government announces the "Third Option" policy of diversifying Canadian trade, but by the end of the decade the total export and import trade tied to the American economy is at an all-time high.

creating a rift in Canada–US relations. The Liberal government elected in 1963 complies with the request.

1976 The G7, the annual meeting of the leaders of the world's seven largest capitalist democracies, is created when Canada joins the G6 countries.

1985 The Macdonald Royal Commission on the Economic Union and Development Prospects for Canada recommends free trade with the United States. The Conservative government of Brian Mulroney approaches the Reagan administration to open free trade talks.

1989 The Canada–US Free Trade Agreement takes effect.

1994 The North American Free Trade Agreement (NAFTA) among Canada, Mexico, and the United States takes effect.

1997 Canada signs the Kyoto Protocol, later ratified in 2002. A decade after signing, Canada's CO2 emissions exceed the Protocol's targets by about 25 per cent.

2000 Over 80 per cent of Canada's imports and exports are tied to the United States and about one-third of Canada's GDP depends on trade with the United States.

2001 After the terrorist attacks of 11 September 2001, movement across the Canada–US border becomes a major issue. As a member of NATO, Canada supports the American-led invasion of Afghanistan to replace the Taliban regime. Eventually, Canada becomes a major contributor of combat forces.

2003 The Liberal government of Jean Chrétien decides not to join the Anglo-American alliance that invades Iraq.

Early 2000s As the possibility of a shipping passage through the Arctic and exploitation of resources increases, the issue of Arctic sovereignty assumes greater urgency. Canada's claim to full sovereignty in the waters of the High Arctic is not accepted by neighbouring nations.

2005 Canada, Mexico, and the United States agree to the Security and Prosperity Partnership, an agreement that appears to pave the way toward greater policy coordination among the three countries.

2008 Canada has 2500 troops stationed in Afghanistan and plays a major combat role within the NATO mission fighting the resurgent Taliban. Canadian public opinion remains divided on Canada's involvement as the number of Canadians killed exceeds 100.

2009 The hundredth anniversary of the Boundary Waters Treaty between Canada and the United States, which created the IJC. Despite some high expectations associated with the treaty and IJC, most policy experts agree that environmental governance now operates largely through agreements and networks of subnational governments.

2009	Barack Obama assumes the presidency of the United States. Canadians have high expectations for the president and his policies. Prime Minister Harper's office announces that the president's first official visit outside the United States will be to Canada.
2011	The Conservative government announces Canada's withdrawal from the Kyoto Protocol and agrees to form an integrated security zone with the United States. Canada fails to win a seat on the UN security council and Canada participates in a nine-month military mission to help end a civil war in Libya.
2013	Canada assumes the chair of the Arctic Council for a two-year term, enabling it to shape the agenda of issues affecting circumpolar nations. Canada and the European Union concludes the Canadian–European

Trade Agreement. This is one of many FTAs negotiated over the previous few years with Panama, Jordan, Peru, and Colombia; negotiations continue with South Korea, India, and Japan.

2014 Canada joins in the Western sanctions directed against Russia for its annexation of Crimea and support for the pro-Russian separatists in eastern Ukraine. Prime Minister Stephen Harper makes his ninth annual visit to Canada's Arctic regions to "show the flag." Canada's military mission in Afghanistan ends.

2015 The Conservative government signs the Trans-Pacific Partnership (TPP) deal on the eve of a general election.

2016 Under Prime Minister Trudeau, Canada recommits to NATO and agrees to participate in a Latvian mission headed by Canada.

The fact remains, however, that while Canadians may have found life with Obama more agreeable than life with Bush, the substance of the Canada–US relationship has changed relatively little. The Obama administration did not take a different line on Canadian claims of sovereignty over the Arctic. Canadian manufacturers and exporters continued to be concerned that the White House and Congress would be protectionist over trade. Although Canadian exporters of oil, gas, and hydroelectric power thought they had little to fear, Obama's 2015 cancellation of the Keystone XL oil pipeline project was a reminder that American administrations continue to be more concerned with domestic politics than with good Canada–US relations.

 Listen to the "Pipeline Politics" podcast at www.oupcanada.com/ BrooksConcise2e.

Summary and Conclusion

The fairest description of Canada's foreign policy in 2016 is that it is undergoing an ideological shift. The Conservative government's 2012 federal budget signalled a move away from multilateralism, with cuts of $319 million in foreign aid and $170 million from Foreign Affairs and

Inside Politics

BOX 12.5 | Rebuilding Canada's International Profile

By 2015, many Canadians and pundits believed that the Harper government's approach to international relations had damaged Canada's reputation abroad with respect to climate change policy, peacekeeping, and immigration. The election of the Trudeau government in late 2015 saw an immediate change in direction in Canadian foreign policy. For example, there was a commitment to participate in programs and treaties to reduce the effect of greenhouse gas emissions on climate change; a push to accept as many as 25,000 Syrian refugees; and a change in the desire and the nature of foreign aid to developing countries. Stephen Toope, while director of the Munk School of Global Affairs, summarized his views on what Canada should do to rebuild its "battered international profile."

1. *Friends and traders.* Canada should

   a. focus greater effort on keeping the Canada–US border open for business
   b. coordinate continental security with the US and Mexico
   c. make a priority of assessing future military needs and joint operations with their armed forces

2. *Energy and innovation.* Canada should

   a. price carbon in a way that lessens our reliance on fossil fuels
   b. find energy alternatives
   c. do a better job of getting its carbon-based fuel to the coasts

   d. at the same time, negotiate and participate with the world in its commitment to slowing the growth of global warming
   e. narrow the productivity gap with the US and other G7 countries caused almost entirely by a lack of business investment in research and development

3. *Democracy, security, migration.* The Charter of Rights and Freedoms is ". . . widely seen [by Canadians] as a precious legacy, connected to our traditions of social inclusion and pluralism. These values mean that Canadians can and should promote the same rights and freedoms for people around the world."

4. *A middling power amid change.* Canada has always been seen as a helpful player in multilateral institutions, but what worked soon after World War II may not be working now. Consider reforming those global institutions that are not "fit for purpose."

5. *From optimism to resilience.* Canada's voice and concrete contributions have and can matter, but we should avoid ". . . patting ourselves on the back about our inclusive society and lecturing others about how many refugees they should take. We should also recognize that many of our friends and allies are under enormous strain. . . . Canada is not a major power. It is now one of quite a few countries with an ability to

help shape events. . . . Canada must conduct an honest assessment of our assets, work to build more diverse relationships, and focus our foreign-policy resources and objectives. In so doing, we can defend and project our interests and values, and play a role of leadership on particular issues that matter in the world."

Source: Adapted from Stephen Toope, "Promises Just Aren't Enough," *The Globe and Mail*, 27 Feb. 2016, F6.

International Trade, the selling of foreign residences, the closing of consulates, and the cutting back of consular staff.[19] And, notwithstanding its participation in the military missions of Afghanistan (2001–2014), Libya (2011), and Iraq (2015), Canada's contributions to peacekeeping activities had been declining for many years.[20] The Liberal government's election on 2015 saw a reversal of the previous government's policies and a renewed commitment to fighting climate change, to NATO in Europe, to accept refugees and to peacekeeping in Africa. These new policies suggested that Canadians could again continue to believe that they were purveyors of human rights values, peace, and international collaboration.

With respect to Canadian democracy's place in the world, the boundaries separating Canadian politics from events and influence from the rest of the world have always been porous, but never so much as they are today in this era of globalization. This truth has been regularly brought to Canadians in fundamental ways with regular terrorist attacks, the unprecedented flood of refugees stemming from political conflicts in the Arab states of North Africa and the Middle East, and the effects of global economic crises. The perpetual dilemma in Canadian politics and in our foreign policy is whether to support multilateralism and the UN policies and mission to deal with international threats to human rights and peace, or to support our allies as global peacekeepers and enforcers. Questions about what promotes and what threatens democracy do not stop at Canada's borders. This becomes clear when Canadians ask themselves what sort of world, governed in what way, is most likely to guarantee the values and interests they cherish.

What could American president Barack Obama have possibly meant, in his 2016 speech to a joint session of the Canadian House of Commons and Senate, when he said: "The world needs more Canada. NATO needs more Canada. We need you."? He was certainly alluding to Canada's declining contribution to NATO. But he was also comparing Canadian democracy to the apparent decline of democratic and human rights practices in countries around the globe. Canadian democracy is an amalgamation of laws, institutions, and accommodations that are inherited, borrowed, or invented by Canadians for Canadians; it is constantly adapting and evolving. Yet, for all its complexity and occasional inelegance, Canadian democracy has allowed Canadians for a century and a half to manage their differences, share their resources, protect their rights, and regularly and peacefully change their governments. President Obama was saying that Canada is an example to the world of how to manage politics. Considering the current levels of political insecurity worldwide, this is no small thing.

Review Exercises

1. Canada participates in a large number of international organizations such as the OECD, NATO, and the WTO. Explain each organization's mandate, Canada's participation, and the leading issues faced by the organization in recent years.
2. How dependent is your community on international trade? To find out, identify the five or six leading employers in your area. Find out how much of their goods or services they export and to what countries, and how many people they employ.
3. Compare Canadian foreign policy initiatives under the Harper government and the Trudeau government. What are the most obvious policy changes to Canadian foreign policy? Are these changes the result of international events or of domestic events? Do these policy changes reflect the ideological values of the party in charge?

Up for Debate

1. Resolved: democracy and human rights are Western concepts.
2. One of the quandaries that Canada faces is whether to intervene (alone or in a coalition) in another country's affairs when a serious human rights violation leads to a humanitarian crisis. Following are a few of the many possible debate topics on this issue.

   a. Should foreign powers be allowed to intervene in another country's affairs or should a country's sovereignty be respected in all cases?
   b. Does the United Nations have an obligation to protect vulnerable citizens?
   c. Where should we draw the line between a state's desire to remain sovereign and the responsibility to protect citizens from human rights abuses?

For some background on humanitarian crises and the kind of debate that occurs every time such intervention is contemplated by the UN, one could look at the following examples: the delivery of humanitarian aid to Somalia in 1992, the prevention of ethnic cleansing in the former Yugoslavia from 1992 to 1995, the invasion of Iraq by the "coalition of the willing" in 2003 and the prevention of human rights violations in Syria from 2014 to 2016.

Starting Points for Research

Bothwell, Robert, and Jean Daudelin, eds. *Canada Among Nations 2008: 100 Years of Canadian Foreign Policy*. Montreal and Kingston: McGill–Queen's University Press, 2008.

Bow, Brian. *The Politics of Linkage: Power, Interdependence, and Ideas in Canada–US Relations.* Vancouver: University of British Columbia Press, 2009.

Cellucci, Paul. *Unquiet Diplomacy.* Toronto: Key Porter, 2007.

Clarkson, Stephen. *Uncle Sam and Us: Globalization, Neoconservatism, and the Canadian State.* Toronto: University of Toronto Press, 2002.

Keating, Tom. *Canada and World Order: The Multilateralist Tradition in Canadian Foreign Policy*, 3rd edn. Toronto: Oxford University Press, 2013.

Knight, W. Andy, and Tom Keating. *Global Politics.* Toronto: Oxford University Press, 2010.

Randall, Stephen, and John Herd Thompson. *Canada and the United States: Ambivalent Allies*, 4th edn. Montreal and Kingston: McGill–Queen's University Press, 2008.

CBC Archives and TVO's *The Agenda*

Visit the companion website for *Canadian Democracy: A Concise Introduction* to follow links to audio and video footage related to the main themes of the chapter: www.oupcanada.com/BrooksConcise2e.

Relevant Websites

Visit the companion website for *Canadian Democracy: A Concise Introduction* to browse a collection of websites featuring material related to the key themes of the chapter, an excellent starting point for research:www.oupcanada.com/BrooksConcise2e.

Glossary

Aboriginal a person who self-identifies as North American Indian, Métis, or Inuit

Aboriginal rights a recognition and a set of guarantees by the state that Indigenous peoples have certain rights such as civil rights and the rights to land, to preservation of culture, and to self-government

advocacy advertising the purchase of newspaper/magazine space or broadcast time to convey a political message

affirmative action the logic and machinery of targeting groups for preferred treatment

alienation apathy, estrangement from the political system, or the belief that politics is systematically biased against one's interests and values; the awareness that the public realm—whose voices are heard and what counts as legitimate political discourse—belongs to others

allophones a term used by Canadian demographers for those whose native language is neither English nor French

anarchy chaos and civil strife

assimilation the absorption of the minority culture into the majority (English) culture

asymmetrical federalism the constitutional recognition of differences in the status and powers of provincial governments

authority the recognition by the compliant party that the person or organization issuing a command has the right to do so and should be obeyed

backbencher an MP who is not a cabinet minister

bicameral legislature a legislature comprising two bodies: in Canada, an elected House of Commons (the lower house) and an appointed Senate (the upper house)

block funding Ottawa's financial contribution geared to the previous year's subsidy plus an amount calculated on the basis of growth in the recipient province's gross product

brokerage politics a strategic choice by a political party to avoid ideological appeals in favour of a flexible centrist style of politics

bureaucracy the political rule by unelected government officials

Canadian Bill of Rights a statutory declaration of rights passed by the Canadian Parliament on 10 August 1960

caucus the body of elected MPs belonging to a particular party

caucus model a system in which party leaders are chosen by other elected MPs of their party

central agency an area of the bureaucracy whose main or only purpose is to support the decision-making activities of cabinet

centre the mainstream of a society's politics

Charlottetown Accord a second round of reforms from 1990 to 1992, called the "Canada round," attempted by the federal government after the Meech Accord failed in 1987; this second attempt also failed

civil liberties or civil rights the rights of citizens to equality and to social and political freedoms

class analysis a theoretical approach that sees the state in capitalist societies as an instrument through which small minorities control most of society's wealth to maintain their social and economic dominance

classical conservatism an ideology based on the importance of tradition and social order and which accepted human inequality—social, political, and economic—as part of the natural order of things

classical liberalism liberalism as it was understood until the middle of the nineteenth century, associated with freedom of religious choice and practice, free enterprise and free trade in business and economics, and freedom of expression and association in politics

classical socialism an ideology based on the principle of equality of condition and radical egalitarianism

coalition government a temporary agreement between two or more political parties to form a government

codified constitution a formal, written constitution found in a unified document

coercion the threat or use of force

communitarianism the belief that active co-operation, including the public mobilization of resources to fulfill group objectives and the recognition of the equality of communities and communal identities, are essential to individual dignity and the maintenance of truly democratic societies

compromise a coming to terms with concessions on two or more sides and a joint decision to abide by an agreement

conservatism an ideology based on the belief that traditions and social order are important and that gradual change is best

constitutional amendment a change in some aspect(s) of the existing constitution, leaving the basic constitutional structure intact

constitutional conventions practices that emerge over time and are generally accepted as binding rules of the political system

constitutional monarchy a system of government with a monarch as a formal head of state that operates within a constitutional framework

constitutional supremacy the concept that the Constitution (the law of laws) is above all else, even the Parliament

constitutionalism a principle that involves predictable governance that has its source in written rules rather than the arbitrary wills of individuals

corporatism a political structure characterized by the direct participation of organizations representing business and labour in public policy making

coup d'état the illegal overthrow of a government by violence or threat of violence

cross-border regions (CBRs) a distinct grouping of neighbouring and nearby provinces and states whose economic, cultural, and institutional linkages create commonalities between the members of this binational (Canada–US) grouping and set it apart from other regions

cultural genocide the destruction of those structures and practices that allow a group to continue as a group

cultural hegemony the ability of society's dominant class to have its values and beliefs accepted as the conventional wisdom in society at large

deliberate discrimination prejudice that one person feels toward the members of some group or groups

democracy a political system based on the formal political equality of all citizens, in which there is a realistic possibility that voters can replace the government, and in which certain basic rights and freedoms are protected

democratic deficit the excessive centralization of power in and around the prime minister and cabinet and the marginalization of the legislature

democratic rights the right of citizens to vote in periodically held elections and to stand for public office

direct democracy government of the citizens by the citizens

distinct society a society noticeably different than other provinces

economic statement a document that provides the government's analysis of the state of the economy and where the government plans to steer it

equality rights rights that embody the rule of law principle that everyone should be treated equally under the law

equalization payment funds paid to a provincial government whose per capita tax revenues falls below the average of the two most affluent provinces

Estimates the detailed spending plans that the government tables in the House of Commons each winter

executive federalism a term sometimes used to describe the relations between cabinet ministers and officials of the two levels of government

extreme poverty an international standard definition of income of less than $1 a day

federal system a form of government with a constitutional authority to make laws and to tax, divided between a national government and some number of regional governments

feminism a theoretical approach that views the state as an inherently patriarchal institution, where politics is not neutral or gender free

fundamental freedoms basic individual political rights (or liberties) that include freedom of religion, belief, expression, the media, assembly, and association

globalization the political, economic, and social integration that comes from the increased international flow of goods, people, capital, and ideas

government the organization of the state and the system of institutions and agencies used to exercise its authority

human rights all the basic rights and freedoms of citizens

ideology a set of interrelated values and beliefs about how society is organized and how it ought to function

influence the ability of A to convince B that a particular action is reasonable or otherwise in B's best interests

Interest group (or pressure group) a private organization that promotes its interest by trying to influence government rather than seeking the election of candidates to manage it

international relations a branch of political science that studies the relationships between states and the international system of governance

intra-state federalism the representation and accommodation of regional interests within national political institutions

judicial independence the principle that judges are to be free from any and all interference in their decision making

judicial restraint a legal concept expressed in the Charter that judges should defer to the legislature when exercising their judicial power

la revanche des berceaux ("revenge of the cradle") the high birth rate that for close to a century enabled French Canada to maintain its numerical strength

la survivance conserving French Canada's religious and linguistic heritage in the face of assimilationist pressures of a dominant culture that was anglicizing, Protestant, materialistic, liberal democratic, and business oriented

language (linguistic) rights guarantees by the state that an individual or a group has the right to choose a particular language for use in private or in public, and to use that language in a given jurisdiction, such as in the educational system, in the government, or in the courts of a given territory

left collectivist and social justice ideas and ideologies, and political parties that advocate social reform

legal rights procedural rights intended to ensure the fair and equal treatment of individuals under the law

legitimacy the rules and institutions that constitute the state and determine how governments are chosen are accepted by most people as being reasonable

liberalism an ideology based on the belief that the state must protect individual liberty, personal choice, and the right to private property

libertarianism an ideology based on the belief that individuals should be allowed the largest possible margin of freedom in all realms of life, including moral choices

lobbying any form of direct or indirect communication with government that is designed to influence public policy

majoritarianism the belief that the opinion of the majority should almost always be considered in decision making

manifest destiny a nineteenth-century American belief that the United States was destined to expand to include all North America

materialism an ideology that places greater stress on economic security and material well-being

Meech Lake Accord a 1987 attempt by the federal government and some provincial governments to reform Canada's Constitution such that, among other things, it would recognize Quebec as a "distinct society."

ministerial responsibility the obligation of a cabinet minister to explain and defend policies and actions carried out in her or his name

minority government a government that depends on the support of another party's MPs in order to win votes in the legislature

mobility rights the rights of citizens to move freely within a country's borders

multiculturalism the idea that cultural diversity not only is good for society, it should also be encouraged

multilateralism the resolution of international differences and conflicts through structures and processes that represent many states

nation building the recent evolution of more powerful and competent provincial administrations which aim to manage socio-economic change in their territories and which are in essential conflict with the central government

National Energy Program (NEP) a scheme brought in by the Liberal government of Pierre Elliott Trudeau to control the cost of energy to the rest of Canada

national standards Canada-wide standards in the delivery of social programs to ensure uniformity of service for all Canadians and create a "national social union"

nationalism a sense of a community defined by its language, ethnic origins, traditions, or unique history; the translation of values and beliefs shared by the people of a territory or a community into a public policy or agenda

neo-institutionalism a perspective on policy making that emphasizes the impact of structures and rules, formal and informal, on political outcomes

notwithstanding clause a feature of the Charter of Rights and Freedoms that enables either Parliament or a provincial legislature to declare that a law shall operate even if it violates the fundamental freedoms, legal rights, or equality rights sections of the Charter. Such a declaration must be renewed after five years; otherwise the Constitution reasserts its supremacy.

open ballot an electoral system whereby voters simply declared their choice publicly at the polls in the presence of a government official

order-in-council an administrative order (appointment, regulation, or legislative order authorized by an existing act of Parliament) issued by cabinet and approved by the Governor General

organization theory the study of how people act within an organization

parliamentary supremacy a principle that Parliament's authority was considered superior to that of all other institutions of government

party discipline a tradition of British parliamentary government, according to which a party's MPs generally vote as a unified block in the legislature

patrimoine the language, the faith, the mores of a community whose roots went back to New France, as well as a leading role for the Church in articulating these values and controlling these structures

patriotism fervent and demonstrative love of country and its symbols

patronage the distribution of favours by a governing politician (e.g., political appointments or government contracts) in exchange for political support

peace, order, and good government of Canada (POGG) an important constitutional principle and emergency power that can provide the constitutional basis for federal actions in special circumstances, but that cannot be used to justify federal laws during "normal" times

plebiscite or **referendum** direct vote of citizens on an important public question

pluralism the understanding of politics as fundamentally a competition between different interests

plurality system or **first-past-the-post system** an electoral system in which the candidate who receives the most votes in a constituency election becomes the member of Parliament (or provincial legislature) for that constituency

policy community a limited set of state and societal actors that is centred on a sub-government; i.e., that set of state institutions and interest groups usually involved in making and implementing policy in some field

policy network the nature of the relationships between the key actors in a policy community

political community a shared sense of belonging to a country whose national integrity is worth preserving

political culture the characteristic values, beliefs, and behaviours of a society's members in regard to politics

political efficacy people's sense of whether their participation in politics matters

political faction a group of citizens whose goals and behaviour are contrary to those of other groups or to the interests of the community as a whole

political party an organization that offers a slate of candidates to voters at election time

politics the management of power and conflict and an activity by which rival claims are settled by public authorities

populism a style of politics that seeks to return power to the common people

post-materialism an ideology that attaches comparatively greater importance to human needs for belonging, self-esteem, and personal fulfillment

postmodernism a theoretical approach that sees the state as an essentially oppressive and even repressive institution

poverty line Statistics Canada's "low-income-cut-offs" (LICOs); the threshold at which a household spends over 20 per cent more of its annual family income on the basic necessities of life (food, clothing, and shelter) than does the average household

power the ability to influence what happens

precarious employment work that is insecure and unskilled, and pays wages that cannot support a household

preferential voting a ranked voting system where voters rank candidates in order of preference

prime ministerial government government where the executive is essentially dominated by the prime minister and the PMO

private realm the areas of life where the state's authority does not extend

Privy Council that part of the executive, made up of the Crown's advisers, in which the power of the monarch resides; it formally includes all members of the present and past cabinets

propaganda the dissemination of selected information or misinformation to the public as a means of spreading a particular ideology or doctrine

proportional representation a method of electing government representatives whereby a party's percentage of the popular votes translates into a corresponding share of seats in the legislature

prorogation a postponement of parliamentary activities without a dissolution of Parliament

Protectionism the theory and practice of protecting domestic industries (the opposite of free trade theory and practice)

province building the phenomenon of powerful provincial governments using the constitutional, legal, and taxation levers to increase their control within their provincial borders and, consequently, their stature vis-à-vis Ottawa; the reinforcing of political administrative needs of governments by the demands of province-oriented economic interests

public agenda the matters identified by opinion leaders in the media and in government as warranting some policy response

public realm the sphere of what is considered to be political; its boundary is located at the limits of the state's authority

public sector the part of the economy that includes those organizations that receive all or a major part of their operating revenues from one or more levels of government

quality of life (QOL) a measure of social and economic prosperity using a combination of objective and subjective determinants

Quiet Revolution a time of many socio-political reforms and changes, and a turning point in the history of Quebec

realignment a situation that occurs when an election or series of elections produces a durable change in the parties' bases of support

reasonable limits legislative limits that can be placed on human rights if it can be established that they are in the best interest of a free and democratic society

receptive bilinguals people who are capable of responding to French communications but do not themselves initiate conversations in French, consume French language media, or seek out opportunities to live in their acquired second language

Red Tory a conservative who believes that government has a responsibility to act as an agent for the collective good, and that this responsibility goes far beyond maintaining law and order

representation by population the principle of "one person—one vote," where all elected members of the legislature should represent approximately the same number of voters

representative bureaucracy a concept and an expectation that the bureaucracy should "represent" the population and reflect in fair proportion certain demographic characteristics of society

representative democracy government carried out by an elected legislature that represents the people

resources things we need for survival or desire for comfort

responsible government the constitutional principle that the prime minister and cabinet require the confidence of the elected House of Commons in order to govern

revenue budget a document that outlines the government's plans to change the tax system

reverse discrimination policies that shift the burden of injustice onto the shoulders of the qualified members of advantaged groups who are not personally responsible for the injustices suffered by minority groups

right ideas and ideologies that advocate social order, protection of private property, economic freedom, and support for capitalism

right wing / left wing labels often used to classify the political ideas that lie behind an action, opinion, or statement

right something that a person is entitled to

Royal Commission a task force or some other consultative body created by the government to study and make recommendations on an issue

rule of law the idea that no public official has the legitimate right to exercise any powers other than those assigned to his or her office by the law; the guarantee that all public authority must be exercised in accordance with the law and that there will be one law for all persons

secularism the separation of church and state

secularization a decline in the belief that religion and religious authorities should be looked to for guidance about behaviour and an increase in the social, cultural, and political influence of elites whose expertise is not based on religious faith

sexism a term coined in the 1960s to label behaviour that treated males and females unequally for no better reason than their sex

shared-cost program a provincially administered program where Ottawa's financial contribution is geared to what the province spends

single-member constituency an electoral system in which each constituency (riding) gets one representative in the House of Commons and/or provincial legislature

social capital norms of interpersonal trust, a sense of civic duty, and a belief that one's involvement in politics and in the life of the community matters; the fabric of connections between members of a community

social learning the process of acquiring knowledge, values, and beliefs about the world and ourselves

social licence the approval by a community or by an alliance of interests or stakeholders for a proposed project

socialism an ideology based on the collective or state ownership of the means of production and the belief in the state's ability to provide social justice, redistribute wealth, and fix social problems

socio-economic mobility the ability of individuals, families, and groups to move from one social or economic position to another

soft power international influence based on intangible or indirect factors that include culture, values, and a sense of legitimacy ascribed to a nation's international aims

sovereignty the ability of a person or entity to act independently without outside interference

sovereignty-association a term generally understood to mean a politically sovereign Quebec that would be linked to Canada through some sort of commercial union or free trade agreement

stare decisis the legal principle of determining the points in litigation according to precedent

state the set of institutions that manage power and conflict for a society within a geographically defined territory

statism a political tradition characterized by a relatively strong political executive and by a population that tends to be deferential toward those in power

substantive equality the principle that individuals should be looked at in terms of their group characteristics and the possible advantages or disadvantages they may have experienced as a result of these attributes

supranational organization an international institution with a purpose that transcends national boundaries and that has acquired some legal authority and decision-making power from its member states in order to achieve that purpose

systemic discrimination the discrimination inherent in traditions, customary practices, rules, and institutions that have the effect of favouring the members of one group over another

Tory a person who believes in deference toward established authority and institutions, acceptance of inequality between classes as the natural condition of society, and a greater stress on preserving social order than on protecting individual freedoms

totalitarianism a system of government that suppresses all dissent in the name of some supreme goal

uncodified constitution the powers of government, as well as the limits to government power, are unwritten or based on precedents, or embedded in the country's laws, conventions, and traditions

unitary state system a form of government where sovereignty or competence resides exclusively with the central government, and regional or local governments are legally and politically subordinate to it

Universal Declaration of Human Rights A declaration passed by the UN in 1948 that provides the basis for various international covenants to which Canada is a signatory, such as the International Covenant on Civil and Political Rights and the International Covenant on Economic, Social and Cultural Rights.

values personal beliefs about what is good or bad, right or wrong, important or trivial, valuable or worthless, and so on

welfare gap the gap that exists between the income that social assistance provides and the cost of living

White Paper a report for discussion on a major piece of legislation being proposed by government, which is based on research by the bureaucracy or the legislature, and serves as a statement of the government's legislative intentions

Notes

1 | An Introduction to Political Life

1. Harris/Decima poll published in *Reader's Digest* magazine, "Trust Issues: Results of RD's 2013 Trust Poll (1/11)," readersdigest.ca, May 2013, http://www.readersdigest.ca/features/heart/trust-issues-results-rds-2013-trust-poll/.
2. World Values Survey, 2000, www.worldvaluessurvey.org.
3. Charles Merriam, *Public and Private Government* (New Haven: Yale University Press, 1944).
4. Bertrand Russell, *Power: A New Social Analysis* (London: Unwin and Allen, 1938), 10, 11.
5. The full exchange may be viewed at www.cbc.ca/archives/categories/politics/civil-unrest/the-october-crisis-civil-liberties-suspended/just-watch-me.html.
6. Leo Panitch, "State," in *The Canadian Encyclopedia*, 2nd edn (Edmonton: Hurtig, 1988), vol. 4, 2071.
7. Victor Davis Hanson, talk at Woodrow Wilson Center, 2 June 2005, Washington, DC.
8. C.B. Macpherson, *The Real World of Democracy* (Toronto: CBC Enterprises, 1965).
9. *CBC Asks*, "Is Politics Broken?" CBC, 25 March 2015, http://www.cbc.ca/news/politics/cbc-asks-is-politics-broken-team-no-weighs-in-1.3003046.
10. Gabriel A. Almond and Sidney Verba, *The Civic Culture* (Princeton, NJ: Princeton University Press, 1963).
11. Quoted in Henry Steele Commager, *Living Ideas in America* (New York: Harper, 1951), 556.
12. Neil Postman, *Amusing Ourselves to Death* (New York: Viking, 1985), 107.
13. "The People Get It Right, on the Whole," *The Economist*, 7 Nov. 1998, 24.
14. https://freedomhouse.org/report/freedom-press-2014/press-freedom-rankings.
15. Eugene Forsey, *How Canadians Govern Themselves*, 6th edn (Ottawa: Library of Parliament, Public Information Office, 2005), 32.

Part I | The Societal Context of Politics

2 | Political Culture

1. R. Kirk, *The Conservative Mind* (London: Faber & Faber, 1953).
2. LEAP Manifesto, https://leapmanifesto.org/en/the-leap-manifesto/.
3. Fernand Ouellet, *Histoire économique et sociale du Québec, 1760–1850* (Paris: Fides, 1966).
4. William Christian and Colin Campbell, *Political Parties and Ideologies in Canada*, 2nd edn (Toronto: McGraw-Hill Ryerson, 1982), 23–5; Gad Horowitz, "Conservatism, Liberalism and Socialism in Canada: An Interpretation," *Canadian Journal of Economics and Political Science* (1966).
5. Kenneth McRae, "The Structure of Canadian History," in Louis Hartz, ed., *The Founding of New Societies* (New York: Harcourt, Brace & World, 1964), 235.
6. David Bell and Lorne Tepperman, *The Roots of Disunity* (Toronto: McClelland & Stewart, 1979), 76–7.
7. Horowitz, "Conservatism, Liberalism and Socialism."
8. Seymour Martin Lipset, *Continental Divide* (Montreal: C.D. Howe Institute, 1989), 1.
9. Bell and Tepperman, *The Roots of Disunity*, 61–2.
10. Reg Whitaker, "Images of the State in Canada," in Leo Panitch, ed., *The Canadian State* (Toronto: University of Toronto Press, 1977), 30.
11. Patricia Marchak, *Ideological Perspectives on Canada* (Toronto: McGraw-Hill Ryerson, 1975), 115.
12. Pierre Trudeau, "Some Obstacles to Democracy in Quebec," in Trudeau, *Federalism and the French Canadians* (Toronto: Macmillan, 1968).
13. In 1951, 80 per cent of Quebec's workforce was in secondary industries (manufacturing and construction) and the service sector, a percentage that was higher than for Canada as a whole (78 per cent).
14. See Kenneth McRoberts, *Quebec: Social Change and Political Crisis*, 3rd edn (Toronto: McClelland & Stewart, 1988), 90–100.
15. W.L. Morton, "The Dualism of Culture and the Federalism of Power," in Richard Abbott, ed., *A New Concept of Confederation*, Proceedings of the Seventh Seminar of the Canadian Union of Students (Ottawa, 1965), 121.
16. Donald Smiley, *The Canadian Political Nationality* (Toronto: Methuen, 1967).
17. Lipset, *Continental Divide*, 136.
18. Pierre Berton, *Why We Act Like Canadians* (Toronto: McClelland & Stewart, 1982), 16.
19. Miles Corak, "Chasing the Same Dream, Climbing Different Ladders: Economic Mobility in the United States and Canada," Economic Mobility Project of the Pew Charitable Trusts, Jan. 2010, www.economicmobility.org.
20. Frank Graves, "The Shifting Public Outlook on Risk and Security," in Karlyn Bowman and Frank Graves, *Threat Perceptions in the United States and Canada: Assessing the Public's Attitudes toward Risk and Security*, One Issue, Two Voices Series, Issue Four (Washington: Canada Institute, Woodrow Wilson Center, Oct. 2005), 10–15.
21. See the summary of studies in Lipset, *Continental Divide*, 155–8.
22. Michael Ignatieff, *True Patriot Love* (Toronto: Viking, 2009).
23. The CEO pay differential data comes from Lawrence Mishel, Jared Bernstein, and Sylvia Allegretto, *The State of Working America 2004/2005* (Ithaca, NY: Cornell University Press, 2005); the data on attitudes is found in Lars Osberg and Timothy Smeeding, "Fair Inequality? An International Comparison of Attitudes toward Pay Differentials," working paper, Russell Sage

Foundation, 2005, 31, www.russellsage.org/programs/main/inequality/workingpapers/051025.267178/.

24. World Values Survey, 2000, www.worldvaluessurvey.org.

25. Pew Research Center, *Economies of Emerging Markets Better Rated during Difficult Times*, 23 May 2013, www.pewglobal.org/files/2013/05/Pew-Global-Attitudes-Economic-Report-FINAL-May-23-20131.pdf.

26. Corak, "Chasing the Same Dream," 14.

27. Canada, Constitution Act, 1982, s. 27.

28. Canada, Constitution Act 1982, s. 15(2).

29. Neil Bissoondath, *Selling Illusions: The Cult of Multiculturalism in Canada* (Toronto: Penguin Books, 1994).

30. Reginald Bibby, *Mosaic Madness: The Poverty and Potential of Life in Canada* (Toronto: Stoddart, 1990).

31. Salim Mansur, *Delectable Lie: A Liberal Repudiation of Multiculturalism* (Mantua Books, 2011).

32. Jeffrey Reitz and Raymond Breton, *The Illusion of Difference* (Toronto: C.D. Howe Institute, 1994), 133.

33. Catalyst, "Women on Boards," October 2014 as reported in the New York Times , http://www.nytimes.com/2015/03/11/upshot/women-on-boards-where-the-us-ranks.html?_r=0.

34. Berton, *Why We Act Like Canadians*, 16–17.

35. Charles Taylor, "Deep Diversity and the Future of Canada," www.uni.ca/taylor.html.

36. Peter C. Newman, *The Canadian Revolution, 1985–1995* (Toronto: Penguin Books, 1995), 12–13.

37. Neil Nevitte, *The Decline of Deference: Canadian Value Change in Cross-National Perspective* (Peterborough, ON: Broadview Press, 1996).

38. Environics Institute, AmericasBarometer, *Canada 2012*, 24, www.vanderbilt.edu/lapop/canada/Canada-2012-Report.pdf.

39. World Values Survey, www.worldvaluessurvey.org.

40. Environics Institute, AmericasBarometer, *Canada 2012*, 24, www.vanderbilt.edu/lapop/canada/Canada-2012-Report.pdf, 12.

3 | The Social and Economic Setting

1. Michael Babad, "Canadians Are Scaling the Income Ladder with the Best of Them," *The Globe and Mail*, 17 July 2015, www.theglobeandmail.com/report-on-business/top-business-stories/canadians-scale-the-income-ladder-with-the-best-of-them/article25533315/.

2. Statistics Canada, Labour Force Survey, Dec. 2010, http://www.statcan.gc.ca/daily-quotidien/120706/dq120706a-eng.htm; 2014 data shows no significant change; see http://www.indexmundi.com/g/g.aspx?c=ca&v=69.

3. Canada Without Poverty, http://www.cwp-csp.ca/poverty/just-the-facts/.

4. World Bank, "Gross National Income per Capita 2012, PPP, " http://databank.worldbank.org/data/download/GNIPC.pdf.

5. Trading Economics, http://www.tradingeconomics.com/canada/unemployment-rate.

6. Bureau of Labor Statistics, http://data.bls.gov/timeseries/LNS14000000.

7. Statistics Canada, Labour Force Survey, Dec. 2010, http://www.statcan.gc.ca/daily-quotidien/120706/dq120706a-eng.htm.

8. Statistics Canada, Labour Force Survey, June 2012, "Employment by class of worker and industry—Seasonally adjusted," http://www.statcan.gc.ca/daily-quotidien/120706/t120706a002-eng.htm.

9. See, for example, Stephen Cohen and John Zysman, *Manufacturing Matters* (New York: Basic Books, 1987).

10. This debate is taken up in Michael Spence, "Globalization and Unemployment," *Foreign Affairs* (July–Aug. 2011), ; and Richard Katz and Robert Lawrence, "Manufacturing Globalization," *Foreign Affairs* (Nov.–Dec. 2011), .

11. According to the OECD and the IMF: "Between 2010 and 2014, Canada Has Been in Second or Third Spot," http://www.cbc.ca/news/politics/spin-cycle-does-canada-s-economic-performance-really-top-the-g7-1.3178235.

12. Environics Institute, *Focus Canada 2012*, 14.

13. Ibid., 53, 55, 56.

14. Professor Wayne Lewchuk, quoted in Chris Sorenson, "The New Underclass," *Maclean's*, 16 Jan. 2013, http://www.macleans.ca/society/life/the-new-underclass/. The article discusses a United Way and McMaster University report called *It's More Than Poverty: Employment Parity and Household Well-Being*, http://www.unitedwaytyr.com/document.doc?id=91.

15. Jason Gilmore, Trends in Dropout Rates and the Labour Market Outcomes of Young Dropouts, Labour Statistics Division, Statistics Canada, 2011. http://www.statcan.gc.ca/pub/81-004-x/2010004/article/11339-eng.htm#a

16. Statistics Canada, "What Has Changed for Young People in Canada?" July 2013, 8, Table 2, .

17. Joseph Berger and Andrew Parkin, *The Value of a Degree: Education, Employment and Earnings in Canada*, p. 7, contactpoint.ca/wp-content/uploads/2013/01/pokvol4_ch1_e.pdf.

18. John Porter, *The Vertical Mosaic* (Toronto: University of Toronto Press, 1965), pp.3-4.

19. Dana Flavelle, "Why the Gap between Rich and Poor in Canada Keeps Growing," *Toronto Star*, 5 Dec. 2011, http://www.thestar.com/business/article/1097055--why-the-gap-between-rich-and-poor-in-canada-keeps-growing.

20. All of the figures in this paragraph are based on the most recent data from Statistics Canada.

21. Nicole M. Fortin et al., "Canadian Inequality: Recent Developments and Policy Options," *Canadian Public Policy* 38, 2 (2012): 121–45.

22. UNESCO, "Poverty," *Learning to Live Together*, http://www.unesco.org/new/en/social-and-human-sciences/themes/international-migration/glossary/poverty/.

23. National Council of Welfare, *A New Poverty Line: Yes, No or Maybe?* (Ottawa: Minister of Public Works and Government Services Canada, 1999), 1.

24. National Aboriginal Economic Development Board, *The Aboriginal Economic Benchmarking Report*, June 2012, www.naedb-cndea.com/wp-content/uploads/TheAboriginal-EconomicBenchmarkingReport2.pdf.

25. Finance Canada, www.fin.gc.ca/fedprov/mtp-eng.asp.

26. Miles Corak, "Chasing the Same Dream, Climbing Different Ladders: Economic Mobility in the United States and Canada," Economic Mobility Project of the Pew Charitable Trusts, Jan. 2010, www.economicmobility.org.

27. Jo Blanden, Paul Gregg, and Stephen Machin, *Intergenerational Mobility in Europe and North America* (London: The Sutton Trust, Apr. 2005).

28. Miles Corak, *Intergenerational Earnings Mobility among the Children of Canadian Immigrants* (Bonn: Institute for the Study of Labor, 2006).

29. Anna Mehler Paperny, "Ontario Now the Worst Place for Educated Immigrants Looking for Work," *Global News*, 30 July 2014.

30. Abdurrahman Aydemir, Wen-Hao Chen, and Miles Corak, *Intergenerational Earnings Mobility among the Children of Canadian Immigrants*, Statistics Canada Catalogue no. 11F0019MIE, no. 267 (Ottawa: Minister of Industry, 2005). See also Statistics Canada, *Educational and Economic Outcomes for Second-Generation Canadians: The Children of Immigrants*, www.statcan.gc.ca/pub/11f0019m/2008319/s9-eng.htm.

31. Porter, *The Vertical Mosaic*; Wallace Clement, *The Canadian Corporate Elite* (Toronto: McClelland & Stewart, 1975).

32. Public Policy Forum, *Edging toward Diversity: A Statistical Breakdown of Canada's 41st Parliament, with Comparisons to the 40th Parliament*, June 2011, www.ppforum.ca/sites/default/files/edging_towards_diversity_final.pdf.

33. Alia Dharssi, "Canada federal election candidates include more visible minorities in 2015 than in the past four votes," *National Post*, 19 Oct. 2015, http://news.nationalpost.com/news/canada/canadian-politics/study-says-canadas-three-major-parties-are-fielding-more-visible-minority-candidates.

34. World Values Survey, 2000, www.worldvaluessurvey.org.

35. Conference Board of Canada, "Life Expectancy," *How Canada Performs 2012*, www.conferenceboard.ca/hcp/details/health/life-expectancy.aspx.

36. Statistics Canada, "Homicides Decline in Most Provinces and Territories in 2012," http://www.statcan.gc.ca/pub/85-002-x/2013001/article/11882-eng.htm#a2.

37. Jan van Dijk et al., *Criminal Victimisation in International Perspective* (Tilburg, Netherlands: Tilburg University and United Nations Office on Drugs and Crime, 2007), 132, Figure 28.

38. Health Canada, *Canadian Addiction Survey 2004*, Mar. 2005, 43, 45, www.ccsa.ca/2005%20CCSA%20Documents/ccsa-004028-2005.pdf.

39. Canadian Alliance to End Homelessness, *The State of Homelessness in Canada 2013*, www.homelesshub.ca/ResourceFiles/SOHC2013.pdf.

40. Food Banks Canada, *Hunger Count 2012*, www.foodbankscanada.ca/getmedia/3b94beb7-fbe2-490e-90dc-4a313dfb97e5/HungerCount2012.pdf.aspx?ext=.pdf.

41. National Council of Welfare, "Welfare Incomes 2004," Revised (Ottawa: Government of Canada, Aug. 2005), 35, http://www.ncw.gc.ca/l.3bd.2t.1ils@-eng.jsp?lid=126.

42. Statistics Canada and Department of Foreign Affairs and International Trade, *State of Trade 2012*, www.international.gc.ca/economist-economiste/assets/pdfs/performance/SoT_2012/SoT_CIdC_2012_Intro-ENG.pdf.

43. The Canadian Journalism Project, 3 Apr. 2013, www.j-source.ca/article/8-10-canadians-read-newspapers-weekly-nadbank-report.

44. Kate Taylor, We Need to Discuss Why Canadian Culture is a Public Good," *The Globe and Mail*, 5 Feb. 2016, http://www.theglobeandmail.com/arts/we-need-to-discuss-why-canadian-culture-is-a-public-good/article28609380/.

45. Jim Stanford, quoted in Lawrence Martin, "Divided against Ourselves," *The Globe and Mail*, 15 May 2012, A11.

46. UNIFOR: *Rhetoric and Reality: Evaluating Canada's Economic Record Under the Harper Government*, July 2015, 2, http://www.unifor.org/sites/default/files/documents/document/909-harper_economic_critique_eng_0.pdf.

4 | Regionalism and Canadian Politics

1. Cited in *The Economist*, special survey of Canada, 15 Feb. 1986, 16.

2. Richard Simeon and David Elkins, "Regional Political Cultures in Canada," *Canadian Journal of Political Science* 7, 3 (Sept. 1974): 397–437.

3. Centre for Research and Information Canada, *The Charter: Dividing or Uniting Canadians?* (Apr. 2002), 30, www.cric.ca.

4. Frank Graves, "The Trust Deficit: What Does It Mean?" Ekos Politics, 14 May 2013, www.ekospolitics.ca.

5. In God We Canadians Trust?" survey conducted by Léger Marketing for the Association for Canadian Studies, Apr. 2012, www.acs-aec.ca/pdf/polls/In%20God%20Canadians%20Trust%20II.pdf.

6. Association of Canadian Studies, "Multiculturalists with Concerns," 8 Oct. 2011, www.acs-aec.ca.

7. Ekos Politics, *Looking Backward, Looking Forward: Five Big Forces Shaping Our Society*, 9 Jan. 2013, p. 31, www.ekos.com/admin/articles/FG-2013-01-09.pdf.

8. Debora VanNijnatten, "Canada–US Relations and the Emergence of Cross-Border Regions," 4, Briefing Notes, Government of Canada, Policy Research Initiatives, 2006, at: www.policyresearch.gc.ca.

9. Stephen Brooks and Barry Rabe, eds, *Transboundary Environmental Governance between Canada and the United States: The Second Century* (Washington: Woodrow Wilson Center, 2009).

10. Roger Gibbins and Sonia Arrison, *Western Visions: Perspectives on the West in Canada* (Peterborough, Ont.: Broadview Press, 1995), 45.

11. W.L. Morton, "The Bias of Prairie Politics," *Transactions of the Royal Society of Canada* series 3, 49 (June 1955): 66.

12. Barry Cooper, "Western Political Consciousness," in Stephen Brooks, ed., *Political Thought in Canada: Contemporary Perspectives* (Toronto: Irwin, 1984), 230.

13. CBC, "Trudeau Campaign Forced to Address 2010 Comments on Alberta," 22 Nov. 2012, www.cbc.ca/news/canada/story/2012/11/22/pol-trudeau-tele-quebec-comments-alberta-quebec.html.

14. Barry Cooper, "Fresh News from Laurentian Canada," Frontier Centre for Public Policy, May 2013, 7, www.fcpp.org/files/1/RW-02Laurentian_AP22F1.pdf.

5 | Language, Diversity, and Aboriginal Politics

1. Information on mother tongue was first collected with the census of 1931. Before then, the census only asked about ethnic origin. Demographer Jacques Henripin suggests that French ethnic origin was probably a good surrogate measure for language group at the time of Confederation.

2. F.H. Leacy, ed., *Historical Statistics of Canada* (Ottawa: Supply and Services, 1983), R1-22, R81–87.

3. Henripin estimated that at the rate of decline experienced in the early 1970s, Quebec would still be 77 per cent French-speaking by 2001.

4. Richard Joy, *Languages in Conflict* (Toronto: McClelland & Stewart, 1972), 58, Table 25.

5. The first experience with immersion education was in 1975 in St Lambert, Quebec.

6. See Peter C. Waite, *Pre-Confederation* (Toronto: Prentice-Hall, 1965), 54–5.

7. These voices included such figures as Gonzalve Doutre, Errol Bouchette, and Olivar Asselin, and the activities of the Institut Canadien.

8. Henri Bourassa, *La langue, guardienne de la foi* (Montreal: Bibliothèque de l'action française, 1918).

9. Quoted by Pierre Trudeau in "Quebec on the Eve of the Asbestos Strike," in Ramsay Cook, ed., *French Canadian Nationalism* (Toronto: Macmillan, 1969), 35–6.

10. Victor Barbeau, *Mesure de notre taille* (1936); Barbeau, *Avenir de notre bourgeoisie* (Montréal: Éditions de l'action canadienne française, 1939); Jacques Melançon, "Retard de croissance de l'entreprise canadienne-francaise," *L'actualité économique* (jan.–mars 1956): 503–22.

11. See Melançon, "Retard de croissance."

12. Lois du Québec, 1974, c. 6.

13. Lois du Québec, 1977, c. 5.

14. See *Attorney General of Quebec v. Blaikie et al.* (1979), 101 D.L.R. (3d) 394 (Supreme Court of Canada).

15. *Ford v. Attorney General of Quebec* (1988), Supreme Court of Canada.

16. See municipalite.herouxville.qc.ca/Standards.pdf.

17. From Consultation Commission on Accommodation Practices Related to Cultural Differences (Bouchard–Taylor Commission), *Building the Future: A Time for Reconciliation*, 2008.

18. From a speech by Premier Jean Charest, 22 May 2008, www.premier-ministre.gouv.qc.ca/salle-de-presse/discours/2008/mai/2008-05-22-en.shtml.

19. Eric Waddell, "State, Language and Society: The Vicissitudes of French in Quebec and Canada," in Alan Cairns and Cynthia Williams, eds, *The Politics of Gender, Ethnicity and Language in Canada*, vol. 34 of the research studies for the Royal Commission on the Economic Union and Development Prospects for Canada (Toronto: University of Toronto Press, 1985), 97.

20. "Francophones in the National Capital Region represent over 35 per cent of the Public Service population but, on average, they work more than 60 per cent of their time in English. In bilingual areas of Ontario the corresponding figures are 23 per cent and 66 per cent; roughly one-quarter of all employees are thus working two-thirds of their time in their second language." Commissioner of Official Languages, *Annual Report 1985* (Ottawa: Supply and Services, 1986), 54.

21. Québec, Commission sur l'avenir politique et constitutionnel du Québec, *Rapport* (Québec, 1991), 17.

22. CRIC Quebec Youth Survey.

23. Environics Poll conducted for the Department of Canadian Heritage, 29 Mar.–18 Apr. 2004.

24. Leslie A. Pal, *Interests of State: The Politics of Language, Multiculturalism, and Feminism in Canada* (Montreal and Kingston: McGill–Queen's University Press, 1993).

25. Ibid., 281.

26. R. Brian Howe and David Johnson, *Restraining Equality: Human Rights Commissions in Canada* (Toronto: University of Toronto Press, 2000).

27. Sylvia Bashevkin, *Toeing the Lines* (Toronto: University of Toronto Press, 1985).

28. Sheila Rowbotham, *Hidden from History* (London: Pluto Press, 1974), 47.

29. Nellie McClung, "Hardy Perennials," in McClung, *In Times Like These* (Toronto: University of Toronto Press, 1972), 56.

30. See the discussion in Penny Kome, *Women of Influence* (Toronto: Doubleday Canada, 1985), ch. 2.

31. Bashevkin, *Toeing the Lines*, 32.

32. Pat Armstrong and Hugh Armstrong, *The Double Ghetto: Canadian Women and Their Segregated Work*, 3rd edn (Toronto: McClelland & Stewart, 1994), 42–3.

33. Penney Kome, *The Taking of Twenty-Eight: Women Challenge the Constitution* (Toronto: Women's Press, 1983).

34. 2002 International Social Survey Program, World Values Survey 2000, www.worldvaluessurvey.org.

35. Statistics Canada, "The Changing Profile of Canada's Labour Force," Catalogue no. 96F0030XIE2001009, 11 Feb. 2003.

36. "Women Now Hold 8.5% of Canada's Top Jobs," *CBC News*, 19 Mar. 2015, http://www.cbc.ca/news/business/women-now-hold-8-5-of-canada-s-top-jobs-1.3001744.

37. Statistics Canada, "Table 282-0072: Labour Force Survey Estimates (LFS), Wages of Employees by Type of Work, North American Industry Classification System (NAICS), Sex and Age Group," CANSIM (2014).

38. The RCAP estimated the difference at 49 per cent for 1992–3. In a study for Infometrica's *Monthly Economic Review* 15, 7 (28 Nov. 1996), a former policy coordinator for the RCAP put the difference at 57 per cent for that same year.

39. *Regina v. Howson* (1894), 1 Terr. L.R. 492 (S.C.N.W.T.), 494.

40. Harvey McCue, "Indian Reserve," *The Canadian Encyclopedia*, 2nd edn (Edmonton: Hurtig, 1988), vol. 2, 1056.

41. Statistics Canada, "Share of First Nations People Who Speak an Aboriginal Language Holds Steady, Even among Younger Generation," 2006 Census: Aboriginal Peoples in Canada in 2006: Inuit, Métis and First Nations, 2006 Census: First Nations People, http://www12.statcan.ca/census-recensement/2006/as-sa/97-558/p19-eng.cfm.

42. Truth and Reconciliation Commission of Canada, *Honouring the Truth, Reconciling for the Future : Summary of the Final Report of the Truth and Reconciliation Commission of Canada*, 1, 21, http://www.trc.ca/websites/trcinstitution/File/2015/Honouring_the_Truth_Reconciling_for_the_Future_July_23_2015.pdf.

43. Harold Cardinal, *The Unjust Society* (Edmonton: Hurtig, 1969), 1.

44. Quoted in Melvin H. Smith, *Our Home or Native Land?* (Toronto: Stoddart, 1995), 143.

45. Peter A. Cumming and Neil H. Mickenberg, eds, *Native Rights in Canada* (Toronto: General Publishing, 1972), 55.

46. Ibid., 4.

47. Cumming and Mickenberg, eds, *Native Rights in Canada*, 53.

48. Gary Granzberg et al., "New Magic for Old: TV in Cree Culture," *Journal of Communication* 27, 4 (1977): 155–77; Gary Granzberg, "Television as Storyteller: The Algonkian Indians of Central Canada," *Journal of Communication* 32, 1 (1982): 43–52.

49. J. Hugh Faulkner, "Pressuring the Executive," *Canadian Public Administration* 25 (Summer 1982): 248.

50. Ninth annual presidential address to the National Indian Brotherhood, Fredericton, New Brunswick, Sept. 1978.

51. J. Rick Ponting and Roger Gibbins, *Out of Irrelevance: A Socio-Political Introduction to Indian Affairs in Canada* (Toronto: Butterworths, 1980).

52. "Today's Letters: Ideas for Solving the 'Native Issue'," *National Post*, 14 Jan. 2013, fullcomment.nationalpost.com/2013/01/14/todays-letters-ideas-for-solving-the-native-issue/.

53. Wab Kinew, "Remarks on Bill C-428," 25 April 2013, http://wabkinew.ca/remarks-on-bill-c-428/.

54. Testifying before the House of Commons Standing Committee on Aboriginal Affairs and Northern Development, 19 Nov. 2013, www.parl.gc.ca/HousePublications/Publ icat ion.px?DocId=6309043&Language=E&Mode=1.

55. See the analysis of Oka in Robert Campbell and Leslie Pal, "Feather and Gun," *The Real Worlds of Canadian Politics*, 2nd edn (Peterborough, ON: Broadview Press, 1991), 267–345.

Part II | The Structures of Governance

6 | The Constitution and Charter of Rights and Freedoms

1. Canada, Constitution Act, 1982, s. 16(1).

2. Pierre Trudeau, *Federalism and the French Canadians* (Toronto: Macmillan, 1968), 187.

3. Constitution Act, 1867, preamble.

4. Constitution Act, 1867, s. 121.

5. Constitution Act, 1867, s. 145 (repealed in 1893).

6. Constitution Act, 1982, s. 36.

7. Supreme Court of Canada, *Reference re Secession of Quebec*, Aug. 1998, at p. 18 of online decisions.

8. *Reference re Secession of Quebec*, 19.

9. Ibid., 20.

10. Ibid., 21.

11. Ibid., 22.

12. Supreme Court of Canada, *R. v. Oakes*, 1986, 1 S.C.R. 103, 136.

13. *Reference re Secession of Quebec*, 22.

14. Ibid., 23.

15. Ibid.

16. Ibid., 25.

17. These are the words used in the "anti-hate" section of Canada's Criminal Code.

18. Constitution Act, 1982, s. 6(3)(6).

19. Constitution Act, 1982, s. 6(4).

20. Supreme Court of Canada, *Morgentaler, Smoling and Scott v. The Queen* (1988), 37 C.C.C. (3rd) 449.

21. Constitution Act, 1982, s. 15(1).

22. Constitution Act, 1982, s. 15(2).

23. Constitution Act, 1867, ss. 96–100.

24. *The Queen v. Beauregard* (1986), 2 S.C.R. 56.

25. This was the basis of a 1986 court action brought against the Quebec government by several Provincial Court judges and the Chief Justice of the Quebec Superior Court.

26. From "Remarks at a Conference on Globalization, Citizenship and Identity," 26 October 2004, http://www.scc-csc.gc.ca/court-cour/ju/spe-dis/bm04-10-26-eng.asp.

27. Philip Resnick, *Parliament vs. People* (Vancouver: New Star Books, 1984), 19.

28. Ibid., 25.

29. Section 91(1). Repealed by the Constitution Act, 1982.

30. Section 92(1). Repealed by the Constitution Act, 1982.

31. Supreme Court of Canada, *Re Constitution of Canada* (1981), 125 D.L.R. (3rd) 1.

32. *Re Attorney General of Quebec and Attorney General of Canada* (1982), 140 D.L.R. (3rd) 385.

33. See "Federal Referendum Legislation" in *Referendums in Canada: The Effect of Populist Decision-Making on Representative Democracy*, http://publications.gc.ca/Collection-R/LoPBdP/BP/bp328-e.htm#A.%20Federal.

34. *Reference re Secession of Quebec*, 26.

35. Ibid., 19.

36. Ibid., 27.

37. Ibid., 35.

38. Ibid., 4.

39. United States Constitution, 14th amendment, 1868.

40. Although many now consider the term "Indian" to be inaccurate and even offensive, it is still used in the Indian Act. See Chapter 5 for a discussion of the term.

41. *R. v. Drybones* (1970), S.C.R. 282.

42. *Ottawa Roman Catholic Separate School Trustees v. Mackell* (1917), A.C. 62; *Protestant School Board of Greater Montreal v. Minister of Education of Quebec* (1978), 83 D.L.R. (3d) 645.

43. *Attorney General of Quebec v. Blaikie* (1979), 2 S.C.R. 1016 (Supreme Court of Canada).

44. *R. v. Oakes* (1986), 26 D.L.R. (4th) 20 (Supreme Court of Canada).

45. Roy Romanow et al., *Canada . . . Notwithstanding: The Making of the Constitution 1976–1982* (Toronto: Carswell, 1984), 211.

46. Alan Borovoy, *When Freedoms Collide: The Case for Our Civil Liberties* (Toronto: Lester & Orpen Dennys, 1988), 211–12.

47. Ibid., 389.

48. *Retail, Wholesale & Department Store Union, Local 580 et al. v. Dolphin Delivery Ltd.* (1986), 33 D.L.R. (4th) 174.

49. Quoted in Mandel, *Charter of Rights*, 204.

50. John Ibbitson, "Charter That Reshaped Canada Becomes a Model to the World," *The Globe and Mail*, 16 Apr. 2012, A1.

51. Kirk Makin, "Why This Year May Prove to Be the Charter's Most Controversial," *The Globe and Mail*, 16 Apr. 2012, A4.

7 | Federalism

1. Pierre Elliott Trudeau, "Federalism, Nationalism and Reason," in Trudeau, *Federalism and the French Canadians* (Toronto: Macmillan, 1968), 195.

2. The term is a translation of "rois nègres," coined by André Laurendeau, in "A Search for Balance," *Canadian Forum* (Apr. 1963): 3–4.

3. Donald Smiley, *The Canadian Political Identity* (Toronto: Methuen, 1967), 30–1.

4. Profiles of Canada 2005, www.cric.ca.

5. Roger Gibbins, *Regionalism: Territorial Politics in Canada and the United States* (Toronto: Butterworths, 1982), 178.

6. Ernest Renan, *What is a Nation?* (Toronto: Tapir Press, 1996), 48.

7. Peter Waite, *The Life and Times of Confederation 1864–1867* (Toronto: University of Toronto Press, 1962), 96.

8. The diversity of expectations was reflected in newspaper accounts of the Confederation agreement. See ibid., 111.

9. There are some exceptions. In *Citizens Insurance Co. v. Parsons; Queen Insurance Co. v. Parsons* (1881), the Judicial Committee of the Privy Council ruled that Ottawa's trade and commerce power did not take pre-eminence over enumerated provincial powers. Why? In the words of Sir Montague Smith, "[The founders] could not have intended that the powers exclusively assigned to the provincial legislature should be absorbed in those given to the dominion parliament." Reproduced in Peter H. Russell,

ed., *Leading Constitutional Decisions*, 4th edn (Ottawa: Carleton University Press, 1987), 35.

10. Ibid., 527, *Re Constitution of Canada* (1981).

11. *Amicus curiae* concerning Certain Questions Relating to the Secession of Quebec, 31 Jan. 1998.

12. See the discussion in Keith G. Banting, *The Welfare State and Canadian Federalism*, 2nd edn (Montreal and Kingston: McGill–Queen's University Press, 1987), 52–4.

13. *Attorney General of Ontario v. Attorney General of Canada* (Local Prohibition case), 1896, in Russell, *Leading Constitutional Decisions*, 59.

14. *Re Board of Commerce Act and Combines and Fair Prices Act*, 1919, 1922, ibid., 75.

15. See Peter Russell, "The Anti-Inflation Case: The Anatomy of a Constitutional Decision," *Canadian Public Administration* 10, 4 (Winter 1977).

16. Constitution Act, 1867, s. 91(2).

17. Constitution Act, 1867, s. 92(13).

18. Russell, *Leading Constitutional Decisions*, 39.

19. *Ontario Farm Products Marketing Reference*, [1957] S.C.R. 198; *R. v. Klassen* (1959), 20 D.L.R. (2nd) 406 (Manitoba Court of Appeal); *Caloil v. A.G. of Canada*, [1971] S.C.R. 543.

20. *General Motors of Canada Ltd. v. City National Leasing*, [1989] 1 S.C.R. 641.

21. Trudeau, "Federalism, Nationalism and Reason," 198.

22. Henri Bourassa, "The French Language and the Future of Our Race," in Ramsay Cook, ed., *French Canadian Nationalism* (Toronto: Macmillan, 1969), 141.

23. Kenneth McRoberts, *Quebec: Social Change and Political Crisis*, 3rd edn (Toronto: McClelland & Stewart, 1988), 214.

24. See Richard Simeon, *Federal–Provincial Diplomacy* (Toronto: University of Toronto Press, 1972), 115–22.

25. Marc Dupont, "November 4, 1981: The Night of the Long Knives—Pierre Trudeau's Strategy," ipolitics.ca, 4 Nov. 2011, https://ipolitics.ca/2011/11/04/marc-dupont-november-4-1981-pierre-trudeaus-strategy-on-the-night-of-the-long-knives/.

26. Quoted in George Woodcock, *Confederation Betrayed!* (Vancouver: Harbour Publishing, 1981), 8.

27. This argument is developed by Barry Cooper in "Western Political Consciousness," in Stephen Brooks, ed., *Political Thought in Canada* (Toronto: Irwin, 1984), 213–38.

28. James Bickerton, *Nova Scotia, Ottawa, and the Politics of Regional Development* (Toronto: University of Toronto Press, 1990).

29. G.V. LaForest, *Disallowance and Reservation of Provincial Legislation* (Ottawa: Department of Justice, 1955).

30. Ottawa ceded control to Manitoba in 1930.

31. Alberta and Saskatchewan also acquired these powers in 1930.

32. Doug Owram, "Reluctant Hinterland," in Larry Pratt and Garth Stevenson, eds, *Western Separatism* (Edmonton: Hurtig, 1981), 61.

33. Loleen Berdahl, *Whither Western Alienation? Shifting Patterns of Western Canadian Discontent with the Federal Government*, Canada West Foundation, Oct. 2010, 9, cwf.ca/pdf-docs/publications/Whither-Western-Alienation.pdf.

34. "Defeated Harper Supporters Call for Independent 'Republic of Western Canada,'" Thinkpol.ca, 21 Oct. 2015, https://thinkpol.ca/2015/10/21/defeated-harper-supporters-call-for-independent-republic-of-western-canada/.

35. Alan Cairns, "The Governments and Societies of Canadian Federalism," in Cairns, *Constitution, Government, and Society in Canada* (Toronto: McClelland & Stewart, 1988), 153–4.

36. John Ibbitson, "Premiers to Face Off against Ottawa over 'Flawed' Job Program," *The Globe and Mail*, 21 July 2013, www.theglobeandmail.com/news/politics/premiers-to-face-off-against-ottawa-over-job-program/article13337953/.

37. Two of the major works using this concept are John Richards and Larry Pratt, *Prairie Capitalism* (Toronto: McClelland & Stewart, 1979), and McRoberts, *Quebec*.

38. R.A. Young, Philippe Faucher, and André Blais, "The Concept of Province-Building: A Critique," *Canadian Journal of Political Science* 17, 4 (Dec. 1984): 785.

39. Privy Council Office, Canadian Intergovernmental Conference Secretariat, www.scics.gc.ca/english/conferences.asp?t=q&y=2013&m=8.

40. Donald Smiley, "An Outsider's Observations of Federal–Provincial Relations," in R.D. Olling and W.M. Westmacott, eds, *Perspectives on Canadian Federalism* (Scarborough, ON: Prentice-Hall Canada, 1988).

41. Jason Fekete, "Why Prime Minister Stephen Harper Steers Clear of Premiers' Meetings," Postmedia, 24 July 2013, o.canada.com/2013/07/24/premiers-meetings-rarely-include-prime-minister-stephen-harper/.

42. Janice McGregor, "Premiers reach 'unprecedented' Canadian free-trade deal in Whitehorse," *CBC News*, 22 July 2016, http://www.cbc.ca/news/politics/premiers-whitehorse-closing-friday-1.3691840.

43. Constitution Act, 1867, s. 118.

44. Ibid., s. 111.

45. Paul Boothe and Derek Hermourtz, "Paying for ACCESS: Province by Province," paper delivered before the Political Economy Research Group, University of Western Ontario, 24 Oct. 1997, Figure 3b.

46. Department of Finance Canada, *Budget 1995: Key Actions and Impacts*, unpaginated.

47. Ibid.

48. Office of the Parliament Budget Office, *Renewing the Canada Health Transfer: Implications for Federal and Provincial–Territorial Fiscal Sustainability*, 12 Oct. 2012, www.pbo-dpb.gc.ca/files/files/Publications/Renewing_CHT.pdf.

49. Konrad Yakabuski, "Provinces Will Feel the Bite When It Comes to Health Care Transfers," *The Globe and Mail*, 28 Mar. 2016, http://www.theglobeandmail.com/opinion/provinces-will-feel-the-bite-in-health-transfers/article29388708/.

8 | How Parliamentary Government Works in Canada

1. "The Executive Government and Authority of and over Canada is hereby declared to continue and be vested in the Queen." Constitution Act, 1867, s. 9.

2. In the provinces, the Crown's authority is exercised through the lieutenant-governors, who are appointed by the Governor General to serve five-year terms.

3. James R. Mallory, *The Structure of Canadian Government*, rev. edn (Toronto: Gage, 1984), 42–3.

4. Constitution Act, 1867, s. 54.

5. Donald Savoie, *Governing from the Centre: The Concentration of Power in Canadian Politics* (Toronto: University of Toronto Press, 1999), ch. 6.

6. Colin Campbell and George Szablowski, *The Super-Bureaucrats: Structure and Behaviour in Central Agencies* (Toronto: Macmillan, 1979).

7. See David A. Good, *The Politics of Anticipation: Making Canadian Federal Tax Policy* (Ottawa: School of Public Administration, 1980).

8. Savoie, *Governing from the Centre*, 189.

9. Ibid., 109.

10. Campbell and Szablowski, *The Super-Bureaucrats*, 29.

11. Gordon Robertson, "The Changing Role of the Privy Council Office," *Canadian Public Administration* 14 (Winter 1971): 506.

12. Savoie, *Governing from the Centre*, 195.

13. Ibid.

14. Robertson, "The Changing Role of the Privy Council Office," 506.

15. Savoie, *Governing from the Centre*, 101.

16. Ibid., 103.

17. Both Donald Savoie in *Governing from the Centre* and Jeffrey Simpson in *The Friendly Dictatorship* (Toronto: McClelland & Stewart, 2001) make the case for this characterization.

18. Simpson, *The Friendly Dictatorship*, 248.

19. Savoie, *Governing from the Centre*, 362.

20. Government of Canada, "Population of the Federal Public Service by Department," http://www.tbs-sct.gc.ca/psm-fpfm/modernizing-modernisation/stats/ssa-pop-eng.asp.

21. Statistics Canada, "Government," Canada Year Book, Cat. no. 11-402-X, [http://www.statcan.gc.ca/pub/11-402-x/2012000/chap/gov-gouv/gov-gouv-eng.htm.

22. ENAP, "Canadian Governments Compared," http://etatscanadiens-canadiangovernments.enap.ca/en/nav.aspx?sortcode=2.0.0.

23. Savoie, *Governing from the Centre*, 248.

24. Robert J. Jackson and Michael A. Atkinson, *The Canadian Legislative System*, 2nd edn (Toronto: Gage, 1980), 22.

25. Savoie, *Governing from the Centre*, 91.

26. Ibid., 92.

27. David C. Docherty, *Mr. Smith Goes to Ottawa: Life in the House of Commons* (Vancouver: University of British Columbia Press, 1998), 234.

28. Geoff Reagan, quoted in John Paul Tasker, "Meet Geoff Regan, the new Speaker of the House of Commons," *CBC News*, 4 Dec. 2015, http://www.cbc.ca/news/politics/speaker-house-geoff-regan-liberal-mp-1.3349744.

29. Savoie, *Governing from the Centre*, 91–2.

30. Docherty, *Mr. Smith Goes to Ottawa*, 204.

31. Ibid., 206.

32. Patti Tamara Lenard and Richard Simeon, eds, *Imperfect Democracies: The Democratic Deficit in Canada and the United States* (Vancouver: University of British Columbia Press, 2013).

33. Michael Chong, *The Increasing Disconnect between Canadians and their Parliament*, Options Politiques, September 2010, 25.

34. See the Constitution Act, 1867, s. 99(1). This phrase, or reference to "misbehaviour," is found in the federal and provincial statutes that govern the removal of judges.

35. Ralph Miliband, *The State in Capitalist Society* (London: Quartet Books, 1973), 124.

36. Judges of county courts and all higher courts are appointed by Ottawa. Provincial court judges are appointed by the provinces. See Figure 8.10 in the text.

37. Canada, Department of Justice, *Canada's System of Justice* (Ottawa: Supply and Services, 1988), 7.

38. Wendy Cukier, *Improving Representation in the Judiciary: A Diversity Strategy*, Ryerson University, Diversity Institute, 27 June 2012. See also Kirk Makin, "Of 100 New Federally Appointed Judges 98 Are White, Globe Finds," *The Globe and Mail*, 17 Apr. 2012.

39. See Marie-Claire Belleau and Rebecca Johnson, "Les femmes juges feront-elles veritablement une difference? Reflexions sur leur presence depuis vingt ans a la Cour supreme du Canada," *Canadian Journal of Women and the Law* 17, 1 (2005): 27–39. The same argument is made for the increased representation of some other under-represented groups, including visible minorities.

40. *Reference re Public Service Employment Relations Act* (Alberta) (1987), 38 D.L.R. (4th) 161.

41. Ibid., 232.

42. Ibid., 200.

43. See Tonda MacCharles, "Top Court Speculation Begins Anew," *Toronto Star*, 19 Jan. 1999.

44. James Mallory, *Social Credit and the Federal Power* (Toronto: University of Toronto Press, 1954).

45. Michael Mandel, *Charter of Rights and the Legalization of Politics in Canada* (Toronto: Thompson Educational Publishing, 1994).

46. Rainer Knopff and Ted Morton, *Charter Politics* (Toronto: Nelson Canada, 1992), 79.

Part III | Participation in Politics

9 | Parties and Elections

1. Susan Delacourt, *Shopping for Votes: How Politicians Choose Us and We Choose Them* (Douglas and McIntyre, 2013), 7.

2. Eugene A. Forsey, *How Canadians Govern Themselves* (Ottawa: Supply and Services Canada, 1982), 32.

3. Leon Epstein, *Political Parties in Western Democracies* (New Brunswick NJ: Transaction Books, 1980 [1967]), 9.

4. John Meisel, "Decline of Party in Canada," in Hugh G. Thorburn, ed., *Party Politics of Canada*, 4th edn (Scarborough, Ont.: Prentice-Hall, 1979).

5. This section was co-authored by Professor A. Brian Tanguay, Wilfrid Laurier University.

6. George M. Hougham, "The Background and Development of National Parties," in Hugh G. Thorburn, ed., *Party Politics in Canada* (Toronto: Prentice-Hall, 1963), 3.

7. Ibid., 13.

8. Escott Reid, "The Rise of National Parties in Canada," in Hugh G. Thorburn, ed., *Party Politics in Canada*, 5th edn (Scarborough, Ont.: Prentice-Hall, 1985), 12. See also Norman Ward, *The Canadian House of Commons* (Toronto: University of Toronto Press, 1950), 157–62.

9. See, in particular, Martin Shefter, "Party and Patronage: Germany, England, and Italy," *Politics and Society* 7, 4 (1977): 403–51; Epstein, *Political Parties in Western Democracies*, ch. 5.

10. André Siegfried, *The Race Question in Canada* (Toronto: McClelland & Stewart, Carleton Library Edition, 1966 [English translation first published 1907]), 114.

11. Siegfried, *The Race Question in Canada*, 136.

12. J.A. Corry, *Democratic Government and Politics*, 2nd edn (Toronto: University of Toronto Press, 1951), 22. Variations on this theme can be found in R.M. Dawson and Norman Ward, *The Government of Canada*, 5th edn (Toronto: University of Toronto Press, 1987), 430–3, and Hugh G. Thorburn, "Interpretations of the Canadian Party System," in Thorburn, ed., *Party Politics in Canada*, 5th edn (Scarborough, Ont.: Prentice-Hall, 1985), 20–40. For a critique of the adequacy of brokerage theory, see Janine Brodie and Jane Jenson, *Crisis, Challenge and Change: Party and Class Revisited* (Ottawa: Carleton University Press, 1988), ch. 1.

13. Robert Alford, *Party and Society* (Westport, Conn.: Greenwood Press, 1963), 250–1. Alford computed his index of class voting by subtracting the percentage of non-manual workers voting for left parties (in Canada, the Liberals and the NDP, according to Alford) from the percentage of manual workers voting for the left parties, on the assumption that a party of the left should receive the bulk of its support from the traditional blue-collar (manual) occupations. See the discussion ibid., chs 4 and 5. Obviously, Alford's index leaves a great deal to be desired and has been subjected to substantial criticism over the years. Many critics of his work are particularly exercised by his classification of the Liberal Party of Canada as a party of the "left."

14. Ibid., 251.

15. Brodie and Jenson, *Crisis, Challenge and Change*.

16. Janine Brodie and Jane Jenson, "Piercing the Smokescreen: Brokerage Parties and Class Politics," in Alain G. Gagnon and A. Brian Tanguay, eds, *Canadian Parties in Transition: Discourse, Organization, and Representation* (Scarborough, Ont.: Nelson, 1989), 28.

17. Canadian Institute of Public Opinion, *The Gallup Report*, "Confidence in Political Parties Declines," 1 Feb. 1989, and "Government Increasingly Becoming Object of Scorn among Canadians," 20 Feb. 1991.

18. Walter Young, *The Anatomy of a Party: The National CCF, 1932–61* (Toronto: University of Toronto Press, 1969), 298, 300.

19. Canada, Royal Commission on Electoral Reform and Party Financing, *Reforming Electoral Democracy*, vol. 7 (Ottawa: Supply and Services Canada, 1991), 221.

20. Andrew Coyne, "Why a Liberal-NDP Coalition Is No Longer Such a Scary Concept for Cautious Centrists," *National Post*, 18 March 2015, http://news.nationalpost.com/news/canada/canadian-politics/why-a-liberal-ndp-coalition-is-no-longer-such-a-scary-concept-for-cautious-centrists.

21. Jeffrey Simpson, "It's Tough to be Ahead," *The Globe and Mail*, 28 Nov. 2006, http://www.theglobeandmail.com/news/politics/its-tough-to-be-ahead/article733087/.

22. Alan Cairns, "The Electoral System and the Party System in Canada, 1921–1965," *Canadian Journal of Political Science* 1, 1 (Mar. 1968): 55–80.

23. William P. Irvine, *Does Canada Need a New Electoral System?* (Kingston, Ont.: Institute of Intergovernmental Relations, Queen's University, 1979), 14.

24. Conference Board of Canada, "Voter Turnout," Jan. 2013, http://www.conferenceboard.ca/hcp/details/society/voter-turnout.aspx.

25. Jon H. Pammett and Lawrence LeDuc, *Explaining the Turnout Decline in Canadian Federal Elections: A New Survey of Non-voters*, Mar. 2003, 2, http://www.elections.ca/res/rec/part/tud/TurnoutDecline.pdf.

26. Elections Canada, "Estimation of Voter Turnout by Age Group and Gender at the 2011 Federal General Election," http://www.elections.ca/content.aspx?section=res&dir=rec/part/estim/41ge&document=report41&lang=e#,p1.

27. Aleksandra Sagan, "Canadian Election: What's the Best Way to Increase Voter Turnout?" *CBC News*, 21 Sept. 2015, http://www.cbc.ca/news/politics/canada-election-2015-voter-turnout-1.3230342.

28. Elections Canada, "Voter Turnout by Age Group, 2015," http://www.elections.ca/content.aspx?section=res&dir=rec/eval/pes2015/vtsa&document=table1&lang=e.

29. Elisabeth Gidengil, "Gender gap and Beyond: Are Women the Key to a Conservative Majority?," idee-ideas.ca, 3 Mar. 2010, http://www.idees-ideas.ca/blog/gender-gap-and-beyond-are-women-key-conservative-majority.

30. "Harper Driving a Wedge between Rural, Urban Canadians, Layton Says," National Post, 4 Apr. 2011, http://news.nationalpost.com/news/canada/canadian-politics/layton-taking-aim-at-canadian-pension-plan.

31. See, e.g., Paul Nesbitt-Larking, cited in Tara Brautigam, "Conservative Urban Shutout Deepens Divide," www.canada.com, 24 Jan. 2006; Allan Gregg, cited in David Warren, "The Urban Angle," *Ottawa Citizen*, 26 Jan. 2006, online edition.

32. Kevin Libin, "The Myth of the Urban-Rural Divide," *National Post*, 10 Apr. 2011, http://news.nationalpost.com/news/canada/kevin-libin-the-myth-of-the-urban-rural-divide.

33. The number of hours per network and the division of time between the parties are determined by the CRTC. In deciding how much time each party receives, the CRTC is guided by a formula weighted according to each party's share of the seats and popular vote in the previous election.

34. Dalton Camp, *Points of Departure* (Toronto: Deneau and Greenberg, 1979), 91.

10 | Interest Groups

1. V.O. Key, *Politics, Parties, and Pressure Groups*, 4th edn (New York: Crowell, 1958), 23.

2. James Madison, *The Federalist Papers*, no. 10 (New York: New American Library, 1961).

3. *Associations Canada* (Toronto: Grey House Publishing, 2013).

4. Estimates based on ibid.

5. E.E. Schattschneider, *The Semi-Sovereign People* (New York: Holt, Rinehart and Winston, 1960), 35.

6. Ibid.

7. Ibid.

8. Charles E. Lindblom, *Politics and Markets* (New York: Basic Books, 1977), especially chs 13–16.

9. Bruno S. Frey, *Modern Political Economy* (New York: John Wiley & Sons, 1978), ch. 11.

10. Business's ideological and academic spokespersons adopt an essentially pluralistic position on the matter of interest-group influence. William Stanbury's remarks are typical: "The relationship between business firms and governments in either positive or normative terms cannot be characterized in a single phrase. It is inevitably plural and diverse. Depending upon the industry, the time, the other issues on the public policy agenda, the individuals involved, and what each 'side' is seeking to do vis-à-vis the other, the relationship might be characterized as adversarial, cooperative, symbiotic,

supportive, or protective." Stanbury, *Business–Government Relations in Canada* (Toronto: Methuen, 1986), 9.

11. Michael Bliss, *Northern Enterprise: Five Centuries of Canadian Business* (Toronto: McClelland & Stewart, 1987), 578.

12. David Vogel, *Fluctuating Fortunes: The Political Power of Business in America* (New York: Basic Books, 1989), 193.

13. James Q. Wilson, "The Politics of Regulation," in Wilson, ed., *The Politics of Regulation* (New York: Basic Books, 1980), 370.

14. Earl Latham, *The Group Basis of Politics* (New York: Octagon Books, 1965), 35.

15. P. Bachrach and M. Baratz, "Two Faces of Power," *American Political Science Review* 56, 4 (1962): 948.

16. This is true of Nicos Poulantzas, *Political Power and Social Classes* (London: New Left Books, 1973); Fred Block, *Revising State Theory* (Philadelphia: Temple University Press, 1987); Bob Jessop, *The Capitalist State* (New York: New York University Press, 1982). Interest groups are given some passing mention in James O'Connor, *The Fiscal Crisis of the State* (New York: St Martin's Press, 1973); Claus Offe, *Contradictions of the Welfare State* (Cambridge, MA: MIT Press, 1984). Among the leading Marxist intellectuals, it is perhaps fair to say that only Ralph Miliband has very much to say on interest groups: see *The State in Capitalist Society* (London: Quartet Books, 1973).

17. The term "political economy" includes three separate streams or meanings today: the Canadian tradition of political economy, which, after Harold Innis's early work, moved squarely to the left; the political economy in the Downs–Buchanan tradition, with a centre of gravity in the United States and a pro-market orientation; and the political economy work among those in international relations, whose focus is globalization and its discontents and whose orientation is more often than not on the left.

18. Miliband, *The State in Capitalist Society*, 131.

19. Jurg Steiner, *European Democracies* (New York: Longman, 1986), 221.

20. It occasionally happens, however, that the CCC is capable of taking a firm position on issues that are more divisive in the business community. Its support for the Canada–US Free Trade Agreement was an example of this.

21. Gerhard Lehmbruch, "Concentration and the Structure of Corporatist Networks," in John Goldthorpe, ed., *Order and Conflict in Contemporary Capitalism* (Oxford: Clarendon, 1984), 65–6.

22. William D. Coleman, *Business and Politics: A Study of Collective Action* (Montreal and Kingston: McGill–Queen's University Press, 1988), ch. 6.

23. Michels's argument was that the specialization of function that accompanies organization inevitably results in domination of the organization by a minority and, therefore, creates the likelihood that the goals pursued by the organization will more closely reflect those of its leadership than its membership. Robert Michels, *Political Parties* (London: Jarrold, 1915).

24. Some of the classics of this literature include Anthony Downs, *An Economic Theory of Democracy* (New York: Harper and Row, 1957); Mancur Olson, *The Logic of Collective Action* (Cambridge, MA: Harvard University Press, 1965); James M. Buchanan and Gordon Tullock, *The Calculus of Consent* (Ann Arbor: University of Michigan Press, 1965); Anthony Downs, *Inside Bureaucracy* (Boston: Little, Brown and Company, 1967).

25. Michael Atkinson, "How Do Institutions Constrain Policy?," paper delivered at the conference "Governing Canada: Political Institutions and Public Policy" (McMaster University, 25 Oct. 1991), 8. A good introduction to this approach and its application to politics is provided by Queen's University economist Dan Usher in *Political Economy* (London: Blackwell, 2003).

26. Alan Cairns, "The Governments and Societies of Canadian Federalism," *Canadian Journal of Political Science* 10, 4 (Dec. 1977): 695–725.

27. James Q. Wilson, *Political Organizations* (New York: Basic Books, 1973), 3–4.

28. These definitions are the ones used in William D. Coleman and Grace Skogstad, "Introduction," in Coleman and Skogstad, eds, *Policy Communities and Public Policy in Canada* (Toronto: Copp Clark Pitman, 1990). They are not, however, agreed upon by everyone who mines this vein.

29. J.L. Granatstein, *The Ottawa Men* (Toronto: Oxford University Press, 1982).

30. O. Mary Hill, *Canada's Salesman to the World: The Department of Trade and Commerce, 1892–1939* (Montreal and Kingston: McGill–Queen's University Press, 1977), 172.

31. Leslie A. Pal, *Interests of State* (Montreal and Kingston: McGill–Queen's University Press, 1992), ch. 6.

32. A. Paul Pross, *Group Politics and Public Policy* (Toronto: University of Toronto Press, 1986), 68–9.

33. See Table 3-2, "Crosswalk between Old and New Multicultural Program Objectives," in Citizenship and Immigration Canada, *Evaluation of the Multicultural Program*, Mar. 2012, 20–1, www.cic.gc.ca/english/pdf/research-stats/multiculturalism.pdf.

34. LEAF, *Voices-voix*, "Women's Legal Education and Action Fund," 15 Nov. 2012, voices-voix.ca/en/facts/profile/womens-legal-education-and-action-fund-leaf. The Conservative government disbanded the Court Challenges Program in 2006 but resurrected part of it in 2008, through the Program to Support Linguistic Rights.

35. Pross, *Group Politics and Public Policy*, 114–16.

36. Michael Geist, "OECD Report Confirms What Canadians Have Long Suspected: Wireless Pricing Among Highest in the World," 15 July 2013, http://www.michaelgeist.ca/2013/07/oecd-on-wireless-pricing/.

37. OECD, *OECD Communications Outlook 2013* (OECD Publishing), DOI:10.1787/comms_outlook-2013-en

38. "Canadian Telecoms Ramp Up Lobbying Efforts Ahead of Verizon's Entry into Canada," *McLean's*, 8 Aug. 2013, http://www.macleans.ca/news/canadian-telecoms-ramp-up-lobbying-efforts-ahead-of-verizons-entry-into-canada/.

39. John W. Kingdon, *Agendas, Alternatives, and Public Policies* (Boston: Little, Brown and Company, 1984), 54–7.

40. Dominque Gross, *Temporary Foreign Workers in Canada: Are They Really Filling Labour Shortages?*, C.D. Howe Institute commentary No. 407 (Apr. 2014), https://www.cdhowe.org/pdf/commentary_407.pdf.

41. Schattschneider, *The Semi-Sovereign People*, 37.

42. Ibid., 38.

43. This literature is brought together in Hugh G. Thorburn, *Interest Groups in the Canadian Federal System*, vol. 69 of the research studies for the Royal Commission on the Economic Union and Development Prospects for Canada (Ottawa: Supply and Services, 1985).

44. Richard J. Schultz, *Federalism, Bureaucracy and Public Policy: The Politics of Highway Transport Regulation* (Montreal and Kingston: McGill–Queen's University Press, 1980), 148.

45. See, for example, M.W. Bucovetsky, "The Mining Industry and the Great Tax Reform Debate," in A. Paul Pross, ed., *Pressure Group Behaviour in Canadian Politics* (Toronto: McGraw-Hill Ryerson, 1975), 89–114.

46. The long-accepted claim that Canada's federal Constitution has led most associations to adopt a federal form of organization is not supported by the facts—at least not in the case of business associations. A survey by William Coleman finds that about three-quarters of business associations have unitary structures. Coleman's conclusion is that Canada's industrial structure has a far greater impact on how business associations organize themselves than does the Constitution. See Coleman, *Business and Politics*, 260.

47. See Schultz, *Federalism, Bureaucracy and Public Policy*, especially ch. 8.

48. Leslie A. Pal, *State, Class, and Bureaucracy* (Montreal and Kingston: McGill–Queen's University Press, 1988).

49. Laura Litvan, "Lobbyists Cash in as Keystone XL Pipeline Slugfest Enters Sixth Year," *Financial Post* (17 Sept. 2013), http://business.financialpost.com/news/energy/fight-over-keystone-xl-pipeline-enters-its-sixth-year.

50. Quoted in Duncan McDowall, ed., *Advocacy Advertising: Propaganda or Democratic Right?* (Ottawa: Conference Board of Canada, 1982), v.

51. For example, a former federal minister of Justice defended his government's advertising on proposed constitutional reforms by saying, "Government is too complex nowadays to rely on policy by press release. Programs must be explained—not by reporters but by people who created them." Ibid., 7. On the subject of government advertising, see Jonathan Rose, *Making "Pictures in Our Heads": Government Advertising in Canada* (Westport, CT: Greenwood Publishing Group, 2000).

52. Privately funded think tanks like the C.D. Howe Institute, the Fraser Institute, and the Conference Board of Canada are another way of promoting group interests, in this case the general interests of business, by producing studies and funding experts whose perspectives and options for public policy are favourable to business interests. Direct-mail campaigns, targeted at selected groups whose opinions and actions may, in turn, affect policy makers is another technique employed mainly by business groups.

53. A fascinating though somewhat dated account of lobbying in Canada is John Sawatsky, *The Insiders: Government, Business, and the Lobbyists* (Toronto: McClelland & Stewart, 1987).

54. Earnscliffe Strategy Group, "Earnscliffe's Clients," www.earnscliffe.ca/clients.php.

55. For specific information on contribution limits, see http://www.elections.ca/content.aspx?section=pol&document=index&dir=lim&lang=e.

56. All this data may be found under "Lobbying Statistics" at the website of the Office of the Commissioner of Lobbying of Canada, ocl-cal.gc.ca.

11 | The Media

1. Neil Postman, *Amusing Ourselves to Death: Public Discourse in the Age of Show Business* (New York: Penguin, 1985).

2. Walter Lippmann, *Public Opinion* (New York: Harcourt, Brace and Company, 1922), 13.

3. See Bureau of Broadcast Measurement data, www.bbm.ca/en/top_programs.html.

4. *Canada Results: 2013 Edelman Trust Barometer*, slides 11 and 14, fr.slideshare.net/EdelmanInsights/canada-results-2013-edelman-trust-barometer.

5. "ITAC Media Choice & Trust Poll," www.itac.ca.

6. The Royal Commission on Newspapers expressed this view, although only the case of newspapers owned by the Irving family in New Brunswick was cited explicitly. See also the comments of the former Premier of Saskatchewan, Allan Blakeney, in Diane Francis, *Controlling Interest: Who Owns Canada?* (Toronto: Macmillan, 1986), 316.

7. Edward Herman and Noam Chomsky, *Manufacturing Consent* (New York: Pantheon, 1988), 8.

8. Walter I. Romanow et al., "Correlates of Newspaper Coverage of the 1979 Canadian Election: Chain Ownership, Competitiveness of Market, and Circulation," study done for the Royal Commission on Newspapers (Ottawa: Supply and Services, 1981).

9. This and all other data reported in this paragraph are found in Oriella PR Network, *Global Digital Journalism Study 2013*, www.oriellaprnetwork.com/sites/default/files/research/Brands2Life_ODJS_v4.pdf.

10. Lawrence Martin, "Canada's Media: A Crisis That Cries Out for a Public Inquiry," *The Globe and Mail*, 2 Feb. 2016, http://www.theglobeandmail.com/opinion/canadas-media-a-crisis-that-cries-out-for-a-public-inquiry/article28494689/.

11. Andrew Coyne, "All the News That's Fit to Pay For," *National Post*, 26 Jan. 2016, http://news.nationalpost.com/full-comment/andrew-coyne-all-the-news-thats-fit-to-pay-for.

12. Polly Mosendz, "How Canada's Newspapers Reported the Ottawa Shooting," *The Atlantic*, 23 Oct. 2014, http://www.theatlantic.com/international/archive/2014/10/how-canada-reported-on-the-ottawa-shooting/381855/.

13. David DiSalvo, "How Netflix Is Changing Our Brains, And Why That May Not Be All Good," *Forbes.com*, 8 June 2014, http://www.forbes.com/sites/daviddisalvo/2014/06/08/how-netflix-is-changing-our-brains-and-why-that-may-not-be-all-good/#73d1e1664d4b.

14. Lippmann, *Public Opinion*, 345.

15. "State of the News Media 2015," Pew Research Center, 29 April 2015, http://www.journalism.org/2015/04/29/state-of-the-news-media-2015/.

16. Pew Research Project for Excellence in Journalism, *The State of the News Media 2013*, http://www.stateofthemedia.org/2013/overview-5/.

17. Ibid.

18. Dean Beeby, "Ottawa Cuts Newspaper Ad Spending Amid Worries about Sector," *CBC News*, 1 Sept. 2016, http://www.cbc.ca/news/politics/newspapers-canadian-heritage-public-policy-forum-digital-news-gathering-internet-1.3743580.

19. Paul Hunter, "Postmedia's big purchase means more Canadian cities like Vancouver," *Toronto Star*, 10 Oct. 2014, https://www.thestar.com/news/insight/2014/10/10/postmedias_big_purchase_means_more_canadian_cities_like_vancouver.html.

20. Robert E. Babe and Jessica Potter, "Media Ownership," *The Canadian Encyclopedia*, 4 March 2015, http://www.thecanadianencyclopedia.ca/en/article/media-ownership/.

21. Dillan Theckedath and Terrence J. Thomas, *Media Ownership and Convergence in Canada*, Industry, Infrastructure and Resources Division, Library of Parliament, 10 April 2012, 3, http://www.parl.gc.ca/content/lop/researchpublications/2012-17-e.pdf.

22. Friends of Canadian Broadcasting, "Split Screen," www.friends.ca/Resource/Publications/publications11019201.

23. See the discussions in Frank Peers, *The Politics of Broadcasting 1920–1951* (Toronto: University of Toronto Press, 1969); and Marc Raboy, *Missed Opportunities: The Story of Canada's Broadcasting Policy* (Montreal and Kingston: McGill–Queen's University Press, 1990).

24. Task Force on Broadcasting Policy, *Report*, Ottawa, 1986, p.433.

25. Marsha Lederman, "TV's New Equation: Content Bonanza Meets Revenue Crisis," *The Globe and Mail*, 15 June 2013, http://www.theglobeandmail.com/arts/television/tvs-new-equation-content-bonanza-meets-revenue-crisis/article12562391/?page=all.

26. Michael Lewis, "CRTC backs off 'Netflix tax,'" *Toronto Star*, 12 Mar. 2015, https://www.thestar.com/business/2015/03/12/crtc-lowering-canadian-content-quotas-to-boost-quality.html.

27. Morris Wolfe, *Jolts: The TV Wasteland and the Canadian Oasis* (Toronto: James Lorimer, 1985), 14.

28. Ibid., 18.

29. Ibid., 262.

30. Ibid.

31. Herman and Chomsky, *Manufacturing Consent*, 19.

32. Edward Jay Epstein, *News from Nowhere: Television and the News* (New York: Random House, 1973),146.

33. Ibid., 147.

34. Stanley Rothman and S. Robert Lichter, "Personality, Ideology and World View: A Comparison of Media and Business Elites," *British Journal of Political Science* 15, 1 (1984): 36.

35. Ibid., 46.

36. Barry Cooper, *Sins of Omission: Shaping the News at CBC TV* (Toronto: University of Toronto Press, 1994), xi.

37. Lydia Miljan and Barry Cooper, *Hidden Agendas: How the Beliefs of Canadian Journalists Influence the News* (Vancouver: University of British Columbia Press, 2003).

38. Blake Andrew, Antonia Maioni, and Stuart Soroka, "Just When You Thought It Was Out, Policy Is Pulled Back In," *Policy Options* (Mar. 2006): 74–9.

39. Derek O'Keefe, "With Just Days until the Federal Election, the Nation's Newspapers Are Lining Up to Offer Their Editorial Endorsements to the Harper Government," Ricochet.com, 16 Oct. 2015, https://ricochet.media/en/671/did-the-owners-of-canadas-national-newspapers-order-them-to-endorse-harper.

40. Ralph Miliband, *The State in Capitalist Society* (London: Quartet Books, 1969), 211.

41. Leon Epstein, *Political Parties in Western Democracies* (New York: Praeger, 1967), 237.

42. Aldous Huxley, *Brave New World Revisited* (New York: Harper & Brothers, 1958), 44.

43. The term is used by Herman and Chomsky in their analysis of the political role of the American media. They, in turn, borrow it from Walter Lippmann, who had in mind, however, government's use of propagandistic techniques to cultivate popular acceptance of their rule.

44. Edward Jay Epstein, *News from Nowhere*, 199.

45. Frank Lloyd Wright, quoted in Henry Peyre, *Writers and their Critics* (Ithaca, New York: Cornell University Press, 1944), 291.

46. Aldous Huxley, *Brave New World Revisited*, Chapter 4, "Propaganda in Democratic Society"(New York: Harper, 1958).

12 | Conclusion: Canada in the World

1. Mark Kingwell, "What Distinguishes Us from the Americans," *National Post*, 5 Mar. 2003, A16.

2. John Ralston Saul, *Reflections of a Siamese Twin: Canada at the End of the Twentieth Century* (Toronto: Penguin, 1997), 171.

3. For more on Canada's early economic development, see Harold Innis's *The Fur Trade in Canada*: An Introduction to Canadian Economic History (Toronto: University of Toronto Press, 1999).

4. Jeffrey Sachs, "Nature, Nurture and Growth," *The Economist*, 14 June 1997, 19–22.

5. Barry Lynn, "Unmade in America: The True Cost of a Global Assembly Line," *Harper's* (June 2002): 37.

6. Office of the United States Trade Representative, U.S. China Trade Facts and U.S.-Canada Trade Facts, 2015, https://ustr.gov/countries-regions/china-mongolia-taiwan/peoples-republic-china & https://ustr.gov/countries-regions/americas/canada.

7. Statistics Canada, "Foreign Direct Investment (Stocks) in Canada," Table 376-0051, April 2015.

8. Statistics Canada, "Canadian Direct Investment Abroad (Stocks)," April 2015, http://www.international.gc.ca/economist-economiste/assets/pdfs/Data/investments-investissements/FDI_by_Country/CDIA_stocks_by_Country-ENG.pdf.

9. Center for North American Studies, American University, *The NAFTA Promise and the North American Reality*, 31 Oct. 2013, slide 15, www.american.edu/sis/cnas/upload/North-America-October-30-1255-pm-FULL-VERSION.pdf.

10. Allan Gotlieb, "Getting Attention," *National Post*, 17 May 2002, A17.

11. Allan Gotlieb, "A Grand Bargain with the U.S.," *National Post*, 5 Mar. 2003, A16.

12. *60 Minutes*, Prime Minister Trudeau, 6 March 2016. To see the interview, visit http://www.cbsnews.com/news/60-minutes-prime-minister-trudeau/.

13. Michael Ignatieff, "Canada in the Age of Terror—Multilateralism Meets a Moment of Truth," *Policy Options* (Feb. 2003), www.irpp.org.

14. Ibid.

15. Joseph Nye, "The Misleading Metaphor of Decline," *The Atlantic* (Mar. 1990): 86–94.

16. Angus Reid poll, cited in Kelly Hobson, "More Than 70% of Canadians Think Liberals' New Refugee Target Is Too High: Poll," *National Post*, 19 Feb. 2016, http://news.nationalpost.com/news/canada/majority-of-canadians-dont-want-to-take-in-more-than-25000-syrian-refugees-new-poll.

17. Care2 Petitions, "Stop resettling 25,000 Syrian refugees in Canada," http://www.thepetitionsite.com/en-gb/790/431/152/stop-settling-25000-syrian-refugees-in-canada/.

18. Michael Ignatieff, "The Burden," *New York Times Magazine*, 5 Jan. 2003, www.nytimes.com/2003/01/05/magazine/05EMPIRE.html.

19. Jeffrey Simpson, "Canada Is 'Back' on the World Stage? Hardly," *The Globe and Mail*, 13 Jun. 2012, http://www.theglobeandmail.com/commentary/canada-is-back-on-the-world-stage-hardly/article4254018/.

20. UN, "Ranking of Military and Police Contributions to UN Operations," http://www.un.org/en/peacekeeping/contributors/2010/sept10_2.pdf.

Index

Note: Page numbers in *italics* refer to figures.